EVERYDAY LAW
MADE E-Z

Edited by Alice K. Helm, LL.B., J.D.

MADE E-Z PRODUCTS, Inc.
Deerfield Beach, Florida / www.MadeE-Z.com

Everyday Law Made E-Z™
Copyright 2000 Made E-Z Products, Inc.
Printed in the United States of America

MADE E-Z
PRODUCTS

384 South Military Trail
Deerfield Beach, FL 33442
Tel. 954-480-8933
Fax 954-480-8906

http://www.MadeE-Z.com

1 2 3 4 5 6 7 8 9 10   CPC   R   10 9 8 7 6 5 4 3 2

This publication is designed to provide accurate and authoritative information in regard to subject matter covered. It is sold with the understanding that neither the publisher nor author is engaged in rendering legal, accounting, or other professional services. If legal advice or other expert assistance is required, the services of a competent professional should be sought. From: *A Declaration of Principles jointly adopted by a Committee of the American Bar Association and a Committee of Publishers.*

Everyday Law Made E-Z™
Edited by Alice K. Helm, LL.B., J.D.

Important Notice

Limited warranty and disclaimer

This self-help product is intended to be used by the consumer for his/her own benefit. It may not be reproduced in whole or in part, resold or used for commercial purposes without written permission from the publisher. In addition to copyright violations, the unauthorized reproduction and use of this product to benefit a second party may be considered the unauthorized practice of law.

This product is designed to provide authoritative and accurate information in regard to the subject matter covered. However, the accuracy of the information is not guaranteed, as laws and regulations may change or be subject to differing interpretations. Consequently, you may be responsible for following alternative procedures, or using material or forms different from those supplied with this product. It is strongly advised that you examine the laws of your state before acting upon any of the material contained in this product.

As with any matter, common sense should determine whether you need the assistance of an attorney. We urge you to consult with an attorney, qualified estate planner, or tax professional, or to seek any other relevant expert advice whenever substantial sums of money are involved, you doubt the suitability of the product you have purchased, or if there is anything about the product that you do not understand including its adequacy to protect you. Even if you are completely satisfied with this product, we encourage you to have your attorney review it.

Neither the author, publisher, distributor nor retailer are engaged in rendering legal, accounting or other professional services. Accordingly, the publisher, author, distributor and retailer shall have neither liability nor responsibility to any party for any loss or damage caused or alleged to be caused by the use of this product.

Copyright Notice

The purchaser of this guide is hereby authorized to reproduce in any form or by any means, electronic or mechanical, including photocopying, all forms and documents contained in this guide, provided it is for non-profit, educational or private use. Such reproduction requires no further permission from the publisher and/or payment of any permission fee.

The reproduction of any form or document in any other publication intended for sale is prohibited without the written permission of the publisher. Publication for nonprofit use should provide proper attribution to Made E-Z Products.

Table of contents

Introduction to Everyday Law Made E-Z™

The primary goal of *Everyday Law Made E-Z* is to give you an understanding of the law as it touches the daily life of an average family. As tenant or landlord, borrower or lender, parent or child, as the maker of a will or the holder of an insurance policy, as the owner of a car or a pet—sooner or later, you are likely to encounter questions of law. It is in these circumstances that you will find it especially helpful to have this book at hand, for it will enable you to discuss your problems intelligently with your lawyer who is, of course, your legal advisor.

Although the law is complex, differing sharply in its details from state to state, general rules do govern your legal rights and responsibilities. In this book, you will learn about such common concerns as your civil rights, the extent of a minor's responsibility for accidents or misbehavior, and how to make a will, as well as more unusual matters like the law of libel and slander, and what you should do if you are arrested. The book explains your rights vis-a-vis the United States government, either as a citizen or as an alien. It explains your Social Security and Medicare rights, and your doctor's legal responsibilities. In many cases, *Everyday Law Made E-Z* will also tell you about major exceptions to prevailing law; in other cases, tables provide a state-by-state catalogue of laws on marriage, divorce, and wills.

Secondarily, but still important, *Everyday Law Made E-Z* hopes to entertain as well as instruct. Although laws are written and enacted by legislatures, their validity is established in the courts, which must consider the law not in the abstract, but in relation to the particular behavior of particular people. To clarify legal points, the book cites hundreds of cases, each of them a small drama of people in conflict. Some of the cases are touching or exciting; a number of them are even comic. Portions of court decisions are quoted to demonstrate the reasoning behind them, and thus to make the law vital and meaningful to you.

Legal terms are explained in this book as they occur in text. To help you still further, however, a *Dictionary of Common Legal Terms* appears at the end of the book, as does an index which enables you to quickly locate the information you seek.

Theodore R. Kupferman, LL.B.
Justice, Supreme Court, Appellate Division

The law of marriage

Chapter 1
The law of marriage

Although the institution of marriage may be considered a holy union, it is governed by numerous rules established by the state. Unless you are aware of them and conform, in the eyes of the civil authorities you will not have a legal relationship. Inasmuch as so many rights are dependent upon its being a valid relationship, it is extremely important that you know your state's regulations.

The state has the welfare of its citizens in mind, and under the Constitution may make rules governing that welfare. It prescribes, among other things, conditions concerning the marriage of blood relatives, the minimum ages for marriage, and requirements concerning the physical and mental health of the parties.

Miscegenation laws

For many years, some states have regulated marriage between persons of different races. These laws are called miscegenation laws. However, the United States Supreme Court has ruled that these laws are unconstitutional. Among the states that had such laws were Alabama, Arkansas, Delaware, Florida, Georgia, Kentucky, Louisiana, Mississippi, Missouri, North Carolina, Oklahoma, South Carolina, Tennessee, Texas, Virginia, and West Virginia. Maryland also had one, but repealed it in 1967.

In 1958, two residents of Virginia, a black woman and a white man named Loving, were married in nearby Washington, D.C., and then returned to Virginia to live. They were charged by the state with violating the state's law banning interracial marriages. They pleaded guilty and their sentences were suspended on the condition that they leave Virginia, and not return for 25 years. They went to the District of Columbia to live, but in 1963 they challenged the judgment and sentence, claiming it was unconstitutional. The case went all the way to the United States Supreme Court. That Court decided that though marriage is a social relationship subject to the state's police power, the state's power to regulate is not unlimited. The restriction, by the state, of the freedom to marry solely because of racial classifications violates the meaning of the equal protection clause of the United States Constitution. Marriage, said the Court, is one of the basic civil rights of man, and the Constitution requires that the freedom of choice to marry not be restricted by racial discrimination. The freedom to marry outside your race is a matter of individual choice and cannot be infringed upon by the state.

Marrying a relative

The reason behind the prohibition of the marriage of near relatives is that harmful physical and mental characteristics are much more likely to appear in the offspring of such close blood relations. Thus, though it is a well recognized rule of law that a marriage which is valid where it is entered into is valid everywhere, an exception is the refusal of some states to recognize the marriage of persons with prohibited degrees of relationship. Relatives as near as sister and brother or aunt and nephew cannot marry in any state. The attempted marriage of a man and woman of closer relationship than first cousins is incest, a crime. In some states this prohibition is extended to include first cousins and first cousins once removed (that is, where one party is a grandchild and the other a great-grandchild of a common ancestor). In a number of states, second cousins may not marry if they are great-grandchildren of a common ancestor.

In an interesting case in New York, a girl named Eva married her father's half-brother, Albert Simms. They signed an antenuptial agreement under which Simms undertook to bequeath $25,000 to Eva (see Chapters 10 and 11 on wills).

The marriage, performed according to the canons of the Jewish faith, was thereafter annulled on the grounds of incest. Subsequently, Simms died and the question before the court was whether the antenuptial agreement was valid and enforceable.

The Domestic Relations Law of the State of New York provides that a marriage between an uncle and niece is incestuous and void. It says nothing about "half blood." However, in prohibiting a marriage between a brother and sister, it covers both the whole and half blood. This leads to the conclusion that half blood in relation to uncle and niece is not interdicted. The agreement, in any event, was held valid because even if in New York the marriage might be considered incestuous, in other jurisdictions it would not be.

Alabama law formerly prohibited a man marrying the widow of his uncle. This had its origins in the Old Testament concepts of marital rules. In an old case in Alabama, the widow of a Dr. Watkins asked to be appointed administratrix of her husband's estate. Years before, when she had become the widow of an uncle of Dr. Watkins, she and the doctor had gone from Alabama to another state to be married and then returned to Alabama, where they lived until the doctor's death.

The penalty for violating this law was imprisonment. By this law the marriage of Dr. Watkins and the widow of his uncle was not a marriage. It was incest, punishable by law. Before the widow's application for her appointment as administratrix was decided, she died, saved thus from the ignominy of possible proceedings branding her a criminal.

A marriage between a man and woman too closely related brought similar censure in a New York court. A 47-year-old woman and her 18-year-old nephew were married in Italy. After the marriage they migrated to New York, where some years later she asked the courts for support from her youthful husband. The court refused to recognize the relationship as a marriage or to grant the relief sought by the woman. Perhaps if the marriage had not also been invalid in Italy, the result might have been different.

Keeping in mind that some states have different interpretations of what a "cousin" is, a consideration of state marriage laws follows:

Marrying a relative

State	First cousins	First cousins once removed	Second cousins
Alabama	Permitted	Permitted	Permitted
Alaska	Permitted	Permitted	Permitted
Arizona	Prohibited	Permitted	Permitted
Arkansas	Prohibited	Permitted	Permitted
California	Permitted	Permitted	Permitted
Colorado	Permitted	Permitted	Permitted
Connecticut	Permitted	Permitted	Permitted
Delaware	Prohibited	Permitted	Permitted
District of Columbia	Permitted	Permitted	Permitted
Florida	Permitted	Permitted	Permitted
Georgia	Permitted	Permitted	Permitted
Hawaii	Permitted	Permitted	Permitted
Idaho	Prohibited	Permitted	Permitted
Illinois	Prohibited	Permitted	Permitted
Indiana	Prohibited	Prohibited	Permitted
Iowa	Prohibited	Permitted	Permitted
Kansas	Prohibited	Permitted	Permitted
Kentucky	Prohibited	Prohibited	Permitted
Louisiana	Prohibited	Permitted	Permitted
Maine	Permitted	Permitted	Permitted
Maryland	Permitted	Permitted	Permitted
Massachusetts	Permitted	Permitted	Permitted
Michigan	Prohibited	Permitted	Permitted
Minnesota	Prohibited	Permitted	Permitted
Mississippi	Prohibited	Permitted	Permitted
Missouri	Prohibited	Permitted	Permitted
Montana	Prohibited	Permitted	Permitted
Nebraska	Prohibited	Permitted	Permitted
Nevada	Prohibited	Prohibited	Permitted
New Hampshire	Prohibited	Permitted	Permitted
New Jersey	Permitted	Permitted	Permitted
New Mexico	Permitted	Permitted	Permitted
New York	Permitted	Permitted	Permitted
North Carolina	Permitted	Permitted	Permitted
North Dakota	Prohibited	Permitted	Permitted
Ohio	Prohibited	Prohibited	Permitted
Oklahoma	Prohibited	Permitted	Permitted
Oregon	Prohibited	Permitted	Permitted
Pennsylvania	Permitted	Permitted	Permitted
Puerto Rico	Prohibited	Permitted	Permitted
Rhode Island	Permitted	Permitted	Permitted
South Carolina	Permitted	Permitted	Permitted

State	First cousins	First cousins once removed	Second cousins
South Dakota	Prohibited	Permitted	Permitted
Tennessee	Permitted	Permitted	Permitted
Texas	Permitted	Permitted	Permitted
Utah	Prohibited	Prohibited	Permitted
Vermont	Permitted	Permitted	Permitted
Virginia	Permitted	Permitted	Permitted
Virgin Islands	Permitted	Permitted	Permitted
Washington	Prohibited	Prohibited	Permitted
West Virginia	Prohibited	Permitted	Permitted
Wisconsin*	Prohibited*	Prohibited*	Permitted
Wyoming	Prohibited	Permitted	Permitted

*Wisconsin—Permits first cousins to marry where the female is older than 55. Obviously this is based on the unlikelihood of conception after that age.

The age of consent

The law fixes the earliest date at which you can marry. Ordinarily, if either the man or woman has not reached that age, there is no marriage. However, with the consent of the parents, marriage is in most instances permitted at an earlier age. The following are the earliest ages at which a couple may marry in the various states, both with the consent of the parents of the girl and boy, and without that consent.

The age of consent

State	Minimum age with parental consent		Minimum age without parental consent	
	Man	Woman	Man	Woman
Alabama	17	14	18	18
Alaska	18*	16*	18	18
Arizona	16*	16*	18	18
Arkansas	17*	16*	18	18
California	None stated	None stated	18	18
Colorado	16*	16*	18	18
Connecticut	16*	16*	18	18
Delaware	18	16	18	18
District of Columbia	16	16	18	18
Florida	None stated	None stated	18	18
Georgia	None stated	None stated	16	16
Hawaii	16*	16*	18	18
Idaho	16*	16*	18	18
Illinois	16	16	18	18
Indiana	17*	17*	18	18
Iowa	None stated	None stated	18	18
Kansas	14	12	18	18
Kentucky	None stated	None stated	18	18

Louisiana	18*	16*	18	18
Maine	16*	16*	18	18
Maryland	16*	16*	18	18
Massachusetts	18*	18*	18	18
Michigan	18	16	18	18
Minnesota	18	16	18	18
Mississippi	17*	15*	17	15
Missouri	15*	15*	18	18
Montana	16	16	18	18
Nebraska	17	17	19	19
Nevada	16*	16*	18	18
New Hampshire	18* **	18* **	18	18
New Jersey	16*	16*	18	18
New Mexico	16*	16*	18	18
New York	16*	14	18	18
North Carolina	16	16	18	18
North Dakota	16	16	18	18
Ohio	18	16	18	18
Oklahoma	16*	16*	18	18
Oregon	17	17	18	18
Pennsylvania	16*	16*	18	18
Puerto Rico	None stated	None stated	18	16
Rhode Island	18*	16*	18	18
South Carolina	16	14	18	18
South Dakota	16	16	18	18
Tennessee	16*	16*	18	18
Texas	14	14	18	18
Utah	14	14	18	18
Vermont	16*	16*	18	18
Virginia	16	16	18	18
Virgin Islands	16	14	18	18
Washington	17*	17*	18	18
West Virginia	18	16	18	18
Wisconsin*	16	16	18	18
Wyoming	16*	16*	18	19

*Lower ages if court approval is obtained.
**Not below 14 for male and 13 female.

Marriage licenses

Since the state must consent to the marriage, in most states you must get a license for your marriage. In the states in which a common-law marriage is binding and legal (see page 24), statutes providing for a marriage license are merely directions. Failure to obtain a license will not affect the legality of the marriage, although it may result in a penalty for the person performing the marriage.

However, in states with laws such as those of Nebraska, which expressly state that a marriage without a license is invalid and illegal, a license is necessary and without it you will not be married.

An Alabama law directed the parties to a marriage to obtain a license but did not state, like the Nebraska law, that a marriage without a license is illegal and is no marriage. In that state, a child 15 years old forged her father's signature to a parental consent to her marriage and with that forged consent obtained a license. The court said that, unless the law clearly stated that a license was necessary for a legal and binding marriage and that without such a license the marriage was void, the marriage without a valid license was binding.

Medical certificates may be required

Since the state is concerned about the health and welfare of its citizens and prospective citizens, medical certificates or sworn statements of freedom from venereal disease (serological tests) are required of applicants for marriage licenses in many states. Moreover, in certain instances there is provision for a waiting period between the time the license application is filed and the license issued. In many instances, a court can modify the waiting time, especially for servicemen.

Requirements for a marriage license

State	Affidavit or medical certificate	Minimum waiting period
Alabama	Required	None
Alaska	Required	None
Arizona	Required	None
Arkansas	Required, but waivable	3 days (waivable)
California	Required, but waivable	None
Colorado	Required	None
Connecticut	Required, but waivable	4 days (waivable)
Delaware	Required, but waivable	1 day for residents 4 days for nonresidents
District of Columbia	Required, but waivable	3 days (waivable)
Florida	Required	3 days
Georgia	Required	3 days except where both over 18 or female pregnant
Hawaii	Required, but waivable	3 days
Idaho	Required, but waivable	None
Illinois	Required, but waivable	1 day (waivable)
Indiana	Required, but waivable	3 days (waivable)
Iowa	Required	3 days (waivable)
Kansas	Required	3 days (waivable)
Kentucky	Required, but waivable	3 days (waivable)
Louisiana	Required	None*
Maine	Required	5 days
Maryland	Not required	2 days (waivable)

Massachusetts	Required	3 days (waivable)
Michigan	Required	3 days (no waiver)
Minnesota	Not required	5 days (waivable)
Mississippi	Required	3 days (waivable)
Missouri	Not required	3 days (waivable)
Montana	Required	3 days (waivable)
Nebraska	Required, but waivable	2 days
Nevada	Not required	None
New Hampshire	Required	5 days (waivable)
New Jersey	Required	3 days (waivable)
New Mexico	Required	None
New York	Required, but waivable	10 days after serological test and 24 hours after issuance of marriage license (waivable)
North Carolina	Required, but waivable	None
North Dakota	Required, but waivable	None
Ohio	Required, but waivable	5 days (waivable)
Oklahoma	Required, but waivable	Non (3 days if below age)
Oregon	Required, but waivable	3 days (waivable)
Pennsylvania	Required, but waivable	3 days (waivable)
Puerto Rico	Required, but waivable	None
Rhode Island	Required, but waivable	None
South Carolina	Not required	1 day
South Dakota	Required	None
Tennessee	Required	3 days, unless both over 18
Texas	Required	None
Utah	Required	
Vermont	Required	None**
Virginia	Required	None
Virgin Islands	Not required	License application must be posted 8 days (waivable)
Washington	Required	3 days
West Virginia	Required, but waivable	3 days (waivable)
Wisconsin*	Required, but waivable	5 days (waivable)
Wyoming	Required, but waivable	None

*Marriage must be delayed for 3 days after issuance of marriage license (waivable).
**Marriage must be delayed for 5 days after issuance of marriage license, except for military personnel or by order of court (waivable).

Ceremonial marriages

Most people are joined in wedlock by a marriage ceremony, although other types of marriages, such as common-law, contract, and proxy marriages, are possible. The clergyman or other official who is empowered to perform your marriage ceremony is usually named in the laws of the state. Generally, the ceremony can be performed by court and city officials and by properly ordained clergymen, priests, rabbis, or other religious authorities.

What is a common-law marriage?

When a man and a woman agree that they are husband and wife, live together in this relationship, and represent it as a marriage to their friends and the public, generally, they are parties to a common-law marriage. Such an agreement is a legal marriage in some states, but in most it receives no recognition by the law.

States where common-law marriages are either valid or recognized

Alabama— valid.

Arizona— may not be contracted within the state but are recognized if valid in the state where entered into; the same is true for Arkansas, Delaware, Maine, Maryland, Michigan, Minnesota, Missouri, Nebraska, New Mexico, New York, North Carolina, Oregon, South Dakota, Tennessee, Utah, Virginia, Virgin Islands, Washington, and West Virginia.

California— valid if entered into prior to 1895. Thereafter, if entered into in another state where valid, will be recognized.

Colorado— valid.

District of Columbia— valid.

Florida— valid if entered into prior to January 1968.

Georgia— valid.

Idaho— valid.

Indiana— valid if entered into prior to January 1958.

Iowa— valid.

Kansas— valid.

Michigan— valid if entered into prior to January 1957.

Minnesota— valid if entered into prior to April 26, 1941.

Mississippi— valid if entered into prior to April 5, 1956.

Missouri— valid if entered into prior to March 31, 1921.

Montana— valid.

Nebraska— valid if entered into prior to 1923.

New Jersey— valid if entered into prior to December 1, 1939.

New York— valid if entered into prior to April 29, 1933.

Ohio— valid.

Oklahoma— valid.

Pennsylvania— valid.

Rhode Island— valid.

South Carolina— valid.

South Dakota— valid if entered into prior to July 1, 1959.

Texas— valid.

Common-law marriages are not recognized in New Hampshire, but out-of-state common-law marriages may possibly be recognized when the parties become permanent residents of the state.

Kansas recognizes them, but the parties are guilty of a misdemeanor. They are not recognized as valid in Kentucky but are considered so for recovery and distribution under certain sections of the Kentucky Worker's Compensation Law; Kentucky recognizes valid marriages of other states.

Improper ceremony

In any state where a common-law marriage is binding, if, for some reason, the marriage ceremony is not performed by a proper official, the omission will not cause the marriage to be illegal. This ruling was established in a famous case decided by the United States Supreme Court. William Mowry in 1844 went from Pittsburgh, Pennsylvania, to the Saginaw Valley in Michigan. There he fell in love with an Indian girl. They were married. Later his wife died and Mowry returned to Pittsburgh.

The law in Michigan, where Mowry and the Indian girl had been married, was that the ceremony must be performed by an ordained minister or a justice of the peace. Long afterward it was discovered that the man who married them was neither a clergyman nor a justice of the peace. With this disclosure arose the question of whether or not Mowry and his Indian bride had been legally married. The court held that whatever might have been the form of the ceremony, or whether there had been any ceremony at all, made no difference. Since the two had agreed to be husband and wife and after that had lived together as husband and wife, there was a legal marriage.

Years after this incident, another case of the same character came before the Supreme Court. In 1865, James Travers, who was living in the District of Columbia, married a West Virginia girl at Alexandria, Virginia. After the marriage they went to New Jersey to live. The girl was an orphan and only seventeen. Four or five years after the marriage she learned that the man who had performed the ceremony was not a minister but merely a friend of her husband. The Court pointed out that in any state where a common-law marriage is valid, the marriage is binding and legal and the parties are husband and wife irrespective of statutes requiring that the marriage be solemnized by a magistrate or clergyman, a license issued, or that the ceremony be performed before witnesses.

State boundaries and marriage

The failure to follow the directions contained in statutes relating to marriage and marriage licenses and ceremonies has no effect on the validity of the marriage in states recognizing common-law marriages. The laws that determine whether a marriage is binding or not are those of the state where the marriage ceremony takes place. If it is legal in the state where it is performed, it is legal everywhere, except when it is void by express provisions of statutes forbidding marriages such as those between persons closely related.

This ruling, that a marriage valid where contracted is valid everywhere, was declared to be the law many years ago in Massachusetts, and it is still the law. In that state a black man married a white woman. The Massachusetts law at the time forbade marriages between persons of the White and the Negro races. This was, however, not the law in Rhode Island. When this couple learned of the Massachusetts prohibition of their marriage, they went to Rhode Island, were married there, and then returned as husband and wife to their home in Massachusetts. When a marriage, said the Massachusetts court in this case, takes place in a state where it is allowed by law, that marriage is good everywhere. If this were not the law, you could dissolve the marriage merely by stepping across a state boundary into another state where the marriage is forbidden. In another instance, a couple traveled from Delaware to New York, went through the wedding ceremony in that state before a notary public, and lived in New York for the next ten years. During three years of the ten that they were in New York, common-law marriages were legal in that state. Later they returned to Delaware, where common-law marriages are not binding.

A few years later, when the wife brought an action for divorce in Delaware, her husband's defense was that they were not married, as the ceremony before a notary public was not a marriage and as common-law marriages were not binding in Delaware, where the divorce action had been brought.

Here again the court held that since their marriage was a binding one in New York, where they had lived as husband and wife, they were still married, following the principle that a marriage that is good in the state where it is made is good everywhere, whatever the state's law.

Marriage in a foreign country

Another case involved a man and woman who were married in Germany in a ceremony that they believed was performed by an official authorized by German law. Thereafter, they lived together as husband and wife in Germany, Austria, and later in St. Paul, Minnesota.

At the death of her husband, the woman asked to be appointed administrator of his estate. Then it appeared for the first time that the ceremony had not been performed by an official authorized under German law, although, in spite of that fact, under German law it was a true marriage.

Brushing aside the question of whether or not the marriage in Germany would be a valid marriage in Minnesota, the court said that since the marriage was valid by the law of the place where it occurred, it was legal everywhere. If the law of any state where the marriage might be questioned should govern its validity, then the marriage might be valid in one state and considered not a marriage in another.

Of course, the prohibition on degrees of relationship, discussed earlier, might be regarded as an exception to this rule.

Contract marriages

The Domestic Relations Law of New York State, although it outlaws common-law marriages consummated after April 1933, provides for marriage by a written contract, after the acquisition of a marriage license, if both parties are over 21. (With the change in the right to vote, 18 may be the more appropriate age.) This contract is signed by the man, the woman, and two witnesses. The residence of the groom, the bride, and the two witnesses are set down, together with the date and place of marriage and the future residence of the married couple. This agreement is acknowledged before a judge of a court of record in a form similar to that needed for recording a deed of real property.

Contract marriages are also recognized in Arkansas, Missouri, Montana, and South Carolina.

Contract-of-marriage form

A form of this civil contract of marriage could be:

> This agreement made this *10th* day of *January, 1958*, by and between *Jane Brown,* residing at *Albany, New York,* and *George Smith*, residing at *Albany, New York.*
>
> Witnesseth, that the said parties have this day mutually and each for himself and herself willingly agreed to become and do hereby declare themselves lawfully united in marriage in accordance with the provisions of the Domestic Relations Law of the State of New York and that on and after the date hereof each for himself and herself undertakes to assume all the obligations attendant upon the relationship of husband and wife and to be controlled in all respects by law in the

same manner and to the same extent as if the marriage of such parties had been officially solemnized by a clergyman, minister, priest, rabbi or public official.

That this contract of marriage has been executed on the above date at *Albany, New York.*

That the witnesses to such marriage are *John Greene,* residing at *Albany, New York,* and *Charles Grant,* residing at *Albany, New York,* and that the undersigned will reside at *Albany, New York.*

Witnesses: (Husband) *George Smith*
Charles Grant   (wife) *Jane Brown*
John Greene
State of New York
County of *Albany*

On this *10th* day of *January, 1958,* before me a Justice of a Court of Record of the State of New York personally appeared *Jane Brown* and *George Smith* and *Charles Grant* and *John Greene* to me personally known and known to me to be the persons described in and who executed the foregoing instrument and they duly and severally acknowledged that they executed the same for the uses and purposes therein mentioned.

David Warner
Justice of the Supreme Court of
the State of New York

Proxy marriages

The conditions created by World War II and subsequent conflicts turned the spotlight squarely on the question of whether one can marry by proxy; that is, does a marriage, to be legal, require the presence of both the man and the woman at the ceremony?

The legislature in Minnesota, in 1945, authorized such marriages until six months after World War II. The Attorney General of Kansas has declared that marriages by proxy are binding marriages in that state. They are valid in Puerto Rico. The Attorney General of New Mexico has said they are valid, but advises the parties to arrange for a regular ceremony to be performed as soon thereafter as possible. In Nebraska, if both parties are members of a religious sect that recognizes proxy marriages and the ceremony is conducted in accordance with the customs of the sect, the proxy marriage is presumably valid. These marriages have frequently occurred in Oklahoma with no adverse effects. In Texas a marriage performed by proxy because the couple are separated by military service is legal.

However, in 32 states marriages by proxy are expressly forbidden by statute.

If you are married in this manner in a foreign country where such a marriage is legal, our courts have repeatedly held the marriage is legal in this country.

Proxy marriage held to be a common-law marriage

During World War II, Margaret was living at Palm Beach, Florida. She had promised Jerry, who was in the armed forces, that she would marry him as soon as her divorce from her husband permitted her to do so. The divorce became final and she was free to marry. In the meantime Jerry had been transferred overseas and was in Scotland.

Under these conditions the two agreed by letter they would be married by proxy, as such a marriage was legal under the laws of Florida. An application for a marriage license was forwarded to Jerry in Scotland. This he filled out and returned to Florida. The application was filed and the license issued. The ceremony was then performed by a county judge, with a friend of Jerry, acting with his authorization, as proxy for the groom. Some months later Jerry died in Europe, never having returned to this country. The question arose whether Margaret was entitled as his wife to his insurance. The Federal court in Florida said the marriage was legal and binding and Margaret was the lawful widow.

However, in Florida, common-law marriages are legal. The marriage between the bride at Palm Beach and the groom in Scotland was legal in that state as a common-law marriage. Whether the proxy marriage would have been legal if common-law marriages were not accepted in the state where the ceremony was performed was not decided.

This proxy marriage held valid

In New York State, where proxy marriages are not valid and where common law marriages are now no longer legal, another case arose involving a young soldier named Raymond. He was with the armed forces outside the country and his fiancée was living in the District of Columbia.

His brother acted as his proxy, and the ceremony was performed by a justice of the United States District Court in Washington, D.C. It should be pointed out that, ordinarily, United States judges have no power to perform a marriage ceremony inasmuch as that is a state function, but in the District of Columbia, the local judges are Federal.

After Raymond was discharged from the army, he and his wife lived together for some months. Then he deserted her and refused to support either his wife or their child. The laws of the District of Columbia do not require both the man and the woman to be present either for the issuance of the marriage license or for the marriage ceremony itself. Nor do they provide that either of the parties may be absent. Nothing in this regard is set out in the statutes.

In the action brought by the wife in New York, the court held that the marriage was binding and that the husband was responsible for the support of his wife and child because all the statutory requirements of the District of Columbia had been met and the proxy marriage ceremony later affirmed and accepted by the husband.

The performance of a marriage ceremony in the absence of either the groom or the bride is as old as history, but new in this country. As an institution, it has not yet stood the test of time, and you should not, unless it is absolutely necessary, adopt this method for a marriage until its validity is better settled and more seasoned by time and use; your lawyer can better advise you on the law of your jurisdiction.

How to make property settlements before marriage

Your wife or husband, when you marry, acquires an interest in any property you have. In many states, a widow has a dower right, a life interest in one-third of all the real property her husband owned during their marriage; the husband has a curtesy right, a life interest in the real property owned by his wife at the time of her death. Further, when either husband or wife dies, the law in most states provides that the other has an interest in the estate of the one who has died no matter what the will of the deceased may provide.

This interest which the law gives to the husband or wife in the property of the other when they marry is often a source of trouble, not only at the death of either of them, but sometimes in the conduct of everyday business affairs.

To avoid this inconvenience, you can enter into a contract or agreement with the man or woman you are planning to marry, before the marriage, which will dispose of these rights in each other's property for all time and leave you free to do with your property after your marriage as you wish. Such instruments are sometimes called prenuptial agreements or in some cases antenuptial agreements.

A representative agreement of this sort, made before a marriage, provided that the property of the husband—if he should die first and there were no children—should belong to his wife. When the husband died, the widow assumed that the property was hers. Her husband's relatives claimed the ownership in spite of the agreement. The court said that an agreement such as this was favored by the courts and would be enforced. The courts have held similar agreements legal and enforceable whenever they were fair and equitable in their terms and entered into in good faith. However, there can be problems so you need legal counsel to prepare the document. A federal government employee's pension forms must be properly filled out and filed and a prenuptial agreement is not adequate. And, in a case in New York, in a prenuptial agreement a publisher named his son as sole beneficiary of his pension. After he died his widow made a claim. The Second Circuit Court of Appeals ruled that she had not waived her claim against the pension by signing the prenuptial agreement during the engagement. Only a spouse can waive such rights so any agreement must be signed after marriage.

Form for property settlement before marriage

Whereas *James Lennox* and *Mary Powers* are about to enter into a contract of marriage, and whereas *James Lennox* is the owner of certain real estate and personal property at this date, and *Mary Powers* is also the owner of certain real estate and personal property at this date, and whereas *James Lennox* and *Mary Powers* may at any time be desirous of disposing of said real estate divested of the curtesy, dower, or other claims of the said *James Lennox* and *Mary Powers*, either by deed or will: now, therefore, in consideration of said *James Lennox* and *Mary Powers* consummating the said contract of marriage, said *James Lennox* and *Mary Powers* hereby agree to waive and release and do hereby waive and release and forever quit claim and renounce all dower, curtesy, and other interest in and to the said real estate and personal property that said *James Lennox* and *Mary Powers* may now have or hereafter acquire by any means whatever. The intention being hereby to leave the absolute disposal of said real estate and other property now owned or hereafter acquired by either of them, unless taken in their joint names, so that at the death of the said *James Lennox* and *Mary Powers,* all of the property of the said *James Lennox* and *Mary Powers*, real, personal, and mixed, shall descend to his or her lawful heirs, released and divested of all claims of dower, curtesy, or other interest that the said *James Lennox* and *Mary Powers* might have as widow or widower. And in consideration of the consummation of said marriage, said *James Lennox and Mary Powers* hereby release, cancel, and waive all claims to all property of said *James Lennox* and *Mary Powers* to which they might be entitled as wife or widow, husband or widower.

Such an agreement, of course, should be properly signed, witnessed, and notarized. Your lawyer will consider with you the other aspects of such an agreement, which does not in itself settle your estate but merely leaves you free to dispose of it by will or otherwise.

Engagement ring

An engagement ring is considered to be in the nature of a pledge for the contract of marriage. Subject to local statutes, the general rule is that if the man breaches the pledge, the girl can keep the ring. However, if she breaks the engagement, she is required, upon demand, to return the ring, on the theory that it constituted a conditional gift. Occasionally one finds an interesting variation on this situation.

A married man sued for the return of a valuable diamond engagement ring, or, in the alternative, for its asserted value of $60,000. He had been living apart from his wife, and they contemplated a divorce. He had given the ring to another woman upon the promise that she would marry him if and when he became free. Shortly after receipt of the ring, she told him that she had "second thoughts" about the matter and decided against the marriage. However, she retained her first thought about keeping the ring. The highest court in New York State held that she could keep the ring because, as long as he was married, it was against the public policy of the State of New York to enforce an arrangement that contemplated a divorce, and accordingly the condition was removed from the gift, and the girl could keep the ring.

For a variation of the foregoing, consider the situation in a New York case where a man arranged to have his girlfriend's apartment decorated. He had already paid a very substantial sum on account, with over $30,000 still to be paid, when he decided to marry someone else. The decorator sued him on the contract, but also sued the girl on the basis of unjust enrichment, asking that she also be responsible for paying the remaining amount due. She contended that it was a gift to her, and that she had no responsibility. However, she had been intimately involved in every step of the arrangements as to color, style, etc., and so the court held that since she was involved in the selection of materials, she was also liable to the decorator, who had done his job, as requested, and had no interest in this almost domestic tableau.

Breach of promise to marry

When you agree to marry, the two of you by this act of agreeing make a contract in the eyes of the law. Here, as with any other contract, the refusal of either person to carry out the agreement to marry is a breach of contract for which damages can be recovered. Lawsuits for breach of marriage promise, by the way, are almost always brought by the woman. In California, Mansell promised Anna he would marry her as soon as his affairs were straightened out. The promise continued for two years. Always the straightening out of his affairs was his excuse for the postponement of the marriage.

Finally, Anna sued him and the case was decided in her favor. Here the court declared not only that the promise of each one to the other made a contract, but that the failure of Mansell to agree to, or set, a definite date for the marriage did not excuse him from carrying out his obligation. Further, even if no date were set, it was implied in the marriage agreement that the ceremony was to take place within a reasonable time. In recent years, actions for damages for breach of promise to marry have come to be looked upon with disfavor by many courts and the public at large. Too often in the past, unscrupulous women have constructed agreements to marry with only their own hopes and wishful thinking as building materials.

Now laws forbidding or modifying actions for breach of promise to marry exist in Alabama, California, Colorado, Florida, Indiana, Maine, Maryland (unless there is a pregnancy), Massachusetts, Michigan, Nevada, New Hampshire, New Jersey, New York, Pennsylvania, and Wyoming. In Illinois, such a law was held unconstitutional in 1946, and thereafter a law limiting damages and restricting the action was enacted. In Tennessee, if there is no written evidence of the contract it must be proved by two disinterested witnesses.

When the statute abolishing suits for breach of promise to marry was passed in New York State, its highest court carefully considered the effect of the statute. It declared that the marriage state ought not to be lightly entered into, since it involves the most profound interests of human life.

"From such a standpoint we view the marriage engagement as a period of probation, so to speak, for both parties—their opportunity for finding one another out; and if that probation results in developing incompatibility of tastes and temperament, coldness, suspicion and incurable repugnance of one to the other, . . . duty requires that the match be broken off." This statement explains why laws are enacted to ban breach of promise suits. While the right to sue for breach of promise has been abolished in some states, as well as a suit for fraud or misrepresentation for a false promise to marry, there may still be an action for deceit in inducing and entering into a marriage that is void because the deceitful party is already married.

Alienation of affections

Although laws abolishing actions for breach of the marriage promise generally also have abolished actions for the alienation of the affections of either party to the marriage through the influence of some third person, cases do arise because adultery by the partners is ever present. Alienation of affections generally is the robbing of husband or wife of the conjugal affection, society, fellowship and comfort which inhere in the normal marriage relation. In Maryland and Virginia the language used is "intentional infliction of emotional harm."

In Iowa, when a husband's affection for his aunt caused a break-up of his marriage, his wife sued the aunt. The aunt paid a money judgment after it was proved she had actively sought her nephew's love. In a Kentucky case a $12,000 award was made to a man for the alienation of his wife's affection.

Domestic violence

Less than a century ago, under the common law, it was legal for a husband to beat his wife. There are today, however, a number of legal avenues that battered spouses can pursue to find protection from physical and emotional abuse. Although most cases involve women, men may also seek protection.

You may file a criminal complaint against the attacker if you have been physically abused. Although the length of the criminal process may discourage a victim of violence from pursuing a criminal case, if the injuries are severe and have been reported, a warrant to arrest the attacker may be issued in order to prevent recurring assaults and injuries. A civil remedy is an alternative. Since 1970, over 30 states have passed legislation that relates to domestic violence. In some jurisdictions, these laws are referred to as the *Intrafamily Offense Act*. Since each state's law may be different, it is important to determine whether the action complained of is covered and whether the victim is protected under the Act. One example might be where a man physically assaults his ex-wife, but the Act only protects a spouse. In that situation, the ex-wife cannot file a charge under the Act.

The remedies allowed under the Act also vary from state to state. Some provide for emergency remedies, such as a temporary restraining order. The selection of a particular legal remedy should be done very carefully in cases of domestic violence since the attacker may respond with further violence.

You may also sue the police department in federal court if they have failed to protect you from your violent spouse. Tracey Thurman won a two million dollar judgement in Connecticut. Connecticut and New Jersey now have laws requiring arrests in domestic assaults regardless of the spouse's wishes.

It may be wise for an abused spouse to seek help and shelter from friends or agencies. If you are suffering from domestic violence check with your community's social service agencies, *Women's Bar Association* or *Legal Aid Society* on your legal course of action. Don't be deterred, even if your spouse is a prominent member of the community.

Further discussion on this issue can be found in Chapter 6, *Wife and Mother* (Spousal abuse).

Interspousal immunity

This is a doctrine which protects spouses from being sued for injury by their partners. It is based on a common law holding that spouses had a single legal existence and you could not sue yourself. There have been a number of cases where the theory has been tested. But you have to know whether your state permits a lawsuit for personal injury against a spouse. A majority of states now allow suit, although 9 states plus the District of Columbia still maintain full interspousal tort immunity. In 5 states, a wife can sue her husband for intentional tort but not mere negligence. This ability to sue is particularly important in cases involving the transmission of the AIDS virus and other infectious diseases, such as genital herpes. What happens if there is fraud and willful nondisclosure of the existence of a disease? Can the marriage be annulled? What about divorce? How does the secret infection affect how marital assets are distributed in a divorce proceeding? What happens if a spouse is falsely accused of having or passing a disease? Can the existence of infection affect child custody?

Generally, there can be an annulment; however, if you continue to cohabit after being informed of the infection, you have waived your rights. The infection can be the basis for an assertion of extreme cruelty or it can work together with other charges of cruelty to justify a divorce. Also, it can be used to show adultery. It can affect a settlement of the marital assets, even in community property states, and it can cause a court to order payment by the errant spouse of all medical expenses of the innocent partner.

As to child custody, the existence of an infectious disease can be used to prove parental unfitness. Or, as in one case, visitation rights of a father carrying the AIDS virus was deemed to be a physical danger to his minor child's well-being and he was denied visitation rights.

Confidential communications

Any communication between spouses is considered confidential and the general rule is that spouses cannot testify, in a court of law, against one another. However, there are exceptions to this rule. For example, in a case where one spouse assaults the other, or where one spouse tries to silence the other by force or with threats, this rule may not hold up. Should a third party hear any of the communication between the spouses, then, of course, it is no longer confidential.

In one particular case, a wife admitted to her husband that she had committed an act of adultery. A New York Court allowed this confidential communication as evidence in their divorce proceeding since the incompetency to testify rule is based on maintaining the marital relationship and the loyalty, affection, and confidence the relationship engenders and none of this was left in that case.

Surrogates

Many married couples cannot have children. Technology now can assist with in vitro fertilization. This has created the surrogate who carries the child. Usually the couple finds a willing surrogate and arranges for the birth for a fee. Sometimes an egg from the woman is placed in the surrogate's womb. Sometimes the spouse donates sperm to the surrogate's own egg. There have been over 20,000 surrogate births. However, the arrangement has spawned public lawsuits over who legally is the parent and much acrimony over the payment of fees for the process.

There are at least 18 states which now have banned or restricted surrogate parenting for profit. Virginia and New York are the two states where the most arrangements have been made. Florida and New Hampshire's laws presume that a child's biological parents are the legal parents but they must go to court to be so declared. In California, the highest court upheld a surrogate contract where a surrogate who carried a couple's test tube baby decided she wanted to keep it. The court said people's intentions are important and the natural mother was the one who intended the birth and intended to raise the child, in this case not the surrogate.

Divorce

Chapter 2
Divorce

Since the state has a special interest in creating the marital relationship, it also provides for its severance. Each jurisdiction sets up its own grounds for divorce and separation (separation is discussed in the next chapter). Two kinds of divorce are provided by law. One is an *absolute divorce* that dissolves the marriage and releases both husband and wife from the obligation of marriage, except for the husband's duty to support his wife and any children. (In this context, it is interesting to note that the state of Florida has ruled that, as of July 1, 1972, such proceedings in that state will no longer be referred to as "divorce," but rather as "dissolution of marriage.") The second type of "divorce" is a *separation by the court*, a separation "from bed and board," with a determination of the amount to be paid by the husband for the support of the wife.

This is an area about which there has been a great deal of controversy through the years. Many critics have felt that the variety of divorce rules has led to divorce shopping, and that only those couples with money could take advantage of divorce statutes.

As a result, a number of states have subscribed to the *Uniform Divorce Recognition Act*, an act that discourages migration in pursuit of divorce. These states, contrary to the usual practice of recognizing the legal actions of sister states, refuse to recognize out-of-state divorces obtained by their own citizens. They are Louisiana, Maine, Massachusetts, Montana, Nebraska, New Hampshire, New Jersey, North Dakota, Rhode Island, South Carolina, Washington, and Wisconsin.

New York has a provision, which many think unenforceable, declaring that if you get a divorce outside the state, but have lived in New York 12 months before and returned within 18 months after, it is evidence that you were domiciled in New York at the time of the out-of-state divorce.

Because of the stringency of some divorce statutes, critics have alleged that fraud is common in the procurement of many divorces. In 1966, the State of New York, where adultery was the only ground, broadened the basis for divorce. A divorce may now be obtained on the grounds of cruel and inhuman treatment, either physical or mental; abandonment for one year or more; confinement in prison for three years or more; adultery; and separation for one year pursuant to a court decree of separation or a written agreement between the parties, filed with the County Clerk.

A famous case interpreting the changed New York law involved Jackie Gleason. Prior to 1966, his wife obtained a separation decree under the new law, Jackie Gleason sued for a divorce based on their living apart for the required period of time, pursuant to the separation decree with which he had complied. The wife objected, contending that it was unfair to allow the new law to be retroactive, especially where it affects the rights of the non-guilty party (here the wife) who obtained the separation decree under the old law. The court decided that the legislative purpose of the new law was to make irrelevant the concept of guilt or innocence. It is the fact of separation pursuant to a decree or written agreement, the terms of which have been complied with, that determines the situation, and the divorce was permitted.

Court decisions in the various states throughout the country differ in their interpretations of the meaning of the grounds for divorce. The facts of adultery for which a wife may be granted a divorce in the state of New York may not sustain a similar decree elsewhere in the country. Likewise, the judicial interpretations of cruelty as a cause for divorce are especially diverse and range from reasons of incompatibility and mental stress to brutal treatment that actually endangers the life and health of the spouse.

Further, grounds that in one state may sustain an absolute divorce may, in other states, be causes for annulment or merely for separation from bed and board.

The causes for which an absolute divorce are granted in the different states are listed on the following pages. Later in this chapter it is explained just what these causes may mean according to the law.

Grounds for divorce

Alabama—Impotency; adultery; abandonment for one year; conviction of felony and imprisonment; sodomy; habitual drunkenness or drug addiction; insanity; undisclosed pregnancy of wife by man other than husband at time of marriage; physical violence; nonsupport for two years; irretrievable breakdown of marriage; complete incompatibility of temperament.

Alaska—Impotency; adultery; conviction of felony; desertion; cruelty; habitual drunkenness or drug addiction; incompatibility.

Arizona—Marriage is irretrievably broken and conciliation requirements have been met.

Arkansas—Impotency; desertion for one year; either party having husband or wife living at time of marriage; conviction of felony; habitual drunkenness for one year; adultery; failure to cohabit for three years; cruel and barbarous treatment endangering life; insanity; indignities; willful nonsupport.

California—Insanity; irreconcilable differences causing irremediable breakdown of marriage.

Colorado—Irretrievable breakdown of marriage.

Connecticut—Adultery; fraudulent contract of marriage; desertion for three years; seven years absence without being heard from; habitual drunkenness; cruelty; conviction of felony; insanity

Delaware—Irretrievable breakdown of marriage.

District of Columbia—Voluntary separation for six months or separation for one year.

Florida—Mental incompetence; irretrievable breakdown of marriage.

Georgia—Husband and wife related within prohibited degree; insanity; impotency; force or fraud in securing marriage; undisclosed pregnancy of wife by man other than husband at time of marriage; adultery; desertion for one year; conviction of felony; habitual drunkenness or use of drugs; cruelty; insanity; irretrievable breakdown of marriage.

Hawaii—Expiration of term in decree of separate bed and board; separation of two years or more under decree of separate maintenance; voluntary separation for two years or more without cohabitation; irretrievable breakdown of marriage.

Idaho—Adultery; cruelty; desertion; nonsupport; habitual drunkenness; conviction of felony; insanity; failure to cohabit for five years; irreconcilable differences.

Illinois—Impotency; either party having husband or wife living at time of marriage; adultery; desertion for one year; habitual drunkenness or use of drugs for two years; cruelty; conviction of felony; communicating venereal disease; attempt by either spouse on life of other.

Indiana—Impotency; conviction of felony; insanity; irretrievable breakdown of marriage.

Iowa—Irretrievable breakdown of marriage.

Kansas—Desertion for one year; adultery; cruelty; habitual drunkenness; nonsupport; conviction of felony; insanity; incompatibility.

Kentucky—Irretrievable breakdown of marriage.

Louisiana—Adultery; conviction of felony; cruelty; public defamation; abandonment; attempt on life of other; nonsupport; separation for one year with no reconciliation during that time; voluntary separation for six months with no reconciliation; fugitive from justice.

Maine—Adultery; impotency; nonsupport; desertion for three years; habitual drunkenness or drug addiction; cruelty; irreconcilable differences.

Maryland—Impotency; insanity; adultery; desertion for 12 months; voluntary separation for 12 months and involuntary separation for three years; either party having husband or wife living at time of marriage; conviction of felony; consanguinity.

Massachusetts—Adultery; impotency; desertion for one year; habitual drunkenness or drug addiction; cruelty; nonsupport; conviction of felony; irretrievable breakdown of marriage.

Michigan—Irretrievable breakdown of marriage.

Minnesota—Irretrievable breakdown of marriage.

Mississippi—Impotency; adultery; conviction of felony; desertion for one year; habitual drunkenness or drug addiction; cruelty; insanity; either party having husband or wife living at time of marriage; undisclosed pregnancy of wife, not by husband, at time of marriage; consanguinity; irreconcilable differences.

Missouri—Irretrievable breakdown of marriage.

Montana—Irretrievable breakdown of marriage.

Nebraska—Irretrievable breakdown of marriage.

Nevada—Insanity; separation for one year; incompatibility.

New Hampshire—Impotency; adultery; cruelty; conviction of felony; violent temper; nonsupport; habitual drunkenness for two years; separation; member of religious sect believing cohabitation unlawful and refusing to cohabit for six months; desertion; absence for two years and not heard from; wife out of state two years; husband abroad intending to become foreign citizen; irreconcilable differences.

New Jersey—Adultery; desertion for one year; cruelty; separation for 18 consecutive months; addiction or habitual drunkenness for one year; institutionalization for mental illness for two years; imprisonment for 18 months; deviate sexual conduct.

New Mexico—Desertion; adultery; cruelty; incompatibility.

New York—Adultery; cruel and inhuman treatment either physical or mental; abandonment for one year; confinement in prison for three years; separation for one year pursuant to court decree or judgment or pursuant to formal written agreement.

North Carolina—Adultery; impotency; undisclosed pregnancy of wife by man other than husband at time of marriage; separation for one year; sodomy; insanity.

North Dakota—Adultery; cruelty; desertion for one year; nonsupport for one year; habitual drunkenness for one year; conviction of felony; insanity; irreconcilable differences.

Ohio—Either party having husband or wife living at time of marriage; desertion for one year; adultery; impotency; cruelty; fraudulent contract of marriage; nonsupport; habitual drunkenness; conviction of felony; divorce by either spouse outside of state; insanity; separation for two years during which time the parties did not live together as husband and wife.

Oklahoma—Either party having obtained a divorce outside of the state; desertion for one year; adultery; impotency; undisclosed pregnancy of wife by man other than husband at time of marriage; cruelty; fraudulent contract of marriage; habitual drunkenness; nonsupport; conviction of felony; insanity; incompatibility.

Oregon—Irretrievable breakdown of marriage.

Pennsylvania—Either party having husband or wife still living at time of marriage; adultery on part of either party; desertion for one year; cruelty; conviction of felony; violent temper; insanity; irretrievable breakdown of marriage.

Puerto Rico—Adultery; conviction of felony; drunkenness or use of drugs; cruelty; desertion for one year; impotency; spouse corrupts or prostitutes children; separation for two years; insanity; divorce by mutual consent recognized by case law in cases where there are no children.

Rhode Island—Impotency; adultery; cruelty; desertion for five years; habitual drunkenness or drug addiction; neglect; conviction of felony; insanity; separation for three years; nonsupport for one year; either party having husband or wife living at time of marriage; under age of consent; related within prohibited degree; gross misbehavior; irretrievable breakdown of marriage.

South Carolina—Adultery; desertion for one year; habitual drunkenness; physical cruelty; habitual drug addiction; separation for one year in which the parties did not live together as husband and wife.

South Dakota—Adultery; cruelty; desertion for one year; nonsupport for one year; habitual drunkenness; conviction of felony; insanity.

Tennessee—Impotency; either party having husband or wife living at time of marriage; adultery; desertion for one year; conviction of felony; violent temper; unnatural behavior; habitual drunkenness or drug abuse; undisclosed pregnancy of wife by man other than husband at time of marriage; nonsupport; cruelty; willful neglect; wife's absence for two years; attempt on life of others; separation for two years; barring spouse from home; irreconcilable differences.

Texas—Cruelty; adultery; desertion for one year; separation for three years; conviction of felony; insanity; irretrievable breakdown of marriage.

Utah—Impotency, adultery; desertion for one year; habitual drunkenness; conviction of felony; cruelty; insanity; nonsupport; separation for three years under court decree.

Vermont—Adultery; conviction of felony; cruelty; desertion or absence for seven years and not heard of during that time; nonsupport; insanity; husband and wife living apart for 6 consecutive months.

Virginia—Adultery; conviction of felony; desertion of one year; sodomy; separation for one year; cruelty.

Virgin Islands—Irretrievable breakdown of marriage.

Washington—Irretrievable breakdown of marriage.

West Virginia—Adultery; conviction of felony; desertion for 6 months; cruelty; attempt by one spouse on life of other; habitual drunkenness or drug addiction; separation for one year; insanity; abuse or neglect of child; irreconcilable differences.

Wisconsin—Irretrievable breakdown of marriage.

Wyoming—Insanity; irreconcilable differences.

"No Fault" Divorce

The prevailing view in America today on divorce is that people who do not wish to remain married should not be forced to do so. With the exception of Illinois and South Dakota, all the other states permit some form of "no fault" divorce, thereby eliminating the necessity of establishing one party's guilt in the breakup of the marriage. For example, some states, like Arizona and Washington, have completely abandoned the notion of fault. In these states, the only ground for divorce is "irretrievable breakdown of marriage." On the other hand, states like Idaho and Kansas have retained many of the traditional fault grounds for divorce, but have added "no fault" grounds like "irreconcilable differences" or "incompatibility."

A New Jersey Case

As in several other states, a couple may obtain a divorce in New Jersey merely by establishing that they have lived "separate and apart" for a period of time established by statute, 18 months in New Jersey. Unfortunately for Mr. Ellam, the New Jersey court was not so liberal in its interpretation of "separate and apart" as the courts in several other states have been.

Mr. Ellam and his wife purchased a home in Elizabeth, New Jersey, in June 1972. One month later, Mr. Ellam moved into his mother's house, which was nearby. Because Mr. and Mrs. Ellam did not want their neighbors to know of their separation, they maintained the appearance of living a normal married life together. On weekday mornings, Mr. Ellam's mother drove him to the marital home where he would let himself in, get the car out of the garage and drive to work. He returned in the evening, staying at the house until 12:30 AM at which time his mother would arrive to pick him up. He occasionally ate his meals there, but always brought the food with him. He spent all his weekends at the marital home, doing odd jobs around the house. Mr. and Mrs. Ellam even continued to accept social engagements as a couple. This continued until May, 1973. At no time during this period did the couple engage in sexual relations. On March 1, 1974, Mr. Ellam petitioned for divorce on the grounds of having lived "separate and apart" for 18 months as required under New Jersey law.

The New Jersey court held that although Mr. and Mrs. Ellam had resided in different habitations for more than the statutory period, they had not been living separate and apart. In order to satisfy the statutory requirement, the parties must have been living apart in such a manner as to show those in the neighborhood that they are not living together. Mr. Ellam's petition for divorce was denied.

One mate at a time

Polygamy was recognized by certain religious groups in our early history; however, present law permits you but one wife or husband at a time. The application of this law in the vast majority of instances is simple.

It is not always simple, however, in a world where wars and revolutions are a frequent occurrence and every generation witnesses the mass migrations of thousands of persons, desperately fleeing for their lives.

An extraordinary situation, involving insoluble doubts, arose some years ago in New York. In May, 1913, Emanuel and Molly Hayden were married at Ekaterinoslav, in Russia. Two years later, at the outbreak of World War I, Emanuel was drafted into the Imperial Russian Army.

He was captured by the Germans at Branowitz, Minsk, made a prisoner of war, and held at Munster, in Westphalia. Before his capture he had written regularly to his wife but never received a reply. In the spring of 1916 a friend and fellow prisoner told him Molly had been murdered in a Russian pogrom. On the day of the Armistice, Emanuel escaped into Holland and there found employment as an attache at the Russian Embassy.

A year later he migrated to the United States and made his home in New York City.

He had continued sending letters to his wife at the place where they had their home. In 1921, six years after his induction into the Russian Army, he heard through another source that both his wife and baby had been killed.

Convinced at last that this was the truth, Emanuel married for a second time and a child was born to him and his new wife. In 1923, he learned that Molly and their baby had escaped the pogrom at Ekaterinoslav and had fled to the city of Kiev, and that his wife had made constant but unsuccessful efforts to find his whereabouts. He immediately forwarded her passage money for herself and the child. At the same time, by mutual agreement, he and his second wife separated. In the action which he later brought for an annulment of this second marriage, the court established the legitimacy of the child with a complete exoneration of the husband.

The tragedy of this family of Russian refugees would gain the sympathy of any court. They were guiltless victims of a world condition in no way of their making.

Cruelty and what it means

The definitions of "cruelty" as a cause for divorce are often so inadequate that they create confusion even in the minds of the courts. The line dividing cruelty that justifies a divorce or separation from the misunderstandings and disagreements to which every family is sometimes heir is not drawn with precision.

While cruelty that is inflicted by either one of a married couple is in most states a cause for divorce, it is not always clear what the legislatures have intended by the use of that term. Cruelty in one instance is not necessarily cruelty in another. Physical abuse is easier to determine. But the mental stresses of a mobile, automated society are not as easily gauged. One harsh and unkind act alone may not be cruel, but the same act, continued over weeks and months, can readily entitle its victim to freedom from the marriage. The cat's suffering was not less because its tail was cut off a little at a time.

Where the divorce is not contested, one finds that the courts are more lenient in accepting certain circumstances as constituting cruelty.

Rudeness is not cruelty

At one end of any catalog of the definitions of cruelty is an often mentioned Illinois case. For three years the husband had been not only a drunkard but a notorious one. He had on occasions torn the dress from his wife, threatened to kill her, repeatedly struck and bruised her face and body, and barred the door of their home against her. The wife was given a divorce.

In another instance in that same state, a husband had failed to provide proper food and shelter. The court said the wife could manage well enough. "Mere austerities of temper, petulance of manners, rudeness of language and want of civil attentions, occasional sallies of passion, denials of little indulgences and particular accommodations, which do not threaten bodily harm, are not legal cruelty." This is generally the rule. You may seek consolation from the "Advice to the Lovelorn" column, but not in the courts.

What is mental cruelty?

In a Florida case the husband, a doctor, became overfond of his nurse and receptionist. He subjected his wife to no physical cruelty, but her suffering over his affair was long and intense. In one instance she followed the automobile of her husband in the car of a friend and observed her husband and the other woman engaging in demonstrations of considerable affection. As a result, she was so sick in mind that she required treatment for hysteria.

The opinion of the court in this case discloses the other extreme cruelty recognized by the courts. "It is a matter of common knowledge that mental pain and suffering, that thing commonly called worry, is one of the major afflictions which result in the destruction of both mental and physical health. It affects every vital organ and probably results in more mental and physical wrecks than any other one affliction."

The wife was granted a divorce because of cruelty. In some states a divorce would have been denied, since physical violence and threats to health and life were lacking.

Physical impotency as a for divorce

The legal definition of impotency is: "Such incurable sexual incapacity of one of the parties at the time of marriage as prevents true and natural copulation. It is such deformity or weakness as prevents the consummation of marriage by sexual intercourse. It is not sterility nor barrenness, nor is it pregnancy by another at the time of marriage."

A recent decision states that not only must this condition exist at the time of the separation preceding the suit for a divorce or annulment of the marriage, but it must also have existed at the time of the marriage and be an incurable condition. The inability of either husband or wife to maintain normal sexual intercourse at the time of their marriage is cause in some jurisdictions for divorce or annulment. On the other hand, barrenness or sterility of which the victim is ignorant provides no ground for such an action.

The ability to become a parent is not, under the law, an essential element of the marriage contract. The ability to maintain normal and complete sexual intercourse is such a condition.

The courts draw a sharp distinction between the inability to procreate children and the inability to maintain sexual intercourse. Were mere sterility, in the absence of fraud, a cause for divorce, the consequences would be disastrous. Such conditions are common after men and women have passed the prime of life. Many marriages are childless.

Courts would inflict great injustice if they deprived a person with such a condition of the privileges of the marriage relationship. However, a fraudulent concealment of sterility known to its sufferer before marriage is ground for annulment or divorce if cohabitation (sexual intercourse) ceases immediately upon the discovery of the condition by the other spouse and court action is not delayed. Such a fraud destroys the marriage agreement itself. Fraud otherwise may be a basis for annulment or divorce.

What about fraud?

A marriage contract, like any other contract, must represent an agreement between the parties.

In everyday business, if a seller leads you to believe you are buying a new product and then delivers a second-hand article and knows he is doing so, he is not selling you what you thought you were buying and the agreement between the two of you is dissolved.

With marriage, too, when an essential condition is known to one party and concealed by him from the other, there is not a completed agreement between the parties. Such an act of concealment is fraud. If it is of enough importance, the courts will annul the marriage, or grant a divorce.

Epilepsy before marriage

A typical case of fraud involved a woman who had suffered from attacks of epilepsy since childhood and married without telling her husband about her condition. He learned about it for the first time 12 years later, when it became necessary for him to place her in an institution for treatment. This act of concealment, according to the court, was a fraud that entitled the husband to a dissolution of the marriage. He had not married the woman he thought he was marrying but the one she knew he was marrying.

At one time, epilepsy was a bar to marriage in some states because it was considered a mental illness. In 1957, Pennsylvania, for example, lifted the restriction, making it unnecessary for epileptics to obtain special judicial permission for marriage. In signing the bill, the Governor said that research showed epilepsy no longer was considered a mental illness. However, it might still be considered as a possible basis for a fraud action, in some jurisdictions, to dissolve the marriage if the situation was such as set forth in the example.

No act of concealment

By way of contrast, let us examine a similar case from which, however, the factor of concealment was missing. A wife, by reason of a physical deformity, was unable to maintain sexual intercourse. Unlike the epileptic girl, she did not know of her condition, never having indulged in sexual intercourse before her marriage. The court held there had been no fraud and under the laws of the state the marriage could not be annulled.

In another case, a young girl was committed to a hospital for the insane and there treated for three months. She was discharged as cured. Later she was again sent to the hospital for seven months and again discharged as cured. For eight years after that she lived a normal, healthy life, with no reason to think her mental illness would recur.

This girl got married. Three years later, in consequence of childbirth, she suffered another attack and was committed to a hospital by her husband. He refused to continue living with her, claiming the marriage was fraudulent and he was no longer liable for her support.

The court refused to set the marriage aside. The girl believed that she had been cured and honestly held that belief when she had married her husband. Insanity, epilepsy, and similar conditions must be known or believed to exist at the time of marriage if, by fraudulent concealment, they are to affect the validity of a marriage. No party to a marriage can be penalized for not disclosing facts that are outside his knowledge.

Undisclosed pregnancy at marriage—a fraud

A woman who is pregnant by a man other than the one she is marrying, if she fails to disclose her condition before the marriage, will be responsible for a fraud for which her marriage may be either annulled or dissolved by a divorce decree.

A case of this sort occurred in New Jersey when an 18-year-old boy was for the first time sexually intimate with a girl a few months younger. Two weeks later she told the boy she was pregnant and that he was the father of her baby. In a week the two were married. Six months afterward the baby was born, a fine and healthy child, normal in every way but conceived, according to medical testimony, three months or more before the intimacy between the boy and the girl he had married.

On this evidence the court annulled the marriage, ruling that the wife was guilty of fraud.

Adulterous pregnancy

Although an undisclosed pregnancy with another man's child at the time in marriage of a marriage voids it or makes it voidable, any child born of lawfully married parents is presumed to be the child of both parents. In some states, however, this can be overcome by proof that the child is the offspring of an adulterous relationship. Still, in every instance, any effort to show the father of the child to be other than the husband of the mother is hedged about with legal safeguards for the protection of the child.

Mental deficiency

The extent to which insanity may be grounds for the dissolution or annulment of a marriage is governed by the statutes of the state in which the parties reside. A below-par mentality is not insanity. The continuation of the marriage relation does not rest on the I.Q. rating of either party. Whether a spouse is a moron or a potential Phi Beta Kappa is a question that does not concern the courts, nor is there any point between these extremes where the law prevents one from becoming a party to a marriage contract.

The necessity for court interference in some instances of mental incapacity, however, clearly appears in a Mississippi action brought on that ground to set aside a marriage.

Annulment on grounds of insanity

Parkinson, a fairly successful businessman, was engaged to be married. The engagement was broken by the girl. The shock and disappointment affected him mentally and he began suffering from delusions of grandeur, holding exalted ideas of his importance. He lost his business and became abnormally excitable and irresponsible. After a couple of years his family had him adjudged insane and confined to a hospital in Mississippi.

At that time he had considerable property. An aunt was appointed his guardian. At the hospital he was considered harmless and allowed to spend weekends at nearby towns. On one of these furloughs he met Eleanor Seay. During the next three months he visited her on these weekend trips. Finally he and Eleanor were married.

When Parkinson had first met this woman, his grandeur complexes had manifested themselves in extravagant statements of his wealth and the extent of his property holdings. Shortly after the ceremony she inaugurated a campaign to obtain control of his property. This ended with an action by the aunt, his guardian, followed by a decree annulling the marriage on the ground of Parkinson's insanity.

Insanity after marriage

A different situation is presented when insanity arises after the marriage. Of such conditions one court has said, summing up the opinions of many:

"No principle of justice or morality will justify the severance of marital ties for any such cause. The judgment and conscience revolt at the thought that such a terrible affliction should be deemed cause for separating the wife from the husband. Divorces are granted not because of misfortune but of fault."

This is the rule in some states, and each instance of this character must be governed by the laws of the state in which the parties live.

Generally in states which by statute allow divorce for post-marital insanity, several years must first elapse.

Adultery has different meanings

In every state adultery is a cause for divorce. There is, in some states, a distinction made in the types of infidelity. A single act of adultery may not be grounds for divorce, but only habitual adultery or "living in adultery."

In one state, the evidence submitted in a divorce trial was that the husband had been repeatedly seen driving in the streets "with a common prostitute and an inmate of a Megowan Street bawdy house." Further, the husband had often been at Megowan Street, spending his time and money with one or another of the occupants of these houses. The statute in that state provides that the wife is entitled to a divorce if her husband "is living in adultery." The facts here show clearly the wife's right to a divorce, as her husband was obviously "living in adultery."

How adultery is proved

Less rigorous proof is demanded by the courts in establishing the occurrence of adultery in a divorce action than in a criminal case. An undefended action in New York showed that the husband had dined with a woman other than his wife; after dinner they had gone to a hotel and registered as "Mr. and Mrs." under an assumed name; they had been assigned to a suite of rooms for one day for which payment had been made in advance, and then had been escorted by the bellboy to the rooms. The boy had left, and the door had closed behind him. On these facts a divorce was granted the wife.

The law relating to the proof of adultery in a divorce action is thus outlined by one court: "It was not necessary to prove him guilty beyond a reasonable doubt but only to establish his adulterous relations with the other woman or women. Persons intending to commit adultery do not in advance proclaim it from the house tops or call in witnesses to the act. On the contrary they court seclusion and secrecy in its commission and hence it must usually be proved by the circumstances that generally attend its commission."

To this might be added a famous conclusion once made in a New York appellate court that: "In the words of an ancient text writer, 'Methinketh they go not to the upper chamber for the sake of saying a paternoster.' " Circumstances that often are used as evidence in the proof of adultery in divorce actions are the entries in hotel registers of assumed names that are preceded by the term of "Mr. and Mrs." in the handwriting of the husband who is accompanied by a woman other than his wife, and the conduct, dress, and environment that are usually associated with adulterous intercourse.

How failure to support is determined

The failure of a husband to support his wife, which is often considered one of the grounds for divorce in many states, is not the same as a mere failure on the part of the husband to pay the amount his wife considers adequate. Important factors are how much the husband is able to contribute, the efforts he is making, and whether the wife is doing her part. The various states have requirements for the duration of nonsupport before it may be considered the ground for an action and basically, the circumstances of each case are considered individually.

Extravagance and nonsupport

One wife's conception of support left a wide wake of unpaid bills. In a filthy home where her husband cooked his own meals, there were a dining room suite for $850, a front room suite for $750, curtains for $300, and expensive carpets and other furnishings, bringing the total to $3,000 for him to pay from his earnings of $10 to $13 a day as a cabinetmaker, when he had employment. His wife's efforts were confined to cabarets and night clubs. Yet she left him, asserting he was not supporting her properly. A divorce was granted the husband, who based his suit on this desertion. The court rejected the wife's claim of nonsupport on the ground that a woman cannot demand more expenditures for support than her husband's income permits.

The desire by the wife for more money than the husband earns does not justify a divorce or a legal separation. This is well illustrated in the following case of a young couple.

A girl of 18 had married a boy whose income was small when she married him and was still small five years later when she sought a divorce for his failure to support her. He owned a little farm, and she had for her own the money she received from the sale of milk, eggs, and butter. She earned a little more by washing clothes, making quilts, and tending a hot dog stand. She lived and dressed as well as the farmers' wives in the vicinity, and her husband was a typical farmer, neither lazy nor aggressive. The food they ate was the meat, poultry, and vegetables that they raised from their own farm.

The court denied this woman's suit. To justify a divorce, the court declared, the failure to support by the husband must be willful and intentional, or of such callous neglect and indifference as to be the equivalent of intentional failure.

When mates are incompatible

Incompatibility pure and simple is not a ground for divorce in most states. The instances where divorces are granted for incompatibility, whether under that name or some such name as mental cruelty, are relatively few. Suppose we look at one case in which the court thought a divorce justified.

In Seattle, Washington, a 23-year-old girl married a man of 53. There were no children. For ten years the couple lived in the man's family home, a big old building lacking modern conveniences and even the comfort and warmth of other homes in the neighborhood. The tastes of the two were different. Their methods of enjoyment were not the same. She liked art, the opera, concerts, and the theater; he was bored and irritated by them. Ultimately their differences became like giants, overshadowing every thought and action.

"Troubles," said the court, "which many couples are able to overcome, and to live harmoniously afterwards, assumed greater proportions through the added difficulty of attempting to mate 'January and May.' It is not only impossible for these parties to live together as husband and wife but it is to their interest and the interest of society that they be divorced."

Much more typical is the case that was tried in a Baltimore court. The wife, bringing suit, complained of the cruelty of the husband, and that he called her "nutty" and "feeble-minded."

The husband's side came out when his attorney cross-examined her concerning certain visits she made to her husband's drugstore.

"Didn't you go in that store and start a quarrel with him?' asked the attorney.

"I had reason to," was the response. "I had no money and the races were going on and I needed money."

"And you would go into his store and make demands on him and do it in a loud tone of voice?' persisted the attorney.

"Yes, and I had reason to."

"Whenever you wanted money you would go to the store and start a quarrel," suggested the attorney.

"Not especially in the store. I needed money and I was not going to spend my money any longer."

The conclusion of the court in relation to this situation, characteristic of legions of marriages, was that no matter how desirable a marriage might be as a moral principle, two people living unhappily together should not be forced by the state to continue such a condition. However, the law did not permit their divorce for such incompatibility. The legislature had unfortunately provided no solution for them. Today there is new thinking on the subject and new legislation either enacted or being considered.

What is desertion?
The desertion of a husband or wife by the other party is

(1) ceasing to live together and have sexual relations,

(2) a refusal to renew such relationship, and

(3) the voluntary separation by one of the parties without the consent of the other and without justification. (Desertion is not a failure to support.)

In some states it is ground for divorce; in others, only for a legal separation. The law in many instances prescribes the period of time the desertion must continue in order to be a cause for divorce.

The wife in a Georgia case claimed she was entitled to a divorce for desertion since her husband had not supported her for six years and had lived apart from her for four years. She failed to obtain her divorce, as she did not show that her husband had been absent without her consent.

A couple married in Maryland had lived together for two years. The wife disappeared and her husband found her in Virginia. The next year she disappeared again, and again he brought her back. The following year she left a third time. When she telephoned him to come and get her he refused. On this refusal she claimed a divorce for desertion.

Refusing to free her from this marriage and to compel her husband to contribute a specific sum for her support, the court declared that her husband had not actually deserted her—this was merely her own interpretation of the incident.

When a wife avoids sexual relations

In an unusual case, a husband and wife lived together for six years and during that time she refused to maintain any sexual relations whatever with her husband. It transpired later, although she did not know it at the time, that the act was physically impossible for her to perform. The husband sought a divorce, basing on the conduct of his wife a claim that by refusing sexual intercourse she had deserted him.

"Desertion consists in a cessation of cohabitation, coupled with a determination in the mind of the offending person not to renew it. Intent is a controlling factor," said the court. "A mere refusal to permit marital intercourse standing by itself and accompanied by no other fact does not constitute desertion."

There must be intention to desert

It is the intention of the party whose conduct is in question that determines whether or not the act of desertion has occurred. A husband who was inducted into the Navy told his wife, after he had entered the armed forces, that he would not live with her again if she were the "last woman on earth." She was granted a divorce. The absence of her husband in the nation's armed forces was, of course, not desertion, but his vehement declaration that he would not return disclosed his firm intention of abandonment and desertion.

Lack of consent

Further, the desertion must be made without the consent of the deserted party. If the husband and wife separated or ceased cohabitation by common consent, tbe legal intent to desert is not present, and a divorce cannot be granted on that ground.

The presumption from continued absence—Enoch Arden Law

When a married person disappears and his whereabouts is unknown for a long period of time, this poses a grave problem for the mate left at home. The statutes in various states make such a disappearance by either husband or wife presumptive proof of death. Unfortunately, such a solution to the problem can hardly be considered satisfactory.

"Enoch Arden," a narrative poem by Alfred Lord Tennyson, published in 1864, is the story of a shipwrecked sailor, lost in the South Seas, who finds, on his return, that his wife has another husband. To avoid complications, he keeps his return secret until his death.

The law in most states in relation to this situation is that any person absent for seven successive years without being heard of is presumed to be dead unless it is shown that he is alive. Irrespective of the statute and the presumption, the one who is absent is either alive or dead. If he is alive, all the presumptions of law from the Babylonian Code of Hammurabi to the statutes enacted by the latest United States Congress cannot make him dead.

Building the hoped-for happiness of a second marriage on a mere presumption of death of the first spouse is like building a house on shifting sands. Either way you court disaster.

The protection of a court decree

The folly of such a presumption was spotlighted in a southern state. Shortly after his marriage, Dan Evans left Mississippi and migrated to Arkansas. No one heard from him. Dan's sister wrote for information to the postmaster at the last place she knew Dan to have been. The reply was that Dan had been drowned. She gave this information to Ollie, his wife. Twenty years after Dan went away, during which time no one had seen him or heard of him, Ollie remarried.

Three children were born of the marriage. After another ten years—30 years after his disappearance—Dan came back to the little Mississippi town where he had once lived. In the meantime, Ollie's second husband had died. When she sought her second husband's life insurance her relatives-in-law, heirs of the deceased husband, produced Dan. The presumption of death from absence was a broken reed, and the court sustained the suit of her relatives-in-law.

As we have seen, the presumption of death from continued absence of the other party to the marriage is set aside by any proof that shows its falsity. When you have such a situation to meet, above all consult a lawyer and obtain a court decree disposing for once and all time of the former marriage and the obligations it imposes. This is the surest way to protect innocent children from the brand of illegitimacy, and their parents from the crime of bigamy.

Residence and domicile

Suits for divorce in the United States have always been actions involving three parties: the husband, the wife, and the state. The state guards the morals of its citizens and the marriage status is a *res*, or thing, over which the state has control. The state therefore has jurisdiction not only of the people involved but of the relationship. States have established what are called *"domicile rules"* for divorce.

Your domicile is that place where you have your true, fixed, and permanent home, your principal establishment to which, whenever you are absent, you intend to return. Domicile is distinguished from residence. A person can have many residences but only one domicile.

Many state statutes will use the word *"residence"* when they set out the jurisdictional requisites for a divorce action, but the word is generally construed to mean domicile. The parties to a divorce are not supposed to create an artificial domicile to facilitate a divorce.

Recently, a new bona fide arrival as a resident of Wisconsin challenged the constitutionality of a state law requiring that before an action for divorce may be commenced, one of the parties must be a "bona fide resident of this state for at least two years." A special three-judge federal court held the residence requirement unconstitutional as being an unfair discrimination to a new bona fide resident. When the argument was made that to eliminate this requirement would make Wisconsin a "quickie divorce mill," the court stated that a jurisdiction which behaves in that manner is one where visitors get divorces, and that Wisconsin would still require that the law of domicile be followed. The question of discrimination against new residents has been considered in other situations, such as the right of a new resident to receive welfare without a waiting period, and the United States Supreme Court has struck down the waiting period in other such cases.

How long must you reside in the state?

The length of time a person seeking a divorce must have resided (be domiciled) within the state in which the action is brought varies in the different states. The time set forth is for general purposes and in many of the states it will vary with the grounds or depend on whether the parties were married there or lived together there or if the grounds for the divorce occurred there. Military service also may be important.

In Alabama the courts have no jurisdiction to grant a divorce if neither party is domiciled in the state. And the mere personal appearance by both parties does not confer jurisdiction. The plaintiff must have resided in Alabama for at least six months if the defendant is a nonresident. However, there is no specific time period of residence for a plaintiff where the court has jurisdiction of both parties and one party is domiciled in Alabama. Until a few years ago, Alabama, because it had no specific time requirement, was a haven for uncontested divorces for those who merely came to Alabama for the divorce.

In general, residence requirements are:

None—Alaska, Louisiana, Washington

6 weeks—Idaho, Nevada, Virgin Islands

60 days—Arkansas, Kansas, Wyoming

3 months—Arizona, Illinois, Missouri, Montana, Utah

6 months—California, Delaware, District of Columbia, Florida, Georgia, Hawaii, Indiana, Kentucky, Maine, Michigan, Minnesota, Mississippi, New Mexico, North Carolina, Ohio, Oklahoma, Oregon, Pennsylvania, Tennessee, Texas, Vermont, Virginia, Wisconsin

One year—Colorado (except where the grounds are adultery or cruelty), Connecticut, Iowa, Maryland, Massachusetts, Nebraska, New Hampshire, New Jersey (except where the grounds are adultery), North Dakota, Puerto Rico, Rhode Island, South Carolina, South Dakota, West Virginia (except where the grounds are adultery)

In many cases there are exceptions: in Illinois, for instance, the time period is one year, but if the offense complained of was committed in Illinois, one party must have resided there for only six months. In Nebraska, the period is one year if the cause arose in the state and two years if it arose outside the state. There are also varying periods for specific grounds like insanity (Vermont, two years). In every situation, the facts and the applicable law should be checked by a local lawyer.

In New York, an action for divorce may be maintained only when the parties were married in the state and either party is a resident and has been for one year when the action commenced *or* both parties have lived in the state as husband and wife and either has been a resident for a year when the action is commenced *or* the cause for the divorce occurred in the state and either party has been a resident for a year or either party has been a resident for at least two years.

Unless there is proper residence in the state where the divorce is granted, it is worthless, and, what is worse, it leaves the parties to the marriage in ignorance of whether they are free and at liberty to remarry or whether the obligations of the marriage still exist. The difficulty lies in the inability to foretell where the courts in your case will determine your legal residence to be.

Such a situation arose in Massachusetts, where a wife sued for support, claiming her husband had deserted her. The court awarded her $20 a week. Two years later the husband went to Nevada; then, after living there for the six weeks prescribed by the

Nevada statute, he sued his wife for divorce, was granted the decree, and returned to Massachusetts.

The next year the wife had him arrested for failing to pay her the $20 a week awarded her by the Massachusetts court. The conclusion of the court shows the uncertainty of divorces involving this feature of residence. "Here it is evident that neither husband nor wife was domiciled in Nevada." This is supplemented by a Massachusetts statute: "If an inhabitant of this commonwealth goes to another jurisdiction to obtain a divorce for a cause occurring here, while the parties reside here, or for a cause which would not authorize a divorce by the laws of this commonwealth, a divorce so obtained shall be of no force and effect in this commonwealth."

Normally, in the United States, full faith and credit and what is called "*comity*" govern divorce decrees obtained in other states. *Comity* is a body of rules that states observe towards one another because of courtesy or mutual convenience. Full faith and credit is required by the United States Constitution, Article IV, to be given by each state to the "public acts, records, and judicial proceedings of every other state." However, some decrees are obtained *ex parte,* that is, without the other party making an appearance. These divorce decrees can be considered initially valid, but inquiry can be made as to whether the sister-state court had jurisdiction of the action. This can sometimes result in the divorce being found deficient. Of course, participation by the other party either by personal appearance, appearance by an attorney, or by petition precludes that party from attacking the decree. A state need not accept the determination of another state court where the other state had no jurisdiction.

Divorce outside the state

In an opinion involving the confusion arising from contradictory state laws and decisions relative to divorce, Justice Jackson of the United States Supreme Court said: "If there is one thing that the people are entitled to expect from their lawmakers, it is rules of law that will enable individuals to tell whether they are married and, if so, to whom. Today many people who have simply lived in more than one state do not know, and the most learned lawyer cannot advise them in confidence."

Gertrude and Joseph Estin had lived their entire married life in New York. Then the wife brought a separation action in that state and was awarded alimony. Three months later the husband went to Nevada, where he brought an action for absolute divorce. In the Nevada suit, the husband was given a divorce and freed of the obligation imposed by the New York court of the payment of alimony.

When the wife sued in New York State to collect her alimony awarded by the courts in that state, the court held that the marriage had been dissolved by the Nevada divorce decree but that the obligation to pay the alimony according to the New York decision was still in force, although the marriage no longer existed. This decision was sustained by the Supreme Court.

Justice Douglas of that court dissented and said of the decision, "The result in this situation is to make the divorce divisible—to give effect to the Nevada decree in so far as it affects the marital status and to make it ineffective on the issue of alimony."

"The court," commented Justice Jackson on this New York decision in a later case before the Supreme Court, "reaches the Solomon-like conclusion that the Nevada decree is half good and half bad under the Full Faith and Credit Clause. I do not see the justice of inventing a compensating confusion in the device of a divisible divorce by which the parties are half bound and half free, and which permits the husband to have a wife who cannot become his widow and to leave a widow who was no longer his wife."

Under the confusion of the law as it now exists in relation to out-of-state divorces, you should consult with your lawyer to determine the practical effect and consequences of any change of residence you make. It may be that, with the more liberal approach to grounds for divorce in each state, there will be fewer attempts to leave the state for the purpose of seeking a divorce.

Divorce and bigamy
In the month of May, a man named Williams left his wife, with whom he had lived for 23 years in North Carolina, and went to Nevada for a divorce. His wife did not go with him and was never in Nevada.

The same month, Lillie Hendrix, who had lived with her husband for 20 years in the same North Carolina town, left him and also went to Nevada, where she was divorced. A few months later Lillie and Williams were married at Las Vegas and returned to North Carolina. Early the following year both were indicted for bigamy by a North Carolina grand jury, tried, convicted and sentenced to imprisonment. Neither had had a legal or actual residence or home in Nevada whereby the courts of that state had authority to grant a valid divorce.

Whether your divorce is legal or worthless depends on your domicile (residence) in the state where you bring your divorce action. This point cannot be overlooked. If you are seeking a divorce outside the state in which the two of you have lived as husband and wife, you must know how your own state will treat your removal and also know the residence requirements of the state where divorce is sought, and observe them scrupulously.

What about divorces in Nevada?
Judging by the decisions of the courts, it would appear to be the law in most states that where a husband and wife have appeared in a Nevada divorce action, the decree is binding on the parties. This principle permits, in effect, a divorce by consent where one spouse institutes the Nevada proceeding and the absent spouse authorizes a Nevada attorney to appear in the action.

A divorce decree will also be valid despite the claim that the plaintiff spouse was not a bona fide resident if such a claim was made in a divorce action and decided against the other spouse.

In general, contesting any issue in a divorce proceeding in any state will make the decision on that issue conclusive and prevent it from being raised in later litigation. Once you have made an appearance in a divorce suit you are bound by what is decided there.

What about Mexican decrees, Ole?

While sister-state decrees are entitled to full faith and credit under the Constitution, those of foreign countries are not. The question usually asked is, "Is it against the public policy of the state to accept the decree of the foreign jurisdiction, or should it be accepted on the ground of comity?' Mexico itself is also a republic made up of states and a Federal District, and it is important to know where in Mexico the divorce was granted, since it too has its more liberal jurisdictions.

The usual procedure in obtaining a Mexican divorce is that one party appears in person in a Mexican state court *with* a local lawyer and the other party appears *by* a Mexican lawyer. In New Jersey, New Mexico, and Ohio a divorce granted in this manner is invalid. In New York, prior to the liberalization of its divorce statute, thousands of New Yorkers went to Mexico for their divorces. The courts then said that although they might disagree with the residence laws established in a state like Chihuahua, Mexico (where Juarez is located, opposite El Paso, Texas), the decree would have to be accepted if the parties complied with the rules. The New York courts were concerned with whether personal jurisdiction had been established over both parties. They knew there was no real intention to establish a domicile in Mexico, but they were willing to accept the decree if both parties complied with the local residence requirements and submitted to the Mexican Court jurisdiction. It was not against the public policy of New York to do so.

However, since September, 1967, with the expansion of the grounds for divorce in New York, questions have been raised about New York treatment of a Mexican divorce decree obtained by a New Yorker. You should consult with your attorney about the situation in any event.

In California, although the Mexican divorce may be invalid as against public policy, if the spouses both participated no complaints will be heard.

It is important to note that "quickie" jurisdiction is no longer accepted in Mexico, so it will not be the site of future such divorces. However, in the Caribbean area, Haiti and the Dominican Republic have adopted laws along the same lines. Extreme caution should be exercised in attempting to take advantage of such laws, with a lawyer being consulted as to the legal aspects.

Mail-order Mexican divorces

These divorces are completely unacceptable. A mail-order divorce is one where neither party appears personally in court, although both agree to submit to the jurisdiction of the court.

Alimony

The traditional view was that a wife was entitled to her husband's support. There is now a middle ground being taken by the courts. With no fault divorces, economic need and the dependent spouse's potential for future self-sufficiency are replacing criteria of behavior and status as the standards for alimony. Many awards of alimony which recently were for shorter terms are being reversed and made permanent, particularly in cases where female spouses are in mid years and unlikely to enter the work force or garner salaries commensurate with their spouse's incomes.

The constitutionality of any state support statute which discriminates on the basis of sex will be reviewed because of the Equal Protection clause of the Fourteenth amendment.

Tax reform and alimony

You should be aware that the *Domestic Relations Tax Reform Act* of 1984 changed the income tax treatment of property transfers between spouses. Six requirements must be met for alimony to be tax deductible to the payor and taxable income to the payee: to qualify as alimony, payments over $10,000 must be made annually for six consecutive years; payments must be in cash, which includes checks or money orders; a divorce decree must not state that the payment is nondeductible by the payor and nontaxable income for the payee; the decree must say that the payor's liability ends at the death of the recipient; the payments can not be treated as child support, and separated or divorced parties can not reside in the same house at the time of payment.

Federal garnishment

Federal, military and District of Columbia employees can have their salaries, awards, bonuses and retirement garnished for child support and alimony payments. The limits are determined by state law. Your attorney will know how to file with the proper government agency.

A New York Case

In a well-publicized New York case, Mrs. Morgan had dropped out of college to have a baby and to support her husband during his last year of college and three years of law school. After graduating from law school and clerking for a federal district court judge, Mr. Morgan went to work for a prominent Wall Street firm. Two months later, he abandoned his wife. Mrs. Morgan returned to college as a pre-med student. In a divorce action, the trial court agreed with Mrs. Morgan that since she had supported him through law school, he should support her through medical school. The Appeals Court reversed, citing established New York law which required the court to deduct the wife's potential earnings from the amount otherwise payable as alimony. Since Mrs. Morgan had a present earning capacity of at least $10,000 a year as a secretary, the alimony was excessive to the extent that it included support for her to attend medical school. The court reduced her alimony to $75.00 a week.

Support during a divorce suit

The alimony that replaces the support that a wife receives under ordinary circumstances still rests on the marriage relationship. No man is liable for the support of a woman who is not his wife. In a celebrated action in New York, a wife sued her husband for support, asking alimony pending the determination of the action. The husband insisted the woman neither was, nor ever had been, his wife. Each of them submitted sworn statements and letters in support of these contrary contentions.

A doctor swore he had attended both parties professionally; that the husband had told him that he and the woman with whom he was living were married but that "for family reasons it was not thought proper to announce it."

The husband, on the other hand, submitted letters from the woman that, according to the court, were "condemnatory of her." The question of whether or not there was a marriage was clearly in dispute. New York's highest court held that the wife was entitled to a temporary allowance for her support during the suit and her expenses in prosecuting it even if the marriage itself was questioned, so long as it was not clearly shown that the marriage was nonexistent.

Custody and support of children

The care of children of divorced parents is the duty of the court that decrees the divorce. The court is, in a sense, the guardian of the child. In its discretion it determines what the care and support shall be and from whom the child shall receive it. A general rule is that the best interest of the child is the prime consideration.

Younger children are ordinarily placed in the custody of the mother, although fathers having custody of children is becoming more common. A few courts have provided for joint custody of children rather than the traditional award of sole custody to one parent. Legislation is pending in some states which would create a presumption in favor of joint custody. In regard to the actual custody, the rights of either the father or the mother are subordinated by the courts to the best interests of the child. Sometimes it is given to persons other than the father or mother. Under such circumstances, ordinarily, near relatives are selected rather than strangers. The preference of a child who has attained the age of discretion will be accorded much weight.

In general, the liability of a father for the support of his minor children continues after a divorce or separation decree until the children come of age.

The obligation to support may continue after the child reaches the legal age of majority if circumstances require. For example, where a child suffered from a dyslexia, a brain defect, requiring psychiatric care and prescription drugs for life, the father was required to support the child beyond the age of majority.

Tuition for children of divorced parents

In many states when parents are financially able, courts order divorced parents to pay college tuition even though child support usually stops when the child comes of age at 18 or 21. In a suit in Pennsylvania brought by a son to require his divorced father to continue paying college tuition, the highest court decided that divorced parents no longer will be required to pay their children's college education. Many other jurisdictions are looking favorably on this decision.

Transsexual parent

A woman who divorced her husband was awarded child custody. In the years that followed she developed masculine characteristics and became a transsexual. She changed her name to Mark and married a woman. The Colorado court which had awarded custody originally set aside its order and awarded custody of the children to their father. The father took the children to Nevada where they were forcibly confined in his home. The children ran away, back to their mother. They were then placed in foster care pending a court determination of custody. At the trial, the mother (Mark) appeared to be a strong healthy male with long sideburns and a mustache. There was testimony at the trial about homosexuality and other sex acts which were denied by Mark. Mark claimed to have established himself as a father image to the children and stated that the children were devoted to himself and his wife. The trial judge interviewed the children. They had been taught about their former mother's sex change and they expressed a desire to live with Mark and his wife. The court concluded that despite social mores and old fashioned attitudes, the welfare of the children would be best served by placing them with their former mother.

Custody to grandparents

Normally parents take precedence over grandparents. However, in a case that aroused national interest and was made into a TV movie, the Supreme Court of Iowa determined custody in a contest between the father and the maternal grandparents. The boy, Mark, was given into the temporary charge of the grandparents at the age of five, after the mother's death. They had provided "stable, dependable, conventional, middle-class background" for the boy, and there was no dispute as to their competence, except that they were 60 years old. The father had remarried and wanted to take the child to California. The father lived an "unconventional, arty, Bohemian" life; he was an agnostic and a political liberal and had no concern for formal religious training. The court stated it was not criticizing the father's way of life, but gave custody to the grandparents because, for the child, a stable relationship was better than "an intellectually stimulating" one.

When parents are separating or divorcing, it is not uncommon for grandparents to seek visitation rights through the courts and win.

Distribution of property

The distribution of property upon the setting aside of a marriage lies, like the custody of the children, in the discretion of the court. In community property jurisdictions, Arizona, California, Idaho, Louisiana, Nevada, New Mexico, Texas, Washington, and Puerto Rico, a wife is entitled to her share in the property that she and her husband have accumulated. "She is entitled to eat and live in as good a style as he is," as a typical decision puts it.

A western farmer, owning a 1,200-acre wheat ranch, a half interest in another tract worth approximately $43,000, and $10,000 in farm equipment, grain, and livestock, was sued by his wife for a divorce for cruelty she had endured for the twenty years of her married life.

Here the wife was given $2,500 in cash, a real estate mortgage for $7,500, a house and lot for her residence worth $3,000, and $75 a month for her own support besides an equal amount for the support of six minor children, to be reduced as each of the children came of age. But no hard-and-fast rule can be given for how the property will be divided in other cases, or how much alimony will be awarded. As already indicated, this depends upon the court.

Putting a husband through school

Some courts have held that a husband's professional license, obtained during marriage with the help and support of the wife, is marital property and that the wife could be compensated for the husband's increased earning capacity in the event of a divorce. Courts are recognizing the concept of "reimbursement alimony" where a wife makes a financial contribution to the household and her husband's college expenses. A recent California State law allows one spouse to be reimbursed if during the marriage he or she contributed to the others' education or training.

The same philosophy has been held to be the law in New York. The appellate court there has also ruled that not only is a license marital property, but an advanced degree obtained during a marriage can be also. Of course the facts must justify the contribution and the enhancement of the earning capacity.

Remarriage after divorce

Except when prohibited by statute, either of the parties to a divorce action is free to remarry upon the granting of a final decree of divorce. In some states, however, there are restrictions on remarriage by either party, prohibiting it for a specified time, or, in the case of the guilty party, absolutely.

As a rule, when a marriage is contracted in violation of these restrictions within the state in which the divorce was granted, it is void. On the other hand, marriages solemnized outside the state before the expiration of the prohibitions against remarriage are in some states recognized as valid on the ground of full faith and credit to the act in the sister state.

Separation and annulment

Chapter 3
Separation and annulment

States in which the power to grant judicial decree of separation is possessed by the courts, and the grounds on which they may grant these decrees, are given below. In some states, however, the only remedy available to a husband and wife seeking a release from their matrimonial contract is an absolute divorce or their own separation arrangements or agreement. In these states the courts have no power to grant separation decrees.

The grounds upon which a separation may be granted in the various states are as follows (their meaning has been explained, in general, in the chapter on divorce, but is always subject to local interpretation):

Grounds for separation

Alabama— The same grounds as for divorce, plus cruelty.

Alaska— No statutory grounds.

Arizona— The same grounds as for divorce, if neither party objects to the decree of separation.

Arkansas— The same grounds as for divorce.

California— Consent of both parties or where one party has failed to make a general appearance.

Colorado— The same grounds as for divorce, and if neither party objects.

Connecticut— The same grounds as for divorce.

Delaware— Legal separation does not exist.

District of Columbia— The same grounds as for divorce, plus cruelty and adultery.

Florida— Statute does not address grounds for separation.

Georgia— No statutory grounds, although private agreements are acceptable.

Hawaii— Temporary disruption of marriage; period of separation not to exceed two years.

Idaho— No statutory grounds.

Illinois— Separate maintenance

Indiana— No statutory grounds.

Iowa— The same grounds as for divorce.

Kansas— The same grounds as for divorce.

Kentucky— Any cause the court may deem sufficient.

Louisiana— The same grounds as for divorce.

Maine— Desertion for one year; separation for one year.

Maryland— Cruelty; desertion; abandonment; excessively vicious conduct; voluntary separation with no expectation of reconciliation.

Massachusetts— Desertion; nonsupport; separation.

Michigan— The same grounds as for divorce.

Minnesota— By mutual consent; or based on necessity as determined by the court.

Mississippi— No statutory grounds.

Missouri— The same grounds as for divorce.

Montana— The same grounds as for divorce, except that one party must request legal separation and the other party must not object.

Nebraska— No statutory grounds.

Nevada— Separate maintenance.

New Hampshire— The same grounds as for divorce.

New Jersey— No statutory grounds.

New Mexico— Separation.

New York— Cruelty; desertion; nonsupport; adultery; unsafe conduct for cohabitation; confinement to prison for three or more years after the marriage.

North Carolina— Cruelty; desertion; habitual drunkenness; violent temper; barring spouse from home.

North Dakota— The same grounds as for divorce.

Ohio— No statutory grounds.

Oklahoma— The same grounds as for divorce.

Oregon— Irreconcilable differences.

Pennsylvania— Separation abolished.

Puerto Rico— No statutory grounds.

Rhode Island— The same grounds as for divorce.

South Carolina— No statutory grounds but allowed by court construction.

South Dakota— The same grounds as for divorce.

Tennessee— Cruelty; nonsupport; desertion; violent temper; barring spouse from home, irreconcilable differences.

Texas— No statutory grounds.

Utah— Desertion; nonsupport; separation.

Vermont— The same grounds as for divorce.

Virginia— Cruelty; desertion; fear of bodily harm.

Virgin Islands— The same grounds as for divorce.

Washington— The same grounds as for divorce.

West Virginia— Separation abolished.

Wisconsin— The same grounds as for divorce.

Wyoming— The same grounds as for divorce.

Divorce or separation?

Sometimes a plaintiff who brings suit for divorce finds that the ground on which the suit is based is sufficient only for a separation.

One case that occurred in Kentucky concerned a husband who was a confirmed drunkard, wasted his property, and treated his wife cruelly, endangering her life and health. He would go on weekend sprees, come home, effect a reconciliation, and then go on another spree. This happened again and again, and finally his wife brought suit for divorce.

These sprees did not constitute drunkenness within the meaning of the statute and hence, the court pointed out, did not permit the wife an absolute divorce, but they did entitle her to a separation from her husband and to support.

Before the change in New York divorce law, when adultery was the only ground, a court decree separating a husband and wife was granted for cruel and inhuman treatment. The wife maintained an intimate association with a man other than her husband, widely displaying her affection in such places as automobiles and the apartment house vestibule. Her conduct was notorious. The evidence showed clearly that her friendship for the man had long since passed the "casual, platonic and sister like" character she claimed for it. But there was no evidence of actual adultery. The only aid and comfort the husband found was a court decree of separation for three years on the ground of cruel and inhuman treatment and a release during that time from his obligation to support his wife.

The law decides

In the laws of South Carolina there was no provision for an absolute divorce prior to 1948. The statutes did, however, provide for a separation of the parties to a marriage "from bed and board" for cruel or barbarous treatment that endangered the life of the other party to the marriage, or such indignities as rendered the victim's life intolerable. In that state a wife stuck an ice pick a couple of inches into her husband's side, poured scalding water over him, shot at him with a pistol, and put his clothes in the back yard. The court found that this man had ample grievance against his wife—it justified a separation, but the parties had to stay married.

These limited divorces or separations from bed and board do not provide more than the parties themselves can arrange by contract if the agreement is made after they have separated. We shall consider the details of such an agreement or contract in the following pages.

When to make separation agreements

Don't make an out-of-court agreement for separation from your wife or husband before the actual separation occurs. The agreement must not be a contract to break up a home. This, the courts in some instances say, is illegal. But if the home is already broken up, you can arrange by this method the details of your future relationship.

In most instances these agreements have survived the onslaughts of litigation between spouses that often follow the execution of such agreements. Sometimes they have not. The law, however, has generally maintained that if you and your wife or husband are actually separated and you no longer live together as husband and wife, any agreement that you make with each other that is fair and that provides for the support of the wife is legal and binding.

Why an agreement may be unenforceable

In Illinois, a husband and wife made a separation agreement by which the wife received $3,000 and the household furniture, and in return released her husband from any further obligation to support her. The court decided this agreement was illegal. It held that the husband could not escape his obligation to support his wife by trading secondhand furniture for a release without the consent of the third party to the marriage, the state.

The duty to support cannot always be avoided by a lump-sum payment. When the money is spent, you may be required to supply support. That is only one reason why consultation with your attorney is necessary for preparation of any separation agreement.

Form for separation agreement

A simple separation agreement for persons who have already separated runs as follows:

> This agreement made and entered into this *10th* day of *February, 1958*, by and between *Charles Graham*, party of the first part, and *Dorothy Graham*, party of the second part, witnesseth:
>
> Whereas the parties are living separate and apart and it is desirous that a settlement of property rights be had, it is mutually agreed as follows:
>
> That the party of the first part will pay to the party of the second part upon the execution of this agreement the sum of *Ten thousand ($10,000.00) Dollars* and the further sum of *One hundred ($100.00) Dollars* per month from the date of this agreement, payable in advance until the death of the party of the second part, said payments to be deposited in the *First National Bank, New York City*, each month to the credit of the party of the second part.
>
> It is further agreed and understood that the estate of the party of the first part shall be holden for said monthly payments until the death of the party of the second part.
>
> The party of the first part agrees to pay to *Charles Haskins*, the attorney for the party of the second part, the sum of $500.00 in full compensation for his services in representing the party of the second part.
>
> The party of the second part does hereby waive, renounce and relinquish all right of inheritance to the property of the party of the first part, and the party of the first part does hereby waive all right of inheritance to the property of the party of the second part.
>
> It is mutually agreed and understood that at the time of the execution of this agreement the parties hereto have actually separated and that this agreement is entered into after actual separation.
>
> This agreement shall bind the heirs, executors and assigns of the parties to the same.
>
> In witness whereof the parties hereto have hereunto set their hands this *10th* day of *February, 1958*.

Charles Graham
Dorothy Graham

State of New York
County of New York } ss:

On this *10th* day of *February, 1958*, before me personally and severally came the within named Charles Graham and Dorothy Graham, his wife, severally known to me and to me known to be the persons described in and who severally executed the within instrument and severally acknowledged that they severally executed the same for the uses and purposes therein named.

Charles Dennis
Notary public

It should be noted that this agreement does not provide for children, household effects, or other property, and is intended only for illustration and so that you will understand what is involved when you consult your lawyer. Tax consequences must also be considered.

Annulment and its grounds

The annulment of a marriage is not a divorce. A divorce dissolves the marriage. After a divorce there is no longer a marriage. An annulment merely confirms that a marriage never existed. However, many states have passed legislation allowing courts to award alimony in annulment actions. The grounds in some states for the annulment of a marriage are the same as for divorce in other states.

The role played by these different grounds in disposing of a marriage varies with the different state laws. Essentially, the ground for the dissolution of a marriage by an annulment is a fraud inflicted on the other by one of the parties to the marriage contract. This element of fraud, the misrepresentation by one party to the other of a material fact, is the major factor in the voiding of the marriage contract by annulment, as it is in voiding of any other contract. This was discussed earlier.

However, the misrepresentation must be of a material fact. It must be made with the intent of inducing the other party to enter into a marriage contract which he would not have done if the true facts had been known.

False representations of previous virginity, intention to have children, intention to perform a religious ceremony, wealth, social position and earnings, as well as concealment of prior divorce or marriage or conviction of crime, are among the grounds for which an annulment may be sought, although a false representation as to some of these, such as wealth and social position alone, may not be sufficient basis. The following are the state laws on annulment:

Grounds for annulment

Alabama— Insanity; fraud; bigamy; incest; miscegenation (probably still true despite the Supreme Court decision).

Alaska— No statutory grounds.

Arizona— Any existing impediment.

Arkansas— Incapacity to consent; fraud; force.

California— Incapacity to consent; impotency; spouse alive; unsound mind; fraud; force.

Colorado— Incapacity to consent; fraud; jest or dare; impotency.

Connecticut— Incest; consanguinity; offense against chastity.

Delaware— Impotency; consanguinity; spouse alive; insanity; fraud; force; incapacity to consent; jest or dare; bigamy.

District of Columbia— Consanguinity; bigamy; insanity; incapacity to consent; impotency; fraud; force.

Florida— No statutory grounds.

Georgia— Incapacity to consent. An annulment cannot be granted on a ground that is also a ground for divorce. Additionally, an annulment cannot be granted where there are children.

Hawaii— Consanguinity; incapacity to consent; force; fraud; Hansen's (leprosy) or other loathsome disease; bigamy; lunacy; impotency.

Idaho— Incapacity to consent; bigamy; unsound mind; fraud; force; impotency.

Illinois— Incapacity to consent; impotency; consanguinity.

Indiana— Fraud; incapacity to consent.

Iowa— Impotency; bigamy; insanity; consanguinity.

Kansas— Bigamy; impotency; fraud.

Kentucky— Force; fraud; incapacity to consent; impotency.

Louisiana— Mistake; incapacity to consent; bigamy; consanguinity.

Maine— Insanity; bigamy; consanguinity.

Maryland— Bigamy; consanguinity.

Massachusetts— Bigamy; incapacity to consent.

Michigan— Incapacity to consent.

Minnesota— Incapacity to consent; force; fraud.

Mississippi— Bigamy; incapacity to consent; pregnant at the time the marriage actually took place; impotency; insanity; force; fraud; invalid license; incest; miscegenation.

Missouri— Duress; fraud; incapacity to consent.

Montana— Incapacity to consent; bigamy; unsound mind; fraud; force; impotency.

Nebraska— Consanguinity; incapacity to consent; fraud; force; insanity or mental retardation; impotency; bigamy.

Nevada— Fraud; incapacity to consent.

Grounds for annulment
New Hampshire— Incapacity to consent.

New Jersey— Bigamy; consanguinity; impotency; fraud; incapacity to consent.

New Mexico— Incapacity to consent.

New York— Bigamy; consanguinity; incapacity to consent; impotency; force; fraud; insanity.

North Carolina— Incapacity to consent.

North Dakota— Incapacity to consent; bigamy; insanity; incest; fraud; force; impotency.

Ohio— Incapacity to consent; bigamy; insanity; fraud; force; marriage never consummated.

Oklahoma— Incapacity to consent.

Oregon— Force; fraud; incapacity to consent.

Pennsylvania— Insanity; consanguinity.

Puerto Rico— Same grounds as for annulment of any contract.

Rhode Island— No statutory grounds. The remedy is divorce.

South Carolina— Incapacity to consent.

South Dakota— Incapacity to consent; bigamy; insanity; fraud; force; impotency.

Tennessee— Incapacity to consent; force; consanguinity; the same grounds as for divorce or separation.

Texas— Impotency and other impediments.

Utah— Incapacity to consent; incest; insanity; bigamy.

Vermont— Incapacity to consent; insanity; force; fraud; impotency.

Virginia— Bigamy; consanguinity; incapacity to consent; impotency; conviction of felony; wife pregnant at time of marriage or a prostitute; husband fathered child out of wedlock; insanity; fraud; duress.

Virgin Islands— Impotency; insanity; force; fraud; incapacity to consent; consanguinity; bigamy.

Washington— Annulment repealed. However, marriage may be declared invalid under certain circumstances: incapacity to consent; bigamy; consanguinity; fraud; force; duress.

West Virginia— Bigamy; consanguinity; insanity; venereal disease; impotency; incapacity to consent; conviction of infamous crime; wife pregnant at time of marriage or a prostitute; husband licentious.

Wisconsin— Impotency; consanguinity; bigamy; force; fraud; incapacity to consent.

Wyoming— Incapacity to consent; force; fraud; impotency; bigamy; insanity; consanguinity.

Marriage by force

In Chicago, some years ago, Margaret Eustice asked a man whom she had known for some time to drive with her in her automobile to a place in the Chicago suburbs, where she was going on an errand. O'Brien accepted her invitation. The two drove gaily toward the outskirts of the city. Soon a big limousine was following. When they stopped for the errand, two men stepped from the other car, tied O'Brien with a rope and set him on the back seat of the limousine.

Next they took him to the residence of a justice of the peace, where Margaret had already arranged the preliminaries for the wedding, and witnesses were waiting. O'Brien was kept in the car while the justice conducted the ceremony through to the pronouncement that they were husband and wife. On their return to the city O'Brien seized the emergency brake, jumped from the car, and fled to a policeman.

In the annulment suit brought later by O'Brien, the court said that this was no marriage. Where consent to a marriage is obtained, as it was here, by force, there is no marriage.

Two husbands at one time

More frequently, however, marriages are annulled for false statements made to get the consent of the other party to the marriage. At Ventura, California, Harold and Ruth Goff were married. She had told him she was a widow and he believed this statement until he learned, about three years after their marriage, that her husband from a previous marriage was still alive and she had not been divorced. Legally, she lacked the ability to wed, and her marriage to Goff was annulled.

When delay is fatal

Conditions for which you can have your marriage annulled cannot be held in reserve like an ammunition stockpile, for use at some future time. If you plan to seek an annulment of your marriage, do it at once. When you discover the grounds for which you can ask for that remedy, it is not wise to wait. Your delay may be a forgiveness of the fraud and you will be compelled to go on with your marriage, with the door for escape closed.

Take the case of a man and a woman who were married in Rhode Island. She did not tell her husband at the time of the marriage that she was suffering from the consequences of a venereal disease. They lived together more than a year, until the woman was forced to enter a Providence hospital for mental diseases. A week later her husband took her from the hospital. Then, for the first time, he learned that the mental condition with which she was afflicted was the consequence of a venereal disease. Nevertheless, he lived with her for more than a year, and it was not until eight years later that he sought to have the marriage annulled.

The court refused to disturb their relationship. "The realization that he was to be burdened with an incurably insane wife seems to have been the motivating cause. He waived whatever right he may have had the day on which he first learned of his wife's blood condition or within a reasonable time thereafter, to have his marriage declared null and void for fraudulent concealment."

Certain aspects of annulment are also discussed in the chapter on divorce, which you should consult. As in all these situations, the facts and circumstances of each individual case are important and you cannot rely on generalization as a solution, but should consult your attorney as to the application of the law to your facts.

Children

Chapter 4
Children

Can an unborn child bring suit?

Childhood or infancy, in law, ends when the child becomes 18 years old, or 21, or whatever other age is set by law. It begins, however, with the life of the child when he is still unborn. By the law of some states a child, for most purposes, is fully as much a person in the nine months before his birth as he is after his birth and his introduction to the family.

An unborn child's rights to a legacy can be seen in the case of Roswell Colt and his daughter. He left a trust fund to be divided amongst his surviving children. He died on May 1; his daughter was born on November 17.

This child, at the time of her father's death, said the court, was as fully a person as some months later when she made her debut into a world of milk, bottles and bassinets. This new little baby girl was entitled to the same rights and consideration and to the same share in that trust income as his other children.

The rule that an unborn child has the legal rights of a child after its birth has exception, however. In some states, actions cannot be brought by children for injuries suffered by them before they were born, unless the statutes specifically provide for such actions. Such states follow the old common law, which holds that an unborn child has no existence apart from its mother.

A typical case of this sort took place in New Jersey. A child sued for injuries from a physician's treatment of its mother six weeks before birth, where, as a consequence of an x-ray examination, the child developed into an idiot. The highest court in New Jersey refused to recognize the child's right to sue. California, on the other hand, would have decided this case differently, as its statutes permit suits of this kind. New York, without a statute, has permitted such a suit. There are some other states in the United States that also permit it.

Now that abortion laws are being liberalized, the arguments about the rights of unborn children are becoming even more noteworthy.

Sexual abuse

The issue of child abuse has become one of the most explosive in the law. It has tarnished the image of the priesthood. It has set children against parents and parents against psychologists and psychotherapists. It has caused states to change their statutes of limitations. It impacted on a multimillion dollar estate.

What has happened is that the abuse, which allegedly occurred in childhood, either surfaces in adulthood or is disclosed by adults who were too traumatized earlier to admit it. Sometimes the recollections occur after years of a dysfunctional life and assistance by therapists. Those who allege abuse have been filing civil suits against their abusers. One woman in Virginia alleged abuse when she was 14 years old by her riding camp director. Another sued the father of her friend for his rape when she was five years old. Former students have sued teachers and former altar boys have sued their priests for sexual abuse and the bishops and the Church for negligence, fraud and conspiracy to cover up. Both the granddaughter and great-granddaughter of millionaire Elmer Bobst, who was a close friend of President Nixon, sued his estate for damages for his repeated sexual abuse.

Courts in at least ten states are allowing abuse claims to be filed years after the events, usually within a specified period after recollection. However, Virginia's law changing the statute of limitations was found to be unconstitutional.

Many parents and others claim they are being falsely accused. They allege the false memory is encouraged by practitioners of "recovered memory" therapy. Although one father who sued therapists obtained substantial damages, there is a legal question of whether anyone other than a patient has standing to sue over the consequences of a doctor-patient relationship. Some patients have sued successfully for malpractice when they were harmed by treatment to unlock their early memories.

When children allegedly are abused, many different people may be involved besides the child and the alleged abuser. There are doctors, social workers, and possibly teachers. When the case comes to court, the child's account of the abuse will be important.

Normally, statements made to others aren't admitted into evidence because they are considered hearsay. These are statements made by a person not in court that might only be their opinion, a rumor, unreliable. The person who made the statements must be in court to be examined and cross examined. Otherwise, it isn't evidence for the jury and cannot be repeated by a witness on the stand who has no personal knowledge. However, there are exceptions to the hearsay rule and one is the *"tender years"* exception. It allows licensed professionals, like doctors, to tell juries what a child told them about the abuse when the child is too young or frightened to testify in person. More than 33 states have a tender years exception. But many states also allow nonprofessionals to testify about the child's account.

Chaperons

Chaperons are vital to almost every trip or event involving children or even teens. But if you volunteer to help, be alert to possible legal consequences. Liability could revolve around the concepts of negligence, due care, inherently dangerous activities, authorized actions or activities, third party involvement or injuries or property damage. Before taking on the responsibility, you should check yours and the organization's insurance coverage, your possible indemnification, the help you will be getting at the event, any rules or regulations which cover it as well as the possible hazards to be encountered not only because of the ages of the participants but because of the type of activity or terrain.

National Childhood Vaccine Injury Act
Many times injuries to a child resulting from a vaccination are not causally related to the vaccine until a later date when links are revealed. There have been vaccines that caused permanent neurological damage, seizures, and death.

Because many vaccines are given to millions of children each year and some are manufactured by a number of drug companies, lawsuits are difficult and the multiplicity of them can burden companies to the point that they stop production. The United States Congress passed this legislation to provide some recompense for injuries sustained and to minimize suits against manufacturers.

If your child sustained an injury because of a vaccine that was administered before October 1, 1988, and you have a lawsuit pending, you can collect up to $30,000 for rehabilitation costs and other expenses if you withdraw your lawsuit. Anyone injured by a vaccine after that date must first make a claim under the Act before filing suit. Accepting compensation precludes the filing of a suit.

You should consult an attorney concerning your most favorable approach to recovery for any vaccine-related injury.

Tax changes on child support
The *Domestic Relations Tax Reform Act* of 1984 changed the rules regarding which parent was entitled to claim dependent children for tax purposes after a divorce. As of January 1, 1985, the parent with custody for the greater part of the year can claim the deduction. There are three exceptions to this: if the custodial parent releases the right by signing a written statement attached to the tax return; if a child support agreement or order was made prior to January 1, 1985, and the noncustodial parent pays at least $600, then that parent can still claim the child; or the "multiple support agreement" under the old law still applies where no one party can meet the exemption regulations.

Also, the new law allows either parent to claim the deduction for medical payments made on behalf of the child.

Enforcement of child support obligations
When a parent doesn't make support payments, the *Uniform Reciprocal Enforcement of Support Act* allows the parent owed child support to sue in the state where the other parent resides. The defaulting parent must appear in court. The Child Support Enforcement Amendments of 1984 require states to collect court-ordered child support payments by withholding wages from the debtor-parent's paycheck when support payments are more than thirty days overdue. It also allows both tax refunds and earned income credits to be withheld by the IRS to satisfy overdue child support payments.

A California woman won a $24,000 settlement from her ex-husband's employer when he fired the husband rather than deduct child support payments from his wages. Courts are taking these laws that affect children very seriously.

Federal garnishments

Child support orders can be enforced against employees of the U.S., the District of Columbia and also military personnel. The governments will deduct various amounts from wages, bonuses, awards and retirement according to the state law. Be sure to consult your lawyer because he or she will know how to file on your behalf.

When childhood ends

The date when the minority of an infant ends is established by law and occurs at different ages in different states and under different circumstances. The age when a boy or girl may make a contract, a valid marriage, when he or she can make a will, all are set by law with different ages prescribed for the performance of different acts and deeds. For most legal purposes, but not all, a person becomes an adult at 21. A recent amendment to the United States Constitution lowered the voting age from 21 to 18 years, and many states have lowered the age of maturity from 21 to 18 years. New Jersey has just recently done this.

The life of a child before becoming of age is under the care of the father or other head of the family. The head of the family has this obligation and responsibility, which is offset by a right to whatever wages the child may earn.

A father's right to his child's earnings

Courts have held that a father is entitled to the earnings of his children until they become of age or until they are emancipated—"on their own." In case of the father's death, the mother is entitled to the earnings of their minor children. When they are no longer supported by their father but earn their own livelihood, children keep whatever wages they receive.

The child who earns his own living

When a child is earning his or her own living, or when the father compels the child to support himself financially, the courts maintain that there is no principle of law that will continue a father's right to receive the earnings of the child's labor.

When the mother is the head of the family

A boy employed by a Connecticut manufacturer died from injuries received in the course of his employment. The mother asked for compensation under the *Worker's Compensation Act* of that state.

Long before this incident, the father had deserted his wife and children. The five children had contributed to the support of their mother for three years. The only money she had had for the maintenance of the home had been their earnings. The award of this compensation was opposed by the state, which contended that since the father was living, compensation should be made to him.

The father, the court held, was disqualified. He had been replaced by the mother of the children as the head of the family and she, not the father, was entitled to the compensation award that represented the boy's wages. "The obligations of a minor to his parents," said the court, "are obedience, subjection, and his earnings, if any, while those of the parent are protection, education, and support."

Contracts of children—are they legal?

The courts consistently extend to children protection from exploitation by their elders. One phase of this protection is the rule that no child or minor is liable for any obligations under a contract. Minors cannot ordinarily be made to pay for anything they buy except such things as are necessary to their health and welfare.

Their contracts are considered voidable at the option of the infant. But an adult cannot avoid a contract with an infant. An infant can compel another party to fulfill his contract.

A minor over 18 who owns his own business and who enters into contracts in connection therewith is bound by them if the contracts are reasonable. This is a special situation.

The consequences of the rule that minors don't have to honor their contracts places on the shoulders of those dealing with youngsters the burden of knowing whether or not they are dealing with minors. In some situations, children may misrepresent their ages. But even if a child does misrepresent his age, this fact still doesn't change his protection. Children are great mail-order devotees, but being minors they can't be made to pay for the merchandise.

However, if a minor disaffirms a contract, he must return the value he has received and he is responsible for depreciation.

A disaffirmance has repercussions

Recently, an honor graduate from a law school in Arizona was almost deprived of the opportunity to practice law because, as a minor, he had disaffirmed a contract involving a substantial sum of money. After reviewing the situation, a committee of the bar association felt that this showed a lack of moral character on the part of the graduate that rendered him unfit to become a member of the bar. The matter was then appealed by the graduate to the court. As a result of the appeal, the decision was reversed to permit admission to the bar since the graduate's disaffirmance as a minor had been legal.

How a child's liability for bills is limited

A minor, says the law, must pay for his "meat, drink, apparel, necessary physic and other such necessaries, and likewise for his good teaching or instruction." Beyond that a child's obligations cease unless after he becomes of age he wishes to pay them. Don't overlook this immunity of minors from any debts except for necessaries. On the death of her father, Doris had agreed with an undertaker in Philadelphia to pay his funeral expenses. Before doing so, she consulted her guardian, the Provident Trust Company, and received its approval. Yet, although the undertaker had earned his money, the court refused her permission to make the payment to him as she had promised.

Real property

When a child is involved in a contract concerning real property, he cannot disaffirm the contract until he reaches majority. If he has given the property away while still an infant, he can, upon reaching majority, get it back.

Can payments be made to children?

In general, debts due a minor, other than wages, should not be paid to the child. Giving the child the money does not pay the debt. Even after the child takes the money, you still owe the debt. When a California insurance company gave a 15-year-old boy the money for a loss they had insured, instead of paying his guardian, the child had the money but the debt of the company had not been paid. The company had neglected the rule of law that a child is not bound by a contract. The court obliged the company to pay the debt over again to the boy's guardian.

This principle of law is to protect children not only from others but also from themselves. "It is a well-settled principle of law," say the courts, "that one deals with infants at his peril."

Injuries to trespassing children

An action brought against the Alabama Power Company showed that an eight-year-old child had trespassed on the company's property, run into a high-voltage wire, and been instantly killed. The conclusion of the court was harsh, but the rule that the wrongdoer cannot complain applies to children as it does to mature men and women. "It must be borne in mind that under our authorities a child may be a trespasser just as well as an adult."

The law of attractive nuisances

The laws in a number of states, however, make the exception that even though children may technically be trespassers, when conditions are such that children are naturally attracted into unsuspected dangers that the owner or person in charge should have foreseen, a liability for any injury to the child exists. The reason often is that this attractiveness is the equivalent of an implied invitation to the child, and the one responsible for the attractiveness is liable for the consequences.

An attractive nuisance exists when an artificial condition is maintained where children are likely to be, where the condition involves an unreasonable risk to such children, where the children don't realize the risks, and when the condition could be remedied without causing the owner too much trouble as compared to the risks to the children.

Some examples of attractive nuisances

Artificial bodies of water are hazards if they have unusual features. A raft in a pond where there is a sudden and hidden drop-off in depth can be an attractive nuisance, as can a large pile of debris near the shore of a canal. An abandoned excavation with debris of a razed residential building in a city was found to be one when a child was injured by a rusty nail on a hidden and loose plank. A junk yard near a public street was found to be one when a child was injured on broken glass from a wrecked car. Another attractive nuisance was a rotting wharf whose holes were covered by piles of sand; it was near a public road frequented by small children. A somewhat unusual example of an attractive nuisance is a mailbox with a spout used to receive mail at curbs from passing vehicles. A five-year-old climbed onto one that wasn't anchored in order to talk into the spout, and was injured. The government was found to be liable.

What is emancipation?

It can be reaching the age of 18 or 21, being married, or earning one's own living. It means independence, freedom from parental control.

When an infant daughter marries an infant husband it is his obligation to support her, and her father is relieved of that responsibility.

Being under 18 or 21 and emancipated, however, doesn't mean that the defense of infancy cannot be used. An emancipated minor can still avoid his contracts.

When is infancy not a barrier?

An infant can have life insurance coverage and be responsible for the premiums; an infant can deal with a credit union and be held responsible for the shares.

A child's liability for injuring someone

While children are not liable for the things they buy, except necessaries, or for any money owed by virtue of a contract, they may be liable for damages they inflict on others. Such obligations do not spring from contract but are torts, or civil wrongs. An infant of tender years may be liable for any tort he is capable of committing. Where malice is necessary, the child must be old enough to have the intent that is legally required for malice. Where negligence is involved, the child is held to the standard of a child of similar age and experience. Some courts say, however, that children under seven years of age are presumed to be incapable of negligence.

A five-year-old was accused of deliberately pulling a chair out from beneath an adult, who was injured. The court found that the child could possibly have the necessary intent. In another case, a four-year-old was accused of negligently pushing and shoving an adult so she fell and was injured. The court held that since a four-year-old was incapable of contributory negligence, he would be incapable of primary negligence.

What about parents' liability?

Usually a parent is not liable for the tort of his child except where the child is an agent or employee; where he entrusts the child with a dangerous instrument; where he knows of any dangerous propensities of the child and doesn't try to protect others from him; or where the parent ratifies the tort of his child—that is, he knows of a wrong the child has done but does nothing to help put things right.

In recent years, there has been support for legislation to make the parents responsible to innocent third parties for the wrongs committed by their children.

More about a child's age

This can be important both in determining whether a child can contribute to an accident to himself and in deciding whether he is old enough to be responsible for an injury to someone else. It is especially important when a crime has been committed.

Children under seven years are usually considered incapable of having the capacity to contribute to a personal injury, although in New York the age is four, and some courts have put the age as low as three. Up to about the age of 14, there is usually a presumption that children are not capable of contributing to their own injuries. However, their intelligence, schooling, and general knowledge are taken into consideration in deciding their maturity and the degree of care required of them in avoiding personal injury. Children must meet a standard just as adults do, and the standard is what can reasonably be expected of the ordinary child of like age, intellectual and physical development, and education or experience under the same or similar circumstances. In Louisiana, a normal child of 12 is presumed to be capable of contributory negligence.

After 14, there is no presumption in favor of the child and the child has no shield against his own negligence.

Can a child sue his parents

There are still states where the rule of parent-child tort immunity governs and an unemancipated child cannot sue the parents in tort for negligence that causes injury. Even then, however, if there has been a willful tort there can be suit.

In Maryland, the state's highest court allowed a wrongful death suit by children against their father who killed their mother. However, it upheld parent-child tort immunity when a daughter tried to sue her mother for causing a car accident in which she was seriously injured. The contrary was the situation in New York when a parent sued her 16-year-old son for negligence in operating a motor vehicle in which she was a passenger. The court held suing a minor child was no different from suing one of legal age.

A child can sue the parents on a contract. And there can be suit against other members of the family for simple negligence. The argument about disruption of "family harmony" because of tort suits doesn't extend much beyond the parental relationship.

Auto accidents of children

Automobile insurance rates are very high for youthful drivers. This is because of the higher incidence of accidents involving young people.

Your son and daughter are liable for payment of the damages arising from their careless automobile driving. When the car they own is driven by someone other than themselves, however, it is often a difficult question to determine. When a minor lets someone else drive his car, any liability he assumes arises from a contract—the driver of the car is his agent, and minors cannot make contracts.

Mildred Scott was 17. Her father had given her an automobile as a birthday present. Dan Brooks was driving this car on a Louisiana highway with Mildred's permission. She herself was in the back seat when Dan hit another auto. As owner of the car, Mildred was sued for the damages. The court held here that a minor is only liable for his or her personal offenses. Since the collision was not Mildred's act and she could not thus be liable, her father was not liable either. Liability merely for ownership is applied by statute in a number of states.

In some states the minor owner of the car would be liable for damage caused by someone else operating it with his consent if in the same situation an adult owner would be liable.

Is a minor liable for fraud?

While a child is not liable under a contract, he may not benefit from his fraudulent acts. The law that a boy or girl cannot be held to a contract to pay for what he or she buys unless it is a necessary is carefully watched by the courts.

Sometimes courts are called upon to protect older and more experienced persons and shield them from frauds perpetrated by legally irresponsible minors. A boy, 17 years old and driving an automobile, hit another car driven by a mature man. This driver asked the boy merely to pay the damages caused by his carelessness. The boy settled the claim by signing a memorandum, "I agree to pay for the doctor's and hospital bills in the sum of $75 at the rate of $2.50 a week." In addition he agreed to pay $500 "for actual property damage." In return the owner of the car agreed he would make no further claims against the youngster.

When the boy was 21, he had paid $240. Then he sued the man he injured for the money he had already paid, on the ground that he was a minor when he had paid it. The court decided against the boy. Although when under 21 the boy was not responsible for contract obligations, it was not proper for him to use this protection for the commission of a fraud in stalling an action for damages caused by an accident that was his responsibility.

In another case, a 19-year-old Creek Indian borrowed $125 from a land company and gave as security a deed of 40 acres of land. Having spent the money, the Native American brought suit to set aside the deed because he was a minor and incapable of executing it.

"Infants have no privilege to cheat men" was the laconic comment of the judge, deciding against the boy. Before the deed could be canceled, the borrowed money had to be repaid.

A child's responsibility for his parents' support

The economic burden of the family does not always rest on the shoulders of the parents. The law at times places on children the care of parents who are helpless, lest they become a public charge.

The support of parents by their children is a subject that has many interesting legal sides to it. A Pennsylvania woman filed a claim against her father-in-law's estate for "board, lodging, nursing and similar services at $5 a week for 72 weeks." She had rendered these services while the old man was living with her and her husband in the house that the father had given his son, her husband.

The food the father had eaten had been from his son, said the court, adding that because it was prepared by the son's wife did not take it out of the rule that when a father or mother comes to live with his or her son, the law implies no promise on the part of the parent to pay for board and lodging and kindred services.

In most of the states, the legislatures have enacted statutes concerning the responsibilities of parents for their children's support, sometimes only until majority. These laws are implemented with penalties for the enforcement of obedience. In most states, too, parents are under legal obligation to support children who are of age if they are impoverished and liable to become a public charge. Some statutes apply this liability also to grandparents, grandchildren, sisters, and brothers.

In Illinois, children are severally liable for the support of their parents if they are in need of such support and likely to become a public charge. When there are two or more children, the court may assess the proportionate ability of each to contribute to such support.

Kids' crimes
Illegal acts by young people have changed drastically. Now there's arson, robbery, murder. Vandalism, graffiti, truancy are comparatively minor offenses. More and more jurisdictions are treating young people, even of so-called tender years, as adult criminals.

And parents are being held more responsible for the misbehavior of their offspring, including abuse of alcohol, truancy, vandalism, shoplifting, burglary, gang involvement. Laws in more than 10 states and multiple local jurisdictions include parental fines, restitution, required counseling, community service and even, on occasion, jail time for the misdeeds of their children. West Virginia, Idaho, Indiana and New Hampshire require parental payment for institutional costs for their juvenile offenders.

Many view these laws as unconstitutional or as interfering with a parent's right of upbringing. But the surge in youth violence is causing a search for solutions.

The Gault Case
In cases where there is delinquency (as compared to more serious criminal behavior) and consequential prosecution, the U. S. Supreme Court, in the case of 15-year-old Arizonian Gerald Gault, established that youths accused of juvenile delinquency are entitled to most of the constitutional rights of adult criminal suspects.

Gerald had been accused of making lewd and offensive phone calls. If an adult had been punished for that offense in Arizona, he would have received a $50 fine and two months in jail. Gerald had a hearing before a regular trial judge sitting as a juvenile court judge, and he was committed to an industrial school for six years, that is, until 21.

The Gault decision applies to juveniles facing delinquency charges who may be confined to a state institution. The juvenile is given the right to remain silent, the right to have an attorney, the right to have full and adequate notice of the misconduct with which he is charged, the right to see the witnesses who will testify against him, and the right to have defense counsel cross-examine witnesses.

In light of the many new laws and attitudes concerning illegal actions by juveniles, you should contact an attorney immediately when your child has been arrested.

Corporal punishment

Corporal punishment is allowed in 42 states. In fact, the law allows more severe beatings of school children by teachers than by parents. Many schools have no legal obligation to inform parents when corporal punishment was used. Many parents reject the notion that such treatment instills discipline. They view it as child abuse and have brought civil suits against school boards. The Piwowars of New York filed a lawsuit alleging that a public school teaching supervisor screamed at their son Anthony, twisted his arms, and banged his head on the floor.

Federal offenses

The United States Attorney General, through local United States Attorneys, handles cases involving federal offenses where the defendant is under 18 years. The majority of cases coming under the *Federal Juvenile Delinquency Act* seem to concern interstate car thefts.

Who has custody?

A United States District Judge in Mississippi became involved in a custody case usually reserved to state courts after two state court officials granted custody to a father who had been accused of sexually abusing his nine-year-old daughter. The case reads like a T.V. drama with a divorce proceeding, custody granted to the mother with visitation rights to the father, accusations of sexual abuse, the mother denying the father visitation and going to jail for contempt, another judge refusing to consider a medical report and giving custody to the father, and the mother dying and the child being sent across country. The child's new guardians asked the federal court to intervene to recognize the medical records showing abuse and protect the child's interests. When the judge would not, a federal appeals court ordered him to hold a hearing on the issues. Thereafter, the federal judge rendered an opinion critical of the state court proceedings and ordered a new custody hearing, banning the state officials from participating.

Illegitimate children—who has custody?

The custody of an illegitimate child is usually determined in court proceedings. A writ is directed to whoever has the custody of the child, ordering the child brought before the court. Then the court determines the person or persons into whose care the child should be placed. The mother is of course entitled to the first consideration, subject, however, to the interests and welfare of the child. Second in consideration is the father.

When the care of the child is given the father, state statutes often prescribe a set of specific conditions the father must meet. By a law of Georgia, the mother is entitled to the custody of her child "unless the father shall legitimate him." The courts invariably maintain that the welfare and happiness of the child is the paramount consideration in a proceeding for his custody.

The harshness and unfairness of this rule has in some instances been set aside by the sympathy of the courts. Some have ruled that the father of an illegitimate child too young to care for itself is under the nonstatutory obligation to support it, which may be enforced in an action brought by the child through its next friend. The state stands in loco parentis (in place of the parents) to see to it that the child is supported, and can pursue the father (if proved so to be) of the illegitimate child.

Rights of an A suit was brought on behalf of illegitimate children for the wrongful illegitimate child death of their mother with whom they had lived and by whom they were supported. The Louisiana court decided that the right of a surviving child to sue did not include an illegitimate child and dismissed the case. The United States Supreme Court reversed this determination on the basis that to deny this right to an illegitimate child would be discrimination in violation of the equal protection clause of the Fourteenth Amendment to the United States Constitution. In a similar case, a Texas mother was denied the right to sue by a Louisiana court for the death of her illegitimate son in an automobile accident in Louisiana. She would have been allowed to sue if the accident occurred in Texas, because the Texas law did not make this distinction. The United States Supreme Court again reversed to put an illegitimate child on a par with a legitimate child for this purpose.

However, a recent United States Supreme Court decision, upholding the right of Louisiana to deny to illegitimate children the same right as legitimate children to inherit from their fathers, appears to cloud the issue as to whether a law that discriminates against illegitimates is unconstitutional. The opinion, upholding the Louisiana court's award of an entire estate to the brothers and sisters of a decedent over his illegitimate child, stated that the Constitution reserved to the states the power to "protect and strengthen family life as well as to regulate the disposition of property."

Adoption—how to adopt a child

The procedure for the adoption of children follows substantially the same pattern in every state. You may adopt an alien under fourteen who can qualify as a non-quota immigrant. See Chapter 8 on *Aliens*. You may also adopt an adult. Forty-four states now have some type of law permitting this. The purpose in most instances is to provide an inheritance device. The procedures are not as complicated as those for adoption of children. There is no duty to support the adult adopted.

A petition must be made to the court by those individuals seeking the adoption. With this petition is submitted the consent of the parents and those who have custody of the child. In cases where the child may have arrived at an age set by the statutes for doing so, the child's consent must also be included.

Is parental consent necessary?

The law concerning adoption has changed from a presumption that the chief consideration in case of dispute should be to return a child to the biological parents to one where the importance is the health and safety of the child.

States have had provisions in regard to adoption that, if the child concerned has a parent/parents or guardian, their full consent shall be obtained. In an older case in Louisiana two unrelated children, ages nine and ten, were in the care of the Children's Home Society. Both children were adopted. The papers were signed by the Superintendent of the Society and the adoptive parents. Twenty years later when the adoptive mother died, a question arose concerning the children's right of inheritance from her estate. Both their natural mothers were still living. Since neither had consented to their adoption, the adoption did not hold up and they could not inherit as proper heirs.

When it comes to children in foster homes or those who have been abused, the Congress has stepped in to change what states can do. They will be required to begin proceedings to terminate the birth parents' rights after a child has spent 15 months in foster care and immediately if a child has been abandoned, tortured, regularly abused whether physically or sexually and where the birth parent/parents have been murdered or assaulted a sibling.

States and courts still look at the case facts, but this will clarify the adoption process for hundreds of children in limbo or at risk.

In New York and Georgia, unwed fathers who have not consented to adoptions are given consideration in an adoption proceeding if they have shown an interest and a willingness to assume custody.

The Minor as mother

In the majority of states and the District of Columbia, a minor mother may, with court approval, place her child for adoption without her parents' knowledge or consent. Michigan, Minnesota, Pennsylvania and Rhode Island require a teen's parents to consent to or receive notice of a hearing on the adoption.

Other requirements

In some instances there may also be a required waiting period prior to adoption. During this preliminary waiting period the adopting parents care for the child, in order to avoid a later objection to the child after the adoption has occurred.

In some states the adopting parents must be residents of the state in which the adoption proceedings are instituted.

The character and social conditions of the adopting parents must of necessity be judged by the court to be suitable, largely from the facts peculiar to each case. The only restrictions are those created by the way the court may interpret the meaning of the word "suitable" in its relation to their financial ability, character, or environment. They must be desirable parents, capable, of giving the child a secure and decent home. The law, however, does contemplate that the adopting parents shall be of suitable age. The mere fact that one has reached an advanced age does not make it impossible for him to adopt a child. Everything depends on the specific facts of who intends to adopt whom.

Some states have religious restrictions for adoptions. In New York, the state constitution provides that when a child is put up for adoption, the child's religion should be matched with that of the foster parents "when practicable." This means that, if all other things are equal, custody will be granted to those of the same religious persuasion, although religious interests will not predominate.

Recently a deaf-mute couple in California were deprived custody of their two-year-old foster son because the court decided that the couple could not provide a normal home for him. The decision was appealed and the appellate court found that, since the couple had another older child who was normal and happy, there was no reason not to allow them to rear the boy also.

During the past century, an essential change has slowly been taking place in family relationships. One feature of this change is the inclination of courts to base their decisions in adoption proceedings less on the natural rights of the parents to their children and more on the interests of the child and society as a whole.

In fact, recently even single women have been permitted to adopt children. In California, the State Department of Social Welfare modified its standing prohibition against placing children with persons who are not married. Usually children who have special problems have been limited in their adoptability by families. It is these special children who are typically considered for adoption by singles. In Oregon a mature bachelor has been allowed to adopt a child. The Department of Welfare of the District of Columbia is also now permitting adoption by single persons, and private social agencies are seriously considering a change in that direction since the results benefit the single individual and more importantly, the child.

In adoption proceedings, be scrupulously careful to follow the statute of the state in which the proceedings are brought and the provisions governing the transfer of the relationship of the child from its natural parents to those who are being substituted. Adoption is no fundamental right as is marriage. This method for changing the parents of a child is created by statute. The natural parent of a child born out of wedlock may later change her mind about her consent to adoption and seek to set it aside.

Failing to obey the statutes
Failure to follow the laws of a state in regard to adoption may, many years later, have serious consequences. Thinking of a child as your own is not enough. Anna, born in Sweden, came to the home of her aunt, Mrs. Carl Brandl, in Kansas, when she was seven years old. For more than fifteen years she was treated as one of the family. When she left Sweden, that country had no adoption procedure and no such proceedings were taken here on her behalf.

Upon the death of her aunt, the settlement of the estate required a determination of her relationship to Mrs. Brandl. The court required that any claim Anna might have for a share of her aunt's estate must be supported by proof of her legal adoption. She was denied the share she sought. There had been no compliance by her aunt with the adoption statute of Kansas.

When adoption decrees become final

The adoption decree of a child had been made by a Michigan court on the last day of July and the consent of the parents properly executed and filed. Under the laws of Michigan and many other states, an adoption decree does not become final and binding until a stated period of time after it has been made. During that time the decree may be changed or modified by the court.

During the ninety-day period provided by the Michigan statute, the child's mother, apparently regretting the loss of her daughter, gave notice of her withdrawal of her consent. The court decided that not only was the mother entitled to withdraw her consent but that, "When the statutory provisions regulating the adoption of children cannot be complied with, the adoption will fail."

Why an adoption decree may be revoked

The decree of the court by which the foster father and mother supplant the natural parents of the child may be revoked or set aside for fraud, such as occurred in one instance where the adopting father was mentally unsound and misrepresented his condition to the court by a statement that he was of a sound and healthy mentality.

Except where the adoption decree is set aside for fraud or misrepresentation of the parties to the proceedings, it possesses the same permanency and finality as any other judgment of a court.

Abrogation of adoption

An adoption can be canceled by mutual consent of all concerned in the procedure, by the court on behalf of the child when the foster parents have been cruel or have refused to support the child, or, in very extreme cases, by the court on behalf of the foster parents for bad behavior by the foster child.

Adoptee's health

A jury in Massachusetts awarded nearly $4 million to a couple who alleged the state did not give them important health and family background information when they adopted an eight-year-old in the early 1970s. At that time it was proper to withhold data. All the state employee told them was that the child was abused, and no medical records existed. Actually, she was retarded and her mother was a schizophrenic. In her 20s at the time of the suit, the daughter had been in and out of psychiatric hospitals. The State changed its policy in 1990 to conform more to the trend elsewhere for disclosure.

Can an adopted child inherit?

Adoption proceedings create an irrevocable relationship between the child and its foster parents. The child does not, however, become a "child of the blood" of its foster parents, unless the statutes of the state expressly provide this in relation to inheritance from relatives of the foster parents.

In all states, however, an adopted child is the legal heir of the foster parents and will inherit the property owned by them at their demise in the absence of contrary provision by will. The rule as to "blood" relationship only extends to property of relatives of the deceased foster parents. Unless the state has a statute permitting it, this rule may prevent the adopted child from representing the foster parent as would a natural child for purposes of inheritance.

Elizabeth was adopted by Will Warr. After the death of Mr. Warr, his sister, Isabel, also died, leaving an estate. Had Warr survived his sister, he would have been entitled to her entire estate. The problem before the court was whether Elizabeth inherited the share in Isabel's estate that would have been her foster father's had he lived.

The inheritance by adopted children from their adoptive parents being governed entirely by the laws of each state, the court, following the state statute, ruled that the property of the deceased, who had died without making a will, should descend to kindred by the blood.

The laws of many states have abolished this discrimination against adopted as contrasted with natural children.

The law of guardian and ward

A guardian has the care and management of the property and rights of another person who for some cause, as infancy or unsound mind, is not capable of caring for himself or administering his own affairs. The natural guardian of a child is its father, or, if the father is deceased or has abandoned the child, then the mother.

The mother is the natural guardian of an illegitimate child. In cases of divorce, the determination of the guardian is made by the court in the award of the custody of the child. Where a child is of tender years, the mother is more frequently entrusted with guardianship.

This guardianship of a child, however, is subject at all times during the minority of the child to the control of the court. The guardian may be removed and replaced by another at any time when, in the opinion of the court, circumstances and the welfare of the child demand such a change.

In most of the states, a child older than fourteen has the right to select his own guardian, subject to the approval of the court.

Upon his appointment, the guardian is notified and must signify his acceptance before assuming the obligations of his trust. This acceptance may be assumed, however, by his performance of his guardianship duties, although in some of the states acceptance must be made within a specified time.

Upon acceptance of the guardianship appointment, the guardian must execute the statutory oath and file with the court a bond as security for the faithful performance of his duties. This security bond is required unless he has been excused from so doing by the court.

Rights and duties of a guardian

A guardian, other than one who is a parent of the child, is not entitled to the child's earnings, nor does he have any personal liability for his ward's support. The maintenance of the ward is solely from the property the guardian holds in trust for him. Its disbursement is subject to the approval of the court by which the guardian was appointed.

The religious instruction of the child is within the control of the court. The court may require the guardian to continue the child in the religious faith of the parents, or may refuse to permit the guardian to change the child from that faith to another.

The proper education of the ward is the obligation of the guardian also.

Where the ward has been accepted as a member of the guardian's own family, it is a general rule that the guardian is entitled to financial compensation in a reasonable amount—to be determined by the court—for the support of the ward.

The guardian's compensation

The compensation of the guardian for the services rendered in the care and custody of the ward and his property is, in most states, governed by statutes. These allow the guardian either a commission on the amount of his receipts and disbursements of the property of his ward, or a reasonable allowance that is determined by the court.

A guardian ad litem

This is a guardian appointed by a court on behalf of an infant to prosecute or defend any suit to which the infant may be a party. Not every state requires that the court appoint a guardian ad litem. Suits by infants are brought also by the infant's next friend, usually a parent acting on his or her behalf.

When guardianship ends

The marriage of a male ward usually terminates the guardianship. Insofar as the property of the ward is concerned, however, the guardianship usually is continued until the ward attains his majority.

When the ward is a girl, upon her marriage the guardianship usually terminates as to her person and, in some states, her property.

Otherwise, guardianship generally ends when the ward reaches the age of twenty-one.

Upon the termination of the relationship of guardian and ward, it becomes the duty of the guardian to account for all receipts and disbursements from any trust fund in his control. Pursuant to the direction of the court, he must turn over whatever property of the trust still remains in his possession.

It is possible that a trust as set up in a will or in a deed of trust may, by its terms, continue beyond the age of twenty-one. However, this can apply only to the property of the ward and involves a relationship that is different from guardian and ward and instead concerns a trustee and a beneficiary of the trust. You may wish to set up a trust fund for your children to gain tax benefits and to be sure of proper estate management. Your lawyer will be able to advise you.

Educational rights and obligations

Under a recent federal law, *Education of the Handicapped Act,* a "free appropriate public education" must be provided to all school age handicapped children, no matter how severe the handicap. The federal government will pay to the states up to 40%, by 1982, of the average per pupil expenditure. Many children who have been unable to attend school or have been forced to go to expensive private schools will be able to share in the fruits of the public school system.

In another area, the Supreme Court ruled that before a student may be temporarily suspended, he or she must first be notified of the charges. Further, if the charges are denied, the student must be given an explanation of the evidence the authorities have and also an opportunity to present his or her side of the matter in an informal hearing. The case arose in Ohio where, after some disturbances, a number of junior and senior students were suspended for ten days.

The Court said that since the state extended to them the right to an education, they could not take it away, even for a short time, without providing certain procedural protections.

Must a parent consent to minor's abortion

Mary Moe, an unmarried pregnant minor challenged the constitutionality of a Massachusetts statute that denied her a legal abortion without parental consent. The statute provided, however, that if either parent refused to give consent, she could petition a superior court to grant its consent. The U.S. Supreme Court held the statute unconstitutional, stating that while Massachusetts could require either parental or judicial consent to an abortion, it had to provide the minor the opportunity to obtain judicial consent without first notifying her parents. Furthermore, the Court stated that if Mary, or anyone else in her situation, could demonstrate that she was sufficiently mature to make her own decision, or if she established that an abortion would be in her best interest, the judge could not withhold consent.

However, in a recent case involving an immature pregnant 15-year-old girl in Utah, the Supreme Court declined to equate notice requirements with consent and held her parents were entitled to notice by a physician before an abortion was performed. Virginia requires notification but Maryland allows a doctor to waive the notice requirement. The topic of abortion is discussed in more detail in the Chapter 6, *Wife and Mother.*

What about contraceptives?

The parents of a 16-year-old female brought suit against the Tri-County Family Planning Center to enjoin it from distributing oral contraceptives to their daughter, and all females similarly situated, without first obtaining parental consent. A federal appeals court in Cincinnati held there was no constitutional obligation on the Center to notify the parents. As with adults, minors possess a constitutional right of privacy including the right to obtain contraceptives.

Are you safe at college?

The Campus Sexual Assault Victims' Bill of Rights gives victims the right to call on off-campus authorities to investigate sexual crimes. *The Student Right-to-Know and Campus Security Act* requires disclosure of crime rates on campuses. All college and universities receiving federal money must publish annually their security and crime reporting policies and make public the number of campus incidents of murder, sexual assault, robbery, burglary, motor vehicle thefts and arrests for weapons possession and offenses related to alcohol and drugs. The data goes to the U.S. Department of Education. Compliance has varied. Victims of campus violence also now can find out more about the criminal record of student violators.

In Loco Parentis

This term means *standing in for parents.* After the 26th Amendment to the Constitution lowered the voting age to 18, states and courts treated college students as adults. The students also wanted total freedom when they were in college. Now the pendulum may be swinging back. How much protection should be provided from crime and personal injury? Is crime foreseeable when prior assaults have occurred in a dark parking lot? What about admitting students with prior histories of sexual assaults? Should there be more security patrols and emergency phones?

Personal injury lawsuits are burgeoning. Students now seem to want protection from their careless behavior. Two students were injured when they ignored signs warning of a dangerous property condition. They sued. One student sued when he was injured after climbing atop a commuter train that stopped at a school owned station. A female student sued after she injured her arm on a broken soap tray in a dorm bathroom while showering with her boyfriend. More courts now are finding a need for universities to safeguard students, as the Delaware Supreme Court did in a fraternity hazing case. Some suits are frivolous, while others have merit. The jury is still out on the return of the doctrine of in loco parentis.

Molestation

The Supreme Court has ruled that students have a Constitutional right under the 14th Amendment to be free from sexual molestation by a teacher and they can sue the school district for damages. However, when fellow students are involved there is no federal complaint since then there is no Constitutional protection, no requirement for school officials to protect high school students from private misconduct.

Father and husband

5

Chapter 5
Father and husband

From time immemorial the legal rule has been that the father and husband is the head of the house. This principle, which in bygone days frequently had crude and even savage applications, has been softened by the greater warmth and informality of present-day family relationships, but it still exists. In everyday life and law, occasions often arise when this fundamental rule becomes of vital importance.

A famous lawyer of this country, James Kent, said of the relationship of a father and his children, "A father's house is always open to his children; and whether they are married or unmarried it is still to them a refuge from evil and a consolation in distress. Natural affection consecrates and establishes this asylum. The father is even under legal obligation to maintain his children and grandchildren, if he be competent and they unable to maintain themselves; it is nature's provision to assist, maintain, and counsel a child." Written more than 125 years ago, this is still a basic statement of the law of this country.

Take the matter of a child's religious instruction, for example. Many times the court's permission is sought to change the religion of a child. In general, however, they will rule that the child shall be brought up in the religion of the father, who has the right to direct and regulate the child's religious education.

The recent movement for the rights of women, which has challenged the traditional positions of husband and wife, has raised legal as well as social questions. While we may expect to see movements for changes in laws that favor the husband, comparatively few such changes have been made.

Can a father chase away his daughter's suitor?
In cases involving the marriage of a child, the father's rights are often brought to the fore. In California, Emory Smith was a suitor of Mildred Kiger. His presence in the home was more than unwelcome to her father, who once pushed Smith to the door, with a "Get out and stay out."

Later, Mildred Kiger and Emory Smith were married secretly. Next came an action for alienation of affection by Smith against his father-in-law. The expulsion of Smith from Kiger's home was part of the evidence at the trial. The court commented that it was settled law that a father had the right to forbid a prospective suitor to call on his daughter; further, that he was under no obligation to permit anyone of whom he did not approve to enter his home.

Can a child sue his father for injuries?
The old rule that allowed a parent to be completely immune from civil liability for any injury he caused to his child has been abandoned in some states.

The immunity has been suspended in cases where there has been grievous injury or where a parent had a responsibility to a group of people, including the child, and the suit was not designed to recover from an insurer. In New York, a child may sue its parents, although in one case there was no recovery when a 4-year-old pulled away from his father and was injured on a department store escalator. The court said that even devoted parents can be guilty of some occasional act resulting in injury, and the threat of civil suit against a remorseful parent for the consequences of his negligence is repugnant. In Virginia however, when a father disciplined his daughter excessively, including dragging her up 2 flights of stairs by her hair, a jury awarded compensatory damages to the child. The court said punishment must not be a cloak for the exercise of uncontrolled passion.

All states have criminal statutes punishing parents for intentionally inflicted serious harm.

Your obligation to support your family

In recent times, the law of child support has evolved so that a wife may be obligated by a court for child support to a former husband who retained custody after the divorce. Both parents may now be required by a court to share the cost of raising their children in accordance with ability to pay.

Most states, though, in order to prevent a child from becoming a public charge still have criminal statutes that punish a father for failure to support a child. The father can be sued by the child. Offspring over 21 and disabled, or otherwise incapable of self-support, must be provided financial support by their parents.

Many parents who owe child support and are in arrears are now affected by liens against property owned by them. The property becomes a security for the payment of the support and there can be no sale, refinancing or receipt of home equity credit until the debt is paid. The federal government, through the Office of Child Support Enforcement, Department of Health and Human Services, oversees a provision in federal law requiring states to implement a system of imposing liens for overdue support. Ten states, including Virginia, have automatic lien laws.

Child support indebtedness now shows up on credit histories which influence mortgage lenders and landlords. Nebraska and Alaska report delinquents to credit bureaus. Virginia and Maryland also report delinquents over $1000.

The Family Support Act was passed to further aid in assuring child support payments are made. It generally covers new support orders. Parents with support responsibility will have the amount automatically withheld from their paychecks starting in January, 1994. Where a custodial parent is on welfare, the law was to be implemented by all states in November, 1990. It is also required that states obtain both parents Social Security numbers at the time a birth certificate is issued so an errant parent can be found. The states are also required to review child support awards to be sure they meet current state guidelines which should reflect inflation, increased costs, and increased incomes.

More information on collecting child support awards can be obtained in the handbook on child support enforcement prepared by the *Federal Office of Child Support Enforcement*, Consumer Information Center, Pueblo, Colorado, 81009.

Illegitimate child

An illegitimate child may not maintain an action against his parents for being born illegitimate. A son who was born illegitimate brought suit against his father claiming that he had seduced his mother by promising to marry her. The father couldn't keep this promise as he was already married. The son sought damages for deprivation of the right to be born legitimate, to inherit from the father's paternal ancestors and for being stigmatized as a bastard. The court acknowledged that the father had committed a willful tort and that the son had suffered an injury but dismissed the case anyway. The court reasoned that to recognize the son's claim would be to create a cause of action for wrongful life. The legal and social implications of this would be enormous.

A Chicago man had lived off and on with a woman for 18 years, and three children were the product of this union. The mother died, and the state denied the father custody because he was not considered the parent under Illinois law. The children automatically became wards of the state. The father contended that he was denied due process of law as he was not given the opportunity at a hearing to show his qualifications. He also contended that he was denied equal protection of the law because an unwed mother would be recognized, where an unwed father would not. A prerequisite in such cases would be to establish the parental relationship.

Paternity tests

Until recently blood tests could only be used to establish that a particular man could not have been the father of a particular child. However, due to advances in technology, these tests, which were based on blood-grouping, have been surpassed by a new and more accurate test known as the Human Leukocyte Antigen (HLA) test. This new test uses a component of the white blood cells to determine that a particular man is the father of a particular child. The Human Leukocyte Antigen test provides definite results, but this test has been shown to be less reliable in Hispanic populations.

Status as father

Recently, the United States Supreme Court stated that fathers of illegitimate children may have a right to retain their legal status as fathers as long as they behave as fathers. The case involved a New York man's effort to block an adoption proceeding which, without notice to him, terminated his relationship to his illegitimate daughter. The father had made no move towards establishing a relationship with the child, had never provided support to the child, and had never offered to marry the child's mother. Meanwhile, the mother married and sought the adoption order to make her husband the child's legal father.

The court held that when an unwed father demonstrates a full commitment to the responsibility of parenthood by coming forward to participate in the rearing of the child, his interest in personal contact with his child acquires substantial protection under the due process clause of the Constitution. Here, since the father had not come forward, he had lost this protection.

Support

Generally speaking, the father's obligation for the support of his wife and children is confined to necessaries alone. "Necessaries," say the courts, is a relative term. It must be defined anew in each instance. *Necessaries* are defined generally as items or services reasonably appropriate for the support of a wife and child. What is "reasonably appropriate" must be decided case-by-case since it depends upon the specific needs of the family and the means of the father.

Some courts have decided that college education expenses are a necessity, given the need for more training for a tight job market. But whatever support has been deemed required by a court, payment must be made. "Deadbeats" no longer will be tolerated. Many states such as Maryland, Florida, and Illinois are taking away drivers' licenses, Virginia and others are seizing professional licenses. There also is the *Federal Child Support Act* that prohibits a father living out of state from falling behind on support payments. One deadbeat dad was given five years of supervised probation as well as ordered to pay his overdue support.

A father whose paternity has been established may not assert as a defense to his support obligation that the mother lied concerning her use of birth control devices. The case before the New York Court of Appeals involved Frank Serpico, the former policeman whose exposure of corruption inspired a motion picture. The family court reduced the amount that Serpico would have otherwise been required to provide because the court felt that the mother's wrongful conduct should weigh in favor of the father in determining the parents' respective support responsibilities. The higher court disagreed. The only factors to be considered in fixing child support are the needs of the child and the resources of the parents. The court also rejected Serpico's argument that his constitutional right to privacy including the decision whether to father a child had been violated.

When a child drives the family car

The advent of the family automobile enlarged the range of liability of the father for the wrongdoing of his children. There is disagreement among different states regarding the broadness of this range. In many states, the rule is that when a father allows any member of his immediate family to drive, all negligence by the driver is imputed to the father. This rule only applies to a child who was using the car for the purpose for which his father lent it to him. An equal number of states have the rule which states that when a father lets his child drive his car, the child is not acting as the agent of the father. They do not hold the father liable for the negligence of the child.

Use of automobiles by minors

In some states the danger from the use of automobiles by minors has been made the subject of special statutes. Typical of these is the one in Idaho stating that the owner of a motor vehicle who causes or knowingly permits a minor under the age of 16 years to drive such a vehicle upon a highway, and any person who gives or furnishes a motor vehicle to such a minor, are liable with the minor for any damage caused by his negligence in driving the car.

Liability here of the father is limited to the negligence of youngsters under the specific age of 16. When the minor is over that age, the father's responsibility is limited to accidents that occur when the boy or girl is acting for him as his agent.

Your responsibility for your child's acts

As a general rule, parents are not responsible for wrongs committed by their children unless the wrongdoing is done with their knowledge and consent.

Parents are liable, however, if a child has a habit of any particular type of mischief. Then, according to the courts, the knowledge of the father and his failure to restrain or supervise the child becomes the equivalent of a consent, and the father is liable for damages. In this respect the law of liability for malicious children is similar to the law with respect to animals.

A father is also liable for the damage that his child does if the father was negligent in allowing the child to use some object or implement. If a father gave his eight-year-old child a loaded gun, for example, and it accidentally went off while the child was playing with it, the father would be responsible for any damage or injury that resulted.

Recovery for adult child's death

Most states bar recovery by parents for the wrongful death of an adult. Florida changed its law to allow it.

Must you pay your wife's debts?

We have emphasized that there is an unquestionable obligation on a husband and father to furnish his family with the necessaries of living. When he fails to meet that obligation, his wife can buy the necessaries on his credit and he must pay the person who furnishes them.

This right that the law gives the wife to buy such goods on the credit of her husband has at times been somewhat overextended by women. What an extravagant wife may consider necessary does not always seem so in the opinion of the courts.

A husband is liable for all items that he has given his wife authority to purchase, on the theory that she is acting as his agent. Whatever goods are bought as necessaries must be bought by the wife on the husband's credit. Again, what may be deemed a "necessary" expense of the wife may depend on the customary standard of living that husband and wife have maintained.

The answers that courts have given to the question of whether a husband is excused from his obligation to provide necessaries for a wife who has independent means have shown a great inconsistency. Some states still require him to support her, while others excuse him from that responsibility.

When the husband's obligation ends

This obligation on the part of the husband for the furnishing of necessaries to his wife ends when the wife leaves the husband or refuses to live with him any longer, or when, for justifiable reasons, such as her adulterous behavior, he refuses to continue living with her. Some states have also enacted legislation that absolves the husband of the support obligation if the parties separate as a result of mutual consent.

The mere fact that the husband has published or given notice that he will not be responsible for goods furnished to his wife will not of itself relieve him from that liability. However, merchants furnishing such goods will be compelled by this notice to show that the husband's liability to them is for necessaries that he has failed to furnish his wife. Such a notice does not in any way affect the husband's obligation to pay for necessaries if he has wrongfully caused the separation.

The debts of a divorced wife

The rule that a husband's liability for his divorced wife's necessaries extends only to the amount a court decrees has sometimes led to legal entanglements, as in the following case. A husband and wife in New York had been separated by a divorce decree. The husband, under this decree, paid his wife a fixed weekly sum until she died. The executor of her estate refused to pay a bill for medical services furnished her after the divorce, claiming it was a charge against her husband. The court held, however, it was not an obligation the husband was bound to pay, and the charge was against the estate of the wife.

A husband is not liable for debts his wife incurs on her own credit—say, a fur coat she buys on her own account when he has specifically denied her one—nor for debts she owed before their marriage. A husband is not responsible for the services of a physician rendered his wife when she was living with an earlier husband, or before marriage.

Can a wife take her husband's funds?

Although a wife is entitled to support, this right does not permit her to appropriate her husband's possessions without his approval. In one case, for example, a wife desired to leave her husband and set up her own home.

When he refused to give her funds for this purpose, she withdrew the entire balance of their joint bank account.

The court held that even though she might have spent this money for necessaries which the husband was legally responsible for providing, she still had no right to help herself to his bank account without his consent.

Joint bank accounts are normally presumed to be half owned by each spouse. However, courts have declared that if there is evidence that one spouse or the other placed all the funds in the account, then the money belongs to that party, unless the depositor expressed a different intention.

Joint ownership may not be desirable

Joint ownership with a right of survivorship may be helpful for a residence that the wife would continue to live in should her husband die. It also may make sense where the property the couple have is not large and they each want the other to have it all on the prior death of one of them. However, when one person purchases property with his or her individual funds and takes title of that property in joint names with right of survivorship, for tax purposes this may be considered a gift, and the value of the gift depends on the state law as to the interest acquired by the joint owner receiving it as a gift.

Where a bank account is concerned, the gift does not take place until the money is withdrawn by the noncontributing joint owner. For estate-tax purposes, the value of all of the jointly owned property is included in the estate of the first one to die, unless the survivor can show what portion he or she contributed to the purchase price. However, for federal estate purposes, in the case of husband and wife, only half the value of a joint account is included in the estate of the first spouse to die.

A man's responsibility for the conduct of his home

Despite the fact that the prerogatives of the husband and father have been modified from what they were in the past, since he still holds the position of head of the house he bears primary responsibility for the conduct of his home and its occupants.

A husband and wife were indicted in Georgia for having whiskey in their possession. Officers found a liquor cache behind the false back of a bookcase.

The house belonged to the wife, and the husband disclaimed any liability. He neither rented nor owned the property.

"As long as the husband and wife are living together," said the judge, "the husband is the head of the family and the house occupied by them may properly be denominated as his house although the wife pays the rent and supports the husband."

An incident that illustrates the rule of law that a husband determines the occupants of his house arose when a man who owned an apartment building brought a suit to put out of the building his wife's granddaughter, who lived there, and a discharged handyman, who slept in the basement.

The man had ordered both to leave, but on his wife's advice they had refused to obey his request. The court held that this man, as master of the household, was acting within his rights. With the obligation to support, maintain, and protect his family, he also had the right to exclude intruders and unwanted visitors from his home despite the whims of his wife.

The situation may change if the husband and wife have marital difficulties. If the husband owns the house, he would still enjoy the same position, as head of the household, that he assumed when the couple were married. He will only be forced to relinquish this position if the wife gains the house in the property settlement.

If the house is owned by the wife, however, many states will give the wife the right to prevent her husband from residing in it.

A newly married Delaware couple moved into an apartment in a building that the wife owned. After two years, during which time the husband paid for improvements in the property around the building, they quarreled and the wife left the premises. The court rejected the argument of the wife that she left him because she feared for her safety, but still ruled "that a wife who leaves her husband without his having given her lawful cause to do so may (still) evict him from possession of all real estate owned by her as her sole property."

When husband and wife own property

The law provides for a convenient arrangement between a husband and wife so that all or any part of the property they own together is owned not only by both but by the survivor when either dies.

Under such a plan, deposits are made in a bank by a husband and wife in the name of both. This fund has a unity of ownership by both husband and wife, and either can make withdrawals.

At the death of either, the deposit in the bank belongs to the one who survives.

Usually banks give a name to a joint bank account which includes the term, "or to the survivor." It is this term that establishes the right of the survivor to the remaining balance on the death of the other joint tenant.

One real-life case involved the ownership of a bank deposit in the name of both the husband and the wife. The checks were signed by either. When the husband died, he was survived not only by his widow but also by a son and daughter. The man left no will. The problem was to determine the ownership of the fund in the bank, and the court's solution was to hold the widow the owner of the entire balance.

An interest in real property held in the name of both husband and wife is sometimes known in legal terminology as a "*tenancy by the entirety*." There are also joint tenancies and tenancies in common.

If the parties each have an undivided interest in the whole, but the survivor does not take the whole interest on the death of the other, it is a tenancy in common. If it is a joint tenancy or a tenancy by the entirety, then the survivor takes the whole interest.

In most jurisdictions, a joint tenancy or tenancy by the entirety cannot be conveyed or mortgaged by only one of the parties; the consent of both is needed.

Previously at common law, the husband was considered the "*entity*" in a tenancy by the entirety and he could sell it if he so wished. However, if his wife survived her husband, she got it back. Now that women have been emancipated, the husband's right to act freely with such property has been curtailed.

The large majority of states allow husbands and wives to contract with each other for all goods and services, except those involving essential aspects of the marital relationship. A husband could not enter into an enforceable contract with his wife to pay for her sexual services. Other types of agreements are allowed, although courts do look closely at any transfers of property between husbands and wives when they are challenged.

The law of community property

Eight states, Arizona, California, Idaho, Louisiana, New Mexico, Nevada, Texas, and Washington, have a system known as *community property*. Under it, property acquired by one or both spouses during their marriage, other than by gift or inheritance, is treated in a manner similar to partnership property.

The husband generally manages the community property and may sell or mortgage it. In some states that part earned by the wife may be managed by her. When either dies, in some states the property is divided and in others the survivor takes it all. If the marriage ends in divorce some states permit an equal division while others require it to be proportioned depending on the cause of the divorce.

What about the property rights of couples living together without marrying? In California the court found that the community property law was not applicable in the case of actor Lee Marvin. Michelle Marvin gave up her career as a singer and entertainer to act as homemaker for Lee in return for his support. They lived together for seven years and when they separated she wanted the property divided according to community property principles.

The court found no contract existed. Therefore, Ms. Marvin was unable to collect a one-half share of the $3.6 million that Lee had earned while they were living together. However, she was awarded $104,000 to help her reestablish herself in a career.

The Supreme Court has ruled that state community property laws cannot cause a child from a first marriage to have a prior claim to inherit pension benefits that otherwise would go to a later spouse.

How a husband becomes his wife's agent

That a husband may be the agent for his wife, and the wife may be the agent of the husband, is a familiar principle of law. This agency of the husband does not arise, however, merely by virtue of the marriage relationship. The agency must be created in the same manner as any other agency between those not so related. According to the law, in cases involving agency, an authority to the agent must be shown to bind the principal party, or there must have been acquiescence in the assertion of authority by the agent or ratification of his act. In general, however, the intimacy and confidence in the relation of husband and wife greatly enhances the possibility of the existence of an agency.

In California, a wife shared in the fraudulent profits of her husband from the sale by him to his partner of a ten-acre tract of land. The fraud arose because he pretended to his partner that he had bought the land from a stranger for $300 an acre, when, actually, it was his own, for which he had paid $35 an acre. Under the law, the wife, who cooperated in the transaction, was equally liable with her husband.

An incident that took place in Massachusetts illustrates another aspect of the responsibility of a wife for her husband's acts as her agent. Anthony Cobuzzy wanted to purchase a house and lot owned by Frank and Mae Parks. Anthony paid $20 down, all he had at that time, and Mrs. Parks took this money. Parks gave him a receipt: "Received from Anthony Cobuzzy deposit of $20 to apply on sale of house at 448 Concord Turnpike, Arlington, Mass. Balance of $1,980 to be paid 30 days from date. Buyer will forfeit deposit if balance of $1,980 is not paid as agreed."

This receipt was signed by Parks with his wife's name at her request, as well as by him in his own name. When Cobuzzy offered the balance, the wife refused to accept it. A better offer had been made for the property, and to justify her refusal she denied she had been a party to the transaction. This excuse the court refused to recognize. It held that in the receipt of the deposit by Mrs. Parks, the execution at her request and in her presence of the memorandum by Parks, and the subsequent conduct of one for the other, each was acting not only in his or her individual capacity but also as agent for the other. Her commitment to Cobuzzy had to be maintained.

Family and Medical Leave Act of 1992 (FMLA)

Thirty-two states, Washington, D.C., and some counties have some form of family leave laws. A few are generous. The issue is a matter of concern to both spouses involving as it does job protection in the face of family emergencies or crises. Employees have had to depend on the good will of a supervisor or company to allow time off without job loss. The leave is over and above leave which is part of employment benefits but not enough to meet the need. It is unpaid and time specific and usually only applies in companies with larger work forces.

The federal law covers companies with 50 or more workers. It requires provision of unpaid leave of up to 12 weeks annually for the birth or adoption of a child, the care of a seriously ill child, spouse or parent or an employee's own serious illness or recuperation. Health care insurance must be continued during the leave and the employee is guaranteed the same or an equivalent job on return.

To qualify, an employee must have worked for the company for at least a year and at least 1,250 hours in the previous year. Employers can ask for medical proof if the leave is for illness. The leave can be taken intermittently, except if it is for child care that must be employer approved. The employee should try to give 30 days notice if at all possible. If an employer is in violation, an employee can get damages in a suit and double damages if there has been bad faith.

Gun dealers beware

The number of persons killed by guns of all types, sizes, and calibers is escalating at a frightening rate. Although local jurisdictions, such as the District of Columbia, states, and Congress, have turned their attention to the problem, the death rate does not abate. There are laws penalizing ownership as well as the use of a gun in the commission of a crime. Waiting periods exist before the sale can be consummated to allow for cooling off time as well as for background checks. There are gun advocates and anti-gun advocates, but there are more guns in circulation now than ever before.

A new theory has developed in recent years. It is to hold gun dealers civilly liable for their negligence when they sell guns that cause damage or death. The cases have all reflected a lack of reasonable care in the circumstances, given that a gun is a deadly weapon. Substantial awards or settlements have been collected by these plaintiffs.

One jury awarded millions to a young woman shot accidentally by a neighbor's gun. The gun dealer was required to contribute to the award because he failed to provide written instructions or demonstrate to the purchaser the safe use and storage of the weapon. In another case, a store sold a shotgun to a drunk who shot an innocent party. The victim's widow received over $2 million.

Another store was responsible for selling a semi-automatic handgun to an adult who was buying it on behalf of a teenager who killed a teacher. In another so-called "strawman" sale, a gun dealer in California was held to be negligent when he sold a semi-automatic pistol to a 19-year-old youth's grandmother. He had tried to buy it and also referred to his grandmother buying it. The boy used it on a dare and killed someone at a party.

In another case, a pawn shop in Georgia failed to do a background check and sold a gun to a mental patient. One gun store clerk was deemed especially culpable when he sold an AK-47, five boxes of extra lead ammunition and three black knit stocking caps to drunk, underage males, one of whom had no I.D. and subsequently shot into a car on the freeway, killing the driver.

Wife and mother

Chapter 6
Wife and mother

Woman's role in society has moved from one of passive acceptance to active participation. Women are entering the ranks of professional and white-collar workers in increasing numbers. Marriage does not change many of the rights and privileges a woman enjoys when she is single. Her earnings are her own. The property she had before her marriage remains her own after she marries. The ancient legal doctrine holding that the members of the family are completely subject to the control and desires of the father and husband is quickly fading from our law.

One survival of the law of yesterday is the rule that substitutes the surname of the husband for the woman's maiden name. A famous incident on this point arose from the laws enacted against Confederate sympathizers during the Civil War. Verina S. Moore had before the Civil War taught school in North Carolina. With the money she had saved she bought stock of the Phoenix National Bank of New York City in 1854. Seven years later she married a Presbyterian minister named Chapman.

In 1864, her stock was seized by the federal government on the complaint that the owner of the stock was a rebel and that the stock "had been bought and taken and was held and used for the purpose of aiding and abetting and promoting insurrection and rebellion."

The papers in this action, however, named "Ver. S. Moore" the owner of the stock. After the war was over, Verina Chapman sued the bank for her loss. Asserting that the name of a married woman after her marriage is no longer the name of her father but of her husband, the court decided the suit in Mrs. Chapman's favor.

Using a maiden name
In Texas, Helen B. McK'y protested against the foreclosure of a tax lien on her land. Before marrying Scot McK'y, she had bought this tract in her maiden name, Helen M. Ball. No taxes had ever been paid by her, and seven years after her marriage a tax suit was brought against "Helen M. Ball." When this suit was instituted there was no Helen M. Ball. The woman of that name who had bought this land seven years before was then Helen B. McK'y—unless she was sued under that, her correct name, the suit was a nullity. Her maiden name of Helen M. Ball, said the court, was not her name.

In a case that went all the way up to the Supreme Court, the validity of an Alabama law was upheld, prohibiting a married woman from using her maiden name on her driver's license. The state law required each driver to secure a license in his or her legal name. The highest court in Alabama ruled that the state had a legitimate interest in requiring women to assume their husband's names. The Alabama court further stated that anyone, including a married woman, could take court action to change his or her name, and therefore there was no valid objection to the requirement that the current legal married name be used.

In Michigan a wife must change her last name if her husband changes his. Cases like these can be used to illustrate the point that you cannot generalize too much from one case. As you will see in Chapter 21 on *Names*, there are other cases that have decided the question of the name used in a lawsuit differently.

Restoration of maiden name

At common law, a person can assume any name that does not interfere with rights of others. Therefore, unless there is a statute to the contrary, a woman who has obtained a divorce may resume her maiden name even without permission in the divorce decree. The decree may also provide for restoration of the maiden name, even where there are children of the marriage.

Spousal abuse

Since the slaying of Nicole Simpson and the publicity about her having been abused by O.J., attention has been refocused on this serious issue. Long ago, under English law, a husband was responsible for his wife's behavior and support. He had a right to chastise her "when necessary." He was the head of the house and his wife's conduct was his responsibility.

There have been cases where the female spouse has chastised the male spouse. However, statistics reflect that when there is domestic violence, usually it is the wife who is the one attacked and injured. Although violence between spouses has occurred for years, it is a recent phenomenon for the battering spouse to be arrested for assault, even when the wife does not press charges. It has been found that arrest and prosecution are the way to stop future assaults. In Virginia domestic assault is a misdemeanor, with penalties ranging up to 12 months in jail and up to a $2,500 fine.

Most police, in the past, have ignored these assaults, although, if they had occurred between strangers, there would have been immediate arrests. Since internal police procedures dealing with domestic violence were vague or allowed on-site discretion by police officers, most officers chose to mediate or remove the offender for a short period.

However, now 7 states, including Virginia and the District of Columbia, require mandatory arrest when there is probable cause to believe that person caused the injury, fear of injury or fear of death. 26 states, including Maryland, have presumptive arrest, giving police some slight discretion. 12 others have hybrid policies. Prosecutors may work out appropriate sentences, including counseling, but the new approach to spousal abuse gives the victim time to resolve his or her future course.

No one should ignore physical abuse or threats. There are private and government agencies that can help you. And if you have been assaulted or threatened, your jurisdiction may now provide for criminal sanctions.

Marital rape

There has been a traditional belief that when a woman gets married she is presumed to have consented to sexual intercourse with her husband. Therefore, an element of the crime of rape, lack of consent, is missing.

The first criminal prosecution of a husband charged with raping his wife while they were living together was brought in Oregon by Greta Rideout. In 1977, Oregon law had invalidated spousal immunity in rape claims. She could bring criminal charges if she'd been forced against her will. Her spouse claimed the Oregon law was unconstitutional in that it denied men equal protection. Greta lost but on other grounds. He was found not guilty because of reasonable doubt, the required standard of proof. However, later he was found guilty of criminal trespass for breaking into Greta's home and for harassing her.

The laws are changing in this area. Thirty-nine states and the District of Columbia, allow women to bring some sort of rape action against their spouses. Maryland and Virginia have removed marriage as a defense. In Maryland, a nurse-wife was almost smothered by a pillow when she refused her husband sex. Another woman was choked and threatened with a knife. Both husbands were criminally prosecuted. In some states, however, the spouse cannot be charged because their laws define rape as "sexual intercourse, accomplished with a female not the wife of the perpetrator." In others the marriage has to formally end. In some where the statute doesn't have explicit exclusions, it has been interpreted has having an implicit exclusion. When Lorena Bobbitt allegedly was raped, she took a different route than bringing criminal charges against John!

A mother who doesn't protect her children

Should a mother be held liable for her spouse's sexual abuse of the children? A Minnesota woman was held liable, together with her husband, for significant damages because her chid, now an adult, was molested by him on a regular basis. A Texan judge has found a mother 50% liable in damages because a stepfather molested her two daughters when they were six and eight years of age. These mothers negligently allowed the abuse. Both the abusers in these cases served time in prison. Although the damage awards in these cases were beyond the defendants' assets, they had homeowners' insurance policies which covered claims for negligence. Their liability is in litigation.

A wife's residence

The determination of where a wife's home will be—not only the neighborhood but the house or apartment as well—is the husband's. The law is substantially the same as the Bible saying: "Whither thou goest, I will go; and where thou lodgest, I will lodge."

When a wife refuses to recognize and conform to this right of the husband by willfully leaving him without a just cause for so doing, she forfeits by such conduct her right to his support, to which she is otherwise entitled. However, in many instances she may decline to live in a residence of her husband's choice if it is considerably inferior to what he can readily afford.

A wife's right to leave her husband's residence

The statute of one state sums up the general law of the land: "The husband is the head of the family. He may choose any reasonable place or mode of living and the wife must conform thereto." But this rule, it has been pointed out in the courts, means that the wife must live where the husband directs so long as the husband behaves himself. When he adopts and persists in a course of conduct that renders it impossible for her to live with him in safety and decency, this prerogative of the head of the family comes to an end.

Are relatives-in-law an excuse for leaving?

Many cases involving the rule of the wife's residence arise because relatives are living with the parties concerned. Here is a good example. A six-room house in Baltimore sheltered not only Adam and his wife Marie but also his mother, an old and penniless widow. Adam and Marie quarreled often over the presence of his mother in the house. Finally Marie declared, "Either that mother of yours leaves this place or I do."

"If that's the way you feel about it," Adam replied, "I suppose you'll have to go. I can't turn my mother out. I'm sorry, but she has no place to go and nothing to live on."

When this quarrel reached the courtroom, the judge said, "The husband has a right to determine the domicile of himself and his family. The wife is compelled to accept as her domicile the place so selected and maintained, and as long as the presence of relatives leaves her under no restraint and mistress of the domicile, this does not constitute abandonment and desertion unless he is financially in a position to provide and support a home for such relatives who are dependent on him."

The law thus laid down by that court is the law accepted generally throughout this country.

A wife's right to her earnings

The ancient idea that the man is the head of the house still casts its shadow on the wife's right to the money she earns. This money is his, except as the old common law has been changed by statute. It has been so changed in most states, and she owns her own property and is free to dispose of it in all states. By law, a husband has a right to his wife's services in the care of the family and maintenance of the home. On the other hand, he cannot force her to work for him if he has a business of his own, nor can he oblige her to work for others.

Discrimination against married women

Job discrimination against women, especially married women, has been successfully challenged in the courts. The United States Supreme Court in a recent case upheld a decision that an airline policy barring married women from jobs as flight attendants constitutes sex discrimination in violation of the *1964 Civil Rights Act*. The Act bars sex bias in employment, unless discrimination is based on a bona fide occupational qualification reasonably necessary to the normal operation of a business.

Can a wife ask wages from her husband?

The employee of an insurance company was injured while engaged in his work and confined to bed for a month. His wife cared for him during his recovery. Later his wife claimed $80 under the *Workmen's Compensation Act* for four weeks' nursing and attendance. The court refused to recognize her claim because a husband is entitled to his wife's services.

In an unusual case that was tried in California, a wife was compelled, because of this same rule, to repay her husband the wages he had previously paid to her.

This woman had worked as nurse for the man she later married. She had told her patient before their marriage that if he would marry her all she would ask from him would be room and board for herself and her child and $80 a month. He married her. During the next three and a half years he paid her under this agreement approximately $3,500. Then she took her child and made her home elsewhere. He sued her for the money he had paid.

The court awarded him the $3,500 he had paid, saying, "It would operate disastrously upon domestic life and breed discord and mischief if a wife could contract with her husband for the payment of services to be rendered for him in his home."

Women's property right

In the 1830s, the first of several versions of the *Married Women's Property Act* was passed in each state, granting married women the right to contract, sue and be sued independently of their husbands, manage their own property, and work and retain their earnings.

However, there are various vestiges of male dominance that still exist today, especially where property is concerned. In common-law states, like New York for example, a woman who works only inside the home never has an opportunity to acquire property. In these cases, the women may only obtain an interest in property through a gift from their husbands.

At his death, a woman in any common-law property state has a right of dower in her husband's estate. This interest, however, can be in real property only. Thus a New Jersey widow has "a right" to one-third of her husband's estate, but if the couple lived in an apartment, this may amount to nothing. Some states, like New York, by statute have ended dower right and given the wife an interest in the husband's estate of which he cannot deprive her and from which he cannot cut her off by his will. For a further discussion, see Chapter 10 on *How to Make a Will* and Chapter 11 on *Death Without a Will*.

In community property states, husband and wife have equal rights in property acquired during the marriage; however, the husband has control. In two of the eight community property states, Texas and Washington, the husband and wife have separate control over property acquired during the marriage. In Louisiana, both spouses now have equal control.

Pension

A divorcing wife can receive a lump sum share of her spouse's pension at the divorce rather than as it is received by the spouse, says the New Mexico court. This follows other community property states of Nevada, Arizona, California. Texas still follows the "pay as it comes" approach. If the spouse can't afford a lump sum, installments can be required. (See also garnishment of a pension in Chapters 2 and 19). The Pension Rights Center in Washington, D.C., has a booklet *"Your Pension Rights at Divorce: What Women Need to Know."*

Who owns a husband's gifts to his wife?

Aside from the common-law dower right and community property, a wife owns, to the exclusion of the heirs of her husband, whatever property he may from time to time have given her during their married life. Clifford Perkins was a successful banker in the East. Whenever he bought securities, he divided them with his wife. He died in New York and his widow moved to California. His son Wallace, the child of a former marriage, survived him. When the widow died in California, Wallace, her stepson, claimed her entire estate, asserting it was the property of his father, of whom he was the only heir.

The laws of New York, where the husband was a resident at the time of his death, allowed the widow, in place of the old dower right, a share of her husband's estate irrespective of whether the estate was land or securities or cash. Consequently, under the settlement of the father's estate, the widow had received a specific sum of money. This was hers in addition to whatever gifts her husband had made her during his life.

The inheritance, as well as the gifts, the California court refused to disturb. These were hers, and her right to them was independent of any interest of her husband's heirs.

Her responsibility for her husband's savings

When the property a wife holds represents the earnings of her husband for her that he has entrusted to her care, the law is far different from what it is in the case of gifts. Savings from a husband's earnings must be carefully accounted for unless it can be proved they were gifts.

For six years a husband gave his wife all his wages. These were to be put aside for their old age. She survived him and claimed this accumulation of money to be her own property. The court disagreed. It maintained that such money was a trust fund in which the heirs of her husband's estate as well as herself were beneficiaries since no evidence was presented that proved the money to be a gift from the husband.

Does a wife have a right to her husband's earnings?

A woman does not have a right to her husband's earnings. Although she assists him in his business, even caring for the money that is the product of their joint labor, this does not make any part of his wages her property.

A Maine physician sought to recover from his wife's estate the money he had earned and given her for saving. She had taken charge of the business side of his work and saved the money he received, but in her own name and for herself.

This woman had had no money of her own except what she had taken of her husband's income. Her estate was $30,000. Half of this she had willed to her husband; the other half to charity.

By the decision of the court, the doctor was entitled to all this money.

How a wife becomes an agent for her husband

The same laws that govern the right of the husband to act as the agent for his wife apply to the wife in acting as the agent for her husband. The mere relationship of husband and wife does not itself create such an agency. There must be acquiescence on the husband's part in her assertion of authority, or ratification of her act. For the agency to be effective, it should be provable that the acts of the wife are binding on the husband.

What a wife can buy as agent

The purchase of food for the home provides the most common example of the wife acting as agent for her husband. A celebrated case was decided on the opinion of the late Justice Cardozo in one laconic sentence: "The husband through his wife, who acted as his agent, bought a loaf of bread."

When a husband and wife are living together, his relation with the neighborhood shops that supply the everyday household needs are in almost every instance carried on through the agency of the wife.

The law permits the wife to purchase the necessaries for the family on her husband's credit. But there the law says she must stop. Such an agency as the purchase of necessaries can be terminated on notice to the seller, as can be the purchase of any other goods on his account. The notice is ineffectual in the purchase of "necessaries" if he has ceased to give her the support he is obliged to by law.

Why notice to terminate agency is important

In some instances, when misunderstandings and trouble occur between a husband and wife, failure to bear in mind the need of a notice to terminate a right that either party has had in acting as the other's agent leads to disastrous consequences for the principal party. This is particularly true where valuable property is concerned.

A bank in Pennsylvania rented a safe-deposit box to a man, and he put some bonds into it. Afterwards, his wife frequently used the box. Six months after it had been rented, she made a visit to it that naturally aroused no suspicion. A few days later the depositor went to his box and found the bonds were gone. After another day or so his wife was gone too. Aside from the depositor, no one but the wife had had access to the box.

Later, when the husband sued the bank for the loss of these bonds, the agency of his wife in the use of the box and her appropriation of its contents were set up by the bank as a defense.

"The relation of principal and agent does not arise from the marital relationship," said the court, absolving the bank from liability for the loss of the securities. "The relationship of agency cannot be inferred from the mere relationship of family ties, but such relationship is competent evidence when considered with other circumstances as tending to establish the facts of the agency."

The "other circumstances" in this case were, of course, the wife's continued access to the box and her use of it with her husband's consent.

Women administrating estates

In 1971, the United States Supreme Court struck down an Idaho law that prefers men over women in administering an estate where two persons are otherwise equal. Mrs. Sally Reid of Ada County, in Idaho, brought a suit against her husband, who was named as administrator of the estate of their 16-year-old adopted son. The couple were divorced in 1958. The state legislature repealed the law in 1971. The Idaho Supreme Court had previously ruled that where persons in the same category, here parents, applied for an administrator's authority a male preference existed. Chief Justice Burger said that "to give a mandatory preference to members of either sex over members of the other merely to accomplish the elimination of hearings on the merits is to make the very kind of arbitrary legislative choice forbidden by the equal protection clause."

A wife giving evidence

At common law and carried over to the law of many states and in the federal courts, neither spouse could testify against the other in any proceeding. The theory behind this rule was to preserve the family relationship. Designed to protect and strengthen the marital bond, it encompasses only those statements that are "confidential," meaning that they are "induced by the relationship and prompted by the affection, loyalty and confidence engendered" thereby.

In New York and other states, by statute, not all communications. between husband and wife are privileged from disclosure. Further, in many states the privilege can be waived. It is clear that these statutes were not designed to forbid inquiry into personal wrongs committed by one spouse against another.

In an old separation and support case in New York, the husband testified that his wife told him of her adulterous relationship with another man. The wife objected to the admissibility of this evidence. The court said that the privilege was never intended "to label as confidential a communication aimed at destroying the marital relation or stamp with a seal of confidence and protect from disclosure an unfounded charge of adultery or, more to the point, a declaration by a wife that she loves another man and has had improper relations with him."

Under the statutory law of New York today, a husband or wife is not competent to testify against the other in an adultery action, "except to prove the marriage, disprove the adultery, or disprove a defense after evidence has been introduced tending to prove such defense."

The statutory law also provides that a husband and wife shall not be required, or, "without consent of the other if living, allowed, to disclose a confidential communication made by one to the other during marriage."

Abortion, contraception, artificial insemination

Scholars from all over the world in the fields of law, medicine, theology, and the social sciences, and laymen from every class in society are debating the subject of abortion as never before. "Abortion" and "miscarriage" are considered equivalent terms. They mean termination of pregnancy.

The effects of a drug called "thalidomide," which caused pregnant women to deliver deformed children, made the issue of legal abortion a widely discussed topic. Many women who had taken the drug and who were fearful of having deformed children sought abortions in the United States. But until very recently, the states prohibited abortions unless the life of the mother was threatened by continuation of the pregnancy.

Typically, in the District of Columbia, abortions were forbidden unless necessary for the mother's life or health. In Virginia, an abortion was only allowed to save the life of the mother. In Maryland, an abortion was permitted when two doctors agreed it was necessary to secure the safety of the mother. This has allowed for some more liberal interpretations.

The states have all had criminal abortion statutes. Some of them, Puerto Rico and the Virgin Islands, referred to acts done with intent to produce an interruption of pregnancy with no legal justification. There were various other rules. Wisconsin had two statutes dealing with illegal or unjustified abortions. One made it a crime, of manslaughter, while the other made it only an offense against morality. The difference is that the Wisconsin courts did not view a child in the womb under four months as a human being. Performing an abortion on a woman only eight weeks pregnant was an offense against morality only, in that particular state.

The child in the womb

It is conceded that pregnancy cannot, as yet, be determined before six to eight days since the tests work only after implantation. The circumstances of pregnancy are that an ovum or female egg is fertilized by a male sperm, and then the egg travels through the Fallopian tube, enters the uterus, and attaches to or implants itself in the uterine wall, where it grows for a period of approximately nine months. The initial stage, before attachment, takes about six to eight days. At this stage 'the child is what is called the "ovum." From the eighth day to about the eighth week, it is called an "embryo," and thereafter a "fetus."

A baby was born in Roanoke, West Virginia, to a mother who had been declared brain-dead and whose body was kept alive by machines for 84 days so she could give birth. The baby was delivered by caesarean section and appeared to be a normal 3 pound, 11 ounce baby. The case is similar to one in San Francisco where a brain-dead mother was kept on life support systems for 64 days until giving birth by caesarean section.

Right to life or invasion of privacy

Some critics of liberalized abortion laws claim that, historically, the unborn child was considered a person. Damages have been awarded for injury to an unborn child, as in Massachusetts, where, because of an accident to the mother, the child was born prematurely and died. Others say, however, that the right to determine when and whether to produce offspring is a private matter, and therefore the state abortion laws are an invasion of privacy. The right to privacy and the use of contraceptives is discussed in detail in the section on contraception.

Abortion reforms

The Scandinavian countries, Japan, and Great Britain are among those nations whose abortion policies are extremely liberal. In the past, many American women who could afford the expense went abroad to have the operation that was prohibited in the United States. Many others had to suffer through illegal operations.

On January 22, 1973, the United States Supreme Court reached an historic decision in the case of *Roe v. Wade*. By a ruling of seven to two, it was decided that states cannot prohibit voluntary abortions during the first three months of pregnancy. In the same decision, the Supreme Court also ruled that in the last ten weeks of pregnancy, abortion may be prohibited unless medical findings indicate that the life of the mother is endangered. However, there can be reasonable state regulations concerning the period between the first three months and the last ten weeks of pregnancy. The Court also ruled that there can be no prohibition directed against out-of-state residents. This historic decision, which affected the abortion laws all over the country, was reaffirmed in 1983.

Since the Roe decision, the issue of abortion has divided the nation into "pro-choice" and "right to life" factions. Thousands of persons march each year in rallies for and against abortion. Clinics which perform abortions have been picketed and bombed. Physicians who perform abortions have been threatened and two were murdered in Florida. Political campaigns have been won and lost on the issue. And state legislatures and courts have addressed varying facets of the issue, many in an attempt to test Roe in the currently more conservative Supreme Court. The Supreme Court has issued a number of opinions since Roe. They have discussed parental consent as compared to notification and that a state cannot place an "undue burden" on a woman's right to an abortion. They allowed an Indiana Court ruling to stand, which held that a husband had no right to veto his wife's decision on whether to have an abortion. She was six weeks pregnant. Not only was his consent not required, there is no judicial consideration of competing constitutional rights. He could not force her compulsory pregnancy and childbirth.

In a case from Kentucky, the Court allowed that state to enforce a 1986 law that required parental consent or a judge's approval for a minor to have an abortion. In 1983, they had struck down an Ohio consent requirement law because it did not contain a clear alternative to parental consent. In 1993, the Court let stand a Mississippi law, similar to ones in Massachusetts and North Dakota, which requires a woman under 18 to obtain both parents permission, or one parent when they are divorced, unmarried, apart or unavailable and containing the "judicial bypass" provision when the teen is unmarried, mature and it is not in her best interest to tell her parents.

Many state legislatures have passed varying forms of restrictive abortion statutes. The territory of Guam passed a very strict statute outlawing almost all abortions and imposing criminal penalties on doctors and women. A federal judge ruled it was unconstitutional and the territory repealed it. Louisiana's strict abortion law was declared unconstitutional. In Pennsylvania, a statute restricts abortions for 24 hours so doctors can give statements designed to discourage the abortion. It also requires spousal consent, which the Supreme Court has rejected. Utah's anti-abortion law was struck down by the 10th Circuit Court of Appeal.

The Supreme Court also has refused to allow Colorado to deny public funds for abortion in cases of rape or incest. Since the state accepts federal Medicaid funds, it cannot deny such funding for abortions. This ruling would also cover laws in Arkansas and Nebraska, restricting Medicaid funding to abortions where life was at stake.

Alternatively, many states have passed laws that follow the language in Roe, while some have put the issue to the voters. In Washington State the voters assured that abortion would be legal even if Roe is overturned in the Supreme Court.

When a doctor refuses to perform an abortion

Is such a refusal medical malpractice? In New Jersey, a child was born blind, deaf, dumb, and mentally retarded after the mother had contracted German measles early in the pregnancy. The mother sued two physicians who had refused to perform an abortion. The court dismissed the suit, since the New Jersey law allowed abortion only when the life of the mother was threatened by continuation of the pregnancy.

Abortion rights provisions

Generally, the typical state statute which allows abortions, permits them to protect the physical or mental health of the woman, allows the pregnancy termination when it is the result of rape or incest, and where there is a possibility of deformity or mental defect in the child. Some few statutes do not limit the basis and minors can seek abortions on their own. Most also provide for appropriate time limits.

Some laws that restrict abortions have some or all of the following provisions: That abortions only be performed in hospitals, not clinics; that physicians or other health care persons may refuse to participate; that they only may be performed, even in the first months, if the mother's life is in danger; that they may not be used for gender control;

that criminal penalties apply to the performing physician and the woman obtaining the abortion.

Because of changes in state laws, court decisions, and the volatile nature of the issue, if you are considering having an abortion, you should check immediately with your physician and an attorney.

Birth control information

A contraceptive is a device to prevent pregnancy. This was another subject that was not discussed publicly until recent years. It has also been an area liberalized after years of test cases and in some areas, commercials for birth control products are allowed to appear on television. However, the states have a variety of laws dealing with the subject of contraception and many cities have ordinances governing the sale and/or the advertising of contraceptives.

Police power

Since as far back as 1873, birth control devices have been regulated. The articles themselves were considered obscene. Congress prevented their possession, gift, or sale in the District of Columbia and all other areas of federal jurisdiction, until doctors were exempted from the provisions. But regulation of contraceptives and of the dissemination of birth control information has generally been considered to be within the police power of the state. It was exercised to preserve the public morals, public health, and safety.

In a New York case, a wife instituted a separation suit against her husband. She sought money for support. During the hearing she admitted that after the birth of their child she refused to have sexual relations with her husband until he agreed to use contraceptives. The court denied the wife support and held that her insistence on the husband's use of contraceptives was contrary to New York public policy and violated the marriage contract.

Then claims were made that the regulation violated freedom of religion, deprived the marital partners of their rights, or interfered with the free practice of the medical profession.

Contraceptives

The United States Supreme Court recently found unconstitutional a Massachusetts law which barred the sale or distribution of birth control devices to single people. It was held that the Constitutional guarantee of equal protection of the law was violated because married people were treated differently than unmarried persons. Back in 1965, the United States Supreme Court invalidated a Connecticut statute which prohibited the use of birth control devices on the ground that it was a matter of privacy in the marital relationship as to whether such items could be used, and that the state had no right to interfere. In this recent case involving Massachusetts law, the court overturned the conviction of a birth control crusader who gave an unmarried woman a package of vaginal foam, and held that unmarried persons have the same rights and could not be treated differently than married persons.

The Massachusetts law involved was a strong anti-contraceptive statute and some other states had similar restrictions, now invalid. Many states repealed theirs after the 1965 Connecticut ruling. New York had a statute which the Supreme Court recently held unconstitutional. The Act made it a crime to sell contraceptives to a minor under 16, for anyone other than a licensed pharmacist to distribute contraceptives, and for anyone, including pharmacists, to advertise or display contraceptives. Other states having similar laws will no longer be able to enforce them. Some states prohibit vending machine sales. An organization called Planned Parenthood can be contacted for information on this subject.

State laws

In 18 states and the Virgin Islands there have been no statutes dealing with the dissemination of contraceptive devices. They are Alabama, Alaska, Florida, Georgia, Illinois, Kansas, New Hampshire, New Mexico, North Carolina, North Dakota, Oklahoma, Rhode Island, South Carolina, Tennessee, Texas, Vermont, Virginia, and West Virginia. However, North Dakota, Vermont, Virginia, and West Virginia did have statutes that prohibited the advertisement of matter concerning venereal disease or referring to persons from whom treatment might be obtained.

Sixteen states and Puerto Rico had statutes regulating the advertising or dissemination of contraceptives and regulating sale by vending machines. They are Arizona, California, Colorado, Hawaii, Indiana, Kentucky, Louisiana, Maine, Maryland, Michigan, Nevada, Pennsylvania, South Dakota, Utah, Washington, and Wyoming.

Eight states prohibited the general sale of contraceptives except for physicians or pharmacists. They are Arkansas, Delaware, Idaho, Iowa, Montana, Ohio, Oregon, and Wisconsin.

In Nebraska and Missouri, the statutes prohibited the sale of contraceptives, but publication of standard medical information containing explanations was permitted, as was the teaching in medical colleges.

In Minnesota, the law prohibits the sale of contraceptive devices although it allows physicians to prescribe articles for the cure or prevention of disease.

In Mississippi, the sale and manufacture of contraceptives are prohibited. But the state does sponsor voluntary birth control clinics.

In recent years the restrictive laws of many states, including New York, Connecticut, and Massachusetts, have either been successfully challenged as unconstitutional or changed by the state legislatures.

The fact that your state may not have a strict rule does not preclude the possibility of substantial regulation at your local level. Many cities do have ordinances governing the sale of such devices. This area of the law that pertains to contraception is in a constant state of flux, and you should consult your lawyer.

Connecticut

This state's statute was the strictest of all. It made it a crime for any person to use any drug or article to prevent conception. So it became the basis for continued litigation. The Connecticut courts denied all claims, telling the parties to abstain rather than use contraceptives to prevent pregnancy. One early case went to the United States Supreme Court, but the Court found that, since contraceptives were being sold in drugstores in Connecticut, the law was not being enforced, so there was no basis for this particular suit.

Then came Mrs. G

The Planned Parenthood League of Connecticut decided to defy the Connecticut state law. They opened a clinic in New Haven with Mrs. G as executive director. She was arrested, as was the medical director, and they were both convicted as accessories under the statute for giving married persons information and medical advice on how to prevent conception and for prescribing contraceptive devices.

The case went to the United States Supreme Court in 1965. It was decided that Mrs. G and the League's doctor had the standing to assert the Constitutional rights of married people not parties to the case. The Court decided that the Connecticut statute forbidding the use of contraceptives was a violation of the right of marital privacy that is within the area of specific guarantees of the Bill of Rights. The marital relationship definitely lies within the zone of privacy created by several fundamental Constitutional guarantees. Another Supreme Court decision indicated that "whatever the rights of the individual to contraceptives may be, the rights must be the same for the married and unmarried alike."

Artificial insemination

This process is sometimes called therapeutic insemination and was presumably first performed in the United States after the Civil War. It is the introduction of semen into the vaginal area of the female by artificial means rather than through sexual intercourse. The semen can come from the husband or from a third-party donor.

Oklahoma was one of the first states to legalize human artificial insemination and to give protection to all parties involved, including legitimatizing the offspring of the procedure. Its statute provides that before the technique can be used, both the husband and wife must give written consent to a physician. A county judge must witness the consent and the physician must attest to the consent. Papers are filed in the same manner as in an adoption proceeding. The child has whatever status and privileges would be accorded to children born as the result of natural conception.

At least 16 other states have similar statutes creating the legal presumption of legitimacy for these children.

Sperm mix-up

A white woman, whose terminally ill husband's sperm was misplaced, sued her doctor and the sperm bank when she gave birth to a child who was black. She settled for a significant sum.

Children are legitimate
In California, prior to the enactment of its statute in 1975, the state Supreme Court held that a man whose wife gave birth to a child as a result of artificial insemination could be held criminally liable for his failure to support the child.

After the birth of the child, the husband and wife divorced. Later, the woman sought child support which the man refused to pay stating he was not the father of the child. The court held that the agreement which he and his wife had signed with the physician imposed upon him the legal responsibilities of fatherhood, including the responsibility of child support.

Rights of the children in other cases
In Illinois, a wife sued her husband for divorce. She claimed that their minor child was conceived by artificial insemination, that the donor was not her husband, and since the husband had never adopted the child he had no right to it. The court granted the divorce but found that the child was illegitimate, and so the husband had no interest in it. The child had not been represented in the proceedings to determine his legitimacy, so he was not bound by the judgment that determined him to be illegitimate. However, of course, the case is a matter of record and in later life he will have to meet the issue.

In New York, a happier solution was reached as far as the children were concerned. A wife obtained a separation agreement in the state that provided for her support and joint custody of the children. At that time there was no question raised concerning their birth. Thereafter, she went to Nevada and obtained a divorce that incorporated the custody arrangements of the separation decree. Sometime later both spouses remarried. However, after the wife's second marriage, something happened and she refused to allow her first husband to see the children. She made the claim that the children were conceived by artificial insemination, and since the donor was not the husband he had no rights. The court was very much concerned about the children, saying that they should not be made pawns of an unhappy marriage nor be made bastards at this late date. Inasmuch as the mother had never raised the issue before, it would not be considered now. The father was allowed his custody and visitation rights.

As a general rule, where the parties are married, there is a presumption of legitimacy for their children.

Artificial insemination is an area of the law that has many uncharted zones. It is certainly important, since there are many couples who cannot have children by any other means. If you are contemplating the procedure, you are strongly advised to confer with your physician and your lawyer before making any arrangements at all.

Wrongful birth and wrongful life
Wrongful birth actions refer to lawsuits by parents against health care providers for a failure to supply information or perform medical procedures with due care, which results in the birth of a defective child. Until recently, medical science had no way of predicting the birth of a defective child. New diagnostic techniques such as amniocentesis and

ultrasonography can now reveal defects in the unborn fetus. A wrongful life action is the child's equivalent of the parent's wrongful birth action.

In a recent New York case, parents of a healthy child claimed that a tubal ligation procedure was negligently performed on the mother. The parents sought damages for the expenses of pregnancy and child rearing. The court held that the birth of a normal child represented no legal harm.

A Washington case

The Washington Supreme Court has joined the California Supreme Court in holding that a child born with birth defects because of his mother's use of a drug during pregnancy may bring a "wrongful life" action to recover extraordinary expenses that will be required because of the congenital defects. The states of Alabama, New Jersey, New York, South Carolina, Texas and Wisconsin have disallowed this type of action. The court also recognized the parent's right to bring a "wrongful birth" action to recover for emotional distress and medical expenses attributable to the child's birth and defective condition. Wrongful birth actions have generally been accepted by all jurisdictions which have considered the issue.

Right to credit

The Equal Credit Opportunity Act passed by Congress in 1975 prohibits discrimination against an applicant because of age, sex, marital status, or because any income comes from public assistance. It also says you may not be discouraged from applying, and you should not be asked personal information about family intentions.

Creditors must, among other things, let you open your own account, use your own first name and surname, consider alimony, child support or any other income in deciding if you are credit worthy and give reasons why credit has been denied. They must also tell you which federal agency supervises their compliance with the law so you can know where to register a complaint. They cannot ask for information about a spouse unless that person will be liable for or use your account or will be providing income to you.

A creditor can be liable for up to $10,000.00 costs, and attorneys' fees if you win the case.

Some states, including New York, have their own Credit Acts. If you have been denied credit by any bank, savings and loan, finance company, retail store or credit card company, consult a lawyer as soon as possible.

Right to be served liquor

A Rhode Island law prohibited certain bars from serving beverages to women. The purpose was to protect women because "bars are rough places." However, what may have been gallantry is now Victorian condescension. The cultural revolution, said the Circuit Court of Appeals which reviewed the suit, is now reflected in the Constitution. They held the statute violated the equal protection clause.

VDT

VDTs are *Video Display Terminals* used with word processors. A number of states, including California, Massachusetts, Wisconsin, New Mexico, Washington, Rhode Island, and Maine, have addressed problems connected with their use including stress, back and eye strain, potential radiation hazards, and possible reproductive risks. Recent legislation in Suffolk County, New York, requires employers to pay for VDT workers' eye examinations as well as contact lenses or glasses.

A study by the National Institute for Occupational Health concluded that the use of VDTs and exposure to their electromagnetic fields were not associated with miscarriages. It did not cover the potential dangers of low frequency fields which can cause cancer.

However, a study done in Finland found that pregnant women working at terminals emitting higher levels of ELF (extremely low frequency) magnetic fields had significant risks of miscarriages. A *milligaus* is the unit of measure for magnetic fields and one milligaus is considered acceptable.

Citizenship

Chapter 7
Citizenship

"Citizenship in this nation is a part of a cooperative affair. Its citizenry is the country and the country is its citizenry." The Supreme Court of the United States made this comment in a recent case involving the loss of United States citizenship.

The Constitution provides that "all persons born or naturalized in the United States and subject to the jurisdiction thereof" are citizens. You can therefore acquire citizenship by birth or through a legal process established by the Congress, called *naturalization*. The words "nationality" and "citizenship" sometimes are used interchangeably.

Who are citizens at birth?
A person is a citizen at birth if he is born in the United States and subject to its laws, or is born outside the United States of parents who are citizens, at least one of whom has a residence in the United States or an outlying possession. Anyone who is born in an outlying possession in the United States of parents, one of whom is a citizen who has been in the United States or one of the outlying possessions of the United States for one year prior to the time of birth, or anyone born outside the United States of parents, one of whom is a citizen who, prior to the birth, was in the United States for periods totaling not less than ten years, is a citizen at birth.

There are also other specific provisions that grant citizenship in particular cases. Children born outside the country are given a certification of birth as citizens from a United States consulate, an office of the Department of State. Sometimes these certifications have been held insufficient, and the American parents must go to the Immigration and Naturalization Service to offer proof of the child's citizenship.

Wong Kim Ark's parents were Chinese aliens. He was born in California and lived there for 17 years. In the early 1900s he went to China for a visit, and when he was 22 he returned to the United States. He was refused permission to enter under the then *Chinese Exclusion Act*. He sued, and the case went to the Supreme Court. It was decided that:

> A child born in the United States of parents of Chinese descent who at the time of his birth are subjects of the Emperor of China but have a permanent residence and domicile in the United States and are there carrying on a business and are not employed in any diplomatic or official capacity under the Emperor of China, becomes at the time of his birth a citizen of the United States.

The Supreme Court's decision reaffirmed that Wong was born in this country and therefore he was a citizen here.

Court Interpreters
The Supreme Court has never found that there is a constitutional right to an interpreter in court proceedings. Some lower federal courts have required them in criminal cases. Most

state court rules require them, in some instances in civil cases also. But their competence is questionable. Being bilingual is not the same as being an interpreter.

One of the men accused and later found guilty in the World Trade Center bombing spoke Arabic. When he was initially arraigned, only an F.B.I. employee was available to interpret. He could only summarize not translate simultaneously and he certainly was not defense oriented.

Tests for certification as an interpreter in federal courts are rigorous but certification is not available even for Japanese. Many state courts don't test or they are very lax. Some interpreters are unfamiliar with dialects. An Indian from Mexico served many years in an Oregon prison for murder because his Spanish language interpreter made errors. Sometimes bilingual people are used who are available, as in the bombing case. In some instances courts have used the husband of abused women or attorneys for their clients, both unreliable practices.

Children born in the United States of alien parents
The rule that if you are born in the United States you are a citizen holds true even though your parents are aliens. There are two minor exceptions: children born to alien parents residing here while on duty for a foreign government ("within the realm of foreign ambassadors"), or while conducting a hostile occupation of the United States, do not become citizens by virtue of birth on our soil.

The courts have declared generally that a child of alien parents born on a vessel of American registry flying the American flag attains the same citizenship as its parents.

What if parents give up their citizenship?
Marie Elg, born in Brooklyn, New York, of Swedish parents, was taken to Sweden when she was four. When she was 15, her father resumed his allegiance to Sweden. Marie remained there until she was of age and then returned to the United States. Six years later the Department of Labor advised her that she was illegally in this country and subject to deportation.

The Supreme Court, however, concluded that just because she acquired Swedish citizenship when her parents resumed theirs does not mean she lost the United States' citizenship she acquired by birth. She could only lose it by operation of a treaty, Congressional enactment or her own voluntary action.

Illegitimate children
Illegitimate children of citizen mothers are granted citizenship if the mother had been continuously present in the U.S. or its outlying possessions for a period of one year at any time before the birth, even if the father is not a citizen.

Derived citizenship
If you hold citizenship only because your parents became citizens through naturalization—you were born in a foreign country—you have "derived" citizenship. If

your parents then lose their citizenship through denaturalization or revocation of citizenship, you also lose your citizenship.

An adopted child

A child adopted by citizens may be naturalized before turning 18 on petition of the adoptive parents. The child must have been lawfully admitted to the United States for permanent residence, must have been younger than 16 when adopted, and must have lived in the United States with his adoptive parents for two years prior to the petition. If one of the adoptive parents is serving overseas, then the two-year-residence requirement is not necessary.

Two nationalities

Some people who are citizens of the United States at birth are also nationals of another country. This is so because some countries where parents are born consider their children to be nationals of the homeland; this was the case of Marie Elg. Such people are called "dual nationals," and Congress has legislated in regard to the conduct of adult dual nationals.

After reaching adulthood they must be careful lest they lose their United States citizenship. If you are a dual national older than 22 and you voluntarily seek benefits from the foreign country and reside within that country for a period in excess of three years, you must periodically take an oath of allegiance to the United States before an American diplomatic or consular officer. Of course, if you are in a foreign country in service, to study, for your health, or on business, this does not apply. Also, if you are more than 60 years of age and have lived for at least 25 years in the United States, you need not worry about taking a regular oath while in the country of your other nationality.

What about the alien who marries the citizen?

Normally, an alien must be a resident for five years before becoming eligible for naturalization. An alien married to a citizen becomes eligible in three years.

In Maryland, a war bride had difficulty in obtaining her citizenship papers. She had married a soldier in 1956 and come to the United States. In 1965, her husband returned to active duty and was killed in Vietnam in April, 1966. In January, 1966, she had applied for citizenship in Kansas, where her husband had been stationed, and had passed her citizenship test. However, the family moved to Maryland before she could take her oath, and three weeks before the ceremony her soldier husband was killed. Since she had applied for citizenship as the wife of a citizen, her affidavits only proved three years residence. With the death of her husband the widow was required to prove a five-year residency. Because of the unusual circumstances of her case an exception was made, and in 1968 the exception became law.

When the citizen is in overseas employment

Anyone married to a United States citizen who is an employee of the federal government or of an American commercial firm and is regularly stationed abroad, needs no prior residence in the United States before making an application for naturalization, if the applicant intends in good faith to become a citizen.

An Air Force captain, stationed during World War II in New Guinea, was married to a girl of Sydney, Australia. After the war the captain and his wife lived for two years in the United States. He was then ordered to Korea and his wife was granted permission to join him in that country.

When his wife applied for citizenship, the provision of the statute quoted above, that the applicant's spouse be "regularly stationed abroad," was cited by the federal court as a basis for granting her petition.

Naturalization

No alien is required to become a citizen and many do not, even after many years of residence in the U.S. However, if you wish to become a naturalized citizen, you should be aware of the prerequisites and adhere to the procedures found in the *Immigration and Naturalization Act (INA)* and the regulations of the *Immigration and Naturalization Service (INS)*.

Naturalization refers to the process by which aliens acquire U.S. citizenship after birth. The 10 requirements for naturalization are:

Lawful admission as a permanent resident of the United States; continuous residence (not to be confused with physical presence) in the United States for at least five years immediately preceding the filing of the petition for naturalization (three years for spouses of United States citizens); physical presence within the United States for an aggregated total of at least one half of the period of residence (two and one-half years for most aliens, one and one-half years for spouses of citizens); residence for at least six months within the state in which the petition for naturalization is filed; ability to read, write, and speak ordinary English; knowledge and understanding of the fundamentals of the history and government of the United States; good moral character, attachment to the principles of the Constitution, and proper disposition to the good order and happiness of the United States; continuous residence (again, not to be equated to physical presence) in the United States from the date of filing the petition for naturalization until actual admission to citizenship; the intention to reside permanently in the United States; attainment of eighteen years of age at the time of filing the petition of naturalization (with exceptions when a child is naturalized with his or her parents).

Procedures

The INS is a part of the U.S. Department of Justice. They have been given the responsibility to deal with persons under the Immigration Acts. All applications, whether for permanent or temporary residence, are handled by them. They also screen candidates for naturalization.

An alien who wants to be naturalized must file a preliminary application with the INS, which should include information to allow them to determine if the applicant meets statutory requirements. After the filing of the application, the alien is scheduled for an interview with an INS naturalization examiner, at which the alien is questioned on the information provided in the application, is tested on his or her oral and written English and knowledge of United States government and history, and executes an oath regarding the affirmations in the application.

Once the interview is complete, the naturalization examiner assists the alien in the preparation and filing of the actual petition for naturalization, which is filed with the court designated for the alien's place of residence. In cases in which the naturalization examiner makes an unfavorable recommendation on the naturalization petition, a preliminary examination is held under the auspices of the court to determine whether the alien should be naturalized. Once the preliminary examination is complete, or in cases in which the naturalization examiner has recommended favorably on the petition, the alien's case is sent to the Attorney General of the United States for decision. Under the *Immigration Act of 1990* (discussed in detail in Chapter 8) the Attorney General is now the sole authority to naturalize persons as citizens. The courts continue to have jurisdiction in cases which were already filed with them or, if a petition for naturalization is denied by the Attorney General, the alien may go to court to have a new judicial review of the denial. An applicant can also go to a U.S. District Court for a hearing if the Attorney General has not acted on the application for 120 days. Once an applicant is successful they must take the oath of allegiance. The Attorney General must administer the oath of allegiance regularly and often and the ceremonies must be conducted as dignified occasions. The new citizen then receives a certificate of naturalization evidencing his or her United States citizenship.

The oath of allegiance

The alien who wishes to be naturalized must pledge that he will support the Constitution, that he will renounce all allegiance to any foreign state or person, that he will defend the Constitution and the laws of the United States, that he will bear true faith and allegiance to the Constitution, and that he will bear arms on behalf of the United States when required by law, or perform noncombatant services. If the petitioner satisfies the court that he is opposed to bearing arms or to performing noncombatant military service by reason of religious training and beliefs, then he need not take the oath on this point. However, he must agree to perform alternative service of importance to the national welfare under civilian direction.

Denial

If a certificate is denied by the Attorney General because of poor moral character and a court hearing rules in the same way, an alien may wait as long as five years before applying again. Denaturalization may also occur. This is discussed at the end of this chapter and in Chapter 8, *Immigration and Aliens*.

Some failures can be remedied

The laws relating to the granting of citizenship are strictly observed.

Oversights, omissions, mistakes, all doubts in relation to these applications are decided in favor of the government. However, a person who fails because of some lack that may be made up in time, like a knowledge of English or the workings of our government, may apply for another hearing when he is able to meet these requirements.

Additionally, the name of the alien can be changed in connection with naturalization proceedings by the court order that admits an alien to citizenship, if the alien so chooses.

Naturalization after service in the army

At one time special citizen benefits had been provided for aliens who have served in the armed forces. Service in the armed forces of the United States during World Wars I and II, and the Korean and Vietnam conflicts, brought citizenship. Today, however, you must hold permanent resident status before you can enlist in any branch of the armed forces. Male aliens who are permanent residents between the ages of 18-26 must register for the draft.

Good moral character

The law is clear that an alien must be of good moral character in order to be eligible for naturalization. But what actions are considered not moral? As regards adultery, the courts have not been uniform in resolution of the issue. In one case a man named Russo had been married for only two weeks when his wife returned to Israel. Thereafter, he had sexual relations with various women, and, at the time of his naturalization hearing, there were paternity and support orders outstanding against him. He was adjudged not to be of good moral character.

In another case, which arose in Illinois, a man had come to the United States leaving his wife, by her own choice, in a Communist country. He started divorce proceedings in this country, but before they were concluded he started to live with another woman. Two months after the divorce he married the woman. Technically, under the law of Illinois, he was an adulterer. But the court hearing his petition for naturalization felt he should not be penalized by being denied citizenship. The judge said that under the social norms of the community he had not exhibited such a lack of moral character as to prevent his attaining citizenship.

Gamblers and addicts

Certain undesirable aliens such as gamblers and addicts would be denied naturalization as being not of good moral character. What about someone who has obtained a Mexican divorce that is not recognized in his state but who has remarried anyway? As a bigamist, he may not be considered to be of good moral character, but the overall circumstances would be considered.

An alien was convicted of murder in California and then was given an unconditional pardon by the Governor. Despite the pardon, the conviction for murder barred his naturalization. This was true in a similar case in Florida. Other courts, however, have granted naturalization after a pardon.

An alien who had disregarded parking regulations on 23 different occasions was not denied naturalization, as the court did not feel this meant that he was against good order.

Anarchists and others

If a petitioner participates in certain proscribed activities during ten years preceding the filing of the naturalization petition, his naturalization will be barred. An anarchist or anyone else involved in activities designed to promote violence and disorder would be barred from citizenship.

Generally, offenses committed prior to the five-year period of residence required for naturalization are not a bar to citizenship, but information and evidence concerning them are received by the court to help the judge decide whether, in fact, the petitioner has conformed to the statutory requirements during the five years. Again you must remember that naturalization is not a right, and the petitioner has the burden of proving he or she is eligible...in all respects.

Bearing arms for the United States

This is part of the oath of allegiance 1 to be taken by a petitioner. An English woman met all the qualifications for naturalization, but she would not swear to take up arms against England. It was her love for her former country and not her religious beliefs that caused her to act as she did. She was denied citizenship.

In a recent case, an avowed pacifist and atheist was granted citizenship despite the fact she would not swear to bear arms. The court accepted her proof that her atheism was not a mere personal code but was a religion, and therefore she could claim it exempted her from the oath.

Losing your citizenship

You can lose your citizenship through involuntary expatriation if you commit certain acts that the law deems sufficient to deprive you of your citizenship.

You can also lose your citizenship through denaturalization after a court proceeding that revokes or cancels the naturalization certificate you received. Renunciation and involuntary expatriation can affect citizens by birth as well as naturalized citizens. Denaturalization can only affect those who were naturalized.

Voluntary expatriation

You must have a voluntary wish to surrender or abandon your citizenship. You abandon it by performing, as the Supreme Court has said, some act that is inconsistent with undiluted allegiance. A minor cannot voluntarily expatriate himself. But when a member of the Fleet Reserve became a citizen of a foreign country, the courts held his act was inconsistent with his oath of allegiance to the United States and was so repugnant to his status as a member of the armed forces that termination of his retirement pay was warranted. If you voluntarily perform some act that the law states can cause loss of citizenship, you must accept the result.

Expatriation under duress

You have the burden of proving that your act was not voluntary. But the courts are very sympathetic to pleas that you were coerced into acting as you did to result in your subsequent loss of citizenship. Coercion can include not only fear of bodily injury, but retaliation, imprisonment, tine, or economic deprivation.

The question of voluntary renunciation of citizenship became very important following World War II. After Pearl Harbor, all Japanese in the United States were forcibly removed from their homes and sent to various internment camps. This included not only Japanese aliens but native-born citizens of Japanese ancestry. In 1951, many thousands of Japanese who had renounced their American citizenship while in certain camps sought to have the renunciations rescinded. They claimed that the conditions of their resettlement and the tension and terror in the camps caused them to lose free will and to execute documents renouncing their citizenship.

The court, after hearing lengthy testimony and reviewing documents that recounted all of the terrible experiences connected with the uprooting of families and their miserable internment for some years, decided that many had, in fact, renounced under duress, and their citizenship was restored.

Expatriation and statelessness

If United States citizenship is lost, and the person is not a dual national, statelessness may result. However, many such persons, although they are considered aliens, have numerous rights while in this country. Even aliens subject to deportation are protected by law.

Anyone whose citizenship is in dispute has access to law to vindicate his status and title to citizenship. If you are abroad, you can apply to the State Department for a certificate of identity to enable you to return to the United States to press your claim. If your claim is rejected by the administrative agency officials, you can bring suit for declaratory judgment to determine whether you are a citizen.

Voting in a foreign election

Until a recent Supreme Court ruling, this was considered a form of voluntary expatriation by accepting the jurisdiction of the foreign country where the voting took place. In a 5-4 decision, the Supreme Court reversed the denial of a passport to a naturalized citizen, holding unconstitutional a statute that took away citizenship for voting in a foreign election.

A Mr. Afroyim was born in Poland and was naturalized in 1926. In 1950, he went to Israel and voted in an election there. In 1960, when he applied for renewal of his United States passport, the State Department refused it on the ground that he had lost his citizenship by voting in a foreign state. Mr. Afroyim sued, and the Supreme Court said, "Citizenship is no light trifle to be jeopardized any moment Congress decides to do so under the name of its general or implied grants of power." Therefore, the Court declared this part of the Immigration and Nationality Act unconstitutional.

Serving in a foreign army

The big question seems to be whether the service was voluntary or whether it was performed under duress. If it was done voluntarily, then the provision in the law that citizenship will be lost will be upheld by the courts. Marks was a native-born American who served with Fidel Castro's army from 1958-1960. After he returned to the United States, he was told he had lost his United States citizenship by such service. His case went to the Supreme Court. The Court found that by 1958 it was clear that Castro was a Communist and Marks' service was voluntary. So he had clearly manifested a lack of allegiance to the United States and his citizenship was rightfully lost.

But in the matter of Joao Camara, it was certainly clear he had been forced to serve in a foreign army. Joao was born at Fall River, Massachusetts, where he lived until he was 12 years old. Then, in 1921, he was taken by his parents to the Azores. At 21 years of age he was drafted into the Portuguese army. Fearful lest he lose his American citizenship, he consulted the American consul, who told him he should get permission to return to this country and join the United States Army as an alternative. He had no money for the return trip, and, on his protest against serving in the Portuguese forces, he was told by the Portuguese officials that either he would serve as he had been ordered or he would go to a concentration camp.

Discharged from the army of Portugal in 1945, Joao found a place as a stowaway on an air transport plane and landed in Massachusetts. When his case came before the federal court in this country, the judge said, "Camara had never forsworn his American citizenship; on the contrary, he had done what he could to assert it and to preserve it. His service as a draftee in the Portuguese army, with a concentration camp as the alternative, was under duress. As soon as he could arrange it, he returned to this country as a stowaway, which attests the intensity of his purpose to retain his American nationality." With this decision of the court, it was clear that Joao Camara was, in fact, a citizen of the United States, and had never voluntarily given up his citizenship.

An oath of allegiance to a foreign state

Taking such an oath is a ground for loss of citizenship. A boy was born of Polish parents in Buffalo, New York. When he was seven years old he was taken by his family to Poland. In 1926, at the age of 21, he entered the Polish military service, continuing to wear its uniform until 1929. During the following year he returned to this country.

His deportation was approved by the federal court because he enlisted in the Polish army after he became 21 years of age and later took an oath of allegiance, thereby becoming expatriated.

Employment by a foreign government

The law states that such employment is a ground for expatriation if nationality in the foreign state is a prerequisite to such employment. Obviously, this does present a problem of divided allegiance, and you would be wise to seek counsel before embarking on any such venture, lest you chance the loss of your most valued citizenship. The nature of the employment will, of course, be a consideration.

Treason, sedition, insurrection

Treason, sedition, and insurrection all are grounds for expatriation of a person who had previously been granted citizenship through naturalization. However, being a member of the Communist Party alone has been held not to be sufficient ground for loss of citizenship unless it can be proved in denaturalization proceedings that when the naturalization oath was taken the petitioner lied, and, at that time, he was fully aware of and was in favor of the party's tenet of overthrowing by force and violence the government of the United States.

Nazis

Many of them came here and were naturalized. But, they have been denaturalized on the basis of their lack of unlawful permanent resident status since they were ineligible for residence at the time they were admitted. They participated in persecutions under the direction of, or in association with, the government of Nazi Germany. They became aliens and were deported as persons excludable at the time of entry.

Denaturalization

Those who have been naturalized can lose their citizenship in two ways: If they lacked a statutory prerequisite for naturalization at the time the Attorney General's or court's order was entered, the naturalization is considered to have been illegally procured. This is easier to prove than a willful misrepresentation or concealment of a material fact, which is another basis for denaturalization. An example of a lack of a statutory prerequisite is the existence of a felony record.

As to willful misrepresentation, the INA contains three bases used as presumptions: If the naturalized citizen, within 10 years of naturalization, refuses to testify before Congress as to subversive activities and has been convicted for contempt for the refusal; if, within 5 years, the person joins an organization that would have barred naturalization if he had belonged then; and if, within 5 years, the citizen goes back to his former country, disposes of U.S. property, and gets involved in business in his native land, a presumption may be made that the person didn't intend to reside permanently in the U.S.

The Attorney General of the U.S. files the petition to denaturalize and the citizen has up to 60 days to reply. There is no time limit on when the government can bring these civil proceedings.

Immigration and aliens

Chapter 8
Immigration and aliens

"Give me your tired, your poor, your huddled masses yearning to breathe free, the wretched refuse of your teeming shore. Send these, the homeless, tempest-tost to me: I lift my lamp beside the golden door." Emma Lazarus wrote these words inscribed on the Statue of Liberty. People from all over the world have come to the United States to visit, to work, and to live. In 1882 the Congress passed the first of our many immigration laws.

Over the ensuing years the Congress passed many laws to control the influx of visitors and people who wanted to settle in the U.S. Some laws were visitor and settler friendly. Others were designed to insulate us from immigrants. The chapter touches on some of these laws. But the main emphasis is on the *1996 Illegal Immigration Reform & Immigrant Responsibility Act (IIRIRA)*, its 1997 refinements and the *1996 Personal Responsibility and Work Opportunity Reconciliation Act,* a companion to the IIRIRA.

Some observers have said that the IIRIRA changed and tainted America's image as a melting pot, the land described by Emma Lazarus. They have said also it is a law curtailing or denying equal rights, due process and traditional access to the courts. Others suggest it was necessary to protect jobs, stop persons from entering on false documents, and save tax-payers from subsidizing more welfare recipients.

In *1952* the *Immigration & Nationality Act (INA)* broadly affected immigration policy. That statute also was known as the McCarran Walter act. It generally established strict grounds for exclusion and deportation. One aspect finally is now being challenged in the Supreme Court. It made a distinction between foreign born children who were the illegitimate children of an American mother and a foreigner. Where the mother was American, the child could claim citizenship. But if the American parent was the father, then the children could claim citizenship only if the father had acknowledged his paternity before the child reached 18. The Supreme Court now will hear a case involving such a situation where the father missed the deadline. The issue is no equal protection based on gender stereotyping, very typical in the 50's.

The INA dealt with *"Aliens,"* a term used throughout all legislation in this field. Aliens could not work in the U.S. without INS authorization. Many who came and worked who had no papers were exploited and threatened with deportation.

Aliens
An alien is a person who is not a citizen or national of the U.S. Aliens who make application for any benefit under the immigration and naturalization laws fall into two categories. They are either immigrants, persons who want to come to the U.S. and live here permanently, or nonimmigrants, who must prove they only want to come temporarily, for travel, work or study. Since so many who come temporarily decide to stay, they have the burden to show they really don't intend to do that.

Visas

With few exceptions, all aliens who enter the U.S. must obtain a visa or an entry permit given to both people who come here temporarily or as permanent residents. There are 18 nonimmigrant or temporary visa categories. The permanent resident visa is the green card. Most nonimmigrant visas are applied for at an American Embassy or consulate in the applicant's own country. A prospective U.S. employer can make an application on behalf of an alien who is waiting abroad.

Refugee Act of 1980

The Refugee Act of 1980 was meant to remove some of the biases that had governed admission of refugees. *Refugees* are persons not yet in the U.S. who apply for admission at U.S. consulates abroad. Previously, persons escaping from Communist or Middle Eastern countries usually were given refugee status. The 1980 Act provided for asylum to any person demonstrating a "well founded fear of persecution." *Asylees* are persons already in the U.S. who are unable to return to their home countries.

Female Genital Mutilation (FGM)

FGM has been recognized by the United Nations and the World Health Organization as a violation of fundamental human rights and harmful to the health and well being of women. The custom has been condemned by leading medical organizations such as the American Medical Association and the International Federation of Gynecology and Obstetrics.

FGM is practiced in more than 40 countries as well as in the U.S. and has affected millions of females all over the world. It has become the basis for requests for asylum, women claiming to be refugees escaping from persecution under the Refugee Act. It covers three different forms of genital mutilation, from circumcision to infibulation. The practice is based on a belief that women are sexual creatures, naturally promiscuous and not only must they be prevented from giving in to their impulses, they must be protected from sexual aggression by others.

The INS determined that under some circumstances FGM may form the basis for asylum. In a case giving rise to that decision, INS found a woman from Togo had established a well founded fear of persecution and that most African women can expect little governmental protection from FGM. Specifically as to Togo, they found she faced danger of persecution throughout the country from police and her tribe because of her desire to avoid FGM.

Because of the prevalence of the practice in the U.S., a number of states including Minnesota, Rhode Island, Delaware and Tennessee have passed legislation criminalizing FGM.

More asylum protection for raped women

There has been more recognition that human rights abuses have been based on gender. There were the mass rapes of females which were part of the ethnic cleansing in Bosnia; there was the systematic use of rape in Haiti by police and soldiers during the coup against Aristide and it was part of domestic violence in Rwanda. Rape is now a form of political persecution and has been recognized as such by the INS. Guidelines have been issued formally recognizing that rape, domestic abuse and similar forms of violent actions against females may be grounds for granting asylum. Earlier this had been thought of as personal conduct.

In a case involving a Jordanian woman, a federal immigration judge granted her political asylum because her government had condoned spousal abuse including her spouse shooting her. The judge stated she had been persecuted for seeking her own identity, espousing Western values, refusing to live in a harem and being at the mercy of her husband, her society and her government.

Not all these type of cases involve females. A young Romanian male homosexual was granted political asylum. Because Romanian law prohibited homosexuality, he was arrested, put in prison and beaten. When he escaped to the U.S., he convinced the authorities his persecution was official government policy.

However, as we shall see later, the 1996 immigration law has radically changed the way these cases are heard and decided.

1986 Immigration Reform and Control Act (IRCA)
In its time this Act was considered a broad reform of the immigration laws.

It was the first federal law to prohibit the hiring of people who were not authorized to work in this country. Employers had to verify the employment eligibility of all new employees. It established penalties for employers who knowingly hired, recruited or referred for a fee aliens not authorized to work. There were legally acceptable documents which could verify both someone's employment authorization and their identity. Job seekers could show a U.S. passport, certificate of U.S. citizenship or various documents from the INS. They also could present a driver's license to prove identity and a Social Security card or certified U.S. birth certificate to establish work authorization. Employers could not discriminate against any job seeker with a valid work authorization on the basis of national origin, citizenship status or because they were foreign looking.

IRCA also provided amnesty to some illegal aliens who had lived in the U.S. continuously from Jan. 1, 1982.

1990 Immigration Act (IMMAC '90)
That act permitted a large number of immigrants to come to the U.S., mainly immigrants sponsored by their families. It allowed work authorization and delayed deportation of spouses and children of any alien who had been given amnesty under IRCA. It also set aside thousands of visas to give permanent residence to millionaires who would invest at least a million dollars in a new business in this country. They had two year conditional residences and could get full citizenship three years later if they created at least 10 jobs. The thrust of this was to bring to the U.S. Hong Kong money people who were worried about the impending takeover of Hong Kong by China.

Another important aspect of IMMAC '90 dealt with broadening the country base for giving asylum to persons fearing persecution. People from El Salvador and other Latin countries, like Guatemala, were not included as refugees under the Refugee Act. But, because of the wars there and America's political involvement, IMMAC designated nationals from El Salvador present in the U.S. as of September 19, 1990, as eligible for what was called "*temporary protected status*" *(TPS)*. This allowed for their stay of deportation and work authorization for 18 months.

TPS also can be given by the Attorney General to nationals who are designated as coming from a country that meets a variety of criteria including an ongoing armed conflict, earthquake, flood, drought, or any conditions preventing their nationals from returning safely to their homeland.

Foreign tourists

IMMAC allowed them to come without the need for a visa for a period not to exceed 90 days. However, they are required by federal regulations to purchase insurance in case they die here or need to be medically evacuated back to their country. Insurance is also required of foreign workers.

Employers

Many jobs have been filled by persons coming from overseas. Employers who wanted to sponsor a foreign national for permanent residence status would show that the individual would not be taking a job from a U.S. worker. They did this by obtaining a labor certification from the *U.S. Department of Labor* (D.O.L.). If the alien was qualified for the labor certified job and met all other INS requirements, permanent resident status was granted.

When IMMAC '90 was passed, it created new categories for employment based immigration and provided for 140,000 such immigrants to enter the U.S. annually. Among the categories of workers were priority workers, who were aliens with extraordinary ability, professors, researchers, executives and managers. The D.O.L. didn't need to certify them. Others were professionals with advanced degrees or abilities in the arts, services or businesses, professionals with bachelor's degrees, skilled workers doing jobs requiring at least two years of experience and unskilled workers performing jobs requiring less than two years experience.

Permanent residence status, the Green Card

There are four principal ways to obtain permanent residence status (the "*green card*"):
1) through sponsorship by a close relative who is a U.S. citizen or a permanent resident;
2) through a petition by an employer;
3) through an application based on "Registry," or
4) through an application for refugee or asylum status.

In addition, there are a limited number of immigrant visas for certain "special immigrants" including the millionaire investors and religious workers.

"*Registry*" which is a procedure whereby an alien who has resided in the U.S. since before January 1, 1972, and is not otherwise inadmissible, may obtain permanent resident status.

The J Visa

This visa has become the most publicized of those granted to aliens who are non-immigrants because of one type of recipient, the *au pair*. The J Visa was established in 1961 pursuant to the *Mutual Educational and Cultural Exchange Act* for non-immigrant bone fide students to study in America in order to increase the mutual understanding between countries. These visas usually have been given to teachers, medical students, and research scholars. They also have been given to airline pilots being trained. In 1986 a program was inaugurated granting visas to au pairs or mother's helpers. They must be between 18 and 25 years old. Originally they came to study and learn about a different culture. In recent years the program has become solely child-care, focusing world attention on the participants in the arrangement as well as the program itself.

The *U.S. Information Agency* (USIA) has been given permanent oversight of the au pair program, although some critics believe that since it is a work program and not a cultural exchange, the U.S. Department of Labor should be the responsible government agency. USIA has granted certification to eight "sponsor" agencies which organize the visits. Employers who hire au pairs do not pay Social Security taxes or send into the IRS the W-2 employer forms required for household help.

Au pairs should not be confused with nannies. The former generally are untrained in child care and receive only a small weekly stipend. Nannies receive extensive child care training, even degrees, have years of experience and are paid a substantial salary.

Death while in the U.S.

It's not a subject everyone thinks about, especially when one has come to do important work in the U.S. But the U.S. government wants to be sure that the taxpayers will not bear the expense of sending a foreigner's body back home. So there are regulations requiring the purchase of insurance.

The *United States Information Agency* is the rule-maker in these cases. Its regulations cover every non-resident alien on a visa, including scholars, teachers, researchers, even au pairs. Everyone must purchase insurance covering the return of their bodies to the country of their choice. In fact, even if the foreign visitor is cremated or buried here, they still must have had insurance.

The insurance generally covers only the minimum legal requirements to ship a body overseas. It does not cover the funeral, an expensive casket, or plane fare for anyone taking the body home. It does cover death certificates, embalming, (or, if the foreign visitor is Jewish, freezing in a wooden casket filled with dry ice) a plain casket and an airline freight ticket for the corpse.

The insurance also must cover a medical evacuation. As shown in Chapter 23, the cost of this service is substantial and so, commensurately, the coverage must be higher.

1996 Illegal Immigration Reform & Immigration Responsibility Act (IIRIRA)

This law affected our immigration policy in a multitude of ways. Persons with problems in this area of law will be well served to seek counsel as soon as possible. Counsel should be versed in immigration law, especially the ramifications of the 1996 Act.

One aspect of IIRIRA, which has been applauded, is its protection for spousal immigrant victims of abuse. Battered immigrant women and their children will not be subjected to deportation if their sponsors delay or refuse to file appropriate immigration documents on their behalf. They need not be intimidated by threats to stay in an abusive relationship in order to change their conditional status. Abused family members, who otherwise would be eligible for permanent residence, will be able to seek it on their own. This implements a provision in the 1994 law, *the Violence Against Women Act* (discussed in Chapter 6). The abused spouse (or child) must be living in the U.S., be of good moral character and have entered into the marriage to the citizen or lawful permanent resident in good faith. They must also provide evidence of the abuse.

Deportation for criminal activity

IIRIRA retroactively expanded the range of crimes for which legal residents now can be deported as being "aggravated felons". Deportation covers aliens already in the country. Before the 1996 law for bases usually were serious felonies such as murder, armed robbery and drug trafficking. Now conviction for a crime such as shoplifting, credit card fraud, or carrying an unregistered weapon is a deportable offense if it was committed within five years of coming to the U.S. and a sentence of one year or more could have been imposed, not necessarily that jail time actually was imposed. The possibility of a waiver, now called "cancellation of removal," no longer is available to residents with these convictions, even those whose lives have been exemplary since the crime and who have U.S. born children. Also the deportation process is considerably shortened.

Homosexuals and deportation

As we saw earlier, a homosexual from Romania was given asylum. Under IIRIRA, since illegal immigrants must prove that deportation would cause extreme hardship to a spouse, child or parent who is a U.S. citizen or permanent resident, it may be almost impossible for a homosexual to remain in the U.S. The laws dealing with marriage work against homosexuals and there are no natural offspring. Also, many come to the U.S. without their parents. In addition many are reluctant to admit their sexual preference. They may not file for asylum to avoid admitting to the type of persecution suffered by the Romanian youth.

Other deportations

Before the IIRIRA, illegal immigrants could hope to stay if they had been here for seven years and could prove deportation would cause them hardship. Now the standard of proof is extreme and exceptional hardship to immediate relatives such as ill children or frail elderly parents who are U.S. citizens or legal residents. Disruption of schooling, bad living or economic conditions in the country of origin or severance of ties with friends or family will not be sufficient to allow an illegal immigrant to remain. Economic hardship such as being the only support for infants or children in the U.S. might be given weight. However, even if one qualifies for a deportation waiver, the numbers are limited to 4,000 a year.

Section 245(i) and the $1,000 fine

Many people who come to the U.S. legally and have been waiting to obtain their green cards reflecting permanent resident status were affected by IIRIRA. Before 1994, green card applicants whose visas lapsed would remain in an illegal status until the applications were approved. They faced no repercussions for their illegal overstays. Once approved they were required to get immigrant visas at a U.S. diplomatic post abroad and reenter the U.S. legally to receive their green cards.

In 1994 the law (Section 245(i)) gave them the option of paying the INS a fine (now $1,000) so they wouldn't have to leave and come back.

IIRIRA changed all that. Under the 1996 law anyone who unlawfully stays in the U.S. more than 180 days over their visa time will be barred from getting a visa overseas and reentering for three years, even if he or she otherwise would be eligible for permanent residence. Anyone overstaying for one year or more will be barred for 10 years. And anyone who has been ordered deported and tries to come back will be barred forever. There are some exceptions, for example, asylum seekers and battered spouses.

Because Section 245(i) allowed the payment of a fine, there was no need to go abroad for a visa. However, that provision required a Congressional extension. Thousands of immigrants were in a state of panic over the potential lapse of the provision since many had overstayed their visa limits waiting for their green card applications to be approved. Once required to go overseas, under IIRIRA they could not reenter.

Section 245(i) was given a temporary extension but only for illegal immigrants for whom family members or employers had filed visa petitions or labor certifications by Jan. 14, 1998. The option to pay a fine will be closed for future illegals. They will have to return to their home countries to wait for their green cards and possibly be barred from returning for the varying lengths of time provided in IIRIRA.

The Congressional action in 1997 temporarily extending Section 245(i) also granted amnesty to Nicaraguans and some Cubans who had come to the U.S. before Dec. 1, 1995. Salvadorans, Guatemalans and some East Europeans were allowed to apply for "suspension of deportation" under the less strict law before IIRIRA. Haitians were not included for amnesty although they may be considered in future Congressional legislation.

Sponsor income

IIRIRA requires that the citizen or legal resident sponsor of a relative who wants to come to the U.S. will have to sign a legally enforceable affidavit promising to support the relative at an income 125 percent of the poverty level until they become a citizen or work for 10 years. The sponsor also must have an income of at least 125 percent of the poverty level for his or her family plus that of the relative. The poverty level presently is $22,000 for a family of four persons. If the sponsor doesn't meet the income requirements, the alien won't be able to become a resident whether or not he or she has resources.

INS authority
Under IIRIRA, immigration officers at points and ports of entry into the U.S. will have the final authority to deport people who arrive with no documents or false documents. They perform an expedited removal and their order is not subject to review by other authority, administrative or judicial. The person involved then cannot come back for five years.

Persons fleeing their country must prove to the officer that they have a credible fear of persecution in order to stop their immediate expulsion and be allowed to apply for asylum. And if they make it in, they must file an asylum application within one year. If they miss the deadline or can be sent to a safe country, they may also be barred from applying for asylum.

Federal court review
The INS no longer will be required to justify most of its decisions to a federal judge. IIRIRA bars review by any court of INS final deportation orders based on criminal convictions as well as discretionary relief decisions by the Attorney General of the U.S., except in cases of asylum. It also prevents a federal court from hearing cases such as those involving visa issuance, detention, asylum adjudication and border enforcement unless they are brought by the government.

The Personal Responsibility and Work Opportunity Reconciliation Act of 1996
The Congress has a way sometimes of telling the country what its purpose is by the titles it gives to the legislation it enacts. This 1996 law was aimed at getting people off welfare and reducing benefits formerly received under a number of government programs.

In connection with legal immigrants, the Act restructured their eligibility for most means tested benefit programs including *Supplemental Security Income* (SSI), which is a form of cash assistance to the needy, blind and disabled, food stamps and Medicaid. It also allows the states, in their discretion, to bar them from state and other programs.

There are a few exceptions including refugees, asylees, active duty military and veterans and their families and legal immigrants who could prove that they, their spouse or parents worked steadily in the U.S. for 10 years.

Immigrants arriving after Aug. 22, 1997, are barred for five years from federal means tested programs except they may receive emergency medical aid, disaster relief, participate in school lunch programs and other protections necessary for life or safety as determined by the Attorney General of the U.S.

Your civil rights

Chapter 9
Your civil rights

The constitutions of the United States and the various state governments, with their amendments, guarantee citizens of the United States an equal opportunity to enjoy life, liberty, and property. These guarantees include the right to own property, freedom of contract, equal protection of the law, and the right to vote without restriction by reason of sex, race, color, religion, or previous condition of servitude.

These civil rights provisions of the federal and state constitutions exercise a wholesome influence by preventing enactment in the various states of legislation that might conflict with the democratic spirit of our nation. These legal safeguards are also used to protect citizens from the abuse of public officials.

There is a law of the United States that has often conflicted with state laws, but which secures a fundamental right enjoyed by all citizens. Any person who, by acts done under state laws, subjects another to the loss of "any rights, privileges, and immunities secured by the Constitution and laws" is liable in damages to the person injured. Such illegal acts, when performed by public officials, are described as committed "under color of law" that is, with a local law to justify them when actually a federal law prohibits them.

This federal civil rights statute has often been invoked in keeping prison officials in check. A typical case involved a prisoner at an Illinois state penitentiary. He complained that he had been struck by a prison attendant with a blackjack, dragged to a sub-basement cellar, chained by his wrists for 18 hours and kept in solitary confinement for 92 days. For six of every seven days during that time, his diet consisted only of bread and water.

The essence of this case, said the court, was that under the civil rights statute the warden had failed to secure to this prisoner immunity from injury—a civil right—while the prisoner was in the custody of the prison officials. The court held that under the conditions outlined by the prisoner he was entitled to damages from the warden for the injuries he had suffered while in solitary confinement.

Rehabilitation Act of 1973, as amended
This Act covers handicapped employment by the federal government and private employers who receive money from the federal government.

Qualified handicapped individuals, which can include alcohol and drug users, cannot be denied employment and reasonable accommodation has to be made for their known physical or mental limitations. Pre-employment medical examinations cannot be limited only to handicapped applicants. A handicapped person can file administrative claims and lawsuits for discrimination. But the Supreme Court has ruled that the government hasn't waived sovereign immunity from money damages so any federal agency violating a law protecting the disabled from discrimination need not pay money damages.

The Supreme Court ruled that discrimination against the handicapped by the federal government and recipients of federal funds extends to those with contagious diseases. The U.S. Department of Justice has said this includes persons with AIDS who are not a direct threat to the health and safety of others.

Birth defects

However, the Second Circuit Court of Appeals in the famous Baby Jane Doe case decided that this Act cannot be used to police the medical treatment of children born with multiple birth defects and prospective severe mental retardation. Such children are not considered handicapped under the Act, nor was Baby Jane discriminated against by the hospital when a consensus was reached not to treat her surgically.

Civil Rights Restoration Act

This Act is linked to some provisions of the *Rehabilitation Act of 1973*. It made the nondiscrimination provisions of the Rehabilitation Act applicable to all activities of a recipient of federal funds, not just the particular part that receives or uses federal money. It also excluded from the definition of handicapped, anyone using drugs or alcohol, who, because of it, is unable to do the job or is a threat to safety or property. It also touched on the issue of contagious diseases which the Supreme Court had discussed in a decision on the Rehabilitation Act. It follows the decision by excluding from the definition of handicapped, those persons with contagious diseases who constitute a direct threat to the health and safety of other persons. But an employer would have to verify all the medical facts of the contagion and transmission before firing any employee.

Americans with Disabilities Act (ADA)

The ADA fills in where the Rehabilitation Act of 1973 left off and extends its protections. Whereas before, only employment by the federal government and those private employers receiving federal funds were covered, the ADA covers almost everyone in private employment and employment with municipal and state governments. It covers more than three million private enterprises that operate more than five million places of public accommodation. Former Attorney General Thornburgh characterized the regulations implementing the ADA as a balancing between the right of persons with disabilities to enter the mainstream of society and the workplace, and the financial and physical limits of the business community and others.

There are over 43 million disabled and they represent the largest minority group in America. More than 28 million are unemployed. This legislation and the regulations implementing it are seen as the means to open the door to use their many skills.

The ADA has been described as the most sweeping civil rights law. since the Civil Rights Act of 1964. It covers the use by the disabled of public and private transportation and structures open to the general public, as well as the employment of the disabled. The access provisions are all-inclusive. It doesn't matter whether it is a Mom-and-Pop deli or the Sheraton Hotel Corporation, whatever entity to which the "able" public has access, now must be useful to the disabled. In providing access to places of public accommodation, there will have to be more than just handicapped parking and a wheelchair-friendly bathroom. The things we deal with daily and take for granted will all have to be rethought in terms of their use and accessibility by the disabled. Barriers, such as turnstiles, steps, and carpeting, may have to be removed entirely or made user-friendly. Display racks, tables, chairs, telephones, paper towel dispensers, and shelves are other barriers that may have to be moved. Automated teller machines may have to be repositioned. Doorways will be widened and Braille dots or voice announcements will be put into all elevators. Interpreters for the deaf or blind will be required. Hotels will install smoke detectors with lights for the hearing impaired. Not only the stations, but busses and trains will have to be accessible.

One provision of the Act is considered of particular importance to the disabled because it gave them more ability to interact. By July 1993, telecommunication services must have been made accessible to persons with hearing or speech impediments so they could contact people who do not have special keyboard devices.

The ADA treats existing structures differently from new ones that will be built. New structures will have to be built with access in mind. Existing structures, not now accessible, must be altered to accommodate the disabled if change is "readily achievable." If not, they must provide relatively achievable alterations.

As to employment, the size of the business is important. Employers of 15 or more persons are included. Discrimination in all facts of the employment relationship is covered. Employers will be required to make reasonable accommodations so that otherwise qualified people with disabilities can perform the necessary function of their job, unless, of course, such action puts hardship (cost) on the employer's business. Implementation is a balancing, as former Attorney General Thomburgh has said.

There are some practices which employers have previously engaged in, that they will not be able to do now. For example, employers will be very limited in their questions of disabled prospective workers regarding past medical history. Medical exams cannot be given only to the disabled prospect. Employers will not be able to exclude the disabled from company pension plans. Employers cannot refuse to hire on the basis that the disabled person lives with someone with AIDS. Former drug users participating in a rehabilitation program are protected. But the ADA does not supersede other laws already in force on drugs and the workplace.

You must first file your claim with the E.E.O.C. They will proceed as they do with cases under Title VII of the CRA of 1964. The remedies are the same, including the award of attorney's fees. Specific time frames must be followed so you should consult an attorney as soon as possible.

Cases which have been filed already cover a variety of problems which are not the traditional discriminatory issues. They include suits for repetitive strain disorders or cumulative trauma disorders, suits by injured workers whose companies won't transfer them to a job that accommodates their injury, a suit against Wendy's, McDonald's and Burger King for allowing smoking thus discriminating against persons with respiratory ailments and lupus and a suit by a woman erroneously regarded as a drug user because of a mistake in drug testing.

AIDS

Many famous people have died from the virus which causes AIDS and many have died who are known only to their families and friends. The virus came to our attention comparatively recently, but its impact has been enormous. Because it is a world-wide killer of monumental proportion, with no known cure, it is frightening. But it is also a misunderstood ailment. Many people do not know how it is transmitted or who is at risk. Widely varied stories are told and believed, though they have no scientific basis. As a result the law dealing with AIDS and the legal rights of the persons who are infected are still in a state of flux.

The virus is the Human Immunodeficiency Virus or HIV. This infection causes AIDS, Acquired Immune Deficiency Syndrome. It weakens the body's immune system so illnesses that normally would not be serious or fatal, cannot be fought by a person's natural disease-fighting system. The HIV cells live in bodily fluids like blood and semen. They are passed to others as these fluids go from one body to another, in sexual contact, blood transfusions, in sharing of needles used during drug abuse, or during pregnancy from mother to child.

Since not everyone who has the HIV virus will quickly develop the symptoms of having AIDS, treatment can help prolong the time until AIDS manifests itself. However, the people who are HIV-positive find that their rights are affected by the perceptions of others concerning their danger to the population. The uninfected public fears the virus and wants to be protected.

The Americans with Disabilities Act, discussed above, will be helpful to persons who are HIV-positive, but they will still continue to face discrimination in employment, insurance, housing, and health care. Some examples—can persons with the infection of AIDS practice their professions if they are in health care and will health care professionals treat persons with AIDS; will emergency aid be denied them; will funeral homes prepare and bury them as they do uninfected persons; will landlords be free to terminate their leases or evict them; will insurance companies be allowed to cut or cap benefits, raise premiums, deny claims, disallow payments for experimental treatments; will criminal penalties be applied to some activities engaged in by an infected person? (This is discussed briefly in Chapter 25.)

The courts will be confronted more and more with these and other issues. But many infected persons may not pursue remedies they may be entitled to because of their desire to maintain secrecy, their lack of funds or stamina, or their lack of quality lifetime to wait for court dockets to catch up.

Thus far, infected persons seem to be successful in cases where their health care is at issue. They are doing a bit better with insurance claims and benefits, but poorly in criminal cases. Employment is a mixed bag of successes and failures. The ADA may help. They will also benefit from a change in Social Security's policy. (See *Insurance*, Chapter 23.)

If you are HIV infected, have AIDS, or are a family member or friend of someone in that condition, and you believe discrimination has been practiced against you or negligence has occurred, you should not delay in contacting an attorney or one of the numerous legal groups that have been established to give you the best and most current advice on your rights and remedies in this area. You should also quickly address concomitant issues such as a will and a durable power of attorney.

Employment "at will"

Employment "at will" means that an employee can be fired anytime by an employer, with no notice, no reason or explanation. There are still many places where that doctrine is accepted, such as in New York, which tends to favor employers' rights. In Alabama, Georgia and Mississippi the doctrine is such that you can be fired if your employer asks you to commit a crime and you refuse.

If you have a written contract that specifies the terms of your employment, you can only be terminated in accordance with those terms. But there are now recognized implied contracts. There can be promises about tenure in personnel manuals or the listing of specific reasons for discharge or having rights to a hearing. Even verbal promises can imply a long-term employment relationship.

Employees are suing for wrongful termination and many are reaping substantial jury awards. Federal laws banning discriminatory dismissals based on sex, color, race, national origin, religion, disability and age have helped (although only workers in businesses with 15 or more employees are covered). Firings for whistle blowing, filing claims for compensation or unfair labor practices are viewed as retaliatory and potentially compensable. And, generally, refusing to participate in immoral or illegal activities cannot be a basis for termination.

If you are fired, you should seek counsel quickly. There have been enough cases all around the country for your lawyer to assess the merits of yours.

Public employees due process

In 1985, the Supreme Court expanded the due process rights of public employees. Before they can be fired, public employees must be given notice of the charges against them, an opportunity to answer these charges, and a right to a hearing.

Retaliation

The Supreme Court has ruled that employers can't retaliate by giving bad references about a former employee who has filed a job discrimination complaint. Those still on the job can't be subject to retaliation but now the Court has interpreted Title VII of *the Civil Rights Act of 1964* also to include past workers. Employers can't retaliate with impunity.

Job discrimination against the obese

A large number of Americans are overweight. Many can lose it with exercise and change of eating habits. However, some obesity is of such duration that it substantially limits a major life activity or is regarded as doing so. The First Circuit Court of Appeals rendered a decision on a Rhode Island woman who suffered from "morbid obesity". She was at least twice the normal weight for her height. They determined that her obesity is a handicap or a perceived handicap, protected under discrimination laws, for which employers must make reasonable accommodation. Her case involved a state institution which received money from the federal government, so she was covered by the *Rehabilitation Act of 1973*. Her damage award of $100,000 was upheld. However, the Supreme Court of California has taken a different view. In a case involving an obese store clerk, the court said obesity is not a handicap when it is an immutable condition beyond a person's control.

Conspiracy of state officials

Arkansas law enforcement officers were indicted and convicted of conspiracy and misuse of power. They had falsely charged citizens with violation of law, held them in jail incommunicado, then tried them in "kangaroo courts" and fined them. The officers had been clothed with authority and their actions taken "under color of" state law were violations of federal and Constitutional law.

Suing a federal agent

The United States Supreme Court ruled in 1971 that federal agents can be sued for violation of Constitutional rights after an arrest or search. Narcotics agents had searched a Bronx apartment and arrested the occupant, who contended that unreasonable force was used in connection with the arrest and that his home had been entered without a warrant. He sued the agents for damages. The court held that federal police officers have no immunity to protect them from damage suits charging violation of Constitutional rights while they are enforcing criminal statutes. However, it is a defense to any such action if the police can prove good faith and reasonable belief in the validity of the arrest and search and the necessity for carrying out the arrest and search in the way it was conducted. This federal rule is quite similar to the general law in state jurisdictions with respect to mistaken arrest.

Trial by due process

Every prisoner is entitled to trial by due process of the law. Law enforcement officials must observe this rule without exception. In a Georgia county, late one night, the sheriff, a policeman, and a deputy sheriff went to the home of a 30-year-old black citizen with a warrant for his arrest. Apparently, the sheriff was nursing a grudge against the man and had threatened to "get" him. The official charge was the theft of an automobile tire. Handcuffed and taken by automobile to the court house, the prisoner was beaten with a blackjack by these three officers when he stepped from the car. Although their prisoner was knocked to the ground, the beating continued until he became unconscious. Dragged into the jail, he was thrown onto the floor and an ambulance called. Within an hour the man died.

These three men were indicted under the federal statute that makes it a crime willfully to subject any person "under color of law" to the deprivation of any rights or privileges, or to different punishments, pains, or penalties by reason of race or color.

They were found guilty and their conviction was appealed to the Supreme Court. Strangely enough, the defense urged it was murder they had done, committed in the official conduct of their duties, not deprivation of Constitutional rights. The court held this defense not valid, and found them guilty.

"Those who decide to take law into their own hands," declared the Supreme Court, "and act as prosecutor, jury, judge, and executioner, plainly act to deprive a prisoner of the trial that due process of law guarantees him."

In 1970, the United States Supreme Court significantly expanded the coverage of federal civil remedies available to victims of private discrimination, stating that the "color of law" provision was not necessary to obtain a federal remedy. A car containing five black people was stopped on a highway in Mississippi during the height of the civil rights activity in July, 1966, by two white residents. Mistaking the driver for a civil rights worker, the two white men severely beat the black passengers, causing bodily and emotional harm. The lower court's finding that the defendants did not act under "color of law," and that therefore plaintiffs were barred from recovery, was reversed by the United States Supreme Court.

Law officers and prosecutors off the hook

The California Supreme Court has, in the view of some authorities, given free rein to rogue cops and prosecutors to arrest and prosecute without good cause.

In one case, an Olympic wrestler hopeful was set up for dealing heroin by an L.A. police officer. When he was cleared after a trial, he sued for the months he was in jail and received over a million dollar judgment. The State Supreme Court overturned it stating the prosecutors were exempt from liability for malicious prosecution by a state law. And the police were civilly responsible only for the time the wrestler was falsely imprisoned by them, between arrest and arraignment, four days.

But in another civil suit on the worth of the four days, a jury doubled the earlier civil award as a rebuke to the Supreme Court.

In a second case, the court said that even though the wrong defendants had been prosecuted "in a blind quest to convict," prosecutors and their counties were exempt from civil suit for damages. Several men were accused of child molestation, convicted and imprisoned for five years. Their convictions were overturned when they proved prosecutors had intimidated and coerced the children into making false statements.

But the Court held that the prosecutors really were state employees and the state is immune from civil suits. Dissenters disagreed, saying they clearly were acting as county employees.

Immunity for members of City Councils and County Commissioners

A unanimous Supreme Court has ruled that these officials now have total immunity from lawsuits for legislative actions. State and federal legislators have always had absolute immunity. However, this does not protect cities from lawsuits.

Here an employee in Fall River, Mass., had been awarded more than $230,000 against former officials whom she accused of racial motives when they abolished her one person city government office. She was the first black administrator in the Health and Human Services Department and she claimed that after she made a racial complaint, the Mayor proposed eliminating her department and the Council agreed. She won in lower courts based on the view their actions were administrative, not legislative.

The Supreme Court focused only on whether the Council and Mayor were acting legislatively. There was a bill introduced to eliminate the Department, it was voted on a signed into law. "The ordinance was discretionary policy making reflecting budgetary priorities and services the city provides to its constituents." This was not a simple hiring and firing decision which would not be protected by immunity.

Immunity of state officials

No one, not even the governor of a state, is immune from violations of the Constitution of the United States.

A husband and wife were charged with using the United States flag in advertising. Efforts for their arrest in New York State were unsuccessful, and application for their extradition was made by New York State to the governor of Pennsylvania. The accused were arrested and returned to New York. Later they sued the governor of Pennsylvania on the ground that he had "unlawfully and maliciously issued purported warrants" for their arrest in violation of their civil rights.

Pennsylvania at that time had a law that the governor of the state, if he acted on the advice of the Pennsylvania Department of State, should be in no way liable for his action. Immunity from violating civil rights secured by the federal Constitution cannot be thus acquired, asserted the federal court. "To federal statute and policy a conflicting state policy and law must yield." This Pennsylvania statute was held unconstitutional and void.

Property rights

The Fourteenth Amendment of the Constitution of the United States has been held to give all citizens of this country the same right to purchase, lease, sell, hold, and convey real estate.

The meaning of this constitutional guarantee has been expanded in a recent Supreme Court case involving the refusal by a realtor in St. Louis to sell property to a black family. The court cited an old law, still in force, that provides that every individual shall have an equal opportunity to purchase property. The opinion stated that this must be upheld if the Thirteenth Amendment, which prohibits slavery, is to be effective. The Court noted that the inability to purchase property is a "badge of slavery," and it therefore ruled that permitting a realtor to refuse to sell to a black family would thwart the purpose of the Constitution.

It is not yet clear whether this decision will mean that property owners will be prohibited in all cases from all discrimination in selling their property. The federal "open housing" statute does specifically prohibit anyone from refusing to sell a home to any person because of his race, creed, color, or national origin, unless the seller owns less than three houses and does not use an agent for the sale. Refusal on other grounds, if they are reasonable, is not prohibited.

What about leasing?

A black family leased a house in a community in Virginia. Under the rules of the community, the owner of the house could also lease his share in a recreational club that was open to homeowners in the area. The corporation that operated the club barred the black family from leasing the membership in the club. The Supreme Court ruled that the play facilities were not private, but that membership in the club was an integral part of the lease to the house. Normally, any person who had a right to live in a house also had a right to join the club. Using the "badge of slavery" argument again, the Court said that to prevent someone from leasing because of his race, creed, color, or national origin is also not permitted.

Can you be denied access to public places?

Federal law does not permit most facilities open to the public to refuse to serve any person because of his race, color, creed, or national origin.

Included among those facilities are public transportation, restaurants, theaters, stadiums and other places of entertainment, gas stations, stores, and all hotels or motels except those with less than six rooms with the proprietor in residence. Facilities that are not open to the general public, such as private clubs, may legally discriminate.

A YMCA in North Carolina that had no stated limit on the size of its membership refused to accept a black member and claimed that it was a private club. In response to a suit by the man to gain admission to the YMCA, the court noted that there were no stated membership limits and that the YMCA did not operate as a private club. The opinion stated that, 'The simplest and most compelling answer is that serving or offering to serve all members of the white population within a defined geographic area (as was done here) is certainly inconsistent with the nature of a truly private club." It was therefore ruled that the YMCA was a public facility and must accept a black as a member.

This federal law does not cover bars, although it does cover soda fountains, and also does not prevent discrimination on the basis of sex. Women may still be excluded, unless local laws have been passed to end that practice. However, the courts have determined that women may not be discriminated against in public facilities. For a further consideration of the rights of females, see Chapter 6 on *Wife and Mother*.

It must be remembered that public facilities may still bar people for other reasons. A California racetrack removed an irate spectator who was intoxicated and was causing a disturbance because he thought that a race was fixed. In a suit for damages for this removal, the judge found for the racetrack, ruling that a public facility has the right to bar a patron on reasonable grounds.

Private clubs

The Supreme Court upheld a New York City law barring sex discrimination in clubs that refused to accept female members. There are tests to determine whether a club is "distinctly private" or a "public accommodation." This decision is in keeping with the former decisions barring discrimination in the all male Jaycees and Rotary Clubs.

The "private" status of two Princeton University eating clubs was challenged. They were "selective eating" clubs choosing their members, similar to fraternities. But the New Jersey Supreme Court stated that, although they were legally and financially independent, they were a part of Princeton, serving as the primary dining halls and could not discriminate against females.

Can people be prevented from voting?

Each state has a right to pass laws regarding voting qualifications. These laws will be upheld if they are based on sound principles. There are, however, certain specific restrictions on preventing people from voting in primaries or elections:

1. Literacy tests and other voting qualifications may be used only if they are applied fairly to all. The federal government will step in if it feels that these tests are being applied in a manner that excludes a specific ethnic group.

2. The poll tax is now illegal. A state or city cannot require you to pay money in order to vote.

A state may invoke requirements that affect a particular group only if the requirements are necessary for the proper operation of an electoral system. Some blacks in Alabama brought a suit because the state had changed many of their electoral districts. They saw this as a means of preventing them from voting. Their suit failed, since the decision was that these changes were necessary and that they were not made with the intention to dilute the voting strength of blacks in Alabama.

Equal rights in schools

Ever since the famous *Brown v. Board of Education* case in the United States Supreme Court in 1954, it has been mandated that schools cannot be segregated. This case has been interpreted to mean that not only the student body but also the faculty and administration of all public schools may not be segregated. The case has also been interpreted to mean that schools must be integrated. This integration has been accomplished in many areas by busing children from their neighborhoods to schools in other neighborhoods. Busing has been held to be constitutional, and, in some cases, mandated in order to achieve desegregation.

Private schools may choose their students on the basis of color and creed. However, if the school receives public monies or is technically considered an operation of a public authority, it must either abolish its discriminatory policy or give up its public funds and affiliation.

Hair length

School regulations in some states provide that the hair length of students may not exceed certain limits prescribed by school officials.

Federal courts in Utah, Colorado, and Oklahoma sustained these rulings, but in New Mexico, a federal court held that students' rights had been violated by the school board. The U.S. Circuit Court of Appeals for the Tenth Circuit, which covers this whole western area, ruled in favor of the school boards and the right to expel or punish a student who would not comply. The United States Supreme Court recently refused to review this determination by the Federal Court of Appeals, which, in effect, means that those school boards may continue to set such standards.

Federal courts in Massachusetts, Pennsylvania, Wisconsin, Illinois, Indiana, Alabama, and other states have held that the First and Fourteenth Amendments to the federal Constitution protect the civil rights of students. This has been interpreted to prevent public schools from excluding students on the basis of the length of their hair.

But recently, the state court of appeals in Texas declined to order a nine-year-old to be returned to his class after the school authorities sent him to be taught in an isolation room because his wispy ponytail violated hair length policy. His family has brought a civil sex-discrimination case alleging the hair length policy applies only to males.

Courts have also upheld the regulation of hair length for other purposes. A recent decision of the Eighth Circuit Court of Appeals, for example, indicates that a state can dictate the hair length of its male park employees based upon the belief that a park official is more likely to be effective when seeking to deter or stop violations when he has short hair.

Beards

Another issue dealing with hair is becoming important but it is in connection with shaving or grooming policy. This is of particular concern to black males who suffer from a skin condition called pseudofolliculitis barbae (PFB), caused when sharp, freshly shaved hair reenters the skin. In earlier years, a federal appeals court rejected an allegation concerning a grocery store clerk who lost his job because he refused to shave since he suffered from PFB.

Many law enforcement agencies require that their employees be clean shaven, ostensibly to command more respect as a part of a paramilitary group. In Maryland, a campus policeman at the University of Baltimore challenged the rule as discriminatory on the basis of his race. The Maryland Commission on Human Relations ruled that a ban on beards without medical exceptions is racially discriminatory under Maryland's civil rights laws. There was no showing of inability to perform his police duties with a small beard.

Although the Marines may adhere to a no beard rule, the other services permit uniformed males to wear a neatly trimmed beard if there is a medical reason.

Generally, on the job grooming codes are upheld except for charges of discrimination. Maryland had also brought a complaint against Dominos Pizza Corporation since its no beard policy constituted religious discrimination against a Sikh.

Nonsmokers' rights

The issue of smoke-free air has become so timely that at one point, forty-eight state legislatures introduced legislation pertaining to tobacco products and smoking. Approximately thirty-one states have passed legislation limiting smoking in public areas such as public buildings, stores, hospitals, public transportation and some government buildings. Of these thirty-one states, twenty-six passed comprehensive "Clear Indoor Air" laws. The remaining five states have more limited smoking laws.

Many other jurisdictions, such as municipalities and counties, have passed legislation regulating smoking in their areas.

Sometimes these local laws are more stringent and comprehensive than the state laws. In a number of instances tobacco industry lobbyists have attempted, in state laws, to preempt the stronger local laws.

Restrictions under these state laws vary. In Connecticut, a person is prohibited from smoking tobacco products in any public area of a restaurant having a seating capacity of seventy-five or more, unless otherwise indicated, as well as in certain health care institutions, in retail food stores, and in any passenger elevator. Nebraska's comprehensive *Clean Indoor Air Act* includes, but is not limited to, prohibiting smoking in restaurants, retail stores, offices, public conveyances, schools, hospitals, nursing homes, auditoriums, arenas, and meeting rooms. In other states, the law may allow smoking in restaurants but require that separate seating areas be designated for smokers and nonsmokers.

In recent years, because of the many scientific studies concerning the dangers of environmental tobacco smoke (ETS) or secondhand smoke, courts have begun to take action to protect persons considered most vulnerable to ETS: children. It has begun to be considered in the same light as alcohol or drug abuse. Many courts have issued orders prohibiting smoking by a parent in the presence of a child. Some consider smoking as a factor in child custody cases when parents divorce. In New York, the judge granted custody to the smoking parent because of other factors, but said it was a legitimate consideration. A Louisiana Court reduced a smoking father's visitation rights because his habit aggravated his child's bronchitis. Others are beginning to view the matter as child abuse or child neglect where a child's medical condition is adversely affected by ETS or it poses a serious health risk as in asthma sufferers.

Smoking and Airlines

Non-smokers on international flights who ask for non-smoking seats and then are put in a smoking section are suing in Small Claims Court. One who sued Air France for breach of contract relying on his boarding pass for a non-smoking seat won $500.

Very soon this issue may be resolved with all international flights originating in the U. S. being smoke free.

Workplace smoking

Because of the change in attitude in regard to smoking in the workplace, an earlier case involving a nonsmoker fired for complaining about smoke may be less likely to occur. June Anderson received $4,500 from a Minnesota jury when she was fired from her Welfare Board position with Anotka County for complaining about "a cloud of smoke hanging from the ceiling" in her office.

Now there are hundreds of companies that are regulating smoking in the workplace by separating smokers from nonsmokers or declaring all their work space environment smoke free. Many show preference in hiring nonsmokers because of office fires caused by cigarettes, health-related leave, insurance costs and lower maintenance costs for smoke free areas. However, when many companies started to regulate the habits of their employees off the job site by hiring only nonsmokers, some states passed laws to forestall what is called "lifestyle discrimination." At least 22 states prohibit employers from penalizing off the job smokers, or what some call after-hours legal activity. As this develops, the arguments will revolve around privacy versus health costs and the relationship between off-duty activity and a worker's ability to perform the duties of the job.

Smokers who lie

If you tell an insurance company you are a nonsmoker in order to qualify for a lower rate, you just might find you are not covered at all if you've been lying. A federal appeals court has joined numerous other courts in ruling that a life insurance company need not pay a death claim even though the cause was unrelated to tobacco addiction. You can never lie about your medical history and now smoking is treated as a medical condition.

There are numerous local groups forming to assist nonsmokers. There is also a national organization located in Washington, D.C. called *Action on Smoking and Health (ASH)*. Contact your local chapter of one of these organizations for more information.

Civil Rights Act of 1964

The Civil Rights Act of 1964 was an historic piece of legislation. It has changed the whole manner of treatment of persons based on their race, color, creed, sex, or national origin. Title VII of the Act was devoted totally to employment practices. It applied to employers, labor unions, and employment. It covered businesses in interstate commerce who employed at least 25 workers for 20 or more calendar weeks in the year.

Amended by the *Equal Employment Opportunity Act in 1962,* it extended coverage to employers with 15 or more employees, the federal government, state and local governments, government agencies, political subdivisions and public and private educational institutions. Exceptions were made for religious corporations, associations, educational institutions or societies employing persons of a particular religion to do their work.

A more general exception concerned employment discrimination with respect to sex and national origin when these characteristics are a *bona fide* occupational qualification (BFOQ) reasonably necessary to normal operation of a particular business. The BFOQ exception has been narrowly construed and will not be acceptable if based on stereotypes, sex-based assumptions or preferences of clients, customers, or co-workers.

Civil Rights Act of 1991

This legislation, perhaps, caused even more animosity among politicians, businesses, and organized civil rights groups than the legislation in 1964. Since 1964, the courts, including the Supreme Court, had developed a number of rules for determining how discrimination in employment should be proved and who should have the burden of proof. Then a more conservative Supreme Court handed down rulings which changed many of the accepted theories. The Congress then attempted to reinstate the Court's prior holdings by legislation. But they also wanted to extend certain rights to groups who had been left out, particularly as to their recovery potential. These persons were those discriminated against on the basis of sex, religion, their national origin or their disability. Although the *Americans with Disabilities Act* (discussed in this chapter) gave a number of new rights to the disabled, it did not clearly cover punitive damages.

Under the *Civil Rights Act of 1991,* employers again have the burden of justifying any hiring or promotion practices, such as job tests, that may unintentionally harm minorities and women in their work-force. Employers' practices again have to be proven related to the job performance of the particular position and necessary to their business, as was the case in earlier Supreme Court decisions.

The provisions in the Act which break new ground, as compared to Title VII of the 1964 Act, are in the area of punitive damages recoverable for discrimination based on sex, religion, national origin and disability. In the 1964 Act, there were no provisions for jury trials, or compensatory or punitive damages. A person could be reinstated in a job, given a promotion and recover lost pay, but could not be reimbursed for any medical bills or recover for pain and suffering or for emotional distress to which people who sue for personal injury are entitled. Racial bias suits under a law passed after the Civil War, the *Civil Rights Act of 1866,* allowed recovery of compensatory and punitive damages with no limit on the amount of recovery. But even this law was said by a recent Supreme Court decision not to cover sexual harassment of a black woman.

The 1991 Act changed that also. But, although it gave a right to sue, it required a compromise to win passage. It limits damage awards in sex, religious, origin and disability suits based on the size of the company being sued. Punitive and compensatory damages up to a limit of $50,000 are allowed for companies with 15-100 employees; $100,00 for those with 101-200 employees; $200,000 for those with 201-500 employees and a $300,000 maximum for larger companies. Most commentators believe that the limits will be raised or eliminated in the future since they apply to a restricted group of persons against whom discrimination is practiced.

Many employment agreements now mandate an alternative to litigating bias claims, settlement through binding arbitration. This method has been upheld by courts in age and sex cases in the security industry. But the employer sets the rules, picks the arbitrator and can limit recoveries. Many believe this alternative is unfair, requiring employees to sign away rights in exchange for a job.

The 1991 Act also allows awards to successful plaintiffs to include reasonable fees for experts who testify or provide other help with the case. This can be very important since experts are expensive but their testimony can be crucial.

It also included two other provisions that extended benefits not included in Title VII and the *Age Discrimination in Employment Act*. On the former, it provided that coverage should extend to U.S. citizens who work abroad for U.S. companies so they can sue for discrimination. As to the ADEA, the *Civil Rights Act of 1991* gives plaintiffs a right to go to court at any time after 60 days from the date they filed charges with the EEOC. Previously, if lawsuits weren't filed within two years of the alleged discrimination, the right to sue was lost.

The Act did not specifically say it could be applied to cases pending at the time of enactment or to pre-Act conduct for which a suit might have been brought after it became law. The Supreme Court now has decided that the presumption against statutory retroactivity is sound and this Act cannot be applied retroactively.

Religion
Both the CRA of 1964 and 1991 prohibited discrimination because of religion. Religious views cannot enter into employment decisions and religious practices must be reasonably accommodated unless there is undue hardship such as changing a seniority system. However, lately, some religious expressions in offices have been taken as impositions on others. There promises to be litigation and possibly further Congressional legislation on this topic.

Punitive damages
Compensatory damages are awarded to reimburse for losses related to the harm caused by the bias. Punitive damages are meant to deter conduct or punish for the biased action, which must be intentional. One such case involved a black male truck driver whose supervisors called him "nigger," told racial jokes, and decreased his work assignments. He sued the company and was awarded both compensatory damages for his disability job-related stress and punitive damages.

Generally, however, if you suffer from discriminatory conduct, you have a more difficult time proving the intent necessary to collect damages. In California, which has its own broad state fair employment law (Ohio and Michigan also have laws broader than the federal law), the appeals court, although allowing employees alleging sexual harassment to seek punitive damages, has required strict standards. In a case where the alleged harassment took place in a hospital, a nurse claimed that a hostile work environment was created by the physician-harasser when he grabbed her co-workers' breasts and made obscene gestures. The Court said the nurse would be entitled to punitive damages even though she may not have been a target, if she can prove that the harassment was in her workplace and was serious, not occasional, sporadic or trivial and was pervasive. She has to show a concerted pattern of conduct.

What about punitive damages in suits not involving discrimination? They can be awarded in a variety of cases including personal injury, fraud, libel and slander, defamation and wrongful discharge. It's a mixed bag. The Supreme Court has said there is no Constitutional limit on the amount of punitive damages a jury can award. Some juries have given substantial punitive damages in discharge cases. One involved a car rental company vice-president, fired with no severance pay or pension. Another involved a female college professor who protested favoritism shown to the school's football players and was fired. Other cases have concerned personal injury. In one case, dozens of plaintiffs sued a manufacturer for alleged injuries received as a result of exposure to something used in the making of its wood preservatives. They were awarded a token of one dollar for their injuries, but millions in punitive damages. When a gas station worker was hurt when an old tire rim exploded in his face, a jury awarded him millions for his actual damages and millions in punitive damages as punishment to the tire manufacturer. Suits against the media for libel and slander generate some punitive damage awards, particularly against publications such as *National Enquirer, Hustler,* and *Penthouse.* One individual who alleged he had been libeled and slandered with untrue accusations by his former employers after he was fired, which reduced his job prospects, sued and won punitive damages.

The other side is that, in California for example, fired workers cannot sue for punitive damages in most wrongful discharge cases except if the firing is for reasons that offend public policy, such as refusing to break a law. In Montana the Supreme Court upheld a state law limiting damages for arbitrary dismissals. In New York, since the courts have tended to favor the rights of employers to terminate employees "at will" (discussed in this chapter), suits for punitive damages are not easily won.

Title VII and Equal Pay Act
Four female matrons at the Washington County, Oregon, jail filed suit in the Federal District Court claiming sex discrimination under Title VII of *the Civil Rights Act of 1964.* They were being paid between $143.99 to $272.00 per month less than male guards. Their jobs were slightly different since they guarded a smaller number of female prisoners only and they also did clerical work.

The District Court rejected their claim. The Court said that a sex-based wage discrimination claim cannot be brought under Title VII if it is counter to another federal law, the *Equal Pay Act*. This Act is limited to wage claims where women are paid less than men for performing substantially equal work on jobs the performance of which requires equal skill, effort and responsibility, performed under similar working conditions. The Court found their work to be sufficiently dissimilar so as not to be covered by the Equal Pay Act and thus they were not entitled to Title VII relief.

However, the Supreme Court disagreed. They found the matrons could allege sex discrimination. Their work was comparable and that was enough to form a basis for a Title VII lawsuit.

Hostile work environment

The full U.S. 4th Circuit Court of Appeals has let stand a lower court ruling that white police officers in Richmond, Va., cannot sue for the creation of a hostile work environment when their supervisor made insulting comments to and about female and black police officers. Nothing was done and the white officers were retaliated against when they complained. They had no standing to sue under Title VII of the Civil Rights Act of 1964 since they were not the targets of the insults.

Title IX

Title IX of the Education Amendments of 1972 covers sex-discrimination, including hiring, in educational institutions which receive federal funds.

Fetal protection

In a landmark case dealing with female employment discrimination, the Supreme Court has ruled that employers may not bar women of childbearing age from certain jobs because of a potential risk to their fetuses. The employers' policies were declared to be "fetal protection." But they were found to be a form of bias on the basis of sex that is prohibited by Title VII of the Civil Rights Act.

The Court said that women should not be required to choose between a higher paying job and childbearing. Males also can be harmed in regard to participation in childbearing by their exposure to hazardous work environments. Warnings are needed as to the risks of exposure to harmful substances at the worksite and provision by the company of appropriate protective and safety gear and devices.

Employers such as DuPont, Monsanto, G.M., and the Johnson Controls car battery manufacturer claim they fear suits for children born with birth defects because of harmful substances in the workplace. But the court said that assumption of a known risk is a defense.

Sexual harassment

Wide attention given to hearings to confirm Clarence Thomas showed how widely varied the perceptions of this subject were. Although the Supreme Court dealt with this issue some years ago and the *Equal Employment Opportunity Commission* (EEOC) issued guidelines on the matter, there is still uncertainty on the part of many as to what constitutes sexual harassment.

Sexual harassment is a form of sexual discrimination that violates Title VII of the Civil Rights Act of 1964, as amended. It can affect both sexes, although it mainly has been directed toward females. The main issue is the action of the person doing the harassing and whether it is unwelcome. The harasser does not have to commit a physical act and the harasser need not be a supervisor, although if job-related retaliation is involved, it is more easily carried forward by a supervising authority.

The EEOC guidelines clearly state sexual harassment: Unwelcome sexual advances, requests for sexual favors, and other verbal or physical conduct of a sexual nature constitute sexual harassment when submission or rejection of this conduct explicitly or implicitly affects an individual's employment, unreasonably interferes with an individual's work performance or creates an intimidating, hostile or offensive work environment. The Supreme Court has ruled that Title IX proscribes maintenance of a sexually hostile educational environment in elementary and secondary schools.

Sexual harassment can occur in a variety of circumstances. For example, the victim as well as the harasser may be a woman or a man; the victim does not have to be of the opposite sex; the harasser can be the victim's supervisor in another area, a co-worker, or a nonemployee; the victim does not have to be the person harassed but could be anyone affected by the offensive conduct. Unlawful sexual harassment may occur without economic injury to, or discharge of, the victim. The Supreme Court has said that plaintiffs need not show the harassment caused severe psychological injury.

Some instances which the courts have viewed as harassment are the making of crude sexual remarks, unseemly gestures, lewd graffiti, posting of nude or pornographic pictures where females work or showing favoritism towards those workers who agree to submit to sex.

It is a victim's responsibility to establish that the harasser's conduct is unwelcome and otherwise impacts on the job performance if it is a work environment claim. If you feel harassed, you should inform the harasser that the conduct must stop. You should use any employer complaint or guidance system provided. There probably will be more in-house avenues to pursue because of heightened interest in the topic. Your employer may be held liable for the acts of sexual harassment regardless of whether the employer knew or should have known of their occurrence. With the Civil Rights Act of 1991 providing for punitive damages (discussed in this chapter), a harasser and/or company may be more receptive to a cessation of the harassment.

If you cannot resolve your situation in-house, you should discuss your complaint with an attorney as soon as possible. There are further actions that can be taken, such as filing a charge with the EEOC and later court action, but there are time limits to be observed and you also will want to be assured you are protected against any reprisals for complaining.

The Ninth Circuit Court of Appeals has ruled that evidence presented in a sexual harassment case must be considered from the point of view of a "reasonable woman." For over 150 years, the standard has been what a "reasonable man" would think the acts described. The Supreme Court says there is a violation when the work environment would reasonably be perceived or is perceived as hostile or abusive.

The Age Discrimination in Employment Act of 1967

In 1967, Congress enacted the *Age Discrimination in Employment Act (ADEA)*. The Act prohibited all forms of employment discrimination against all individuals who are at least 40 years of age, but less than 70. It is a violation of the Act to discriminate by age in wage benefits, hours worked, or availability of overtime. Unions and employers may not discriminate against those in the protected age group in providing fringe benefits, such as education or training programs, career development, vacations, and sick leave. The statute also prohibits printing, publishing or causing to be published notices or advertisements indicating a preference, limitation, or description based on age. The Labor Department has determined that employment advertisements indicating a preference for young people over older ones, such as *"girls," "boys," "students,"* or *"recent graduates"* are illegal. A federal appeals court has ruled that the use of the term and concept of being *"over qualified"* can also be a basis for an age discrimination lawsuit. This can be considered a code word for being too old, especially if the position is given to a younger person who may not command as high a salary.

The Supreme Court has allowed collection of double damages for willful violation by proving the company knew it was breaking the law or showed reckless disregard of it. Evidence of employer motivation is unnecessary. Any back pay or money damages are subject to federal income tax.

There have been some amendments to the ADEA. The age cap of 70 has been removed. And, in 1990 the Congress passed *the Older Workers Benefit Protection Act (OWBP)*, also known as the *"Betts Bill,"* named for a plaintiff in a Supreme Court case. After two decades of law on the ADEA, the Supreme Court changed it with a ruling in the case of June Betts. She was a state employee who was denied a disability pension after she had to retire at 61 because of Alzheimer's disease.

The state barred disability to workers over 60 so Mrs. Betts only received her regular pension. The Supreme Court said that the ADEA was not applicable to employee benefit plans such as disability and health insurance. The "Betts Bill" restored employee benefits requiring employers to give older workers benefits of equal value or equal cost as those given to younger employees. However, it allows employers to "integrate benefits" such as disability and retirement or health insurance and severance pay. They don't have to pay both or can effect a deduction. The OWBP Act also prevents employers from coercing older employees to waive their ADEA rights in layoffs or early retirement programs. The individual's signing must be "knowing and voluntary" and waivers must meet seven requirements.

The Supreme Court has rejected equating pension status with age. There is no age discrimination when someone is fired as a pension is about to vest. The *Employee Retirement Income Security Act (ERISA),* which protects against interference with pension rights, should cover the case.

The Supreme Court also has ruled that a worker alleging age discrimination after losing a job to someone younger still can sue when the replacement is 40 or older. The issue is job loss based on their age.

Under the ADEA, if you claim age bias in a state that has its own age discrimination law, you must file a charge with the state agency. But now the Supreme Court has held that even if the state agency rules against you, you can file a suit in federal court.

The new Civil Rights Act of 1991 also helped persons being discriminated against on the basis of age. It allows suits after 60 days of filing charges with the EEOC. Thousands of older cases filed with the EEOC lapsed because the Commission didn't pursue remedies.

Use of the streets

Not only can the public use streets and parks to express their views, but, in addition, people have a right to choose what street or park they wish to use to exercise their First Amendment right to freedom of expression. Furthermore, the federal courts have ruled that one group can't be restricted from expressing views in a particular public place if another previously was allowed to do so in that same place.

Freedom to speak and assemble is not absolute, however. The government can place reasonable restrictions as to time, place and manner on persons who express their beliefs in a public place in order to maintain peace and good order. But the government cannot abridge speech just because it may be controversial or insulting to some people.

Skokie and the Nazis

The Village of Skokie denied the Nazi group permission to demonstrate. The organization brought suit in the Federal District Court challenging the constitutionality of three village ordinances.

The Nazis claimed that the Skokie ordinances deprived them of their constitutional right to use the streets and the parks for communication. The Court decided that all three ordinances illegally restricted the Nazis' freedom to speak and assemble recognizing that although freedom of expression and assembly is subject to reasonable regulation, it "must not, in the guise of regulation, be abridged or denied."

The District Court also adopted a standard set down by the Supreme Court years ago. No matter how controversial or offensive speech may be, an organization has a constitutional right to speak and assemble in a public place unless the speaker has the intent to incite the public to "imminent lawless action" likely to produce such action. Since that was not found to be the situation in Skokie, the speech and assembly were constitutionally protected.

Loitering

A local law recently declared unconstitutional by the United States Supreme Court provided that it was unlawful for three or more people to assemble (except at a public meeting of citizens) on sidewalks, street corners, or the mouths of alleys and parks "and there conduct themselves in a manner annoying to persons passing by." The law was held unconstitutionally vague because a violation "may entirely depend on whether a policeman is annoyed." This was said to be "an invitation to discriminatory enforcement" because a gathering of whatever individuals might be considered annoying for "their ideas, their life-style or their physical appearance" could be resented by others.

Right of privacy

Among the civil rights enjoyed generally is a right that has been termed by Justice Brandeis as "the right to be let alone." Under the New York law this right is embodied in a civil rights law forbidding the use of the picture or name of a person for commercial purposes except with the written consent of the person involved. In other states, the law forbids the exploitation of the private life of individuals, or episodes that have occurred in their experience, for commercial purposes without their consent. These laws are known generally as *laws of the "right of privacy,"* although in some states the recognition of this principle is refused.

The United States Supreme Court has upheld the right of a citizen to have obscene material in the privacy of his own home. However, the Court has also held that there is no comparable right to distribute or sell obscene material through the mails to willing adult recipients.

Lie detector tests

As a job applicant or employee, you may be required to take a lie detector test or submit to a psychological stress evaluator (PSE). The lie detector measures changes in your blood pressure and breathing. The PSE can be hidden in a phone and records voice changes produced by stress. Because of reliability and privacy questions, 17 states and the District of Columbia ban such tests. One employee of a Florida firm won a $250,000 judgement because the polygraph company relied on by the employer to get evidence so they could dismiss the employee had not done its job properly.

Transsexuals

Transsexuals are not protected by state sex discrimination laws according to many authorities. And every federal court that has considered the matter has determined that discrimination against transsexuals is not cognizable under Title VII of the Civil Rights Act of 1964 as sex discrimination. However, a settlement was achieved for a transsexual in his suit against the Postal Service under the Rehabilitation Act and the Equal Protection Clause of the Constitution.

Homosexuals

The Ninth Circuit Court of Appeals ordered the Army to reinstate Sgt. Perry Watkins who had been discharged because he was a homosexual. He had been allowed to reenlist on prior occasions although the service knew about his sexual preference. A prior ruling by the Court on constitutional grounds, which said homosexuals should be treated like racial minorities, was vacated. The services usually are given broad authority. For example, in 1986, it was decided that the Air Force could bar an Orthodox Jewish officer from wearing a yarmulke (skull cap) since uniformity outweighed the First Amendment's guarantee of religious freedom.

The Supreme Court has not extended the private sphere of individual liberty to encompass homosexual activity. It has consistently upheld state anti-sodomy laws. The Supreme Court declared unconstitutional a Colorado state provision that nullified civil rights protections for homosexuals. Eleven states, including New Hampshire and Maine, offer protection against discrimination to homosexuals.

Gay marriages

When two gay males were refused a marriage license in the District of Columbia, they filed a discrimination suit under the city's *Human Rights Act*, which prohibits discrimination based on sexual orientation. The court said it wasn't because of orientation but because marriage requires a male and female. The Congress has passed the *"Defense of Marriage Act"* defining marriage for federal purposes in the same way and authorizing states to refuse to recognize same sex marriages performed in other states. They are banned in 18 states. But some localities, like San Francisco, require that organizations doing business with the city extend benefits received by spouses to workers with same sex partners.

Searches, seizures, and fingerprinting

The Fourth Amendment to the Constitution, which has been held applicable to the states, protects persons against unreasonable search and states warrants shall issue only probable cause describing the place, persons, and things involved. Thus, evidence obtained in the home of an accused person is suppressed and not permitted to be used against him at a criminal trial, unless there is adherence to the Constitutional requirements. See Chapter 25 on *Criminal Law.*

The United States Supreme Court has held that the police could not make investigatory detentions for the purpose of fingerprinting suspects in the absence of probable cause to arrest. Fingerprinting does not involve as much interference with personal rights as other forms of invasion and search. Fingerprinting involves none of the probing into an individual's private life and thoughts that marks an interrogation or search. Nor can fingerprinting detention be employed repeatedly to harass any individual, since the police need only one set of each person's prints. Furthermore, fingerprinting is an inherently more reliable and effective crime-solving tool than eyewitness identifications or confessions and is not subject to such abuses as the improper line-up and the "third degree."

The Pregnancy Discrimination Act

Discrimination on the basis of pregnancy, childbirth or related medical conditions constitutes unlawful sex discrimination under Title VII of the Civil Rights Act of 1964. It covers refusal to hire because of pregnancy although the person can perform the major functions of the job. It requires similar treatment for pregnancy related workers as for others in regard to a variety of work matters including performance, leave, holding the job open, health insurance and fringe benefits. Child care leave is not covered by the Act although Title VII requires that this leave be treated as is other leave for non-medical reasons. Pregnancy benefits are not to be limited to married employees.

If you believe you have been discriminated against, you should consult an attorney as soon as possible. There probably are internal administrative procedures to be followed and counsel can advise you on the EEOC's procedures as well as your options for a lawsuit. You will need information from your workplace as to treatment which you received which was different from that given to others similarly situated. This is called "disparate treatment." You will need to provide your counsel with comparison information so it can be reasonably inferred that an employment decision was made which, for discriminatory reasons, was different from decisions relating to persons who were not pregnant. For example, you had asked for a reassignment to avoid heavy lifting. You were given work at odd hours which you refused because of interference with child care responsibility. You were fired. You will need to show that other, non-pregnant employees who were reassigned for medical reasons and objected to the new assignment were not fired.

After acquired evidence

The Supreme Court ruled that when an employee loses a job as a result of discrimination, the well founded claim cannot be voided by a later discovery of some earlier misconduct which would have caused the dismissal if known then. Unauthorized review of files, removing company files or lying on a job application could be considered in deciding on a remedy such as reinstatement, future wages or the amount of back pay. But the employer has the burden of establishing the severity of the wrongdoing.

How to make a will

10

Chapter 10
How to make a will

"Say not you know another entirely until you have divided an inheritance with him," said Johann Kaspar Lavater, an 18th-century writer.

You must always remember that the right to make a will and to dispose of your property as you wish at your death is given you by the state in which you reside. The conditions and limitations to this right are embodied in the statutes of your state and must be observed if your will is to be fully effective.

You must also remember that your financial condition may change through the years and that your family may grow larger or smaller. What may have been a proper disposition under a will made years ago may not now reflect your true circumstances or intent. No will, or a poorly drafted will (homemade), may also create "bad will," hard feelings, and legal rifts, and may dredge up unknown relatives.

A number of important terms, whose meanings you should know because they are often used in connection with wills, are defined below:

Administrator/Administratrix: the man or woman appointed by the Court who takes charge of the distribution of your property when there is no valid will or there is no executor provided for in the will.

Attest: certify by signature or oath.

Bequest: the gift, under a will, of personal property.

Codicil: a separately executed later addition or modification of a will.

Devise: the gift, under a will, of real property.

Executor/Executrix: the man or woman appointed in a will to carry out the terms of that will.

Legacy: a gift, by will, of property.

Legatee: the person to whom a legacy is given.

To probate: the act or process of proving a will in court.

Testator/Testatrix: the maker of a will.

Capacity to make a will

The right to provide by will for the disposition of one's property at death is withheld only from those who are not sufficiently sound of mind to apprehend and understand the ordinary affairs of life, which include the nature, extent, and character of their own property.

Use of drugs or intoxicants

A mere use of drugs or intoxicants is not in itself sufficient to prove that a person does not possess the capacity to make a will. A person is considered to be deprived of that capacity, however, if he uses drugs or intoxicants to such an extent that it can be determined as a fact that he lacks the mental capacity to comprehend the extent of his property and the purpose of his acts in making a will.

The effect of senility on a will's validity

It is a mistake to think that because a man is old and forgetful he is incapable of making a will that will prove acceptable to the courts despite the allegations of relatives that he was mentally incompetent when he made it.

A will was made by an 80-year-old man. After his death the will was contested, and it was pointed out in court that he had behaved peculiarly during the period in which he made it. Only at rare intervals, testimony established, would he show sufficient interest to reply to questions; at other times he said nothing. He often failed to recognize acquaintances. Some of them considered that he was "not normal."

"There was nothing in the evidence," said the court in asserting the will of the old man to be a valid one, "that showed more than old age and a weakness of intellect resulting therefrom, and this does not constitute mental incapacity to make a will unless the weakness amounts to imbecility."

The probate of the will of a Michigan man was objected to for this same mental incapacity. Eighteen months after he had made the will, the man had been placed in the psychopathic ward of a hospital, a victim of senile dementia. One physician testified the man was mentally incompetent when the will was made.

The conclusion in this case demonstrates the attitude of some courts toward claims of weakened mentality and incapacity. "The entire testimony shows the case of a man who, after working hard at his trade of blacksmith the greater part of his life, finally became old and had the usual infirmities of age, forgetfulness, untidiness, and who eighteen months after the will in question was executed was committed to an institution as a senile dementia patient. Such facts alone are not sufficient to set aside a will. Weakness of mind and forgetfulness are not sufficient to invalidate a will if it appears that the testator's mind was capable of attention and exertion when aroused and was not imposed upon. The weak have the same right as the prudent and the strong-minded to dispose of their property."

Recently, a very old and infirm man married his nurse, a much-married younger woman who had at one time been accused of murder. The man died soon afterward, leaving a considerable fortune to his widow. There was no proof that she had coerced him into the marriage or that he had died of causes other than age, so his family's objections to her collecting his estate were not sustained. If she had been found guilty of his murder, for example, she would not have been permitted to receive his estate. A court will not lightly set aside the wishes of a testator set forth in the will, unless incapacity to make the will is clear.

Undue influence and how it is proved

Sometimes one person possesses so much influence over another that he is able to substitute his own private aims for the other's wishes. This problem is of particular interest to us in connection with wills. When the victim is driven far from the course that would be charted by his own reason and fairness, this influence is labeled "undue" and is condemned by the law.

To prove a case of undue influence upon the maker of a will, the following factors must generally be shown to be present:
(1) a person unquestionably subject to such influence,
(2) opportunity to exercise such influence and effect the wrongful purpose, and
(3) a disposition to influence unduly for the purpose of procuring an improper favor.

A clear-cut case of undue influence

Amalia Feeley, injured in a railway accident, for six years preceding her death suffered from delusions. Under their influence she committed such acts as tearing a mattress into pieces to secure filling for her house mop, throwing rugs out of her home, using an axe to remove a door that displeased her.

For 20 years preceding her accident, she and her husband had lived peaceably together in Chicago in a three-family house, which they owned. Evidently concerned about her health, her relatives invited her to Wisconsin for treatment. Eight days after her arrival in Wisconsin she made a will, naming her sisters and mother her sole beneficiaries, with no provision whatever for her husband. At the same time she transferred the bank account in which were the savings of her husband and herself into a joint account with her sister.

When her husband came to Wisconsin to see her, he was ordered from the house by her relatives, and did not see his wife again until he attended her funeral four months later.

The court refused to accept this will, holding that it was the product of the influence of the mother and sisters on the weakened mind of the maker.

When objections are not valid

A different story is told by a New Jersey case, where objections were raised on the ground of undue influence upon a father for the benefit of his daughter.

Morris Alper was an invalid for 16 or 17 years. During that time, his daughter Theresa cared for him and his property, collecting the rents, superintending repairs, and carrying on various tasks for her father that were necessary from time to time.

Two years before Morris died, speaking to some friends of this daughter, he said, "She is a very good girl. She has given her life for me. I am worried about her. The other girls are married. They have homes, children—they have families and Theresa hasn't. But I provided for her. I took care of her, so if I go, she won't have much worry."

When Morris died, 60 percent of his estate had been willed to seven children and grandchildren and the other 40 percent to Theresa. It was claimed that the will was the result of undue influence exercised by Theresa over her father.

"The will," said the court, "is neither unnatural nor unjust. This is not to suggest that a testator may not dispose of his estate unnaturally or unjustly, but in the instant case neither criticism may be leveled at his will. It is for him, and him alone, to weigh those circumstances and influences which, in his mind and consciousness, justify such fairness in bounty as he chooses to denote."

Describe property in a will accurately

Beware of loose or incomplete wording in your will. Be specific and detailed in your legacies, particularly where they are valuable. For a valid gift of property under a will there must be a description of the property given sufficient for its identification. Otherwise the devise or bequest may be void.

How charitable bequests are limited

When you make your will, be sure that you are familiar with the state laws about gifts by will to charities and charitable institutions. Also be sure about the validity of forms provided for bequests to charities and associations. The forms you find in magazines and brochures may not be accurate. You should consult with your lawyer about the appropriate form for any bequest to such groups.

Many states restrict such bequests both in the period of time that must elapse between the execution of the will and the death, and in the proportion of the total estate that can be thus bequeathed when there are surviving relatives.

The laws of California, for example, provide that, where there are near relatives, charitable bequests are valid only when the will has been executed at least 30 days before the death of its maker, and the charitable bequests cannot amount to more than one-third of the entire estate. Any excess over the total of one-third is void, and each charitable bequest is reduced pro rata.

Cy pres

If a trust, devise, or bequest for charity is or becomes illegal, impossible, or impracticable of fulfillment at the time it is intended to become effective, a court may order settlement cy pres—"as nearly as possible"—to fulfill the general charitable intention. But the testator must show an intention to devote the property to charity.

In a New York case, a legacy was left in trust for an Italian religious institution. But it could not be paid because the institution had been discontinued by the time of the testatrix's death. The court applied the cy pres doctrine, and the money was given to a cathedral that was also an object of the testatrix's bounty.

In another case, money was left to the Society for the Prevention of Cruelty to Children in Richmond, Virginia. However, the Society was not capable of taking a testamentary gift, so it was determined that the Children's Home Society of Virginia, being an organization operating in the same locality and furnishing the same sort of charitable aid, would receive the money.

Cy pres could not be applied in a Connecticut case. There the testator wanted to create a public charity for the benefit of aged, respectable, indigent men over 65 who had been residents of New London. The existing facilities, however, already exceeded the need at the time of the death of the testator. The court said that since the testator was so definite in his terms for the bequest, no enlargement of the class of beneficiaries could be made.

If you leave money for an educational purpose, cy pres cannot be applied to divert it to a religious purpose or for the sick. It is best for a testator to provide his own alternatives in the event a primary wish cannot be fulfilled.

As was said in the beginning, periodic review of your testament will solve many problems and save expensive litigation after your death. Many estates have been dissipated because of suits to clarify a testator's wishes.

Form of a will

The following is a very simple will. In most cases it should be more elaborate and involved, generally providing for setting up trust funds, giving bequests, and naming successor executors, legatees, etc. Your attorney will go over the details with you so that your testament genuinely reflects your wishes and your family circumstances:

> I, Lewis Helm, residing in the City of Denver, State of Colorado, do hereby make, publish and declare this to be my last will and testament, hereby revoking any and all former wills and codicils by me at any time heretofore made.
>
> First: I direct that all my just debts and funeral expenses be paid as soon after my death as may be practicable.
>
> Second: I give and bequeath to my cousin James Marshall of Adams, Massachusetts, the sum of One Thousand Dollars.
>
> Third: All the rest, residue and remainder of my estate, of whatever kind or nature it may be, of which I shall die seized or possessed or to which I may be entitled at the time of my death not otherwise effectively disposed of (including any property over which I have power of

appointment) I direct my Executor, hereinafter named, to divide into two equal parts, which I give, devise and bequeath as follows:

A. to my beloved wife Alice, her heirs, executors, administrators and assigns, absolutely and forever, one of said parts but in no event less than $10,000;

B. to my son, David Helm, his heirs, executors, administrators and assigns, absolutely and forever, the second of said two parts.

Fourth: I name, constitute and appoint John Romer of Denver, Colorado, executor of this my last will and testament and direct that he be not required to give any bond as such executor.

In witness whereof I have hereunto signed my name this 15th day of December, 1971.

(Signed) Lewis Helm

Follow this with the attestation clause:

The foregoing instrument was subscribed, published and declared by Lewis Helm, the testator above named, as and for his last will and testament in our presence and in the presence of each other, and we at the same time and at his request and in his presence and in the presence of each other have hereunto subscribed our names as witnesses hereto this 15th day of December, 1971.

This attestation should be signed by three witnesses, with their addresses following their names in each instance, after the maker has duly declared this to be his last will and requested the three persons to sign as his official witnesses.

Rules for executing your will

Carefully follow the directions of the statutes of your state in executing your will. If you fail, it may be valid but it may not. The defects will be discovered when you are no longer here to correct them.

Always follow two major rules in the execution of a will: first, sign the will at the end; second, sign it preferably before three witnesses, always before two, and ask them to add their names to the attestation clause at the end, with their addresses.

The law requires three witnesses in Connecticut, Maine, Massachusetts, New Hampshire, South Carolina and Vermont. In the rest of the states, only two are needed. But should you happen to own real estate in any of the states requiring three witnesses and have but two witnesses to your will, the property there will go as though you had made no will. Also, you might some day move to one of those states.

None of the witnesses to a will can be a beneficiary, or have an interest under it. If they do, at best they will receive only what they would have received if there had been no will. Also, it may be a reason for invalidating the will.

Intent of the maker

It has long been the law that the courts will direct their efforts to carrying out the wishes of the maker of a will. Nevertheless, the document must conform to the law—it must be a will. A typical situation where the intent of the maker of the will controlled occurred in Massachusetts where the ink in a fountain pen used in the writing of the will became exhausted and the will was finished in lead pencil, and part of the will was on one sheet of paper and part on another.

"The will was not drawn with precision," said the court, "but as it was duly executed and as the intention can be ascertained it was effectual to pass her property."

Signatures of Witnesses

Witnesses to a will in the District of Columbia signed their names before it had been signed by the maker. Because of this omission the validity of the will was disputed. The court held the will was good and refused to deny it probate "merely because the testator signed after the witnesses in the same transaction where the will was in all respects according to the provisions of the statute."

This suggestion, however, was added: "It is of course preferable as well as usual for the testator to sign first but we think the validity of the will should not depend upon who signs it first, provided of course all sign at substantially the same time and in each other's presence."

How signatures can vary

Courts may be liberal in recognizing wills as valid when the maker fails to comply strictly with the law that he must sign at the end of the will. However, it is dangerous to rely on a liberal construction and best to comply strictly with the law.

The will of a New York woman was prepared for her execution when she was too ill to undertake the physical task of signing her name. She asked her husband to sign her name, which he did in her presence.

This will was accepted by the New York court. "While the provisions of the law seem to contemplate that the testamentary instrument must be 'subscribed' at the end thereof by the testator in person, the common-law rule that performance of the physical act may be delegated to another is impliedly recognized."

Leniency was shown by the court in a Virginia will case where the signature was "M. Calvin Lafew—X" (his mark). The meaning of signature is not restricted to the written name. Where the testator puts his mark (X) to the instrument in the presence of the required number of witnesses, this is a sufficient signing within the meaning of the statute.

If you fail to follow the statute

The following will was offered for probate in California:

Knowing we all must depart from this life someday, I want all my debts paid. I want all my insurance put on my funeral. The home I am buying at 2125 West 29th Street, Los Angeles, I want Clifton Muldrow to have. If I have not finished paying for it I want him to finish paying it out. I want Clifton Muldrow to have part of my household goods and Wayman More part of the household goods. Clifton Muldrow must pay all of my debtors' bills if there be any, and all of my other debts. (*Witnesses*) Mrs. Bobbie Rodgers Rhodes, Alphonse E. Cain. (*Signed*) Wretha Jordan.

P.S. I want Clifton Muldrow to send my brother Wash. Fatheree $20.00, my brother Rice Fatheree $20.00, and my niece Ina Jenkins $20.00, if they are alive. Clifton Muldrow is to be executor of my estate without bond. Anyone contesting this will will be paid one dollar and one cent. Subscribed and sworn to before me, a notary public in and for the county of Los Angeles, state of California, this 11th day of November, 1945. Hazel A. Macbeth.

The court here excluded the portion of the will written after the signatures of the witnesses, because it did not follow the law of the state giving the requirements for the execution of such a document.

What are codicils?

When you make a will and later want to change some of the provisions, you may do so by making a codicil instead of rewriting the entire will. This codicil must be executed and witnessed in every detail exactly as in the making of the original will.

A good definition of this term, embodying legal requirements, is: "A codicil is a clause added to a will after its execution, the purpose of which is to alter, enlarge, or restrict the provisions of the will, or to explain, confirm, or republish it. It does not supersede the will as an after-made will would do, but is a part of it, to be considered with it as one entire instrument."

Modifying a will by codicil

The will of Charles Clark of St. Louis, Missouri, set up a trust in real estate. From the income of this trust there was to be paid each month an allowance to Clark's son "in such proportions as the trustee named may deem advisable." Five months after he had made this will, Clark provided in a codicil, "Whereas I am of the opinion that an annual income of $6,000 is amply sufficient for his support and maintenance and that a greater income would be harmful, this income is curtailed to that amount."

This modification by the codicil was accepted by the court. "Viewing the will and the codicil as one instrument," the court said, "the testator intended the subsequent clear plan and unequivocal direction in the codicil should govern. The explicit direction erased, took away, and left no room for the discretionary power given the trustee."

The court's statement clearly shows the purpose of a codicil and its effect. It is part of the original will, but changes the effect of the will to the extent indicated.

Effect of a faulty codicil

A resident of Philadelphia created by his will a trust fund for the benefit of an adopted 15-year-old daughter. The income from this trust fund of $50,000 was to be paid quarterly after she had become 21 years old. When she became 35, the principal of the trust was to be paid to her.

When the daughter became 22, the maker of the will made a codicil saying, "I revoke the trust fund in favor of my daughter Mildred and substitute a lump sum of _____ dollars in cash." The space left by the testator for the amount was never filled in by him.

By this man's will, his widow was entitled to the bulk of his estate, less this bequest. She contended that the codicil canceled the trust and that the daughter received nothing. Allowing the amount of the principal of the trust fund as the amount intended to be filled in the blank space, the court made this explanation:

"The general scheme of the will is not to be overborne by modifying directions that are incomplete, ambiguous, or equivocal." The codicil did not "destroy or change the dispositions of the will further than is necessary to give effect to the provisions of the codicil. We cannot conceive that by one short, incomplete sentence the testator intended to strike down all he had so thoughtfully constructed in the will."

Where to keep your will

After execution, the original of your will can be left with a number of reliable persons including your attorney or a trustee of your bank. In some states there is provision for its deposit with the Surrogate Court for a small one time fee. You might also wish to give a copy to the executor named in the will. Your attorney should be consulted on the procedures to safeguard it.

Automatic cancellation of wills

The law in many of the states is that when a person marries and becomes the parent of a child or children, these occurrences revoke, to the extent that such spouse or child would inherit in the absence of a will, any will made before the marriage and birth of the children occurred. This, however, does not apply when a provision is made in the will for a surviving wife by a marriage subsequent to the execution of the will, or for children born subsequent to the execution of the will. Several states also recognize that while divorce alone is not enough to automatically revoke a will, divorce accompanied by a property settlement may be sufficient.

Two wills

If a testator leaves two executed wills, it is generally an open question as to which one controls. Where the language of the later will does not indicate that the prior will is revoked, and the provisions of the later instrument are not so inconsistent with the previous will, a New York court has stated that both documents can be probated together as a last will and testament. It is always best to revoke specifically all prior wills by either completely defacing them or by specifically referring to revocation in the later will. Never leave an ambiguous will, which can cause more confusion than comfort.

Signs of revocation of a will

Whether the maker of a will attempted to cancel the document after its execution is determined by three factors: (1) the intent of the maker, (2) the efforts made for cancellation, and (3) the statutes of the state in which the maker lives that relate to the revocation of wills.

A woman in the District of Columbia made a will that was found after her death with pencil cross marks over the face of the will itself. The first page was completely defaced. Three pencil lines were drawn through the attestation clause. The signatures of the witnesses were torn.

The statute of the District of Columbia, like that of many other states, declares that a will may be revoked by another will, a codicil, or "by burning, canceling, tearing or obliterating the same" by or under the instructions of the maker. The court accordingly held that the marks manifested an intention of the maker to revoke the will, and although the marks were in pencil, it had been obvious that the woman had intentionally altered her will and upheld this document.

Incomplete revocation

The New York statute says that no will in writing shall be revoked except by some other will in writing, or some writing of the maker declaring such a revocation, which must be executed in the same manner as a will, "unless such will be burned, torn, canceled, obliterated or destroyed" with the intent to revoke it.

In one case in New York, the maker of a will made cross marks on the face of the document and, opposite, in the margin, wrote, "See codicil."

A proposed codicil was found among his papers that had been signed but never formally executed. Here the court decided the marks were insufficient to effect a revocation of the will since no codicil had been executed.

How to make a revocation unmistakable

In West Virginia, a man made a will naming his wife, who had been married twice before, as his sole beneficiary. Four years later he was divorced from her, and at his death she was living with her fifth husband.

During the last days of his married life with this woman, the man had at one time crumpled up his will and thrown it into the waste basket. His wife recovered the will.

According to his version of the incident, quoted in court, "In order to have her clear of him he gave her $1,000 and she promised to burn the will."

She didn't.

When he died she offered the will to the court for its acceptance in a "crinkled" and "crumpled" condition. The intent of the maker of the will became the major feature in the determination by the court of whether or not there had been a revocation. His statement quoted above showed clearly what he desired, and the court refused to recognize the will as valid.

When you wish to revoke your will, do it in a regular manner. Have your lawyer draw up another document, and sign it and execute it in exactly the manner you would a will. Then there can be no mistake or misunderstanding of your intent, or any possibility that your wishes will remain unfulfilled.

Joint wills

Although this document normally involves spouses, individuals otherwise related may also have one. It is a single will executed by two persons which they both sign. It can be deemed a mutual will when the parties agree to dispose of their combined property in a particular manner.

A joint will may create problems, such as, can a survivor make a new will or is the original one irrevocable? It also can create a tax disadvantage. If property left to a spouse in a joint will is determined to be a life estate and a contractual agreement, then it will not qualify for the tax free marital deduction.

Mutual wills

When two people, most frequently husband and wife, each make a separate will that is part of a mutual plan or compact for the distribution of their property at death, the transaction has the legal features of a contract.

These wills have a phase that is peculiar to them and that is not a feature of ordinary wills executed by only one person. When a husband and wife execute mutual wills, each making the other the beneficiary with a proviso for disposition of the property at the death of the survivor, then the survivor, upon receiving the benefits under the will of the other, must carry out his part of the agreement. He is not allowed to revoke the will or to make disposition contrary to its provisions.

A contract for mutual wills must be clear

A mutual will agreement must be free of doubt and uncertainty as to its existence. The mere fact that wills appear to have been made under such a compact is not sufficient proof that such a compact existed. A contract of this sort might well be expressed in the wills themselves or in a separate agreement made and executed by those concerned.

An effort to enforce such an agreement was made in California in a case where the contents of two wills were practically identical. The sameness in itself proved nothing. "The mere fact that the wills are reciprocal or contain similar or identical provisions or

181

that they are executed at the same time and before the same witnesses is not of itself sufficient evidence of an agreement."

Attempt to evade a mutual will

Anthony and Amanda Myers, husband and wife, made their wills, each leaving everything to the other. At the death of the survivor, their property was to go to a Grace McGrew, who had lived with the couple since she had been a child, done the housework, and helped them in many ways.

Anthony died first. Then Amanda changed her mind in regard to Grace and in the presence of a friend threw into the stove the will she had executed under her agreement with her husband.

The provisions of the will she destroyed were part of a binding contract that she could not evade, the court declared. There was an agreement with her husband and he had performed his part. The court required the agreement to be carried out, since the wife had accepted its benefits.

When husband and wife die simultaneously in a common disaster

With air and high-speed automobile travel, it is not unusual for an accident to take the lives of both spouses. When this happens, sometimes there is no way to determine which one lived the longer and who, therefore, inherited the family property.

New York has adopted statutory provisions similar to *the Uniform Simultaneous Death Act* that disposes of property when there is no will and when there is insufficient evidence that the people involved have died other than simultaneously. What happens is that the property of each person will be disposed of as if he had been the one to survive. However, if there is a will, but no provision in it to take care of a simultaneous death situation, and if the disposition of the property depends on one surviving the other, the statute says that all the assets will be pooled and then equally divided amongst all properly designated beneficiaries.

Be aware of the fact that there is no presumption that a particular person survived because of an age difference, or sex, or even relative physical condition. So if you wish to avoid your state's statutory provisions on the subject or the lack of any statute, you should make provision in your will for the disposition of all property in the event that death comes to you and your spouse, or other family member with whom you share assets, at the same instant of time. Your lawyer can help you to decide how best to dispose of your estate in this eventuality.

Holographic wills

A holographic will is one written entirely in the handwriting of the maker and is valid only when it complies with the statutes of the state in which it is executed. The ordinary attestation clause and declaration before attesting witnesses may be omitted in most instances.

Will by a member of armed forces

In some states, active service in the armed forces is essential to the legality of a holographic will; in other states, it is not. The New York law, for example, says in substance that a holographic will, to be legal, must be entirely in his own handwriting and made by (1) a member of the armed forces in actual service during war or armed conflict in which the member of the armed services was involved, or (2) a person who is attached to armed services in armed conflict, or (3) a mariner while at sea; that it is valid for a year after his discharge, and in the case of a mariner for three years after the date of the will; thereupon it ceases to be recognized as a will unless he is unable at that time to make one in the ordinary form, and then it remains valid until one year after such person is capable of making a will.

In Alabama, holographic wills are not recognized, but if a will is written in the handwriting of the testator and is attested to by at least two witnesses, it is not considered a holographic will.

Where holographic wills are valid
State—Number of witnesses as to validity of writing and signature:

Alaska— none
Arizona— none
Arkansas— three
California— none
Colorado— none
Idaho— none
Iowa— must be executed as regular testament (two witnesses)
Kentucky— none
Louisiana— none
Maryland*— none
Michigan— none
Mississippi— none
Montana— none
Nevada— none
New Jersey— none
New York*— none
North Carolina (1)— none
North Dakota— none
Oklahoma— none
Pennsylvania— none
Puerto Rico (2)— none
Rhode Island (3)— none
South Dakota— none
Tennessee— two
Texas (4)— none
Utah— none
Vermont— must be executed as regular testament
Virginia— two

Virgin Islands*— none
West Virginia— none
Wyoming— none

*In Maryland it is valid only if made outside the U.S. by a person serving in the United States Armed Forces, but it is not effective more than one year after his discharge if he then has the capacity to make a will.

In New York it is the same as above, for (1) a soldier or sailor in actual service while in actual combat, (2) a person accompanying the military in actual combat, or (3) a mariner at sea. For (3), the will is valid for three years from its date.

In the Virgin Islands, valid only if made by person in military or naval service or by mariner at sea. Not effective more than one year after discharge if he then has the capacity to make a will.

1. In North Carolina not only must the testator's handwriting be proved by three witnesses, but the will must be found among his valuable papers or put into someone's safekeeping.

2. In Puerto Rico the testator must be of age, the date made must be clear, and the will must be probated within five years of the date of death.

3. Rhode Island recognizes it only for the soldier and sailor and the mariner at sea.

4. In Texas the testator must add an affidavit that the instrument is his last will and that he was 18 years of age at the time of its execution (or, if younger than 18, that he was married or in the armed forces or maritime service), and that he was of sound mind. Otherwise two witnesses are needed as to proof of the handwriting.

In Connecticut, Hawaii, Maine, and Washington, a holographic will made in a state where it is valid will be accepted.

Witness to wills

In many states, when a holographic will is probated, at least two disinterested witnesses identifying the testator's signature are required. For attested wills, identification of the testator's signature by witnesses is usually not necessary. Beneficiaries of an attested will may act as witness to a testator's signature. This is not the case for holographic wills.

An unsigned will—why the court accepted it

An unsigned holographic will probated in California, where the law makes no provision that the maker of the will must be in the military service, read:

> Compton, Calif., March 10th, 1947. I, Mrs. Estelle Gardener, 433 West Laurel Street, do give, devise and bequeath Mrs. Dorothy Mathews and Mrs. Eleatra Hyatt of Compton all of my belongings, should they outlive me, consisting of house, lot, all household furnishings, trunk and clothing now situated at 433 West Laurel Street, Compton, Calif. I hold

possession and life tenancy of the property during my lifetime. My only last will and testament. Signed this 10th day of March, 1947. Compton, Calif., 433 West Laurel St.

The court held this a valid holographic will although unsigned. "An inspection of the document shows it to have been written with care and that it is a complete declaration of the desires of the testator." Normally, however, the probate law of California requires that a will entirely in the testator's writing be signed and dated by him.

A hole in a holographic will

Someone said there can be a hole in a holographic will. This is because the writer may have his own personal quirks, and they may not be explainable after his death. In a New York case, a will written by the testator in his own hand bequeathed the sum of "twenty five ($2,500) dollars" to a nephew. Did the uncle mean $25 or $2,500? In some states, when the written lettered amount disagrees with the numbers, the former prevails. In this case, however, the nephew received $2,500.

Wills by word-of-mouth

Wills passed by word-of-mouth are called *oral* or *nuncupative wills* and are recognized by law. However, the law does not favor them except where the makers are soldiers in active service or sailors at sea. They are in many cases permitted for civilians, but their validity is strictly held to the provisions of the statutes of the state in which the maker has his residence. As a general rule, these wills can be made only in a "last illness," although this phrase is subject to various interpretations by the courts of the different states.

During World War I, George Mallery, who was with the American army in France, declared to some of the men with whom he was associated, "If I should not come back, I want my father and mother and no one else but them, no matter what happens, to get all I have coming from the government, and I want to tell this to enough of you boys from around home so some of you will go back to tell what I want, in case I don't."

Mallery died in France, still in the army. Accepting this oral declaration as a will, the court remarked that since Mallery's statement of his wishes was made in substantially identical terms upon two occasions, each time to a single witness, it was a sufficient compliance with the statute.

In World War II, a similar will was "executed" by Stanley Knapp, who was captured by the Japanese on Mindanao and imprisoned on Amboina, where he died. Knapp told two of the men with him in the Japanese prison that "he wanted his mother to get everything he had, nothing to go to his father." This statement was accepted by a New York court as a nuncupative will, since it was made during active military duty and before two witnesses, as the statute requires.

Typical restrictions on oral wills

The law in Idaho carries a further restriction—that a nuncupative will, to be accepted as a will, must be proved within six months after the testamentary words are spoken.

It is a vital essential under the Kansas law in the making of a nuncupative will that the maker declare the statement is intended as his will. The mere statement of wishes not declared as a will does not suffice. A patient in a Kansas hospital told a hospital nurse, the day before he died, the disposition he wished made of his property. The court refused to accept this statement as a will because he did not call upon those present, at the time of orally declaring his will, to bear witness that it was his will.

State laws on oral wills

Alabama— Valid when made by soldiers on active duty or sailors at sea. For civilians, personal property bequeathed can be only $500 or less in value, and the will must be made during the testator's last illness at his residence or where he has resided for ten days or more, or when he becomes fatally ill and dies elsewhere. Testator must have asked persons present to bear witness that such was his will.

Arizona— Not recognized.

Alaska— May be made by mariner at sea or a soldier in military service, as at common law to dispose of personal property only. If oral, the words must be reduced to writing within 30 days and must be proved within six months.

Arkansas— When the Probate Code was enacted in 1949, provisions for oral wills were eliminated.

California— Valid when value of personal property does not exceed $1,000 and the will is spoken before two witnesses, one of whom is asked by the testator to witness the statement as his will. Testator, at the time of his declaration, must be in military service and in peril of death or must expect it from injury received on the day of making the will. The verbal statement of the deceased must be written down within 30 days after the making and filed for probate within six months.

Colorado— Does not recognize them.

Connecticut— Invalid.

Delaware— Not recognized—all wills must be in writing.

District of Columbia— Valid only for servicemen on active duty or mariners at sea during last sickness. Valid only for personal property disposal. Must be acknowledged before two witnesses and written down within ten days.

Florida— Invalid.

Georgia— Valid only if made during last illness and must be proved by oaths of two witnesses, written down within 30 days, and application for probate must be made within six months.

Hawaii— No provisions on this type of will.

Idaho— Valid when written down within 30 days of its declaration, and probated not less than 14 days after death and not more than six months after oral testament.

Illinois— Not valid.

Indiana— Valid for personal property not exceeding $1,000, except that soldiers on active service or mariners at sea may dispose of $10,000.

Iowa— Does not recognize them.

Kansas— Valid for personal property when made in last sickness if acknowledged and declared as the final will before two witnesses and written down within 30 days.

Kentucky— Not valid—must be in writing.

Louisiana— Can be made by public act or privately. To be done publicly, it must be received by a notary public with three persons dwelling in the place where the will is executed as witnesses or by five nonresidents. The testament must be written by the notary and signed by the testator and all witnesses. Privately, it must be written by the testator himself or anyone else from his dictation, in the presence of five witnesses residing in the place where executed or seven nonresidents; or the testator can declare to the five or the seven that the paper written out of their presence is his will. It must be read to all and signed by the testator and witnesses. If it is done in the country rather than the city, there can be three witnesses in residence or five nonresidents.

Maine— Valid for personal property of soldiers on active duty or sailors at sea. For civilians, valid for personal property not exceeding $100 unless three witnesses present. Must be made in the deceased's last illness at home or at the place where he resided for ten days before the making. If words not written down within six days, must be proved in court within six months.

Maryland— nvalid.

Massachusetts— Valid for the personal property of soldiers on active duty or sailors at sea.

Michigan— Invalid.

Minnesota— Invalid.

Mississippi— Valid only if made during last illness at the residence where lived for ten days prior. If property exceeds $100 in value, the will must be acknowledged by the testator before two persons he asks to act as witnesses. Probate must wait 14 days to allow for notice to kin but must be accomplished within six months unless testament reduced to writing within six days after spoken.

Missouri— Valid for personal property of not more than $500 in value. It must be made in the last illness of testator, acknowledged before two witnesses, and proved within six months after death and written down within 30 days of the making of the will.

Montana— Valid for servicemen on active duty and for their property not exceeding $1,000 in value. It must be made before two witnesses when testator is in fear of death or with death imminent from an injury suffered the same day. It must be written down within 30 days and proved not less than 14 days after death nor more than six months after testament.

Nebraska— Valid for wages or personal property of soldiers or sailors, or for property exceeding $150 when acknowledged before three persons called by the testator as witnesses and made during his last illness at home or when sick elsewhere. Probate is not allowed for 14 days to permit process to be issued to the widow and others interested so they may contest. Probate must be completed within six months unless oral testament written down within six days.

Nevada— Valid for property not exceeding $1,000 if made during the last illness and proved by two witnesses to the making within six months. Must be reduced to writing within 30 days after spoken.

New Hampshire— Valid for property not exceeding $100 unless acknowledged by the testator before three persons called by him as witnesses, or made during his last illness at his dwelling place or when fatally ill away from home. It must be written down within six days and proved within six months of the testament.

New Jersey— Invalid.

New Mexico— Not recognized.

New York— Valid for personal property for members of the armed forces on active duty in actual combat or mariners at sea when made before and proved by two witnesses. Invalid and unenforceable after one year following discharge if a soldier or sailor and if he has capacity to make a will at that time. See the discussion on holographic wills in New York State.

North Carolina— Valid when proved by two witnesses to the making of the will in the last illness of the deceased where he lives. After six months it is invalid unless it is written down within ten days of being spoken. Cannot be proved until there has been publication for four weeks in newspapers to call the widow's and kin's attention to it so they may contest.

North Dakota— Valid if the deceased was on active duty if a soldier, or at sea if a sailor, and feared death or was in imminent peril of death from injuries suffered the same day he made the will. For property not exceeding $1,000. Must be proved by two witnesses to the making of the will, one of whom was asked by the deceased to bear witness that such was his will. Testament must be reduced to writing within 30 days.

Ohio— Valid when made in the final illness, and written and signed by two witnesses, not mentioned in the will, within ten days and proved within six months.

Oklahoma— Valid for soldiers in the field or sailors at sea who have reason to fear imminent death, or expect it from injuries suffered that day. Valid for property not exceeding $1,000 in value, when proved by two witnesses present at the making of the will, one of whom was asked by the testator to bear witness that such was his will.

Oregon— Not recognized.

Pennsylvania— Invalid.

Puerto Rico— It must be shown it was impossible to write the will. Where the testator was in imminent danger of death, the will may be executed (without a notary) before five witnesses. The testator must die within three months of making the will; it must be probated within three months of death. Also, it must have been reduced to a public instrument according to the law of civil procedure.

Rhode Island— A soldier, sailor, or airman may dispose of his personal estate as he might have done at common law.

South Carolina— Valid, except that if property exceeds $50 in value the will must be proved by three or more witnesses to the making who were requested by the maker to act as witnesses. The will must be made in the last illness in the house or place where the testator dies, and the will must be proved within six months. This period is extended to one year if the will is written down within six days of the making. The widow must be notified before probate.

South Dakota— Valid for property not exceeding $1,000 in value for soldiers in the field or sailors at sea, when in imminent peril of death or expecting it from injuries suffered that day. Two witnesses present at the making of the will are required to prove it, one of whom was requested by the testator to be witness, and the will must be written down within 30 days of the making. It must be filed for probate not less than 14 days after death and not more than six months.

Tennessee— Valid only for personal property when made in imminent peril of death from which death resulted. Must be made before two witnesses and reduced to writing by one of them within 30 days of the testament and proved within six months of death. Limited to $10,000 for military personnel in active service during war and $1,000

189

otherwise. There can be no probate for 14 days, and the will must have four weeks of publication in newspapers to alert widow and kin.

Texas— Valid when spoken during last illness at the home of testator, or elsewhere if his last illness occurred away from home, except that when personal property exceeds $30 in value the will must be proved by three witnesses within six months after it was made. This proviso is waived if the will is written down not more than six days after it was made. Probate must wait for 14 days, and heirs must be summoned to contest. Soldiers on active duty may dispose of chattels without regard to the rules on wills.

Utah— No provision for this type of will.

Vermont— Valid for personal property for a soldier and for a mariner at sea, but not exceeding $200 in value for anyone else and only when written down by a witness to the making of the will in the six days following the making and presented for probate within six months.

Virginia— Valid for the personal property of soldiers on active duty and sailors at sea.

Virgin Islands— May be made by a soldier or sailor in actual military or naval service. Must be made within the hearing of two persons and the execution and tenor thereof proved by at least two witnesses. Invalid after one year.

Washington— Valid only for personal property not exceeding $1,000 when made during the last illness and proved by two persons who witnessed it at the bidding of the testator, provided the words have been written down and the will is proved within six months. Service personnel or merchant mariners may dispose of wages and personal property in this manner. The widow must be given notice to enable her to contest. No real estate may be devised by such a will.

West Virginia— Valid only for the personal property of servicemen on active duty and mariners at sea.

Wisconsin— Invalid.

Wyoming— Not recognized.

Taxes

Taxes are an integral part of life but, unfortunately, most people do not take them into consideration when they are creating a will and deciding what to do with their estate once they are gone. It is very important that you consider the tax implications of any bequests that you make in your will. It doesn't matter whether the estate is large or small because even with small estates many possibilities for tax savings exist. When planning your will it is best to consult your attorney. He or she is familiar with the laws and will be able to advise you on these potential tax savings.

There are a number of options available. For example, your attorney may suggest that gifts be made during your lifetime rather than at death. In any event, do not overlook this tax aspect when you are ready to formally set down your wishes in your will. You want your beneficiaries to receive all that they are entitled to and by taking the time to investigate the tax savings possibilities now, you will be able to make a difference later.

How to avoid probate

Another aspect of wills that should be considered when you are deciding what to do with your estate is probate. Probate can cause delays for your beneficiaries that you may not want. If you consult with your attorney, he or she will be able to suggest a few of the options available that will enable you to avoid probate.

You can set up an *inter vivos* (during your lifetime) trust providing for the principal sum to be held by a trustee with the income to be paid to you during your lifetime, and then on your death paid over in full to someone else. A living trust must be revocable. You can hold your real estate or stocks and bonds in joint names so that the whole will belong to the survivor. A bank account can be set up payable on death to a named party. Life insurance can be payable to named beneficiaries instead of to your estate. If you give away the ownership right in the policy when you take it out, not only can you avoid having the proceeds in your estate and avoid an estate tax, you may also be able to avoid a gift tax, because the policy has no cash value when you take it out.

Trusts

Although the living trust can be advantageous, there are some potential drawbacks. It will not save either income or estate taxes. And can be costly because of fees attendant on its administration.

In addition to *inter vivos* trusts, there are also testamentary (covered by your will) trusts. These are helpful as a means of postponing the vesting of the principal sum in any beneficiary. By using a trust, the principal can be held intact, and the trustee pays over the income to the person or persons designated—or the income can be accumulated to build up the capital.

A trust is especially helpful when there are minor children involved because they must have a guardian, and administering minors' assets can be difficult, expensive, and subject to Court supervision unless there is a trust fund. Of course, one must be sure to comply with the laws of one's state as to the length of the trust and any accumulation. Be sure to consult with your attorney when contemplating a trust. By doing so, you can be sure that the trust will comply with local laws. The law has long been opposed to the "dead hand" controlling property for too many generations. Usually a trust must be measured (have the length) of no longer than the lives of people who are alive at the time the trust takes effect.

Death without a will

11

Chapter 11
Death without a will

Should you make a will?
Don't state laws take care of designating who gets your property after you die? If you are not very rich, does it still pay to have a will? The answer to all three questions is, "Yes;" however, the reasons for the answer may not seem apparent at first.

If you could tell where and when you were going to die, it would not be very difficult to put your affairs in order and have your estate distributed as you wish. There are, however, many little things that do not seem important now but which may create problems when you are dead. Your joint bank account may expire (be spent) before you do; property you presently own may be sold; you may buy additional property before you die.

State laws, which are substantially the same, provide for the distribution of your property in the event you die without a valid will (intestate). However, what the law decides is the legal way to distribute your property may be a far cry from what you would want.

If you have a wife and minor children, the law generally requires that your children receive the lion's share of your property and that a guardian—generally your wife—be appointed by a court. Your wife (or other guardian) would be required to furnish a bond and comply with statutory guidelines for the use of your children's share of your estate. Your wife would be unable to use any portion of your children's share except for their welfare and would require permission from the court, from time to time, even to use the funds on behalf of your children. In addition, your wife would be required to file a statement of account for all of the funds that were set aside for your children.

There is nothing in the United States Constitution that forbids a state legislature to limit, condition, or even abolish a person's power to dispose of his property by will anywhere within the state's jurisdiction. The right to inherit the property of a dead person is created by statute.

If you leave no heirs whatsoever—recognizable under the law—then, by statute, your property reverts to the state.

A wife is never the heir of her husband, legally speaking. Only a blood relative is an heir in the traditional sense of the law. The wife's position, however, has been improved from what it was in earlier times by new legislation that has followed today's tendency to place husband and wife on an equal plane in every respect, including property rights.

The widow's rights
Formerly, when the ownership of real estate represented a greater portion of the husband's wealth, she had her dower right in an interest for life in a third of his land. Today such a provision is considered inadequate and unjust because a husband may be outstandingly wealthy in securities and cash, and own no real estate whatever. Under the

old law, in such a situation, a man could leave his wife destitute by the simple expedient of making a will in favor of other persons.

Nowadays, in New York, for example, a widow is entitled to a portion of her husband's estate that is fixed by statute. If he has made provision for her in his will, she has a right of election—a right to choose either the legacy under his will or the portion allowed her by the statute.

A surviving wife, when there are children and her husband dies leaving no will, receives in many states generally one-third or one-half of her husband's personal property, depending on the amount of the property, in addition to an interest in any real property he may have owned during their marriage or at his death. The other one-half or two-thirds of the personal property and the real property, not affected by the wife's interest, is divided in equal shares among the children.

How a man attempted to defraud his widow
The attitude of legislatures and courts, in thus giving material protection to a wife, is apparent in a court decision on a case involving a man who sought to arrange his personal affairs so that there would be no estate in which his wife could claim a share. The man had four children by a former marriage. He transferred his property to them during his life, while at the same time retaining control of the property thus transferred.

The court, in its decision, struck directly at this evasion of the rights of the wife. It declared they may not be destroyed by transfers under which the grantor deprives the widow of these rights, and the attempt to elude them is a fraud. As a consequence, the husband, with respect to the widow, must be regarded at the time of his death as being the owner of the property in question. If the husband had given the property away without retaining control, the decision would have been different.

The rights of the surviving husband
The rights of a husband in the estate of his wife are, in general, comparable to those of the wife in the property of her husband when she is the survivor. The details of these rights are provided for in the statutes of the different states where the spouses have their residence.

A husband is no more the "heir" of his wife than she is of her husband except as either is made so by the statutes of the state where they reside. In general, throughout the states, if there is no will and there are no surviving children or parents, the husband receives the wife's entire estate. If there is a will, he has his choice of taking what is left him under the will or of taking the share the state law permits him to elect.

The husband's share when there are heirs
The law in some states is, if there are heirs, the husband has the use for his life of a third of the property his wife owns at the time of her death. When he dies, the property in which he has this interest passes to the heirs of the deceased wife according to the provisions of her will. If there is no will, it goes to the heirs who inherit her property

under the statute. This right of the husband is much like the old *"right of curtesy,"* where the husband had a life interest in the property that his wife owned at her death.

The children's share

When a parent dies without a will, one-half or two-thirds of his estate (the exact amount varies in the different states) is apportioned in equal shares among his children. The remaining part of the estate is divided among his spouse and parents, as we shall explain later.

Children born after the father's death

The law in relation to a child that is born after the death of his father is that for all beneficial purposes of his birth, the child is legally the issue and heir of his father.

The right of an unborn child is shown in a case that took place in Montana. When Charles Normandin died, he left behind him a wife and an unborn child. Immediately upon Charles' death, his brother, Peter, seized his property and kept it as his own. Eight months after Charles died, his daughter, Agnes, was born. Twenty years later, Peter died. Two months after Peter's death, Agnes presented her claim to the executrix of Peter's estate for the half of the estate of her father to which she was entitled and which Peter had appropriated.

"Agnes," said the court, "is deemed to have been living at the time of her father's death, although she was not born until eight months thereafter. She enjoyed all the rights of inheritance conferred upon living persons." Accordingly, Agnes received the portion of her deceased father's estate that was rightfully due her.

Can unborn children have heirs?

An unusual situation occurred in Alabama when, two months after the death of Frank Pinkston, his child was born, only to die within a few hours, the child's mother also dying soon afterward. Pinkston had a half-interest in a tract of land and at his death the property, under the law, went to his heirs. Claim to this interest was made by the heirs of Pinkston's wife on the ground that the mother had inherited this share of the property through the child, being the heir of the child unborn at the time of Pinkston's death.

Posthumous children (children born after their parent's death) have the same right of inheritance of property as the parents, and the same right of inheritance is vested in their heirs. This unborn child, the court ruled, was a living person "for most purposes of property."

The rights of adopted children

The law has had to provide for a peculiar circumstance in the case of adopted children. These children often have two sets of parents—the foster parents who adopted them legally, and the natural parents whose offspring they are. Adopted children are favored by the law.

The modern trend is to treat the adopted child as a member of the adoptive family and terminate all rights of inheritance from the natural family except where the child is adopted by the spouse of one of the natural parents. See Chapter 4 on *Children* for their right to inherit from others.

How children share in their grandparents' estate

When children die before their parents, the law generally gives to their children or grandchildren the share in the parents' estate which the children would have received if they had survived their parents.

Iowa's statute in relation to the share of grandchildren in the estate of grandparents dying without a will is typical of state laws throughout the country. It says that when the parents of the grandchildren die before the grandparents, the grandchildren's portion of the estate is the share their parents would have received had they outlived the grandparents and died in possession of their share.

A further provision is that, if there are no children, the inheritance passes back to the parents or other ancestors of the deceased, and then on to their descendants.

Who inherits an illegitimate child's estate?

What happens to the estate of a child of illegitimate birth who dies without a will? The following case provides a good illustration.

An illegitimate son died in Minnesota, leaving no wife, parents, brothers, or sisters. At his mother's death he had inherited all her property. He was survived by her brothers and sisters, and children of these brothers and sisters.

The Minnesota law is essentially the same as the law of most other states. It says that if any illegitimate child dies without a will (intestate) and without spouse or issue who inherit under the law, his estate shall descend to his mother, or, if she is dead, to her heirs.

The word "*heirs*," as used in a statute providing that the property of an illegitimate child shall pass to the heirs of the mother in case of her death, in general includes those persons to whom the law would give title to the mother's estate by way of descent if she should die without a will. By virtue of being the persons designated by the statute, the heirs of the mother inherited the property of the illegitimate child.

Under the old law an illegitimate son or daughter had no heirs except his or her children. To overcome this injustice statutes such as this have been enacted. It is still the law that an illegitimate child does not inherit from a father who does not leave a will. In many states if the father formally acknowledges the illegitimate child, that child can inherit.

The line of inheritance

The order in which property is passed to the various blood relatives upon the death of its owner without a will demands the application of the rules of the statutes of each state in every instance. There is, however, a general scheme followed by all these statutes.

Interestingly enough, it parallels pretty closely the ancient course of descent of the kingship to English sovereigns.

When spouse and parents survive

A typical statute, in California, provides that if the deceased leaves a surviving spouse and no issue, one-half the estate goes to that spouse and one-half to the parents of the deceased in equal shares. If either parent is dead, his portion goes to the survivor, or if both are dead, to their issue.

In case there are no children or spouse, the parents receive the whole estate. If they are dead, the brothers and sisters of the deceased get equal shares in the estate, and if these too are dead, their children inherit.

Going back to earlier generations

We see, then, that although the course of the descent of property tends downward, through one's children, it may swing up and down again, among the several generations. When there are no children, grandchildren, or other descendants, the right of inheritance shifts to the parents, and if they are deceased, the inheritance goes down to brothers and sisters or to their descendants, and so on.

If there are no descendants of the grandparents who may be recognized as heirs, the right of inheritance swings upward to preceding generations and down to their descendants until it ultimately finds a resting place.

Common ancestors become heirs

The rules of descent and distribution of the property of those dying without wills have the rigidity of mathematics, while on the other hand the conditions and circumstances to which these rules must be applied are of infinite variation. In some instances they are bewildering.

In Pennsylvania, a tract of land was owned by James Custer. Later, James died, leaving no wife, children, brothers or sisters. His father survived him, but the property had been inherited by James from his mother and, under the law in Pennsylvania, "No person who is not of the blood of the ancestors or other relations from whom any real estate descended, or by whom it was given or devised to the intestate, shall take any estate of inheritance therein."

Under that prohibition the father had no claim to the land. By ancient law, the court pointed out, property goes back under such conditions to a common ancestor of the man who has died. Then from that ancestor it passes down.

By this computation, James Davis, a great-grandfather of James Custer, was his next of kin and entitled to the estate, and from him it descended to his heirs.

This rule has since been abolished by statute in Pennsylvania.

Many of the old English rules such as this requirement that the one inheriting land be of the whole blood, or *primogeniture*—the rule that the eldest son inherits all the land—have been abolished in the United States.

When there are no heirs

Our law today retains an ancient provision that when there is no one to inherit the property left by a man or woman dying without a will, the property passes or "*escheats*" to the state. In England, long ago, property to which there were no heirs eventually reverted to the local lord or the Crown; in the United States, our states have assumed this position of a final heir.

If you make no will, or if it is found invalid, then the Probate Court, sometimes called the Surrogate's Court, will appoint an administrator to dispose of your estate in accordance with the laws of intestate succession, which means in accordance with the way the State Legislature has thought people would want their worldly goods distributed. The Administrator will undoubtedly be required to post a bond to insure the faithful performance of duties; the bond is an expense against the estate.

Only a will carefully drawn can give you any security as to a disposition of your estate in accordance with your desires. And while considering the means of disposition, thought can also be given to the very important aspect of the tax situation and how to provide for it and what will be left in the estate after payment of the estate taxes.

Common legal problems of death

12

Chapter 12
Common legal problems of death

When you die, it is hoped that your relatives will not immediately fight over your property. It is also hoped they will be more concerned about an appropriate funeral and burial in the fashion you would like. The law, however, is not very helpful in these areas.

The law must offer guidance amid the conflicting desires and claims of those who survive. The law is often compelled to determine precisely when a death occurred. In disasters or cases of continued absence, the layman is likely to presume death without proof of its actual occurrence, but the law must make the final decision. The law, too, is called upon to determine by whom the funeral and burial solemnization shall be arranged, and whether the body of the deceased may be transferred to another resting place. We already discussed some of the problems that death may raise; here, we examine other common after-death problems.

The body of a dead person belongs to no one under any property right. The great weight of authority in this country is that a person can dispose of his own body by will. Further, a wife or husband who survives or those who are the nearest relatives have the right to determine who shall have the custody of the body in preparation for burial.

Autopsy
When there is doubt as to the cause of death, the law requires an autopsy before a death certificate can be issued. In general, an autopsy must be made before burial, unless good and sufficient reason can be given to the court why a body should be disinterred. Serious suspicion of murder is such a good reason, but most other reasons will not be sustained.

The consent of surviving relatives is required for the performance of an autopsy by hospital authorities, as it is for all other autopsies, unless performed by a coroner. Generally, when an autopsy is performed, the results are not available to the public. They are available only to the authorities if there is reason to suspect a crime, and to the surviving relatives.

Funeral reform
A funeral is likely to be one of the largest purchases that many of us will ever have to make. Over $5.2 billion is spent each year by American consumers for funeral arrangements, with the cost of the average funeral being $2500.

Since 1972, U.S. Federal Trade Commission (F.T.C.) has been trying to protect the consumer from certain business practices of funeral providers which hamper bereaved relatives at the time they are making funeral arrangements. Among the F.T.C.'s chief concerns is the industry-wide practice of using either single-unit or bi-unit pricing. This means that the purchaser generally must pick either a complete package or one that separates out only the casket price and then lumps all other services together, regardless of whether they are wanted or needed.

As of April 1984, the F.T.C. required funeral homes to tell the consumer about the cost of each service being purchased such as embalming, casket, flowers, music, before a contract is signed. Also, prices must be quoted over the phone. Another provision makes it illegal for the funeral home to misrepresent to the consumer state requirements concerning the necessity of items such as a casket or embalming. Nor can they require the purchase of a casket if a body is cremated.

Emotional distress

An appellate court in California has broken new ground in allowing damage claims for emotional distress by third parties. When the family of a deceased told the funeral home it was not their relative in the casket, the funeral home denied the problem and proceeded with the funeral. A few days later, another funeral home discovered it had the real deceased. This required a second funeral. The widow received a settlement from the first funeral home, but the lawsuit by other relatives was dismissed since the lower court said they did not have a contract with the funeral home. However, the appellate court said that was too narrow an approach since the others also suffered from this mix-up.

Removing a dead body

The problems involving a dead body do not stop with the funeral. In Georgia a few years ago, a husband purchased a cemetery lot he believed suitable for the burial of his wife; he himself wished to be interred in the adjoining lot. After his wife was buried, however, he learned that the second lot had already been purchased by another.

He asked for a permit to transfer his wife's body to another lot. The Supreme Court commented on his plea. "To permit the husband to reinter the body is but to grant him the right to exercise his choice to a place of burial on the lot owned by him, which would permit his body, when his own death occurs, to be placed nearby. He seeks now no profanation nor any indignity to the dead, but merely the fulfillment of his original purpose." His request was granted.

How the courts decide on disinterment

The factors involved in the granting of permission by courts for the disinterment and removal of a body already buried are, first, the wishes of the dead person, second, those of the surviving spouse and, last, those of the next of kin.

For 20 years Major Koon of the United States Army made his home in Detroit, with his wife, Velma Doan Koon, and her family at Richmond.

He died and was buried in the cemetery lot of the Doan family at Richmond. Then for the first time Velma and her family learned that Koon had been divorced long ago and there were children of that marriage.

None of these children attended their father's funeral, but over a year later they asked to disinter the body, cremate it, and ship the ashes to California. On the ground that the Major was properly buried where he would probably have chosen to be, and that the widow's wishes were paramount, the court refused to grant the children's request.

The courts, as we have noted, are loath to disturb the quiet of the grave unless there are good reasons to decide otherwise. The presumption is against a change.

Surviving relatives are prone to forget the wishes of the deceased, and to regard his body as their property. Not so the courts. In Virginia, a widow sought to shift the family burial plot to follow her changing religious beliefs. The courts did not favor her suit.

The controlling factors were different in the case of a woman who died and was buried in Kansas, after living most of her life there. Before her death she had expressed the wish to be buried in California. When one of her daughters applied for the right to remove her mother's body to Los Angeles, the court granted her permission. All the governing rules were satisfied: (1) It was the wish of the deceased; (2) the wish of the next of kin (no spouse survived); (3) the rules of the cemetery (which must be considered when made a part of the contract of purchase of the plot) did not forbid it; and (4) the tenets and usages of the religious body conferring the right of burial likewise did not forbid it. It should be noted, however, that ecclesiastical rules and regulations are not controlling, at least where they come into conflict with principles of equity and other pertinent matters.

Death presumed from absence

When a person disappears, leaving no information of his whereabouts, a legal determination of his death or continued survival often becomes necessary. This occurs not only when the remaining spouse wants the marriage dissolved, but also in many business relationships where the fact of death is of outstanding importance.

A typical case

Arrested for a violation of the Virginia state liquor law, a man named Sherrill Goodwin was released on bail pending his trial. Several days before the date set for the trial, Goodwin packed his bag and disappeared, leaving a note telling his wife that he was going away, but that he would send her some money as soon as he secured work, and that he loved his family as he always had. At the trial he was found guilty and sentenced to sixty days of hard labor with the convict road force. Nine years later, Goodwin's wife sued for the insurance payable at his death on the policies he had carried.

In all states, the death of a person is presumed—unless the contrary can be shown—if he has disappeared and has not been heard from for a prolonged period. The statute in Virginia, which is the common law rule applicable in most states, says that any person residing in the state who goes away or disappears for seven successive years and is not heard from shall be presumed to be dead in any case where his death shall come in question unless it can be shown that he was alive during that period.

Whether Goodwin was alive or dead was for the jury to decide. Their verdict was that he was dead, and his widow was entitled to the insurance.

How death is presumed from imminent peril

The problem of deciding whether a missing person may be presumed dead, and when he met his death, is relatively simple in cases involving "imminent peril." What this term means is clearly shown in the case that follows.

The *Sixeola*, with a Coast Guard crew aboard, was torpedoed in World War II. Two weeks after the catastrophe, the wife of one of the Sixeolak crew members received a telegram from the commandant of the Coast Guard, saying that her husband was missing following action in the performance of his duty. The commandant promised to furnish her with further information as soon as possible.

This telegram was followed six months later by a letter saying that 28 members of the crew, including the woman's husband, were reported missing. "Due to the length of time and the circumstances of the attack these missing crew members are presumed lost."

In the suit brought to recover the insurance on the life of the missing man, these facts were held to be sufficient proof that he had died at that time.

Not in all cases is the law of imminent peril applied so readily as those affecting military personnel presumed killed in action. The following case is an illustration of a typical incident.

A forest fire was ravaging the country around Spokane, Washington. Many had lost their lives and volunteers were striving to check the flames. Thomas Fanning told a friend in Spokane that he was going to volunteer to fight the fire. The next day Fanning could not be found at his boarding house and he was never seen again.

Fanning's absence and the lack of any information of his whereabouts set the date of his death, by law, at the end of seven years. In this case the imminent peril of the forest fire showed the probability of his death, as the submarine attack on the vessel with the Coast Guard crew showed the probable death of those who did not survive, but the date of Fanning's death was determined by the legal presumption in the absence of supporting evidence.

Proximate peril

The minister of a church in Idaho was happily married and had two children to whom he was devoted. He was a healthy optimist, 32-years-old, of exemplary habits, and with a fondness for fishing.

One afternoon he rented a small rowboat, pushed off from the shore, and rowed out into a neighborhood lake. He was last seen late in the afternoon a quarter to a half mile out. The next morning he had not returned. The boat was found off shore, the minister's coat hanging over the side, one oar missing. A two-week search for his body was unsuccessful.

When his widow sued for the insurance on her husband's life, the court held she was entitled to collect. Summarizing the cases where death is presumed upon the occurrence of an approximate peril, it said: "Two settled principles applicable to a case of this nature are: That a person who was alive when last seen is presumed to continue living until the contrary is shown; and that one who disappears and remains unheard of for seven years and whose absence is unexplained, is presumed to be dead. Where the proof shows that the absentee encountered some specific peril to which it may reasonably be thought he had succumbed, death may be inferred short of the expiration of the seven-year period."

Circumstantial evidence of death

The perils from which the law infers death are not merely physical ones. Nowadays, situations of emotional or mental stress are widely recognized as a basis for presumption of death.

The disappearance of a resident of Bangor, Maine, was marked by no physical peril. The man's home life had been happy, but during the closing years of the Depression of the thirties he had become despondent. He was insolvent. His home was mortgaged. He had borrowed from friends, relatives, and banks.

"I realize if I live much longer I'll not have much of a good time. It wouldn't bother me if I were to die tomorrow," he remarked to a friend. He left Bangor for Boston, hoping to obtain financial help. Later his wife received a wire from him stating: "No luck. Leaving tonight. Boat. New York party. Home Friday. Love."

This man's personal luggage was found a few days afterward in his room on the boat, but he was missing. These facts, in conjunction with his disappearance and his mental attitude at the time, established his death in the suit brought later by his widow to recover his life insurance.

According to the law, while the presumption of life continues, the fact of mere disappearance does not prove death. But disappearance where there is no information about the absentee, although search and inquiry are made, together with other circumstantial facts, such as the evidence of suicide in this case, may be sufficient to establish death.

Patient dumping

A federal law, the *Emergency Medical Treatment and Active Labor Act,* was passed to meet the problem of poor people being refused hospital treatment. Hospitals that receive federal funds (most under Medicare and Medicaid) must take anyone who "comes" to an emergency room. Many poor people use emergency rooms as their only contact with medicine and their care is very expensive. What of those who have to use rescue vehicles to get there?

In a case in Chicago, a parent called for the paramedics to help a baby in cardiac arrest. When the medics contacted a hospital nearby, they were rerouted somewhere else. The second hospital had no facilities for children and she was taken to another hospital where she died. The nearby hospital was sued. A Federal Appeals Court decided that the hospital normally would be required to give emergency stabilizing treatment, but this child did not "come" to the hospital. The hospital's "telemetry system" was not considered to be the emergency room.

The problem of relatives killed in a common disaster

The order in which the deaths of a husband and wife occur when they perish in a common disaster, such as the sinking of a ship, a fire, or an automobile accident, determines who inherits their property. But the answer to the question of who dies first is in most instances of this kind really a conjecture. The only adequate solution to the problem is a provision for such contingencies in the wills of both the husband and the wife.

If the husband dies first, the wife inherits the widow's share of his estate, however short the time may be by which she survives him. Then, at her death, whatever property she possesses, together with what part of her husband's estate she is entitled to, passes not to his heirs but to hers.

A father, mother, and two daughters were driving by automobile from Chicago to Bowling Green, Kentucky. The road was wet and slippery. The car skidded and turned over. There was a flaming explosion of gasoline and all four occupants of the car were burned to death with no witnesses of the tragedy.

All the victims were considered to have perished at the same time. No circumstances existed to contradict this presumption.

The claims were decided by the rule that is generally followed in such instances. In case of the death of two or more persons in a common disaster, according to this rule, there is no presumption either of survivorship or simultaneous death. In other words, representatives of the wife's estate, if they claimed the insurance, had to show that she survived her husband. If they could not, the property of the husband passed to his heirs, as it would if she had not survived.

Exceptions: Louisiana and California

Some of the legal principles of survivorship in the state of Louisiana are exceptions to the general rule of law in this country that all in a common disaster are supposed to perish at the same time unless the contrary can be shown. The laws of this state follow the legal codes of France. By these laws, the youngest is presumed to live the longest, and the oldest to die first. A man is presumed to survive a woman when both perish in a common disaster. California, following the laws of Spain, formerly had a rule similar to that of Louisiana.

A Louisiana case

On board the steamship *La Bourgogne* that sailed from New York for France in July, 1898, were a mother and daughter from New Orleans. Each had made a will giving all her property to the other, with an alternative disposition if neither survived the other.

In mid-ocean the *La Bourgogne* collided with another vessel and sank. No facts existed for determining whether mother or daughter survived the other. Both perished.

Under the law of Louisiana, which is an exception to the general rule in this country, it is provided that if several persons respectively entitled to inherit from one another happen to perish in the same event and it cannot be ascertained who died first, the circumstances of the fact determine the presumption of survivorship. If those who perish together are older than age 15 and younger than age 60, the male must be presumed to have survived where there is an equality of age or a difference in ages of less than one year. Otherwise, the younger person, regardless of sex, is presumed to survive the older.

In deciding the controversy that arose from the *La Bourgogne* tragedy, the Louisiana court said that it must be presumed that the daughter survived the mother since she was the younger, and they were older than 15 and younger than 60.

Transplants

Leading into the next chapter on *Gifts* is a problem usually associated with death, although it is a gift that might be made by a living person, and that is the problem of anatomical gifts, a form of transplantation.

Because of the world-wide interest stemming from the fast human heart transplant performed by Dr. Christiaan Barnard in 1967 at Capetown, South Africa, studies were done on the legal aspects of the use of human organs, tissue, and blood for the purpose of implanting them in another human. The laws of all 50 states and the District of Columbia now recognize organ donation as established under *the Uniform Anatomical Gift Act*. However, because of major advances in transplantation and the continuing need for donors, the *National Organ Transplant Act* was passed in 1984. It provided for establishment of a Registry to include potential organ recipients, donors and a matching system with 24-hour capability. It also provided for start-up grants to non-profit organ procurement organizations, and it prohibited the interstate sale of human organs.

If you wish to make an anatomical gift, the law allows any person 18 or older to donate all or part of their body after death for research, transplantation, or placement in a tissue bank. A donor's gift takes precedence over the rights of others, except where a state autopsy law may prevail. If a donor does not make arrangements, his survivors, in a specified order of priority, may. Doctors who accept gifts of organs or tissues, relying in good faith on a donation document, are protected from lawsuits. However, the fact of death must be determined by a doctor who is not also involved in the transplant. A donor may revoke a gift and the gift may also be rejected. A donation may be made by a will (without waiting for probate) or other written and witnessed document, such as a card designed to be carried on the person. The document may specify a recipient such as a hospital, medical school, or individual needing the gift.

The Office of Organ Transplantation in the Department of Health and Human Services, Washington, D.C. can be helpful.

Patient's right to die

Courts in the states of New Jersey, Massachusetts, Ohio, Delaware, New York, and Washington have recognized the right of a patient to refuse life sustaining treatment in circumstances where the patient's condition is irreversible and incurable. These courts have found that an adult who is terminally ill has a constitutional right of privacy and the right to be free from bodily invasion which includes the right to refuse treatment that serves only to prolong life.

The landmark case of *In Re Quinlan* set up general guidelines which must be followed in the difficult decision as to whether "to pull the plug" when the patient cannot participate in the decision. Upon the concurrence of the guardian and family of the patient, the attending physician must be consulted and must conclude that there is no reasonable possibility of the patient emerging from the present condition to a cognitive, sapient state and that life support apparatus should be discontinued. The hospital ethics committee must also be consulted. If that body agrees that there is no reasonable possibility of recovery, the life support system may be withdrawn without any civil or criminal liability on the part of any participant in the decision.

Karen Ann Quinlan's life-support system was removed in 1976. She died in 1985.

Withholding food and water

Recently there has been controversy in connection with the right to reject food and water by patient or family. Twenty-one states allow withdrawal of artificial feeding, 12 are ambiguous and 8 have laws prohibiting the withholding even in a living will. Oklahoma prohibits it unless it causes severe pain, a patient requests it or death is imminent. In Missouri, the Supreme Court rejected efforts by parents of a comatose woman to end artificial feeding she had since 1983. The New York Court of Appeals ordered continued artificial feeding of a 77-year-old mental incompetent despite testimony that she had often said she didn't want it. The Court wanted a detailed living will.

Patient not terminal

A quadriplegic in Colorado desired to cut off all life sustaining assistance even though he had no terminal illness. His wish was granted by the County Judge. Although Hector Rodas had an indefinite life expectancy he saw himself as living in total and unmitigated misery, a form of prison and he had a right to decide to die by starvation.

Living will

Living wills sometimes are called health care proxies, or advance directives. All states recognize them. They can involve 'do not resuscitate' orders. If upon a terminal illness you do not want extraordinary measures used to prolong life, you need a statement signed, dated and witnessed by two adults. It should be detailed and specific. Even then, however, sometimes your desires may not be carried out. In an Ohio hospital a man was revived by a defibrillator despite clear contrary instructions. He then suffered a stroke and was incapacitated. His family sued after his death to recover hospital expenses claiming negligence. The hospital said there's no action for continued living. The court said it was a mistake.

Durable power of attorney

This is a document wherein you appoint someone (or two persons to be sure of one's availability) to make health care decisions for you in the event you are incapable. At least 24 states authorize a surrogate to make a decision concerning ending life support treatment.

In 22 states the courts have decided that family members or a legal guardian can be your surrogate if you have given specific power to someone to act on your behalf. However, in some states, such as Maine, Missouri, and New York, the court will not accept a surrogate's decision unless the patient previously clearly and convincingly had indicated a wish not to receive artificial aids to prolong life.

Your lawyer can help you draw up a document that conforms to your wishes and your state's laws.

Which should you have?

You may wonder whether you need both a living will and a durable power of attorney. Many people feel they need both and your lawyer can do both at the same time. You may want to outline all your particular desires to avoid any misunderstanding, and you may want to have a trustworthy representative help carry out your wishes. You may need that person to deal with medical people or mediate amongst family who disagree about your wishes.

It is very important that any document that is prepared is not locked away, but is widely distributed to your family, physician, and spiritual leader. This is so that your wishes can be implemented at the appropriate time, especially in an emergency.

If you do not have an advance directive, in California no conclusion can be drawn from this omission concerning your desires. However, in New York, Missouri and other states, if you have none and the hospital won't end treatment, very strong evidence is required in court to prove your intentions.

And if you are a female with no directive, your prior comments may not be taken as seriously by the courts. In some cases they have characterized them as "casual, informal, general" and let others make the decision on care.

Patient Self-Determination Act

A new federal law will now require that all patients entering a health care facility, such as a hospital or nursing home, be informed about their right under state law to choose or refuse treatment if they are incapacitated or terminally ill. As discussed above, there is more widespread recognition of a person's right to decide how much medical treatment they want. Some people are afraid to discuss the matter or just do not know how explicit they have to be or to whom they should address their preferences.

Now the issue will have to be confronted, at least when you become a patient at a medical facility. It is the hospital or nursing home staff that will have the responsibility to alert incoming patients of their rights. It is not a requirement for patients to provide an "advance directive." However, they must be informed by a hospital, nursing home, hospice or health maintenance organization (HMO) which receives Medicare or Medicaid funds, that they may refuse treatment. Also, the medical records must show whether the patient has an advance medical directive.

Of course, if you are not incompetent or unconscious, your direct consultation on your case will override any document on file.

Wrongful life suit

Edward Winter saw his wife die a slow and agonizing death when she suffered brain damage after shock resuscitation from a heart attack. When he suffered a heart attack, he told his family and physician he didn't want that for himself. But his wishes were not recorded on his heart monitor and he was revived by a nurse after he suffered another attack. He later had a stroke, which left him partially paralyzed, sad, and angry. His medical bills soared.

He sued the hospital in Ohio for "wrongful life." He had wanted to die in peace. He did die a few years after his attack, but it was not the life or death he thought he had assured with his verbal statements. It may have been different had he written out his wishes earlier and appointed someone to assure that everyone in the care facility was aware of his desires. If the new law had been in effect, the hospital personnel would have been more knowledgeable about his desires.

Liability of an estate

Courts have been nearly unanimous in not allowing punitive damages to be awarded against the estate of a dead tort-feasor. Some have based their decision on the fact that their state's survival or wrongful death statute expressly prohibited such an award. Others reasoned that the only purpose of punishment is to deter and punish persons who have committed wrongful acts and a dead person can no longer be punished. However, the West Virginia Supreme Court of Appeals has recently decided that since punitive damages serve other important functions, going beyond mere punishment of the wrongdoer, they should be allowed. The court recognized that punitive damages also deter others from following a like course of conduct and provide additional compensation to the injured Party.

Death of a twin

There are about three million sets of twins in the country and there is evidence that multiple births are on the rise.

When a twin is injured or dies because of negligence, is the survivor entitled to more compensation because of the special relationship? Some courts and juries think so. In a Minnesota case when a twin was burned, the uninjured twin recovered a quarter of a million dollars because he'd suffered "a loss of twin-ship." In a Michigan case when a twin died, the survivor received as much for "loss of society" as did the deceased's spouse.

Posse Comitatus

This is a 13th Century doctrine whereby civilians are called upon to assist law enforcement. When an off duty officer in Virginia Beach came upon a crash on a highway, he stopped a female civilian to ask her help. They were both killed when a speeding car hit them. Her family filed and received workers compensation, claiming she had been deputized and would have been guilty of a misdemeanor if she had refused to help.

Gifts

Chapter 13
Gifts

An English court, many years ago, attempted to formulate a legal doctrine in light of ordinary human reactions by stating that, "There cannot be a gift without a giving and taking."

This simplest concept of ownership is, thus, materialistic and identified with physical control. When young children trade things, the standard way to "transfer title" is to hand over the item. A child who no longer physically possessed the item would not derive comfort from the fact that he or she was still the lawful owner. Following this line of thinking the owner is the one with physical possession. To make someone else owner you physically transfer the property; and, if you lose possession you are no longer the owner. Very few people are interested in hearing about a legal distinction between "title" and "possession."

The modern notion of ownership shifts the emphasis to the functional criteria of what the law requires before putting one man in the shoes of another with reference to any particular property. Thousands of gifts are made daily in this country by people with only the simplest ideas of ownership, and generally without legal advice. Many people who would not think of considering a will without going to an attorney do not even realize that a legal problem exists in gifts of personal property. People have been making gifts all their lives without legal advice, and giving, to most of them, means delivering possession.

The necessity of delivery in gifts of personal property has always been adhered to in the United States. The typical law would therefore be as follows: to succeed in effectuating a gift, the claimant must show:
(1) the alleged donor's intent to give, and
(2) delivery of either (a) the gift, e.g., cash, or (b) an instrument of gift, e.g., a stock certificate.

A gift or not a gift?
Remember, when you make a gift, it is not a gift if you reserve a right to take it back. The giving must be complete—there is no halfway ground. It is either a gift or it is not a gift.

Twelve hundred dollars and 40 shares of stock were transferred to Wilma MacPherson by her aunt one month before she died. Later, the executor of the aunt's estate claimed that both the cash and stock Wilma had received were not gifts.

The aunt was over 70-years-old, with no children or relatives except some nieces and nephews. Of these, Wilma had been the only one to show any kindness to the old lady, and during every illness had cared for her. The assignment of the stock had been carefully prepared and executed, and the aunt herself had withdrawn the cash from the bank and deposited it to Wilma's credit.

The transfer of this money and stock was a valid gift, the court declared. Such a transfer must be intended as a gift—and as a gift in the present, not in the future. Further, it must give to the one who receives it full ownership and control. There is not a valid gift without a complete delivery, even though every other step essential to the validity of the gift has been taken. If the gift is not actually delivered, it is not a gift. "Intention cannot supply it; actions cannot supply it; it is an indispensable requisite without which a gift fails."

False "gifts"

By way of contrast, let us examine the facts of a case that came before the federal court in Florida, where for 15 years a father had made so-called gifts of the stock of his business to his children. In every instance, he endorsed the stock certificates before witnesses, declaring them to be gifts to his children. Then he had taken the certificates and put them into his own safe-deposit box. He kept the dividends for himself, while he gave his children promissory notes for an equivalent amount, and deducted these dividends from his income tax returns because they were "gifts."

According to the law, the court said, these transfers were not gifts. One who makes a gift must do everything possible to give the ownership and control of the gift to the person receiving it. The father here had made no delivery of the stock to his children. He continued to deal with the securities and the income as his own; hence, this income was taxable to him.

A vital element in many such attempts at making gifts is the trait deep rooted in every possessor of property to hang on to the possession of it—the wish to be a giver and still keep the gift.

A gift with a condition

For many years Louise Johnson was a close friend of Augusta Scharf, an old lady in poor health. One day, when Louise Johnson called, Mrs. Scharf handed her the following note: "I give Mrs. Henry Johnson [Louise Johnson] the sole right to my bonds, all of them, for my expenses in case I pass away. Augusta L. Scharf."

Below this she had written, "If Mrs. Scharf should get well and strong again, I will return to her the four bonds as she requested. If she passes away, I am to give Anna Zalinski the $1,000 bond, a gift to her for her services during her poor health during the last three years. She was always willing and kind through very trying circumstances. Louise, the expenses I want you to pay are Anna [Anna Zalinski], and have my name put on my tombstone. My funeral expenses must come from the house as well as other bills when the house is sold."

With this memorandum Mrs. Scharf gave her friend the four bonds she had mentioned. Since Louise Johnson accepted them, her signature to the document was not necessary. Two weeks later Mrs. Scharf died. Mrs. Scharf's attempt to make a gift failed. The cause was the all too human trait already mentioned, the desire to hold on to one's property even though one gives it away. It cannot be emphasized too strongly. For a gift between living persons to be valid there must be a giving up of possession, a relinquishment of all control both present and future. The gift must be placed beyond the power of the giver to recall it.

A gift must be accepted

The law requires in the making of a gift not only that the giver release all ownership and control but, more, that the one to whom the gift is made should accept it. Before the gift is accepted, if the giver changes his mind, or dies, the gift is revoked. It cannot be revoked once the gift has been accepted. Acceptance of a gift is as essential in the eyes of the law as is the offer by the giver. Not until there is an acceptance by the one who receives the gift does ownership pass.

When gifts are a burden

The courts will not infer, in the absence of proof, that a designated recipient has accepted a gift or legacy which is not only without any monetary value but which would be a millstone around his neck.

A resident of Pennsylvania died, willing his property to his wife. The estate was hopelessly insolvent. The holder of a mortgage on land that was part of the estate sued the widow for the past due taxes on this property. The property was already mortgaged far in excess of its value. According to the court that tried the case, the widow could not have accepted such property as a gift and so she bore no responsibility for it.

Showing acceptance

The receiver for a Michigan bank sued the widow and children of a stockholder for assessments made on the stock which they received from him. They had received and spent the dividends two years before the assessments were levied. By accepting the dividends, they showed they had accepted the stock and were therefore liable for payment of the assessments.

The necessity for acceptance before a gift can be complete is similar to the acceptance of an offer before a contract becomes a binding obligation.

Gift of bank deposits

When you decide to make a gift or a gift is made to you, always keep in mind the rule that the object of the gift must pass completely from the control of the giver and be entirely within the control of the receiver of the gift. In the gift of bank deposits and the determination of whether such gifts are valid, the courts emphasize this transfer of ownership more than any other feature of the transaction.

Intention to make a gift

An old lady in California, realizing she had only a short time to live, decided to transfer her bank account into a joint bank account in the name of her sister, her nephew, and herself. She signed the necessary papers for this purpose and gave them to the teller of the bank on a Friday afternoon after banking hours. Before the bank opened the following Monday the old lady was dead.

Because she had delivered to the teller of the bank both her bankbook and the withdrawal order for the transfer of the account, the gift was complete. The required delivery, actual or symbolic, to one to whom the gift was made, or to someone for his benefit, with the intent to make the gift, had taken place. The deposit here had passed from the control of the old lady and was under the control of the three owners of the account. A gift may be made although the giver still retains some interest in it.

When a gift by check becomes complete

A gift by check is complete when the check is received and paid by the bank on which it is drawn. When this is done, the check is removed from circulation and canceled, and the transaction is closed.

The victim of a California automobile accident, who was close to death, gave to a friend a check payable to a third person, asking that it be deposited immediately to that person's account. At closing time of the bank that day the check was deposited. A few hours later the man who had signed the check was dead. Nevertheless, the gift was complete. The check had been deposited and paid before the death of the giver.

Giving an engagement ring

The engagement ring has the character of a pledge—it binds the contract to marry. With the dissolution of the bargain by the woman, her right to the ring disappears. By the law of some states, she can be obliged to return it.

The other side of this problem is shown in a case that took place in Kentucky, where a couple were engaged to be married. "Shortly thereafter," according to the county judge, "pursuant to a custom, to the origin of which the mind of man runneth not, the man presented a gift to the woman, the diamond ring here in question." Then later, the man broke the engagement.

Later, these two went squirrel hunting. Sitting under a tree, the woman had her engagement ring in her hand. The man took the ring and put it in his pocket, where it stayed until that judge decided the case and the woman received back her ring.

When a woman receives an engagement ring and then refuses to fulfill the conditions of the gift—to marry the giver—she must return the ring.

On the other hand, when the man refuses to carry out the marriage agreement, he forfeits the rights to the return of the engagement ring. However, in some states that have outlawed actions for breach of promise to marry, you may not be able to force return of the gift regardless of who is at fault. See more on this in Chapter 1 on *The Law of Marriage*.

Who owns the engagement ring of a dead woman?

In Illinois, on a Christmas eve, a man gave a dinner ring to the woman he had promised to marry, and later he gave her two other rings. Afterward she died, and he demanded that the rings be returned to him since the marriage had not taken place.

When the woman died she owned the jewelry, said the court. It was hers. She had broken no marriage contract nor had she refused to marry him. The man had no claim to the jewelry.

Other gifts during engagement
When gifts are made during an engagement—be they rings or any other objects—and they are gifts pure and simple and not part of the engagement pledge, or used to seal the promise to marry implicit in it, the general rule is that they remain the property of the recipient if the engagement should be broken off.

Making a gift of land
A gift of real estate, like any other gift, is not a gift until the transfer is complete. The land must be out of the giver's control and in the control of the one who receives the gift. This can best be done by the giving of the deed to the land, properly signed and authenticated.

Gift by word of mouth
A transfer of land cannot be made by word of mouth. There must be a delivery of possession or some act symbolizing that delivery. Further, there must be an acceptance of the gift and acts of the receiver of the gift in reliance on the validity of the gift, such as the making of improvements to the extent that it would be a substantial injustice if the gift were revoked. This is because arrangements with respect to land are required by law to be in writing to be enforceable.

Improving a gift of land
In North Dakota, a mother gave her son and daughter-in-law some land, making the gift by word of mouth. The son and his wife made investments in building improvements. However, they paid the mother no rent for the land. When she ordered them to vacate, the son obeyed, but the daughter-in-law refused. Suit was brought to oust her, but these efforts proved to be in vain. There had been a reliance by the son and his wife on the gift of the land by word of mouth. They had taken possession and spent money on its improvement and development. To hold the gift void under such circumstances would have been a substantial injustice.

When a gift is irrevocable
A situation similar in many details occurred in Maryland, except that in this case the gift was conveyed by a written document. A father executed and delivered to his daughter deeds of two houses he owned in Baltimore. Later, the father remarried and wanted his land back. The daughter, not in sympathy with her father's new marriage venture, refused to reconvey the property. The father sued to recover it, but he did not succeed. The gift of land, being in writing, was complete and irrevocable.

If delivery is postponed
The circumstances are different when delivery or possession of a gift is postponed. An elderly woman had her attorney prepare a deed of her property to a close friend and instructed him, when she executed the deed, not to deliver it to her friend until she gave

him further orders. Here, there was no gift. The owner never delivered the deed, nor did her friend have the opportunity of accepting it.

Conditional gifts

A gift with conditions tagged to it, we have seen, may lose its character as a gift because of these conditions. However, if, by the transaction, the gift immediately becomes the property of the one to whom it is given, it is a legal gift.

Possession does not always make a gift

To the rule set forth in the preceding paragraph there are certain exceptions that must be explained. One of them is illustrated in the following case. A husband and wife in New York State signed the statement, "I give into the possession of my wife 90 shares of Bethlehem Steel common to hold in her possession until after my death. After my death, that 90 shares of Bethlehem Steel common are to become the personal property of my said wife, Jennie, but in case I should survive her, then, after her death these 90 shares of Bethlehem Steel common are to be returned to me and become part of my estate."

This was no gift. The wife was merely to act as custodian of the stock unless her husband died first. There was a delivery and an acceptance but there was no intent to make a gift except if the husband's death should occur before his wife's.

What power to revoke means

A very similar case concerned stock given with the understanding that the giver should receive all the dividends, and if he survived the person he gave the stock to, then the stock should be returned to him.

Such a plan, said the court, constituted no gift. The stock was merely held for the owner's lifetime with an agreement that the holder could transfer it to himself if the giver were the first to die. The giver could have revoked the transaction at any time during his life, for until he had been divested of all title, dominion, and control, the gift could be revoked. If a gift can be revoked or nullified, there is no gift.

Interest retained in a gift

The retention by the giver of a beneficial interest in property, or a right to share in the income or proceeds from it, is held by the courts not to be inconsistent with a valid gift.

Geraldyne Pratt was the daughter of a western railroad president. She lived with her parents and had only a small income of her own. Her mother wrote her the following letter:

> Dear Geraldyne: I have transferred to you 200 shares of Texas Oil Company stock as a gift—with this reservation—that when you sell the stock you invest the proceeds in United States government securities to so remain during your life, with the further understanding that no part of the principal shall be disposed of either by sale or used for a loan. The income, use as your best judgment may dictate. Should death occur to you

before either your father or myself, then the securities will revert to me, otherwise to him. If married and no issue, the preceding paragraph will prevail. If issue, the securities will be left in trust for the issue. Your mother. Mrs. J. A. Edson.

In a federal court action concerning the income taxes on the securities involved in the transfer, the court said that here was an unmistakable gift. In regard to the provision for the return of the securities on the daughter's death, it was pointed out that all the factors that make a gift were present: (1) a giver competent to make a gift; (2) a clear and unmistakable intention on her part to make it; (3) a person capable of taking the gift; (4) a conveyance, assignment, or transfer to the receiver of the gift with no power of revocation by the giver; and (5) a relinquishment of the control of the gift.

Gifts in contemplation of death

Another and frequent type of conditional gift is one that becomes effective at the death of the giver—gifts *causa mortis*. Such a gift made in contemplation of death by the giver is valid although it is intended to be a revocable gift if the giver should not die.

The essential features of such gifts are as follows:

(1) the gift must be of personal property;

(2) possession of the property must be delivered at the time of the gift to the donee (recipient) or someone for him and the gift must be accepted by the donee; and

(3) the title to the property must vest in the donee at the time of the gift. To constitute a gift *causa mortis* it must also be shown in addition to the above elements that the gift was made from a premonition of death from present sickness.

There is an essential distinction that should be stressed here between gifts of this character and gifts in general. Ordinarily, once a gift is made, the ownership of the gift is in the person receiving it. Here ownership is conditioned on the death of the giver. If the giver recovers from the illness that gives him the premonition of death under which the gift is made, the transaction is revoked and the giver becomes again the owner.

These rules were laid down in a case concerning the estate of a Mr. J. M. Thomas of Danville, Virginia. Mr. Thomas had put in his safe-deposit box an envelope containing securities, and on the envelope, with a list of the contents, was endorsed, "The personal property of my wife, Florence Thomas." He had been seriously ill and knew "he was down for good for some time."

He gave his wife a key to the safe-deposit box. Shortly before his death he asked, "Florence, where are your keys? Remember those keys are very precious for you to hold, for you might need them in order to get in the box in my safe to get possession of what I told you I have left you in the box." This statement was important evidence in the case.

In concluding its opinion on this case, the court said, "Looking at the evidence in connection with the surrounding circumstances, we think it shows that Mr. Thomas intended to make his wife a gift *causa mortis* of the stock and bonds in question and the same should be upheld."

A gift by a person not then expecting death, but which is to have effect on his death, is not valid. The reason is that such a disposition is testamentary, or similar to one made by will, and therefore requires all the legal formalities necessary to execute a will.

Gift taxes

Tax law is very complicated and changes are made frequently. There have been amendments recently dealing with gifts to a spouse as well as charitable gifts. You should know that the law provides for a $10,000.00 annual tax exclusion for gifts to each person. This tax is progressive, based upon the total gifts made over the donor's lifetime. Gifts between spouses usually are not subject to gift tax due to the current 100% marital deduction.

When one spouse buys savings bonds in both names, there is a gift when the proceeds are received by the other spouse. When there is a joint bank account there is a gift when the spouse who does not contribute makes a withdrawal.

Gifts to charities

You may have a church, school, fraternal order or other group you wish to assist. You can contribute to the fostering of national or international sports competition. You can give money, land, personal property, or income from property. You may wish to set up a trust for this purpose. However, you should be careful that the rights of family members are considered since persons whose expectations are not fulfilled may make claims. Consultation with counsel will result in your getting all the tax advantages you are entitled to and assure compliance with the law.

An interest in undivided property

When a part of a property is given as a gift and the whole property remains undivided, a special problem is created for which the law provides. How this provision operates is shown in the following case, concerning an interest in bonds of great value.

A Mr. Collins of Chattanooga told his wife that he intended to give her half of the bonds he possessed. They went to the bank where he had the bonds and he turned half of them over to her. She clipped the coupons of her half. Some she deposited in the box and the rest she cashed, spending the proceeds. Collins gave her a key to the box, and her share was left with the other half, which Collins retained as his own. This disposition of the securities continued until Collins died two and a half years later.

At that time the state collected an inheritance tax on all the bonds, and the administrator of Collins' estate sued to recover as much of his tax as was represented by the bonds belonging to the widow.

This transfer by Collins to his wife of an undivided half of these securities was held a valid gift even though it was an undivided portion of the property.

Generally there can be no physical delivery of an interest in undivided property. If a half were separated by delivery, there would be a gift of half, not of an undivided interest in the whole. Further, the gift of many chattels (property, except real estate), such as an animal, is not susceptible to division. The physical delivery of a part interest in a living animal would be impossible. An undivided interest in a chattel or in a claim against some third person can be the subject of a valid gift and, though delivery is necessary to complete a gift, a "constructive" delivery, such as delivery of a deed or bill of sale in place of the property itself, will be sufficient.

The mentally ill and the law

14

Chapter 14
The mentally ill and the law

The law gives to the word "incompetent" a special meaning that is different from our everyday usage of the term. Legally, an incompetent is a person incapable of managing his own affairs in his own interest. One person may be more keenly alive than another, more aware or more intelligent, yet both are unquestionably competent in the eyes of the law if they can conduct their own business in a relatively capable manner.

There is, so far as the law is concerned, no rule of mathematical precision that enables us to measure exactly how competent or incompetent an individual may be. The law's definition of "incompetent" is adequate for most practical purposes. A typical state statute declares this term to mean "any person who, though not insane, is by reason of old age, disease, weakness of mind or from any other cause incapable, unassisted, to properly manage and take care of himself and his property, and by reason thereof would be likely to be deceived or imposed upon by artful or designing persons." This definition is applicable in all states.

As might be expected, the question of whether or not a person is incompetent arises often in connection with the transfer of property.

Some years ago, in California, a mother of nine children deeded to one of her boys a parcel of land worth between $4,000 and $6,000 from the property she owned, which had a total value of ten times that amount. The other children made an effort to have their mother adjudged incompetent and the transfer of this land set aside.

While the mother was unable to state exactly the amount of her net income, she did remember clearly the various tracts of land she owned. As for her lack of business judgment in the management of her property, criticized by those of the family who sought to have the transfer to her son set aside, the court said that she was the owner of the property and had the right to manage it as she pleased. She could dispose of it, the court declared, as she thought fit, unless she was liable mentally to be deceived or imposed upon by "artful or designing persons."

A lower court had appointed a guardian for her. This appointment was canceled with the statement that, "Generally speaking an adult person has the right to control his own person and affairs and that right should not be taken from him except upon a showing that the statutory grounds warranting a restriction of his liberty of action was for his own protection."

Lack of judgment and incompetency

The courts, as you see, demand evidence of a very substantial nature before they will decide a person is incompetent. More must be shown than a demonstration that a person is eccentric or holds unusual beliefs.

Nor can the mere existence of a physical ailment or condition be dispositive on questions of competence. Decisions should be based on specific mental function deficiencies. California has enacted a comprehensive competency law, *the Due Process in Competence Determination Act*. It includes specific medical factors judges should consider.

In a competency case involving a woman of 76 who married a 45 year old man (her third marriage), a doctor testified she was credulous, showed a lack of judgment and an intelligence defect. The court, however, stated that her arrangement with the man to manage and care for her ranch and be her chauffeur for a half interest in the property might be poor business judgment. But that doesn't establish incompetency.

What the law presumes

Every man is supposed, legally, to be sane and mentally sound and to continue so until the contrary is shown. When the court decides he is insane or incompetent, then he is presumed legally to remain in that condition until the court determines that he has regained his sanity. No consistent pattern has developed regarding the acceptance by one state of the decision of another state that an individual is incompetent. Some states will accept the decision of another jurisdiction, while other states choose to make their own determination of the issue.

Can an incompetent change his will?

A resident of North Carolina made his will. More than 20 years later, he was legally declared an incompetent, unfit to manage his own affairs because of his age and infirm condition.

At the time this man was found to be incompetent, he asked his wife for his will. He wanted to destroy it and allow his estate to be distributed as if there were no will. This woman was his second wife, and he had children living born of a first marriage. The will he wished to destroy provided that his property should go at his death only to the wife and children of the second marriage. He had made no provision in his will for the children of the first marriage.

His wife refused to give up the will. The man died and the children of the first marriage sought to show he had revoked the will by seeking to destroy it. The court refused to set the will aside, however, following the legal rule that if a person is too feeble mentally to make a will, he is too feeble to revoke one already made. Further, the court pointed out that when a person has been found incompetent, this condition is supposed to continue until a court finds a different condition to exist.

Can an incompetent commit adultery?

If incompetency or insanity prevents a person from appreciating the nature and effects of his acts, it constitutes a strong defense against any accusation. Mentally incompetent persons are not convicted under any criminal law—they are placed under proper medical supervision and control. The law has come to look upon legally incompetent individuals as sick people. Persons considered legally insane are not held responsible for their actions. Therefore, such persons cannot be convicted of crimes.

A decision by a New York court some years ago involved the adultery of a woman who had been declared mentally ill. In a divorce action the infidelity was admitted but excused by the court on the ground that the woman was legally irresponsible.

This decision followed one handed down more than 100 years ago with a ruling that is still the law of this country. The old case concerned an Alabama wife who committed adulterous acts for several months. At that time, she was mentally ill, suffering from hallucinations, and for a long period of time had enjoyed no lucid intervals. Under such conditions there could be no more a forfeiture of her marital rights, said the court, than if advantage had been taken of her by drugs or force.

However, in many states, the showing of some mental illness is not automatically an adequate defense in a divorce action based on adultery, unless it is shown that the party who committed the adulterous act was not actually capable of understanding the nature and consequences of the act when it was committed. A number of courts throughout the country have rejected the argument that a history of mental illness and disorder is sufficient evidence to excuse the adultery. These states require additional proof that demonstrates that the party was actually unaware of the consequences of the act.

Recovery from insanity

We have said that when a man is declared to be legally incompetent, the law presumes this condition to continue until it is shown to be otherwise. For a restoration of his rights, it must be proved to the satisfaction of the court that he has recovered his sanity.

The explanation of this rule is that incapacity is a fact likely to continue to exist. When the victim asks for a change of his status, he must prove that it is different from what it was. Otherwise he could impose upon those trying to protect him and put upon them the burden of proving his incapacity as often as he saw fit to file a petition for his release from these limitations.

A typical case that came under this rule concerned two brothers who had been found by a Massachusetts court to be incompetent. Later they made an effort to obtain their release. The court asserted that after they had been found to be insane it became their task to prove they were competent and sane—not the task of those opposing their release to prove in each instance that they were incompetent. Their suit was denied by the court because they could not prove sanity.

An appeal of the decision regarding the legal competency of an individual may be brought on behalf of the person involved by a friend or relative. Courts have discretionary power to grant to the person bringing the appeal the costs of the action. These funds can be taken from the property of the individual who had been declared incompetent.

How guardians of incompetents are chosen

The choice of the person to be appointed guardian of an incompetent, to care for his welfare and property, is generally left to the court's discretion.

It is the court that decides whether the management of the incompetent's property shall be entrusted to the guardian appointed for his personal custody or by still another person. Most frequently, the person who takes care of an incompetent is a close relative or friend, while the custodian of his property must have a special qualification—he should be possessed of the judgment and experience necessary to administer properly the incompetent's funds. The welfare of incompetent persons and the matter of their property are objects of particular care and attention on the part of the courts.

Alternatives to guardianship

There are ways to provide for your care and the protection of your property and avoid the appointment by a court of a guardian in the event of incapacitation and inability to make decisions. You can establish a revocable living trust, which provides funds to you on a regular basis during your lifetime. You can give an individual of your choice a durable power of attorney to make treatment decisions on your behalf. You can write a living will and outline your wishes on extraordinary methods to be taken if you are terminally ill.

You should consult your attorney to be sure any document reflects your wishes and is valid in your state.

Objectionable guardians

A close relative is not always the most desirable guardian for an incompetent, as the facts in the following case show. In a case in the state of Washington, a son sought to be appointed his mother's guardian. Evidence was presented that proved the relationship between the mother and son was not particularly close. The father had objections too. Consequently, the son was not appointed. The court, as the law provides, used its own discretion in its selection of a guardian.

Ordinarily, a person who is indebted to an incompetent is not selected to be his guardian, but such a choice is not impossible, being subject to the general rule that appointments be made in the sound discretion of the court and with the incompetent's happiness and material welfare as the paramount consideration.

Why appointments are revoked

The court's interest in an incompetent does not end with the appointment of a guardian. If a guardian becomes guilty of fraud or misconduct, is found unqualified for his position, or applies for relief from the trust, the court will appoint a new guardian.

The manner in which a Kentucky court exercised its discretion in one case was clearly open to criticism. It appointed an 86-year-old man, confined to his bed with a fractured leg, as the guardian of his incompetent sister who was 83-years-old. Such a man was obviously incapable of fulfilling the duties of a guardian, and when other persons who had an interest in the situation brought it to the attention of the higher court, this appointment was set aside.

In another case, where a wife and children, acting with the assistance of an attorney, arranged for the appointment of the attorney as the guardian of the aged husband and father, they did this in an effort to secure a division of his property among themselves, rather than because of concern for the mental and economic welfare of their incompetent family member. This appointment, which conflicted with the aim of the law, was also set aside.

When the incompetent is not notified

When a guardian dies, resigns, or becomes unable any longer to fulfill his role, a successor may be named without giving notice to the incompetent. Since the incompetent is incapable of caring for himself or his property, or representing himself, such notice would be useless. So the court decided, when an attempt was made to set aside the appointment of a guardian chosen by the court without notifying the incompetent. The court stressed the governing factor in these cases: "The matter of who is to act as guardian lies very largely in the sound discretion of the court making the appointment."

Who owns an incompetent's property?

The problem frequently arises of who has title to the property of an incompetent. Ordinarily, when someone dies, title to his personal property belongs to the executor. His real property belongs to the heirs, subject to sale for the debts of the deceased. Does the ownership of an incompetent's property pass to his guardian, the way a dead man's personal property passes to his executor? The answer is often of vital importance, not only in the management of the incompetent's property, but in the enforcement of his rights.

The law says that a guardian is merely the custodian of the real and personal property of his ward. The incompetent still owns his property. He is merely deprived during his incompetency of its management and control.

When a property needs immediate attention during a competency proceeding, courts often appoint a temporary receiver.

A guardian, or "committee," as he is sometimes known, was appointed for a man committed to a hospital for the insane in Virginia. Two years later the court decided this man had regained his sanity. The guardian, however, refused to return his property. Here the situation was governed by the rule that the incompetent still owned his property and had been merely deprived of its control during his illness. When he was declared sane, he automatically regained his rights to its control, and the duties and authority of the guardian were dissolved.

How an incompetent is committed

The liberty of all is protected by Constitutional and legislative guarantees. This protection is supposed to be extended to the victim of a mental malady to the same extent as it is to a person endowed with physical and mental health. A person whose competency is being considered in a legal procedure is therefore entitled to the same protection as one who is charged with a criminal offense. The laws of the various states prescribe the different ways a mentally ill person may be committed to a mental hospital. Sometimes these laws have been found to operate in situations in a manner that effectively denies the full protection of the law to possible incompetents.

Recently, a Federal court in Pennsylvania found that thousands of mental patients had been placed in that state's mental institutions under a procedure that violated due process of law. All these patients were committed by their families, with the concurrence of two doctors, but without a court order and against their will. Due process of law was violated because the persons involved had no chance to present evidence of their competency.

Each state now has its own method of committing incompetents. A trial may be required, or an examination before a committing magistrate, or some other procedure involving a legal hearing. Evidence is presented that is made part of the record. The evidence consists of the testimony of physicians and psychiatrists, as well as of ordinary witnesses. The statutes governing the procedure must be obeyed down to the last detail.

A woman inmate of a state hospital was brought before a court for a determination of the legality of her confinement. The person seeking to obtain her release was her 18-year-old son, her sole support. It was revealed that the woman had not even been present at the hearing when she was determined insane and ordered confined in an asylum. The commitment had been made on the mere conclusion of a social worker that the woman was in need of treatment in a mental hospital. This was a violation of the law, and the woman was released.

One alleged to be an incompetent has a right to a lawyer. The court must appoint one for him, unless the court feels that he has made an intelligent judgment not to have one, which is difficult for an alleged incompetent. If a person is improperly committed, he is generally entitled to sue the state for damages.

When a hearing is not given

However loosely the statutes in this area may be interpreted, then, they do not permit a person to be deprived of liberty without legal due process. If a court permits a person to be confined in a mental hospital without strictly following the required procedure, there is always recourse to a higher court. Some form of trial or hearing is always required before a person can be declared an incompetent.

Are contracts of incompetents valid?

There is no hard-and-fast rule covering this question. The decision will rest largely on whether the party who dealt with the incompetent acted in good faith. If that party did not realize that he was dealing with an incompetent, the contract is more likely to be upheld.

A man who was to be confined to a mental institution was negotiating for the purchase of a hotel in Atlantic City, New Jersey. His wife and son, under advice from their attorney, wrote to the real estate broker for the hotel, notifying him of the mental condition of the man with whom he was dealing. Nevertheless, the hotel owner closed the deal. The New Jersey Supreme Court, in an action to set aside the purchase, ruled that, even if the sale was fair, it was invalid. The judge said that the wording of the letter, which was sent by the buyer's family and which the hotel owner had seen, "was plainly such as would lead a prudent person to the belief of (the man's) insanity."

A person furnishing livelihood to an incompetent is entitled to recompense, as if he were furnishing it under an agreement. Board and care were given for 11 years by a son to his father, a speechless paralytic. The older man was not confined to his bed, but was mentally infirm.

Another son had been appointed custodian of the father's property. When the father died, this son was asked by the first for payment, out of the father's estate, of the expenses he had incurred over the 11 years he had cared for his father. The custodian refused to give him such sum, but the courts awarded it to him.

The principle that a mentally ill person is not responsible for his contracts is a shield for that person only so long as he actually is mentally ill. The occurrence of the illness may have been long before a formal court ruling of incompetency, and the court decision can be applied retroactively to nullify contracts made between the inception of the incompetency and the date of the court's decision. The shield dissolves as soon as the person recovers sanity. This may also occur long before a court ruling.

In Minnesota, a woman borrowed some money. When effort was made by the lender to recover this money, the woman pleaded incompetency.

She had long before been restored to full mental health, but she pointed out that the guardianship she was under—her husband's, in this case—had not officially been terminated. The court refused to release the borrower from her obligation to pay.

When an incompetent commits a crime

We have seen that a mentally ill person is incapable of committing a crime in the eyes of the law since he lacks the necessary intent. However, merely showing that the person involved was not in control of all his faculties at the time the crime was committed will not protect him. He must meet the accepted standard of being "legally insane" at the time the crime was committed in order to avoid punishment. The elements of this standard vary from state to state. The rule of "not knowing right from wrong" is still prevalent in most jurisdictions, although it has come under much criticism lately.

The protection afforded by the law extends beyond the rule that the defendant had to have had the necessary intent at the time he committed the crime. If he is mentally ill at the time of his trial, he cannot be tried even if he was sane when the crime was committed. The case is postponed until he recovers from his disability. The law says that an incompetent can neither plead to an arraignment, be subject to trial, receive judgment after trial, nor undergo punishment as a criminal.

Until the prisoner does recover, he is kept in a mental hospital or other prescribed place of detention.

Not guilty by reason of insanity

When John Hinckley was found not guilty of attempting to assassinate the president because he was insane, there was a public outcry. Several states have responded by enacting statutes which allow the jury to find the defendant *guilty but mentally ill* (GBMI). A person who was not insane but was suffering from a "mental illness" at the time of the commission of a crime may be found guilty but mentally ill. These statutes generally provide that upon a finding of GBMI the court may impose any sentence appropriate for the offense charged. If the defendant is sent to jail, there must be periodic examinations and appropriate psychiatric care. Such statutes provide mental health care to convicts while serving society's need to protect itself and society's right to punish criminals.

Presumption of sanity

When a person has once been legally adjudged an incompetent or insane, the presumption of sanity enjoyed by every normal individual is gone. In its place is a presumption of insanity, and the recovery of sanity must be proved before the incompetent can again be held responsible for his acts or permitted to defend himself in a criminal trial.

Recovery of damages

The rule governing the recovery of damages for injuries inflicted by a mentally ill person represents a clear appraisal of both sides of the situation. There is a seeming hardship in compelling one who is unaware of his irrational acts to pay for their consequences. Yet it would be unjust to deny redress to the one who has suffered damage and is in no way responsible for it. Hence, the rule is that an insane person is liable in damages for wrongs he commits to the same extent as any normal person.

Does an incompetent pay punitive damages?

A barn on a Wisconsin farm was set on fire by a man subsequently committed to a state hospital for the criminally insane. In an action by the owner against this incompetent's guardian, the court followed the rule of the lunatic's liability for damages for his wrongdoing. The cost of the barn had to be paid out of his estate.

It should be pointed out, however, that in a case brought against an incompetent the courts will not award punitive damages—that is, damages a wrongdoer is obliged to pay as punishment, rather than as compensation. No suit will be sustained where a malicious intent on the part of the defendant is a necessary element to recovery of damages, since this cannot be shown to be present in a person mentally ill.

An incompetent's liability for murder

When a mentally ill person kills someone, the liability that is owed the next of kin of the victim is governed by the general rule on wrongdoing. In an Illinois tragedy, a lunatic killed another man, then shot himself. The victim's next of kin were awarded damages for the loss they suffered by the violent and untimely death of their relative.

An insane person—to cite the court's opinion—has no will; for that reason, he cannot commit a crime. Nevertheless, his estate is liable for the damages he inflicts.

Slander by a deranged person

A false accusation of stealing was made in Tennessee by a deranged man. The victim of this slander brought suit against his accuser. In deciding the case, the court stressed the fact that intention is an element of slander. The defendant, it decided, could not be liable in damages because "the insanity of the incompetent at the time of speaking the words complained of is a complete excuse when the speaker is entirely insane and, when partially insane, that fact is considered in mitigation of the damages awarded."

Is an incompetent responsible for any damage he causes?

A man in West Virginia, who had gone insane, shot his friend. The injured man was taken to a hospital where, after a month, he died. No criminal prosecution for murder could be initiated, since the man responsible for the killing was insane. However, a civil action was brought for the suffering caused to the deceased man and for the potential income he could have earned had he remained alive.

The court, in upholding a verdict of $20,000 against the insane man, ruled that although no punitive damages could be charged against the defendant, an award for damages actually suffered by the dead man and his family could be made. The reason for allowing such recovery of damages against the incompetent was that while both the killer and the deceased were legally innocent, the responsibility for the loss was placed on the one who caused the action involved.

Is the marriage of an incompetent valid?

A California man took part in a wedding ceremony that was held in an old garage. He had to be prompted continually during the ceremony for his responses. In an action to have the marriage declared invalid, the judge noted that the evidence presented indicated that the man "was unaware of the fact that he was being married and he interjected remarks concerning matters foreign to such a solemn occasion." Evidence was also presented that revealed that the man's new wife began stealing his property immediately after the ceremony. The court annulled the marriage, declaring that such evidence was ample to show that the man was not of sufficiently sound mind to engage in a legal marriage ceremony.

The rule employed in most states is that the validity of the marriage depends upon whether the parties understand the nature of the marriage contract when they enter into it. This includes an understanding of the duties and responsibilities it creates. If a person who has been deemed incompetent may be said to have understood these matters at the time of the ceremony, then the marriage is considered legal.

In some jurisdictions across the country, "marriages" of persons who have been ruled unable, legally, to engage in a valid wedding ceremony may become legal if the incompetent cohabits with his spouse after he regains his competency or during his sane periods.

How dependents of incompetents are supported

Many states have rules providing that people must support certain close relatives if they are able to, even though those relatives are adults.

Applying these rules to the care of the family of the incompetent, the law holds that the family is entitled to maintenance from the income of his property. Beyond that, the court has the power to make provision out of the surplus of such an estate for those whom it supposes the incompetent would have provided for had he been sane.

A famous case of the right of a guardian, with the approval of the court, to contribute from an incompetent's estate to the support of the relatives was that involving Ida A. Flagler. Seventy-eight years old and incurably insane, this woman possessed an estate with a value of more than $11,000,000, which produced an annual income of approximately $500,000.

A second cousin of the incompetent Mrs. Flagler was a woman of middle age who had an unemployed husband and an adopted daughter. The only income of this family was $15 a week, which was earned by the wife. Coal bills, doctors' bills, and house repair charges had all piled high.

"If Mrs. Flagler today could decide upon the disposition of her great estate, moral or charitable considerations would dictate her decision only to the extent that she felt their force," was the comment of the court on the application of this family for an allowance from the estate of Mrs. Flagler.

"Her great affluence might impel her to relieve the distress of her cousin; the law would not compel her to do so if she decided otherwise. The court may not be moved by its own generous impulses in the disposal of the income of the incompetent. In reaching a decision the court may give to moral or charitable considerations only such weight as it finds that the incompetent herself would have given them. Allowances for the support of collateral relatives of the incompetent have been made upon the theory that the lunatic would in all probability have made such payments if he had been of sound mind."

On this opinion, provision was made by the court for relieving the destitution of these relatives of Mrs. Flagler.

If allowances are made to adult children

The general rule is that when allowances are made by guardians to adult children capable of supporting themselves, any sums will constitute an advance against any inheritance to be received on the death of the incompetent.

Medical records

Many physicians and other health care professionals do not think that patients should be able to see their records. This is particularly true for psychiatric patients. However, a poll at a mental hospital in Washington State found that a very high percentage of these patients wanted to see them and believed they would be helpful and therapeutic tools.

There are many states that have laws guaranteeing you, as a patient, access to your charts in your physician's files. Some have exceptions for mental health records. But, even where you cannot look at your records, or make copies, if you change doctors and request a transfer to a new physician, the former doctor must transfer them. This is only reasonable given a need for proper care and information concerning diagnoses and treatments.

The American Medical Association has an opinion on professional conduct which states that, in regard to records "they should not be withheld because of an unpaid bill for medical services."

Mix-up in medical records

Open heart surgery was performed on a woman with no heart problems when her name was erroneously placed on a report of a patient who had a serious heart valve defect. It was not until she was in surgery that the doctor noted her valve was normal and sewed her up.

If you encounter difficulty in either reviewing your records or having them transferred, there are some steps that you can take. You can call or write to the *American Medical Records Association* in Chicago; you may enlist the aid of your state health department; or your attorney can write on your behalf. Some states mandate access to records if a lawyer makes the request. If they still are not forthcoming, you should consult your counsel to see if a lawsuit is in your best interest.

The law of slander and libel

15

Chapter 15
The law of slander and libel

"Sticks and stones may break my bones, but names will never harm me," runs an old saying. It is far from true. Name calling, under certain conditions, can damage one's reputation seriously. Then it becomes slander or libel, and the ground for a legal action to collect damages. Any retraction of the statement must clearly indicate that the statement was incorrect. However, the damage may be done.

Libel and slander are two different offenses. Libel is restricted basically to written statements, but it can be committed by means of signs, pictures, or other representations of a person or his acts. Slander is limited to statements made by word of mouth. In their basic conditions they sometimes overlap.

Because it is in more permanent form and so presumably more harmful, written defamation is actionable without proof of special damage. All that must be shown is that the words were written and that they were defamatory to the person to whom they referred. As to spoken defamation, unless the slander is of a certain class, it is not actionable without proof of damages. Those falling within the special class of slander are known as "*per se,*" meaning harmful "by itself."

The courts have been considering whether a spoken television broadcast is libel or slander. While not permanent as in writing, broadcasting reaches many more persons and can be more harmful than a mere spoken statement. If it is not libel, then it must fall within the specified class to be actionable without proof of damages.

A New York court has given a definition of libel that expresses, in general, the law of this country. It says: "Any written or printed article is libelous or actionable if it tends to expose the subject to public contempt, ridicule, aversion, or disgrace, or induce an evil opinion of him in the minds of right-thinking persons and to deprive him of their friendly intercourse in society." It must also be shown that the words were understandable to the general public and were meant to be understood in a derogatory sense. The party who was the subject of the statement has an advantage in that he or she does not have to show that people actually took the words to be true.

To any charge of defamation there is one very important defense: It is the defense of truth. A case of defamation, generally, does not exist when the statement on which it is based is true from start to finish. The burden of proving the truth of a defamatory statement, however, rests on the defendant in a suit. To mitigate the damages that may be allowed, the defendant is permitted to show that the plaintiff has a bad character and reputation.

Where the defamer is shown to have been motivated by ill will or malice, courts and juries may award punitive damages—damages as a punishment—in addition to those actually incurred.

The Internet, The Web, E-Mail, Cyberspace

A whole new era of technology is upon us. It brings possibilities for fraud, loss of privacy and causing harm to reputations with consequential law-suits. Where will the suits be brought when the people involved are all over the world?

A Virginia police detective has filed suit for defamation against a woman he stopped for a traffic violation, her son and a compiler of data for a web site. The son sent an E-Mail message alleging that the policeman had insulted and beaten his mother. The message was then posted on a Web site titled the *"Police Brutality Page."* The policeman said he was humiliated and his reputation was injured.

This is defamation in cyberspace. Cases are just beginning to surface. Most have been against companies providing the service. One high profile libel suit for $30 million was filed by an assistant to the President against an online gossip columnist, Matt Drudge, for his allegations on the Drudge Report as well as against America Online (AOL), the company that carries his gossip. Drudge reported that the assistant had a spousal abuse past that had been covered up. It was untrue and a day later Drudge took the item off his World Wide Web site and apologized.

A Federal District Court judge has ruled that AOL and other Internet services, unlike publishers, are immune from civil actions resulting from their comments. The judge said Congress exempted them when it passed the *Communications Decency Act of 1996.* They disseminate material created by others and the speed of the dissemination prevents regulating information content. This is different from other information providers such as newspapers, magazines or TV.

The judge wanted to hold AOL to the standard applied to publishers, libraries and bookstore owners but he said Congress has acted in the matter. The Blumenthals plan to appeal.

The law for the new technology will take quite a while to be settled since it covers a whole range of business and social communications including chat sessions, advertising, and marketing. There even have been solicitations to provide bogus term papers. Be aware of the risks of communicating in a technology that has the immediate potential of worldwide dissemination.

Food disparagement laws

Food producers now have laws in at least 14 states and they are pushing in 8 more allowing them to sue anyone spreading false and damaging information about food products. The laws have been dubbed *banana bills*. They are likened to SLAPP suits discussed in this chapter. They chill speech and debate about possible harmful products. Producers point to the apple Alar scare. Critics say they don't allow for good faith speech. A Texas rancher sued Oprah for comments she made about Mad Cow Disease and not eating hamburger. After her show cattle prices dropped. The court ruled against him.

Truth and libel

A resident of Louisiana complained to the court that "his good name, fame, credit, and reputation" had been injured in the sum of $25,000 by a letter sent not only to him but to his sisters and brothers also. This letter, which referred to one written by the plaintiff, declared:

"One can expect such a letter as you have written, in view of the fact that you failed in the filial devotion that you owed your late mother by refusing to pay your 1/5th percentage of her funeral bill. Your excuse for not paying this bill was the ridiculous statement that you had not been consulted in making the funeral arrangements."

The plaintiff asserted that although he had on several occasions refused to pay the bill, since he had ultimately done so, the letter was libelous.

In dismissing this action, the court declared that the truth was a complete defense. This so-called libelous letter did not deny he had ultimately contributed his share of the funeral expenses, but stated simply that he had once refused to. Since he admitted this, there was no libel.

The consequences of a libel suit

"In this man quackery reaches its apotheosis. He continues to demonstrate of a libel suit his astuteness in shaking shillings from the pockets of credulous Americans notwithstanding the efforts of various governmental departments and agencies." So ran the leading paragraph of an article in a prominent monthly magazine, which went on to describe at length its further objections to this individual.

In the libel suit the man brought against the publication, the testimony amounted to more than 1,000 printed pages. It revealed the background of this "charlatan" much more fully than the magazine article had done. Not only had he received his medical degree from a "diploma mill"—for 16 years he had performed sexual rejuvenation operations on from 5,000 to 6,000 persons, charging them from nothing to $750 apiece.

He had enjoyed a monthly gross income of approximately $100,000, and stimulated this medical practice by pamphlets, newspapers, and radio broadcasts. Then both his medical license and his license for an independently operated radio broadcast station had been revoked.

It was further shown in court that he had been indicted in California for the illegal practice of medicine. At the time of the publication of the I article for which this libel suit was brought, the evidence pointed out, he was advertising by Mexican radio broadcasts that he would treat prostatic troubles by letter at two dollars a case.

Said the court: "We think the facts are sufficient to support a reasonable and honest opinion that he should be considered a charlatan and quack in the ordinary and well-understood meaning of the words."

This case, like many other libel suits, illustrates the folly of seeking to repair damage to one's reputation by taking court action. Even if one wins a libel suit—which this man did not—the public airing of the testimony often does further damage to the character of those concerned, whether that testimony is true or whether it is false.

Libel in a few words

A daily newspaper published a paragraph that declared that a well-known actress, who had been married for six years to a man of good reputation, was the "latest lady love" of another. The publication of this statement, said the court, was considered to be a libel. It was established that the lady concerned was of good reputation, and the newspaper report, the court ruled, had unnecessarily brought to its victim humiliation and mental suffering.

No ground for libel

In another instance, a large, metropolitan daily newspaper printed the story of a woman named Catherine, who ran a boarding house. The newspaper reported that Catherine had been courted by a man who, although she did not know it at the time, was wanted by the police in Chicago because he was suspected of the murder of his wife five days before. This man was later apprehended, tried, and hanged for his crime.

Catherine sued the paper, claiming she was libeled by the article, that she was held up to public scorn and ridicule. But the court pointed out that all the paper had said was that Catherine had been courted by a murderer five days after he had committed the crime. Although the man was described as a murderer and an archfiend, there was in the entire article not one word of discrediting comments on Catherine's own character or conduct. She did not have a valid case in the eyes of the law.

Insinuation as libel

A New England newspaper published an article about a candidate who was running for public office. It said that a neighbor of this candidate had built his house with two driveways on one side and none on the other, and had planted trees in the space between the two driveways as a screen against the candidate's prying eyes, to protect the housemaid from annoyance.

This insinuation, that the candidate spent his time as a "Peeping Tom," was held to be a libel by the court, reflecting as it did on his reputability as a member of the community. He was resting his claim for public office on the respect and confidence of his fellow-citizens, which the newspaper article tended to take away from him.

The court must make the decision as to whether the words were used in such a manner as to be defamatory. The person who claims to be defamed cannot lift words out of context. The entire setting in which the words were used must be considered in the decision.

False and malicious publication

An Alabama paper provided the ground for a libel suit when it published an article declaring that "An Arabian sheik asked a friend here to buy him an American girl for his harem," and named the friend. It went on to say that while this American friend "will not take the responsibility of selecting Sheik Iman's chief wife, he will be glad to make contact with the Arabian for those interested," and it included the friend's telephone number and post office address.

"The very idea of a harem," said the court, "is as repulsive as is the purchase of a girl to be carried from America to some distant country to complete a harem of four wives." A false and malicious publication that anyone stood ready and willing to abet such a program was held an actionable libel.

Incomplete insinuation is not libel

A practicing physician in Chicago who was a former citizen of Warsaw incurred the ill-will of a Polish-American publication by accepting a cross as a decoration from the Polish government. Referring to him, it wrote in its columns that "For some years former 'honor vivas' [complimentary decorations] of this kind have emitted a specific stench. Characteristic of them is an epigram of Pushkin, one of the greatest of Russian poets."

Libel award in Britain not enforced in U.S.

Although the United States gives full faith and credit to the laws and decisions in other jurisdictions, in the case of a British Court's decision on a libel case involving two former Soviet Union journalists, the highest court in Maryland refused to enforce a finding awarding one of them over $400,000.

Both had engaged in a bitter exchange of letters in a London newspaper. One criticized the B.B.C. for its hiring practices of Russian correspondents and the other accused the former of a "racialist recipe," which the former interpreted as being called a racist and antisemite and sued for libel.

Because of looser libel laws in Britain, the Russian journalist plaintiff won. When the defendant moved to Maryland, the plaintiff asked that the judgment be enforced. But the Court of Appeals in Maryland refused, saying the plaintiff had not had to prove that the letter contained false statements or was written with malicious intent. They stated they could not uphold the award unless they ignored our First Amendments's guarantee of the free flow of ideas and opinions on matters of public concern. The offending letter was simply the "rhetorical hyperbole" of a "vigorous public debate" written on the occasion of giving a high decoration to one of the Russian dignitaries who had served the government well during his tenure as an official representative of his country.

"Oh Lord God Jesus Christ
You have used a thief on the cross
And now you have new trouble
To save a cross on a thief "

The word "*thief*" in this poem was not intended to charge the individual who received the medal with such a crime. His act was not one of larceny. Unless that specific word was used to convey the idea that the doctor was a thief and therefore guilty of a crime, said the court, there was no libel.

What is slander per se?

Slander relates solely to spoken words. An assertion, to be slanderous per se, that is, to be ruled slanderous without showing any evidence besides the fact that a third party heard the statement, must come within one or more of these classes:

(1) words imputing the commission of a crime;

(2) words imputing infection by a loathsome or contagious disease that excludes the person from society;

(3) words proclaiming unfitness for office or employment or words derogatory of a person's fitness for a trade or profession; and

(4) words imputing unchastity (spoken of a woman).

As with libel, a statement cannot be considered slanderous if it is actually true. However, jurisdictions in certain states across the country will not admit the truth as a defense if malice is shown to be an element in the statement and on which the accusation of defamation is based.

When the defamatory words are not slander per se, then proof of special damage is necessary in order to have a case. The special damage must involve monetary loss. If the defamed person can demonstrate that his business fell off because of the slander, or that it resulted in the loss of some particular contract, then he can recover for the damage. But the fact that the defamed person was humiliated by the statement, or that his friends avoided him, is not sufficient evidence.

A statement might appear on its face not to be defamatory, but may be ruled slanderous per se when additional facts are shown. This could be the case, for example, if a person spreads a false story that a certain woman gave birth to a son. If it is proven that the woman was unmarried and those who heard the story were aware of this fact, then the statement becomes slanderous per se. This seemingly nondefamatory report actually imputed unchastity to the woman. A few states, however, always require the showing of special damages in any defamation case in which apparently innocent words are shown to be defamatory.

False accusation of a crime

A rancher published a report in which he falsely accused one of his neighbors of poisoning cattle and added that "if he thereafter is known to be guilty of any more villainous conduct or any more stock poisoning, he will be dealt with as justice may demand." The court found the rancher's statement to be defamatory, and thus would not allow the rancher to introduce additional evidence of other crimes as an indication that the neighbor was a criminal. The judge in this particular case stated that "I am aware of no rule of law which would allow proof to be made of specific offenses and particular acts of dishonesty, not connected with the transactions under investigation."

An essential condition of slander

Words, to be considered either slander or libel, must actually be made public—in other words, they must be communicated to, and understood by, at least one person other than the one of whom they are spoken or written. Condemning another to himself alone may breed trouble, but it is neither slander nor libel.

An employee of an oil company, during World War II, made remarks on the conduct of the war that were offensive to his associates. "He wished Hitler would take the European countries and come on over here and take the United States," was a typical comment. The superintendent of the company told the man he was being discharged for these un-American speeches. Whatever the superintendent said was heard by no one except the employee. The suit brought by this employee for slander was unsuccessful. There had been no publication of these statements, and no third person heard them—hence, there was no case of slander.

No witness, no slander

The manager of an Ohio hotel discharged an employee. "You stole the butter and that is not the only thing you ever stole around here." This statement, like that of the oil company superintendent, was heard by no one but the discharged waiter; hence, there was no injury other than the discomfort and hurt feelings of the man who lost his job.

Slander with others present

In North Carolina, the manager of a grocery company called an employee into his office. "Last week two boxes of bananas went out of the warehouse. They went out on trucks. It shows you are letting the drivers take them out and sell them—then split with you. The drivers you have over there are crooks."

The manager was sitting with his back to the doorway of his office and, in the doorway, unseen by the manager, was another employee. Here was a publication of words imputing a crime that sustained the employee's suit for damages.

Repetition of a defamatory statement

A newspaper that subscribed to a press service printed an article, which it attributed to the press service, stating that a respected resident of the area had just defaulted on thousands of dollars worth of loans. The story was untrue, but the person described was hurt in his business. The court found that the newspaper was guilty of libel, even though it attributed the article to another party. The fact that the newspaper printed the article was sufficient grounds for a finding of defamation. (However, newspapers sometimes have a defense of "fair comment," which is discussed later in this chapter.)

Every repetition of a defamatory statement is also a further defamation.

SLAPP suits

These suits are *Strategic Lawsuits Against Public Participation* (SLAPP). They typically are filed by developers or business enterprises against environmental or public interest groups or individuals who have expressed opposition to their plans, such as clearing land, building, or expanding. The suits can be for libel based on letters sent to legislative bodies, who have authority over the development, to the Editor or urge testimony in public hearings or on leaflets opposing the project or enterprise.

Defendants claim the suits are to intimidate and stifle legitimate political expression. What is involved is part of the First Amendment to the Constitution, the right to petition. These suits can be costly. Some defendants have "SLAPPed back," filed counter suits for conspiracy to violate their Constitutional right of free speech.

Twelve states including New York and Washington State have anti-SLAPP laws that allow the suits to be dismissed more quickly. Should a citizen testifying before the state legislature have an absolute privilege? The statements legitimately should relate to the grievance from which they are seeking relief said a Maryland court. But there is no comprehensive immunity from liability for libel for comments by citizens exercising their right to petition or on their attacks against the private enterprises.

Some courts have taken up the citizens' cause, especially in allowing "SLAPP back" counter suits. In New York, a developer lost a suit against the Nature Conservancy. The judge found the suit was retribution for the Conservancy's opposition to his development plans and an effort to "chill" their future exercise of First Amendment rights.

When you speak out make sure your facts are correct, complete and your view of the result is reasonable. Be sure that even when you have good facts you don't create a false impression that tarnishes an individual or company's reputation or image. That's called *libel by implication*. Some groups who are involved in land use issues are establishing defense funds against SLAPP suits. But you'll probably be David with a slingshot until your state legislature passes SLAPP suit protection.

Defamation of deceased

It is the general rule that a libel or slander upon the memory of a deceased person, which makes no direct reflection upon his living relatives, gives them no cause of action for defamation either on their own behalf or on behalf of the deceased. However, if the words, by implication, defame a living person, they may be actionable. For example, the statement that a deceased person was never married may be grounds for a claim by his daughter that she was defamed.

Words that are slanderous

An installment furniture merchant, repossessing his merchandise on a default of the buyer in payment, said in the presence of another man and two small children, "You damned old bitch, you—I'm going to take my stuff and I'll beat you with my cane before I get out of here." This statement in the presence of others, and the fact that the legal definition of "*bitch*," when used in this manner, is a lewd woman or common prostitute, constituted a slander for which the woman so addressed was allowed to recover damages.

The term *"rat"* was once applied to an opposing attorney. Though ill-chosen and harsh, said the court, this invective did not constitute slander. The word *"rat,"* in itself, did not impute a crime, unchastity, a loathsome disease, or dishonesty.

The general standard used for words that are slanderous is that the person spoken about must be defamed in the eyes of an important and respectable group in the community in which he lives. Each state has its own standard of what constitutes "an important and respectable group."

Imputing a disease to someone

The element of libel and slander in the imputation of disease does not arise when there are merely general reports of pestilence or disease and of public-spirited efforts to rid the community of such scourges, as in a newspaper. It is only where the words represent an effort to destroy the happiness and community standing of the person concerned that valid grounds are supplied for a lawsuit.

In general, slander or libel, to be such, must not refer to a minor disease, but to a serious contagious infection, like leprosy or syphilis.

Libel of a class of people

A prominent sportswriter made the following statement in an article about boxing that appeared in a national magazine: "I must be truthful. Boxing is the garbage pile of sports. The few who transcend it have my respect. Still it damages more young men than it helps. It is the sanctuary of the scoundrel and it always has been a toy of the rogue."

A professional boxer sued the writer for defamation. The court ruled that "the article contains matter highly defamatory of various unnamed characters in professional boxing. That is no basis for libel because an impersonal reproach of an indeterminate class is not actionable."

To obtain a judgment for a defamation that refers to a group or class of people, a person must show that he was in the class that was defamed and that he can be specifically identified as one to whom the statement has particular application. The writer here referred to the sport of boxing in general. This one boxer could not prove that he was one of the people to whom the derogatory remarks of the writer referred.

Venereal disease and slander

An insurance investigator, calling on a woman in relation to the payment of the insurance on her husband's life, said, in the presence of a third party, "Our association is absolutely not going to pay your husband's claim because the company has proof that you and your husband have syphilis." This untruthful statement charged these people with a loathsome disease and was actionable slander.

A more virulent assault was made by an Iowa woman on her son's wife. Among other remarks, she said of the younger woman, "She's nothing but a whore. She runs around with other men, has a bad disease, and is nothing but dirty trash."

The daughter-in-law answered with an action for slander in which the jury awarded her $3,000. The mother-in-law appealed. The higher court refused to change or modify the verdict, and added that the jury under such circumstances might well have added "exemplary" damages—a punishment for the wanton attempt to injure the character of the daughter-in-law.

When a man's business is injured by defamation

A charge that a person is unfit in his trade or profession can do more than injure his reputation. It can also be expected to interfere with his earnings and to alienate persons who would otherwise patronize or employ him. Therefore, this is perhaps the most serious category of libel or slander from the viewpoint of actual damages.

A business may be defamed by words that cast aspersions on the character of the firm, or upon the character of its employees, if the words refer to its method of doing business. But businesses cannot be defamed by words that would affect the purely personal reputation of an individual.

Libel by a business service

Dun & Bradstreet, the financial reporting service, erroneously reported that an electrical supply company in Kansas had filed for bankruptcy. The company sued for libel and received a substantial damage award from a jury, and the Federal Court of Appeals for the Tenth Circuit affirmed the judgment. The United States Supreme Court refused to consider the matter, which means, in effect, that the freedom of the press privilege heretofore discussed does not extend to financial reporting services.

Fair criticism

A magazine article criticized the publications of a psychiatrist about soap opera broadcasts of various networks. These programs the psychiatrist had analyzed in psychiatric terms that were long and unflattering. The title of the offending magazine article was *"Dusting off Dr. B."*

"If Dr. B. can find nothing wrong in publicizing the miseries of the doomed, the drugged and the damned through the medium of books and motion pictures," the magazine observed, "why don't he let radio have a frustration or two? There ain't nobody here but us chickens, boys. If we may break a metaphor over the reader's head, it seems much as if radio and Dr. B. were in the same bed except that Dr. B. is working the other side of the street."

Then, in reference to his psychiatric studies, the article said, "In any case, it seems quite possible that Dr. B. will contrive to turn the entire trilogy into a trauma of obfustication [*sic*], full of big words that us poor folks in radio don't hardly know the meaning of—just another teleological concatenation of sesquipedalian lucubrating—all whizz and canal water."

Offended at this ridicule, the doctor sued the magazine, but his action was unsuccessful. The article was held not libelous because it did not exceed the bounds of fair criticism to which any other person of public prominence may be subjected with impunity, nor did it shame or disgrace the author, in the court's opinion.

There is a famous legal maxim that says that an individual has a right to swing his arms—but that right ends where the next man's nose begins. Fair and unbiased criticism is healthful. But when the criticism goes beyond the bounds of truth and fairness, it goes beyond the point "where the next man's nose begins."

How Congressmen are protected

Congressmen have certain immunity under the Constitution of the United States. Remarks that they make as part of official meetings of the Senate or the House of Representatives, or the committees of either, may not be made the basis of a slander or a libel suit, even though they may seem scurrilous. On the other hand, defamatory remarks made by the same persons in other places may be grounds for a suit.

Major officials in the executive branches of state and local governments and all federal employees have recently also been granted immunity from suits for defamation. However, this immunity only extends to statements that are fair comment made in the legitimate course of their jobs.

The right of fair comment

The New York Times carried a full-page advertisement charging that the Commissioner of Public Affairs of a Southern city was responsible for illegal actions by the police force of that city. Some of the statements made in the advertisement were untrue. The Commissioner sued the newspaper and those who paid for the ad for defamation. The Supreme Court, in an effort to promote what it called "uninhibited, robust and wide-open" debate on public issues, ruled that the Commissioner could not recover for defamation, since the free speech guarantees of the Constitution "prohibit a public official from recovering damages for a defamatory falsehood relating to his official conduct unless he proves that the statement was made with 'actual malice'—that is, with knowledge that it was false or with reckless disregard of whether it was false or not." If the person accused of defamation felt that the statement was true when he made it, he is thereby protected from a charge of defamation.

The rule was recently put very succinctly by Justice White of the United States Supreme Court as follows:

> For public officers and public figures to recover for damage to their reputations for libelous falsehoods, they must prove either knowing or reckless disregard of the truth All other plaintiffs must prove at least negligent falsehood, but if the publication about them was in an area of legitimate public interest, then they too must prove deliberate or reckless error. In all actions for libel or slander, actual damages must be proved, and awards of punitive damages will be strictly limited.

Privilege and malice

A well-established principle of law is that a person may publish defamatory statements in the performance of a legal or moral duty—when he believes such statements true—if the publication is made without malice. Such privileged communications include those of an attorney to his client, a doctor to his patient, a priest to his communicant, public officials to their superiors, or witnesses in a trial to a judge and jury. They also include the communications of a husband to his wife on matters involving their household or marital relationship, or of parents to their children. A businessman enjoys the same privilege in communicating with his partner.

Fact versus opinion

Shortly before Pearl Harbor, a book called *The Trojan Horse of America* was published. It contained numerous comments about a magazine *"Southern Progress,"* likening it to a Communist or Nazi Trojan horse by quoting source of its text, such as that "Adolf Hitler is the George Washington of Germany." The magazine owner sued for libel. Whether the magazine was an advocate of the Nazi party was a matter of opinion. Whether a book is worthless or helps a cause is an opinion. Since only opinions and not misrepresentation of fact were involved the action for libel failed.

Book reviews

An author sued the *New York Times* for its book reviewer's libel of his book on organized crime and football. The reviewer had called the book "sloppy journalism" giving examples from the text. The author claimed the review was inaccurate and hurt his livelihood. The Federal Appeals Court for Washington, D.C. said the reviewer was expected to make "evaluative judgements." Readers have expectations for reviews and critics must be given Constitutional "breathing space" as appropriate. The commentary is actionable only when the interpretations are insupportable by reference to the written work.

Calling someone a Communist

Changed public opinion can make statements slanderous or libelous that, at a former time, would not have exposed the person so charged to public contempt or ridicule.

With the close of World War II began a new phase in the law of libel, that no man should call another a Communist, unless he was such in truth, without being prepared to pay damages.

Before World War II, communist wasn't a bad word. In a 1939 libel action based on a statement that a man was affiliated with the Communist Party, the New York Court said, "The Communist Party under existing law may function as a political party. . . It may like any other established political party proclaim its principles and invite public approval of them. At least while it possesses that status and those rights it cannot be held that it is defamatory per se to say of one that he is affiliated with or a member of the Communist Party any more than it would be to say that he is a member of any other legally recognized political party."

After the war, unless someone was a Communist, calling him one could result in a damage award. In 1945, the U.S. Circuit Court of Appeals was asked to decide whether a magazine article contained a libel of a Massachusetts lawyer because it said that "The Political Action Committee has hired as its legislative agent one S.G., who but recently was a legislative representative for the Massachusetts Communist Party."

They agreed it was a libel, "unless there is a difference between saying that a man is a Communist and saying that he is an agent for the party or sympathizes with its objectives and methods." It added that "any difference is one of degree only."

A later ruling said, "Having regard for current public attitude—transitory as it may be—the courts have held that a false charge that one is a Communist is basis for a libel action. And it is of little moment whether the statement describes plaintiff as a Communist or as one having communistic sympathies and affiliations."

Now that the cold war is over and there is no longer a Soviet Union enemy, the implications of association with the communist system are very different. However, statements about another ideology or perceived danger or comments about loyalty may come along for the courts to judge about the public's perception.

Slandering a fired employee

"Compelled self-publication" is a new doctrine which is having mixed reviews in the courts. California, Minnesota, Texas, and New York judges have accepted it. Typically, in defamation suits, you have to have a publicizing of the defamatory remarks. Employees who are fired now say since they have to tell the reasons they were terminated, they are compelled to publish their former employer's statements. If an employer is willing to minimize the reason for the firing, then an employer is less likely to prevail.

Employees suing for wrongful dismissal are also alleging slander. A prospective employer calls to check about the former employee and is told he was fired for some wrongdoing. If it is egregious, such as sexual harassment, drug abuse, theft, the damage can be substantial. Even gross insubordination is harmful. However, the courts look to see whether the employer recklessly disregarded the truth about the employee in dismissing him. So although some of these cases have produced large damage awards it is an evolving area of the law.

Defamatory statements made in political broadcasts

A candidate for the U.S. Senate in North Dakota, who was granted equal time on television, accused his opponents of disloyalty. The station let him make the statement because the law requires that all candidates be given equal time to speak on radio and television. One of the other candidates sued the station for defamation.

The Supreme Court stated that "while denying all candidates use of stations would protect broadcasters from liability, it would also withdraw political discussion from the air. If a station owner could protect himself from liability in no other way but by refusing to broadcast candidates' speeches, the necessary effect would be to hamper the congressional plan to develop broadcasting as a political outlet, rather than to foster it." The Court therefore ruled that no claim can result from any statement that is made by a candidate during a political broadcast.

Defamation recovery not tax free

When a Maryland plaintiff received $500,000 in a settlement of a defamation suit against her former employer who had accused her of embezzlement, the IRS wanted to tax it. The settlement had not specified whether it was for compensatory or punitive damages. On the appeal to the Tax Court, they ruled the payment was for a personal injury which defamation is, under Maryland law, and rejected the IRS's contention that punitive damages were taxable. However, the IRS appealed to the U.S. Fourth Circuit Court and they agreed with them that punitive damages are intended as punishment, not compensation for an injury.

Punitive damages are also discussed in connection with the Civil Rights Act of 1991 in Chapter 9.

Real estate

Chapter 16
Real estate

Buying and selling real estate involves many legal considerations in which almost everyone, at some point in his life, is involved. The technical aspects of a real estate transaction are complicated; however, a general understanding of the nature of such a transaction can help avoid many financial and emotional mistakes.

There are numerous terms associated with buying and selling real estate that a prospective purchaser should know, such as deed, binder, tenancy by the entirety, covenant, title, easement, mortgage, eminent domain, and condemnation, to name a few.

The purchase and sale of any piece of real estate usually begins with a contract of sale.

The binder
The purchase of a house frequently begins with the prospective purchaser signing a written memorandum of the transaction, called a *"binder,"* at the time he pays the deposit. The contents of the binder can be very important and may be used against the purchaser in connection with the preparation of the formal contract of sale.

Binders are generally not enforceable unless they contain the minimum terms of the transaction, namely:
 (1) the parties involved
 (2) a description of the property
 (3) the purchase price, and
 (4) the method of payment.

Even if a binder refers to a contract, it can, in itself, be a contract and a very unsatisfactory one at that. If a deposit is necessary, let your check serve as the receipt and sign no papers without the services of an attorney.

Formal contract of sale
Once the parties have agreed to consummate a real estate transaction, they should sign a contract of sale providing for the delivery of the property or "closing of title" at some specified time. The purpose of the contract of sale is to embody all of the aspects of the transaction in a written document and to enable the buyer to arrange for financing and to insure that the seller has proper title to the property before title actually passes from the seller to the buyer. Whatever is left out of the written contract of sale, be it oral assurances or "understandings," is unenforceable and has no effect after the contract is signed.

Unmarried buyers
Many adults who are living together and decide to buy a home do not have a contract between them. This is a mistake since most states have no rules concerning singles. Some of the issues you should cover in a contract are: What happens if one partner wants to sell and the other doesn't; the relationship is severed but both are making the mortgage

payments; one co-owner dies; one wants to buy out the other but their appraisals are far apart. You should also decide if you want to hold the property as tenants in common, so the shares will go to the individual estates rather than the co-owner's, and whether you want insurance to cover the mortgage payments.

Tenancy by the entirety

It is common practice for a husband and wife to purchase or take title to a house in their joint names. A deed that lists the buyers as "Robert Jones and Jane Jones, his wife" creates such a tenancy by the entirety whereby each possesses the entire property and after the death of one the survivor takes the whole property. There are estate tax considerations in taking property in the form of a tenancy by the entirety, and a husband and wife should contact their attorney before signing a real estate contract in this form.

Description of the property

Before you buy property you should be fully aware of what you are buying. If the description of the property being purchased is inaccurate or incomplete, you may be buying less than what you think, or may end up using someone else's property, or your neighbor may be using property that, in fact, belongs to you. It is always advisable to obtain a survey so that the buyer knows the real estate building that he is buying. In many cases, the seller has a survey and will deliver it to the buyer.

What is the actual purchase price?

The contract of sale should clearly state the amount of money to be paid and the method of payment. If the purchase price is listed at $40,000 and a separate clause refers to a mortgage of $20,000, it is unclear whether the buyer will have to pay $40,000 or $60,000. Great care should be taken to avoid any such ambiguity in connection with an existing mortgage and to make it clear that the purchaser is to be credited with any existing mortgage or *purchase-money mortgage* (a mortgage given by the seller to the buyer to secure the unpaid balance of the purchase price).

The purchaser should be careful when purchasing property with a preexisting mortgage to have competent assistance to review all of the terms of the mortgage and to receive satisfactory proof from the seller showing the reduced amount of principal, the interest rate, and maturity date, so that the purchaser knows how much he actually has to pay on the existing mortgage.

Closing title

The time and place for paying the purchase price and delivering the deed (a document signed by the seller transferring title to the property to the buyer) are also set forth in the contract of sale. At the closing of title, adjustments should be made in any fees, taxes on property, principal, costs, interest, or other expenses.

The deed

There are a number of essential facts you should always bear in mind when you take part in a transfer of land. First of all, you should make or receive a deed to establish the transfer—or conveyance, as it is often called at law. The deed represents or symbolizes the land itself. When a deed is delivered, it is, effectively, the delivery of the land.

It is indispensable that this deed be in writing. It must be properly signed and should be witnessed. Make certain, also, that it is acknowledged before a notary public and entered in the official records of your locality. Copying of the deed into the public records gives legal notice of ownership to all who may be concerned with the land in the present or the future.

Land deeds fall, roughly speaking, into three classes: (1) warranty deeds, (2) bargain and sale deeds, and (3) quitclaim deeds. Each of these is different from the others. Each has a different purpose and each has different requirements.

A *warranty deed* not only conveys the property, but contains a covenant by the seller that he owns the property and that his title is free of any liens or encumbrances other than those specifically set out in the deed. Should the buyer find, after he makes the purchase, that there are encumbrances or liens other than those specified in the deed, he is entitled to recover from the seller whatever he is compelled to spend in satisfying these claims, which the grantor or seller represented to him as not existing.

Bargain and sale deeds are simple conveyances of title to land by the owner, but contain no representations or warranties such as those set out in warranty deeds, except possibly a warranty that the seller himself has done nothing to encumber or create a lien against the property. With this form, the purchaser gets, in addition to the rights of the seller, the benefit of any rights an innocent third party purchaser may have against creditors of the seller who didn't record their mortgages, etc.

A *quitclaim deed* is generally used where there may be some claim against a parcel of land, resulting from the complexities of descent or similar conditions. It conveys simply whatever ownership, however qualified, the seller may possess in the property.

Warranty deed
A covenant of warranty and of "quiet enjoyment" runs with the land—it is a warranty of title and quiet enjoyment not just to the immediate purchaser but to all subsequent owners of the property.

In states where the wife still has her dower right in her husband's property she must join him in signing it and be a party to the deed.

These deeds can be prepared by your counsel according to the particular statute of your state.

The protection a warranty affords
A deed of Alabama property contained provisions warranting title and quiet enjoyment, and that the property was free from encumbrances—all the standard guarantees. Later the purchaser died and the property passed to his heirs. They in turn conveyed the property to

a man named Poyner. At that time, six years after the original conveyance, it was discovered that when the first deed was made, the city had a lien on the property for street paving expenses.

Poyner, the owner of the property, sued and recovered an amount sufficient to satisfy the lien. The court pointed out that such a warranty covenant runs with the land into the hands of the heirs and any assignees and may be the grounds for suit when the breach of such a covenant occurs.

The home buyer gets a break

There now are rules which end some abusive practices of lenders over-charging borrowers when it comes to escrow accounts. When you pay your mortgage monthly, it includes principal, interest and some for the escrow account. Federal law requires the escrow contribution to be one-twelfth of the total of taxes, premiums and other charges "reasonably anticipated" each year. It also allows a "cushion" equal to two months worth of escrow payments, in case of increases in taxes or whatever. There's no requirement for a cushion.

Now at settlement lenders have to give you an initial escrow account disclosure statement telling you how much you'll have to pay each month, including the cushion, which could be zero. Once you go through the payments, if there's a difference in the initial estimate with an overage in the escrow account of $50 or more, the lender must send you a check for it within 30 days. If there is a shortfall you work out a make up arrangement.

Also now all lenders must use the same accounting method to compute escrow contributions. The nationally prescribed method results in lower monthly payments. And there cannot be higher escrow charges for the early collection of sums to pay taxes not due till later in the year. This saves you subsidizing the "float."

Know your rights and ask you lender the right questions.

Handicapped accessibility

The *Fair Housing Act* has been discussed in Chapter 22 dealing with leases or rentals. It also covers condos and home builders who have paid insufficient attention to the Act's design requirements. Noncompliance with handicapped accessibility is nationwide. It cannot and should not be tolerated.

The Act's handicapped accessibility rules cover all residential dwellings with four or more living units constructed for first occupancy after March, 1991. This would include attached single family town houses and condominium developments. There must be wheelchair accessible entryways, accessible public and common use areas, extra wide doorways, bathroom walls to accommodate grab bars and kitchens the handicapped can use.

One handicapped person who bought a condo under construction asked for changes to make it accessible. She was asked to pay more. She complained and the developer settled. Another person asked his condo board for a ramp to allow access. After the board refused, an investigation revealed the whole complex lacked appropriate features under the Act. Negotiations are in progress.

If you have an access problem, complain to the Justice Department and the Department of *Housing and Urban Development* (HUD), both of which agencies are pressing enforcement actions.

Handicapped parking

Although the handicapped are covered in the *Fair Housing Act* when it comes to residential accessibility, it is another story when parking in common areas of condo properties is concerned. The by-laws of the condo association seem to take precedence. If they provide that the parking places belong to all the residents and are available only on a first come basis, a handicapped owner is stuck in the dilemma between civil rights and property rights. Of course, if the condo board is willing to propose an amendment to the by-laws for handicapped parking and the requisite support is given by the owners, the problem is solved. However, it could take a long time to happen or it may never happen.

The Department of Housing and Urban Development (HUD) is well aware of the issue. So are some state commissions on human relations who also are recipients of complaints. The problem was solved in Maryland when a law was passed giving condo associations the power to override their by-laws to create handicapped parking spaces.

Condo boards' responsibilities

All members of the board have a responsibility to the owners. If you, as an owner, have problems with board inaction, such as unannounced meetings, or action, such as possible fraudulent dealings with contractors, you should check your state's condominium law as well as the by-laws and other documents under which the board operates for possible remedies. If meetings must be announced and open, you can complain. Also there are quorum requirements to make Board action legal. And, minutes must disclose the actions upon which votes were taken.

Maryland law required open meetings except in regard to personnel matters. Other states may also. If there is a possibility of fraud with contractors, that would affect all owners, not only as to their fees but, potentially, on the safety of items such as elevators. You should seek legal counsel on this immediately and let your representative speak for you to avoid potential slander or libel. Your action could trigger broader condo owner support. Everyone would want to protect the significant investment in their unit.

Good faith estimates

When you contract to buy a home, every lender of a federally related mortgage loan is required under *the Real Estate Settlement Procedures Act* (RESPA) to provide you with an information pamphlet explaining the upcoming settlement procedures and also tell you what the "good faith estimate" is of the probable charges you will incur for the various settlement services. This estimate, under regulations issued by the Department of

Housing and Urban Development (HUD), must be provided no later than three business days after the lender receives your loan application.

The purpose of all this information is to give you, the buyer and borrower, a pretty good idea of what you will have to spend up front on your house purchase. If the estimate of settlement and closing costs is higher than you expected, you may have to borrow or otherwise rethink the purchase, a problem if you've signed a contract.

If the lender has not conformed to the terms of RESPA or HUD's regulations, you may want to complain to a variety of agencies including the Federal Trade Commission, the Comptroller of the Currency, the Federal Reserve Board, or your State Attorney General. But, ultimately, it's up to you to decide on whether you want another lender.

What is best is for you to ascertain all the costs of the house before you sign the contract. Your real estate broker should be the one to turn to for this.

Senior housing can bar children

Although the Fair Housing Act made discrimination against children illegal, there is another federal law dealing with residences where seniors live that creates an exception. It allows a no-child policy when 80 percent of the units in rental buildings, condos, planned unit developments and mobile home parks are occupied by people 55 or older. The sites do not have to provide significant services and facilities for elderly residents. Occupancy is the criterion.

Satellite dishes

Local governments, homeowner and condo associations cannot prevent homeowners from having a TV antennae or small satellite dish on their property. The *Telecommunications Act* gave authority to the Federal Communications Commission (FCC) to encourage television viewers' extended access. There can be local rules dealing with safety (such as no dishes on fire escapes), historic preservation districts and architecture and design but they must not interfere with installation or reception or cause an unreasonable increase in cost. The FCC still must resolve the question of whether renters can put equipment in places they don't own.

The devil will be in the details of what will be considered interference or what is unreasonable cost. But the basic right of the homeowner to high tech TV reception seems to have been resolved.

Private mortgage insurance (PMI)

Millions of homeowners pay for mortgage insurance. It is part of the monthly payment to their lender. A settlement of a class action lawsuit has impacted the need for insurance. But, Congress can't agree on federal legislation to save homeowners from continuing to make payments for insurance when there no longer is a risk to the lender.

The premiums have added hundreds of dollars yearly to mortgage loan repayments. Once a borrower has paid down 20% of the value or the resale value of the home is such that the risk of loss to the lender from default is minimal, why continue the insurance?

The class action settlement with Banc One Corp might mean other mortgage companies will follow and automatically cancel mortgage insurance coverage on loans when the borrower's equity exceeds 20%. The settlement also provided that new borrowers would be given written disclosure statements explaining about mortgage insurance and that customers would be sent an annual statement on how and when they can ask for a cancellation of the premium payments.

Some states have varying laws on this issue. Some require disclosure to alert homeowners of the possibility of cancellation. Some require termination. Fannie Mae and Freddie Mac (government insurance) permit cancellation but don't alert their borrowers to the potential. FHA borrowers sadly have to pay premiums for the life of the loan. The Congress wants to address the issue but can't agree on how to handle when you can cancel, whether your equity is pay down or increased value, and who should decide. Also, as is usual with federal legislation, the issue of preemption arises. Should the federal law preempt or take precedence over a state's law or should a state be able to pass a law stricter than a possibly weak federal law?

If you have significant equity in your house, check your mortgage immediately to see whether you have any cancellation potential of your private mortgage insurance.

Bargain and sale deed

As in the execution of the warranty deed, in states where the wife still retains her dower right in her husband's property, she must join in, and be a party to, the conveyance.

Your lawyer will follow your state statute in drawing up an appropriate form of this class of deed.

What is a quitclaim deed?

A quitclaim deed does not necessarily convey the land, but simply the right, title, and interest of the seller or grantor, if any, in the land. As in the other types of conveyance of land, the wife should join in the deed and be a party to the conveyance where she still retains her dower right in her husband's property.

Are oral deeds legal?

Do not accept an oral transfer of ownership of land. The law does not recognize such a conveyance as a deed. A typical state statute in relation to the execution of deeds says: "An estate in real property other than an estate at will or for a term not exceeding one year, can be transferred only by operation of law or by an instrument in writing subscribed by the party disposing of the same . . ." All states have similar "statutes of fraud" requiring that conveyances of real estate be in writing. They are intended to prevent "fraud" in testimony about oral transactions.

How a deed should be executed
In Indiana, the boundaries of a tract of land were not clear. The owners involved settled upon their titles by an oral agreement, but no deeds were exchanged.

Here, the court laid down the rule that is accepted as the law of the country in relation to the execution of deeds: that an instrument to transfer the title to land must not only have a grantor, a grantee, and a "thing granted"—it must also be signed by the grantor or someone he directs to sign for him. Further, it should be witnessed and acknowledged before a notary or other public officer as required by the statute and delivered to the grantee. Some courts, following their statutes, will not insist upon the witnessing or acknowledgment, but for your own protection you should always have these.

Signing with an X
An aged owner, nearly deaf and blind, wished to deed property in Oklahoma to his son. Unable to sign the deed himself, he used an X for his signature before witnesses and acknowledged the document to be his deed before a notary public. Later the validity of this deed was questioned because it had been executed by a cross rather than the signature of the owner of the land.

This objection did not prevail. Where there has been an acknowledgment and the grantor is able to make a deed, the conveyance is secure against any defects in its execution, said the court. Further, when a document in the form of a deed is attested and delivered, the courts consider it a deed if the control of the property passes from the original owner on the delivery of this deed.

An X signature by one who is unable to write his name is always valid in the eyes of the law.

Acknowledging a deed
The acknowledgment of a deed—a document of the statement made by the grantor of land before a notary public or other officer authorized to certify to such statements that the execution of the deed is the free act of the grantor—is not generally necessary insofar as the actual transfer of the property is concerned.

A rule laid down by the court in one case where no acknowledgment was made in the conveyance of real estate says that a deed to real property that has been executed and delivered is valid between the parties to the transaction although neither actually acknowledged nor witnessed the transaction itself.

In another case the court held that a deed that was signed and delivered, although it was not acknowledged before a notary public, was adequate to transfer the title to the property to the new owner.

When acknowledgment is necessary
A similar decision was made in a case where a deed was neither acknowledged nor witnessed. Here, however, the court indicated that an acknowledgment is necessary for the recording of a conveyance for notice of the conveyance to later purchasers. This is a

point you cannot afford to overlook. Suppose a deed is made and delivered by a grantor, and later this same grantor makes a second deed of the same land and delivers this second deed to another grantee. The grantor is committing a fraud, but if the first deed has not been recorded and the second grantee is innocent of the fraud and has no knowledge of the previous deed, when he records his deed he acquires legal title to the land. The first grantee has no such title.

An acknowledgment of a deed by a grantor, the court explained, is not essential to pass legal title between the parties to the instrument. Attestation and acknowledgment are formalities required by the statute to entitle the deed to be recorded so as to operate as notice to subsequent purchasers, but are not essential to transfer the title between the parties.

A deed must be delivered
The delivery of a deed is necessary for the transfer of the ownership of real property. While the delivery to the grantee personally is not necessary, there must be some act of the one conveying the land that signifies a surrender of his ownership and control of the property. Such an act is known as a "*constructive delivery*." The word "constructive" is applied at law to a condition or act the court assumes on the basis of other conditions or acts that have actually taken place.

If you take part in a transaction involving a deed, be sure that it is delivered. That is the safest course. However, the courts have declared that a valid transfer of real property can occur without the knowledge of the grantee. The case that follows provides an illustration of this rule.

An example of constructive delivery
A woman owning land in California made a deed of land to her brother and herself as joint owners. She left this deed with the notary before whom she had acknowledged it, and asked him to have it returned to her.

The brother to whom the joint interest in this property was thus conveyed had no knowledge of the transfer until three years later, when his sister died. There was no necessity to show acceptance. "There may be a constructive delivery as well as an actual delivery so long as acts are shown to indicate the intention of the grantor to vest title by the instrument."

Delivery by an agent
The owner of some real estate in Georgia wrote the following letter: "Dear Brother: Am not feeling so well. Asthma is bothering me. Am in town having a paper fixed up. If anything happens to me you have this paper recorded at once and turn over to Stella (his wife) if she is living. Mark the envelope so you will know what it is and take care of it. Am mailing it to you. Your loving brother, J.W.C."

A properly executed deed was enclosed in the letter. Less than a year later, C. died. Two days after his death his brother had the deed recorded and left instructions that it be returned, after recording, to Stella, the wife. This was done.

The brothers and sisters of the man who had died sued to set aside the deed on the ground that it had never been delivered by the grantor. Deciding in their favor, that there had been no delivery of the deed and that title and ownership of this land had not passed to the wife, the court explained that when the deed was sent by C. to his brother, he made his brother an agent to have the deed recorded and delivered to his wife. When C. died, his death revoked that agency and the authority of his brother to act for him ended. Hence, there was no delivery of the deed, either physically or constructively, and the effort of C. to convey the land to his wife failed. The letter could not, of course, operate as a valid will, either.

There is a significant lesson here. A deed is an important document. Any matters pertaining to it should be taken care of directly, without relying on a person who is not an attorney.

Recording of deeds

The deed you receive when you buy real estate should be recorded immediately—that is, delivered to the proper officer of the county where the land is located, with instructions to put the deed on record. This officer is sometimes known as the County Register or Registrar and sometimes as the County Clerk.

There is an old adage that a man may be honest but he should be kept honest. We have referred to the fact that when the owner of land has given deeds of the same land to two different grantees, the second deed is obviously a fraud—because by that act the grantor is selling something that he no longer owns, and if the second grantee has his deed recorded before the first grantee records his, the land belongs to the second grantee unless he is in some way a party to this fraud or had knowledge of the earlier conveyance.

"The basic purpose which led to the enactment of the recording acts was to prevent persons owning lands from selling them more than once," is the laconic observation of a New York court.

Before a purchaser can assert a claim on such a second grant, it must be made clear that he is innocent of any knowledge or of any wrongdoing. This statement was first made over 100 years ago. This opinion resulted from a case that concerned a person who purchased some land at a sheriff's sale and then sought to put off that land a grantee under a previously executed but still unrecorded deed of the land. Here, the purchaser from the sheriff knew in advance that the deed was not recorded. He was a party to the fraud and thus acquired nothing by his purchase.

What is a covenant?

A covenant is an agreement to do or not to do a particular act, according to the courts. Covenants may stipulate the character of the buildings or improvements that may be made on the land, as well as those that may not be made. They may state who may live in the buildings on the land, or what use may be made of the land. They may contain a wide range of restrictions and yet be a basic condition of the conveyance.

If you, as a grantee of land, fail to do as you have agreed under the covenants in the deed of your land, you may be penalized by the loss of the property, by damages for your violation of the covenant, or by a prohibition by the court—known as an injunction—against the continuance of the violation. What the penalty will be depends on the nature of the covenant and the judgment of the court.

A typical covenant

Typical of covenants of this sort was one in a deed of Connecticut property that said: "For a period of twenty years from and after the date hereof the grantee will not erect or maintain or permit to be erected or maintained any building except a one-family dwelling."

First, the grantee of this deed received into his house three "paying guests." Next, he rearranged the interior of the home and inaugurated what was considered a boarding house in the full meaning of the expression. This use of the house violated the covenant in his deed restricting the use of the building to one family, and an injunction was issued against a continuance of this use.

Injunction granted

The covenant in a deed of land in Oklahoma restricted the use of the property to residential purposes. "No building shall ever be used or occupied for any purpose except for that of private residence exclusively, nor shall any part or portion thereof be used for business or trade of any kind whatsoever."

The residents on this tract objected to the construction there of a gasoline filling station by an oil company, and sought an injunction. They declared such a use of the property was contrary to the covenant into which all the adjacent landowners had entered, and it was on this ground that the injunction was granted.

Covenants binding in the future

An agreement was made by the owner of property on the bay at Mobile, Alabama, not to use his property for any public or commercial purpose except for the reasonable and proper use for bathing by his family. Two years later the owner adopted a plan of renting the beach for public picnics and bathing parties.

Such an agreement that restricts the use of land "runs with the land," was the decision of the court, and is binding on all who have notice or knowledge of the restriction. Furthermore, by the execution of such an agreement the owners of the property bind not only themselves but also succeeding owners of the property. By recording deeds that contain restricting covenants, you give legal notice of them to all subsequent purchasers or grantees when purchasing property that is intended for a particular use. It is important, therefore, that the land records be searched for the existence of any such restrictions when you purchase any piece of property.

Forfeiture of title

A deed of property at Beverly Hills, California, provided: "All buildings to be erected on Doheny Drive shall be exclusively for private residence." It contained the further provision that a breach of this condition after 30 days' notice and a failure to remedy the breach would forfeit title to the property—it would then revert to the original grantor, leaving the succeeding grantee without his property.

This covenant was later challenged, but to no avail. Restrictions governing the character, location, and cost of buildings to be constructed in accordance with the general plan for a specific neighborhood in cities have been universally held to be valid and binding. Also, provisions for forfeiture of title by the owner for failure to comply with such restrictions may cost him his property.

How covenants are abandoned

After covenants of this character are made, conditions often arise that justify the courts in holding the restrictions abandoned because of changes in the character of the neighborhood. A typical case concerning such a condition is the one that follows.

In Pasadena, California, various real estate owners made a contract or covenant by which they bound themselves to restrict to "persons of the Caucasian race" the use of a neighborhood owned by them. Later there was an influx of people of other races into this neighborhood. When some of the owners protested against these violations of the covenants in the deeds, the court refused to interfere.

Such interference, the court declared, would serve only to harass and injure those living in the vicinity. The enforcement of this covenant was not justified when the character of the neighborhood had changed by virtue of altered conditions in no way connected with these covenants. Today, of course, such a limitation is unenforceable. See Chapter 9 on *Your Civil Rights*.

When restrictions are unenforceable

In 1855, a deed made for the conveyance of property in Baltimore, Maryland, contained a covenant restricting it for small private residences. The houses in this vicinity were at the time occupied by single families, and the yards were filled with flowers, shrubbery, and trees. Thirty years later these families were gone. In the place of the onetime homes were rooming and tenement houses, a gasoline filling station, and a used car lot.

The courts, when requested to, refused to enforce the restrictions. It was held that they had been inserted into deeds to maintain the locality as a residential district. The vicinity no longer had that character—the restrictions were no longer reasonable or enforceable, now that the reason for their imposition was gone.

In general, restrictions of this type can exist for no longer a time than the nature of the circumstances and the purpose of their imposition indicates them to be reasonable. Unreasonable restrictions, in the light of changed economic or other conditions, will not be enforced by courts through issuance of an injunction.

The meaning of easements

An easement is an acquired right or a privilege to enjoy or use land belonging to another. A path across the land of another used so long by the public that there is a right to its uninterrupted use, a roadway through another's lot, the protection afforded by the eaves of a house overhanging the land of another—all these are easements. That is why an easement has been called "a privilege without a profit."

If, for example, your walkway to the beach cuts across your neighbor's property, and you have always used that walkway, and to reroute your steps would be a significant inconvenience, this would come under the heading of an easement.

For 30 years, near the town of Bear Creek, in California, a man named Mr. Peck had made use of a lane over another owner's land, that lay adjacent to his own. One day Mr. Peck found that the road had been barred by the neighbor. Across the land Mr. Peck found a locked gate.

The court maintained that Mr. Peck had a right to the use of this path. That right had been acquired by him as well as by others by an "open, visible, continuous, and uninterrupted" use for 30 years. The neighbor, though the owner of the land, had no right to bar others from the use of the path that they had grown accustomed to.

What makes an easement?

The use of another's property by one who claims an easement must be "adverse" to the owner of that property. Passing across a field on the express invitation or consent of the owner creates no easement. Doing so for 20 years (the period of time usually prescribed in which an easement will accrue), will create such a right, provided the exercise of that right has been "open, adverse, and continuous," for all that time. An easement is said to arise thus by *prescription*—that is, continued use against the legal rights of the landowner to prevent it if he chooses.

Easement in the use of a building

An easement also arises from the use of common stairs and hallways by those passing through a building. In Lowell, Massachusetts, John and Thomas Nesmith built adjoining buildings and provided for a common entrance, landings, and stairways. Half of the space so used was allotted to the property of one and half to that of the other.

All went well until a successor to one of these owners wished to tear-down the building. The other owner refused to give his permission for this action. The court was called upon to decide which of the owners had the law on his side.

"If the structure ceases to exist," reads the decision in this case, "the right ends as there is nothing upon which it can be exercised. This is because the owner of the building is not obliged to replace it when it ceases to exist by reason of decay, earthquake, tornado, fire, or its destruction otherwise caused without fault or act of the owner."

This is the general viewpoint of the law on this matter. However, the question of whether the owner of the property subject to an easement of this character is free voluntarily to destroy the building and not restore the easement is not uniformly decided. The court here held that the owner of the land was free to demolish the building without obligation for the restoration of the hall and stairways for the use of the adjoining owner. In some states a contrary rule has been established.

The best solution to this problem is to follow the method usually adopted by owners who want to prevent easements—closing the passageway for an appreciable length of time at not too infrequent intervals. By closing the pathway for a substantial amount of time you break the continuity that is an essential feature in the establishment of a right of way or easement of this character.

Easement by implication

Easements are in some instances recognized by the courts as arising by implication. The following is a good example of such an easement. When part of a tract of land is sold to another, and there is no other reasonable way of access available to the purchaser, the seller by implication gives to the grantee a right of way across his own land to the plot sold.

How a mortgage operates

A mortgage of real estate is simply equivalent to the deposit of land by its owner (or mortgagor) as collateral for the payment of a loan. A mortgage is merely security for a debt. You buy land and pay, let us say, half the purchase price in cash. The payment of the remaining half of the price that you still owe, you secure to the person who puts up the money (the mortgagee) by giving a mortgage on the property for that amount. This loan or mortgage you pay off as stipulated in an agreement, which may or may not be a part of the mortgage. When it has been paid off, the lender's interest in the property ends.

It is of fundamental importance, when payments are completed under a mortgage, that the mortgagor obtain and file a "satisfaction piece" from the mortgagee. Otherwise he may have no clear proof that his title to the property is free of encumbrances. A "satisfaction piece" is merely legal terminology for a formal document that the mortgage has been paid and the lien released.

Kinds of mortgages

Mortgages that are held on land, as well as mortgages that are held on the buildings situated on the land that, in terms of the law, are considered a part of the realty, may be as many as there are lenders to the owner of the money thus secured. These mortgages, however, are entitled to priority in payment in the order in which they are given. They are generally designated as a first mortgage, a second mortgage, and sometimes even a third mortgage.

A mortgage given in part payment of the purchase price of property is a *"purchase money mortgage"* and has priority in payment over any subsequent mortgage other than those already on the land when it was purchased.

Appraisals

Whether it's for a loan for a new home or the refinancing of your present dwelling, the lender must know the value, so the property is appraised. Under an amendment to the *Equal Credit Opportunity Act* (discussed in Chapter 6), as a loan applicant who has paid for the appraisal used to evaluate your application, you are entitled to a copy of the report if you request it in writing. You should get it whether your loan is approved or not to use as you wish.

Escrow accounts

Millions of homeowners have escrow accounts with their mortgage lenders. They accumulate the funds to cover items such as real estate taxes and hazard insurance. A mortgagee usually sends one monthly payment covering loan principal and interest plus the added sums the lender has indicated to cover the other recurring expenses. However, many problems can ensue from escrow accounts, particularly when they are transferred to other lenders when institutions fail or merge. Bankers want escrow accounts to be sure taxes and insurance are paid on time. But the money in them accounts for a tremendous accumulation on which no interest may be paid. This is the bankers' "float."

You should know that if you have a "Fannie Mae" or "Freddie Mac" mortgage, you are not required to pay into an escrow account if you and your lender agree. Your state's law may guarantee your right without a lender's permission if you meet their criteria. If you want to reduce your monthly mortgage payment and can qualify, find out what your lender's rules are and if your state law is applicable.

National Affordable Housing Act

This law was passed to remedy abuses in mortgage servicing transfers by bankers and other lenders. Mortgage servicing, as homeowners know, is the collection of monthly payments of principal and interest and maintaining escrow accounts for taxes and insurance. Whereas in the past you sent your payment to the same institution that made you your home loan, now servicing rights are sold to mortgage bankers who do it for a fee. The servicing can be resold many times. This has resulted in escrow padding, bad recordkeeping that caused late fees for wrong addresses, lenders not notifying the borrowers of the transfers, and servicers who were lax in paying taxes and insurance which caused homeowners to suffer.

HUD regulations help home buyers

The Act required HUD to issue regulations to protect home buyers from servicing abuses. The penalties for failure to comply are very stiff including compensation to borrowers for damages. There are new consumer disclosure forms which must be signed before closing on a property. You must be told that you will be given notice before your loan service is sold or transferred, and that the new servicer must confirm the transfer quickly. The notice must also give you details including who the new firm is, their toll-free number and names of persons at your original lender and the new servicer who can answer your queries. For 60 days after a transfer, if you happen to send your payments to the wrong address, you cannot be charged a late fee. Also, when you write about a service-related matter, you must receive a quick acknowledgement and the matter must be rectified within 60 days. During this period, your credit records cannot be changed.

The regulations also give you an opportunity to compare lenders since the lender must also tell you whether your loan service is likely to be sold or transferred by them. Of course, in hard times lenders may be difficult to find. But if this issue is of importance to you, you now are entitled to have the absolute right to have your prospective lender protect you against the consequences of any servicing abuses.

Improving property already mortgaged
Should improvements be made to the property, buildings erected, or similar additions made that enhance the value, the mortgage covers these as well, and the security of the mortgagee is correspondingly greater unless such improvements are expressly excepted from the lien of the mortgage by agreement between the mortgagor and the mortgagee.

Who inherits a mortgage?
A real estate mortgage is personal property, as is any other form of security, such as a bond, or a stock, or bank deposits. Upon the death of the owner of the mortgage, it passes to the beneficiaries under the will of the mortgagee as would any other debt owed to the estate.

Foreclosure of real property mortgage
The foreclosure of a mortgage is made to collect money that has been lent the owner of the property, when he fails to repay the holder of the mortgage as stipulated. In such an action the property is taken from the owner and sold at auction. From the proceeds of the sale, after payment of the court and sale expenses, the debt for which the mortgage was given as security is paid.

In some instances, where property is rented to tenants and is producing a current income for the owner, a receiver is appointed by the court to collect these rents and hold them until the final disposition of the proceeds of the sale. However, when the value of the land is sufficient for the payment of the mortgage debt, this remedy is seldom granted by the court, nor is it granted when it is apparent that the income from the property is already being paid on the taxes and interest, and in reduction of the mortgage.

The foreclosure decree, made by the court, determines the amount of the debt, makes provision for the payment of attorney fees and costs, and orders the sale of the property with directions as to the notice of sale, the place where the notice must be given, and the time allowed between the giving of the notice and the date of the sale. This decree will also specify the time and place for the sale, or leave these details to the decision of the master or referee—the officer appointed by the court for the conduct of subsequent proceedings until the making of the final foreclosure decree, after the sale.

The foreclosure sale

A public notice of the place and time of the mortgage foreclosure sale must be given in accordance with the decree or, in some states, with the provisions of the statute. This notice is often given by publication in a newspaper "printed in the county" or "of general circulation," or by posting the notice in a specific and prominent place.

The foreclosure sale is made by public auction. If no bidder appears, the auctioneer adjourns the sale to another date.

If the proceeds do not cover the mortgage

In some, but not all, states, if the mortgage contains an agreement by the mortgagor to pay the debt—or if the debt is represented by a separate written obligation, called a bond—there is a personal liability on the mortgagor that goes beyond the proceeds of the foreclosure sale. It requires payment by him personally of any deficiency that may occur. In other states the right of the mortgagee to this deficiency judgment is not recognized. If the foreclosure sale yields proceeds in excess of the mortgage and fees, this money belongs to the mortgagor.

As a rule, the right of the individual who is the mortgagor to redeem the mortgage is ordinarily closed and ended with the sale on foreclosure. It is, however, sometimes held by the courts that the mortgagor may be permitted to redeem the mortgage after the initial sale but before the final foreclosure decree is made by the court.

When a deed is given as a mortgage

A mortgage of land is, in practical effect, a conveyance of the land to whoever lends the money, while the person making the mortgage continues in possession of the land, with an agreement that if and when the money is repaid to the lender, as agreed, the conveyance is void and of no effect.

Often an absolute deed is given as security for the repayment of a loan on real property, by agreement or understanding between the owner of the property and the lender of the money that the deed will be returned or canceled when the money is repaid. When such an arrangement is made, the legal problem of what the instrument is—deed or mortgage—may arise, particularly at the time the borrower attempts to exercise ownership or the lender attempts to foreclose.

An individual who was the purchaser of a piece of real estate in Florida erected on his land a two-story brick building. Shortly before the building was completed, the owner mortgaged it and the lot for a loan. Sometime later, when the owner was unable to reduce the mortgage, he gave the lender a deed of the property. In this deed was the agreement that the lender manage the property, collect the rents, and apply them to this unpaid loan.

Six years later the borrower asked for an account of the money that had been collected and the balance that he owed on the loan. The creditor refused to honor this request, saying that he had taken the deed in payment of the loan.

Here, the court asserted that "an instrument given for the purpose or with the intention of securing the payment of money is a mortgage."

If the mortgagee buys the property

The mortgage does not pay the debt; it is simply security for its payment. As we have already indicated, if the proceeds from the sale of the security are not enough for the payment of the balance, the deficiency remains as the borrower's obligation, which he must pay, just as he must pay any other debt he owes.

An owner of property in Philadelphia borrowed $4,500 and gave as security a mortgage on her property. When she failed to pay, the property was sold at foreclosure and bought by the lender of the money. Later, after the borrower had died, the administrator paid the deficiency and demanded the return of the property. This the court refused to order.

A mortgage not fully paid on a foreclosure sale of the property can be a personal claim against the mortgagor for the deficiency, even if the mortgagee himself buys the property at the sale.

How a mortgagee's claims are limited

State statutes, however, in many instances impose limitations on the amount of the judgment or claim that may be granted the mortgagee after the foreclosure and sale of the property and the credit of the proceeds on the mortgage, for which he looks for payment to the mortgagor.

Real property taxes

The power to levy a tax on real property is generally delegated by the state legislature to local authorities—such as the city, county, or town—and is subject to whatever limitations or restrictions the legislature may see fit to impose on those officials. The levy is made for either the calendar or the fiscal year.

A notice of the assessment against each taxpayer must be posted or advertised by the local authorities. The officials frequently do this by making the tax rolls or books in which the assessments are listed available to an inspection by the public—and to the individual taxpayers particularly—at a designated public office during business hours on certain days.

Should any taxpayer feel aggrieved by the assessment against his property, he has the opportunity, within a stated time, to file objections with the tax authorities and be heard on his complaint. After this hearing, the tax may be reduced or left undisturbed, although it is still subject to review by the courts at the instance of the aggrieved taxpayer.

The usual grounds upon which complaints are made by taxpayers is that their property has been overvalued and the amount that they have been assessed is unjust and inaccurate.

How real estate value is assessed

The highest price the property would bring free of encumbrances at a fair and voluntary private sale for cash, or its fair cash market value, is ordinarily the criterion of its value. In estimating the value of land, the assessors take into consideration the location, quality, conditions, improvements, and use—all the factors that affect the market value or that would influence the minds of purchasers. Original purchase price and recent resales also are considered in fixing value.

Foreclosure sale for taxes

On and after a named date in the statute, unpaid taxes on a real estate become a lien on the land. Substantially, these taxes are a first mortgage. If the tax is not paid within the time set by the law, the land may be sold for the nonpayment of the taxes.

The statutory requirement is that the tax collector shall make a list of the lands on which taxes remain unpaid, with a description, in each instance, of the property and the name of the owner. After the list has been advertised, either by posting in some prominent place or by publication in a newspaper, or both, the land is sold at public auction and the unpaid taxes deducted from the proceeds.

After a sale, the former owner has a specific period of time in which to pay the taxes, expenses of the sale, interest, advertising and other charges to get the property back. The time varies by state statute, but if everything isn't paid in time, the property goes to the auction purchaser.

Seller's responsibility

"Caveat emptor," let the buyer beware, is changing in regard to defects in homes. There is more sympathy for buyers who are hurt by sellers knowledgeable about hidden defects. These include environmental problems, illegal construction or alterations that violate codes, rezoning plans, neighborhood construction or crimes which occurred in the house (murders need not be disclosed), any of which could affect price and desirability.

Lenders protect themselves with title searches and title insurance. Buyers can have an inspection but not find hidden, potentially big ticket problems. Realtors are legally required to reveal defects they know about. But, how are buyers really protected? In California and Maine it is against the law for a seller to conceal a defect that affects the property's value or desirability. Over 32 states only have voluntary disclosure plans. Buyers are fighting back, suing sellers for fraud and refusing to complete the purchase or asking for damages post sale. Courts are listening. Check with your attorney if your house has turned into a lemon.

Condemnation and eminent domain

An owner of real property may have proper title, pay all necessary taxes, mortgage payments, or whatever and still lose his property. The right of the federal or local governments to take property for the public interest upon payment of just compensation is inherent in government. Under the Fifth Amendment to the United States Constitution, the government may exercise its power of eminent domain as long as it pays the owner just compensation, a policy that is especially current because of ecological concerns.

The laws governing eminent domain generally derive from the late 19th century when open lands were plentiful and were being claimed for canals, roads, and railroads. Now, with a highly urbanized society and many more agencies with the power of eminent domain, vast amounts of private property have been claimed for interstate highways, urban renewal projects, schools, parks, and many other public-interest uses. The value of the property being condemned has led to numerous lawsuits and hardships to private property owners. The owner of real property must realize that his rights of ownership are subject to a higher state authority that may, on occasion, require the owner of property to give his specific property for the interest of the public at large, but with just compensation.

What is "just compensation" becomes a question of expert opinion as to values and comparison with other property in the vicinity.

In one case, the owner of property had protested a high valuation or assessment of his property for tax purposes and had succeeded in having the value reduced. Thereafter, the government had taken his property in eminent domain proceedings for a public purpose of slum clearance. The owner now wanted a much higher valuation for his compensation.

The court determined that the value for tax purposes and the value for condemnation purposes were not necessarily the same, because different factors were involved. It is common knowledge, for example, that in many areas of the country, for tax purposes, property is underassessed.

Air rights

Urbanization has also led to many modifications of classic real estate concepts, one of the latest being the development of air rights. The first air rights law was adopted by Illinois in 1927, allowing railroads owning real estate to sell, convey, and lease estates above and below the surface. Increasing pressure for usable building space in urban areas led to the enactment by Congress in 1958 of a law granting to the Interstate Highway System the right to establish parking facilities for motor vehicles above and below the highways of the system. Both federal and local governments expanded the use of air rights and established a trend toward treating air rights as real property subject to the same treatment as other real property.

Air rights are described as air space or development rights to above a specified horizontal place and such surface rights and land needed for support and access for the street and to ensure compatibility with subsurface use.

In 1970, New York City amended its zoning law to allow the transfer of unused and/or development rights from a site that could not use such rights to one that could, thus creating a greater economic use of limited space.

Examples of air rights projects are: the Pan American Building over Grand Central Station, and Madison Square Garden and Pennsylvania Plaza over Pennsylvania Station, both in New York City; the Prudential Center in Boston; the Chicago Merchandise Mart of the Marshall Field Company over the Chicago and North Western Railway tracks; and the Chicago Daily News Building over the Chicago Union Station.

Condominiums and cooperatives

Another form of development is the condominium concept of owning real property. This ancient concept, known since the Roman Empire, has taken on new life since the end of World War II. A *condominium* is the term for a form of real estate ownership whereby an individual acquires a title in fee to an apartment in a multiple dwelling while having a right to participate in the use of common facilities. It is an attempt to make apartment ownership similar to private home ownership. Owners buy and sell freely, subject only to contract arrangement with other owners of condominium apartments. Each owner arranges for his own financing and mortgage with the previous owner. Owners of condominium apartments are subject to real estate taxes and other real property expenses, in addition to fees to maintain common aspects of the building, such as heating, and maintenance of hallways, lobbies, and the exterior of the building. However, unit owners may also deduct state and local real property taxes that are assessed against the unit. And, upon a subsequent sale of the unit, an owner may deduct from gross income up to 60% of any gain from the sale. This could be quite a substantial sum due to the recent rapid appreciation rate of condominium property in certain areas of the country.

The sudden boom in the demand for condominiums and the problems associated with condo conversions, such as tenant displacements and decrease in the availability of rental units, have prompted many municipalities to enact regulations governing conversions. Regulatory methods include prohibition on conversions for a specified period of time, restrictions on tenant displacement and the imposition of a conversion tax on the initial sale. The constitutionality of some of these regulations is still unsettled.

One federal district court judge in Illinois has held that a total moratorium on conversions violates the fundamental right to buy and sell land. In a case in the District of Columbia the D.C. Appeals Court stated that while the City Council could enact a 90-day moratorium on condominium conversions in the face of a serious shortage of rental housing, it could not enforce the moratorium beyond the 90 days without resorting to permanent legislative procedures.

If you are faced with the prospect of a conversion, you may wish to form a tenants' association and seek legal counsel to assist you.

Cooperative apartments

A variation of the condominium approach to owning an apartment is the cooperative building. In a cooperative, a group of people come together to purchase a whole building and allocate the apartments or areas of the building to the respective purchasers in accordance with the financial responsibility of each owner. The usual form of a cooperative involves separate shares or interests in the common facilities and leases of specific apartments. The two types, that is, shares and leases, usually must be transferred together. The owners of the shares then elect a governing board to set policy and rules for the running of the building, and it generally functions as a private, closely held corporation.

An individual who is the owner of a cooperative apartment, however, does not "own" the apartment itself in the usual ownership sense. In this case, ownership is more like being a stockholder in a corporation with a right to possession of an apartment as long as you remain such a stockholder. You can sell your interest in the cooperative, the purchaser being subject to approval of the board of directors (pursuant to the corporate charter and by-laws), and with it goes the right to possession of the apartment allocated to those shares. There are tax advantages to this type of arrangement, because local real estate taxes and interest on a building mortgage are deductible, to the extent applicable, from income tax. Any mortgage is on the whole building and not on the individual apartment in a cooperative, so the corporation and not an individual owner-tenant, makes the arrangements for the mortgage. If you borrow money to buy your cooperative, it is a personal loan and not a real estate loan. However, some states, like New York, where cooperatives are in vogue, have recent statutes allowing loans tied into a specific cooperative apartment.

How do you treat the purchase of shares of stock and a proprietary lease in a cooperative apartment?

In a recent case in the state of New York, the purchaser defaulted because of a downturn in his business conditions and wanted his deposit back, subject to any actual damage. The seller claimed it was like an interest in real property. The court held that the stock certificate and lease were more like personal property, partly on the basis that, without proof of actual damage, forfeiture of a deposit is like a penalty and a penalty is unfair unless clearly required by law.

Condominium board and security

Condos are governed by a Board of Directors according to by-laws of the condo association established at the time of the inception or conversion. If there are security problems in the building such as thefts from the laundry room or muggings in the parking area, does anyone have any responsibility to the owners? The California Supreme Court in a recent case involving an owner who had been raped said that the condo association is held to the same standard of care as though it were a landlord. If they knew of security problems and did nothing, they would be liable. In addition, the individual directors of the condominium board were held personally liable since they knew of hazardous conditions and took no action. The existence of the association could not insulate them from their tortious conduct.

If you are a director of a condominium board you should be sure that the condo association obtains adequate insurance that will cover you in the event of a suit.

Condo building

There have been a number of cases involving the ownership aspects of the condo building. Much of it is in response to the desire to reduce the authority of the condominium board of directors who take action that the owners may not want. In cases in the District of Columbia and Virginia, the condo boards began expensive renovations of their buildings' windows which caused a high assessment on the owners. The owners sued and the courts in both jurisdictions determined that the windows actually belonged to the owners of the individual units, and did not belong to the condominium association.

You need to check your association documents carefully to see what is included in the common elements that belong to the association.

Condo records

A condo owner in Virginia wanted to see the Association's records on the salaries of the staff. When the Association refused he sued. The Virginia Supreme court, in interpreting the State's condominium law, which many states have followed, found for the owner. The Association had argued that privacy issues were involved. The law allows Association records of expenditures to be available to all unit owners. The Association could not exclude salary information by passing a resolution.

Noise

A state appellate court has held that noise may constitute a nuisance if it is unreasonable in its degree. Property owners can have it stopped and also collect damages.

Some landowners in Indiana sued the owners of a nearby property to stop them from letting it be used as a summer camp for high school marching bands. The groups arrived on Sunday afternoons and practiced from 8:00 a.m. to 10:00 p.m. seven days a week. The neighbors claimed they had to keep their doors and windows closed, they could not hear their TV or have a decent conversation. They lost sleep and their property lost value.

The court restricted the bands' playing time to weekdays, 8:00 a.m. to 5:00 p.m., and awarded $600.00 in damages.

"House for Sale" sign cannot be banned

Willingboro township, a Levitt community near Fort Dix, New Jersey, tried to prevent property owners from placing "sale" signs on their lawns. The Town Council noticed a decline in the white population and being interested in stable, racially integrated housing and believing the signs spurred panic, they passed an ordinance banning their use.

The Supreme Court decided that society has an interest in the free flow of commercial information that is neither false or misleading. Therefore, they invalidated the law. The Supreme Court also has struck down an ordinance that banned all signs except "for sale" and "sold" signs from homes and lawns of a wealthy St. Louis suburb. Residents can post signs on their own property.

Can I get my down payment back?

In an ordinary real estate transaction, the down payment on a purchase that is not completed is not refundable to the purchaser unless the contract specifically provides for a refund. This is so even if the seller sustains no damage. For example, when the purchaser does not go through with the deal, the seller may possibly sell to someone else at a higher price, but he can still keep the down payment even though there was no loss to him. If you are making a sizable down payment on a property, or if you have any question with regard to your ability to complete the transaction, it would be advisable to work with your attorney or real estate agent to make sure beforehand that you can recover your down payment should you be forced to change your mind for whatever reason. Sometimes circumstances arise that are out of your control—not being able to sell the house you already own, losing your job, family emergencies. It is best to be prepared for these eventualities.

The rule as it applies to personal property matters, however, is the opposite. The down payment must be refunded (unless the contract provides otherwise) by the seller, but the seller is allowed to show the damages that have been sustained by virtue of the failure of the purchaser to go through with the deal, which damages may be covered by the down payment.

House raffles run afoul of the law

If you find that you are unable to make your mortgage payments due to high interest rates and you fear that you won't be able to sell your house due to a tight real estate market caused by an unstable economy, you should think twice before considering a house raffle as a solution to your problem. Many such contests violate the various state and local gambling laws. If the contest involves selling or advertising name tickets through the mail, you may also be in violation of federal law. In addition, there are many problems in the conveyance of real estate by games of chance. For example, a family in the state of New York discovered that they could not sell a house that they had won in a raffle since they did not have clear title to the house in question. You could wind up with a house you can't live in and one which you can't sell.

Pesticides

Recently, the largest lawn care company in the United States, Chemlawn, has been charged by the New York Attorney General with false and misleading ads about the safety of its pesticides and other substances that it uses. It is also being sued by individuals as well as in a class action. Another lawn care firm, Diamond Shamrock, settled a suit in the state of Virginia for the death of a United States Navy lieutenant, allegedly caused by his exposure to their chemical DACONIL. The pesticide company, Orkin, has been fined $500,000 by a Virginia Court for a fumigation that resulted in the death of a couple. Orkin did not monitor the air in the house and were found negligent about poisonous gas that was trapped in a mattress cover.

Trees
What happens when a tree comes between you and your next door neighbor? Local laws govern the rights and obligations concerning overhanging branches, dead limbs, expanding roots.

Generally, when you own property you own it all the way up and all the way down. If a tree from next door extends into your yard, it's in your space and you can cut the branches or take out the roots, but only to your own property line. This is self help. In many states you can't bring a lawsuit on this issue. The courts say take care of it yourself!

A limited exception is for so called "noxious" trees a neighbor won't remove. Then you can sue to require that he does it. A broader exception applies to dead trees that pose a danger. You can sue to require their removal.

What about trees falling during a storm? A general rule is the property owner whose house is hit by a tree is the one to claim damage on the homeowner policy. Tree removal expenses are covered only when a structure is hit. Otherwise removal is maintenance.

Mortgagee protection
The Truth in Lending Act (discussed in Chapter 19) now will help homeowners who get home improvement loans and consumer financing which targets persons with poor credit but real estate equity. It also will aid seniors who sign up for reverse mortgages.

A reverse mortgage is a way for a senior with a paid up mortgage to live off its equity. A lender pays the homeowner based on the worth of the property either in installments or as in a line of credit. A problem arises when the owner dies or sells the home early on. The fees and interest costs, which reduce the total worth, can be extremely high. Under the new law, all reverse mortgage loan applicants will receive truth in lending disclosures that spell out all risks, such as a projected total cost forecast. There also is a provision for cancellation of the transaction. As for high cost home equity loans for credit purposes, disclosure is required on the annual percentage rate for which the borrower is signing. There's also a cancellation provision even though a loan application has been signed. The law also bans balloon payments (lump sum payoffs) on all high cost mortgages with terms under five years and negative amortization plans that allow buildup of debt by adding unpaid interest into the principal balance.

Beware of telemarketing pitches for lump sum payments to be invested. The service company takes a high commission off the top and may direct you to companies selling bad annuities.

Your personal property

17

Chapter 17
Your personal property rights

As a general rule, the term *"real property"* includes land and buildings. All other forms of property or assets are *"personal property."* If property is movable, it is likely to be considered as personal property. This class includes animals, ships, furniture, merchandise, and the like, as well as such things as stocks, bonds, patents, copyrights, claims for damages, etc. It even includes debts.

This distinction between personal and real property becomes vital in the settlement of estates and the payment of debts, as it is the personal property of a deceased person that is used first in the satisfaction of claims and the payment of funeral and administration expenses.

The same distinction is also important in determining what is included by deeds of real estate and the traditional phrase used in them: "Together with the appurtenances and all the estates and rights of the party of the first part in and to said premises."

The definition of personal property by a typical state statute is: "The words 'personal property' include money, goods, chattels, things in action, and evidences of debt." ("Things in action" means claims or rights that have a monetary value—we shall discuss these items further along in this chapter.)

This definition determined the meaning of a clause in an agreement between a father and his son that, in return for the support and care of the father for the remaining years of his life, the son should have all the personal property of the father at his death.

The contract was made shortly before the entrance of this country into World War I, and the father died a few months after that war ended. One of the things the father owned was a farm. During the period between the execution of the agreement and the death of the father, receipts from farm products reached an unprecedented amount, due to the high food prices of that time. This definition that personal property included money compelled the court to determine adversely the claims of other members of the family that the accumulation of money, since it was derived from the farm, was not personal property and not included in this agreement.

Suing data processing manufacturers

What normally would be workers' compensation claims are turning into claims under the ADA (see discussion in *Civil Rights* chapter) and product liability. Early claims for physical problems from repetitive tasks used to come from assembly line workers, laborers, or butchers. But now there are thousands of cases in ten states filed against data processing manufacturers for repetitive strain or stress injuries or cumulative trauma disorders such as carpal tunnel syndrome. Plaintiffs range from secretaries and supermarket checkers to stock brokers, doctors and hundreds of employees of the New York Times. They are alleging that the manufacturers knew they were putting poorly designed products on the market and failed to notify the consumer.

Cases have gone both ways on liability. IBM has won a number of cases in Minnesota, Missouri, Pennsylvania and New York. But multi-millions were awarded by a jury in Brooklyn to three women who sued Digital Equipment Company. They had been cited for injuries to their own workers in 1989 and then they lost the customer injury case. California has approved a narrow law on repetitive motion injuries. Many companies are adopting "ergonomic" programs on their own by designing tools and jobs to eliminate repetitive injuries.

Is timber personal property?

A landowner in Arkansas contended that a lien on his land for unpaid taxes did not apply to standing timber but solely to the soil—that standing timber was personal property.

The term "land," the court declared, meant not just the land itself but everything that was attached to it "by the process of nature or art." The standing timber was attached to the land and was as much a part of the land as was the soil itself. This is also the case with growing crops, as we shall see later.

On the other hand, a purchaser of land in Georgia claimed ownership of pulp wood cut from his tract months before he took title to the property. But the law holds that timber, when cut down, is personal property and does not pass under a deed of the property. "Anything detached from the realty," said the court, "becomes personal immediately upon being detached therefrom."

Property in its full meaning

The boundary line that courts and legislatures have drawn for the man in the street as a clear distinction between what he can own to the exclusion of all others, and what belongs to everyone to the exclusion of none, often disappears in a fog of uncertainty. In general, we may say that property includes practically all valuable rights—the term relates to every possible interest a person may have, tangible or intangible. For example, a Georgia state court recently held that the right to practice law is a property right.

Is a professional name property?

A name, too, can be property. Two men, whose names had acquired a notable advertising value in radio, assigned to a broadcasting company the exclusive management of their services, their trade names, and their productions, and agreed they would make no contracts with other broadcasting companies.

They then proceeded to make another contract for the publication of their broadcast material under their own names. The court forbade the use by them of either their names or the script, as these rights had been assigned to the broadcasting company, and were property rights belonging to the company and entitled to protection by the court.

In this same category of property rights may be placed the trademarks and trade names of the business world in general.

Franchising

Nearly one-third of our nation's retail trade is conducted through franchise, involving more than forty industries and employing millions of people. McDonald's and Kentucky Fried Chicken are two of the most famous franchise operations in the U.S.

A person who purchases a franchise is known as the franchisee. The person from whom the franchise is purchased is known as the franchiser. The mechanism for accomplishing the purchase of a franchise is known as a franchise agreement.

The franchiser is typically a successful business with a well recognized logo, such as Colonel Sanders. The franchiser will have gone to the expense of making a thorough cost analysis and will have formalized the theory of success. Throughout the franchise agreement, the franchiser agrees to allow the franchisee to use the logo and other ingredients and to provide the franchisee with assistance, training, and expertise in the franchiser's methods. In return for this, the franchisee must compensate the franchiser. Compensation generally involves payment of an initial fee ranging from $5,000 to $50,000 dollars and up. In addition, the franchisee may be required to pay the franchiser a percentage of the profits ranging from one to 15 percent or more of gross sales.

A Federal Trade Commission (FTC) rule requires that the franchise seller provide the potential buyer with a detailed disclosure statement at least 10 days before the agreement to purchase. This document has 20 categories of information required including: the names and addresses of other purchasers; the seller's fully-audited financial statement; the cost to start and maintain the business; and the obligations of the buyer and seller. You should get the seller's promises in writing and consult a lawyer before entering into any franchise agreement.

However, there is another problem you should be aware of and that is the possibility that the company may be merged or sold. A federal appeals court in Ohio ruled that the franchiser is not obligated to tell a franchisee about plans to sell or even to disclose long-term corporate strategy. The case came up in connection with a Burger Chef System, Inc. franchise and the sale of Burger Chef by General Foods to Hardees.

There have been a number of recent developments in the evolution of franchising. Lawsuits based on the negligent acts or omissions of franchisees have caused problems for their franchisers even though franchisees are supposed to be independent contractors. A lot depends on how much control the franchiser has over the franchisee. Dominos paid out multi-millions because of their fast delivery promise when a franchisee's driver injured someone.

Franchisees have gotten a tax break. The U.S. Tax Court said a buyer's fee for an existing franchise which is higher than the seller's original purchase fee can be deductible and won't be considered as goodwill, which is not deductible. The IRS had tried to make the difference non-deductible goodwill.

Iowa law has turned franchise agreements upside down by allowing rewriting of existing contracts to favor franchisees. McDonald's is challenging the law based on the Constitution which says states can't impair contracts. Even if the law is struck down for present agreements, it signals a trend which will include broader rights of sale by franchisees, competing if the franchise ends, and absolute renewal rights.

Patents, trademarks, and copyrights

This area is a specialty in the law, so much so that lawyers are permitted to state that they specialize in this field. The Constitution of the United States provides in Article I, Section 8, Clause 8 that Congress shall have Power

> To promote the Progress of Science and useful Arts, by securing for Limited Times to Authors and Inventors the exclusive Right to their respective Writings and Discoveries;

This covers patents for inventors and copyrights for authors. It does not cover trademarks, the authority for which comes from the power of Congress "to regulate Commerce."

Trademarks and how to register them

A trademark is a name, symbol, sign, or device attached or applied to goods for sale in the market. It serves to distinguish these goods from similar ones made by others, and is a means by which they may be identified with their particular manufacturer or producer.

The courts have based their prohibition of the infringement of trademarks on the ground that the trademark owner has an exclusive property right in the mark. They have also based it on the ground that the public is entitled to protection against fraud by the false representations of unscrupulous merchants or manufacturers seeking to "palm off" on the public their own products as those of another.

Generally any phrase, mark, word, or device that will serve to identify the origin or ownership of the goods to which it is applied may be adopted as a trademark. On the other hand, it can be used only if it will not prejudice the rights of others who may already have established the same or a similar symbol as a trademark. Further, it must not be a word in common or general use which is descriptive of the product.

The Supreme Court has ruled that color alone can uniquely identify a product so companies can register a product's distinctive color as a trademark. A bottle shape (Coke) and a sound (NBC's chimes) have been registered so why not color.

The *Federal Trademark Act*, also known as the *Lanham Act*, provides for the registration of trademarks by owners who have acquired their title by virtue of actual use in interstate commerce. The application for trademark registration must be made to the Commissioner of Patents, be signed by the applicant, and specify the name, domicile, location, and citizenship of the applicant or, in the case of a firm or corporation, the place of business. Further, this application must state the class of merchandise and provide a particular description of the goods comprised in the class for which the trademark is appropriated, and the length of time the mark has been used, as well as a description of the mark itself. The application must be accompanied by a drawing of the trademark, signed by the applicant, and five additional specimens of the mark as actually used and as are required by the Patent Commissioner, together with a fee of $35.

Such a federal trademark when issued has a term of 20 years, provided that during the sixth year an affidavit is filed to the effect that the trademark is in use or explaining its non-use. It may be renewed for additional 20-year terms within the six months prior to expiration by showing of continued use. The renewal fee is $25.

In addition to federal registration, there are state trademark acts and rights at common law for trademarks.

Trademarks are not protected in foreign countries. Anyone doing business overseas must look to that country's laws for registration and steps should be taken quickly to get counsel so that protection can be gained as soon as possible. Eventually for the European Community (EC), there may only be a need to register once under a Community Trademark.

What happens when trademarks conflict?

If it appears that the trademark owner is entitled to registration, the mark is published in the official Patent Office publication. When, however, an application is made for the registration of a trademark that is substantially identical with a trademark already registered for other goods, or has such close similarity to a mark already in use as to be likely to be mistaken for it, it is termed an interference. For the purpose of determining priority rights under such circumstances, any person believing his rights damaged may oppose the registration of the mark by filing a statement of the grounds on which he bases his objections.

If the trademark will not result in confusion, the Commissioner has the duty to grant registration. But where the prior user shows that his interests would be injured by the registration of the mark, then the opposition will be sustained and registration refused.

In court actions for infringement of trademark, the United States Circuit Court of Appeals for the Second Circuit, covering New York, Connecticut, and Vermont, stated that many factors are taken into consideration.

"The prior owner's chance of success is a function of many variables: the strength of his mark, the degree of similarity between the two marks, the proximity of the products, the likelihood that the prior owner will bridge the gap, actual confusion, and the reciprocal of defendant's good faith in adopting its own mark, the quality of defendant's product, and the sophistication of the buyers. Even this extensive catalogue does not exhaust the possibilities—the court may have to take still other variables into account."

Patents

An inventor has a right, separate and distinct from any rights under the Patent Law, not only to use and sell his invention but to deprive the public of its use by keeping his invention a secret. He will be protected by the courts in this right, which we shall discuss further along in this chapter.

Aside from his right in a secret process or invention, any exclusive right to the production and sale of an invention can be secured by an inventor only from the government through letters patent.

The law states that (a) "any new and useful process, machine, manufacture, or composition of matter, or any new and useful improvement thereof," (b) any asexually reproduced "distinct and new variety of plant other than a tuberpropagated plant" and (c) "any new, original or ornamental design for an article of manufacture" can be patented.

No patent can be obtained for any method or device that lacks the essential feature of innovation or discovery. The mere alteration of shape or form is not sufficient.

In an interesting situation reported in the press, an application for a patent to raise sunken ships by pumping polystyrene foam pellets into compartments of the ship's hull in order to displace water until the buoyancy was sufficient to raise the hull, was thwarted by Donald Duck. It seems that a while before in a Donald Duck comic strip a similar method was used but instead of polystyrene it was ping-pong balls. Accordingly, there was nothing novel or original to the basis of a patent.

In relation to designs, the thing to be patented must have the essential feature of novelty. The term for a design patent is at most 14 years, while for a regular patent it is 17 years.

The right to a patent is granted by Congress only to the inventor, and letters patents issued to one who is not the inventor are void. In order for anyone to be the original inventor, he must have conceived it. However, a mere conception of the mind is not an invention, and it does not become an invention or a patentable object until it is represented by some physical implement demonstrating its practical efficiency and utility. The idea must be reduced to a thing. Mere suggestions are not inventions.

The obtaining of a patent is by an application for letters patent to *the Commissioner of Patents* in Washington. The application must be in writing, signed by the inventor or by his representative, and must consist of a petition, specifications, oath, drawings, and a fee of $65.

Patent applications and claims for patents are complex and written in a manner which requires special knowledge. A patent attorney should be consulted in this connection.

The petition must be addressed to the Commissioner of Patents, must be written in English, and must state the name, residence, and post office address of the petitioner. It must designate by title the invention sought to be patented, contain a reference to the specifications for a full disclosure of the invention, and be signed by the applicant or his representative.

The specifications must be a written description of the invention and point out the part or combination which is claimed the discovery. The patent may be assigned by its owner to another person, but a record of the transfer should be promptly filed with the Patent Office. If not filed within three months, the assignment is void against a later innocent assignee who paid something of value.

Literary property and copyright

The exclusive right of printing or otherwise multiplying copies of an intellectual production and publishing and selling them is defined as copyright. This right is available, however, only by virtue of the provisions of the *Copyright Act*. Under the law this exclusive right is granted to the author—not only to make copies and sell them, but to translate, dramatize, perform, represent, or deliver dramatizations in public, or to make records or means for their mechanical reproduction.

Further, under the new copyright law, effective January 1, 1978, an author has a property right in his work before it is published. He will be granted relief by the courts against anyone who either deprives him of that right or, by fraudulently obtaining possession of the results of his work, attempts to use or publish it without his consent.

The first Federal Copyright Act was enacted by Congress in 1790 and the last comprehensive revision was effective as of January 1, 1978. Besides both the published and unpublished works of an author, it now includes books, maps, charts, dramatic and musical compositions, engravings, cuts, prints, photographs and their negatives, paintings, drawings, chromes, statuary, and medals or designs.

Until recently there was no copyright available for a recording because the recording was not considered a work in itself, but rather, only a means of reproduction. But as Marshall McLuhan said, "the Medium becomes the Message," and so "sound recordings" published after February 15, 1972 are protected.

While musical compositions, in order to be copyrighted, must be original, copyright is not confined to productions that are essentially new, but may be extended to any arrangement or adaptation of older compositions. The arrangement for a pianoforte of an orchestral score of an opera is an original composition within the purview of this law. The size of a painting is not material, nor whether any pictorial production is a work of art. Nor will the fact that a work of art is also utilitarian prevent it from being copyrightable.

There is no power under the Constitution by which Congress may grant a perpetual copyright. The term for which this right has been granted prior to January 1, 1978 in the United States had been divided into an original and a renewal period. This provided for a 28-year term with a renewal for a further period of the same length obtained by filing for it in the 28th year of the first term.

The Congress of the United States passed a new comprehensive copyright law effective January 1, 1978. Among other things, it changed the term of copyright for new works to the life of the author plus 50 years in order to be in accord with the European practice, and to extend the copyright term in subsisting works to 75 years. For this reason, there have been extensions of the renewal term for works still protected by the old copyright law so that they would not go into the public domain. The extension applies only to works already in the renewal term. This means that if you are interested in copying without permission a work in the public domain in the United States, you must look to see when it was first copyrighted. As a rule of thumb, if it was in 1905 or before, you are safe to use it. Adding 56 years (28-year first term and 28-year possible renewal term) to 1905 gives us 1961, and the extension did not start until September 19, 1962.

Copyright forms and instructions are available from *the Register of Copyrights, Library of Congress, Washington, D.C.* For registering a work published in the United States, the form must be filled out and sent with two copies of the work and 10 dollars.

Copyright is actually obtained for a published work by the fact of making the work available to the general public and by providing therein a proper copyright notice, which for a book consists of the word "Copyright" or letter "c" in a circle, thus, ©, plus the year of publication and the name of the copyright owner. This notice must be in a prominent place. which for a book is best on the title page or page thereafter.

For a sound recording you use the letter "p" in a circle, thus, ℗.

Copyright registration is a mere formality coming after copyright has been obtained as described.

The letter "c" in a circle, ©, gives protection under the *Universal Copyright Convention* (U.C.C.) which came into force September 16, 1955, to which the United States and now some 60 other countries are parties. A work first published in countries which are not members of the U.C.C. and with which the United States has no treaty, is not protected in the United States.

Before 1973, the U.S. had no treaty with Russia. So Dmitry Shostakovich, the famous composer, had no copyright protection to stop Twentieth Century Fox from using his music in the movie *"Iron Curtain"* about Soviet espionage.

The U.S. now is a member of the Berne Convention for the Protection of Literary and Artistic Works. Any work copyrighted in any country is protected in all other signatory countries, giving broader international protection than under the U.C.C.

With the information highway have come new issues involving technology such as computer software. Conferences are being held to determine how international legal protection can be resolved.

Visual Artists Rights Act/Architectural Works Copyright Protection Act/Computer Software Rental Amendments Act

The Copyright Act has been amended to give more protection in these areas. On visual works of art including art pieces and photos, it applies to those created after 1991 or to those creators who still had title in 1991. It expanded copyright protection to architectural works such as plans and buildings. Software programs now can't be copied for commercial advantage. Video games are exempt.

The right of ownership

The ownership of real or personal property carries rights of exclusion for its possession, use and enjoyment. The U.S. Constitution guarantees this against both the United States and individual states.

Stolen property cannot be transferred

Certificates of railroad stock that were made out in the name of two children were pledged by their guardian with a bank at Pittsfield for a loan on behalf of the children. Three days after the loan was made, the cashier of this bank stole the certificates and pledged them elsewhere as security for a loan that he took out for himself.

Five months later the guardian paid her loan and left, as she supposed, the stock certificates in the custody of the bank. A year later the persons who were holding these certificates as collateral for the cashier's loan sought to transfer them to their own names. This action was refused because of the lack of a court order permitting such a disposition of the stock by the guardian who had endorsed them. They then asked the cashier to obtain the necessary probate decree authorizing the sale of the stock. This he did by forging the petition, and by this fraud the stock was transferred.

Two years later the cashier committed suicide and his theft of the stock certificates was then disclosed. The children were the actual owners of the stock. They had never parted with its ownership. Those who had made the loan to the cashier pleaded their right, but they could not secure ownership from a thief since the thief held no title. "A bona fide purchaser for value from one who has taken property in such a way acquires no title to it," said the court, in its decision decreeing in the children's favor.

Title to stolen money

The rule in most jurisdictions, that the owner of personal property cannot lose title without his consent, has been the law for many years. There is, however, an exception to this rule for currency and negotiable instruments. One who has given value to acquire stolen money or negotiable instruments and who took the stolen property honestly, without knowledge that it was stolen, normally acquires the right to that property.

Stolen bankbook

In a recent case that went to the highest court in the state of New York, a marine engineering officer, returning from a voyage, stayed at a hotel in New York City, and on awakening discovered that his personal effects had been tampered with and that, among other things, his bankbook for an account with a New York City bank had been stolen.

First thing the next morning he appeared at the bank to inform them and discovered that $12,000 had been withdrawn from his account. He sued the bank for the money, and the defense was that the signature had been carefully compared and found virtually identical with the one on file.

Unlike the situation with a negotiable instrument, where those who honor such a signature do so at their own peril and are accountable to the person whose name is forged, in the absence of legislation, the rule for a bankbook is whether the bank was negligent. The jury decided in favor of the depositor, and the bank appealed. The highest court in the state of New York stated that evidence merely of comparison of signatures was not sufficient, and that under the circumstances the withdrawal of $12,000 out of a balance of $12,700 required that the bank establish that they followed prudent banking practices, which would involve additional inquiries, comparison of personal data in its records, etc.

When personal property becomes real property

Property often lies astride the boundary line set by law between real and personal property. A dwelling built on a permanent foundation is unquestionably real property. The material of which the building is constructed was personal property before it was assembled into a building. The point when it ceases to be in one class and becomes property in the other is carefully indicated by the law, but so many special cases arise that special interpretations are often required.

The general rule

The general rule used to determine whether fixtures are a part of the real estate or are chattels is demonstrated in the following case.

The owner of a house bought a heating furnace under an installment contract providing that the seller owned the heater until the price was fully paid. This contract also stated that the heater remained personal property and did not become a part of the house in which it was installed until payment was completed. The owner failed to make the payments not only on this contract but on the mortgage on the house which he owned.

The seller's efforts to recover this heating plant met with the opposition of the owner of the mortgage, who claimed the furnace was a part of the house by which his mortgage was secured. In its decision that the furnace was a part of the real estate and beyond the power of the conditional seller to recover, the court gave three tests by which it could be determined when property thus attached to land or a building becomes real estate and loses its character as personal property.

First, the property must be annexed to the land.

Second, it must have "an appropriate application to the use of purpose of the realty to which it is attached."

Third, the owner must have an actual or apparent intention to make it a permanent part of the realty.

Is it detachable?

A gasoline tank and pump used by a garage were not the property of a purchaser of the land on which they were situated. The removal of the tank, said the court, could be effected by digging, and of the pump by unscrewing a few bolts. The equipment was neither essential nor a permanent part of the garage of which it was an adjunct, as was the heating plant in the previous case.

In general, the rule in the majority of states is that if the attached property (such as heating plant, refrigerator, stove, air conditioner, lighting fixtures, etc.) can be detached from the building without damage to the land or building, then it keeps its character as personal property and does not become real estate by reason of its original installation.

A rather interesting question regarding this issue was recently decided by a New York court. That court ruled that the rights in a cooperative apartment were personal property, not real property, since they were to terminate after a certain number of years. See the chapter on *Real Property*.

Ideas as personal property

Under some circumstances ideas are property, and the owner of an idea is entitled to protection against its exploitation by others. A leading case which established this principle declared that "when an idea, which may be neither patentable nor subject to copyright is more than a mere abstraction, and is reduced to detailed form, and is novel, the law gives effect to a property right in it." Here there is a striking analogy between the ownership of ideas and the ownership of wild animals. Capture an animal in the woods and keep it in a cage—then it is your property and no one but yourself has a right to its possession. Let the animal escape to the woods whence it came, and it again becomes the property of whomever takes it for his own.

Secret ideas or processes which are undisclosed to the public and "know how" withheld in confidence by its possessors are similar in the application of the law. The employees of an organization engaged in chemical research had the exclusive possession and knowledge of secret formulas for production. Some of the employees engaged in the use of these formulas left the company and organized a competing business. Commenting on their use of these secrets, a New York court pointed out the well-established law that property rights exist in secret formulas and former employees who learned them in confidence would be enjoined from their use in competition with the owner. In the absence of a prior agreement to the contrary, an owner of a shop or factory generally owns the right to the use of any discoveries made by his employees while they are working for him. To preserve these property rights, however, the processes and formulas must be kept secret. When a knowledge of them comes into the possession of the general public, the property right evaporates. The right of a person to his ideas as property so long as they are secret or fended from public exploitation by agreements to that end is illustrated by a decision of the highest court of New York State some years ago in an action brought against the Equitable Life Assurance Society for their use of an advertising idea where ownership of the idea was claimed by another. The suit was unsuccessful, for the plaintiff had revealed his idea before making any agreement with the Society.

In this case, the essentials that must exist for an exclusive property right in ideas were outlined as follows: "Without denying that there may be property in an idea or trade system or secret, it is obvious that its originator or proprietor must himself protect it from escape or discovery. If it cannot be sold or negotiated or used without discovery, it would seem proper that some contract should guard or regulate the disclosure. Otherwise it must follow the law of ideas and become the acquisition of whomever receives it."

Courts have ruled that by revealing an idea on a confidential basis the originator does not lose his rights in it.

If you wish to protect a valuable idea, therefore, be sure that it is not disclosed to the prospective user until you have entered into a contract providing for your compensation on its use. An attorney should be consulted immediately, if you have a valuable idea or secret, which another person is using without your permission.

Discoveries and inventions

This same rule of law governs the ownership of discoveries and inventions. A suit was brought to prevent the use of certain inventions in petroleum production by competitors. While the process may not be one entitled to protection as a patent, suggested the court, it may still be entitled to protection as a trade secret.

Facts of great value, like a lost purse on the highway, declared the court, may lie long unnoticed upon the public commons. Hundreds pass them by until one more observant than the rest makes a discovery. The inventor and the discoverer are both entitled to protection, one by the patent law, the other by injunction against the violation of this secrecy by which the owner holds his discovery in captivity. However, protection is given only against those who have learned the secret because of a confidential relationship with its owner. There is no protection against a person who honestly and through independent investigation acquires the same secret.

One of the early decisions in this country was that a "secret art" is property and that a contract can be made that the receiver of any knowledge of this "secret art" will not divulge his information.

Registered mail

One problem is proving you created your idea at the date you claim and showing what was in the idea. One way to do this and keep a record of it, is to enclose a copy of your expressed idea in an envelope and send it to yourself by registered mail. When received, the registered letter is put away in a safe place without breaking the Post Office seals on the envelope. The date on the envelope will show that the content was conceived and at least expressed by that date and the seals will demonstrate that the content was then as you now claim and not a later substitution.

Are crops personal property?

While crops are growing, they are *land*. When they are harvested, they are *personal property*.

Growing crops ordinarily pass with a conveyance of the land. They may, however, be sold separately from the land as may standing timber. A lawsuit was brought in Arkansas against the Western Union Telegraph Company for damages to crops. A levee had been weakened because a hole was dug in it for a pole to hold the wires of the company. As a consequence the riverbank gave way and the overflowing river destroyed the crops in the adjacent fields.

The company's defense was that the destroyed crops were real property and for that reason the lawsuit must be in the county where the land was located. This contention was sustained by the court in holding that the unmatured crops were part of the land.

If a non-owner raises crops

The law relating to the status of crops raised by one who is not an owner of the land was featured in a suit in the state of Washington. Stanfield and Dodge, in possession of land in Chelan County, had raised and harvested a fruit crop which they sold to the Fruit Production Company. In May of that year Harrison had bought this land. While he had never been in actual possession or occupation of the land, he nevertheless gave the Pacific Fruit and Produce Company a chattel mortgage on this growing fruit crop.

In determining the ownership of this crop the court asserted that the owner of the land, when he is not in possession of it and it is cultivated by a stranger, has no right or title to crops harvested before he takes possession; that it makes no difference whether the one growing and harvesting the crops is in possession or is a trespasser.

Can a trespasser own crops?

In the state of Missouri, Claude McCullock raised a seven-acre crop of corn on a large section of land that belonged to other people. McCullock had been a tenant of a former owner, and continued in possession of the land after its sale in February of the year in which he raised and harvested this crop.

When the owner of the land sued him for the value of the corn, the court held that McCullock himself was the owner of the crop. "Where one in possession of land, even as a mere trespasser, cultivates and brings to maturity a crop and severs it from the soil, he thereby becomes the owner of the crop. But if he abandons the possession of the land before the crop is matured and severed from the soil, it then becomes the property of the owner."

Other states, however, have not been as lenient toward such trespassers as was the state of Missouri. In California, for example, all rights which a tenant has to crops that he is raising normally end at the time of the termination of his leasehold. In New York, a trespasser does not have a right to possession of the crops he has raised against any party who was an owner of the property while the crops were being grown. He does have title superior to anyone who acquires the property after the crops have been harvested.

Claims and rights of action

The law, we have seen, classifies property as real and personal—land and the improvements that are a part of the land are real property—all other property is personal. Personal property includes not only things themselves—as money, household goods, wearing apparel—but it also includes the right to the possession of these things. Your wages or salary are personal property. The right you have to wages or salaries that are earned but not paid to you is also personal property. Claims for damages or for anything with a money equivalent are also your property. Claims and demands are known in the law as "chooses in action," or "things in action."

Certificates of deposit—personal property

The will of an Alabama resident contained the following: "I also will to my said wife all other personal property of which I may die seized or possessed except any notes or mortgages that may be payable to me." Part of the property of this man were certificates of deposit of a local bank, amounting to $6,000. (Certificates of deposit are a bank's written statements or acknowledgments of the deposit of specific sums of money.)

His relative claimed these certificates were notes and mortgages which he had excluded in his will from the property he had bequeathed his wife. The court, however, held them to be personal property represented by a right to the collection of the money at their maturity.

Conditional and installment sales

Goods bought and sold in the usual way belong to the buyer when they are delivered to him. The difference between an ordinary sale and a conditional sale is that by a conditional sale the goods do not belong to the buyer until he has paid for them, and the contract for the sale states this. The buyer has possession of the article but the seller owns it. It is his security for the price the buyer has agreed to pay.

If you do not keep up installments

The remedies of the seller when the buyer's payments are not made as agreed are:

(1) the seller may retake the property and end the contract;

(2) he may retake the property, sell it, apply the proceeds of the sale to the amount remaining unpaid and sue for the balance, if any; or

(3) he may bring a lawsuit for the unpaid balance.

What is a chattel mortgage?

A chattel mortgage is a mortgage on personal property. Like the conditional sales agreement, it is often used by a seller to obtain the payment of the purchase price by the buyer.

The following provision or its equivalent will usually be found in chattel mortgages: "For the purpose of securing payment of the amount set forth herein, the mortgagor does hereby grant, bargain, sell and mortgage unto the said mortgagee the above described property, provided that if said mortgagor shall well and truly pay the said sum, then this instrument shall be void, otherwise to remain in full force and effect."

Some states also require that certain specific information be included in all chattel mortgages. Before any such document is prepared, care should be taken to see that it is not unenforceable because of failure to comply with the technical requirements of the jurisdiction in which it is drawn.

Why recording is necessary

A chattel mortgage leaves the legal title with the mortgagor. As a result, it gives the mortgagee only a security title.

Under a *conditional sales agreement*, the seller may retake the goods. Under a chattel mortgage, if he retakes the property, he normally sells it and applies the proceeds of the sale to the unpaid balance and then brings suit for whatever remains unpaid. This unpaid balance may include the costs of reclaiming, storing, and reselling the property.

Care should be taken, when the document creating the chattel mortgage is drawn, to make it clear that it is indeed a chattel mortgage and not a conditional sales contract.

In 1952, a *Uniform Commercial Code* was approved by the National Conference of Commissioners on Uniform State Laws, who work to improve and to simplify the state statutes in various fields. The purpose of this Code was to simplify, clarify, and modernize the laws governing commercial transactions. Over the years, it has been adopted in every state of the Union, and in the Virgin Islands. In New York State, its effective date was September 27, 1964, which made it applicable to all business transactions entered into or occurring after that date. Instruments or agreements, such as chattel mortgages and conditional sales contracts, are now "security agreements."

The statutes in most of the states require that, when security agreements, conditional sales or chattel mortgages are made, the contract or a copy be filed on the public record as directed by the statutes. Unless it is recorded in this way, the seller loses any rights he has to retake possession of his property if it is seized or levied on by others for the buyer's debts.

The place of record is generally the office of the village, town, or county clerk, or the office where deeds and mortgages of real estate are recorded.

What happens when a conditional sales agreement is not recorded is illustrated by a case that occurred in Colorado.

A bond and mortgage company bought $1,000 worth of office furniture under a conditional sales contract, paying $300 down and agreeing to pay the balance in monthly installments of $56.

The landlord of the building the company occupied had inserted a clause in his lease that he had a lien for any unpaid rent on all the tenant's property. The company neglected to pay the furniture merchant and overlooked paying the landlord. The landlord changed the lock on the office door and took the furniture. Thereupon, the furniture merchant sued the landlord for his furniture.

The merchant had failed, however, to put his conditional sales agreement on record. For that reason, as far as the landlord was concerned, the agreement whereby the merchant reserved the right of retaking his goods was void. For his remissness, the merchant, and not the landlord, suffered the loss.

Because of many consumer complaints of advantage being taken by sellers, the law in a number of states is now in a state of flux on the right of sellers to enforce the sales contract. See more on this subject in Chapter 19 on *Loans, Lenders, and Credit.*

One of the problems has been that of the "holder in due course" or the "bona fide purchaser." Suppose you are sold shoddy merchandise under a chattel mortgage periodic payment plan with notes that you signed for payment. When the time comes for you to make a payment, you refuse and stand ready to defend on the ground that the merchandise is almost worthless. However, you find that you are sued on your notes by a bank that acquired the notes by paying your seller for them. You cannot raise the defense against this bona fide purchaser, and so you have the burden of starting a suit against the original sellers if you can find them. Some states like New Jersey are changing this rule and making the bona fide purchaser in this kind of a situation subject to the defenses you would have had against the original sellers.

Another problem is the door-to-door salesman who catches you off-guard and makes a quick sale. In some states, like New York, you now have a period of time to cancel the agreement on more mature and reflective thought.

Cognovit note
The United States Supreme Court recently declared that a "cognovit note" did not violate the provision of the Fourteenth Amendment to the U.S. Constitution which prevents deprivation of property without due process of law.

The cognovit is an ancient legal device by which a debtor consents in advance to the holder's obtaining a judgment without notice of hearing and possibly even with the appearance on the debtor's behalf of an attorney designated by the holder. The idea of it is to permit the holder of a note to obtain a judgment without trial on possible defenses which the signer of the note might assert. It is somewhat similar to a "confession of judgment." The cognovit note goes back to the time of Blackstone and was even mentioned by Charles Dickens in his *Pickwick Papers*. There has been a great deal of critical comment with respect to it because it means that the debtor is waiving the opportunity to raise proper legal questions and defenses against the collection of the note. Some states specifically authorize the cognovit, such as Ohio from which the challenge arose to its constitutionality on which the U.S. Supreme Court ruled. Other states disallow it and some make it a crime to have it signed, for example, Indiana, New Mexico, and Rhode Island. The majority of states, for example, Connecticut, Michigan, and Minnesota, however, regulate its use, and many prohibit the device in small loans and consumer sales, because that is where it has its most objectionable use. The U.S. Supreme Court stated that the use of such a note was not per se unconstitutional, where the facts of the commercial transaction showed that there was a proper use of it. However, the Court indicated that the debtor should still have an opportunity, even if in a separate action, to raise his claims against the creditor. Also, it stated that if there were defenses such as prior payment or mistaken identity, those could be asserted in any event.

Abandonment of property

Personal property is considered to be abandoned when two conditions are satisfied:
(1) the owner intends to abandon the property; and
(2) he actually leaves or throws it away.
Under such circumstances the property belongs to whomever finds it.

Telephone Consumer Protection Act

This new law was passed to help telephone subscribers who do not want to be annoyed by unwanted sales pitches at all hours. The U.S. Federal Communication Commission's regulations implementing the Act restrict the use of autodialers to informational calls, sales calls to consumers with whom there is an existing business relationship and to businesses. You can't be called before 8 a.m. or after 9 p.m. and the telemarketers must identify themselves and give an address and phone number where they can be reached. If after the first call you do not wish to be bothered further, you can get on a do not call list. If they continue to call you can file suit in Small Claims Court for up to $500 per call and for more money for "willful" violations. The law also bans all unsolicited ads to fax machines.

You should keep a record of all calls you receive and stop requests and any calls made thereafter contrary to your stated wishes. This record will assist in any lawsuit.

The Center for the Study of Commercialism in Washington, D.C., sued Citibank in Small Claims Court for unwanted calls. A settlement was negotiated for $750.

If you don't want to sue, you should ask your State Attorney General to bring a civil suit against the telemarketing firm on your behalf.

The care you owe another's property

The kind of care required of someone in the possession of another's personal property has been defined as follows:
(1) *extreme care,* when the use of the property is solely for the benefit of the one to whom it is loaned;

(2) *ordinary care,* when it is for the benefit of both owner and user; and

(3) *nominal care,* with a liability only for gross negligence, when the property is put into the custody of one not the owner solely for the benefit of the owner.

Telemarketing and Consumer Fraud and Abuse Act

It is a start to protecting consumers against telephone scams. It allows state attorneys general to sue telemarketers in federal courts so they can get out of state swindlers. Con artists can't mislead about their product or service. They can be liable for bogus contests and goods never delivered. But many states are enacting stronger laws to register and ban telemarketers, prevent couriers from coming to pick up payments and require written authorization to debit a consumer's bank account for a purchase. Beware of fraud over the phone.

Your responsibility for rented property

Road contractors in Massachusetts rented construction machinery. While this property was in use, they claimed it continually "broke down." On return of the equipment to the owners, parts were found broken, others missing, and the entire machinery was in serious disrepair.

The owner of the machinery, asserted the court, was entitled to the return of his machinery in as good condition as it was when leased to the contractor except for "ordinary wear and tear." When the contractor failed to return it in that condition he became liable for the repairs necessitated by his improper use of the property.

If property in your care is stolen

An old legal adage says that one who has in his custody the property of another is not liable for "thefts, acts of God or the public enemy, or where goods are taken by violence." This old rule has been somewhat modified, but it is still the law—the user of another's personal property is not an insurer against loss by theft or fire.

The owner of an automobile left his car in a garage on a Saturday. Monday morning the car was found overturned in a ditch in a neighboring town.

The garage proprietor, the preceding week, had hired a 16-year-old boy. He had inquired of the boy's former employer and had been told that the boy was "Absolutely O.K. as far as he was concerned. Good worker. No trouble as to dishonesty and would rehire him if he needed help."

This boy and two others had broken into the garage, found the ignition key to the car, and driven it to a nearby town, where they turned it over in a ditch and left it. The next morning they were arrested by the state police.

The garage owner was exonerated of any liability to the car owner for the theft and damage. Saturday he had closed and locked his garage. No one was in the building when he left. The boys had entered by the commission of an act of burglary in forcing open the window. The garage owner was not an insurer of the car, but liable only for the exercise of reasonable and prudent care, which he had used.

Hirer is not an insurer

The owner of a nightclub at Evansville, Wyoming, rented a roulette table, checks, chairs, dice table, "21" table, and other furnishings for the club. Later, the building was destroyed by fire and the rented gambling paraphernalia badly damaged. The court absolved the nightclub owner of any liability, basing its decision on the universally accepted rule that "A hirer is bound only to ordinary or reasonable care."

Goods placed in the care of a person other than their owner require the same care the custodian would exercise over his own property, that is, the ordinary diligence of a prudent person. If he fails to return them, or returns them in a damaged condition, it is his duty to furnish an explanation of what has happened. But if the loss or damage does not arise as a consequence of his negligence, the owner himself must bear the loss.

Power of attorney

To handle your property, or to act for you in other ways, you may appoint an agent orally or in a written document which is signed and notarized. It is preferable to have a power of attorney as an official authorization of your agent.

Any person who is legally capable to act for himself may act as an attorney. Of course this excludes an incompetent or mentally ill person. Children may act as agents, too, provided they have reached the age of discretion.

The person given the power of attorney acts in your place. He has your authority. It is, legally, as though he were you. So, one must be careful that wishes are expressed clearly and narrowly to avoid unexpected results. The authorization should contain all the instructions, performance of one or two acts or many, depending on how you wish the power to be worded. Within these limits, you are liable for the acts performed by the person who holds the document.

Washington, D.C., Maryland and Virginia are among the many jurisdictions which now permit a power of attorney to convey property. This includes sales and mortgages, so borrowers can appoint someone to execute documents on their behalf.

An attorney's power to act for his principal may be revoked by the principal's appropriate giving notice to the attorney. Those persons who are dealing with the attorney should also be notified of the revocation, if the acts defined by the document have not yet been concluded. If you do not notify all concerned in a revocation, you may be responsible for any acts that your attorney may perform honestly under the power originally conveyed to him.

A power of attorney is revoked automatically by the death of his principal, by the conclusion of the acts described in the document, or by the expiration of any limit of time set forth in the document. If the principal is declared incompetent, revocation is also considered automatic. However, you may wish to include in the power of attorney a written statement that it shall not terminate on the disability of the principal.

Proxies

In the conduct of stockholders' meetings in a corporation, every holder of stock has a vote for each of his shares. Often it is difficult for the individual stockholder to attend the meetings personally. In order that his vote can be taken in the election of directors and in other matters requiring the consent of the stockholders, he is permitted to execute a proxy allowing another to represent him and his interests. In other words, a proxy is a power of attorney for the purpose of voting. It may be restricted to one meeting or more. You should read your proxy form very carefully, follow the instructions and be sure you are giving your vote to persons who will represent your wishes at the meeting or as to the policies of the corporation.

Downsizing

Many new terms are in use now for what used to be called layoffs. Now it's downsizing or "reengineering." When companies plan to get leaner in their workforce, they may offer buyouts as an incentive in getting people to retire early. The federal government is using it extensively. However, sometimes employees who ask about buyouts are given misinformation. Then, after they retire, there's a buyout and they don't benefit. Many have sued. Some courts of appeal have ruled that retirees who weren't told of the buyout plans can sue to obtain the benefits. But other federal appeals courts have decided they missed the boat and have no standing. The issue may turn on when a company "seriously" discussed the plan so that when it misinforms or denies, it is violating ERISA (discussed in Chapter 23 on *Insurance*) and the company's fiduciary duties.

If there's employee money in a company pension and benefit plan, there is a very high level requirement of disclosure and not to misrepresent proposed changes.

Truth in hiring

Persons without employment contracts who allegedly are terminated wrongfully usually are not permitted to sue in most states, except for discrimination. Terminations at will generally are still acceptable. (See discussion in Chapter 9, *Civil Rights*.) However, that rule is being modified in many courts for suits based upon employee reliance on promises made by an employer. They are made during recruitment and hiring and are pufferies about the particular work the employee will be doing, the work experience they will get, the company's business prospects or financial stability. If a company has exaggerated its status or fraudulently misled a prospect causing the employee to leave a job, turn down or not seek another job or lose valuable work experience, the terminated or laid off employee can sue and recover substantial damages. This is so even in New York, which has broad restrictions on claims against employers. Cases have been won also in Connecticut, Vermont and Minnesota.

Beware of rent-to-own scams

Items such as appliances, TVs and furniture can be taken home and paid for in installments. The weekly payments may be modest but you should be aware that the interest rate charged can be over 200%, making the cost of the item four or five times its actual cost. And a missed payment causes repossession. Many states grant these purchases exemptions from laws covering installment purchases. California requires disclosure of all fees and the total sales price, but doesn't limit the interest rate. Pennsylvania calls a rent-to-own contract a credit sale rather than a lease arrangement so there is an 18% interest rate cap. Courts in New Jersey, Minnesota and Wisconsin have defined the arrangement also as a credit agreement limiting interest rates.

Taxes

It is said that the only things certain are death and taxes. Taxes are levied by every level of government: federal, state, and local. There are taxes on income, estates, inheritances, autos, and purchases. The statute providing for the tax discusses any deductions, exemptions, times for payment, and other details for compliance. Taxpayers are always complaining about the complicated tax structure and politicians are always advocating simplification. You need to keep good records and consult someone knowledgeable in the field to be sure you are getting all the benefits to which you are entitled and meeting all the requirements of the law. Penalties can be severe.

Since this field is so complicated, only a few topics will be mentioned. The Supreme Court has ruled that punitive damages awarded in personal injury cases are subject to federal income tax. A woman died of toxic shock syndrome from use of tampons. Her family brought a product liability suit against the tampon manufacturer and won not only high actual damages but $10 million in punitive damages, punishment for reprehensible conduct and to deter a future occurrence. The court said the tax law only excluded from taxes compensatory damages received on account of personal injuries or sickness. The Congress also has exempted most punitive damages from the no tax provision.

The *Taxpayer Relief Act of 1997* continues to provide for the deductibility of mortgage loan points under conditions set by the IRS, which must be strictly observed. Points are fees charged by mortgage lenders to increase their annual percentage rate. Each point amounts to one percent of the mortgage. The points paid by a home buyer generally are fully deductible for the tax year in which they are paid. (When you refinance, deductions for points are based on their amortization for the life of the mortgage.) Points paid by the seller also are deductible.

Taxpayers can exclude from taxable income up to $250,000 gained from the sale of a principal residence or $500,000 for married couples filing jointly. The exclusion can be taken once every two years. The once in a lifetime exclusion of $125,000 has been eliminated. However, you will receive no deduction if you sell your house for a loss, a more likely prospect than selling for the high amount.

If you are very wealthy, over the next 10 years the amount of your assets you can transfer without incurring estate taxes will go up to $1 million. However, the increments are a hodge podge ($25,000 in some years, none in some others and $50,000 in 2006). And the rate structure is high for overage, from 37% to 55%. As for gift taxes, the $10,000 a year gift free of tax will now be indexed to inflation. (Spouses can give $20,000 each year tax free.)

If you are receiving long term care at home or in a nursing home, you should consult a tax advisor before filing your return to see about any deductions you may have for uninsured costs, whether the insured payments are taxable income and what tax form must be used to report.

You still can keep all the income you can get from renting out your "dwelling unit" for 14 days or less in any one year. If you own property in a resort area, a place that caters to conventions or one a movie company wants to use, you can rent it out and never even have to report the proceeds on your tax return. "Dwelling units" can be houses, cabins, condo apartments, mobile homes or boats, as long as they have a sleeping space, toilet and cooking facility. Aside from the time factor the only other limit is that you can't write off any rental expenses such as housecleaning.

If you are unable to meet your tax payment deadline because of a Presidentially declared natural disaster, there's no penalty for three months but interest will continue. And starting in 1999, you will be able to pay your taxes using a credit card.

Taxpayers Bill of Rights

The IRS (Internal Revenue Service) is a most unpopular federal agency. People fear and hate it. Some of its tactics and agents hake been exposed in Congressional hearings and there will be overhauls. However, many people are not aware of legislation called the Taxpayer Bill of Rights, which gives taxpayers some protection against arbitrary and capricious action by the IRS. It has been updated and provides, among other things: Suits are allowed for unwarranted collection action with damages collectible up to $1 million. When the taxpayer wins a suit, there is now a presumption the IRS case should not have been brought so the burden is on them to justify themselves or they pay costs including attorney's fees at $110 an hour. The IRS ombudsman (taxpayer advocate) now can require the agency to help the taxpayer. Installment payment plan agreements can't just be terminated by the IRS if the taxpayer falls behind. The agency must notify the payer first about a planned termination, explain why and give 30 days for response before canceling. Notification is required for former or separated spouses if the IRS is going to collect jointly owed back taxes. They can't be blind-sided by a judgment.

Private delivery service of returns and other documents are now allowed, not just using a postmark to verify a date. Time stamps of UPS or Federal Express are acceptable. The IRS now can more easily lift a tax lien on an asset. The IRS is required to notify you annually of overdue taxes to avoid accumulation of interest and contact you within 60 days when it receives a payment it can't match with your account. You can sue anyone who has filed a fraudulent W-2 or Form 1099 causing you tax problems. If the IRS gives you incorrect data in writing which you rely upon to your detriment you owe no penalty. They can't take enforcement action resulting in significant hardship. These and many more rights are now yours. Consult counsel immediately when you have a problem with the IRS.

Read the fine print

Be careful when you sign up for a product or service when it's an advertised special, a "freebie," or part of a contest. Many marketing firms have hidden specific requirements for cancellation, charges just for entering or other complicated disclaimer provisions in small print which you ignore at your peril. L'Eggs pantyhose offered a free pair through a mailer "just for the asking." When it arrived, the package included four other pairs and a bill. The purchaser had unwittingly enrolled in a pantyhose program. She had not read the disclaimer on the back of the mailer. America Online has had a free 50 hour trial offer. But the hard to read print underneath contained a number of qualifiers about time limits and cancellation. A sweepstakes in Florida giving away a car caused thousands who signed up to be responsible for charges for voice mail. The entry form had fine print on the back authorizing the organization sponsor to add a monthly fee to the entrant's phone bill.

If you signed up and don't want to participate, get in touch immediately with the company involved. They are responsive to complaints. If not, write to your state's Attorney General. That office probably heard from others similarly situated and may already be investigating.

Source tax

A federal law now bars states from taxing the pensions of former residents. People who worked in one place but moved after retirement to states that have no state taxes have been taxed by the state where they resided and worked. Many states still have these source taxes but won't be enforcing them now.

Innocent spouse

Most people hurt by faulty joint tax returns are female homemakers who sign the form prepared by their spouse or a tax preparer. If the IRS disallows items or the spouse preparer leaves, the IRS can step in and take the house, bank accounts, whatever. But under certain circumstances the unknowing spouse can claim "innocence" and escape liability. Now 19 states allow the claim if you had no reason to know a deduction wasn't legitimate or that there was some other error. But you will need a lawyer and you should find one with good tax experience.

Damages for wrongful dismissal are taxable

The Third Circuit Court of Appeals in case involving a woman in New Jersey and the Sixth Circuit Court of Appeals in a case involving women employees of the T.V.A. had decided that although awards for settlement of discrimination complaints were based on lost pay, they were damages derived from personal injuries and therefore non-taxable. The I.R.S. had wanted to collect income tax on their discrimination awards. The Supreme Court reversed these lower courts and ruled that Congress wrote Title VII to restore fully taxable wages to discrimination victims.

If you have received an award and didn't pay a tax, you should get counsel on the retroactive application of this decision.

Social Security

This topic is discussed here and in Chapter 23 on *Insurance*. Although almost all jobs in the U.S. are covered by Social Security, there are special rules which apply to some. You should check with your local office if: You work in someone's home doing housecleaning, gardening, babysitting; you are a student and are also employed by your school; you own, operate or work on a farm; you are a member of a religious order (some who have taken a vow of poverty will qualify for a fixed minimum benefit if they first became eligible before 1992); you have a job where you get cash tips; you are an employee of an international organization; or you work outside the U.S. As of January 1984, coverage was extended to all employees of non-profit organizations, and to new U.S. government employees.

- *Credits*
  Before you can qualify for benefits and hospital insurance you need credit for work under Social Security.

- You should check with your local Social Security Office to see what the current requirements are for credits.

- *Retirement benefits*
  Age 65 is when you are eligible for full retirement benefits. But you can start receiving reduced benefits as early as 62, as can your spouse. If your child is under 16 or disabled, receiving Social Security benefits and is in your care, you can receive a spouse's benefits regardless of your age. Divorced spouses generally are eligible at 62 and, under certain conditions, children may be eligible for benefits based on grandparent's earnings.

  U.S. citizens can receive benefits outside the country as can eligible dependents and survivors. Non-citizens should contact the Administration because of differing rules for certain countries.

- *Benefit amounts*
  They are based on your age when you apply and your lifetime earnings on which you paid Social Security taxes. Basic pay you earned from active duty or active duty for training in the military since 1957 is counted. Inactive duty payments have counted as wages beginning on January 1, 1988. Other earnings and income is not used to calculate your benefit. Spousal benefits may depend on earnings after retirement.

- *Survivor benefits*
  As you work and pay Social Security taxes, your family becomes eligible for monthly benefits when you die. They are paid to: Widows or widowers at age 60, at 50 if disabled, or at any age (including those divorced) if they have care of a child under 16 or disabled and who is receiving benefits; unmarried children under 18 (under 19 if in high school) or at any age if disabled; dependent parents who are 62 or older.

- *Disability benefits*

   Based on your age, the work credits needed will vary. But, generally, you need to have paid Social Security taxes for 5 of the 10 years before you became disabled. Also, your disability has to be expected to last for a year or result in death and the condition must be so severe that it prevents you not only from doing your previous work but any kind of substantial work.

- *Benefits*

   They can be reduced by worker's compensation, a disability benefit paid by federal, state, or local government, or a pension based on work not covered by Social Security. The amount your spouse receives also may be reduced, if he or she is receiving a government pension.

   In addition, if you continue to work, there is a limit to the amount you can earn and not have your benefits affected.

   Congress in *the Senior Citizens Freedom to Work Act* increased the amount you can earn if you are 65-69 to $14,500 a year. ($8,280 for retirees 62-64.) By 2002 the limit on earnings will rise to $30,000 a year. At age 70 and older you can earn any amount and not incur a reduction in your Social Security benefit.

Medicare

Medicare is a two-part federal health insurance program for persons 65 or older, people of any age with permanent kidney failure, and certain disabled people. The two parts are Part A for hospital insurance, which pays for inpatient hospital care, skilled nursing facility care, and home health services, and Part B, which is *Supplementary Medical Insurance* covering physician fees, most outpatient hospital services, and other related services. Everyone 65 or older who gets monthly Social Security or Railroad Retirement benefits is eligible for hospital insurance. Others may qualify if they worked long enough in federal employment or to be insured under Social Security or Railroad Retirement. Spouses, widows, widowers, or dependent parents at 65, or disabled spouses and children over 18 may be eligible. Hospital insurance benefits include inpatient care, skilled nursing facility care, and home health care under certain conditions.

Almost anyone who is 65 or older or who is eligible for hospital insurance can enroll for medical insurance. You have to pay a monthly premium for it.

Although Medicare has been of tremendous help, the Congress changed it in recent times to allow for additional coverage (Medigap policies are discussed in Chapter 23 on *Insurance*) as well as options in receiving the services. The program will be called *Medicare Plus Choices*. All beneficiaries continue to pay their monthly premium for Part B. Each year, however, you receive a booklet that explains what plans are available and you must pick or change plans. Each will have to offer all covered Medicare services such as annual mammograms (for all beneficiaries 40 and over), X-rays, radiation treatments, ambulance transportation. Some will be better and some you will have to pay for yourself. Some will follow Medicare's fee schedule and, in others, the charges can be higher.

The plans will be traditional Medicare (a fee for service plan), Medicare HMOs, Medicare Preferred Provider Organizations (medical people join an existing plan), Provider Sponsored Organizations (HMO's organized by local physicians and hospitals), Point of Service, which are HMO's with a fee for service option. In addition, some doctors who don't want to deal with Medicare will be able to write a contract with a patient which allows for an agreed upon fee, presently an illegal arrangement. All the plans will ban "*gag clauses,*" which restrict doctors from advising about more costly treatments and be required to cover emergency room treatments.

If you work past the age of 65, if you and your spouse are between the ages of 65 and 69, and if your employer has 20 or more employees, his group health benefit plan must be offered to you. If you are under that plan, then whatever Medicare plan you decide upon will be your secondary health insurance payer.

As you near the age of 65, you should begin to inquire about government health coverage, your eligibility, enrollment periods, and plan switching options.

Doctors' fees
Because of the changes in Medicare, some doctors will be allowed to charge more if they opt not to participate in Medicare. In the past, for patients covered by Medicare, the law required doctors to file claims for patients and not treat you as a privately paying patient. Also, Medicare paid 80% of approved or reasonable charges of medical bills. Participating doctors agreed to take the approved amounts in full payment. And non-participating doctors could not bill more than 15% above the approved amounts. Doctors violating fee schedules and billings limits could be fined or banned from the program.

Of course, if you choose a Medicare plan that is the same as it has been, your doctor will have to conform. However, for doctors who do not wish to deal with Medicare and write contracts with patients, the 15% overage will not apply. The costs will be yours or those of any private health plan you can carry.

Is there a right to one's privacy?
Many states adopted laws which grant certain protections to individuals to enable them to maintain control over knowledge about them. A magazine once published an unauthorized, somewhat embarrassing, photograph of a female movie personality in connection with a false story regarding a crime which was unrelated to the picture. The photograph was authentic, but it was obtained using devious means. In a suit for damages, the court ruled that the actress' right of privacy had been invaded, since the picture was both unauthorized and could not have been taken in public.

Part-time home health care services
The agency which administers Medicare, the *Health Care Financing Administration* (HCFA), is part of the U.S. Department of Health and Human Services. Recently, it

changed its rules on part-time home health care in response to a federal court decision. Before, part-time services paid by Medicare were limited to a maximum of 28 hours a week but only during four days. If you needed an aide on the fifth, or other day, you were out of luck. The court considered this arbitrary. Now you can spread the hours over seven days.

If your claim for services was rejected under the old rule, make an inquiry immediately to be sure your case is being reviewed.

Nursing homes

Nursing homes have become big business in the last decade. People go there temporarily for recuperation or therapy or they go to live out their lives when family cannot care for them. Before going into a home you need to sign an admissions agreement. You should have an attorney review it beforehand. It can contain many provisions some of which may be illegal, such as their absolving themselves of responsibility for your injury. Or it may burden you with costs you don't want such as charges for laundry.

There are some very good homes but, generally, nursing homes have mixed reputations. Because of horror stories of abuses, Congress, as part of the budget process for the U.S. Department of Health and Human Services, included provisions covering nursing home reform requirements.

You should be aware of some of the rights nursing home residents now have. Of most interest is the freedom from physical or mental abuse and from any restraints not medically required. A graphic example came out in Texas where an 84-year-old woman strangled when she became entangled and suspended on the side of her bed with a vest-like restraint wrapped under her arms and neck. Her children charged the geriatric center, where the mother lived, with negligence. A jury rendered a verdict in favor of the children with a substantial award for damages.

Other requirements that homes must adhere to is giving the resident a right to privacy and confidentiality of their records, more compatible roommates, and more precision in the use of drugs. Many times drugs were used for restraint, to control the patient rather than treat a specific symptom or illness. The law also requires additional training for nurses' aides and a registered nurse on duty at least eight hours daily.

Questions remain about whether stronger state laws will take precedence and exactly what additional legal rights to sue, if any, are given by the federal law. However, if you or your family believe that a relative has not been treated properly, you should consult an attorney without delay. The person in the home may be at risk and is dependent upon caring outsiders for protection and to make the stay bearable.

IRA (Individual Retirement Account)

An IRA generally is a tax deferred savings account set up to provide retirement income although now there's one allowing contributions up to $500 for children's higher education expenses. It requires a *trustee*, which can be a bank or brokerage firm. Anyone younger than $70\frac{1}{2}$ (the time when you generally are required to begin withdrawing IRA money) with working income can contribute $2,250 although now non-working spouses can contribute up to $2,000 to an IRA. You can withdraw money from your IRA account for certain levels of medical expenses without paying a penalty, which usually happens when you withdraw before age $59\frac{1}{2}$. The tax ramifications to IRA's are complicated. You have to be careful about moving your IRA account in a timely manner from one investment to another.

The IRS publishes booklets 575 and 590 which can tell you more about the IRAs available and how to avoid errors and penalties.

Lost property

Chapter 18
Lost property

Lost property, according to the law of many states, is entirely different from property that is mislaid or left behind unintentionally. In general, the courts hold that property is lost when the owner has deprived himself of its possession by accident, neglect, forgetfulness, or by any other means, without any intention to put it down or abandon it. Property is not "lost," however, when its owner voluntarily puts it down somewhere with the intention of picking it up, and afterwards does not remember where he left it. Such property is mislaid or "left."

As you can readily see, to determine where the dividing line lies between "*lost*" and "*mislaid*" property is at times difficult. Basic definitions vary in the laws and decisions of the different states. New York State found the distinction too vague and now treats both lost and mislaid property as "lost" property. Other states still retain the distinction.

A pocketbook was thoughtlessly left by a customer in a barber shop at Lebanon, Tennessee. The barber picked up the pocketbook, spent the money in it, and was arrested and convicted of larceny. Here the pocketbook was not lost, nor was the barber a finder within the meaning of the law. The pocketbook was "left," not "lost," said the court that tried the case. "To lose is not to place or put anything carefully and voluntarily in the place you intended and then forget it—it is casually and involuntarily to part from the possession."

Who owns lost property?

A different situation involving lost property occurred some years ago in Missouri. A wrecking company in Kansas City purchased an old residence and proceeded to demolish it. The demolition work disclosed a metal box that had been concealed in one of the walls. The box held money, gold certificates, and other valuables, with a total value of $12,700. No one knew when or by whom the box had been placed in the wall. In this instance, the box and its contents were unquestionably "lost property." The wrecking company was the tinder and entitled to possession.

An old decision sums up the conditions under which lost personal property belongs to the finder. It says that a stray animal or other thing found, to come under the law providing for the disposal of such things, must appear to be without an owner, like the wild animals that range in the forests or fields. Where the owner is known, the strayed animal or other lost thing cannot properly fall within the legal meaning of the term "lost goods."

The general rule is that the finder has a sufficient right of possession to enable him to retain the property against all but the rightful owner. If there are two or more finders, and the original owner is unknown, those who found the property have equal rights in it.

Anyone to whom the tinder sells the lost property acquires the same rights in it that the finder had; that is, he has a superior title to it against all but the original owner.

Finding money in the street

On a February afternoon, some years ago, H. L. McDonald, walking along Figueroa Street in Los Angeles, found seven $1,000 bills lying on the sidewalk. He proceeded to the Turf Club, changed one of the bills, made a new acquaintance with whom he was soon fast friends, and told him of his find. Leaving this "friend," he returned to the hotel where he lived, shortly after midnight.

A few minutes later there was a knock at the door. A man named Paul Beach entered, showed a detective's badge, and demanded the money McDonald had found. McDonald surrendered four of the $1,000 bills and told Beach there were no more. The next morning Beach called again with a woman companion whom he introduced as the daughter of the man who had lost the $7,000. McDonald gave up the other $3,000. A few days later Beach was arrested for grand larceny and was convicted and sentenced to prison. The money was the legal property of McDonald since the owner was unknown. He had a right to its possession against all except the true owner.

The finder's duty

While the finder of lost property owns what he has found against all but the true owner, the law places on him the duty of making an effort to discover the true owner. The phrase commonly found in the statutes of the different states is that the finder must make a "reasonable effort" to ascertain who the true owner is. What specific efforts the finder shall make, the statutes either leave to his own judgment and determination of what is a reasonable effort, or they specify the procedure that should be followed in attempting to find the original owner. In any case, the person who finds the property must always take reasonable care to see that the property is maintained in adequate condition.

There is sometimes a penalty attached to failure to comply in those states, which require some search for the rightful owner. A typical provision of the law concerning the finder says: "A person who finds lost property under circumstances which give him knowledge or means of inquiring as to the true owner, and who appropriates such property to his own use or to the use of another person who is not entitled thereto without having made every reasonable effort to find the owner and restore the property to him, is guilty of larceny."

A man who was mentally unbalanced, laboring under the delusion that people were trying to take his money from him, drew $600 from a Wisconsin bank, then boarded a train. At a station stop he jumped through the car window, fled along the tracks, and hid the roll of bills under one of the rails. One of those who helped to apprehend the incompetent found this money and retained part of it. He was convicted of larceny.

Who takes charge of mislaid property?

On a public desk in the National Exchange Bank at Albany, New York, a careless depositor left $50 in bills. A man named Loucks picked up the money and gave it to the cashier for safekeeping until it was claimed by the owner. Two years later the money had not been claimed and Loucks demanded its return to him. The bank refused.

Deciding Loucks was not entitled to the money, the court called attention to the distinction made by the law where lost articles have been dropped on a shop floor, left in a public hotel room, or on a railway train. When articles are left in such places under circumstances that suggest that the true owner will later return to claim them, they are not "lost," and the proprietor of the shop or other person in charge is the proper custodian. If the property remains unclaimed, it goes to this custodian.

This right of the person in charge of a place to take custody of, and eventually title to, lost objects found on the premises under his care has its limits. A plain, unmarked, white envelope in which was enclosed $500 in currency was found by the employee of a bank in Toledo, Ohio, on the floor of a lobby near the bank's safe-deposit vaults. She turned the money over to a bank official. Years later she sued the bank for this money.

The money, asserted the court, was found on the floor of an entryway through which passed not only customers of the bank and of the safe-deposit company but those who were customers of neither organization. If a lost object is found in a public or semi-public place, the proprietor, or neighboring proprietor, does not automatically become its custodian on behalf of the true owner. The right of possession and custody of the finder was superior to that of the bank or shopkeeper. This was held to be the law even when the finder is an employee of the owner or proprietor of the premises.

Finders are not always keepers

When lost property is found, it must be taken into custody of the finder. Otherwise the property remains in the public domain, available to the ownership of whoever else claims it.

The steamship *America*, with a cargo of lead, sank in the Mississippi. Between 25 and 30 years later, a wrecker named Brazelton located the wreck. To establish his company's claim, he fastened a buoy to the ship by a weight resting on the submerged hull, postponing the work of raising the vessel until a later period. Before he had taken possession of the property, others took over the wreck and claimed the right to both cargo and ship.

These last claimants were awarded possession of the property under the rule that "To be able to acquire possession of property, two distinct things are required: the intention of possessing it as owner and the corporeal possession of the thing."

Establishing proof of ownership

It is an accepted rule of law that no one can be deprived, without his consent, of lost property that he has found in a place common to all—except by the true owner. However, suppose the true owner does turn up. He indeed has a claim to his property, but he must first establish his right of ownership. When property that is in the possession of someone who is not its real owner cannot be readily identified, as, say, an automobile can by its serial number, it is not always easy for the real owner to establish his right. Often, the property in question is money, and there is no proof of ownership except the circumstances under which it has been lost and found.

A specific case involves World War I veteran Christopher Williams. Mr. Williams was discharged from the United States Army and confined to a hospital as a tuberculosis patient for eight years, until his death. He lived frugally and saved much of the government compensation that he received during these years. Two months before he died he withdrew from the bank $2,112.71 in gold certificates. At the time of his death the hospital authorities took charge of his personal effects, which included an old traveling bag. This bag, along with other personal items, was forwarded to Mr. Williams' home in Kentucky. Four years later the brother of Christopher Williams sold the bag to Virgil Baugh.

After Baugh had used the bag for five years, his wife one day appeared at the bank with $1,040 in gold certificates and asked for their exchange into silver certificates. She explained that she had been cleaning an old traveling bag that her husband owned. After feeling something bulky in the bottom, she investigated and found inside the lining a hole covered with adhesive tape; in it she found $2,140 in $20 and $50 gold certificates. She related the circumstances under which her husband had acquired the bag from Christopher Williams' brother.

The news of the find spread through the town. Then the administrator of the veteran's estate sued to recover the money. The defense was interposed that the money had not actually been identified as Williams' property. However, the evidence of its original ownership was considered by the court as amply establishing the right of the administrator to recover the money.

This incident is typical of many similar cases. Lacking positive identification, the owner's proof of possession must rest on circumstantial evidence, in this case, the story of the road the property traveled from its disappearance until it was found.

Rewards and expenses of finder

If a reward is offered for the recovery of lost property, the finder who returns the property may sue to collect the reward money. The law considers that a contract exists between the original owner and the finder when the lost item is produced in response to an offer of a reward. Most states, however, do not give the finder a lien on the lost property. He must return the item and then sue if the reward is not paid.

When recompense is made

In the early days, in Oregon, two horses were lost while their owner was crossing the plains. A man named Watts found the horses, but the court refused him any allowance for his expenses or labor in their care. The court declared that no principle of law was better settled than that the finder of lost property could claim no recompense for either his services or his expenses except when this had been promised.

This rule sometimes makes the restoration of lost property to the rightful owner a serious burden. Nor does it become less by a principle announced by another judge: "Where one person gratuitously performs an act of kindness for another, the law, as a general rule, does not recognize the right to compensation for such an act."

In some states, however, statutes have been enacted providing for recompense to finders of lost property for expenses they have incurred in its care and return. In Iowa, for example, originally the laws expressly provided that a finder of lost property was entitled to no reward unless the reward was voluntarily given. A later statute is that the finder is entitled to "ten percent upon the value thereof," and may demand that amount as a condition for the return by him of the property to the owner.

Who owns "treasure trove?"

Treasure trove is money or coin, gold, silver, plate, or bullion found hidden in the earth or in a house or other private place. It may also be concealed in other articles, such as bureaus or safes. Its original owner must be unknown, and it must have been hidden or concealed long enough to indicate that the owner is probably dead or impossible to locate. Treasure trove is not lost property in the sense we have been discussing. Under ancient law, when found, it belonged to the king, but if he who had hidden the treasure was afterwards discovered the original owner and not the king was entitled to it. In the United States, the right of the state or federal government to property of this character has seldom or never been claimed. The finder is entitled to such treasure against anyone but the true owner, in the absence of a statute to the contrary. However, much depends on where the treasure is found, and whether it is actually treasure trove or simply lost property. The distinction between these two categories has been maintained in several states, while others now group all lost property under one set of laws.

When buried treasure is found

A celebrated case concerned two boys, Hugh Gray and Darwin Yoran, who found under a plank in a barn two tin cans, each containing $1,000 in currency. They took these cans to the father of one of the boys, who deposited the money with the county treasurer and advertised its finding in the state journal. This advertisement did not turn up the original owner. However, the owner of the barn in which the money had been found sued to obtain it under the lost-property law, claiming it should be his since it was discovered on his property.

The court in this state decided to maintain the separate treasure trove category and declared that the statutes pertaining to lost property did not apply in this case. The money was treasure trove, the court said, since its original owner was unknown and it had been hidden for a long time. It belonged to the boys who had found it.

But a person who merely finds articles of value embedded in the soil, which are not considered treasure trove, acquires no superior title to the property. There is an assumption made by the law that the owner of the property on which the item is found is the rightful owner of the article.

If you lose property in a restaurant

In 1958, New York State enacted the *Lost and Found Property Act*. The Act abolished the old common-law distinctions between "lost property," "mislaid property," "abandoned property" and "treasure trove." It also eliminated distinctions between "public" and "private" premises and set up a procedure for the return of found property to the true owner. It also gave authority to the Police Department to take custody of found property and after a reasonable period of time to distribute it where there was no contest as to who should receive it. The general intent was to give the finder a right superior to everyone but the true owner, regardless of where the property was found. There were certain exceptions. If the finder's presence on the property where something was found by him was a crime (e.g., a thief), the finder's rights, if any, would belong to the person properly in possession of the premises. If a public employee or official found property during the course of his duties, the group or entity for whom he worked was considered the finder, and the same could be the case for an employee who should have delivered the lost property to his employer.

In 1969, an interesting case reached the Court of Appeals, the highest court in the State of New York. A contractor had been employed to remodel the basement of a private home. He found almost $5,000 in small bills concealed under an old wash basin, which had been there for some time. The owners of the house did not know of the money, although they had been in the house for some ten years.

In considering the question of whether the contractor or the house owner should receive the money, the Court reviewed the early common-law rule to the effect that if property was found in a private place, the owner or occupant of the premises where the property was discovered had the right to it, except as against the true owner. But the Court held that the new rule applied, and that it was the finder who now had the right superior to all except the true owner, rather than the owner of the premises.

New York lost and found

The proprietor of a restaurant is not liable for the loss of the coat and hat of a customer unless it is checked with a restaurant employee or the employee acknowledges that he will take care of it in some other manner. The proprietor may also be liable if his employees are negligent in their general care of the property of patrons that is temporarily laid aside.

A customer failed to give his overcoat to the waiter or check it at the coat and hat stand, but hung it on a hook near his table. At the end of his meal he found his coat gone. The restaurant owner was not liable for this loss. He would have been, however, if the overcoat had been given into the custody of a restaurant employee.

Another case involved a restaurant where there was no checking place for patrons; however, along the walls and around four columns in the center of the room were rows of hooks for hanging coats and hats. On the walls were placards saying, "Not Responsible for Hats and Coats." These were not noticed by a customer who hung his overcoat on one of the hooks about two feet from his table. After finishing his meal, he noticed that his coat had disappeared. He sued the restaurant.

If the customer wished to retain control over his overcoat, said the court in deciding the action, the hooks were there for his convenience. On the other hand, if he wished to give it to the exclusive possession of the proprietor and so place on him any liability for its loss, he could have done so. But, he could not keep control of his coat and hold the proprietor of the restaurant liable for its safety. Under the circumstances, the restaurant was not liable.

Situations such as these are commonplace. Proprietors of restaurants, by the very nature of their duties, cannot stand guard over coats and hats hanging unchecked about the room. In most restaurants of any size, checking stands are provided, thus relieving guests of the burden and worry of coats, hats, umbrellas, wraps, and other apparel. By using these facilities, the customer makes the proprietor liable for any loss that occurs through neglect or failure to return the apparel to its owner.

When baggage gets lost

When you travel by air, train, bus, or boat and give your luggage to the agent or check it for delivery at your destination, the carrier to whom you entrusted it is responsible for its delivery. He is liable to you for its value in almost all cases in which it is lost, provided that you do not contribute to its loss. The exceptions to this rule are for losses, which result from such extraordinary incidents as acts of God or from special actions taken by a governmental authority. Even in these exceptional cases, if negligence on the part of the carrier placed the baggage in the position where the loss occurred, the passenger may still be able to recover.

A woman checked her bag and its contents with a bus agent. When she reached the end of her journey, the bag was missing. If the passenger has control of baggage to the exclusion of the carrier, said the court that heard her case, then the railway or bus company is not liable for the loss. But when a passenger delivers a bag or suitcase to a bus agent, as in this instance, the Bus Company and not the passenger must bear the loss.

Custody of baggage determines liability

The baggage delivered before a passenger bought his ticket comes under the same rule of law with the same liability of the carrier, unless the carrier lets the passenger know of special liability limitations, such as the fact that it will not become responsible for the baggage until the passenger pays his fare. A passenger normally has the right to deliver his baggage to a bus or railroad in order that he may have a reasonable time before the departure of the train or plane, or before the sailing of a boat, for obtaining a ticket. From the time the luggage is delivered to the carrier, the responsibility for its safety no longer belongs to the passenger.

The owner of a trunk reserved space on a train from Detroit to Cleveland and left it with the railway baggage agent about six hours before the time of departure. An hour after he left this luggage with the railroad, it disappeared. For the loss of the trunk and its content, the railroad was held liable in the suit brought by the traveler for its value.

On the other hand, if the owner of baggage does not deliver it to the carrier but retains it in his custody, he cannot hold the bus or railroad liable for his loss. A woman boarded a bus at Pulaski, Tennessee, for Birmingham, Alabama. She had with her a bag which she left hanging from an arm of the seat. Later she discovered it was missing. The court held she was not entitled to recover for this loss from the bus company.

In another lost-baggage incident, the bus driver requested the passengers to leave the bus, saying he would hand them their luggage and asking that each passenger identify his bag as it was handed out. When almost all the passengers received their baggage, one woman was offered a bag not her own—her bag had disappeared.

The court, deciding in her favor, pointed out that, if the driver asked the passengers to leave the bus and to let him distribute their luggage, he assumed control of it and the company became responsible for any loss.

Traveling on different trains

When baggage is checked for a trip through and over connecting railroad or bus lines and is lost, it is impossible for the owner to know by which bus or railway company the baggage was lost. Under these circumstances, the owner of the baggage can always seek recovery from his loss from the first carrier. Under the law, the initial carrier, the first bus or railway line on which the owner travels—the one to which the baggage is delivered at the beginning of the journey—is liable for any loss of baggage that may occur on the trip, regardless of any different or connecting railway or bus lines over which the traveler may proceed. The first carrier sells the passenger a through ticket and checks the passenger's luggage to his destination and, irrespective of where the loss occurs, it is liable for the passenger's loss.

How liability for loss of baggage may be limited

It is a general rule that a railroad, airline, or bus company may limit its liability for a failure to perform its contract for the safe transportation of a passenger's luggage. This limitation of liability for the loss of luggage is stated on the baggage receipt. An extra charge is made when baggage is valued at an unusual amount or at a greater value than a specified sum. If it is not paid, the carrier's liability for loss is limited to the stated maximum.

This limitation for liability, however, cannot be made by the bus or railroad except with the consent of the passenger. While the courts have in some instances held that the liability for loss may be limited by a general notice—on the baggage receipt, for example—that notice nevertheless must be brought to the attention of the passenger.

Are hotels liable for lost or stolen property?

Many jurisdictions hold a hotel proprietor responsible for the safekeeping of the goods of his guests. They make him almost the insurer of the baggage of those who stay at his hotel, unless the property is lost by an extraordinary incident, such as an act of God, or by the negligence of the guest himself.

The liability is based on the right of the hotel proprietor to charge for the accommodations of the guest. It is one aspect of those accommodations. Jurisdictions which apply this liability feel that whoever stays at a hotel and pays for a room is entitled to this protection of his property.

This rule originated long ago when the roads and country were infested by thieves and highwaymen. In those times, the innkeepers, frequently in collusion with the thieves, would set traps for unsuspecting wayfarers. By establishing this liability, the courts gave protection to travelers, who, being unfamiliar with the neighborhood, were not in a position to judge the character of the innkeeper from whom they sought lodging.

In other jurisdictions, a hotel owner is only liable for losses if he failed to exercise "adequate" care of the property of his guests. While these jurisdictions demand that less precaution be taken by the proprietor, they will still require that he be extremely careful with the property of his guests before absolving him of liability for any loss.

A sign, displayed either in the room of the guest or in public places about the hotel and which states that the establishment will only be responsible for valuables that are checked with it, may be adequate notice in all jurisdictions to relieve the proprietor of liability for the loss of all valuables that are not checked.

Regulations regarding the depositing of valuables with the proprietor for safekeeping do not apply to the clothing and articles which guests normally use daily, nor do they apply to money in reasonable amounts needed for ordinary expenses. These would normally not be checked and the proprietor may, therefore, still be responsible for them.

Regardless of whether the hotel owner is held to be responsible for a high standard of care or just adequate care, there may be statutory limits of liability.

Who is liable for parking lot losses?

An automobile owner, when he leaves his car in a parking lot, should always read the stub he receives for the return of his car. Frequently, these stubs carry printed notice of limitations to the liability the proprietor assumes in the care of the car left in his custody.

On one such stub was printed, "Parking Contract. Read it. We are not responsible for the car, its accessories, or contents while parked in our lot. No employee has any authority to vary or increase our liability. Additional parking charge begins at 7 A.M. No attendant on duty after 6 PM."

The car owner who had received this stub in the morning returned for his car after six o'clock that evening. He could find no one on duty at the parking lot, and his car was gone. He had paid the charges in advance, and at the request of the parking lot attendant had left the keys of the automobile in the ignition switch so that the car might be moved for the convenience of the attendant.

The court held, in the suit brought by the car owner to recover his loss, that when the owner left the ignition key with the attendant, at the latter's request, the proprietor of the lot assumed the responsibility of taking the same care of this car that a reasonably careful man would take in the care of his own automobile. Since he had failed to do so, he had to make good the loss of the car.

The keys decide the responsibility.

The law is different, however, when the owner of a car pays the parking fee and leaves his car in whatever place is designated, taking his keys away with him. In such a case the parking lot proprietor is not liable for the loss of the car by theft. The reason for this is that the owner of the car has the custody of his car when he enters the parking lot, and by retaining the keys he never surrenders possession of the car to the lot proprietor.

There are exceptions to this rule, as the following case shows. A car owner left his car in a parking lot. This lot was about 200 feet square, enclosed by an eight-foot wooden fence that had but one exit. There was an attendant on duty 24 hours a day. The car was gone when its owner called for it. The car owner, the court held, was entitled to recover the value of the car irrespective of whether or not he had left his keys. He had a right to expect, from the equipment of the lot, that his car would receive the care and watchfulness he was led to believe he was paying for. There is, the court declared, an implied obligation on the part of a parking lot proprietor to keep safely and return the property which he has taken into his custody, except when the property is lost or damaged without negligence on his part, as from a disastrous fire.

As you can see, the resolution of such a case depends, to a large extent, upon the facts of the case. Not all courts, however, will view the same facts in the same way. The interpretation of each case will vary from jurisdiction to jurisdiction. To simplify the rule of law governing the responsibility for the safekeeping of an automobile in a parking lot, however, you should understand this premise: the liability follows the keys. If you give your car keys to the parking lot employee, then the parking lot proprietor is liable for the safekeeping of your vehicle. If, on the other hand, you keep the keys yourself, you assume the risk, unless you can show negligence on the part of the parking lot owner or his employee.

Loans, lenders, and credit

19

Chapter 19
Loans, lenders, and credit

Most people do not adhere to Shakespeare's admonition "neither a borrower or a lender be." We borrow from friends and family, We borrow from banks or other institutions such as credit unions and S & L's, who have recovered from their debacle. People borrow from companies whose only purpose is lending, such as loan companies and pawnbrokers. Foolish people borrow from loan sharks and suffer the consequences.

However, from whatever source, you need to know what your borrowing will cost you. Interest rates vary, the way it is figured can be complicated and different laws apply.

Usury is the charging of a rate of interest higher than the law allows. The usual rate of interest charged on an ordinary loan for every $100 borrowed varies from state to state. The maximum rate is fixed by state law. A lower rate may be agreed upon between the borrower and the lender. In the case of pawnbrokers and money-lenders, however, a part of the transaction is the pledge of jewelry, household goods, and personal property, and it is in transactions of this character that a greater rate of interest is permitted by law.

Banks
In the case of banks or savings and loan associations, loans may be made on salaries or wages for any amount that the earning ability of the borrower justifies. In many jurisdictions, it is illegal to assign, as security for a loan, any wages that are to be earned in the future.

The interest rate varies depending upon the credit rating of the borrower. That amount is often deducted at the time the loan is made. For example, on a loan of $100 for a year with interest at the rate of 6% per year, the borrower receives $94 and at the end of the year pays the bank back $100. Thus, the actual rate is greater than the stated annual rate of 6% since the interest is actually being paid on a loan of only $94.

Loan companies
The interest rates charged by loan companies and pawn brokers vary in the different states and with the size of the loans. You should check very carefully before finalizing any loan agreement and do some comparison shopping. Interest rates change periodically depending on what the Federal Reserve Board does, what the economy is like, and whether inflation is up or down.

Mortgage contracts are complicated documents. Sometimes there are clauses such as *escalator rate, variable rate, adjustable rate*, which can affect the interest to be paid and your ability to meet your monthly budget. Before entering into any loan agreement which might have a long term effect on your home ownership you should seek legal advice.

Fair Debt Collection Practices Act
This Act was passed in 1977 to stop debt collectors from using abusive and deceptive tactics to collect overdue bills. The Federal Trade Commission (FTC) oversees its

enforcement. The Act covers collection agencies and collection attorneys used by creditors when they cannot collect a debt. The Act exempts creditors who have their own in-house collection department. State laws govern them and many states have limited or no coverage of them.

Although debts should be paid in a timely manner, collection agencies are not allowed to harass debtors, pose as lawyers, or make obscene calls to encourage payment. The law gives a debtor 30 days to respond to a request for payment, forbids calls before 8 a.m. and after 9 p.m. and prohibits collectors from threatening action they do not intend or are unlikely to carry out, such as having the debtors arrested.

If you are being harassed, you should notify your State Attorney General or the FTC. You also should consult legal counsel if you believe the collection tactics were too extreme.

Credit Bureaus

Credit Bureaus develop credit reports. There are 3 major credit reporting companies, *Equifax, TRW* and *Trans Union*. These companies collect and compile information about your business transactions. It comes from banks, stores, car dealers, everyone with whom you have a credit card and payment history. Their reports can help you obtain credit or they can hurt you, particularly when they contain errors. Congress has made getting errors corrected easier for consumers.

In the past, under the *Fair Credit Reporting Act*, consumers had rights to information. But many times the practice didn't comport to the paper requirement. Now the law has been strengthened. Credit bureaus must have toll free numbers with live people answering your queries. They must investigate your complaints within 30 days and notify you of the result. They must provide you with a free copy of your credit report if you have had any of broad range of adverse consequences as to credit. They also must make the reports easier to understand and give you most data about you, except they do not have to give you what are called "risk scores". They are what banks and stores use to gauge how good a credit risk you are. You also must be told who has received a copy of your report and show all inquiries received.

The new law also governs actions by the users of the reports, including any employer, who must ask your permission first to obtain it, and people who provide the information. They can be liable for damages if they don't correct mistakes.

If you aren't getting a free report, credit bureaus can't charge for a copy of a report more than what a state law says can be charged or if a state doesn't state a charge, then no more than $8.00. You should assure yourself that your credit report is accurate. Call *Equifax* at 1-800-685-1111, *TRW* 1-800-682-7654, or *Trans Union* 1-312-408-1050 to see which company has your file and what it says.

Debit card

These cards are also known as check cards. They are used instead of checks, (so no ID is required) instead of money, (so less cash is needed) and instead of traditional credit cards (so no interest or late payment fines attach). However, balancing the benefits is the risk that theft of this card could mean a total depletion of your bank account. Losses from credit card thefts are capped at $50. For debit cards it goes to $500 if reported past 2 days and unlimited if not reported for 50 days. You can't stop payment on a check card. And after a report and while an investigation goes on, your account is still out of what the thief debited. You may like their convenience but be aware of the downside.

Government agency contracts

Veterans Administration and Federal Housing Administration insured mortgages do not contain escalator clauses.

Small loans

These are loans for under a specified amount, usually less than $1,000, which are strictly controlled by statute. They carry a fixed rate of interest, and some states provide that the interest need not be payable in advance. The statutes are aimed at protecting borrowers of small sums who may not fully appreciate all of the intricacies in the world of finance.

The lender must be licensed and must deliver to the borrower at the time of the loan a statement showing in clear terms the amount and date of the loan and the time of maturity, the nature of the security, if any, the name and address of the borrower and the lender, and the rate of interest charged. The borrower must receive receipts for all payments which must indicate the amount applied to interest and any of the money that is being applied to reduce the principal. The receipt must also show how much of the loan remains unpaid. Some small-loan statutes will not allow a lender to have more than one contract of indebtedness with the same person or with a husband and wife together.

Fees in addition

Some statutes allow the lender to charge fees over and above the loan, such as notary fees and recording fees of the security for the loan. But these additions are very few in order not to overburden the debtor.

What about insurance?

Sometimes a lender will require that a borrower, before getting the loan, purchase insurance as security for the loan. However, if it is not reasonably necessary, then the loan can be considered usurious, since adding the insurance premium on to the payments causes the interest rate to be higher than allowed by law. What makes the insurance unnecessary is that the borrower already has assets exceeding the amount of the loan.

Some lenders say that they will procure insurance for the borrower, charge the borrower for it, but then fail to buy the insurance policy. These loans are also considered usurious.

Attorneys' fees

Attorneys' fees incurred by a lender through a delay by the borrower in making his payments are often made an additional charge. This method is seized upon by some money-lenders as a ready means for securing a greater return on loans than the interest which the law allows. There may actually be no attorney involved, or a greater charge made than the attorneys' fee requires. Statutes have been enacted to control dishonesty in fixing this charge on loans.

A small-loan note given in New Jersey contained a clause that on the entry of judgment there should be included reasonable costs including attorneys' fees of $15 plus 15 percent of the amount of the judgment. The borrower challenged these fees.

The statute in New Jersey, which is typical of laws of this kind, says: "In addition to the interest herein provided for, no further or other charge or amount for any examination, service, brokerage, commission, expense, fee, or bonus . . . shall be directly or indirectly charged . bonus . . . except on actual sale of the security in foreclosure proceedings or upon the entry of judgment." The right of the money-lender in this state to additional charges was confirmed by the court with these words: "The statute itself puts no limit to either the amount or character of the charges upon the entry of judgment."

The lenders here had scrupulously followed the provisions of the statute for no charge in addition to the note and interest until the entry of judgment. In other instances in this state, these additional charges were made on the default of the debtor irrespective of suit or the entry of judgment. The penalty for this violation of the statute was the loss by the money-lender of the money he had loaned.

Collection charges

Another incident that is fairly common in connection with this type of transaction occurred in Louisiana. The Unity Plan Finance Company, a small-loan organization in Louisiana, had inserted a special clause in the notes they issued. It said that, should the borrower fail in making his payments promptly as agreed, he must pay the company, as liquidated damages, five cents for each dollar in arrears. This was "to cover the cost of collection without employment of attorney."

The Louisiana courts held that if this additional amount, together with the interest payable by the borrower, exceeded the $3\frac{1}{2}\%$ allowed by the statute, the money-lender could not recover his loan. However, when such additional charges represent attorneys' fees paid for the bringing of suit and the entry of judgment arising from the borrower's default in payment, the rule is that such a stipulation is valid and enforceable.

But when these charges are made before suit is brought, they are a violation of the statute if the additional charges and interest exceed the interest rate allowed by law.

However, the courts in Pennsylvania, Connecticut, and Massachusetts have determined that their Small Loan Acts prohibit the charging of attorneys' fees as well as of other charges or fees.

Other loans

Many people borrow money on personal property, by means of chattel mortgages, as well as on real estate. Insurance policies are often made the basis of a loan for the policyholder. These subjects are discussed elsewhere throughout this book, and you should consult the table of contents under the appropriate topic, such as *Your Personal Property Rights* or *What You Should Know About Insurance*.

Credit cards, plastic money

Credit cards became a way of life in the United States in the 1960s and since then, personal debt has soared. But, buying on credit has helped to stimulate the economy and cause business expansion. There is no problem when persons with cards are able to repay on their purchases. But, when a recession comes along, people lose jobs or cut back on spending, and they are not able to meet their credit card obligations. Many credit cards are issued by banks; bad credit risks can hurt their standing.

Anyone who has a credit card now knows more about their obligations and rights than they did before laws were passed creating greater consumer awareness. The first one is called the *Consumer Credit Protection Act,* or the *Truth in Lending Act.* That Act required, among other things, disclosure of credit terms in almost every type of consumer transaction, including disclosure of credit terms in advertising. All credit card companies had to make you aware of all charges connected with your purchases using their card. The Act also dealt with extortion-type credit transactions. Most states have set ceilings on the maximum interest rate that can be charged on credit transactions. The Act also limited the garnishment (which is the withholding of a portion of an individual's salary to pay a debt) of wages.

Because of that law, you now know that if you lose your card or if it is stolen, you must take certain steps to report it and limit your liability for unauthorized use. Generally, your total liability is $50.00 per card if the unauthorized use occurred before you notified the company of the loss or theft. You are not liable for anything after notification. There are heavy criminal penalties for the fraudulent use of credit cards.

What the Act did not do was to require that all the information given to consumers be understandable in layman's language. There were so many interpretations of the Truth in Lending Act that disclosure forms were lengthy and complex and barely comprehensible to the average consumer. So a new law was passed called *Truth in Lending Simplification and Reform Act.* All forms had to be made clearer.

Thereafter, the Federal Reserve Board, which governs the banks and their activities, adopted regulations that required credit card issuers to disclose their interest rates, annual fees, monthly fees, any grace periods for repayment, and other terms in a chart on the application used to sign up customers. Once the Truth in Lending Law was passed, all credit card companies could no longer just send out cards. They had to receive a request from you, and the data you needed to decide whether you wanted that particular card could be printed on your application. The Federal Reserve Board's rules applied to all cards such as *Visa, Master-Card,* and *Discover*, all department store cards, and to charge cards such as American Express.

Problems remain, however, and card comparisons are difficult. Some cards require full payment each month; others have high interest rates, but may not charge an annual fee; some give insurance protection; some have no grace period, assessing interest as an item is purchased; some bank cards require you maintain a checking account with high monthly service charges; some offer rebates on purchases, but have higher interest rates. Some of these requirements or benefits are done in combination. The consumer must always be on the alert.

Late fees on credit cards

With every mail delivery someone somewhere is being solicited by a bank to apply for a credit card. But before signing up you should be very careful to check to see where the issuing bank has been chartered to do business. A Supreme Court ruling can impact on you if you are late in repaying your charges. You not only have to pay interest at the rate allowed by law but the Court said banks also can charge you whatever late payment fee is allowed in their home state. Most of the credit card issuers operate out of South Dakota or Delaware, which do not limit the amount the lender can charge.

Late fees may not seem like much each time, usually $15 a cycle, but they add up. Citibank charges $15 every 15 days after the due date. *Discover* charges $20 for every 20 days late. Some banks are more liberal like *AT&T Universal* and *First USA*. So if you expect you may not pay on time, shop around for the least disadvantageous late fee.

Credit contracts sold

Many times a retailer will extend credit to a purchaser and then sell that credit contract to a finance company, thereby absolving himself from any further responsibility to the customer. The customer then must pay the finance company, and will be forced to continue paying even if the product or services is defective or inadequate. Of course the finance company does not service the item, and the customer may be left holding the bag. Before you buy any item on credit, especially one that will need to be repaired from time to time, you should ascertain what provision the retailer makes for repairs. It may be better to do without the item than to be taken in by an easy credit seller. (See more on this in Chapter 17 on *Your Personal Property Rights*.)

Holder in due course

A legal doctrine known as the "*holder in due course doctrine*" allows a finance company to take over your installment sales contract without taking over the responsibility of correcting any defect on your purchase. For example, if you buy a used car from a dealer on the installment plan, he can immediately turn your note over to a finance company. If your car is defective and you have the dealer's guarantee, you are still required to pay the finance company.

In light of these abuses, many states, including New Jersey, Connecticut, Massachusetts, Utah, and Vermont, have eliminated the holder in due course for the home improvement industry, if not for all goods. The Consumer Credit Code, described above, prohibits the use of negotiable promissory notes.

Debt consolidation agencies

What happens when you get in over your head in charges, credits, loans? Many agencies have advertised themselves as the solution to debtors' problems. These agencies are also called debt consolidators, managers, liquidators, poolers, pro-rators.

They claim that they will pool all your debts and, with a small regular payment made in your behalf to your creditors, pay off your obligations over a stated period of time.

At present, there are 21 states that outlaw these agencies, and many cities do also. These states include: Arkansas, Delaware, Florida, Georgia, Kansas, Maine, Massachusetts, Missouri, New Jersey, New Mexico, New York, North Carolina, Ohio, Oklahoma, Pennsylvania, Rhode Island, South Carolina, Texas, Virginia, West Virginia, and Wyoming. A number of states regulate the business dealings of these agencies, and many state legislatures are considering their prohibition.

Before you sign any agreement with a debt consolidation agency, you should be fully apprised of all their charges, how much they will be taking as a fee and how much of your payments will go to your creditors, and how able they are to deal with your creditors and the long-term progress of your debt reduction. You should also check with your local Better Business Bureau for any information they may have on the company. They may be able to tell you whether the people you owe will deal with such a company.

Repossession

Most states allow a seller to sue for a deficiency judgment even though the deficiency may be small, with the result that after all expenses are included the costs may be substantially greater than the original purchase price and, in addition, the property is taken away from you. An example of this is where a finance company repossesses a car after the buyer had paid almost the total purchase price, say, $2,000 on a $2,500 car. The finance company then resells the car to the original dealer for $400, and the buyer still must pay the unpaid balance even though an open negotiated sale of the car may have netted close to $1,000.

If ever you suffer a repossession, be certain to send the finance company a certified or registered letter that requests its representative to use his best efforts to get a fair price. If possible, attend the sale, with a friend or a lawyer for support.

Garnishment

This is a means used by creditors to obtain repayment of debts. A creditor will make a claim on the debtor's property that may be in the hands of a third party, or on monies owed by a third party to the debtor. Usually it is used to reach unpaid wages of an employee who is in debt. A creditor garnishees, or causes a summons to be issued to, an employer ordering him to pay to the creditor some of the wages owed the debtor. Needless to say, this creates ill feeling on the job, since it is a nuisance for an employer to make out two paychecks. Also, it lets the employer know how much in debt his employee is, and, unfortunately, this can sometimes lead to the employee being fired.

The states have laws that regulate the amount of money that can be garnisheed. These laws differ from state to state. In Arizona, the law permits the garnishment of 100% of both a husband's and a wife's wages. But since this means that there is then no income left for normal living expenses, the debtor can petition the court and have 50% of his salary paid to him. Pennsylvania and Texas exempt all wages from garnishment; Florida exempts the wages of the head of the family; Illinois exempts 85% of wages; New York exempts 90% of wages; Wisconsin exempts 60% or a maximum of $100. If there are dependents, the exemption cannot exceed 75% of all family income; Kentucky exempts a maximum of $67.50 a month; New Hampshire exempts $20 a week; Iowa exempts $35 a week plus $3 for each dependent.

Workers benefit plans
The Supreme Court recently ruled that creditors may garnish benefits owed to workers in private plans regulated by federal labor laws. These include health, vacation and job training benefits. Any state law barring garnishment, such as the law in the Georgia case in the Supreme Court, is preempted by the federal law permitting it.

Being in debt is a hard enough row to hoe. But having your salary garnisheed does indeed make life difficult. Sometimes it is possible to work out a satisfactory repayment plan with your creditors. However, be very careful of the agreement that you sign to be sure you will not be paying back more than you owe. Also, on occasion, creditors will print up their own summonses and not file them with the court; the court, therefore, does not exercise its protective control of the garnishment process. If your wages are being garnisheed, it will pay you to see someone at your local Legal Aid Society to be sure that everything is in order.

Can a wife garnishee her husband's pension?
Some states, for example, Pennsylvania, have declared that pension funds are free and exempt from claims of creditors. But is a wife who has a valid support agreement a creditor? Some states will not allow a wife to attach her husband's pension, but others say that a wife must not become a public charge and that if the husband has pension rights, he can be made to exercise them and obtain the cash surrender value of the plan in order to meet the wife's support needs.

Federal employees
The law on garnishment of the retirement monies of federal, military and District of Columbia employees is mentioned briefly in Chapter 2 on *Divorce*. In addition, a recent law now also allows garnishment of the salaries of federal employees including Members of Congress, the military and the Postal Service, to pay for debts owed landlords and other creditors as ordered by the Court. Twenty-five percent of the worker's disposable earnings will be withheld for this purpose. The only exception will be for those employees in states that prohibit garnishment.

What is a co-maker?

Sometimes a lending organization requires an endorsement of a borrower's note by a person who knows the borrower. Before you become an endorser or co-maker of such a note, consider your responsibility. Borrower and co-maker are identical in the liability they assume for the payment of the loan. The co-maker signs the note and the borrower signs the note. The lender may demand and collect from either or both.

Time limitations on recovery

In every instance where there is the right to bring a suit for the enforcement of a remedy, the collection of money, the recovery of damages, or where there is any other claim or cause of action, the law prescribes a period of time within which such a suit must be brought. This is called a statute of limitation. The object of these laws is to prevent an unscrupulous person, long after the records and recollection of the transaction are lost and forgotten, from bringing a lawsuit that either would be impossible to defend adequately or would not be susceptible of a fair decision. These laws do not extinguish the claim. After the collection of a loan of money is barred by the statute of limitations, you may still owe the money, but the law prevents the lender from collecting by bringing a suit.

The periods of time allowed for bringing suits differ, both in different states and in different transactions. Actions for money loaned or other simple contract debts are ordinarily barred after the expiration of six years from the time the action could be instituted.

However, the promise by the borrower to pay the loan, or a partial payment, in many instances removes any limitation of this character that may then exist, and the period in which the action may be brought is renewed after such an acknowledgment of the debt for another corresponding period.

Loopholes in the law of usury

State laws impose penalties for an overcharge of interest. However, sometimes borrowers can't always benefit from the redress the laws afford.

A Washington, D.C. couple borrowed $300 from a moneylender. He charged them interest that amounted to 67 percent or $200 a year on the $300 loan.

After the note had been made, the money-lender sold it, before it was due, to a third person, who paid value for it and knew nothing of the usurious interest charge.

The negotiable instrument law is substantially the same in every state, and the buyer of a note before it becomes due, if he pays value and has no notice of any defenses of the maker, such as usury, holds it free of such a defense.

This was the position of the buyer of this note. The court, deciding the borrowers must pay, and pay in full, said that however unfortunate it might be, they were helpless to defend themselves against this outrageous transaction, since there was no law that afforded them relief. The liability for payment of the entire amount was theirs to meet.

In Nebraska, the usury statutes were amended to read that the debt involved would not be canceled if usurious interest was charged. The principal would be due but not the interest, and if it has already been paid the borrower is entitled to a return of the usurious interest or charges after paying the loan. In a case that came up under the statute, the borrower wanted the court to void his contract to buy a mobile home and award him title to it since there was usurious interest involved. On an installment contract the payments made usually go first to pay off the interest and then the principal. The court said in this case that the money would be applied wholly to principal because of the usury.

When you pawn a valuable

A pawnbroker is not liable to the owner of a pawned object for its loss by fire, robbery, or any other cause unless this loss is a result of negligence on his part. A money-lender is not an insurer—he is merely a custodian.

Over 75 years ago, a man named George Frederick had a pawnshop on Bleecker Street in New York City. Susan Abbett borrowed money from him and gave as security a gold brooch, two silver watches, a pair of earrings, and a pair of silver cuff links. Three weeks later the pawnshop was robbed and this jewelry, with other pledges, was stolen. Susan Abbett sued the pawnbroker.

Said the court: All that has ever been required by the law on the part of a pawnbroker has been that which is required of warehousemen, the exercise of ordinary diligence and care. Since the pawnbroker in this case had taken reasonable care of the pledged property, he bore no responsibility for its loss.

Pawned objects destroyed by fire

In New Orleans, Frank Monrose summed up a transaction with Elisha Cracker in this receipt: "Received of Elisha Cracker $312 to be repaid in 60 days from this date, and as collateral security for the repayment I do hereby place into his hands the following articles, viz., one pair diamond earrings, two diamond rings, one diamond breast pin, two pair gold buckles, one pair gold earrings with breast pin. Signed, F. Monrose."

Before the 60 days had expired, Cracker's house and its contents were wholly destroyed by fire. The statutes of Louisiana, conforming substantially to those of the rest of the country, say that the lender with whom the property is pledged is only responsible "for loss or decay of the pledge which may happen through his fault." The money-lender here was not liable for this loss since in no way could it be blamed on his lack of care of the pledge.

Can a pledged article be withheld?

Does the pawnbroker have a right to withhold an article that has been pledged upon payment of the loan with interest and surrender of the receipt or pawn ticket?

Martha Buchanan pledged jewelry with the Provident Loan Society in New York as security for a loan of $2,000. Later she offered the Society her receipt or pawn ticket and the amount due on the loan with interest. The pawnbroker refused to deliver the jewelry, claiming others had an interest in it. Under such circumstances, declared the court, the Society was liable for the value of the goods.

Is notice of sale necessary?

A ring was pawned at New Haven, Connecticut, for a loan payable in six months, and the borrower received a pawn ticket endorsed: "Goods pawned will not be kept longer than six months from the date of the ticket, but will be sold at private sale, and no further notice will be given."

The pawnbroker held the ring for eight months. When it had not been redeemed by the borrower in that time, the pawnbroker put the ring on sale and disposed of it in the usual course of business. Three months later, 11 months after the ring had been pawned, the borrower sought to redeem his ring but found it had been sold.

The pawnbroker contended the loan had been made on the terms endorsed on the pawn ticket. The borrower insisted there was an agreement that the ring would be sold only at public auction after notice to the borrower and that the endorsement of the pawn ticket did not apply and had been waived.

The court held that a contract with a pawnbroker gives him the right to sell the property pawned if the loan is not paid within the time agreed. In the absence of any agreement to the contrary, the property pledged must be sold at a public sale after notice has been given to the borrower not only of the intention to sell the pledge, but of the time and place when the sale is scheduled to occur.

Observe your redemption date

Observe closely the time within which a loan must be repaid as well as any provisions for "days of grace" given the borrower by statute, which extend the time for payment beyond the period agreed upon. Under some statutes, 60 days beyond the due date is allowed as "days of grace" before the pledge can be sold. However, the number of days varies with the state.

If you borrow money and promise to repay it, the obligation is not less if the agreement is written down informally in the form of an IOU. It is valid evidence of a contract of a loan and a promise to repay.

Gambling debts

An IOU for a gambling debt incurred illegally cannot be used to enforce payment. However, many gambling debts, although not enforceable legally, are enforced by physical abuse or threats. Be wary of entering into any such agreement.

Electronic funds transfer

Under the *Electronic Funds Transfer Act* of November 10, 1978, banks offering this service are required to disclose to their customers all the relevant terms and conditions of transfers, including the customer's liability for unauthorized transfers. For instance, under the Act, if you discover your access card has been stolen or lost and you report the loss to the bank within 2 business days, your liability is limited to no more than $50.00. If you fail to act within this period, you could be liable for as much as $500.00. You should check with your bank for additional information as to your rights and obligations.

Expedited Funds Availability Act

In 1987, Congress enacted this Act which, among other things, limits the length of time a bank may hold the money you have deposited before you can make a withdrawal. The Federal Reserve Board issued regulations effective September 1988, requiring your bank to tell you its policies. Generally, you should be able to take out money the day after your deposit. If your deposit check is on an out-of-town institution there can be a delay. But your bank must let you have some money the next day.

Truth in Savings Act

This law became effective in 1993 and helps consumers by requiring more disclosure from banks, S & L's and credit unions. Institutions that advertise free checking now have to say for how long and they can't charge monthly maintenance fees or per check charges. They can't advertise a higher rate on interest bearing accounts than is actually paid, such as only paying on the lowest balance in the account. All terms are to be standardized such as annual percentage yield (APY) and customers must understand all terms and receive information on the APY on their statements.

On certificates of deposit (CD's), customers must be notified before the CD matures and any rate changes over its lifetime must be reflected in the APY so the average return per year figuring all the rates will be clear.

Credit unions are regulated by the *National Credit Union Administration*. They won't have to comply with the Act until 1995. They don't pay interest but "dividends" on shares. Many credit unions have been paying dividends only on $5.00 increments to accounts, not every dollar. Also they may not be paying dividends for money deposited after the 10th of the month until the following month, (known as "*rollback*"). In 1995 their advertised rates will be what their actual rates are comporting with their fellow depository institutions.

Bankruptcy

Economic hard times cause more people to declare bankruptcy. They find that their liabilities exceed their assets and they cannot pay their debts as they come due. This has become true more and more because many individuals and business have been living on credit or "plastic" and when called upon, cannot answer with sufficient liquid assets.

There are federal laws that regulate the manner in which debtors can declare themselves unable to repay debts and what can be kept from creditors. The Bankruptcy Code, which was reformed and modernized in 1979, has provisions known as "*chapters*." You file your bankruptcy under Chapter 7 or Chapter 11 or Chapter 13.

If you are without any assets at all, you probably would file under Chapter 7 of the Bankruptcy Code, which is known as a liquidation. In this case, you are relieved of most of your debts except your taxes, and any alimony or child support that you are legally required to pay. You are able to avoid liens on 'household goods' held primarily for personal, family or household use of the debtor or a dependant. What that generally includes is your residence, auto, pension, and tools of your trade. Recently, a Court of Appeals has said that it means "something typically found in or around a home and also something used to support and facilitate daily life within the house."

If you have an income and want to keep your assets, you can negotiate your terms under Chapter 13 of the Bankruptcy Code. This is a debt retrenching that allows you to pay your creditors a percentage of your debts over a specified period of years. A trustee is usually appointed by the court; you pay this trustee your agreed amount and the trustee in turn pays your creditors. However, you have to have a certain high level of secured debts and a lower level of unsecured debts to qualify for Chapter 13 bankruptcy. If you have more debts than would fit under the terms of Chapter 13, you can file under Chapter 11, which is used for business reorganization. However, the United States Supreme Court has said that both individuals and businesses can now file under Chapter 11. No trustee is involved in Chapter 11, but you will probably have to negotiate a higher repayment schedule with your creditors. Filings under this chapter have mushroomed in recent years because of the recessionary economy and widespread unemployment throughout the country.

State laws

State laws govern what their citizens can protect in bankruptcy. Some states such as Florida and Texas, have exceptionally liberal laws. They prevent seizure of a residence regardless of its value. So you can shelter a three-million dollar estate in Florida or Texas. Whereas in New York the shelter is about $10,000 in a homestead, and in California it is $75,000 for a family home. Florida also exempts all wages, IRA's, life insurance policies and profit sharing benefits.

Bankruptcy and divorce

Alimony payments that have been ordered by the court cannot be wiped out or discharged by bankruptcy. Now the United States Supreme Court has decided that a property settlement is in that same category. Mr. Faney and Mrs. Faney divorced and she received an equity in their house. Mr. Faney was to pay his ex-wife the equity amount that was due her in two installments; Mrs. Faney had a lien on the house. He never paid the equity obligation and, when he declared bankruptcy, he got to keep the house, thinking that he had wiped out his debt to her. But the Supreme Court said that her lien survived the bankruptcy.

It is very important that in any divorce proceedings where there is a structured settlement, that is, where one party has agreed to pay the other party a specified amount over a period of time, the issue of bankruptcy be taken into account. Your lawyer can protect your interest not only when it comes to real property and alimony, but also with regard to pensions, IRAs, and other savings and retirement plans.

Your lawyer may suggest to you that you and your spouse see a divorce mediator. This individual, who can be a lawyer or can also be a qualified therapist, can help the two of you reach a settlement that is agreeable to both of you. The mediator will also help you cope with the intense feelings that arise from a divorce, which can affect the outcome of any financial settlement. Always make sure, however, that you are comfortable with the professionals you hire, and feel that your best interests are being considered.

Animals

20

Chapter 20
Animals

In the eyes of the law, animals are personal property. However, the law makes a distinction between wild animals and tame ones. The bear cub or the rabbit in the forest—animals in their wild state—belong to nobody. For them to become your property, you must catch them and keep them. If they escape and become wild again, your right of ownership comes to an end. The next person to capture the animals has a right of ownership that is superior to yours.

However, if you capture a wild animal that escapes from a zoo or a circus, or one that has been tamed, it is a well-established principle of law that you do not become its owner. By this principle, if you keep rabbits in your backyard and they escape into the street or a neighbor's yard, they do not become the property of the person who catches them.

No one has a right to enter your land to hunt wild animals. Such entering, without permission, is trespassing.

Bees are property, too, if you have caught them or have them in your possession. If they leave your land, they are yours as long as you know where they are. Still, you have no right to trespass on someone else's land to recover bees that have escaped.

Tame animals—chickens, ducks, and other barnyard fowl, as well as sheep, cattle, horses, goats, and other animals used for food or labor—rank unquestionably as personal property, and, in general, they enjoy all the protection of the law afforded such property. The case is different with dogs, however.

Dogs

Dogs are generally considered domestic animals, or personal property, but they are not in exactly the same class as horses, sheep, and cows. They are, rather, classed with monkeys, parrots, singing birds, and "similar animals kept for pleasure, curiosity, and caprice," to quote the words of the Supreme Court. Cats belong in the same class.

Of dogs, Justice Brown of that court wrote: "They differ among themselves more widely than any other class of animals and can hardly be said to have any characteristics that are common to the entire breed. While the highest breeds rank among the noblest representatives of the animal kingdom and are justly estimated for their intelligence, sagacity, fidelity, watchfulness, affection and, above all, for their natural companionship with man, others are afflicted with such infirmities of temper as to be little better than a public nuisance."

For these reasons, there are special rules of law that have been developed regarding the behavior of dogs.

Why your dog should be licensed

Cities and states generally provide, either by ordinances or statutes, that the owner of a dog must file with the town or city clerk, or a similar officer, a statement of his ownership and a description of the dog. The owner must also pay a license fee for the privilege of keeping the dog for a stipulated period, usually a year, and for this a tag is issued that is attached to the collar of the dog. Failure to register a dog and pay a license fee is penalized by fine or by withholding legal protection of the dog. Or the municipal authorities may have the right to impound or kill the dog if they find it to be unlicensed.

Damages for an unlicensed dog

A Newfoundland dog renowned for pedigree and pups and named in the *American Kennel Blue Book*, Countess Lona lived with her master in New Orleans. Following him along the street one day, she stopped on a railroad track and, failing to notice an oncoming train, was hit and instantly killed.

At that time, in New Orleans, a city ordinance provided that no dog should be at large unless provided with a tag furnished annually by the city treasurer for $2. The Countess had no tag. By this ordinance of the city, she was an outlaw.

Her owner, a man named Sentall, sued the railroad for his damages for the loss of the dog and recovered. That judgment was reversed by the Louisiana appellate court and ultimately came before the Supreme Court of the United States. The Supreme Court affirmed the decision of the Louisiana appellate court that Countess Lona without her tag was outside the protection of the law and that her owner could not recover damages for her death.

In brief, the fate of a dog and the protection of the law will be determined by the specific provisions of the law of the locality.

If a dog is killed negligently

A pole on which was strung a lead cable was maintained by a telephone company in a yard used as a run for two hunting dogs, Nancy and Pooch. The telephone company made some repairs on this cable. Four weeks after the repair work was done, Nancy died from lead poisoning. During that time Pooch, too, became sick, and the week after Nancy's death he died. A search of the yard where the telephone company had done its repair work disclosed quantities of lead parings and bits of solder. The owner of the dogs brought suit against the company.

A statute saying that no action could be maintained for the loss of a dog not equipped with a tax tag was invoked by the telephone company in its defense. That statute, the court held in this case, cannot be intended to exonerate persons who kill or injure dogs through negligence. The telephone company was liable for the value of the dogs.

Dogs have not been given the overall protection of such domestic animals as horses and cattle, but they nevertheless are property and, when equipped with tax and license tags, have their own right to legal protection.

Pick-up trucks

A number of states have enacted or are considering legislation prohibiting dogs from riding in the flat bed of open pick-up trucks. The practice is dangerous for the animal and traffic. If you have a truck, you should check with your local animal control agency before putting your dog in the open back or you may face local penalties.

Dog enticement

Two valuable hunting dogs died after eating poisoned bait which had been placed on a ranch in Montana. The owner had requested the Department of the Interior to place the bait to kill coyotes. A hunter who had no permission to be in the area with his dogs claimed that nevertheless he should be paid damages for the loss of the dogs since the bait odor was detectable for 200 to 300 yards and his dogs had been enticed by it. The court said that the bait was attractive to the dogs, but that there had been care to post the area, warning of the poison, and that if the hunter had obtained permission to hunt on the ranch, he would have been further aware of the danger. The moral is that some things do entice animals just as there are attractions for small and unwary children, but you, as the owner, may not be able to collect damages for your loss if there has been no negligent conduct or if you have been at fault.

There are some courts that have allowed recovery on any injury caused by a wild animal. But yet some other courts have required a showing that the owner of the animal was negligent or that the injured party did not incite the animal.

Dangerous animals

If an owner knows his animal is dangerous, he is obligated to exercise due care to control it. "Dangerous" could mean playfulness. When a 105lb. "over friendly" Great Dane jumped on his owner's housekeeper and she fell and was injured, she was allowed to recover damages since the owner was aware of this dog's characteristics and he was negligent in not controlling him.

In a recent case, Hayward Tumipseed was convicted by a Georgia Court of involuntary manslaughter and sentenced to 5 years in prison for the death of a child caused by his 3 pit bull terriers. His was irresponsible pet ownership. His dogs were known to be vicious yet they had easy access not only to the outside of the house but to the outside of his property. Mr. Tumipseed also has been sued by the parents of the child for the wrongful death.

Vicious dog legislation has been passed in Washington State and proposed elsewhere, making it easier for communities to deal with aggressive animals and irresponsible owners.

Ten states including Maryland and the District of Columbia view the hybrid wolf dog as a wild animal and dangerous and have banned them. They cannot be vaccinated against rabies.

If an animal is normally peaceable and attacks under provocation the owner is not responsible.

Cows on the highway

In some of the southwestern and western states, where cattle-raising is a major industry, cows are permitted to run at large, and the owner of land cannot recover for the damages they may cause to his property unless he had it fenced. In other words, the duty in these states is to fence the cattle out, not to fence them in. This, however, is not the rule in the industrial states of the East, and those states with large manufacturing centers. The old bucolic rule is illustrated by the following case:

An automobile driver on an Alabama highway collided with a cow, then sued the animal's owner for the damage his car had suffered.

"The common-law rule that animals must be on the owner's premises is not the law in this state. The rule is rather reversed," said the Alabama court. "Animals are permitted to run at large unless prohibited by statute."

The court held the cow owner not responsible for the damage. The cow had a right, as did the automobile owner, to be on the highway, and her owner was not negligent because she was there unless he knew she had propensities that would result in damage.

This is no longer the rule in Alabama, which now provides for impounding animals running at large on state and federal highways.

In many states, which have open-range policies, when a motorist injures a cow, he not only cannot collect for his damages but he must also pay for the cow at the going beef rate.

When a hired animal causes injury

The owner of an animal, when he hires it out to you for use, is responsible for the damages caused by the animal's viciousness if he knows or should have known that the animal was vicious. In general, he is under an obligation to find out whether an animal is inclined to be dangerous, and to give you such information about the animal. He is also under an obligation to furnish you a reasonably safe animal. If the owner informs you that the animal has vicious tendencies and you use it anyhow, you assume the risk of the consequences.

Horseback riding at one's risk

At a riding school, a woman who had lived on a farm and had been familiar with horses all her life was offered a mount she had difficulty in controlling. Another mount was offered her, but she refused it. Finally, when she was riding the first horse, he reared and wheeled; the woman, unable to keep her seat, was thrown to the ground.

This woman was not a novice, said the court when she brought suit against the owner. In order for her to recover damages for her injuries, it had to be shown that the owner of the horse had a knowledge of his vicious propensities, which knowledge the rider did not possess. Since before her accident, the plaintiff had a clear idea of how the horse would behave, she had no claim against the owner and could not recover damages.

In another case, a young, inexperienced rider was given a horse at a riding stable. It was regularly used by youngsters frequenting the stable. The horse reared soon after the youngster mounted him, and the boy was thrown to the ground, breaking his arm. His parents sued. They might have been able to recover, since the boy was a novice and the court conceivably would have said the stable was under a duty to give him a calm horse. However, it was determined that the horse reared because the boy kicked it. Since the boy incited the horse, no recovery was allowed.

The normal hazards of sports
A 13-year-old girl receiving instruction at a riding academy brushed against a tree while riding a horse and was hurt. The horse was calm, well-behaved, and had no vicious habits.

The court held that there was no fault on the part of the owner and that the girl could not recover damages for these injuries. The owner did not agree to become an insurer against every accident that might occur, the court pointed out, and there is always some hazard in horseback riding, as in most sports. One who participates in any activity voluntarily must be charged with assuming all normal risks of that activity. The animal was reasonably safe, so no charge could be leveled against the owner.

Animals that may be destroyed
A mad dog or any other vicious or dangerous animal that is running at large and menacing the lives of others is a public menace and may lawfully be killed.

Statutes, local laws, and ordinances have recently been adopted throughout the country for the destruction of cattle affected by tuberculosis. The United States Supreme Court has already asserted that the police powers of the states justify the destruction or abatement of whatever may be regarded as a public nuisance. Within this power lies the right to condemn infected cattle, on which the welfare and health of the people depend.

A California act, for example, provides that cattle infected by tuberculosis should immediately be segregated and each animal appraised and slaughtered within 30 days. The owner is then reimbursed by the state for one-third of the difference between the proceeds of the sale of the salvage and the appraised value, but not more than $75.

Cruelty to animals is punishable
The old English law from which our own has grown held little or no concern for the sufferings of animals and the prevention of the cruelties inflicted upon them. A few centuries ago, men could torture animals with impunity. The situation is different today, and states have laws that protect animals and provide for the punishment of those who treat them cruelly.

In addition to the damages for which one is liable when the animal is another's property, the punishment under the criminal laws for cruelty of this character extends from offenses for which a fine is imposed to imprisonment at hard labor. In fact, there are at least 17 states where animal cruelty crimes are classified as felonies.

Under a statute in California relating to these offenses, a man who had maliciously placed poison in a water trough for use by horses received a prison term. Recovery has also been allowed against persons who negligently leave poisonous substances on streets or highways, or who spray or dust plants, if injury to animals results.

What "cruelty" means

What constitutes cruelty to animals? A famous court decision set a definition that has long served as a guidepost. "The torture must consist in some violent, wanton, and cruel act necessarily producing pain and suffering to the animal." Cruelty may refer to a wide range of acts. It may be beating an animal, or it may be failing to take care, in a civilized way, of an animal in your charge. If you do not provide your dog with proper food, drink, or shelter, for example, this is generally considered cruelty, depending on the circumstances, and particularly the suffering inflicted on the dog.

A typical case of cruelty was based on a complaint lodged against a man in Indiana charging that he had imprisoned dogs in a wagon. There was not enough space for them in it, and he failed to supply them with sufficient food and water. They became sick, and some of them died. Found guilty, the owner had to pay a fine.

Unusual treatment is not always cruel

Complaints of cruelty are often made without any basis in fact. Animals may be treated in an unusual way, but if it does not involve "wanton and unnecessary torture," it may not be cruelty under the law.

A store temporarily lodged a two-week-old chick in a glass container as an advertising feature. This container was 19 inches high. Inside was food, water, and a wire netting on which the chicken could stand. There was also three-way ventilation.

A society for the prevention of cruelty to animals complained to the courts of the cruelty this treatment inflicted on the chicken. The manager of the store was arrested and tried as the responsible party. It was shown that the chicken weighed twice the standard weight of its contemporaries, and a university expert testified that it was in good health. The case resulted in no conviction, since cruelty normally involves the wanton and unnecessary torture of an animal.

Many humane groups have sought to enjoin rodeo performances because they allege that the animals are cruelly treated. Bullfighting has also been banned in the United States because of the alleged cruel and inhumane treatment accorded the participating animals.

Trespassing domestic animals

Two families lived on adjoining lots in North Carolina. Each had a flock of chickens. After the garden peas and other vegetables had been planted, the chickens of each family became increasingly irksome to the other. In one of the families was a small boy who displayed sadistic tendencies in ridding his father's garden of the neighboring chickens. One of the chickens he chased into a brush pile, where he grabbed it by its legs and crushed its head with his heel. He pulled off the head of the next. Another he impaled on a sharp stick.

"This boy had no more right to destroy the trespassing chickens," said the court, "than he had to destroy his neighbor's cattle. The remedy is by impounding them till the damage is paid or by action for damages." This, in general, is the law regarding animals that trespass. Ordinarily, one cannot freely kill or injure trespassing animals. However, many jurisdictions have held that, unlike in this North Carolina case, a person has a right to kill a trespassing animal if in defense of the person, his family, or his property.

Killing an animal nuisance

A dog racing through a sheep pasture was shot and killed by a boy who believed that the dog was after the sheep, since, in the past, the dog had made periodic raids on them. The owner maintained that this time the dog had actually been innocent, engaged solely in a hunt for rabbits.

The killing, however, was held justified by the court, irrespective of whether at the moment the dog was after sheep or otherwise employed. "When a dog acquires the egg-sucking or sheep-killing habit," the court declared, "he becomes a nuisance and may be destroyed as such."

There is, however, no rule against trespassing by a dog, provided he does no harm. The point in this specific case, on the other hand, is that there was good reason for regarding the dog as a menace.

When wild animals cause injury

Earlier in this chapter we said that animals are assigned by law to two classes, tame and wild. If you have the custody of wild animals, you are required to exercise extreme care—much more than you have to with tame animals, unless these are known to have a vicious disposition.

At a Virginia resort, two bears, both wild and vicious, were kept on the premises, and the guests were encouraged to feed them sweets and soft drinks. The proprietors gave no warning of the vicious dispositions of the bears. They were kept in a pen of two layers of poultry wire reinforced by hog wire.

A guest was standing with his back to the pen. One of the bears sprang to the fence, forced his paw through the wire, and severely scratched and tore the face and clothing of the guest.

The court held that, while there may have been some contributory negligence on the part of this guest, "the keeper should have exercised a very high degree of care in the manner and place of keeping such animals." Damages were awarded the injured guest.

Wild animals in the national parks

The United States has been sued for injuries sustained as a result of encounters with bears in some of the national parks. In one case a man was bitten on his arm while he was dozing in his car. He and his family had gone to Wyoming on a cattle-buying trip and were returning to Nebraska by way of a sightseeing trip through Yellowstone National Park. The wife was driving, the children were in the back seat, and the car was in a line of traffic which was stopped to watch some frolicking bear cubs. The family did not see the adult bear approach the car and bite the father. The man sued for his injuries, claiming that he should have been warned not to have his window rolled down, and that the park rangers should have taken measures to see that the bear was taken to a remote part of the park. The court did not feel there was any negligence. The government was not in the same position as a private person who has a choice whether to harbor a wild animal. Keeping the park in its natural state is in the public interest, and therefore having the park bears roam at will is not negligence. The rangers had no notice that this bear was dangerous, and there were many warnings posted to the effect that bears are wild animals and that tourists were not to feed or encourage them. Here, because of the overriding public benefit, there was only a duty of ordinary and reasonable care.

In another case, a small child was visiting the National Zoo in Washington, D.C. She was with her grandfather, from whom she became separated momentarily. They were in the lion house. The child slipped past a guard rail and got too near one of the cages. In roughly playing with her, the lion injured her fatally. At that time there were no wires to prevent the lion from reaching outside the cage, although there were warning signs in the area. The case was settled out of court, but it did result in added precautions being taken to prevent another such tragedy.

Downed animals

Thousands of food animals (cattle, pigs, sheep) go "down" outside slaughter houses and auction facilities from illness, including bacterial or antibiotic residue or a variant of Mad Cow Disease, injuries received during transport and stress. *Downers* are animals unable to walk in or out of the transport vehicles or into the facilities. They are prodded or dragged into the facility or, if not responsive, left to die in trash piles. Three states, California, Colorado and Illinois passed laws banning cruelty to downers. Cincinnati has an ordinance prohibiting transportation or delivery of any downed animal in its jurisdiction.

Puppy Lemon Law

Pennsylvania is one of 15 states to protect pet purchases. Its law protects only people who purchase puppies or dogs from U.S. Department of Agriculture and Pennsylvania state licensed kennels or pet shops, not unlicensed kennels. It does not deal with other pets. You must be notified of the law at the time of purchase. Each violation can subject the seller to a $1,000 civil fine.

The protections are pretty broad. The dog must have a health certificate signed by a veterinarian or a health guarantee must be signed by the seller. If the puppy becomes ill within 10 days from a contagious or infectious disease, or 30 days from a congenital or hereditary defect, you have three options which are: return the dog and get your money back; exchange the dog for another dog; or if you want to keep the dog, you would receive vet costs up to the purchase price, provided the dog can be cured.

You as the buyer must notify the seller of the veterinarian's examination within two business days and the seller shall give the refund, replacement or reimbursement within 14 days. If it is a registered puppy, the papers must be sent to you within 120 days (four months) or you can return the dog for either a refund or keep the dog and receive one half of the purchase price.

An accident despite reasonable care

A carload of cattle was being shipped from Houston, Texas, to its final destination in Tennessee. The car was unloaded overnight into a cattle pen at Vicksburg, Mississippi. The next morning, while the cattle were being reloaded, a steer escaped and, while running at large in a suburb, attacked and gored a small child.

This steer, contended those acting on behalf of the child, was a wild animal, savage and vicious. "Cattle," answered the court, "emerged from the classification of wild animals into that of domestic animals centuries ago. Whether such a domestic animal may return to the classification of wild animals is not before the court."

The court found that since reasonable care had been taken and the misfortune did not arise from the negligence of the employees of the railroad or the stockyard, the case did not provide grounds for the recovery of damages for the child's injuries.

Handlers must be skilled

Some animals were on exhibition at the Cleveland Brookside Park. Among them was Osa, a onetime wild elephant who, with a veneer of civilization, still retained the habits of the jungle. A boy bought a ticket for a ride in the howdah on her back, but, when he was seated there, Osa reared on her hind legs and, trumpeting loudly, she bolted for the gateway to the elephant house. The howdah was torn from her back and her passenger was hurled to the ground. The elephant attendant, who lacked training, had been unable to control her.

The rule emphasized by the court in this case—the rule that governs in all such instances involving damages from the behavior of wild animals—is that a superior skill and knowledge is demanded of a keeper of wild animals. Since Osa's attendant was untrained, the proprietors of the exhibition were liable for damages.

Photographs of an animal

A dog owner arranged to have photographs of her dog taken and paid the photographer for them. The photographer who took the pictures made copies of the photos available to an advertising agency for a fee. The agency used the pictures in advertisements that it produced for its own clients. The court held that the dog had no right of privacy, but that the right in the specific pictures by contract belonged to the dog owner, who had paid for them, and she could prevent use of the pictures against her wishes by innocent parties such as the advertising agency and client and, in addition, collect damages from the photographer.

Care by a veterinarian

Your veterinarian must use such reasonable skill, diligence, and attention in his care of your pet as may ordinarily be expected of careful, skillful, and trustworthy persons in any other profession. If he does not, then he can be held responsible for the consequences that result from his want of skill or care. Even if he is not a graduate of an accredited school of veterinary medicine, if he is a licensed practicing veterinarian he will be expected to conform to the proper level of treatment. He can also be liable for an improper diagnosis.

Nuisances

Dogs, regardless of how many they are in number and whether they are kept by their owners for pleasure, profit, or as a public service, may become a private nuisance, and the court will issue an injunction against the nuisance. The word "nuisance" means the use of property by someone so as to interfere unduly with the property or enjoyment of someone else. Anyone who is keeping noisy, odorous, mischievous, or annoying dogs may be subjecting his neighbors to a private nuisance if the comfortable enjoyment of their homes is lessened, or if the value of their property is substantially diminished as a result of the animals' behavior. You must be a person of normal sensibilities, however, to claim that you have been offended. If you ask for an injunction, the court's decision will not depend on whether you have complained about the nuisance earlier, or whether your other neighbors agree with you that there is a nuisance. What is important is that you can identify to the court the offending dog or dogs and can show that you are a normal person.

A family in Louisiana was awakened every morning between 4 and 6:30 A.M. by the barking of a neighbor's German shepherd, who was kept in a fenced backyard. Other neighbors testified that they had a feeling of security with a watchdog in the area, but nevertheless the court found that the dog was a nuisance, and the owner was enjoined from allowing his dog to bark early in the morning. The court suggested that he keep him in the house.

In another case, a pharmaceutical company kept laboratory dogs in order to test drugs that are used in the treatment of animal diseases. There were odors and noises from the kennels and runs, and some owners of summer homes in the area have sought to have an injunction issued against the company. In this case the court found that the business had a right that was superior to that of the homeowners, since the company had tried to keep the dogs quiet and since the animals were involved in scientific development.

In each such case, the court will weigh the considerations on both sides to determine whether to order a removal of the animals.

What about pets in an apartment?

If you have a lease which forbids animals, then you had better adhere to it; the courts hold that provisions like this are not unreasonable. If you breach the provision, the landlord may be able to repossess the premises.

Sometimes the landlord will consent to the breach. Where the lease requires written permission, the landlord can give oral permission for you to keep a pet. Also, if he has knowingly allowed your pet in the apartment for a long period of time, the court may consider that he has waived the requirement that you obtain permission. If he has asked you to move because you have a pet and then accepts rent for a time past your notice to vacate, he will be considered to have waived the provision, and you will not have to move.

Read your lease and be sure of provisions concerning pets, be they dogs, birds, or even snakes. Permission once given may be revoked if your dog and your landlord do not get along.

However apartment complexes that receive federal money, such as those where the rents are subsidized for seniors or the disabled, cannot bar pets. Six states also have extended the law to apartment complexes receiving state subsidies.

What about your companion animal if you live in a condominium, which you own? You may encounter problems with the rules of the condo association. (See discussion about Condominiums in Chapter 16, *Real Estate*.) The California Supreme Court agreed with the Lakeside Village Condominium Association whose regulations banned cats and other pets (though not birds) from the complex. Owners, said the Court, rely on the regulations when they buy into the complex and individuals cannot be exempt without showing the burden outweighs the benefit for everyone else.

Charitable trusts

The courts have held that a charitable trust or bequest established by a competent person for the care and protection of pets is valid and will be enforced.

Names

Chapter 21
Names

The purpose of a name is to designate a person. You may be known by a variety of names, none of which appears on your birth certificate. Yet, under the law, any of these names generally will be valid. You may collect money due you, sue, or be sued under these names, so long as they are names by which you are known.

A policy was issued in Alabama by the *National Life and Accident Insurance Company* on the life of Mary Sloan. Her husband was the son of a man named Hartley and also the stepson of a man named Sloan. He was known to his acquaintances by either surname, and his wife's name naturally followed the same changes as her husband's among their friends.

When she died, the insurance company objected to paying the policy on the ground that she was really named Mary Hartley, while the name of the woman it had insured was Mary Sloan.

The court held the company liable for the payment of the insurance since the name in the policy was one by which the woman was known. The general rule is that insurance companies may only be absolved of their obligation to pay in such cases if the use of an incorrect name led them to believe that they were insuring a person other than the deceased. Otherwise, the use of an incorrect name is considered inconsequential. The same rule applies to disputes over grants of property and to contracts. There again, if the designated party is clearly identified by the name used, a minor error will be inconsequential.

Using the wrong name in a lawsuit
A Mrs. Fern Kirk rented property at Dewitt, Arkansas, to W. H. Bonner. When her tenant was in arrears for his rent for over a year, she brought suit. The woman had used interchangeably the names Kirk and Kirkpatrick. She had signed the lease of the property with the name Fern Kirk, but she brought suit for the recovery of the rent in the name of Kirkpatrick. On this discrepancy of names the tenant sought to avoid his liability in the defense of the suit.

The purpose of an individual's name, the court pointed out, is to designate the individual, and whatever name the woman used was immaterial, so long as it served that purpose.

Once it is realized that a minor mistake in the name was made, it is a mere formality to have it changed on the record.

Names and voting
This judicial tolerance toward the use of names stops short of the names to be used by voters at the polls. Courts cannot lend their aid to voters concealing their identity under the cloak of an assumed name.

A few years ago a woman in New Jersey asked the court for an order that her vote be accepted under the name of Love Faith. This was a new name she had adopted, and she had refused to disclose to election officials what her real or previous name had been before she changed it.

Denying her this right, the court ruled, "There is no more reason why the individual who now chooses to be known among her associates by the name of 'Love Faith' should fail to disclose her past identity by registering under her previous, ordinary name than should the members of the Roman Catholic sisterhoods, all of whom carry out their civil voting privileges under their ordinary civil names."

Many people these days take different names for religious or other reasons—witness Muhammed Ali, originally known as Cassius Clay. Names may be changed by legal procedure or simply by use. When the latter, whether the change will be recognized depends on the law of the jurisdiction involved and on whether the change has a fraudulent purpose.

How the law views middle names

In general, middle names have no special importance to the law. The courts find one Christian name sufficient. If a middle name or initial is inserted, omitted, or even used incorrectly, whether in a criminal or a civil proceeding, the courts pay no attention to the matter, as a rule.

A confession of burglary made to a district attorney in Texas was signed *"T. L. Gallagher"* and submitted as the confession of Tommie Gallagher. An effort was later made to set aside the conviction on this discrepancy of names.

The court held that the middle initial was of no consequence in terms of the confession, according to the well-established rule that the law recognizes the use of only one Christian name.

Incorrect middle initial

Frank E. Coxe was named in a suit over the collection of taxes assessed against property owned by Frank Coxe. This discrepancy in the presence or absence of the middle initial was disregarded by the court with the comment, "Middle name and middle initials are immaterial."

Omitting a middle initial on a check

Lewis L. Wagner, losing some money in a dice game at Miami, Florida, paid his obligations with a check signed "Lewis Wagner." He omitted his middle initial deliberately, anticipating that the bank would refuse to pay the check since his usual signature included the initial. The bank paid the check. He sued the bank to recover the sum involved, but lost the suit. The law, the court indicated, regarding the insertion or omission of L in his signature was, in this instance, of no moment.

Error in a title or degree

Names are often accompanied by titles like *Doctor, Professor, M.D., Reverend* and so on. They are no more a part of a name than *Colonel, Governor,* or *Honorable.* While they are descriptive of the person, a name is the name received at birth. The law holds that any variation in name, with or without title, is not material unless, as may happen in some court cases, it can mislead a jury to do some substantial injury to the accused.

Is "Mrs." part of a name?

The name of a married woman is her given or Christian name, her family name before marriage, and the family name of her husband, which she acquires upon marriage. Thus, if her maiden name is Isabelle Smith and she marries a man named Brown, her full legal name is Isabel Smith Brown. For convenience and the information of others, she may precede her name with "Mrs." but this prefix is not part of her name.

Courts have held, in a few cases, however, that a married woman could legally use her maiden name while still married if her husband had abandoned her. It is normally preferable for a woman to use her married name, even if she is separated from her husband, at least until she is legally divorced.

On the other hand, a woman can normally choose to use "Mrs." Even after she is divorced. But some courts have prohibited women from using their married name, although not from using the prefix "Mrs.," if they were divorced as a result of their adultery.

One court has made the typical observation that "Mrs." is not a name but a mere title and, not being used exclusively by married women, raises no presumption that the person using this title is married at the time. "It includes widows and divorcees as well as married women. It indicates that the party using it is a woman who has been married, but leaves it doubtful whether she is married at the time or not." Of course, the new form "Ms." deliberately leaves the identification of marital status as vague as "Mr." does for the male.

"Junior" and "Senior"—parts of a name?

The suffixes "Junior" and "Senior" are also merely descriptive and not part of the user's name. To omit or add such a suffix is normally a harmless error in civil and criminal proceedings. The use of these suffixes may be necessary if there would otherwise be confusion regarding whether the father or the son is being designated.

Abbreviations

Under most circumstances, abbreviations are recognized by the courts as synonymous with the names from which they are derived. For example, in one case, when "Ed" was used for the Christian name of Edwin P. Gaston, and this use was challenged, the court held that the "ordinary and commonly used abbreviations of Christian names" are permissible.

This, however, does not apply in all instances to the use of the mere initial. A letter of the alphabet, one court observed, does not make a name. However, the use of the initial letter to represent a name is so common that it can generally be regarded as the abbreviation of the Christian name.

A check was written by Mary A. Wall, signed "The Mining Securities Company, by M. A. Wall," payable to Mary A. Wall, and cashed at the bank on which it was drawn. The woman was not entitled to the money, and the company sued for its recovery. The defense asserted that nothing before the court showed that the M. A. Wall who had signed the check and the Mary A. Wall who received the money were the same person.

"It is sufficient to describe a person by any known or acceptable abbreviation of his Christian name," declared the court, holding that in the Wall case the name and the initials represented identical names.

Compare this situation with that in the Clifford Irving case, where McGraw-Hill, a publishing firm, in payment for rights to an alleged autobiography of Howard Hughes, made out a check in a very substantial amount to H. Hughes, which check was endorsed "Helga" Hughes, who turned out in reality to be Clifford Irving's wife Edith.

Exceptions to this rule have been made. In these exceptional cases, evidence, in addition to the mere similarity of names must be presented to indicate who was the person that was actually designated.

The rule consistently held by all the states under all circumstances involving names is, as we have observed earlier, that the name is the correct Christian and family name with either the correct initials or full middle name.

Is a misspelled name valid at law?
The correct name of a man involved in a summons and a suit for the partition of land in Minnesota was Albert B. Geilfuss, while the name that had been used was Albert B. Guilfuss. The question which ultimately came before the Supreme Court for determination was whether or not this irregularity was vital. The Supreme Court held that the mistake in the name did not affect the validity of the Minnesota court's decision. The due process clause of the Constitution that requires notice to be given to a party to a suit, the Supreme Court said, "does not impose an unattainable standard of accuracy. If a person is served personally with process in which his name is misspelled he cannot safely ignore it."

This is the general rule. Court rules of procedure permit corrections in misspelled names of plaintiffs or defendants so long as the proper person has been served with the process or writ.

Nicknames

A nickname obviously derived from a Christian name may be used as the correct and legal designation of an individual. However, as mentioned earlier, it is better to use the actual Christian name and avoid possible misunderstanding.

A woman named Mary Elizabeth Hedges was known to her business associates as Elizabeth Hedges and also as Bess Hedges. She had dropped her first name, Mary, and had retained her middle name, Elizabeth.

A creditor secured a judgment against Bess Hedges. Elizabeth Hedges owned real estate in the county in which the judgment was recovered. If it could be assumed that the person against whom this judgment had been recovered and the owner of the land were identical, the judgment was a lien on the property.

The New York court was called upon to determine whether or not this judgment against Bess Hedges was a lien on land owned by Elizabeth Hedges. Some names, the court said, have nicknames that are synonymous with the names themselves; others, such as Cliff for Radcliffe, Ganz for Gansevoort, Will for Wilbur or Wilfred, are not. On the other hand, Bess and Elizabeth have been equivalents for centuries, and a judgment against Bess Hedges was indeed considered a lien on property owned by Elizabeth Hedges.

The deciding factor in each case will be the extent to which the use of the name clearly identifies a particular person. If there is still some question regarding the identity of a specific individual, extrinsic evidence will have to be presented to indicate who is the actual party involved.

The rule laid down on the use and misuse of names and nicknames, to quote the words of one authority, is, "If two names are in original derivation the same, and are taken promiscuously to be the same in common use, though they differ in sound, yet there is no variance." This is the rule that is generally applied by the courts.

Other names held to be similar equivalents are Willie and William, Bill and William, Charlie and Charles, Dan and Daniel, Frank and Francis, Jack and John, Ed and Edward and Bob and Robert.

Fraud to and change of name

The law is well settled in this country that a person's name is his change or continue as he may see fit, except where there may be statutory restrictions on such action or where a name is changed for the perpetration of a fraud.

The substitution of a name that serves to implement a fraud comes under the same condemnation of the law as does the fraud itself. Dewey Librizzi, having been convicted of crime in New Jersey, later changed his name and became to his acquaintances and business associates Dewey La Rose. Under this name he operated a garage, made agreements with supply firms, leased property, and carried his bank account. With his original name already on the state list of drivers whose licenses had been revoked, he made a new application under the name of Dewey La Rose. In support of his application he asserted that he had never had his license revoked or suspended.

Faced with the charge of having made a false motor vehicle license application, he contended he had a right to change his name under the law. The law is clear, answered the court, that in the absence of a statute or judicial determination to the contrary, there is nothing in the common law which prohibits a person from taking or assuming another name. If this is done for the purpose of committing a fraud, it is illegal, the court pointed out, rejecting La Rose's plea.

Changing your name by court process

In a majority of the states, statutes have been enacted prescribing the method by which you may change your name other than by simply adopting and being known by a new name. You accomplish a statutory change generally by filing an application with the court named in the law, which thereupon makes an order changing your name as you request.

Your request, however, is not granted by the courts as a matter of right, but rests in the discretion of the court to which you apply. In one instance, a man named Taminosian made an application asking that his name be changed to Mohammed Nadir. His application was rejected when this change was opposed bitterly by the wife and children, who, said the court, were entitled to consideration, especially when no sufficient cause for the change had been shown.

A court order changing your name has the advantage of furnishing an official record of the change which will establish beyond question your identity under either the old or the new name, should this be necessary.

In a few instances it has been held that once the change is effected by court procedure under a statute, the person must be known by his new name and by no other. Under such circumstances, any further change must be made by application to the courts, and the right to a voluntary change without this procedure is lost.

The New York law outlines the usual form for an application to change one's name. The applicant must state his name, age, and residence, the name he wishes to assume, whether or not he is a citizen of the United States, whether married or single, whether any judgments have been recorded against him under the name he is seeking to change, whether he is a party to any pending legal action, and whether he has any monetary obligations under the name he is seeking to abandon.

Some other states also require that the reason for the change be given and that the petitioner state whether he has been convicted of a crime under his present name. Most courts will allow the name change unless there is a substantial reason to deny it.

When the application for a change of name is made by an infant, the child must be represented by one or both parents, depending on the state, or by a guardian. When the parents disagree on the change, the welfare of the child is considered by the court.

A father generally has a superior interest in maintaining the parental surname in the child, even if the mother has custody. However, courts will allow a change in the last name of the child against the wishes of the father in cases where the use of the father's last name may be embarrassing or harmful to the child, as, for example, when the father is an infamous criminal.

Your rights and remedies under your lease

22

Chapter 22
Your rights and remedies under your lease

The lease of an apartment or house is simply a contract between two parties, the owner of a building, called the "*landlord*," and a "*tenant*." The tenant agrees to pay a specific sum, called "rent," generally in equal monthly installments, and the landlord agrees that the tenant may have the use and possession of the apartment or house for the time stated in the lease. The landlord is known as the *lessor*, and the tenant as the *lessee*.

There have been many situations across the country over the years where people have been discriminated against in regard to their leasing apartments or houses. The main basis has been race, but many have also involved bias against the handicapped or persons with children. Amendments to the *Fair Housing Act* in 1988 made discrimination against children and handicapped persons illegal. The new *Americans with Disabilities Act* (discussed in detail in Chapter 9), therefore, did not need to cover this issue. Recently, in Cleveland, the Amendments bore fruit for two families with children. They received an excellent settlement of their suits which alleged discrimination against them because they had children. One family alleged that when they had a baby, the landlord would not renew their lease. The other litigant was a potential renter of an apartment in a suburban complex. He complained that he could not rent because he had a teen-aged son. The settlement included payment of a substantial sum and requirements that the landlords build a playground and advertise using language encouraging families.

Generally, in situations where discrimination is not an issue, you just have someone desiring to rent an apartment or house who is confronted with a landlord who has a standard form of a lease and refuses to alter its terms. It can amount to a take-it-or-leave-it situation and, if you want the place, you may justify signing. However, if you can insert a few beneficial clauses, you should try to do so. A few items for your consideration are that you obtain (1) possession of the premises at the agreed time; (2) in the condition specified and; if possible, (3) a right to sublet or assign all or a part of your interest in the lease.

A mass of law has grown up governing the mutual obligations and duties of both parties to a contract of this type. A breach of this contract, however, does not in every instance create a forfeiture of the contract. When a tenant agrees to pay his rent in advance on the first day of each month, his failure to pay until some later date does not permit the landlord to take possession immediately and leave the tenant homeless. The only punishment the tenant may suffer is dispossess proceedings, or a legal action by the landlord which requires the tenant to pay his rent, with the only penalty being the additional dollars for the legal expenses the landlord has incurred on his account.

The landlord on his part may fail to furnish the heat, the water, or the service that the tenant has anticipated or that are stipulated in the lease. For many of the minor inconveniences of this character, the tenant's only remedy is to select another dwelling when his lease expires.

Statutes, however, generally provide that the landlord is criminally liable for a failure to furnish adequate heat, water, or sanitary conditions, besides providing the various services that the legislatures of the different states have imposed upon apartment-house or multiple-dwelling owners. For failure to comply with these requirements, various penalties are handed down to the property owners.

Although the ordinary lease of a dwelling contains conditions and obligations to which both tenant and landlord agree, when you sign your lease and pay your rent you have virtually complete control of the premises for the period of occupancy set out in your lease. No one can interfere with your enjoyment or possession of the premises or your access to them, any more than anyone can interfere with your occupancy of a dwelling for which you have paid in full.

No obligation to rent

A recent decision of an appeals court in the state of California protected a Roman Catholic couple who refused to rent an apartment to an unmarried couple. The Catholic couple's constitutional right to the free exercise of their religion was deemed more important than their violation of a state law that prohibits discrimination against unmarried cohabitating couples. This issue will probably receive further attention in California and elsewhere in the country where there are many unmarried couples living together, including both heterosexual and homosexual pairs.

How to protect your deposit

A prospective tenant is often asked to give a landlord a deposit of, usually, one or two months' rent as security for the fulfillment of the tenant's obligations under a lease. Such an agreement for security is legal and enforceable. The tenant should, however, always arrange the terms of his lease so that he will receive value for the money he advances or deposits. The money should be on account of an obligation that is discharged by the payment of deposit—for example, it might serve as the payment of the last few months' rent—and the lease should say this. Such an arrangement keeps the tenant from losing his money or being obliged to go to law to recover it if there is a change of landlords.

As of September 1, 1970, New York State required that a landlord deposit all security for rental payments on residential real estate in interest-bearing accounts in the name of the tenant.

Where governmental rent controls are in effect, there is usually a provision, as part of the control on rents, limiting the deposit to one or two months' rent.

Must the landlord oust trespassers?

A tenant signing a lease of an apartment or house naturally assumes, when he pays the first month's rent, that the landlord is obliged to give him possession. This assumption is correct, but only within certain limits. The landlord is not obliged to evict a former tenant or a trespassing third party who has no right to possession of the premises.

At Hempstead, New York, Abe and Dorothy Fergang had leased a store; the lease expired on June 30. A man named Teitelbaum had leased this store for a term to begin the following day. The Fergangs refused to vacate. Teitelbaum brought eviction proceedings, was unsuccessful in the lower court, appealed, was granted a new trial, and finally, when the Fergangs did not appear for the new trial, he secured a warrant of eviction for them. The premises were vacated the following January, six months after his tenancy had begun.

Teitelbaum then sued his landlord for the damages he had suffered because of the landlord's failure to give him possession. The court held that since there was no implied obligation on the part of the landlord to oust a trespasser, his failure to do so did not make him liable in damages to the tenant.

The tenant, by virtue of his lease, has title to the property leased, and it is his duty to make full use of the remedies the law affords for gaining the possession he is entitled to under the law.

A number of states have modified this general rule to provide for certain rights of the tenant against the landlord who has failed to give possession, such as the right to cancel the lease. In reality, the tenant has bargained for possession and not the right to sue someone.

Should rent be paid in advance

The payment of rent by a tenant is a discharge of his obligation under the lease for the possession of the property. Rent is not an obligation or a debt until it becomes due and payable by the terms of the lease.

The attempt of a landlord to collect rent that would accrue in the future under a lease, but had not yet become due, was denied by the court. The rent was no debt, the court declared, until the future time when it became payable, and even that event was not a certainty.

For this reason, any incident that deprives the tenant of possession will end his obligation to make rental payments unless there is some provision to the contrary in the lease.

This principle makes an advance payment of rent to a landlord a hazardous concession. After such a payment has been made, but before it becomes due, the landlord may sell the property or he may lose possession and ownership through foreclosure of a mortgage; there may be a fire or some other unforeseen contingency. Then the tenant has to sue the landlord to recover his money.

In the case of a mortgage foreclosure or the sale of the property, the tenant may readily become liable to the new landlord for the payment of rent as it becomes due, despite advance payments.

When rent is due

A written lease generally provides that the rent shall be paid in advance, usually on the first day of the month. It is an almost universal rule of law, however, that unless a lease expressly provides for payment of rent in advance, the rent will be payable at the end of the period for which it is reserved, whether it be a week, a month, a quarter, a year, or longer. If, as is usual, the rent is due monthly and the lease does not call for payment in advance, it will be due at the end of the month. The actual use of the premises is what the tenant agrees to pay rent for. Consequently, until this period of use is complete, no rent is payable unless it is otherwise agreed.

If no date is set

A lease of property for a term of years provided for a total rent of $20,000. Stipulated payment dates for $19,000 of this sum were set out in the lease, but no time for the payment of the remaining $1,000 was set under the lease. The payment of this $1,000, the court held, was for this reason not payable until the tenant's term of occupancy expired.

Refund in eviction cases

When rent is paid in advance, and a tenant is evicted, he is entitled to a partial refund. This refund should be equal to the rent-paid period of residence he is deprived of by his eviction. For example, if a tenant pays rent on the first of the month and is evicted on the fifteenth, he is entitled to a refund of the rental for the rest of the month after the fifteenth. Of course, this assumes the tenant has no further liability under a lease.

Accidental destruction of premises

The accidental destruction of the premises does not release a tenant from his liability for rent unless the lease provides for this. However, in the absence of a clause providing for no further payment of rent, if the premises are destroyed, an obvious injustice is inflicted on the tenant. For this reason, in many of the states, statutes have been enacted relieving him of the need to continue paying rent in such a situation.

Your duty to pay promptly

In most instances, rent is made payable on the first day of each month. Failure to pay on this date is a breach of contract, and the landlord is entitled to evict. However, if payment is made later in the month and the landlord accepts it without protest, this is a waiver that deprives him of the right to base eviction proceedings on nonpayment on the first. However, he can reinstate this provision for payment on the first by a demand to that effect in advance of a subsequent payment date.

Who must make repairs?

Under the common law—our traditional law, derived from England—a tenant takes the apartment or house he has leased as is. The common law still prevails in a majority of the states, and landlords are not obliged to make any repairs on the property. However, in some states the common law has been modified by statute, and landlords must make repairs. Also, in the absence of provision for repairs, the tenant covenants to make repairs in the tenant area and the landlord's duty to make repairs extends only to portions of the premises over which he retains control, e.g., common hallways, lobbies, elevators.

If a building becomes uninhabitable due to lack of repair, the tenant, at common law, could vacate the premises and in an action for nonpayment of rent assert the defense that the landlord caused the premises to become unfit for occupancy. This is referred to as a "*constructive eviction*." In 1971, a New York City tenant challenged this doctrine when, without moving from the premises, he alleged that the landlord breached the covenant of habitability and fitness for use by his failure to repair and maintain the building. The court ruled in favor of the tenant, citing the contemporary housing conditions in New York City and the chronic housing shortage. Under these conditions, the remedy of "constructive eviction," under which the tenant can claim that the premises have become uninhabitable and that therefore he has the right to move and to refuse to pay future rent, is an illusory remedy. As long as the tenant is required to move out to have this defense, he is in an unfortunate position, because there is no place to which to move. In these situations, the tenant seeks only habitable housing and not a defense against a lawsuit for rent.

In a recent case, the United States Supreme Court denied the right of tenants to withhold rent from a landlord who fails to make repairs. In a case involving the Oregon law, two tenants in Portland sued in the federal court to have a state law held unconstitutional which allowed the eviction of tenants who failed to pay rent. They had stopped paying their $100 per month rent because the landlord had failed to make the repairs after city officials had declared the premises unfit for habitation.

In a 5-2 decision (Justices Lewis F. Powell, Jr., and William H. Rehnquist, recently appointed to the Supreme Court, did not take part in the decision), the Court made it clear that it was not prepared to assist the legal reformers who had helped to liberalize landlord-tenant laws. Justice Byron R. White, writing for the majority, stated: "The Constitution does not provide judicial remedies for every social and economic ill. We are unable to perceive in that document any constitutional guarantees of access to dwellings of a particular quality or any recognition of the right of a tenant to occupy the real property of his landlord beyond the term of his lease without the payment of rent."

The Court made it clear that "The assurance of adequate housing and the definition of landlord-tenant relationships is a legislative, not a judicial, function."

Some jurisdictions allow a tenant to make repairs and offset them against the rent due the landlord. In New York, where a landlord had refused to repair a toilet in a residential apartment, the tenant was forced to hire a repairman at her own expense. The tenant was held entitled to offset the cost of the repairs against the rent due. The Court stressed that the traditional doctrine that distinguishes a landlord's right to receive rent from his duty to repair and maintain a building in accordance with local housing codes had received increased criticism, and it rejected the common law idea of the landlord/tenant relationship for a more modern doctrine based upon mutual rights and obligations.

TV antennas and air conditioners

When you rent an apartment it does not include rights outside the premises unless specified. So, unless your lease so provides or unless rent control rules apply, you do not have the right to install a television antenna on the roof or an air conditioner which extends much beyond the window frame.

Control of rented premises

The control of the premises is the tenant's, and the responsibility for the welfare and safety of passers-by that might be imperiled by the improper use of the premises can be placed on the tenant and, in some cases, on the owner also.

Building security

Tenants and visitors who are robbed, raped or otherwise assaulted in apartment building laundry rooms, lobbies, stairwells are suing apartment building owners, managers and landlords for negligence in not providing adequate security. They are winning sizable judgments. Some of the alleged breaches include faulty locks, shoddy doors, poor lighting, no patrols, unsecured patio doors and the hiring of workers who have prior histories of violent conduct. The suits also allege failure to alert tenants about crimes on the premises or giving false assurances about safety measures. One woman collected when, after she asked for an inside locking deadbolt and was refused, she was raped by an intruder who had stolen her key from the manager's office. Courts have been taking into account the overall crime history of the complex and crime in the surrounding area to judge the foreseeability of crime and whether the security was reasonable.

Is a landlord liable for injuries?

In one of our southern states, a store building was leased. This building had a parapet wall of 8 to 14 feet. An adjoining building, which was 10 or 12 feet higher than the leased building, was destroyed by a fire which weakened the parapet wall. The tenants complained to the landlord of the danger from a collapse of this wall, but he made no repairs. In a severe wind storm, a month after the fire, the wall collapsed, crashing through the roof and the two upper floors of the rented store building, and killing one of the occupants on the first floor.

In the suit that followed, the court pointed out that under the common law, where there is no statute to the contrary, the landlord is not under any obligation to make repairs. In the absence of such a statute, a landlord is not liable to his tenant for personal injuries sustained because of the defective condition of the leased premises. However, if there is an agreement to make repairs which the landlord undertakes to fulfill and he does his work negligently, to the injury of the tenant, he bears the responsibility. This is the law, and it is enforced even if the landlord makes the repairs voluntarily, at the tenant's request. If the landlord, after agreeing to make repairs, fails to do so, and the tenant is injured, the landlord is liable.

Under a statute which required a landlord to keep the building and every part thereof in good repair, a landlord was held liable for $10,000 damages for the rape of a girl by an intruder who was presumed to have gained access to her apartment through a broken window. The landlord had been notified numerous times of the defective window and, since the window was part of the building and the landlord had sufficient time to make repairs, he was held liable. The judge said that failure to repair the broken window was a cause of the admission of the rapist.

Mr. Becker, a tenant in a California apartment complex, was injured by falling through a shower door of untempered glass. A door of tempered glass would have reduced the risk of injury. The landlord denied knowledge of the untempered glass and argued that no other such accident had occurred. The California court held the landlord liable for latent defects existing at the time the premises were rented.

A tenant sued and settled a sexual harassment case allowed under a little known provision of the *Fair Housing Act*. She alleged she had been groped by the superintendent and when the building management firm and owners didn't fire the culprit a hostile living environment was created.

A landlord's agreement to make limited repairs
Sometimes a landlord agrees to make certain repairs of a limited nature. This agreement does not bind him to make any other repairs. The extent of repairs determines also his liability for negligence or personal injury.

For example, a landlord in Massachusetts agreed to make some repairs to a house, but did not agree to repair a piazza railing. Later the tenant was severely injured by a fall when this railing collapsed.

The landlord was not liable for the injury. He had not agreed to do this particular repair work, and could not be called negligent because he failed to make repairs that he had never agreed to make. The mere fact that he had made some repairs was no evidence that he would make more.

May you withhold rent?
In signing a lease, a tenant agrees to make periodic payments—usually monthly—of rent, and the landlord, on the other hand, agrees that he will furnish the tenant with various services, including adequate heat. Suppose the landlord fails to do his job—what recourse do you as a tenant have? The laws in the various states are not uniform on whether rent may be withheld when the landlord fails to furnish some of the services he has promised. In some cases the tenant is required to pay the rent either to a court or to an escrow agent who will hold the money, pending the determination of the court. Recently, tenants in many states have been withholding their rents in what have been called *"rent strikes."* When, as a consequence, the landlord brings action for eviction for nonpayment of rent, the tenants will assert the landlord's defect of service either as a defense to the suit or as a counterclaim. If your landlord disregards your complaint about lack of services, such as heat, ask the local health authorities or your lawyer for advice.

How to end lease early
If your landlord is willing, you can end your lease before the stated date a by making an oral agreement with him. No formal writing is needed. You merely leave the premises and return the keys to the landlord, who accepts possession. However, it is always safer

to have a statement in writing from the landlord that you are released from your rental obligation in order to avoid later claims. Most leases provide for rent to continue, even if you move out before their expiration.

When rent ends

During the last years of World War II, Barbara King occupied a one-family house. Her landlord sold the property, and the next August the new owner told her he wanted it for his own use and asked her to vacate. At the time, she was unable to do so, and she remained in the house, paying her rent regularly. On the following December 8, she sent the owner a check for eight days' rent, moved out, and gave him the keys. On her check for the rent she had endorsed, "Final payment in full for rent." The landlord, still holding her check, sued for $110, the full rent for the month of December.

The rent had been paid in full to the termination of tenancy, said the court. The landlord was not entitled to rent for the portion of the month that remained after the tenant had surrendered—and the landlord accepted—possession of the premises.

How the landlord's acceptance is proved

In general, the best possible token of a landlord's acceptance of surrender of premises is shown by his taking possession of the property and again assuming all the authority of an owner in possession.

In one case, a tenant told his landlord that he had an opportunity to buy a house and asked if a surrender of the rented premises would be acceptable for the unexpired term of his lease. The landlord apparently consented to the suggestion. The tenant moved out in November, gave the keys to the landlord, and paid the rent until the end of the month Later the landlord sued him for the balance of the rent under the lease.

The court held that the landlord, in taking possession of the property and seeking a new tenant, "without any agreement express or implied that the tenant's rent was to continue, released the tenant from further liability."

Oral agreement to end lease

A plumbing store in Franklin, Kentucky, was rented for five years at $35 a month during World War II. After some months the tenant told his landlord that, with plumbing and heating fixtures "frozen" by the government, he could not continue the lease of the store unless the rent was reduced to $15 a month. The landlord replied, "If you can't pay the $35 a month, you can move out and I'll go into business myself."

The tenant replied, "I'll move out." To this the landlord answered, "All right."

In the suit the landlord brought later for the rent that accrued after the tenant vacated the premises, the court held the offer of the tenant and the consent of the landlord represented a surrender and acceptance of the lease, and that the landlord's action for the subsequent rent could not be maintained.

What holdover tenancy means

When you have to make arrangements with your landlord for the continuation of your tenancy because your lease is going to expire, be sure to make them a reasonable length of time before the date of expiration. Do not leave such arrangements to chance and do not leave them to the last minute. The courts of the various states have laid down different rules of law to govern the liability of a tenant under such circumstances, and not all are what you might desire.

Most states have a rule that when a tenant voluntarily continues in possession of property after a lease for one year or more has expired, and does so with the consent of the landlord, a tenancy for an additional year is created. This is known as a *"holdover tenancy."* Such a tenancy may be ended on notice of either landlord or tenant prior to the end of the year. The length of time between the giving of notice and the termination of the tenancy is governed in some cases by statute. The tenancy is also ended if the tenant moves out at the end of any holdover year, according to the rule in the majority of states. In some states the rule is that when a tenant continues to occupy premises with the landlord's consent after the lease has terminated, the tenant becomes automatically a tenant from year to year, and his tenancy can be terminated only on notice.

In a few states the rule is that when a tenant holds over after his lease expires, a tenancy at will or sufferance is created which can be ended with a notice by either the landlord or tenant to the other.

In most instances, the termination of these holdover tenancies is governed by statutes that prescribe when and how notice must be given. It is important to follow these rules to the letter.

When notice is not adequate

For six and one-half years a tenant had occupied premises. On October 1, he gave notice to his landlord that he was vacating the premises on the following January 1. The law of the state required a six-month notice rather than the notice of three months which the tenant gave. As a consequence, the notice was ineffectual, and the tenant was liable for the rent for another year. This emphasizes the care a tenant must take under such circumstances to follow the statutes of the state in which the property is located.

Restriction on landlord

The holdover rule works both ways. The landlord is bound to another one-year term if he accepts rent after the expiration of the original lease term. He cannot then evict the tenant during the additional term created by the holdover.

The rule about holdover for one year also applies to leases for a term of months or weeks or any period less than a year. In such cases the hold-over and the payment and acceptance of rent after the end of the original lease creates a new term for one month or one week, as the case may be.

Rent control and holdovers

This doctrine of holdover tenancy has no application if, when the original lease term expires, the tenant is authorized to continue in possession by any federal, state, or local rent control laws. In these cases he becomes what is known as a "statutory tenant," and the tenancy can be terminated at any time without further liability by his removal from the premises.

The reason for this exception is that the rent control laws prevent the landlord from dispossessing the tenant at the end of the lease term, and hence he is not held by the courts to have given his implied consent to the holdover by the acceptance of the tenant's rent.

Subletting and assignment

If your lease prohibits you from the subletting or assigning of your premises, you must obey this provision. If your lease contains no such provision, you are free to sublet all or part of the premises. A sublease is a transfer of only a part of the lessee's estate or interest in the premises, with a right to take it back at some time before the term of the lease expires; an assignment, on the other hand, is a transfer by the lessee of his entire interest remaining in the lease. When a tenant sublets or assigns his interest in the lease, generally he is still primarily liable for all of the covenants and terms of the lease, and only upon specific agreement with the landlord can the tenant be relieved of this liability.

The only restriction imposed by law on a tenant who sublets is that the use of the property by a subtenant or assignee of the lease shall not be of a different character than that provided by the lease. In other words, the subtenant must observe all the terms and restrictions of the lease just as the original tenant would.

Subletting against landlord's wishes

Generally, if you assign or sublet your premises when the lease prohibits you to, this act does not in and of itself terminate the lease. It merely gives the landlord a right to terminate the lease if he so chooses. However, the landlord still must do this in the manner prescribed in the lease. On the other hand, the violation of a provision against subletting will not permit the landlord to declare the assignment or sublease void and at the same time allow him to continue the exercise of his rights under the original lease.

In other words, the landlord may terminate the lease and thereby release the tenant of any further obligation for the payment of this rent. However, if this is the case, the landlord cannot collect rent from the tenant and at the same time deny the tenant the benefits of the lease under which he is collecting that rent.

How a landlord waives the sub-letting restriction

A landlord may waive his right to withhold his consent to an assignment or sublease. He may even give his consent after a specifically prohibited assignment or sublease has been made. The landlord's waiver may be made either by words or acts that clearly evidence his consent. The law finds a waiver when the landlord, having knowledge of the subletting in violation of the lease terms, accepts rent from the tenant.

Taking in roomers

Some of the rooms in an apartment in the District of Columbia were rented by the tenant to roomers or lodgers. The landlord demanded the eviction of the tenant, claiming this use of the apartment for roomers was a violation of such a clause against subletting contained in the lease.

A roomer or lodger, asserted the court, is not a tenant. The letting of a room to a lodger is not a subletting that entitles the owner to possession as a breach of the covenant against subletting. The tenant here had the exclusive possession of the apartment in which she rented rooms to lodgers. The lodger had only a right to use or occupy the room—a mere license to use it which gave him no control of the premises, such as would be enjoyed by a tenant under a sublease.

License or lease?

A case involving two businessmen illustrates further the difference between a lease and a license. A wholesale shoe manufacturer consigned to a retailer a stock of shoes under an agreement that the shoe manufacturer should "lease a sufficient amount of space in the store and the store windows for the sale and fitting" of his shoes.

The retailer failed to pay the rent of the store. The landlord seized the stock of shoes for the unpaid balance, claiming that the manufacturer was a subtenant and his goods subject to the landlord's lien for rent.

Calling this arrangement between the shoe manufacturer and the storekeeper a lease did not make it so, asserted the court. When the use and occupation of premises is given for a special purpose in which the owner is concerned, and the owner retains control and legal possession, no tenancy is created. This rule applies equally to the relation of lodgers and proprietors of rooming houses.

The tenant's obligations after eviction

A lease provided that should the tenant be dispossessed or evicted, he should pay a sum equivalent to the rent still due—which should be applied to the expense of obtaining possession, then to the payment of the rent and he should be liable for any deficiency.

The tenant who received this lease deposited $800 in security. Eventually, he was evicted. In this situation, not only was he deprived of possession of the property, but the security he had deposited was applied to rent that accrued after he had been dispossessed.

When this tenant sued to recover his money, the court pointed out that the obligation of the tenant to pay rent for the full-lease term may be made to survive a notice of termination or eviction, while the landlord retains the security to cover this obligation.

The tenant, we have said, is entitled to a credit for any rent received from another person to whom the landlord lets the premises. It is not the landlord's obligation, however, to find another tenant.

Rent control and statutory tenancy

It is important to bear in mind that the rules of law set forth in this chapter are the general rules concerning the landlord and tenant.

These rules have been temporarily modified by rent control statutes, primarily for the benefit of tenants, which usually deprive landlords of the right to dispossess tenants except for nonpayment of rent and in certain other specified circumstances, such as use of the premises for himself or his immediate family, demolition of the building, etc. Landlords also are deprived of the right, where the premises are subject to rent control, to set the terms of the tenancy.

There is no standard national rule in matters of this kind, and your local rent office, or your attorney, should be consulted.

Live-in lover is grounds for eviction

The New York Court of Appeals has recently held that landlords have the right to evict unrelated people who are sharing an apartment without the landlord's knowledge. A landlord sought to evict a tenant because she had violated her lease by allowing her boyfriend to live with her. The tenant accused the landlord of discrimination on the basis of her marital status in violation of state and city human rights laws. The Court of Appeals concluded that the landlord was not evicting the couple because they were unmarried but rather because the tenant had allowed an unrelated person to move in with her in violation of her lease agreement. In the lease the landlord had reserved the right to limit occupancy and the tenant had agreed to this. The court said that the fact that the additional tenant was the woman's lover was immaterial. Even if the additional tenant had been an unrelated female the lease would still have been violated.

Bias in renting

Can a couple who are unmarried and want to rent an apartment sue for discrimination when they are refused on religious grounds? Courts are divided and this issue may very well get to the U.S. Supreme Court. The Alaska Supreme Court said landlords cannot use their religious beliefs as legal justification for refusing to rent to unmarried couples. But courts in Illinois, California, Wisconsin, Minnesota and Massachusetts have disagreed.

Is it fornication against God's law or discrimination against potential tenants based on their marital status? Does enforcement of the fair housing laws deprive a landlord of the right to free exercise of religion? Will this lead to discrimination on other bases such as against couples who drink or dance or whatever else may violate a landlord's beliefs? Are landlords in commerce or worship?

Other types of bias cases have been won against both property managers and property owners when there is discrimination by the managers. The U.S. Fourth Circuit Court of Appeals found discrimination against the owners even when they directed their manager not to discriminate. She had refused to rent to a single mother.

What you should know about your insurance

23

Chapter 23
What you should know about insurance

There are various types of insurance which you come in contact with in your day-to-day activity. Life insurance, accident insurance, health insurance, and unemployment insurance are probably the best known and most widely used. If you own a house, you probably have liability, property, and fire insurance. Most car owners carry personal liability, fire and theft, and collision insurance, even if these are not required by state law. This chapter outlines basic information to help you understand the purpose and coverage of insurance.

An insurance policy is a contract and, like any other contract, may be void if it is made with fraudulent misrepresentations by either of the parties. The insurance company cannot be held to indemnify you against a loss when the risk it agrees to indemnify under its policy is not the actual risk as it was represented by you in your application.

Not all misrepresentations will deprive a person of his right to benefits. Many people misunderstand the questions in the applications and thus supply faulty answers, or they forget to include details that may later turn out to be significant. Omissions and other misrepresentations may be minor or major, and their effect on the right to collect depends on the circumstances, as the cases that follow will show.

A life insurance policy was issued on the life of a man who, less than six months afterward, died of cancer. In his application for this insurance, he had represented to the company that for 12 years previous he had consulted no physicians except in one instance—when he was ill with influenza. The court, in holding the company not liable for the face amount of the policy, pointed out that his failure to mention this cancerous condition in his application was a concealment of a material fact that might well have been a contributory cause to his death, and increased the risk assumed by the company.

"Whether the misrepresentation relates to health or to some other fact or condition, the final test is whether there was an increase in risk, " the court declared.

Viatical settlement
People with terminal illnesses expecting death within two years may need immediate cash. A viatical settlement involves the sale of a life insurance policy to companies that will pay you a percentage of the policy's face value. You assign the policy, the company pays the premiums and collects the death benefit. Before you take this step you should check your policy to see if it allows early payment, consult with your beneficiaries, check out different companies for their solvency and licensing, if required, and look into estate and tax consequences. (Some states allow these settlements to be tax free.)

Volunteer Protection Act of 1997
This law provides some limited liability protection for certain negligent acts to persons who provide uncompensated help to non-profit, charitable, civic, educational, religious or welfare organizations. In a civil suit volunteers still remain liable for non-economic

losses such as pain and suffering and other non-pecuniary losses unless a state law provides additional protection. If you are a volunteer director, officer or other level, you should consult your organization about any insurance coverage they have for their unpaid helpers.

Health Coverage Availability and Affordability Act of 1996

This Act gives some tax help to persons who buy federally qualified *long term care insurance* (LTC). (Long term care tax issues also are discussed in Chapter 17.) Part of the premiums may be deductible as a medical expense and the deduction is higher the older you are. If you are self-employed, you will have to be aware of the special rule for you on deductibility. Also, if you are a dependent on your spouse's plan, you still may be able to purchase your own long term care insurance and take a deduction.

All LTC insurance policies issued before January 1997, were federally qualified if approved by the buyer's state insurance department. New ones will be qualified if they contain certain provisions, including that you, your spouse or covered dependent, in order to be beneficiaries, will have to be certified to be chronically ill or disabled for at least 90 days.

When there is a minor misrepresentation

An application for an accident and health policy failed to state that, a year before the application, the applicant had suffered an injury to his foot. Two days after the policy was issued, the insured, while working for an engineering organization, fell and was seriously injured. The insurance company maintained he was guilty of a misrepresentation in the application because he had omitted any mention of the foot injury.

It could not be proved that the foot injury was responsible for the man's fall. The omission was therefore held by the court not to be a material misrepresentation that would justify the company's refusing to pay benefits to the insured.

Each decision, when there is a charge of misrepresentation, depends, as we have said, upon the facts of the particular case, and even though each case often depends on the subjective interpretation of the insurance adjustor, it is necessary to include all pertinent information.

An innocent misrepresentation may be damaging

A warranty in your policy is a material statement and is vital to the contract. Breach a warranty, and the insurance company can void your policy. If your policy says that any declaration you make concerning your health is a warranty, and you give inaccurate information about your health, you are endangering your right to collect, even if the misrepresentation is unwitting. Here is an unfortunate example of how a person may be penalized even though he is innocent:

Many years before Ettman applied for a disability insurance policy, he was unable to read the writing on the blackboard at school. His mother took him to an eminent eye specialist. This doctor found that the boy was suffering from a disease that would eventually cause him to lose his sight. But at the request of the boy's mother, the doctor withheld this information from him.

During World War I, Ettman's eye condition prevented him from serving in the armed forces. His statement at the time he applied for his disability insurance policy was that he was nearsighted. Asked why the Army had rejected him, he said, "I knew I was nearsighted, and I didn't think they would use anybody in the Army that had glasses."

Later, when his sight failed him, he sought to collect benefits. The company contested his right, alleging misrepresentation when he originally applied.

The court held that this man could not recover under his policy. His statements about his health in the application for insurance were warranties, or material statements. Though the insured might have had no knowledge of their falsity or of his condition, his statements were a breach of warranty.

Reinstating a policy

A year before his death, a man who held a life insurance policy was afflicted with Hodgkin's disease, a serious, and potentially life-threatening, illness. Six months later, his policy lapsed because of nonpayment of premiums. In his application for its reinstatement, the following question appeared: "Within the past two years have you had any illness or have you consulted or been treated by any physician or physicians?' He answered it with a "no."

When the insurance company refused to pay benefits and a suit was brought against it, the court declared this man's answer in the application "was patently untrue and for more than two months prior thereto the insured was a 'sick man.' The misrepresentation of the insured that he had not consulted a physician had the effect of increasing the risk." For this reason, the decision favored the company.

An important exception

There is an important exception to this right of an insurance company to refuse to pay benefits under a policy when it has been secured through misrepresentations by the insured. This right may be automatically waived if the company continues to accept premiums paid after it has notice or knowledge of such misrepresentation.

A man suffering with ulcers applied for and was granted a policy of life insurance. Five months later he developed severe symptoms. He was taken to a hospital, where he died in a few months.

The insurance company contended his death was caused by a condition that had existed for over ten years. However, while the insured was confined to the hospital, his wife, who had been paying the premiums on his policy, told a representative of the company about her husband's condition. She also told this agent that her husband had made misrepresentations when he applied to have his policy reinstated after it had lapsed because of nonpayment of premiums a few months before. She asked the agent if his company would continue the policy and accept her future payments. After this conversation, three premiums were paid by her and accepted by the company before her husband's death.

Legally, when the company received, in the person of its agent, notice of the misrepresentations of the insured, it possessed grounds for the forfeiture of the policy. Whether or not the agent conveyed this information to the office of the company was immaterial. Before the law, a company and its agent are the same thing. When the company continued to accept the premiums and allowed the matter to rest without doing anything further, its right to forfeit the policy was lost.

The difference between brokers and agents

The average person often assumes, to his grief, that the insurance broker is the agent of the insurance company by which he is insured and that the transactions he has with the broker are transactions with the company. While it is true that under some circumstances the broker is the agent of the insurance company, in others he is solely the agent of the insured. Do not take anything for granted. Get written assurance from the company that your broker is their authorized representative. If he is not, conduct insurance transactions directly with the company itself. Pay your premiums to the company directly. Send proofs of loss to the company yourself and make your requests for changes or modifications of your policy to the company. In this way you will eliminate the question that often vexes even the courts—whether the broker is the agent of the insurance company or of the person who is insured.

Whose agent is he?

The proprietor of a lunchroom asked a friend who was an insurance broker to secure for his automobile a policy of fire and theft insurance and also a policy of property damage. The broker applied for both policies, but the property damage policy could not be issued until after an investigation. The broker, however, did not tell the insured of the delay in the issuance of the property damage policy. Two days later a property damage loss occurred.

The lunchroom proprietor, in suing for the damages that he had suffered, contended that the property damage risk had been accepted by the company through the broker as its agent. He was acting on the erroneous assumption that most laymen have that such a relationship exists between an insurance broker and the insurance company he represents.

The court held the lunchroom proprietor had no claim against the insurance company since the broker was the agent not for the insurance company but for the lunchroom proprietor. Here a distinction was made by the court that is of vital importance in transactions like this:

"Ordinarily the relation between the insured and the broker is that between principal and agent. An insurance broker is ordinarily employed by a person seeking insurance, and one so employed is to be distinguished from the ordinary insurance agent who is employed by insurance companies to solicit and write insurance by and in the company."

When the broker is the company's agent

It is a general law, as the courts have pointed out, that a broker is the agent of the policy holder and not of the insurer. Generally, he acts for you. However, when he receives the executed policy for delivery to you, he becomes for that purpose the agent of the company.

Another general rule of law about insurance brokers is that, when a company gives a policy of insurance to a broker for delivery to the insured, the broker is authorized to collect the premium on the policy at the time he delivers the policy. To that extent a broker may be the agent of the company.

Who can be the beneficiary

If you take out an insurance policy, to collect benefits you must have an insurable interest in the person or property it covers. This means simply an interest in any person whose death or injury, or any property whose loss or destruction would cause you serious disadvantage or direct financial loss.

This basic rule of law has eliminated to a large degree speculation in the buying and selling of insurance policies. Also, before this rule was established, it was objected that policies were often nothing more than wagering or gambling policies, by which any disinterested insurer stood to profit if the event he insured against, and in the hope of which he paid premiums, happened to take place. Moreover, it used to be alleged that if a person named as a beneficiary in a life insurance policy had no serious interest in the continued welfare of the one insured, there was created a serious temptation to take human life in order to receive the benefits of the policy.

What is an insurable interest in life insurance?

In line with this rule, two safeguards are imposed on the issuance of life insurance policies. The person taking out insurance naming himself as beneficiary must stand in a close family or financial relationship to the person whose life is the subject of the policy. The beneficiary must also acquire the insurance with the consent of the person insured. Everyone may rightfully and legally provide in his insurance policy for those who are related by ties of blood or affection, not excluding illegitimate children.

As a general rule a person may lawfully take out a life insurance policy on his own life and make it payable to whomsoever he wishes even though the beneficiary has no insurable interest, provided the insured party acts in good faith without intent to defraud the insurance company. When the insurance is taken out on the life of another, an insurable interest must exist.

The purpose of requiring an insurable interest is to prevent insurance being a lottery in which a person may bet on the probability that a certain event will occur. The idea of insurance is to protect people against substantial loss, not to give them a chance on a windfall.

In a recent case in New York, a man took insurance on an automobile; when the automobile was stolen, the insurance company refused to pay on the ground that the man had no insurable interest in the automobile, because, when he bought it, it was a stolen car. Now if he knew it was stolen when he bought it, he obviously would not be entitled to collect insurance when it was stolen from him. If, however, he was an innocent purchaser without knowledge that the car was "hot" property, was this possession sufficient to give him an insurable interest? The court stated that he had a substantial economic interest in the vehicle and that he had the right of ownership as against everyone but the true owner, and that this gave him a sufficient interest to make it insurable.

Insurance may be taken out on the life of a debtor, but it must be reasonably proportioned to the amount of his obligation to his creditor.

In one case, a brother attempted to collect the proceeds of an insurance policy that he had taken out on the life of his sister.

"A brother has no insurable interest in the life of his sister merely because of the relationship," was the ruling of the court that rejected his claim. "In order for a brother to have such an insurable interest, it must appear that he is her heir at law or dependent on her in some way, or that the relation of debtor and creditor exists between them."

Can business associates insure each other?
An agreement between C.G. Cooper and Clarence Lebus provided that Lebus was to construct a restaurant building and a filling station, and Cooper was to conduct the business. The profits were to be divided equally between the two men. Also, an insurance policy was issued on Cooper's life for the benefit of Lebus.

At Cooper's death, the proceeds of the policy were paid to the administrators of the estate of Lebus, who had also died. The administrators of Cooper's estate sought to recover the money on the claim of no insurable interest on the part of Lebus.

Holding that the administrators of Cooper's estate were not entitled to this money and that Lebus had an insurable interest in Cooper's life, the court asserted that any person had such an interest in the life of another when he was a creditor and had a financial interest in the preservation of the life of the insured.

It is common, therefore, in accordance with this law, for business partners to insure their lives, each for the benefit of the other. This is especially important where the success of a business is dependent on both or all partners. Such policies are also used in order to permit the heirs of the deceased partner to be paid the value of his share in the enterprise so that the surviving partner can continue the business without division of the company's assets.

Study your policy

Before you accept a life insurance policy, read it through carefully. Pay particular attention to the exceptions, the causes from which death may result that are not covered by the insurance. If there is any doubt or uncertainty, insist that the company write its policy in clear and unequivocal terms in every respect, specifying precisely under what circumstances they will pay the death benefit, and under what circumstances they will not.

Such a clear and well-defined statement of the circumstances under which your beneficiaries will receive the money you wish to provide may spare them considerable difficulty later on. Your insurance company agent will usually help you with the policy, but you should be certain that you have taken all the necessary steps yourself.

Double indemnity

Many life insurance policies provide for double indemnity—payment of double the face value of the policy—when the death of the policy holder occurs through an accident.

Across the cover page of one policy was stamped in purple ink "Double indemnity for fatal accident." In the body of the policy this provision for double indemnity was limited to occasions when the death "has resulted directly and independently of all other causes, from bodily injury effected solely through external, violent, and accidental means, provided, however, that such double indemnity shall not be payable if the insured's death has resulted directly or indirectly from the taking of poison or inhaling gas, whether voluntarily or otherwise."

The insured was killed by the inhalation of carbon monoxide gas. The court criticized the glaring ambiguity and the contradiction in the representation stamped in purple ink on the cover of the policy and the terms of coverage set forth in the body of the instrument. It pointed out that the insurer could easily have avoided ambiguity by adding to the stamped matter some brief expression calling attention to the limitations.

"Even a careful reading of the whole instrument," the court declared, "would probably leave in the uninitiated mind the belief that the especially stamped phraseology was intended to afford a measure of protection broader than that indicated in the printed matter of the policy." The insured was therefore held entitled to the double indemnity provided by the policy. "The stamped matter must be taken as part of the policy."

The usual rule when there is ambiguity is to construe the document against those who prepared it.

What accidental death means

The child of a policy holder was a patient in a hospital. She urgently needed a blood transfusion for her recovery. His blood being found suitable, the policy holder offered it for the transfusion. A preliminary examination showed his heart to be normal.

While the insured was on the operating table, and before any blood had been withdrawn, he died. The court held that the beneficiary under the life insurance policy of this man was entitled to the double indemnity provided when death was caused by "external, violent, and accidental means."

"The interpretation," said the court, "must be that of the average man who would say that a death has been caused by accidental means when the deceased died in such a way that his death is spoken of as accidental."

Suicide

As a matter of general law, on an ordinary life insurance policy, the burden of proof to sustain any exception is on the insurance company. There is also a presumption against death by suicide, so that if the insurance company contends that the accidental death was due to suicide, they have the burden of proving that the insured took his or her own life. However, where double indemnity is involved, the beneficiary has the burden of proof to show that the provision applies.

If you pay your premium late

The details in the carrying out of insurance contracts are governed very largely by the provisions of the policy itself. In the payment of premiums the time and method is usually specified in the policy. Whether or not you are late in paying your premium, and therefore whether or not your policy has lapsed, will depend on the postmark of the envelope in which the premium was sent, the receipt, or on any other stipulation that has been made a provision of the policy.

How soon the company is liable

How soon the company becomes liable under a new policy is also governed by its provisions. The liability may exist when the first premium is paid or it may exist independent of the payment of this premium; the policy may be delivered and the company become liable for the risk with a time provision for the payment.

In the absence of a statute or provision in the policy or application to the contrary, payment of the first premium is not generally necessary to make the contract of insurance valid or effective.

When a lapsed policy still has value

Many life insurance policies contain provisions against forfeiture. In other words, in the event that you should fail to pay the premium on your policy, the insurance contract is not canceled, but rather you are given a lesser amount of insurance, that is, paid in full. The value of the insurance policy is figured by computing the amounts previously received by the company in premiums—although this value may be only a fraction of the face of the policy when it was originally issued to you.

By contract or statute a grace period may be provided covering the time between the date the premium is due and cancellation of the policy.

Can creditors claim your insurance?

A policy of life insurance naming someone other than the insured as beneficiary is ordinarily considered the property of the beneficiary. For example, when the amount of the policy is for the benefit of the wife, the husband is considered to have made the payments as the agent of the wife. In many instances, however, the amount that may thus be allocated for the benefit of the wife, in the event of interference by creditors of the husband, is limited by statute.

When the policy is payable to the estate of the insured it is his property. It is subject to the claims of his creditors, and to his own disposition as security for any loans or similar business uses which he may undertake.

Ordinary or whole life insurance

This type of insurance allows the insured to accumulate a portion of the premium and give the policy some intrinsic or surrender value, which increases over time, in addition to the amount of insurance which is payable on death and which is reflected in the face value of the policy.

Ordinary life insurance costs about three times as much as term insurance in the same face amount, which has no value unless you die. There are beneficial aspects in an ordinary life insurance policy in addition to surrender value. The interest component of ordinary life insurance is neither taxed to the insured or the beneficiary. Once an ordinary life insurance policy has been issued, the insured need never take another physical examination, and as long as the conditions of the policy are met, the insurance company cannot cancel your policy.

Term insurance

This is a form of life insurance, effective only for the term or period for which the premium is paid, with, possibly, the option of continuing the insurance from term to term. But at the end of the term the liability of the company ceases.

Under these policies, the company retains the right to decline a renewal.

Since term insurance is for a stated period—a number of months or whatever time is presented by the premium which is paid—the premiums are lower in amount than for a regular life insurance policy and the coverage of the policy is limited. Term insurance is pure death insurance with no intrinsic value.

Endowment insurance

The contract for this type of insurance is that the insurance company will pay a specific sum to the insured when and if he attains the age stated in the policy, or, if he dies before that time, the company agrees to pay the sum to the beneficiary named in the policy. Actually, it is insurance for the continuance of life rather than its ending, and it is an investment and a form of saving as well as life insurance.

There is no "best" type of insurance. Everyone differs in his needs and requires different protection. It is always best to discuss your insurance needs with a reputable broker or agent, or your lawyer, who can help you evaluate the various aspects of different types of life insurance.

Homeowner's insurance

Can a policy insure a parent for sex abuse of his child? A child sued her father in Maryland for assault, emotional distress and negligence. During the years she suffered abuse the Nationwide Mutual Fire Insurance Co. covered the home with two policies. The father wanted the company to defend him under one policy, on the daughter's negligence assertion, since the terms provided they would pay damages that the insured was legally obligated to pay due to an occurrence. However, it excluded "damages expected or intended by the insured." Nationwide refused to defend and filed suit in Maryland to get a court to spell out its obligations under the policy. The father claimed he never intended her injury. The Maryland Appeals Court, however, said sex with one's daughter has to be intentional injury. Other courts in Arkansas, Minnesota, California, Michigan, Illinois and Washington have all agreed that the homeowner's insurance policy does not insure against abusive conduct.

Bias in underwriting homeowners' insurance was found by a Midwestern appellate judge to be covered by the federal Fair Housing Act of 1968, as amended. The Supreme Court denied review of the decision so it stands.

The American Family Mutual Insurance Co. was sued by the NAACP for *"redlining,"* which is the denial of coverage on the basis of geographic location, generally minority living areas. They also were alleged to be charging minorities higher premiums than whites.

The federal law dealt with discriminatory mortgage lending and renting and real estate practices. It did not mention insurance. However, the Seventh Circuit Court said that lack of property insurance affects housing opportunities. "No insurance, no loan; no loan, no house."

Property damage—automobiles

A fundamental rule about policies indemnifying damages to property is that, when their clauses are doubtful in meaning, they are interpreted in favor of the insured. Such policy clauses, however, must be interpreted in such a way that each clause is given effect, as far as possible.

The difficulties and misunderstandings that can arise out of ambiguous clauses are many, and often cannot be foreseen. The wisest course in selecting a policy is to look for a broad and general coverage restricted by as few exceptions as possible.

This is as true of policies covering automobiles as it is of policies covering other kinds of property.

Car damaged by unknown cause

A parked automobile insured under a casualty insurance policy was damaged by an unknown cause while the owner was absent. The policy contained a provision making the insuring company liable "for any loss of or damage to the automobile and the equipment usually attached thereto . . . except that this company shall not be liable for loss by collision."

The insured sought to establish that the damage was not from collision.

This the court refused to concede. "A collision," it was pointed out, "implies an impact. Both bodies may be in motion or one in motion and the other stationary. Clearly it matters not whether the car or the other object is in motion. The damage to the insured car was caused by collision with another object."

When a car is used as a public conveyance

Frequently, policies covering liability for property damage to autos contain a clause saying something like there will be no liability if the auto is "used as a public or livery conveyance for carrying passengers for compensation."

The courts have been careful to construe this to mean that a vehicle is held out to the public as a mode of transportation available for use by a wide class of people. Use of a vehicle for a limited class of people selected by a predetermined standard does not make the vehicle a public conveyance. In Missouri, a driver who used a vehicle to commute with a group of friends who contributed toward driving expenses was not held to be driving a public vehicle. In New York, a personal car operated by a woman to transfer her children with other children to and from a day camp was held not a public conveyance.

Despite the fact that the use of a vehicle was restricted to the members of a country club, a California court found that any member of the public could patronize the club, thus eliminating the selectivity of the group and placing the vehicle in the class of a public conveyance.

In determining whether a conveyance is public or private, the importance of charging a fare varies from state to state. In Louisiana, the charging of a fare is essential in determining a conveyance to be a public conveyance; in California, the charging of a fare is not an essential element.

Collecting twice

More than half the states allow plaintiffs to make a double recovery in law suits, that is to be reimbursed from their own insurance and get damages from the defendant. Defendants are prevented from introducing evidence that a plaintiff has insurance or other sources of compensation. But if a defendant has been negligent, why should he not have to be responsible?

Automobile collision and casualty insurance

A company insured an automobile owner against damages from collision. However, the policy stated the company would not pay if the collision occurred when the automobile was driven by a person violating the provisions of the law relating to age or occupation.

In this case, the policy holder's car was involved in a collision when it was being driven by his daughter. Since she was only 15 years old and had not received a driver's license, he could not recover his damages.

Another policy insured against loss or damage to an automobile from collision or upset or from the "stranding, sinking, or burning or derailment of any conveyance in or upon which the automobile was being transported."

The owner of the policy, driving his truck and trailer onto a ferryboat, was directed by a ferry employee to stop. He did so. In some way the stopping of his large vehicle loosened the stakes to which the ferryboat was tied. The boat drifted into midstream, and the truck and trailer, left thus half on and half off the boat, dropped into the river.

The insurance company contended that the accident was not one covered by the policy. The court, however, held that it was, since the damage was ultimately caused by the ferry and its employee, and the driver was entitled to recover the amount of his damage.

One automobile insurance policy provided for indemnity "for any loss or damage to the automobile except by collision, breakage of glass, loss caused by missiles, falling objects, theft, explosion, earthquake, wind storm, hail, water, flood, vandalism, riot, or civil commotion."

The policy holder's car was parked on a steep grade facing downhill, the front wheel turned against the curb, the hand brake set, and the gears engaged. A three-and-one-half-year-old child crawled into the car and managed to release the brake. The car rolled down the hill, collided with a parked car, and stopped. The damages resulting from the acts of this child, the court held here, were covered by the insurance policy and the accident was not within the exceptions made to its coverage.

No-fault insurance

After many years of discussion a number of states have adopted "no-fault" automobile insurance. States' plans vary, but basically they provide that an insured victim can collect out-of-pocket losses from his own insurance company, whether or not he was negligent, quickly and with little additional expense. Traditionally, drivers carry liability insurance protecting them in case they negligently injure someone. Victims recover damages only when they can prove that an accident was not their fault—often a costly and time—consuming task.

When you carry liability insurance—and in many states it is compulsory—you are protecting yourself against your own fault. In any suit brought for injuries or property damage suffered because of another person's fault, the victim, in order to recover damages, must show, first, that the other person was negligent, and, second, that he (the victim) did not contribute to the accident by his own negligence. If the victim establishes his case, the compensation he receives is paid by the other person's insurance company.

The theory behind no-fault insurance is that, in view of the great number of automobile accidents and in view of the difficulty of apportioning responsibility, payment of damages should be dealt with in the manner of workmen's compensation cases. Under no-fault plans, the victim is compensated regardless of whose fault the accident was. The amount, however, is generally limited to loss of income and out-of-pocket medical and hospital expenses. (In traditional automobile negligence suits, there are, apart from these basic costs, often additional grounds for recovery of damages, such as those caused by pain and suffering. The determination of monetary compensation for such nebulous damages may be relatively difficult, but the resulting awards may be substantial.)

One exception to the rule requiring freedom from negligence is where the victim has died, because it is too difficult in this situation to prove freedom from negligence. Another exception is where the victim has lost his memory. In a recent case in New York, a trailer truck negligently blocked a thruway. An automobile collided with the trailer truck, and as a result, the driver of the automobile suffered loss of memory, among other injuries. He was in no position to testify as to his freedom from negligence, and under the circumstances the court treaded lightly on the obligation to show such due care on the victim's part.

Accident insurance

As we indicated earlier in this chapter, the words "accident" and "accidental" have no technical legal meaning but are used by the courts in the ordinary sense in which they are understood by the average man. Justice Blatchford of the Supreme Court once defined an accident in the following way: "If a result is such as follows from ordinary means voluntarily employed in a not unusual or accepted way, it cannot be a result effected by accidental means; but if, in the act which precedes the injury, something unforeseen, unexpected, and unusual occurs which produces the injury, then the injury has resulted through accidental means."

It is against injuries arising from these "unforeseen, unexpected, and unusual" occurrences that accident insurance indemnifies the policy holder.

What is total disability?

A common provision in accident insurance policies is that benefits are payable only when the injuries "wholly and continuously disable the insured from performing any and every duty pertaining to his occupation."

A meat cleaver slipped and cut off the right-hand thumb of a butcher insured by such a policy. With this injury, he was unable to carry on his work as usual. He could do only such minor jobs as grinding sausage and cutting coarse meats.

The insurance company refused to pay under their policy, claiming he was not prevented from "performing any and every duty pertaining to his work," as provided in the policy.

The rule prevailing in most of the states in such a case is that the total disability contemplated by an accident policy is not to be interpreted according to the strict meaning of the phrase. The courts generally do not require the insured to be in a state of absolute helplessness for benefits to be payable. Rather, the phrase means "an inability to do all the substantial and material acts necessary to the prosecution of the insured's business in a customary and usual manner," say the courts.

In the butcher's case, the court held that the injury entitled him to the benefits payable under the total disability clause in his policy, for there was a substantial interference in the pursuit of his trade.

Benefits while under a physician's care
Another phrase in ordinary use in accident policies restricts the payment of benefits to the period in which the insured "shall be under the regular care of a legally qualified physician or surgeon."

An injured man was told by a surgeon to massage his injured hand and soak it in hot water, and with this advice the doctor discontinued his treatment. The man insisted that by following these instructions he was "under the regular care of a physician." But the court ruled this self-treatment was not the equivalent of being under the regular care of a physician, and denied the man a recovery of benefits.

"Continuously confined within the house"
Some accident policies provide for the payment of benefits only during the period in which the insured is "continuously confined within the house." An oil contractor was disabled by acute inflammatory arthritis. He had, however, taken automobile trips for his health and in a few instances had transacted some business on these trips. Defending his right to benefits under this clause in his accident insurance policy, he said, "All I did on those trips was just to ride in the car; somebody else always did the driving."

"Continuous confinement," as used in such clauses of accident insurance policies, does not mean actual confinement within a house. "The mere fact that he went out occasionally for the purpose of taking exercise and fresh air under the advice of his physician," said the court, deciding in his favor, "would not be sufficient to prevent recovery of benefits."

Fire insurance
A fire insurance policy is a contract by which an insurance company agrees to indemnify the owner of property, or anyone who has an insurable interest in property, against damage to it by fire. It is a contract with the policy holder alone and does not run with the property. However, when the property is sold, the policy may ordinarily be assigned to the purchaser, provided the consent of the insurance company is obtained. If this assignment is not ratified by the company, the purchaser has no rights under the policy.

As with other types of insurance, the person for whose benefit fire insurance is written must have what we have called an insurable interest in the property insured. You have an insurable interest in property when you will be benefited by its continued existence and will suffer a financial loss if it is destroyed. An executor, a receiver, a person owning merely an interest in a building, or any person in rightful possession has such an interest. But a mere trespasser has no interest that would sustain his recovery for any loss.

It is to your advantage to have the policy describe the property in comprehensive or in general terms. However, the description will not be extended to cover property outside what you and the insurance company had in mind when the policy was drawn up.

Any misstatement of fact by the insured that might induce the company more readily to write the policy and accept the risk will void the policy.

When a fire loss occurs, the usual requirement of the fire insurance company is that notice of the loss be given it immediately. No particular form of proof of loss is required, unless provided by the policy, but the proofs furnished should contain all the information available to the insured. Under such circumstances, you should bear in mind that the statements you include in any proofs of loss are binding. If you make them carelessly or inaccurately, this may prejudice your right to recover the insurance to which you are otherwise entitled.

The Wisconsin Supreme Court has held that a wife whose estranged husband burned down their jointly owned home was able to recover on a fire insurance policy. The insurance company argued that they should not be held liable since there were cases which said that an insured who is innocent of any wrongdoing cannot reap the benefits on an insurance policy when the intentional acts of another insured caused the damage. The Wisconsin court felt that denying coverage would be contrary to basic notions of fair play in that it would be imputing the guilt of the arsonist to the innocent insured party.

Two kinds of fires

Surprising as it may seem, the courts distinguish between "hostile" and "friendly" fires. A fire insurance policy always insures against damages from a hostile fire, as distinguished from a friendly fire such as one in a furnace or stove.

When a "friendly fire" causes damage

A store building was heated by a furnace that became overheated one night. Smoke and soot poured from the furnace room, and the showrooms of the store were covered with ashes and dust. In the lawsuit against the insurance company for the damages from this fire, the court held this is a friendly fire. Also, nothing was burned.

If you drop an object into a fire

A package of antique jewelry accidentally left on the floor of a jewelry store was swept up by employees and thrown with the day's accumulation of trash and rubbish into an incinerator. The fire policy insured against "all direct loss or damage by fire." Under this clause, an attempt was made to collect damages.

In deciding the case, the court referred to the principle of nonrecovery for damages due to a friendly fire. The policy did not insure against a loss of this kind.

If a fire is for the ordinary purpose of heating, lighting, manufacturing, or incinerating, it is not a fire within the meaning of a fire policy. Had fire escaped from the stove and burned the jewelry, damages could have been collected.

Fire as a proximate cause of damage

The Ohio River had overflowed its banks at Cincinnati. A gasoline tank was torn from its moorings by the flood and exploded in flames 500 yards from the building of the insured. The fire spread rapidly in the direction of the building, and employees of the insured who were working in his store were ordered by the police and fire departments to vacate it. The inundating water reached a depth of five feet in the store, damaging the merchandise. However, none of the property was damaged directly by the tire or by the use of water in checking the fire. Still, it was because of the fire that the employees had not been permitted to remain and save the merchandise.

The court held that the fire was the "proximate" cause of the loss. "The phrase 'all direct loss or damage by fire,' or 'loss or damage by fire caused by order of civil authority,' is not restricted to a fire on the premises, and a loss will be held to be within such policies where a fire was the means or agency in causing the loss."

Thus damage to premises caused in combating a fire in adjoining or nearby premises can be within the coverage of the policy.

Extended coverage with a fire insurance policy

A fire insurance policy excepted from its coverage "loss by explosion or lightning unless fire ensue and in that event for loss or damage by fire only. If a building or a material part thereof fall except as a result of fire, all insurance by this policy on such building or its contents shall immediately cease." Most do not exclude lightning.

An explosion occurred, followed by a fire in which some additions to the building collapsed. The defense of the insurance company was that the collapse of these additions released the company from liability.

The court said that the doubts and ambiguities in an insurance policy must be interpreted in favor of the policy holder and that the company was liable here for whatever damages occurred to the building as a consequence of the fire.

Coverage for such accidents not involving fire is known as "extended coverage." It is obtainable by a rider to the fire insurance policy upon payment of an additional premium which is much less than the premium for fire coverage alone.

Theft

The phrases used in some theft insurance policies are not always as clear as they could be. Lack of uniformity in the decisions of the courts makes it hard to predict how they will decide in certain cases. As with other policies, follow this rule: Beware of words in your theft policy that can be considered "weasel words." These terms can take on unforeseen shades of meaning under the stresses and strains of a court suit and can often be used to the insurance company's advantage.

Robbery is not "trickery"

What is or is not a robbery generally depends upon the meaning given the word by the insurance policy. It is important to study policy definitions carefully, as the following case shows.

The theft policy of a pawnbroker had a provision that "robbery as used in this policy shall mean a felonious and forcible taking of property: (a) by violence inflicted on a custodian; (b) by putting him in fear of violence; or (c) by an overt felonious act committed in the presence of a custodian and of which he was actually cognizant."

One day, shortly before noon, a well-dressed man came into the policy holder's pawnshop and asked to see an unset diamond—he had heard about it through an acquaintance of the pawnbroker. In a small room of the shop the diamond was laid on a flat-top desk for exhibition. After some conversation the stranger picked up the diamond and, while inspecting it, attempted to light a cigarette. As he did so, there dropped from his hands to the desk an object resembling the diamond, but which later proved to be a mere bit of glass. The stranger left without making a purchase and, shortly afterwards, the pawnbroker discovered the real gem was gone. He tried unsuccessfully to overtake the thief with the aid of the police, but no trace of the man was ever found.

When the pawnbroker sued to recover the value of the stolen diamond, the insurance company claimed he had no right to collect since his suit was based on the clause in the policy insuring against loss through "an overt felonious act committed in the presence of the custodian." According to the company, the crime was one of trickery, and not robbery.

If the company had not defined robbery the way it did in phrase (c) of the policy, observed the court, its argument about trickery would have made more sense. But "no amount of argument, no matter how well presented, can alter the plain reading of the company's undertaking." The taking of the diamond was held to be an overt and felonious act against which the company had insured the pawnbroker.

Other courts might have decided this case differently, giving more weight to the part of phrase (c) which limits the felonious act to one of which the custodian is "actually cognizant." The lesson is clear—make certain what the actual meaning of the words in your policy are.

Theft and the unlawful use of an automobile

A boy was employed by the owner of an automobile to clean the car and entrusted with the keys of the car for that purpose. With some other boys he drove the car into the country and left it wrecked in a ditch.

399

The insurance company contended that it was not liable for damages. It said the boy's possession was lawful, and consequently his taking the car was not a theft. The court answered this defense with a quotation from the Supreme Court: "The phraseology of contracts of insurance is that chosen by the insurer, and the contract in fixed form is tendered to the prospective policy holder, who is often without technical training and who rarely accepts it with a lawyer at his elbow." The company was held liable under its policy for the theft of the automobile.

In another instance with almost the same circumstances, a boy who had been employed to clean and polish a car took it for a joy ride and wrecked it. In this case a different court held that the result of the boy's acts was not a loss for which the insurance company was actually liable under its policy of theft insurance.

Contradictory decisions such as these emphasize again the vital need of an automobile owner to have the coverage so clearly expressed in his policy that a layman as well as an insurance expert may be certain of its meaning and of the extent of its coverage.

Burglary insurance

An insurance policy against loss by burglary is interpreted by the definition of "burglary" under the statutes of the state in which the insured premises are located. Burglary, in general, is said to occur when a house is broken into by force at night for the purpose of stealing. The term "burglary" has been extended to daytime as well, and in buildings other than dwellings. Whether or not you can collect damages under your policy depends on the precise definition your state has made concerning burglary, and on other details of the statute.

For payment of benefits, burglary insurance policies sometimes require visible marks on the premises as proof of actual force made in entering the building. These requirements are not a limitation of liability, but are used only for the purpose of preventing fraudulent claims by policy holders. Sometimes there are losses with no evidence of burglary— probably the result of pilfering by clerks or the like. These cannot be considered losses by burglary, which requires entry by the use of force or fraud.

It is the rule that, where the policy may be interpreted in more than one way, the interpretation most favorable to the insured will be adopted by the courts, but a court will not make a new contract by a forced construction of the terms of the contract. For this reason a person taking out a policy should read its terms carefully and critically before accepting it and paying the premium.

In one instance of this sort, a court said, "The insured was not obliged to accept the contract of insurance; she might have secured more liberal terms elsewhere, but the courts are not at liberty to extend by construction the plain and well-understood meaning of the language."

One insurance policy provided that there should be no claim for loss when the theft was the deed of members of the insured's household. Similarly, a loss caused by theft when others were introduced into the premise by a member of the household was also not to be recoverable under the policy by reason of this exception.

In many burglary policies the insurance company reserves the right to replace the stolen property. Furthermore, where the loss has been adjusted and paid by the insurance company, the insured cannot recover for additional items which later may be found missing but which he failed to include in his original claim.

Pregnancy medical coverage

The Supreme Court has recently ruled that employer health insurance plans which fully insure spouses for other medical needs cannot limit or deny them pregnancy coverage. A shipbuilding company's insurance policy covered its female workers for pregnancy and fully covered their spouses for most medical needs. However, it only covered a small portion of the childbirth costs of the wives of male workers. The court said that such practices discriminate against male employees by giving them less comprehensive coverage than their female counterparts.

In 1978, Congress enacted the *Pregnancy Discrimination Act* to protect female employees from discrimination in insurance coverage when they became pregnant. This court ruling extends this protection to the spouses of male workers. The court reasoned that Congress enacted the 1978 law to make sure that employers treated pregnancy no differently from any other medical condition. Employers, however, will not be required to provide benefits for the pregnancies of an employee's dependents other than for the pregnancy of a spouse.

Credit insurance

Under a credit insurance policy, for a stipulated sum the insurance company guarantees a creditor up to a specific amount against losses from the insolvency of his customers.

Credit insurance policies classify losses into two groups. The first is the initial loss up to a certain amount, which the insured agrees to bear. The second is the loss in excess of this amount, but up to a certain limit. It is against this loss that the insurer agrees to indemnify the policy holder. In other words, the insuring company indemnifies the insured for an amount above a named minimum and below a stipulated maximum sum.

The usual form of credit insurance limits the losses against which the insured is indemnified to those from customers who have received a certain rating by credit mercantile companies. Also, by some policies the losses against which the insured is indemnified are confined to those on sales to customers with whom the merchant has previously had business transactions.

For a clearer picture of what such a policy is, let us look at the terms of a typical one that came into court. It contained, in part, provisions that if the insured, by reason of the insolvency of those to whom he had sold merchandise on credit, suffered losses in excess of $1\frac{3}{4}\%$ of his total sales, but not more than \$5,000, the insuring company would pay these losses. This agreement also provided that the credit extended by the insured should not exceed 30% of the capital rating of the customer, and that this rating should be above a specified amount.

A contract such as this is essentially the same as any other insurance contract insuring against a risk. It is a policy of indemnity against the loss of property. The peril of loss through insolvency is as definite and real to the merchant as the peril of fire, accident, or theft, except that he faces it much more frequently.

Under most of these policies, provision is made that the insured give notice to the insuring company within a certain period of time after learning of the insolvency of the customer. The purpose of this preliminary notice is to afford the insurer information that will enable it to investigate and take whatever precautionary measures may be possible to limit its loss.

Fidelity insurance

A fidelity insurance contract is an agreement by an insurance company to or indemnity bond indemnify the policy holder against losses he may suffer through lack of honesty, integrity, or fidelity on the part of his employees or officers of his organization.

The usual fidelity insurance policy provides that the company will pay to the employer or the person insured the amount of any loss of funds or damage to property he shall incur through the dishonesty of the employees insured against. This coverage includes loss through any act performed in bad faith by an employee, or—also in bad faith—any failure to perform a necessary act. It does not include losses through mere negligence, incompetency, or error of judgment on the employee's part. It is immaterial whether or not the loss occurs in the performance of any duty or trust especially assigned to the employee. The loss may involve the insured's own property, or property in his custody.

Frequently this type of insurance is in the form of an indemnity bond. But whatever the form—insurance policy or indemnity bond—the insurer guarantees the fidelity of the employees.

Where the policy covers losses from fraud or dishonesty, or from larceny or embezzlement, the liability of the company will not extend beyond losses from such causes. The frequently used terms of "fraud" and "dishonesty," however, extend beyond criminal acts, and the general rule is that when an agent collects money belonging to his employer and either uses it for his own purpose or refuses to turn it in, the insurance company is liable. On the other hand, when there are mutual demands of employer and employee against each other, and the employee's refusal to turn in money is made with the honest belief that his employer owes him an equal amount, the employee cannot be considered to be acting either fraudulently or dishonestly.

The policy or indemnity bond requires, as a general rule, that, in case of loss, notice shall be given to the insuring company in writing within a reasonable amount of time. The employer is not required to report mere suspicions unless they are strong enough in his opinion to justify the discharge of the employee.

In the application for insurance of this kind, statements are asked for about the character, past habits, and conduct of the person or persons insured against. If these representations are false, and known to be false by the insured, they may serve to release the insuring company from liability in the event of loss.

State unemployment insurance

The unemployment insurance laws, which have been enacted generally throughout the states, provide for a payroll tax by the state. The money acquired through this tax is devoted to the aid of those who are unemployed and who meet the qualifications set up by statute for receiving benefits.

Any worker, except those specifically excepted from the operation of these statutes, should immediately upon the loss of employment apply to the unemployment bureau of his state for information and forms necessary to file his claim for a share of these benefits.

The applicant must be wholly unemployed—that is, he must be free to accept any employment that may be offered him through state agencies. Further, he is obliged to report regularly for assignment to any work in his field for which the bureau of the state has been requested to supply workers. If he obtains a job on his own initiative, he must bring this fact to the attention of the bureau at once. It is illegal to continue to collect unemployment checks while working, and a penalty will be imposed.

A worker becomes disqualified for unemployment benefits if he refuses, without good cause, any offer of employment for which he is reasonably fitted by his training and experience. Depending upon your state law, the grounds on which he may refuse work in his field offered by the unemployment bureau and still retain unemployment benefits usually are:
(1) if the employment suggested to him has, as a condition, membership in a company labor union that would interfere with membership he may have in another union;
(2) when there is a strike or similar industrial disturbance in the organization in which this employment is offered him;
(3) when the place of employment is an unreasonable distance from his residence; or
(4) when the wages offered are substantially less than those prevailing in the locality for that or similar work.

The tax for unemployment insurance is not levied against government payrolls and payrolls of nonprofit organizations operated exclusively for religious, charitable, scientific, literary, and educational purposes. Consequently, unemployed workers from these organizations are not usually entitled to benefits.

Benefits are continued for a stipulated period, except when the recipient is successful in securing employment. The amount of benefits is based on the wages or salary he enjoyed during the time of his employment.

The unemployment insurance system is now an established part of our social and economic structure. Yet when it was first introduced, there were some objections raised to it. In justification of the *New York Unemployment Insurance Statute*, which is typical of those throughout the country, the highest court in New York pointed out that in 1936 (the year in which many of these statutes were enacted) unemployment had increased enormously in every part of the country. When such a condition becomes general and affects the whole country, said the court, the situation demands the exercise of the power of the state. During the Depression years, tremendous sums of both state and federal money were expended in keeping housed and alive the families of the unemployed.

"Such help was absolutely necessary and it would be a strange kind of government, in fact no government at all, which would not give help in such trouble," said the court.

Liability insurance

This type of insurance is an indemnity against liability for bodily injuries or for damages inflicted upon the property of others. It has a wide application both in industry and in private activities.

The hazards of modern industry have created such risks for employers that a tremendous demand has arisen for liability insurance that will protect them against losses from causes beyond their control.

In this class of insurance are included the so-called public liability policies, which provide insurance against loss from the bodily injury or death of persons who were not employed by the insured, but who were involved in an accident through the negligence of his employees or others engaged in his business.

Liability insurance compensates an employer for damages he must pay to people injured due to the negligent acts of his employees. (Employees themselves are covered by Worker's Compensation, discussed later in this chapter.) The premiums for injuries to employees are ordinarily figured as a percentage of the compensation paid to them, and are computed on the payroll of the insured at specific rates that are proportional to the risk assumed by the employees, such as office workers, drivers, machine operators, and so on.

The various functions of liability insurance extend to the liability of contractors, elevator liability, risks borne by landlords, losses from strikes, as well as from many of the infinite activities of everyday life. Liability coverage is also issued to physicians, dentists, and lawyers, and covers losses arising from error or mistake. These are known as "*malpractice*" policies and can be quite expensive.

Patient rights

When patients are hospitalized, they have a right, after reading their consent forms, to edit them. For example, many times when a patient is scheduled for minor surgery and a specific condition is found, even though that situation may not be an emergency, further surgery is performed because the patient is already on the table. You can require beforehand that no other procedure is done unless it is an emergency so you can have time later to review your options.

You should always inform the hospital of any drug allergies you have and any medications you are currently using since, otherwise, untoward results might not be the hospital's responsibility.

Auto liability policy

An automobile liability policy provides indemnity against loss through injuries to others arising from the operation of the insured's vehicle by himself, by members of his family, or by others with his consent. Such a policy, however, does not indemnify the owner against damage to his own car by others. That is usually covered by the other person's policy.

Casualty insurance

Insurance of this kind ordinarily provides for payment of loss for damage arising from accident or some other unanticipated event. Usually it provides benefits to compensate for damages to property from cyclones, hail, hurricanes, or lightning; the loss of domestic animals; breaking of plate glass; boiler explosions, and the like.

Essential facts about Social Security

This topic has been discussed, in part, in Chapter 17 on *Personal Property Rights*.

Whether you are employed or not, everyone aged 5 or older must have a Social Security number. Parents fill out application Form SS-5 to obtain one for each child. You will need their birth certificate and other identification and proof of your relationship. You must also now list your dependent children's numbers on your tax return.

The Federal Social Security Act provides that after December 31, 1939, every individual who is considered "fully insured," who has attained the age of 65 and who has filed an application for the benefits provided by that law, is entitled to monthly payments from the time he becomes eligible for them until he dies.

Starting in the year 2000, the age at which full benefits are payable will be increased in gradual steps until it reaches 67. This will affect people born in 1938 and later. Reduced benefits will be payable at 62 but the reduction will be larger.

If you plan to retire before you reach the age of 65, you should apply for monthly benefits no later than the last day of the month you want benefits to begin. Generally, benefits payable for months before the age of 65 can begin no earlier than the month you apply. This is the same for widows and widowers who will receive benefits before they turn 65. However, they can apply in the month after the worker's death and still get a benefit for the month of death.

If you apply after you reach 65, back payments can be made for some months before the month you apply for retirement or survivor's benefits. You can apply up to 3 months before the month you want benefits to start.

Lost cards and change of name
If you lose your Social Security card, contact a local office to apply for a duplicate. You must have evidence of your identity. If you change your name, you must apply for a new card and you must have evidence that identifies you under both the old and new names.

Disability provisions
It is now possible to receive disability benefits as part of Social Security. Any worker who becomes severely disabled is eligible for monthly benefits under Social Security if he has worked long enough and recently enough, regardless of age. While a worker is disabled, payments can also be made to certain members of his family. A person disabled before the age of 18 does not have to qualify for disability benefits if his parents have worked.

Contact your local Social Security Office for assistance as soon as disability occurs. They will tell you how many credits you must have and how recent they have to be.

AIDS Virus
There are new Social Security disability rules allowing people infected with the AIDS virus to qualify for benefits earlier than they would have before. The coverage is for persons not yet of retirement age who apply for benefits or persons under the *Supplemental Security Income (SSI)* program for low income persons. There are now more conditions allowing you to qualify as automatically disabled and eligible. If you tested positive for the HIV virus and have some symptoms, such as fatigue or an inability to take public transportation, or diseases associated with AIDS such as a low white cell count, pneumonia, persistent unresponsive diarrhea, or inflammation of the heart lining, you can receive benefits. You will no longer have to show you are incapable of working.

If you tested positive or have a friend or relative who has, you should apply to take advantage of the more lenient government rules. The AIDS virus and your civil rights are covered in detail in Chapter 9.

Relatives who can collect benefits
Retirement or disability payments can be paid to spouses 62 or over, spouses under 62 if caring for a child 16 or disabled, who is getting a benefit based on the retired or disabled worker's earnings, unmarried children under 18 (or under 19 if full time high school students), unmarried children 18 or over who were severely disabled before 22 and who continued to be disabled.

Survivor payments can be made to the children as noted above, widow, widower, or surviving divorced mother or father if caring for the worker's child under 16 or disabled, who is getting a benefit, widow or widower 50 or older who becomes disabled not later than 7 years after the worker's death, dependent parents 62 or older when there is no spouse or children. Survivor benefits can also go to a divorced spouse 62 or over or to a surviving divorced spouse at 60 or a disabled surviving divorced spouse age 50 or older if the marriage lasted 10 years or more. Grandparents' earnings may also benefit children in some circumstances.

Self-employed

You and your employer each pay an equal share of Social Security taxes (FICA). If you are self-employed you pay taxes for retirement, survivors' disability and hospital insurance at a rate twice the employee rate. Self-employed people have received a credit against the self-employment Social Security tax rate of 2.0% of self-employment income for 1986-1989. After 1989, this credit was replaced with deductions designed to treat the self-employed in much the same manner as employees and employers.

Taxes

You now may have to pay a federal income tax on up to one half of your benefits in any year in which your adjusted gross income for federal tax purposes plus non-taxable interest income and one half of your Social Security benefit exceeds a base amount. If you have other income you should consult a Social Security Office or the Internal Revenue Service for a free booklet explaining it.

If you work after 65

If you return to work after you started getting your retirement checks, your added earnings could result in higher benefits since Social Security will refigure your benefit after the additional earnings are credited to your record. In addition, there is a special credit that could mean a larger benefit. It is called a delayed retirement credit. Starting for workers who reached 65 in 1990, this credit will be increased gradually.

However, you must also be aware that if you are employed after starting to receive benefits, the level of your earnings may cause a reduction in your benefits. The exempt amount you may earn now is different if you are under or over 65 or 70, as is discussed in Chapter 17. In 1990, $1 in benefits will be withheld for each $3 in earnings above the limit for people 65 and over. Beginning in the year 2000, the age at which this withholding rate applies will increase as the retirement age increases.

Some outside sources of income such as V.A. benefits, income from savings, most investments, insurance, pensions based on work covered by Social Security, non-governmental disability compensation and rents received if you are not in the real estate business are not considered wages or earnings and will not affect your monthly payments.

Check up on your account

You should get in touch with your Social Security Office if:

- You are unable to work because of an illness or injury that is expected to last a year or longer;
- you are 62 or older and plan to retire;
- you are within 3 months of 65 even if you don't plan to retire;
- someone in the family dies;

- you, your spouse or children suffer permanent kidney failure.

You also should get in touch every few years to get a statement of their record of your earnings upon which Social Security taxes were paid and to see the amount of Social Security taxes.

Errors have been known to occur in the Administration's records, or the employer may not regularly be sending in the tax. If rectification is not made within a few years of the date of the error, it cannot be made at all, and the loss is the employee's. The field offices of the Social Security Administration have a special form available for requesting a statement of your account. Only this form can be used.

No one entitled to benefits under this statute can transfer or assign any of the monies that may become due or payable under it, nor are any of these benefits subject to claims or attachments by creditors, or to the operation of any bankruptcy or insolvency statutes.

When and how to apply for benefits

Application for the benefits under the Social Security Act must be made on the forms prescribed by the commissioner and may be obtained from any office of the bureau. The amount of wages and the dates of payments may be established by any applicant by the records of the Administration or by any other acceptable evidence.

When you apply you should have with you: Your Social Security card or a record of your number. If your claim is on another person's record you should have their card or number. You should also have:
- Proof of your age, such as a birth or baptismal certificate;
- marriage certificate, if applying for those benefits;
- child's birth certificate for their benefits;
- W-2 forms or tax returns for the last 2 years so these earnings can be included for benefits;
- medical data, if applying for disability benefits; and
- proof of support by the worker, if applying for benefits as a dependent.

If you are missing any papers, don't delay your application. Social Security will help you to look for alternative proofs.

Hospice benefits

The first American hospice was established in 1974. Hospice care is a coordinated program of palliative and supportive services for the terminally ill with very limited life expectancy. It is covered as a benefit under Medicare, Part A. (Medicare is discussed in Chapter 17.) Home care is provided along with certain inpatient care and services not otherwise covered by Medicare. The patient must be eligible for Medicare Part A, the life expectancy must be 6 months or less and care must be provided by a Medicare approved hospice program including a public or private agency primarily engaged in service provision to terminal persons. You can find an agency by calling your Social Security

Office. The agency will give you all the information on length of care, type of care and services not paid for.

The hospice may also arrange for short term respite care, that is providing someone to give the regular provider time off, a respite or temporary relief. Some charge is attached to this service.

Mammograms

Because breast cancer is the second most common form of cancer to affect women, and mammograms are an excellent tool for detecting a cancer in the early stages when it is more curable, mammography screening will continue to be covered by Medicare.

However, now payment will be made for annual screenings for all female beneficiaries 40 and over. The Part B deductible for screening is waived, but beneficiaries must still pay 20% for screening mammography and any unmet deductible and 20% coinsurance for diagnostic mammography.

Medigap insurance

These are policies which are meant to supplement Medicare. There are about 10 benefit policies and they must all have standard provisions. Their language must be simple and the labels must be the same for similar benefits. They must clearly delineate what the policy pays as compared to Medicare's payment and your costs.

Standard coverage includes payment of your 20% share of Medicare approved doctors' fees and your contributions to the cost of a lengthy hospitalization. Additional benefits are available at added costs such as for foreign travel emergencies, prescription drugs and the hospital deductible.

Medigap policies can be purchased within 6 months of turning 65 despite some technical overlaps with another private health policy you may have. You also can get a Medigap policy even with a pre-existing health problem if you apply within 6 months of turning 65. But if you are older, you are out of luck.

If you are disabled and on Medicare, you also can get a Medigap policy if you apply within 6 months of turning 65 and you won't be disqualified by prior medical problems.

Uniformed Services Former Spouses Protection Act

Divorced spouses had problems receiving a share of the retirement benefits of the covered working spouse. In 1981, the Supreme Court held that even after 19 years of marriage, the ex-wife of an Army Officer could not receive a share of his Army retirement as part of their divorce settlement since it had been given to him as an inducement for his enlistment.

However, the Congress changed this when they enacted *the Uniformed Services Former Spouses Protection Act*. It allows the courts to treat retired pay as property of the serviceperson or of the serviceperson and the spouse. The treatment depends on the divorce and property laws of the jurisdiction where the divorce occurred. The total payment may not exceed fifty per cent. There is no minimum duration of the marriage needed unless otherwise noted.

Civil Service retirement benefits and foreign service retirement benefits may also be paid to an ex-spouse.

Workers' Compensation Acts

These state statutes have been enacted for payment to an injured employee or family of a specific amount for injuries "arising out of and in connection with" employment, if they are incapacitating, either temporarily or permanently. Their underlying principle is that of insurance. Workers' Compensation is a substitute for other remedies the worker may have against the employer such as a negligence action.

Many workers are trying to bring negligence actions for a higher recovery, particularly in cases where employers, aware of a work hazard, willfully or wantonly fail to take precautions. Other employees, with long term exposure to work hazards or injuries occurring away from a job site but job connected are trying to be covered by compensation.

Workers' Compensation is proportioned to the amount of a worker's earnings and the gravity of the injuries. The application for benefits should be made by the worker, or someone acting on his behalf, to the state labor bureau, or whatever corresponds to it, in the state in which the applicant resides or has been employed. They will help on the preparation and filing of the claim with the proper state authorities.

Workers' Compensation cases are fact rather than law related. What is or is not job related is the issue. A truck driver delivering jet fuel spilled some on himself and when he lit a match in his home and was burned, a court in New Jersey said his injury arose out of his employment.

By receiving Workers' Compensation you do not waive any claim you may have against a third party, not your employer, for negligence causing your injury. You can sue them, although your employer may have an interest in anything you collect because of the compensation you receive.

Stress

Recently, claims for injuries related to stress suffered on the job have increased. Massachusetts has barred compensation for mental stress resulting from transfers, layoffs and personnel decisions. Oregon disallows stress claims related to employer actions such as firing, discipline, and employee evaluations, if they are reasonable. In Michigan the stress must be significant and arise out of actual events at work. In the District of Columbia workers must not have had a predisposition to psychological harm. However, in Maryland, fire fighters and police are given a presumption that their stress is caused by the job.

Federal Employee Group Life Insurance Act (FEGLIA)

When state law conflicts with federal law, children in divorce actions may suffer. FEGLIA guarantees that federal employees can change their life insurance policy beneficiaries at any time. But it requires that the name of any new one must be in writing, witnessed and filed with the employee's agency. If no beneficiary is listed, the proceeds go the surviving spouse.

In a decision by a federal appeals court in Illinois, a divorce decree which specified that children of a federal employee father would be his life policy beneficiaries was not enforceable. His new wife collected when he died because he'd never listed any beneficiary. Courts in Georgia and Colorado follow this rationale.

Kennedy-Kassebaum Health Insurance Reform Act

Thousands of employees who change jobs no longer will lose health insurance coverage. The so-called Kennedy-Kassebaum bill, named after the two Senators who were the chief sponsors, guarantees insurability in the new job's health plan to workers who were covered in their former job for at least a year. Pre-existing conditions also are covered.

The law helps those who are starting their own business or joining one that has no existing health plan. In that event, although you will be guaranteed access to insurance, you have to buy and pay for it yourself, perhaps at steep cost depending on age and medical condition. There's no assurance the available insurance will be comprehensive. But, there won't be a waiting period for pre-existing conditions, including pregnancy. For this coverage you will have had to have a former policy for 18 months.

Medicaid funded nursing home care ineligibility

Anyone who reduces his or her net worth by transferring assets for less than fair market value within three years of applying for Medicaid is ineligible for nursing home care covered by Medicaid. The ineligible period would be the number of months in a home for which the assets would have paid. Persons who charge to help the transferor are liable for criminal prosecution.

Any transfer of property or other assets can be complicated and have tax and other ramifications. It is important to seek legal advice for estate planning.

ERISA (Employee Retirement Income Security Act) and HMO's

ERISA, enacted in 1974, was designed to protect pensions and other benefits. But with the rise of managed care and HMO's (health maintenance organizations) ERISA has been hurting employees. It's prevented successful lawsuits when an employer's health care plan insurer denies coverage for an operation or procedure, and the employee or family suffers as a result. It has helped HMO's in their position that ERISA takes precedence over state laws so the case must go to federal court where ERISA prevents suits against health care organizations. So it's been a Catch 22 for employees. ERISA also doesn't allow compensatory or punitive damages.

Some federal courts of appeal have decided that ERISA does not necessarily protect HMO's and have allowed them to be sued for malpractice in state courts as doctors can be. If you have a problem with your employer's HMO not allowing a medical procedure, you should obtain another opinion as to its worth for your health, try to renegotiate with them and then seek legal counsel. It could mean your life or that of a loved one.

ERISA and trickery

The Supreme Court has ruled that workers who are tricked by employers into giving up their benefits can sue to have their coverage restored. The theory before was that ERISA, the Act passed to protect employee pensions and other benefits, did not permit suits brought for the benefit of employees but only on behalf of the benefit plan itself.

In the case in the Supreme Court hundreds of workers were induced to transfer from a solvent company to a subsidiary which folded. That left them and thousands of retirees without health care coverage.

The company claimed ERISA did not permit employees to sue on their own behalf. But the Court said ERISA gave workers access to the federal courts and was meant to insure that administrators of benefit plans acted solely in the interest of participants and beneficiaries. The Court felt the parent company deceived their workers by assuring them they were transferring to a company with a bright future when they knew the new company had debts and was unprofitable.

Insurance discrimination against battered women

Spousal abuse has been discussed in Chapter 6. But many people have been unaware that the abuse has been the basis for denial of coverage for health, life and disability insurance to the victim. Insurers are not required to disclose the reasons for denial.

Forty states have a mandatory requirement that doctors document and report evidence of domestic violence. Medical records as well as police and court reports are reviewed by insurers. As a consequence, companies in New York, Pennsylvania and elsewhere have used them to make underwriting decisions unfavorable to victims. Domestic violence has been like a preexisting medical condition.

The American Bar Association advocates state and federal legislation ensuring non-denial of benefits. Five states already have legislation prohibiting the use of abuse status, abuse related conditions and a history of abuse related claims as a basis for insurance coverage. There are other states where similar bills are under consideration. State Farm Insurance Companies have stated they no longer will use domestic violence to determine an insurance applicant's eligibility.

Motor vehicles, drivers, and related matters

24

Chapter 24
Motor vehicles, drivers, and related matters

Before you sign a contract to buy a car, be sure to read it carefully. Check for fringe charges, a dollar-a-day late charge on your payments, etc. Also, you will be wise to get all guarantees specifically set down by the seller in writing. Such guarantees are known as "*express warranties*," and the seller must back them up. If he fails to do so, you may bring an action to recover damages or, if you have not yet paid the purchase price, you may return the car and cancel the agreement.

Do not rely on the mere word of a salesperson that a car is in good condition. The court may consider that what he said was just personal opinion and not a commitment on the part of the company he represents. You need an official statement from the company or the individual seller if your complaint is to stand up in court.

In a recent case in a French court, a car buyer sued because his car got only 16 miles to a gallon of gasoline, whereas the car salesman had assured him he would get 24 miles to a gallon. The Paris judge ruled that gas consumption is one of the most important qualities of an automobile and is one of the most convincing sales arguments. The excessive consumption of gas made the car defective. The owner obtained a $1,000 judgment from the car dealer. Such substantial misrepresentations may be grounds for a successful suit by the buyer.

A manufacturer of automobiles or a dealer who handles cars as a business sells the product with certain implied guarantees, as well as the ones which are stated in the sales contract. Failure of any of these guarantees will be grounds for a suit. Among these implied warranties is the promise that the product is in acceptable condition for use, unless the manufacturer or dealer indicates any particular dangers or defects which he knows or should know about and which are not obvious to the buyer. This particular implied guarantee will not apply, however, if the buyer had an opportunity to inspect the product before the sale and could have found the defect upon inspection.

Perhaps the most important implied guarantee is for the general operating fitness of the car. This will apply, unless the seller specifically disclaims it.

All potential buyers should understand that if the car is bought from someone other than a dealer, such as the original owner of a used car, these implied guarantees are much less strict and particular caution should be used. You should always road-test a used car before considering buying it. In all cases, be sure to read the contract carefully before you sign. These rules for the purchase of automobiles apply to almost all other new and used products as well. While the movement for consumer protection is gaining strength, there are many areas in which the buyer is still unprotected.

An interesting extension of the doctrine of implied warranty with respect to a new product involved a man who was working in a sewer and using an oxygen-producing mask made by the defendant. He died of asphyxiation because the mask did not work properly. The plaintiffs in the case were members of his repair crew, and they were injured while rushing into the sewer to save him. They sued the defendant manufacturer on the "danger invites rescue" theory based on the original wrong of breach of implied warranty that the mask would be acceptable for use. The court stated that whether they were suing on breach of implied warranty or on negligence in manufacture was not significant, because both were wrongful acts. The manufacture and sale of the defective mask placed the man in peril and invited his rescue by those who worked with him, and the defendant was held liable for damages sustained by the rescuers in their attempt to aid the victim.

If the product proves unsatisfactory

A buyer can bring action against the seller for failure of the product to meet either the stated contract guarantees or the implied guarantees, if he has notified the seller of the failure within a reasonable time after he discovers, or should have discovered, the defect. What a "reasonable" time is will depend on the nature of the defect. The first step that should be taken, if the defect has been discovered soon after purchase and the payment was by check, is to stop the check. If the buyer cannot get satisfaction from the seller, he may take any of the three following possible actions:

1. resell the product, if possible (noting the defects to the new buyer, of course), and obtain the difference from the original seller, between the price he would have received on resale if the product had been satisfactory, and what he actually did receive, or

2. sue for the difference between the actual value of the product with the defect and the original purchase price, or

3. if he cannot resell the product and does not want to keep the defective one, he can try to force the original seller to furnish a product which is in proper condition.

False advertising

Describing an automobile or any other product in glowing terms, particularly in a context in which it should be obvious to the prospective buyer and seller that an effort is made primarily to glorify the product, is usually acceptable. Untrue or fraudulent statements, however, may be grounds for an action in fraud and deceit by the buyer. The decision in each case will depend upon how the court feels the remark should have been interpreted by the buyer.

A bicycle manufacturer described his product as "having been subjected to the most severe practical tests." He added that "we guarantee them to be all that is claimed—perfect of their kind, unsurpassed and unsurpassable." A buyer of one of these bikes brought an action when the product did not prove to be of excellent quality. The decision in the case was in favor of the manufacturer. The court stated that merely to advertise an article as "perfect of its kind" or "unsurpassed and unsurpassable" is not such a representation as to be classified a guarantee of performance. The judge in this case added that these statements are "nothing more than the extravagant phrases with which dealers are prone to recommend their wares." He felt the buyer should have understood them in this context.

All states except Arkansas and South Dakota have *"lemon laws,"* which establish arbitration procedures to make it easier for owners of hopelessly defective cars to get a replacement or a refund. Thirteen states run the arbitration and you are more likely to be satisfied. The rest use procedures sponsored by private groups (Better Business Bureau, AAA) or the auto makers. Get copies of your state's law from your State Attorney General's office for help on procedure, time limits for filing and your options if unhappy with the arbitration. Also contact the *Center for Auto Safety* in Washington, D.C. for their many publications. You should know that "lemons" bought back can turn up on the used car market, especially out of state. Buyer beware!

How to transfer title to a car

When you purchase a car, used or new, apply at the most convenient motor vehicle license bureau for the transfer of its registration to you.

The name under which the car is registered is the name of the legal owner of record. In the event of loss or mishap, your ability to prove your ownership and your right to possession of the car becomes of paramount importance. A correct entry in the official records is the best way of proving your title. Almost every state now requires that, before any car can be sold, the potential buyer must obtain the formal certificate of ownership (which motor vehicle authorities maintain). This protects the new buyer. If it turns out that the car was sold by someone who stole it, the new buyer would not have priority of ownership over the rightful owner. He would also not have priority over a party who has a lien against the car, and any existing secured interest in the automobile would be indicated on the certificate of ownership.

Financing the purchase of your car

The purchase of an automobile made other than for cash may be financed with the assistance of an automobile-financing company, a loan company, a bank, or a credit union.

Under all circumstances, if the money needed for the purchase of a car can be obtained from a reputable bank or credit union, by all means borrow money from one of them. The bank lends a portion of the money needed for the purchase, and the borrower supplies the balance. The bank secures its loan by a chattel mortgage on the car. If you cannot meet the payments, the bank may start proceedings to repossess it. But aside from the interest that will be deducted from the face of the loan when it is made there is no other charge, or only a small one.

In financing the purchase through the aid of a finance company, be careful to check the amount you are asked to pay for interest. Examine with special care the "charges" over and above the interest. Carrying charges are today regulated in most of the states by statute. Federal law now requires that the actual interest you agree to pay be made clear to you. Do not accept a chart indicating repayments as a substitute for a simple statement of the interest rates.

Can you sell a mortgaged car?

With the consent of the mortgagee or lender of the money, in the event the loan is secured by a chattel mortgage, you are free to sell your car before the payments are fully made, under any arrangement that meets with the expressed approval of the lender of the money. It is a penal offense to attempt to sell an automobile or any other property that is mortgaged unless you first obtain the consent of the mortgage holder. Such a consent must always be set out in writing, signed by the lender, and made a part, preferably, of the bill of sale to your buyer.

What to do in an accident

If you are involved in an accident, do not make the mistake of failing to obtain the names and addresses of all or as many as possible of the witnesses. If you are insured against the casualty, immediately notify your insurance company. Further, be careful, when arranging for the repair of the damages done to your car, to have no work done other than the repairs made necessary by the accident. In this way you obtain a clear statement of your damages that will require no explanation in court of other charges, and will open no door for a cross-examination belittling the expense you have incurred. The opposing attorney will also be unable to create for the jury the implication that your claim included additional and outside items.

Damages

A suit to collect damages resulting from an automobile accident must be brought within a reasonable time of the date of the accident. Generally the time limit is three years. The laws of your state will mandate the exact statute of limitation.

Not all discomfort, nor every bruise that may occur, is a ground for the collection of damages. The operation of a bus or of a private car may be the cause of slight injuries to passengers by a too abrupt stop, but the way the driver handled the vehicle may have provided escape from greater injuries. If a too abrupt stop causes the passengers to be bruised or injured, and it is due to the operator's careless driving, then there is unquestionable ground for claims for injuries. If, however, the operator was not negligent—if the sudden stop and the injuries occurred in the proper and honest exercise of skill demanded to avoid an accident—there is certainly no liability on the driver or the owner of the automobile. A driver is not an insurer of the safety of others, nor can any operator guarantee to his passengers an absolute freedom from injury or discomfort that may be the consequence not of his own negligence but that of others.

What "negligence" means

Negligence, a factor commonly encountered in suits arising from automobile collisions, has been defined as "the omission to do something which a reasonable person guided by those considerations which ordinarily regulate the conduct of human affairs would do, or to do something which a prudent and reasonable man would not do. Negligence is the absence of care."

What is contributory negligence?

Contributory negligence is the act or omission amounting to a want of ordinary care on the part of the injured or complaining party which, concurring with the defendant's negligence, caused the injury. Without such cooperating negligence, the injury would not have occurred.

Where the parties to an accident have both violated the rules of the road, and both violations contribute to the injury, a person may be barred from recovery because of contributory negligence.

Comparative negligence

An alternative doctrine is called comparative negligence. It would merely reduce the plaintiff's recovery to reflect the comparative fault of the parties rather than bar the action completely. The plaintiff may recover a portion of the damages suffered equal to the other party's fault, at least where the plaintiff's negligence is less than the defendant's and, in some states, even where the plaintiff's fault equals or exceeds that of the defendant.

When an accident is unavoidable

When a person driving a vehicle has taken every precaution possible and yet is still involved in an accident, he cannot in general be held responsible for damages that result from that accident.

The car of a woman driving along a highway was suddenly struck by another automobile. The collision threw her car out of control so that for an instant it was diagonally across the highway and in the path of a third car, which hit it. The court ruled there was no liability on her part for the damages suffered by the driver of the third car, since the accident was not her fault. Said the court: "Where is the absence of care or what did she do which a prudent and reasonable person would not have done? There is not the slightest evidence tending to show any negligence on her part."

A passenger's rights and responsibilities

The injuries or damages that may be inflicted on others by someone operating a borrowed car are, in most states, the responsibility of the owner who loaned it. Where this is not the law, in order to prove that the owner is liable, it must be shown that the lending was in itself negligent—for example, the car was loaned to a child or an incompetent driver.

A driver normally must be reasonably careful of his passengers, and he is liable for injuries suffered by them as a result of his failure to observe such reasonable care.

However, the majority of states have passed *guest statutes,* which permit a passenger to recover for only those injuries resulting from reckless or willful conduct or gross negligence on the part of the driver of the car in which he is a passenger. A demonstration that the driver failed to exercise reasonable care will not be sufficient in guest statute states to allow injured passengers to sue the driver successfully. The idea behind the guest statutes is that, since the passenger is not paying for the ride, the host should not be held to a high standard of care.

In none of the states does the law permit a passenger to recover for his injuries if he failed to point out imminent dangers which he should have realized the driver would not notice. Legally, a passenger in this situation is said to have contributed to the accident and cannot recover for damages which resulted.

Data at the Motor Vehicle Administration (MVA)

For years the information on your license, including your name and address as well as data about your driving record, has been made available by over 30 states to anyone for a fee. Many bulk mail and marketing firms wanted it as well as attorneys and insurance companies. Many people were unaware their Motor Vehicle Administrations were selling this information. Now, there is a federal requirement that states give people the option of closing their driving records to the public at large.

Maryland enacted a law which gives people privacy protection. It allows individuals to request that information such as name, address and personal description be removed from inspection. They also can block dissemination of car tag number, make and model of all owned cars and any traffic violations received in the last three years. No Social Security numbers were ever released so there was no need to address that in the law. If you are concerned about the privacy of your data, given the amount of it accessible from so many sources, you should check to see if your state's MVA sells it and what they plan to do about changing that practice.

Joint adventure

An adventure in law can also be called a joint venture or a joint enterprise. It is a joint undertaking by two or more people, and a determination of who controls the undertaking is of the utmost importance in defining it as a joint adventure. If both parties in a vehicle have a common destination, are making a trip for a common purpose, are sharing expenses, and can equally direct which route will be taken on the trip, then a court may very well decide that the trip was a joint adventure, and the driver's negligence will be imputed to the passenger just as though he were driving. It does not matter, in such a case, that the passenger might not know how to drive. If it is demonstrated that he can exercise control over the driver and the operation of the car, then he too can be considered negligent.

Some courts have applied the term "*joint adventure*" only to situations where there is a business or financial interest in the trip or the use of the car. But most courts still say the use can be for pleasure as well.

Many courts do not like to use the term where married people are concerned, since the marital relationship is something special and has about it a general commonness of purpose. However, you should be aware that many courts will find a joint adventure even if the parties in question are legally married.

Members of a joint enterprise or adventure can sue one another and recover damages based only on allegations of simple negligence. This is an exception to the requirements of the states' guest statutes previously discussed.

Moving companies

Interstate moving companies which transport your household goods across state lines are required to give you binding estimates or guaranteed prices. *The Household Goods Transportation Act* makes it easier for you to know what your moving costs will be. This helps you avoid the trauma at the time your furniture is to be unloaded of finding the estimate that you counted on is not even close to the actual price. The Act, however, does not cover intrastate or local moves.

Car pools

Share-the-ride arrangements abound, and there is no general rule governing them. In some cases you will be considered a guest, and in others you will be considered an invitee, to whom is owed the duty of ordinary care. One thing that the courts consider in assigning responsibility is whether the purpose of the arrangement is social or whether the driver is simply being accommodating. In the latter situation, the passenger will probably be held to be a guest.

Another important factor is whether the passenger pays for the ride. Suppose you drive your car some days and ride with others the rest of the time. Payment can be money, services, or other benefits. The point is that you have an obligation either to pay for your rides or to reciprocate in kind. It is also important that you have a definite rather than a casual arrangement, and also that you pay regularly and in some fixed amount. Another aspect that the courts will look to in deciding whether the passenger is a guest is the relationship between the driver and the passenger. If there is a family relationship, the courts tend to find that the passenger was a guest.

The plaintiff was injured while riding in an automobile under an arrangement that he had made with six fellow employees. Five employees had cars and alternated driving, while the sixth, who had no car, paid 75 cents a week to be transported. When the plaintiff, a regular driver, sued his driver, the court held that the plaintiff was a guest since the arrangement was "simply the exchange of amenities between fellow employees." The plaintiff lost his case because he could not prove his driver was grossly negligent.

In another case, a woman was injured while riding to work with her son-in-law. She rode with him regularly and from time to time gave him $1 for gasoline. She was held to be a guest.

In each case, the court will view the particular arrangement involved to determine whether a guest relationship existed.

What about taking the kids?

In a typical arrangement, neighboring parents agreed to take turns driving each other's children to school. There was an accident and a lawsuit. The court found that there was "a definite business relationship whereby each party was saved time and expense in the task of transporting her child to and from school." So the driver was held to the duty of ordinary care.

What about pleasure or vacation trips?

Sharing the expense of gas and oil consumed on a trip when that trip is taken for joint pleasure or social purposes is nothing more than an exchange of social amenities, and a passenger is still considered a guest. It might be different if payment constituted an important element for the giving of the transportation.

Two friends went to a bowling tournament out of state. They had made similar trips in the past and had alternated using cars and sharing travel expenses. In the suit that followed an accident, the court held that the plaintiff, who was injured while in his friend's car, was his guest. "Balancing of expenditures for mutual auto trips does not constitute payment for transportation."

The rules of the road

These days it is imperative that a driver drive defensively and that he obey the "rules of the road," not only for his own safety but to avoid penalties. The law of the road has been defined as "the custom or practice which has become crystallized into an accepted system of rules regulating travel on the highways." Legislative enactments have established these rules of the road officially in an effort to reduce accidents resulting in death, injury, and the destruction of property. However, not all drivers know these rules, nor do they know how the law views them under varying circumstances. Here we shall consider some of the common problems you may face, and what your rights and responsibilities may be when you are involved in different kinds of accidents.

The right of way when entering a highway

Under the statutes governing the right of way, the driver of a vehicle about to enter a highway from a private drive must yield the right of way to all vehicles on the highway.

At the intersection of a private road and a common highway, a truck and a bicycle collided. The boy on the bicycle had come from the private driveway. Before leaving it, he had seen the truck approaching, but, believing he would have time to travel a hundred feet on the road and turn to the left into another street before he would be overtaken by the truck, he had shot ahead. He was hit by the truck, knocked from his bicycle, and injured.

When this boy sought to collect damages, they were denied him. The traveler on the highway has the right to assume—although not absolutely—that the other traveler, about to enter his path of travel from a private driveway, will yield to him.

Right of way and how it is limited

Right of way, when its abuse can lead to an accident, is a relative thing. The duty to avoid accidents or collisions at street intersections rests on all travelers who find themselves there at the same time.

When two automobiles collided at a street intersection, one of the drivers protested that the other had been negligent in not reducing his speed, irrespective of his right of way.

In its comment on this criticism, the court observed that not only is there no universal rule requiring a motorist who has the right of way to reduce the speed of his car under all circumstances at a street intersection, but that also, there is nothing in the law that entitles a motorist to proceed across a street intersection regardless of other circumstances. "The right of way possessed by a motorist is, like a 'green light,' not a command to proceed but a qualified permission to do so."

Another court has stated this rule to be that every traveler must take heed at a street intersection and that, even though he is first at the intersection or has the technical right of way, such facts are not of controlling importance.

Right of way and negligence

Late on a winter night a car was traveling an icy road between Battle Creek and Lansing in Michigan, where "slow" signals warned of danger. At a street intersection the driver stopped, glanced along an intersecting street and, since no other vehicle was in sight, he started his car. However, trees had obstructed his view. A cab was approaching. He noticed it when it was 150 feet away, and the ice of the pavement made it impossible either to stop or to speed ahead. The cars collided.

An effort was made by the cab driver to reverse the judgment awarded against him. He contended that the passenger-car driver had been guilty of contributory negligence in not exercising greater care at the street intersection.

Refusing to disturb the verdict of the court below, the appellate court said that no hard and fast rule exists that speed or statutory right of way determines negligence. Each driver must use such care as obvious conditions require.

Pedestrian right of way

Late on a misty afternoon a brickyard employee was returning home from work. The yard was on the north side of a highway, and the workman, starting to cross along a path used by his fellow workers for many years, glanced to the east and west for approaching automobiles. About one-eighth of a mile to the east was an approaching car—another was coming from the west about twenty feet away. Confident that he could reach the center of the street before the arrival of the nearer car, he started across and had reached the center line safely when this oncoming car swerved to the left, hitting the man, knocking him to the ground, and rendering him unconscious.

The automobile driver's defense was contributory negligence on the part of the injured man—since he had glanced only once at the oncoming car. The defendant also declared that "pedestrians are obligated to yield the right of way to all vehicles on the roadway." However, the court held the rule of the road to be that the right of way is relative and not absolute and that it does not absolve anyone from the duty of exercising due care to avoid accidents.

In some places the right of way always belongs to the pedestrian, except where signals control traffic.

Signals and warnings

The rule of the road is, in general, that anyone traveling on a street or highway must cooperate with others. Those on the road possess mutual rights. A driver of an automobile has no rights on a highway superior to the rights of others engaged in the lawful use of the road. When a driver engages in an act that involves the safety of others on the road, he must give them a timely warning by a proper sign or signal, mechanically or by hand, as the situation requires.

Sounding the horn by a highway

An automobile driver approaching a highway from a private roadway or drive must sound his horn and give a signal that he intends to enter the highway.

A motorcycle, with its exhaust explosions audible at 400 feet, was traveling a highway at 35 miles an hour. An automobile entered the highway from a service station and gave no signal. It collided with the motorcycle. The motorcycle operator, said the court, had the right to assume that the driver of the automobile would not take the right of way without first giving warning of an intention to do so. It was the motorcycle operator's duty to sound a warning "only in the event it appeared necessary to give a warning."

Failing to sound a horn for pedestrian

One winter morning an elderly farmer started on foot to a nearby town leading a gentle seven-year-old cow by a four-foot lead rope. Another farmer was driving his car at 20 miles an hour. Looking ahead, the driver saw the man and the cow on the right side of the road. When he overtook them he slowed down to about five miles an hour and passed about 11 feet on their left, not sounding his horn, as this seemed unnecessary to him. Suddenly, when the automobile was abreast of the man and the cow, the cow gave a lunge, knocking her owner to the ground. His fall resulted in a fractured hip.

The trial court held there was no negligence, and that the automobile driver was under no obligation to give any warning of his approach. The cow owner appealed, and the appellate court declared this omission might or might not have been negligence—it was a question of fact for a jury to determine.

"A timely warning would not have been a vain thing," said the appellate court. "It would have given notice of a close approach of danger which the owner of the cow had no special reason to apprehend."

Another pedestrian

In a fairly similar incident, a pedestrian was walking on the right side of a highway. The driver of an automobile proceeding in the same direction attempted to pass on the left side about eight feet from the pedestrian without sounding his horn. Startled by the sound of the car, he jumped in front of it and was injured. Under the law of that jurisdiction, a pedestrian on a highway was required to travel on the left side of a highway. However, although he was walking where he should not have been, the court held that this violation did not mean that he could be run down at will. The law is that a motorist has a duty to exercise the care and precaution that circumstances require, and by all means to sound a warning on approaching a pedestrian.

When a horn is not sounded properly

An 11-year-old boy, riding a bicycle along a highway, was overtaken by an automobile which collided with him. He was thrown to the ground and killed. At the time of the accident, a strong wind was blowing in a direction away from the boy on the bicycle. The driver of the car had sounded his horn when he was 175 feet in the rear of the bicycle, but the wind apparently prevented the signal from reaching the boy's ears. The court held the driver of the car liable in damages for the death of the boy. "He was negligent in failing to give an audible warning as he approached and undertook to pass the bicycle."

Rear red lights and stopping

The driver of a truck stopped without giving any signal that he intended to do so. His negligence was responsible for an accident. Sued for damages, he based his defense on the fact that the red signal lights displayed when he applied the brakes were adequate notice to the car following in the rear.

The court held the truck driver guilty of negligence. A signal made by holding out a hand, said the court, "is not subject to speculation, but definitely advises the following driver of the intention to stop. Causing the red stoplight to go on is not the equivalent of the stop signal, and failure to give it is negligence."

Today, however, directional signals and flashing red lights are generally accepted as proper notification of a driver's intentions.

Lack of signals on turning

A truck driver, without checking his rear-view mirror to see if any car was behind him, made a left turn without turning on his directional signal or using his hand. At that very moment, the driver of an automobile that was going in the same direction was attempting, after sounding his horn, to pass the truck. The two vehicles collided. In deciding the suit that the automobile driver brought, the court pointed out that a driver, before starting, stopping, backing, or turning from a direct line, must assure himself that he can act with safety and, when another vehicle is affected, he must give a signal of his intention to turn.

Although the judgment of the trial court favored the driver of the passenger car, this decision was reversed on appeal and remanded to the trial court. The automobile driver's attempt to pass had been made at a street intersection. If the jury should determine this to be contributory negligence on his part, the appellate court declared, he could not recover damages for his losses.

Failing to signal at an intersection

A heavy truck was traveling on the right side of a highway at 15 miles an hour. At a crossroad, without giving any signal, the driver swung his truck sharply to the left. He had not seen a passenger car less than 75 feet behind him, going 30 miles an hour.

The driver of the passenger car sounded his horn and undertook to pass on the left at the intersection of the roads—it was too late for him to stop when he saw the truck driver make his turn to the left. The passenger car driver swerved farther to the left. The passenger vehicle then skidded from the pavement all the way over to the shoulder of the road and finally stopped when it hit a telephone pole.

In the suit by the owner of the passenger car, the court pointed out that the driver of any vehicle on a highway must signal his intention to turn from a direct line, or to start, stop, or back, by extending his hand and arm horizontally beyond the vehicle's left side.

Here, however, the driver of the passenger car failed to recover damages. He had been guilty of contributory negligence when he attempted to pass the leading truck at a street intersection.

Signaling to cars in the rear

When two or more cars are one behind the other on the road, the leading vehicle has no better legal position than the cars that follow it. The driver of each must take care not to stop, slow up, or swerve from his course without giving notice of his intention to those behind.

A bus followed by a truck at a distance of 100 feet was traveling about 45 miles an hour. The bus suddenly and without warning turned to the left and stopped. The truck crashed into the bus, overturned, and caught fire. Its driver was killed.

The court that tried the suit brought by the bus company decided in its favor. The owner of the truck appealed, because the question of negligence on the bus driver's part had not been submitted to the determination of the jury. Because it was shown that the bus driver had not signaled, the court reversed the judgment.

This court made a fundamental observation about cars traveling one behind the other. They must all observe the rules of the road, of course. However, the court said, "Just how close to a vehicle in the lead a following vehicle ought, in the exercise of ordinary care, to be driven; just what precautions the driver of such a vehicle must, in the exercise of ordinary care, take to avoid colliding with the leading vehicle which slows, stops, or swerves in front of him; just what signals or warnings the driver of the leading vehicle must, in the exercise of due care, give, before stopping or slowing up, of his intention to do so, may not be laid down in any hard-and-fast or general rule." Such issues are for a jury to decide after hearing all the evidence.

Reducing speed at crossings

A pedestrian at two o'clock on a winter morning was hit by an automobile while crossing intersecting streets and later died.

"I heard a crash like a thud," testified one witness. "I looked around and saw something flying around in the air that looked like a piece of cardboard. It hit the ground and it was a man."

The driver of the car appealed from the verdict against him. He claimed he had the right of way and that the man he killed had been guilty of contributory negligence. He contended that when two or more persons traveling in different directions approach at a crossing, the one having the preference is entitled to the first use of the crossing—that it is the duty of others to give him a reasonable opportunity to use it.

The court refused to disturb the decision of the court below. "It was incumbent on the driver of the automobile to be continually watchful for the possible presence of persons on the crossing," declared the court, "and to have the speed of the car so reduced and controlled that it would be readily stopped or diverted in time to avoid collision with pedestrians who might be exposed to such danger."

Making a left turn

Many accidents arise from the making of left turns in the face of opposing traffic. One of the most common hazards faced by the driver making such a turn is that he often cannot properly appraise the speed of the approaching car. At what distance can he make such a turn and be within the law?

Two automobiles were approaching each other when the driver of one of them made a left turn. They collided, and this driver was severely injured. The testimony of the injured man was that he had made the turn 300 yards from the approaching car. The testimony of the driver of the other car was that his turn had been made at less than 50 yards.

Here was a question of fact that a jury would have to determine. But the appellate court remarked that it was unwilling to hold, as a matter of law, that it is negligent to cross to the left in front of another car 300 yards away. On the other hand, said the court, if the approaching car was less than 50 yards from the one driven by the injured man when he turned to the left, he was clearly negligent. If the other driver was farther away than fifty yards, whether the driver making the turn could make it prudently would depend on the apparent speed of the oncoming car, and whether its driver saw and recognized a signal of the other driver.

When you back on a highway

An automobile owner had parked his car parallel with the curb between two other parked cars. In maneuvering his car free, he backed into the pathway of an oncoming car. The cars collided. Before backing, the man in the parked car had looked and seen no approaching cars and, believing the road was clear, he had given no warning signal with his hand.

The court charged that this man's failure to give the hand signal as he was required to by law was negligence. Nevertheless, such a failure did not entitle the suing automobile owner to recover damages unless there had been no negligence on his own part.

Be careful when backing

A four-year-old child was playing in the yard of a Portland, Maine, tenement house used as a playground by the tenants' children. In the same yard Joe Balzamo was cleaning an automobile. When he finished his work, he started to back the car into the street and ran over the child, crushing his leg.

Damages were awarded for the injury. The court commented that since, in backing a closed car, a driver is greatly hampered because the lower edge of the rear window limits his field of vision, he must take further precautions or give a warning signal. Otherwise he is guilty of negligence.

When you drive a motorcycle

More than half of our states require motorcyclists to wear safety helmets, since many motorcycle accidents result in head injuries. Other states are likely to pass similar laws to protect cyclists. Check your state's driving code before venturing out on a motorcycle as a driver or a passenger.

Parking

If you stop your car on a public highway just for a little while, to let passengers off, this is generally not considered parking. However, you are parking if you leave your car for a period longer than necessary, say, to load or unload passengers or freight, and there is no one in the car who can operate it.

Street lot owners and their rights

What are your rights if your city installs parking meters in front of your property?

The owner of property facing on a street brought an action to restrain the city from using the street as a parking-meter zone. He asserted the existence of the parking meters was an illegal interference with his right of access to his property.

The court held, however, that whatever right of access the owner possessed was subordinate to the rights of the public. He had no remedy or right to compensation, unless a special statute should be passed.

On this subject, all courts do not agree. In other instances it has been held that the owner's right of access to his property includes "passage, accessibility, and stopping briefly and reasonably in front of premises without unnecessarily inconveniencing the passage of the general public. The owner of property on the street has the right to have his family, guests, or customers come and go within reasonable limitations and, further, the owner has the right to park alongside his own property within reasonable limitations without the exaction of a parking tax."

Can an injured bus passenger always sue the carrier?

A Greyhound bus and a truck, each going in opposite directions, collided.

The driver of the truck, traveling on the wrong side of the road, had refused to surrender a proper share of the highway. In a suit brought by a passenger of the bus for the injuries which she received, the court held the bus company was neither guilty of negligence nor liable for the injuries of its passenger. The driver of the bus, said the court, had the right to presume that the approaching vehicle, which was on the wrong side of the road, would go over to its proper side and the bus driver could not be expected to anticipate that it would not.

However, since the truck driver was definitely negligent, the injured passenger was entitled to bring suit against him.

Your duty toward children

A child running across a road was hit by an automobile and suffered substantial injuries. The verdict of the jury awarding damages to the child was reversed on appeal. The reason was that the jury had not been asked to determine whether the automobile horn was sounded by the driver of the car at a sufficient distance from the running child to be heard, since "it was the duty of the driver of the car to give a timely warning."

The specific facts are of great importance in all these cases. However, the courts of the different states have set various ages under which they hold a child is not capable of proper appreciation of dangers. But it is generally held that while age is a factor, and an important one, it is not the only factor. The capacity of a child to exercise care must be determined by a consideration, also, of his intelligence, experience, discretion, training, and other characteristics, as well as the nature of the danger itself. Nevertheless, unless a child is so young as to be incapable of using any care, he is responsible for a degree of care that can be determined only by the circumstances of each case.

The general rule is well summed up by one legal authority. "While it cannot be said as a general rule that all infants above the age of seven are required to exercise the same degree of care as an adult, such a one is required to exercise such degree of care as a person of like age, intelligence, experience, and capacity for understanding and avoiding the danger might reasonably be expected to exercise under similar circumstances and surroundings."

Parental responsibility

When an adult accompanies a pedestrian child, the duty of the driver is changed. In Alabama, a three-year-old was killed by a postal truck. The accident occurred near a rural mail box. The child's father was working on an auto nearby when the truck pulled up. Two older children went for the mail and the tot followed. He was in front of the truck when it started. Before moving, the driver had looked around but the tot was too small to be seen. The family sued the United States for negligence.

The court found that since the family was close by, the mailman would not expect the child to be in a place of danger. The father's contributory negligence in not exercising care prevented him from recovering damages for the loss of the child.

Car seats

Many state statutes now require that infants and small children be placed in safety-regulated car seats. Contact your local government as to the specific requirements of your jurisdiction.

Nonresident motorist act

State statutes provide for "*constructive*" or "*substituted*" service on a non-resident motorist. This is to be used when such motorist becomes involved in an accident while using the highways in the state where the statute has been enacted and leaves before any court action can be commenced.

Typically, the statute provides for serving a state official, such as the Secretary of the State or the Director of Motor Vehicles, with a copy of the process, and also for mailing to the nonresident motorist a copy of the same process and a notice of the service on the state official. The rationale behind the statutes allowing substituted service is that the motorist, when he drove into the state, consented to all the automobile laws of that state, including those governing the procedures for any action at law.

These statutes differ from state to state in the requirements they provide for mailing notices. Some states allow the notice simply to be sent by ordinary mail. Others require that it be sent by registered mail and that the return receipt be filed with the other papers in the case. It is important that the proper procedure be followed. Cases have been won or lost on points such as the notice being addressed to the wrong party or improperly addressed. Sometimes the party to whom the notice is sent refuses to accept the letter, which is why you need proof of registered mailing.

What if the accident occurs on private property?

Many of the nonresident motorist acts have been broadened to include accidents that occur "within the state" rather than just on the public highways. They may also include vehicles which are not in motion at the time of the accident.

If your state statute uses the word "*highway*," then if you have an accident that occurs in a parking lot, service station, or drive-in movie, you cannot sue the out-of-state driver by substituted service. The word "*highway*," however, can include the street, so a pedestrian area may be included within the terms of the statute. It is wise to consult an attorney immediately who can advise you about the state's regulations.

What is a motor vehicle?

Of course, an automobile is such a vehicle; but what about a motorcycle? A nonresident motorcyclist who gets involved in an accident out of his state can in fact be served under the same statutes that pertain to automobiles. However, a crane, tractor trailer, or semi-trailer is generally not considered a motor vehicle under these acts. It is obviously important to consult an attorney when you are involved in an accident with an out-of-state vehicle, or if you yourself are the out-of-state driver. In this way you can be sure that all your rights will be fully protected.

Financial responsibility laws

These are statutes which most states have enacted to protect the public against the operation of motor vehicles by financially irresponsible persons. Usually the statutes provide that, within a stated period of time following the report of an auto accident to the Motor Vehicle Department, which accident involved significant property damage or serious personal injury, the operators or owners of all the vehicles must furnish reasonable security to satisfy any judgments and give proof of financial responsibility for the future. If security is not given, the driving licenses and registrations of those delinquent are suspended. If there is automobile insurance, then the statute does not apply.

In a recent case that went to the United States Supreme Court, a Georgia motor vehicle safety responsibility statute was found to be faulty. Under the statute, a motorist who did not have insurance and who was involved in an accident had to post security to cover the amount of damages claimed by the people injured, and failing to do so, his motor vehicle registration and driver's license were subject to suspension.

An uninsured motorist, who was a clergyman, was involved in an accident where a girl rode her bicycle into his automobile. He did not post the security required, and at the hearing held by the Georgia Director of Public Safety, the motorist's offer to prove he could not be liable for the accident was rejected, and he was told to post the security. The United States Supreme Court decided that before the license and registration could be suspended, due process of law required that there be a determination that there was a reasonable possibility of a judgment being rendered against the motorist as a result of the accident, because, if there was no such possibility of liability, it was unfair that he be required to post security.

On the other hand, in a similar situation in a Utah case that went to the United States Supreme Court, it was held that, even though the motorist was not granted a hearing on the question of reasonable possibility of fault, such a hearing had been given in the district court in Utah, and the suspension had been delayed pending the determination of that court. Accordingly, the Court ruled that the motorist had had a meaningful hearing and therefore the financial responsibility law could be applied.

Compulsory auto insurance

This is in effect in Massachusetts, New York, and North Carolina, and in Rhode Island for minors only. Under the New York law, no vehicle may be registered unless the application is accompanied by proof of financial responsibility such as liability insurance, a bond, or a deposit of a stated large sum of money. If a driver is involved in an accident while uninsured, the penalties are severe. The New York law applies to both resident and nonresident motorists. The Massachusetts law operates only as to cars registered in the state and to out-of-state vehicles operated in Massachusetts for more than 30 days. The

Massachusetts statute does not apply when accidents occur on private property or to guest occupants of vehicles.

Intoxication tests

Many states have enacted statutes on the subject of chemical tests to determine whether a driver is intoxicated. Alcohol in the brain causes intoxication, and the amount of alcohol in the brain is determined by the amount of alcohol in the blood. Opinions vary as to what percentage of alcohol must be in the blood for a determination of intoxication or being under the influence. Given our high speed society, legislatures have been reducing the blood alcohol level to stem the tide of accidents. Virginia and ten other states have a low level of .08 blood alcohol. In Virginia, for drivers under 21, it is .02 blood alcohol. In Maryland it is .10 for everyone.

Liability for serving drunks

There have been several court cases holding third parties liable for injuries caused by drunk drivers. Under so-called *"dram shop" laws*, bars and restaurants are liable for serving liquor to intoxicated adults or to minors. A few states have *"host liability" laws* allowing recovery against hosts serving liquor or drunken guests.

The California Supreme Court upheld damages against a San Mateo apartment manager who gave a cocktail party for tenants. One of the tenants got drunk and caused a car crash. In Missouri, a tavern giving away beer and a radio station advertising the free beer paid $92,000 to a couple whose son was killed by a drunk driver who had patronized the tavern.

The return of dram shop laws and the growing use of police check points to test drivers for alcohol abuse is largely due to the efforts of antidrunk driving groups. *Mothers Against Drunk Drivers (MADD)* has chapters in 47 states and lobbies for strict laws and penalties involving drunk drivers.

In contrast to these cases, the Washington State Supreme Court did not find state and county officials liable for failing to revoke the license of an oft-arrested drunk driver. While the driver caused the death of a woman, the court held that the failure to revoke the license, under the *Washington Habitual Traffic Offenders Act*, was too remote from the accident to impose liability.

Must you take a drunk test?

Chemical tests may include the blood test, the breath test, the saliva test, or the urine test. Not all states are equipped to give a driver each test. The tests have been upheld as constitutional in that they do not involve an unreasonable search or violate a person's privilege against self-incrimination. This is because the operation of a motor vehicle on the roads of a state is not a right but a privilege. There have been challenges to all these tests as violations of the constitutional right against unreasonable search and seizure, but none of these has been successful.

New York was the first state to enact a law which says that any driver of a vehicle shall be deemed to have given his consent to a chemical test for alcohol content in the blood. If the driver does not consent, then he can lose his license. Other states that provide for revocation of the driver's license for refusal to be tested are Idaho, Iowa, Kansas, Nebraska, North Dakota, and Utah. Certain prescribed procedures must be followed, however, before a license is revoked, including a hearing.

Can you get your own doctor to do the test?

Yes, at your own expense, of course. However, if your doctor cannot come, his absence is not sufficient reason to refuse to take the test.

Do you have a choice of tests?

The type of sobriety test to be given a driver is determined by the arresting officer. In Kansas, a driver said he was diabetic and wanted to choose the type of test. When he refused to take the test proposed, his license was revoked. The court later said he had no right to refuse since there was no proof he was a diabetic. The same results were reached in a case involving a man who claimed he had a heart condition, and in a situation where the driver refused to take the test claiming he had a rare blood disease. You should let police officers know if you prefer a particular test, or if you think the first one they gave you was not accurate. The officers are not obliged to comply with your wishes, but in several cases they have agreed to this expressed preference.

In many states, such as Georgia, Maine, Minnesota, New Jersey, Oklahoma, Oregon, Rhode Island, Texas, Washington, and the District of Columbia, refusal to take a sobriety test is not admissible in criminal proceedings. In New York, if you refuse to be tested for blood alcohol content, you cannot be required to submit to a test, and a refusal is not admissible as evidence in criminal proceedings. However, you can lose your driver's license.

In a New York case, a defendant was charged with driving while his ability was impaired. He refused to take a test, and at his trial he pleaded not guilty. The charge was dismissed, as there was insufficient evidence for conviction. The defendant then tried to use the criminal dismissal to block the revocation of his license, but since he had refused to take a test, he could not block the revocation.

Having your license suspended or revoked

The U.S. Supreme Court has ruled that having a driver's license is not a constitutional right. In order to stop drivers who drink and drive, states not only have been lowering the blood alcohol content for a determination of legal intoxication, they are taking away licenses immediately on the road if a driver fails a breath test or refuses to take one. The courts have been supportive.

Virginia, the District of Columbia, Maryland and over 30 other states have curbside suspensions. Some give temporary licenses until a court hearing. Others require waiting for an expedited hearing at which time the judge decides on suspensions according to the state's law.

Aviation accidents

These days, with highjacking of airplanes almost as common an occurrence as the highjacking of contraband liquor by rum-runners, one from another, during the days of prohibition*, we should consider claims involving accidents on airplanes. (*The 18th Amendment to the United States Constitution, passed in 1919, prohibited the sale of liquor. It was repealed by the 21st Amendment in 1933.)

Unlike the other usual accident cases, problems with air travel can be worldwide. First, you have the problem of venue, or where should you sue? Possible choices include the place of the accident, or where the plaintiff lives, or where the defendant corporation is incorporated or has its home office, or, possibly, if your lawyer thinks it is the fault of the manufacturer of the plane or the maintenance company, as well as of the operating airline, where those others are located. Naturally, your lawyer will try to select the place where the law and the damage claim can be most favorable. For example, we have heretofore considered for the automobile the problem of "guest statutes," where approximately 17 states prohibit recovery against the host for ordinary negligence. Suppose you are a guest in a private airplane taking off from a state with such a statute, and the accident occurs in another state. These are all complicated situations that require expert legal analysis.

In a case that went to the highest court of the State of New York, a New York resident took off from a New York airport as a passenger of a well-known airline. The plane crashed in Nantucket, Massachusetts. The suit was brought in New York. If the law of Massachusetts, where the accident occurred, was applied, the amount that could be recovered for negligently causing a passenger's death would be limited, as the Massachusetts law then provided, to no more than $15,000. The New York Court refused to apply the Massachusetts limitation in this action for wrongful death against a common carrier. If the suit had been brought in Massachusetts, the result would have been different.

Back in 1929, an international diplomatic conference was held in Warsaw, Poland. The United States did not participate in this conference, but it did have observers. Out of this came the Warsaw Convention, to which the United States became a party in 1934. This Convention limited the liability of an airline to 125,000 French francs or the equivalent of $8,300 in American money. Regardless of whether the airline was negligent or not, you could collect up to $8,300 and no more, if your flight was an international flight. This means that if you, an American, leave Los Angeles on your way to London and have an accident over the United States, the Warsaw Convention will apply. Not all of the countries of the world are parties to this Convention, and therefore, if you are flying to one of those countries, the Convention does not apply.

In order to avoid the $8,300 limitation, it is possible to show willful misconduct by the airline. Let us say that an employee mechanic deliberately puts sand in the fuel pump, then the limitation would not apply. Today, the $8,300 figure is no longer relevant because most of the airlines have accepted a $75,000 limitation. Because there was so much dissatisfaction with the $8,300 figure, in 1955 there was a meeting at The Hague, which became known as *The Hague Protocol*. This raised the amount to $16,600 or double the old figure. The United States participated in the Hague meeting and its delegates accepted the new figure, but it was never ratified by the U.S. Senate because it was clearly an insufficient sum. Finally, the United States was prepared to withdraw from the Warsaw Convention, when the airlines of the world agreed to the Montreal agreement, which required that they waive the limitation on damages from $8,300 up to the new limitation of $75,000. Most of the airlines outside of the United States are government lines, and so it was really government policy that was involved. There is an agreement called the *Guatemala City Protocol*, prepared in 1971, with a $100,000 limitation and with no exception for willful misconduct, etc. However, the United States has taken no action with respect thereto, although its delegates to Guatemala accepted it.

One way to protect yourself against the limitations imposed by the Warsaw Convention or the problems of what law applies in connection with your suit for negligence, is to purchase your own insurance. Then your only problem is whether the insurance you purchase covers the accident you have. In one case in New York, a man purchased insurance at the airport to cover his flight, as he indicated on the form, from New York to Los Angeles and his return from Los Angeles to New York. He took a helicopter from Los Angeles to Disneyland and on the way back, the helicopter crashed. Did his insurance cover this side trip? If, when he purchased his insurance, he had indicated that he was going to Disneyland, he definitely would have been covered. However, the insurance company contended that this was now a separate flight for which he should have purchased a new insurance policy. The members of the Court divided, with some taking the position that at the airline insurance counter one is not too careful in indicating the terminus of the flight and could very well have meant Los Angeles to include Disneyland. See the specific chapter for the general subject of Insurance.

Drive-in theaters

What about movies containing nudity which are visible to passing motorists? The Supreme Court said that a Jacksonville, Florida, ordinance making the exhibition of such films a nuisance would be acceptable as a traffic regulation since breasts and buttocks are distractions. But the ordinance applied to movies that could be viewed from any public place. The right of free speech was more important and a citizen could avert his eyes if he found the scenes offensive. The law was held to be unconstitutional.

Motor homes

In 1985 the Supreme Court ruled that police do not need a warrant to search the interior of motor houses. Because such vehicles are mobile and subject to local government regulation, the Court found they fall into the "vehicle exception" to the warrant requirement. If however, the vehicle is stationary or connected to utilities, the Court acknowledged that the motor home may be really a home and not a vehicle.

Tired workers

Working overtime may be profitable to an employee but it can cause fatigue that, in turn, can cause accidents. Examples of fatigue related mishaps include medical personnel prescribing the wrong medicines, train operators missing warning signals, ships beaching because the Master had been up too long and auto crashes.

A McDonald's in Oregon was sued when an employee, who had worked two successive length shifts and had also attended a regular school day, was involved in a fatal car crash. The basis for the suit was the employer's alleged negligence for allowing the student to drive after he had been on the job for an unreasonable period of time. This rationale is similar to that used to put liability on persons who serve too many drinks and the drinker then causes an accident. Of significance in any case would be that an employee complains of fatigue to a supervisor.

Of course, if the employee himself is injured, that could be considered a work-related injury covered by Workers' Compensation. The employee then could not recover in a lawsuit. (See *Workers' Compensations Acts* discussed in Chapter 23.)

Zone of danger test

The courts in New Jersey and Wisconsin have relaxed the rule to allow some bystanders to sue for negligent infliction of emotional distress. The Supreme Court still applies the rule, the zone of danger test, but now allows suits even when non-family members endure emotional distress.

The test was that any bystander alleging such distress had to have been in the way of the danger that harmed the actual victim. This test was applied to limit fraudulent claims. But when a woman in New Jersey who saw her fiancée killed in a traffic accident sued for negligent infliction of emotional distress, the court agreed she was entitled. In Wisconsin the mother of an accident victim didn't see the accident, only the horrible consequences. She sued and won.

The closer the relationship to the victim and the site the better the chances of recovery. But the issue is still in flux.

Criminal law

25

Chapter 25
Criminal law

One object of criminal law is to punish those who are found guilty of crimes; a more important goal, however, under our system of justice, is to protect the rights of the innocent.

A civil action is based on an offense against an individual rather than against the community, and the plaintiff prosecutes the action himself, generally through a lawyer whom he retains. A criminal action is based on an offense against the state or the community and is conducted by the official prosecutor. To be guilty of a criminal act, one must either have intended to cause the action which occurred, or he must have acted in a manner that was so negligent or reckless that willfulness is implied by the law, which therefore recognizes no legal defense for committing the act.

Generally speaking, the word "*crime*" includes both felonies and misdemeanors. *Felonies* are offenses of a more serious nature which are defined by the statutes and constitutions of the states as offenses punishable by imprisonment in a penitentiary or state prison, or by death. *Misdemeanors*, on the other hand, are "faults and omissions" of less consequence, and are punished less severely.

For example, murder is a felony, while the violation of a traffic law or municipal ordinance is a misdemeanor; both are generally classified as crimes. A felony is sometimes defined as a crime which carries a punishment of imprisonment for one year or longer, and a misdemeanor is defined as a crime for which imprisonment is less than one year. A parking violation is not considered to be in the crime category. It is usually called an "offense."

In all felonies, the accused is entitled to trial by jury as a constitutional right. This is not true of all misdemeanors, which can be tried by a justice of the peace, a magistrate, or some special court composed only of judges, provided that the penalty is not more than six months imprisonment. If more, then the United States Supreme Court has ruled that a jury trial must be provided.

Although the guilty verdict of a jury normally is the final word for the trial phase, defense lawyers usually ask the court to throw it out or declare a new trial. Some states, including Massachusetts, Virginia, the District of Columbia, and Puerto Rico, allow a judge to change a verdict, usually because of judicial error.

Warrants

A warrant is an order signed by a magistrate or a judge. It is made on a complaint by someone, and it charges that you committed a crime.

In 1983, the United States Supreme Court abandoned search guidelines that it established twenty years ago. The former guidelines required that before magistrates could issue a warrant based on knowledge which police officers obtained from informants, the magistrate was required to consider the informant's basis of knowledge and the informant's trustworthiness and reliability. Under newly established criteria, the magistrate may issue a warrant if, after a common sense evaluation of all the circumstances, it appears that there is a fair probability that contraband or other evidence will be found in a certain place.

The warrant must list the charge against you. It also must direct the police officer to make the arrest and to bring you before a magistrate or judge. If a police officer has a warrant for your arrest, he must tell you he has it. You have the right to ask to see it. If you ask, he must show the warrant to you. Even when a police officer has a warrant, the Supreme Court has held that he may be liable for damages if he acted unreasonably in obtaining the warrant without probable cause.

A police officer can arrest a person without a warrant, however, if he sees that person commit a criminal offense. In nearly half of the states, a private person can make a citizen's arrest if he observes a criminal offense.

Recently, the United States Supreme Court ruled that a warrant is required for nonemergency inspection of your residence or place of business by city health or fire inspectors without your consent. However, in order to obtain a warrant, these officials need not prove that there is or may be a violation of the law as to your premises. A warrant will be issued based on their reasonable need to conduct periodic inspections for health and safety purposes.

Search and seizure

The Constitution has provided that any search of your person or your home must be reasonable. It is reasonable if it is conducted incidentally to a lawful arrest, if it is done with your consent, or if it is done pursuant to a legal search warrant.

Even with a warrant, the Supreme Court has ruled that the police are constitutionally required in many cases to knock and announce their presence before entering a home to conduct a search. It is not a rigid rule and need not be applicable in cases where there is a threat of physical violence or a danger of destruction of evidence. Lower courts will decide when unannounced police searches will be allowed. The states which imposed "no knock" and announce requirements will have to change.

If a search is improper, then any evidence seized, however incriminating, cannot be used against you.

Recently, this constitutional rule was said by the Supreme Court to be enforceable against searches and seizures by state authorities.

Strip search

If you are arrested, there is a substantial chance that you may be asked to submit to the humiliation and embarrassment of a strip search. The reason for such search is that dangerous arms and contraband can be concealed in underwear or body cavities.

However, if the offense for which you have been detained is a minor one, such as eating a sandwich in a no food area, searches may be a violation of your constitutional protections against unreasonable searches and seizures.

If you find yourself in custody and are ordered to strip, the best thing to do is protest to the jail supervisor, threaten to file a lawsuit and try to contact your lawyer to have it stopped.

Canine sniffing in schools

The Courts of Appeal for the Fifth, Seventh and Tenth Circuits recently reached decisions regarding the use of dogs to sniff out drugs in students' cars and lockers. They adopted a doctrine of "public smell" analogous to the doctrine of "public view." If a police officer is in a place which is proper and smells marijuana, no search has occurred since the smell coming from the property is considered exposed to public view and therefore unprotected. The courts concluded that the use of dogs merely enhances the police officer's ability to smell in the same way that a flashlight enhances the eyesight.

The use of trained dogs to sniff the students themselves is less clear. The Court of Appeals for the Fifth Circuit found such searches to be unreasonable where the person searched is not under suspicion. The Seventh Circuit is the only circuit to have concluded that the sniffing of school children is not a search.

Stop and frisk

The Supreme Court has ruled that persons whom the police reasonably suspect might be engaged in criminal activity may be detained for a short period of time, and questioned, but only for the purpose of checking the suspicious behavior. If the stop lasts for more than a temporary period of time, it will likely be considered to be an arrest. If during the stop the police have a reasonable suspicion that the person is armed, they are allowed to "frisk" the suspect for weapons. The frisk is limited to a pat down of the person and can only be directed at weapons, and not at other items of suspicion.

Traffic violations

A police officer may require a car to pull to the side of the road if the officer reasonably suspects that a traffic violation, or other violation of law, has occurred. The officer may also require a person in the car to get out of the vehicle for further questioning.

Vehicular searches

In earlier years, when there was no warrant for the search of a vehicle or closed contents in it, the questions were, were you searching an auto that coincidentally turns up a container, or a container that coincidentally turns up in an auto? The rule has been that when police have probable cause to believe a vehicle contains something illegal, they could search the vehicle without a warrant.

The Supreme Court has ruled that drugs found in a car by D.C. Vice Officers during a traffic violation stop could be admitted as evidence. The local rules restricted traffic enforcement to uniformed officers, a rule or law in many jurisdictions. In the case at issue the violation was a right turn without signaling. The officers admitted that enforcing the traffic laws was a pretext for the arrest. Given this decision almost any set of circumstances could justify a search by any duly authorized law enforcement personnel.

What about any closed container in the car? Until recently, the authorities needed a warrant to search it. However, now the Supreme Court has said there is no distinction. The police may search an automobile and any closed containers in it without a warrant when they have probable cause to believe there is contraband or evidence in the container.

The hearing

The first step in the judicial process is normally a hearing at which witnesses are examined, and you have the right, but not the obligation, to testify. You can ask that this hearing be adjourned until your lawyer can be present. For certain misdemeanors, this hearing constitutes a trial; the presiding magistrate will dispose of the case directly and either dismiss the charge or find you guilty. In other cases, where he cannot try the charge himself, the magistrate decides only whether there is a reasonable basis for finding that you have committed the offense charged. In such case, you may waive the hearing. If you are charged with a misdemeanor, the magistrate will hold you for trial by another court. If a felony is involved, he will hold you for action by a grand jury.

Grand jury

A felony indictment can only be made by a grand jury, which is larger than a normal jury and hears evidence in secret session. You have the right to consult a lawyer at a grand jury, although he cannot be present in the jury room. You also have the right to ask to appear before the grand jury when it is considering your case, but you should not make this request without the advice of your lawyer. The trial itself is held before what is called a petit jury composed of 12 members. In many jurisdictions, a jury of six members is being used, and has been held constitutional by the United States Supreme Court.

Jury duty

As a citizen and resident of your community, you have the duty to answer the call to serve on the jury. Of course, when hardship is involved, the court will usually excuse your service. Sometimes you will not get to sit on a case because your presence may be challenged by the respective attorneys. There are two different types of challenges. You can be challenged with no reason given—this is called a *peremptory challenge*—or you can be *challenged for cause*, which means that there is something that would make your service unsuitable, such as your relationship to the defendant, your prior knowledge of the case, or your prejudgment of the issues. However, the Supreme Court has said that the Constitution's guarantee of equal protection bars the exclusion of potential jurors on the basis of their sex as it does to prevent peremptory challenges to weed out jurors on the basis of race. They have not yet decided on that principle for religion.

Ignorance of the law

The presumption is that everyone knows the law, and from this springs the legal maxim that ignorance of the law is no excuse. If, for example, you do not know that your city has an ordinance forbidding you to litter the streets, you cannot, when charged with this misconduct, make your lack of knowledge a defense.

However, it is only to the law of your own country and state that this presumption relates.

When there are special circumstances in a case involving ignorance of the law, the court can at its discretion impose a lighter sentence.

When you are arrested

A police officer may arrest you without a warrant if he sees you commit or sees you try to commit a violation of the law. He can also arrest you without a warrant if a felony has been committed and he has reason to believe that you did it, even though he was not actually present at the time.

It is a crime to resist an officer who lawfully arrests you. If you believe you are not to blame, you can assert your rights through your attorney at the proper time. If you have been arrested without a legal basis, you have recourse through civil action. If the arrest was proper, the fact that you are innocent will not give you the right to collect damages.

Mr. Gideon

Gideon was charged in Florida with having broken into a poolroom with the intent to commit a misdemeanor. He had no money, and when he appeared in court he asked that a lawyer be appointed to defend him. However, the Florida law permitted the court appointment of counsel for indigent defendants only in cases involving the death penalty. Gideon conducted his own defense and was convicted and sentenced to five years in prison. He appealed while in prison, and his case went to the United States Supreme Court. The Court held that the right of an indigent defendant in a criminal trial to have the assistance of counsel is a fundamental constitutional right, one essential to the conduct of a fair trial. The Sixth Amendment to the Constitution has provided that counsel must be appointed for poor defendants in criminal cases in the federal courts, and now that right applies in state court criminal cases where the defendant is charged with a crime subject to a significant penalty of more than six months in jail.

Mr. Mallory

At about six o'clock one April evening in 1954 a woman was raped in the laundry room of her apartment house in Washington, D.C. Mallory was arrested the next day at about two o'clock in the afternoon. He was questioned and given a lie-detector test. He was the half-brother of the house janitor and had been helping in the laundry room. He was not told of his right to counsel or of his right to a preliminary hearing before a magistrate. He was not warned of his right to keep silent or that any statement he made could be used against him. At about 9 P.M. he confessed to the rape. He was taken before a magistrate the next morning and charged with the crime. After a trial, he was convicted and sentenced to death.

On appeal, Mallory claimed his confession should not have been admitted in evidence against him. The appellate court found that there had been an unnecessary delay between the time of his arrest and his being brought before the magistrate. An earlier arraignment meant he would have been advised of his right to remain silent. Therefore, his confession was held to have been obtained illegally, and Mallory's conviction was reversed.

Mr. Escobedo
Danny Escobedo was 22 years old. He was arrested, along with his sister, in connection with the fatal shooting of his brother-in-law 11 days earlier.

He had been arrested shortly after the shooting, but he obtained a lawyer and he was released. His second arrest came as a result of a statement by an alleged accomplice who implicated Escobedo. At the time of the second arrest, Escobedo asked to see his attorney, who was at the police station and asking to see his client. No meeting was permitted. During questioning, Escobedo made damaging statements connecting himself to the shooting and at the trial these were admitted in evidence, and he was convicted.

Escobedo's appeal went to the Supreme Court, and it held that it is unconstitutional to deny the right of counsel to an accused person who is no longer the object of a general inquiry, but who has become a particular suspect. When the police are no longer investigating, but are accusing and are seeking to obtain a confession, the accused must be permitted to consult with his lawyer.

Mr. Miranda
Ernesto Miranda was a 23-year-old indigent Mexican with a ninth-grade education living in Phoenix, Arizona. A girl was raped and kidnapped, and Miranda was arrested. He was taken to the station house and questioned for about two hours. He then wrote a confession. He was later convicted and sentenced to 20 to 30 years in prison. He appealed, and his case went to the Supreme Court.

The Court stated that the rights of an accused in a criminal case must be protected, and it set out certain rules for the authorities to follow. When a person is taken into police custody, he must be given certain warnings concerning his rights. If these are not given, then any statements made during police questioning cannot be used in evidence at a trial. An accused must first be in custody or deprived of his freedom of action, but once he is, then he must be told he has the right to remain silent, that any statements he does make may be used as evidence against him, that he has the right to the advice of an attorney.

Exceptions to Miranda
Recently, in two cases, the Supreme Court carved out exceptions to Miranda. In a New York case, the Court held that the police need not give warnings before questioning where they believe the public is endangered by the suspect's concealment of a weapon. In an Oregon case, the Court decided that if a suspect confesses before being given his rights, the confession can be used if he again confesses after subsequent warnings.

Asking for a lawyer and further questioning
Robert Edwards was charged with robbery, burglary and first-degree murder. He was arrested and taken to the police station in Arizona. Edwards was informed of his rights as

required by the Miranda decision. He stated that he understood his rights and was willing to submit to questioning. Edwards was questioned until he said he wanted an attorney present. He was then held overnight without further questioning until the police officers returned. They then began to question him but again informed Edwards of his Miranda rights. He confessed to the crime and was thereafter convicted.

The Arizona Supreme Court held that on the second day Edwards voluntarily waived his right to remain silent and his right to an attorney when he voluntarily confessed after again being informed of his Miranda rights. On appeal, the U.S. Supreme Court reversed the state court's decision and overturned his conviction. The Court stated that after an accused in a criminal case asks to have an attorney present during questioning, his request must be granted before any further questions are put to him, unless the accused himself initiates further communications with the police.

What about a spontaneous statement?

A man walked into a California police station and confessed to a crime he had committed in Oklahoma. This confession was allowed in evidence since the authorities were unaware of any crime until his confession. But remember, if you are under arrest or are placed under compulsion by the authorities, the Miranda warnings must be given. As soon as you are placed in custody, you are entitled to a lawyer.

In 1960, Mr. Killough strangled his wife and concealed her body in the city dump in Washington, D.C. She remained there undiscovered for two weeks until he took the police to the spot. He had been arrested on suspicion, since all anyone knew was that Mrs. Killough had disappeared and that blood was found in the Killough car. After being in custody for 34 hours, Killough confessed and was then taken before a United States Commissioner and charged.

After trial and conviction, Killough appealed. On appeal, Killough's confession was found to have been illegally obtained. However, Killough was retried and the government used another confession in evidence. This one had been made by Killough while in jail, to a graduate student who worked at the jail obtaining statistical information from the prisoners. Killough again appealed, and the second confession was also found to have been improper, since Killough had not been warned that his comments could not be kept confidential.

Shoplifting

In California, a food store security agent saw a man steal some meat and go through the checkstand without paying. He arrested the man outside the store and took him to a room in the market where the man confessed. At his trial, the man claimed he had not been warned of his rights, but the court, unlike in the preceding Oregon case, said that the Supreme Court rules did not apply, since the store officer was a private person.

Retail stores have suffered billions in losses due to shoplifting. Statistics show that half of all shoplifting occurs in the last three months of the year. The total cost of such thefts amounts to almost 7% of the gross sales of merchandise.

Although stores have developed surveillance and other techniques, there are limitations on what they can do to protect themselves.

In New York, for example, security personnel may only take measures against suspected shoplifters that are calculated to lead to an arrest or the collection of evidence. This means that they cannot do things that are designed solely to intimidate customers; this would include taking fingerprints or photos or compiling a blacklist of suspected shoplifters to be circulated to other stores in the area.

A model code proposed by the *National Coalition to Prevent Shoplifting* has been used to strengthen existing laws in California, Washington, D.C., West Virginia, and Wisconsin. Michigan, Missouri, New York, Tennessee and Texas are studying the code.

Unlike most state laws, it defines shoplifting as a crime distinct from ordinary theft and it provides for mandatory fines and prison sentences for repeat offenders.

Under the code, shoplifting is committed when a person, with intent to appropriate merchandise without paying the merchant's stated price, alone or with another person knowingly conceals the merchandise or (2) removes, takes possession of or causes the removal of merchandise or (3) alters, transfers, or removes any price marking or any other marking that aids in the determination of value affixed to the merchandise or (4) transfers the merchandise from one container to another or (5) causes the cash register or other sales recording device to reflect less than the merchant's stated price for the merchandise.

The code expressly applies to the theft of shopping carts and also creates a civil cause of action allowing for recovery beyond the value of the stolen item.

Handwriting samples and fingerprints

You can be made to give your fingerprints, stand in a line-up, or give a sample of your blood for comparison purposes. These investigative actions are not considered violations of the rule against self-incrimination. However, the courts have compared the taking of handwriting samples to the giving of a confession. If the samples are not obtained voluntarily, they cannot be used in evidence. You are also entitled to legal counsel if you must participate in a line-up.

The accessory to a crime

The accessory or accomplice to a felony is anyone who directly or indirectly assists in the commission of the offense.

An accessory before the fact is a person who uses his influence to have a crime committed, gets someone else to commit it, or participates in the crime before it happens, by planning it or in some other way. An accessory after the fact is a person who, with knowledge of a crime that has been committed, conceals it from the authorities and protects the one who is charged with committing the offense.

Solicitation to commit a crime

The law generally provides that anyone who solicits another person to commit a crime shall, if the crime is committed, be considered an accessory and punished severely. If the crime is not committed, the offense is generally punishable as a misdemeanor.

The publisher of a periodical which called for revolution and murder, naming poison and dynamite as the agencies to be used, was punished for the commission of a misdemeanor. On the other hand, had revolution and murder actually been accomplished in the way the periodical recommended, the publisher's crime would have been a felony.

When a child commits a crime

Children now are committing violent acts with knives and guns. The states are taking hard lines against younger perpetrators. A child, or an adult for that matter, to be guilty of a crime must be capable of criminal intent. This usually means distinguishing between right and wrong. But for a child he or she must know more than the difference between good and evil. They must realize the illegality of the particular act.

Almost all 50 states have changed their laws allowing juveniles to be tried as adults, thus recognizing the change of perception and behavior on the part of young perpetrators. The law in Virginia is similar to new laws in many of the states. It leaves no discretion to courts or prosecutors. When violent acts such as murder are committed by youngsters 14 and older, they will be prosecuted and punished as adults. Other crimes such as armed robbery also lead to adult prosecution. Florida allows prosecutors alone to decide whether 14 year olds can be tried as adults.

There also has been a change of attitude concerning even younger children. Cases have arisen when even 6 year olds killed. Under the English common law anyone under 7 could not be charged with a crime; those 7 to 14 were protected by *a "presumption of infancy."* The rush to change the juvenile court system and incarceration may even reach down to the youngest.

Is adultery a crime

Under the ancient common law, adultery was not an indictable offense but was punished in the church courts. Now, in half the states adultery is a crime. In at least five, Massachusetts, Idaho, Wisconsin, Oklahoma and Michigan, it's a felony. In Maryland, it is a misdemeanor. In three states, there's no adultery statute at all.

In some of the states, only the married person is guilty; if the other party is single, the offense of that person is not adultery but may be considered fornication. However, fornication is a crime in only about a third of the states. With no fault divorce now possible in all states, adultery no longer is even considered.

Arson

Arson, a felony, is the deliberate burning of another's building. However, in many states, criminal statutes include the burning of a building owned by the offender, although under the ancient law this did not constitute the crime of arson. If anyone is killed while in the fire, the crime is murder.

Assault and battery

Assault is the attempt made, within striking distance, to strike or injure another person—an attempt which, if not prevented, would result in a battery. Battery is the infliction of an unlawful beating or other physical violence on another without his consent.

Assault, then, is the threat to commit battery, and can be committed without actual physical contact. Battery requires some touching or contact.

Thus, if someone violently pushes you, he may be guilty of assault and battery. If he threatens to strike you, and you have good cause to believe he will carry out his threat, he may be guilty of assault.

Carjacking

This is now a federal crime under the *Anti-Car Theft Act*. But, is the law constitutional? Congress justified passage because they can intervene in matters affecting interstate commerce. Courts in Pennsylvania and Wisconsin have said it is. But a Tennessee court said it's unconstitutional. They also complained that Saturn owners aren't protected since those cars are manufactured instate.

Conspiracy

The Berrigan trial in Pennsylvania and the trial in Chicago (*The Chicago 7*), as an aftermath of the Democratic Convention of 1968, revived interest in the crime of conspiracy. In general, an unlawful combination or agreement by two or more people to do an unlawful act, or to do a lawful act by unlawful means, constitutes a conspiracy. Four elements are needed for the crime of conspiracy: an agreement, specific intent, an unlawful object, and an overt act.

The criminal act is the understanding or agreement itself. If a new party concurs in plans formed before he became a member of the conspiracy, and he comes in to aid in the execution of it, he becomes a fellow conspirator, and each conspirator is liable for the acts of every other member done to carry out the conspiratorial plan. This is what makes the crime of conspiracy so all-encompassing, because once you are part of it, acts of the others become your problem as well. The reason for the requirement of an overt act is to have the dividing line between act and talk, so that the opportunity is provided to avoid liability by withdrawing before any action has been taken to further the arrangement.

Bigamy

A bigamist is a married person who, while his marriage partner is alive and undivorced, marries another person.

Bigamy is not always committed knowingly. A few months after the marriage of Lloyd C. and Sarah L., Sarah disappeared, eloping with another man. Five years later, Lloyd, hearing that Sarah was dead, married Frankie. After this second marriage he learned to his surprise that Sarah was still alive. He immediately obtained a divorce from her and again married Frankie.

Shortly after his first marriage to Frankie, he was indicted for bigamy and convicted. The appellate court sustained the bigamy conviction, but added that the good faith of the offender should be considered in mitigation of his punishment.

In a number of states, the law is that a person is not guilty of bigamy when, at the time of entering into the second marriage, he reasonably believed that the former marriage had been dissolved by divorce, annulment, or death. In other states, this belief will not excuse the offense of bigamy.

Blackmail

In the law, "blackmail" has a wider meaning than popular usage gives it. The full range of the term was aptly shown by a New York court, which defined this felony as "equivalent to, and synonymous with, extortion—the exaction of money either for the performance of a duty, the prevention of an injury, or the exercise of an influence." It supposes the service to be unlawful and the payment unlawful.

"Not infrequently, it is extorted by threats or by operating upon the fears or the credulity, or by promises to conceal or offers to expose the weakness, the faults, or the crimes of the victim."

Bribery and extortion

A justice of the peace was convicted of accepting a dollar from a prisoner as consideration for dismissing and setting aside a warrant of arrest. The court that tried him supplied this definition of bribery:

"A voluntary giving or receiving of anything of value in corrupt payment for an official act done or to be done. The distinction between bribery and extortion seems to be that the former offense consists in offering a present or receiving one, the latter in demanding a fee or present by color of office."

Color of office means the pretense of acting in the capacity of a public official, and in a legal sense "extortion" is applied only to the acts of an officer.

One of the most publicized bribery cases of recent times involved Jimmy Hoffa, the former president of the Teamsters' Union. He was convicted of bribery because he attempted to have members of a jury vote for his acquittal in return for the payment of money. In this case, the jury members were performing an official act by making their decision.

Burglary—whether successful or not

This crime, as considered under an ancient law, was defined as "breaking and entering a dwelling house of another in the nighttime with intent to commit a felony therein, whether the felonious purpose be accomplished or not." This old definition is now generally modified by statute. A typical law now says, "A person is guilty of a burglary if he enters a non-abandoned building . . . or separately secured section therein, unless the premises are at the time open to the public or the actor is licensed or privileged to enter therein."

The factors of entry and intent are important here, and the crime is punishable even if nothing is stolen.

When worthless checks are passed

In most states, the giving of a worthless check with the knowledge that it is worthless is included as a crime in the broad category of obtaining money or property by false pretenses. In a few states, however, if a person merely gives a check without representing that there is money to cover it in the bank, it is not a criminal offense. Several jurisdictions are now beginning to pass legislation which also makes it a crime to use another's credit card if the rightful owner has not given his permission.

Disorderly conduct

Under the common law, these offenses were called breaches of the peace and were generally categorized as loud and unseemly noises, disturbing the peace and quiet of the neighborhood, collecting a noisy crowd, or disturbing a meeting or religious worship. Now the offenses are governed by local statutes and can include such actions as spitting on the sidewalk, public drunkenness, and begging without a license. One court said, "The gist of the crime of disorderly conduct is the doing, or saying, or both, of that which offends, disturbs, incites or tends to incite a number of people gathered in the same area."

Some states have now also passed laws which make anyone who engages in, or solicits another to engage in, lewd public conduct, guilty of this crime.

Sometimes an arrest under such a statute can be considered a violation of a person's constitutional rights. In Connecticut, a member of Jehovah's Witnesses played a phonograph record attacking the Catholic Church. He was arrested and convicted for inciting a breach of the peace, but the conviction was reversed when the court found that his freedom of religion had been violated.

In Louisiana in 1965, over 2,000 college students went to the local courthouse to protest some convictions in cases with racial overtones. Many of the marchers were arrested and charged with disturbing the peace under a Louisiana statute which forbade pickets and parades near a courthouse with the intent of interfering with the administration of justice. The students appealed their times, and the United States Appellate Court said that, although freedom of speech and assembly are basic rights, not everyone with opinions or beliefs to express may do so at any time and at any place. The court would not sanction even peaceful conduct which conflicted with statutes drawn to protect basic governmental functions.

With demonstrations becoming quite common. and at times causing disruption of traffic, business, and governmental affairs, the courts must answer the question in each case of which interest—the right to free expression or the threat to normal safety—will prevail. Much will depend on the extent to which the disturbance interferes with other activities. This should be kept in mind if you plan to engage in a demonstration. The right to free speech has its limits.

See Chapter 9 on *Your Civil Rights* for more on this subject.

Drunkenness

Most states and cities have laws against public drunkenness. Some statutes refer to the common drunkard as someone who offends peace and order. In Wisconsin and Virginia, one can be convicted of being a common drunkard regardless of where the arrest occurs. But other jurisdictions only punish, as disorderly conduct, public misconduct or acts done while in a state of intoxication which are deemed harmful to society.

Drunkenness is not always synonymous with intoxication. There is also the expression "under the influence." Statutes which use this term do so in connection with driving. When someone is under the influence, he has decreased his driving ability so as to lose his normal control. Driving in this condition is a criminal offense in those states.

There are also particular laws involving drunkenness, such as the statute, which many states have passed, making it a misdemeanor for a physician to be intoxicated while acting in his professional capacity.

Embezzlement

A captain of the United States Army Field Artillery was in command of a Reserve Officers Training Corps unit. Among the stores in his custody were 4,221 blankets. These blankets were sold at public auction and, since the government had no depository in that vicinity, the captain deposited the proceeds of the sale in his personal bank account. Later, when he had failed to account for this money or pay it over to the government, he was indicted for embezzlement.

The court, in deciding this case, gave a good basic definition of "embezzlement" and how it can be proved to the satisfaction of the law. It said that embezzlement is established by proof that property came lawfully into the embezzler's possession under circumstances which create a relation of trust between him and the owner, and that there was a breach of trust or unlawful appropriation of the property to the embezzler's use.

Since the blankets were sold, and since the captain received the proceeds and failed to pay over the money or account for it, he was guilty of embezzlement.

The crime of embezzlement can be committed by any individual who is an employee of any type of business or a public official to whom money or property is entrusted for safekeeping during the course of his or her term of employment in office.

Abduction

This crime is the taking away of any child or woman by fraud, persuasion, or violence. Many of the statements speak of a taking for immoral purposes.

A woman persuaded her younger sister, a child under 14, to accompany her to a house of ill fame for the purpose of prostitution. For this offense she was convicted of abduction. Had she taken the child across a state line, she would have faced a charge under the federal *Mann Act*, which we shall discuss later.

Compounding a felony

This means agreeing, for money or some other valuable consideration, to refrain from prosecuting a criminal, or to show some favor to him so that he may escape conviction. For example, a man was given a worthless check in a state where this is a statutory crime. Then a number of persons associated with the issuer of the check made an agreement with the defrauded man to pay him the amount of the check if he would conceal the offense from the county attorney and abstain from prosecution. They were found guilty of compounding the felony.

Forgery

Forgery is committed when someone, with the intent to defraud, makes or materially alters a writing which, if it were genuine, would have legal force. The offense is not limited to handwriting, but may also include: printing, engraving, etc. Another definition is the fraudulent making or altering of a writing to the prejudice of another's right. Not limited to the writing or altering of signatures, it applies to any part of a written instrument. For example, altering the sum of another's check is forgery.

Forgery can also be committed by using or negotiating a written instrument known to have been forged.

Homicide—with or without intent

"The unlawful killing of a human being with malice aforethought," was the phrase used in the indictment describing the offense for which a soldier named Myers was convicted in Texas for the murder of another soldier. Myers had been drinking heavily, and was irritable and quarrelsome. After a little altercation he went to his tent, loaded a pistol, and shot and killed the other man. He was convicted of murder in the first degree. His sentence was imprisonment for life.

Where the homicide, or killing, is done with prior deliberation or "malice aforethought," the legal term for a deliberate act, as in the Myers case, it may constitute murder in the first degree.

Where the homicide is committed with the intent to kill but the intent did not exist until the moment of the act, it is murder in the second degree. This applies to murder committed in a sudden fit of passion. For example, in the case just described, had the soldier, instead of going out and bringing back his gun, suddenly struck his victim down with a makeshift weapon, he would have been guilty of murder in the second degree. This crime never carries the death penalty.

Any killing that occurs during the commission of a felony—such as robbery, arson, or rape—is murder and is called felony-murder. Any person who was involved in the commission of the felony is deemed guilty of the murder, even if he did not do the actual killing.

To justify homicide in the defense of a home, it must appear that no greater force was used than was necessary. When, however, someone is seeking to break into a house at night, the owner may without penalty resort to the extremity of taking life.

Manslaughter, a still less serious crime, is different from both of these offenses. In general, manslaughter means killing without malice or intent, as in the heat of passion or by gross negligence.

Insanity

Before punishment may be exacted, it must be shown that the offender was to blame for the act. In a civilized and ordered society, people must assume responsibility for their deeds. But, what about the defendant who is insane? What is insanity? It used to mean wildness or possession by the devil. Now it can mean that someone is neurotic or psychotic.

In 1843, in England, a rule was set down by the court in a case involving a man called Daniel M'Naghten and ever since it has been called the *M'Naghten Rule*. It has been the basis for the finding of criminal insanity in most homicide cases to this day. What the court said then was that, if a defendant is found to be suffering from some mental disability or derangement of his mental processes of such severity as to render him incapable of knowing the nature and quality of his act, or from knowing that the act was wrong, he will be found not to be responsible for his crime. It has been called the "right and wrong" test.

Some courts in the United States felt that this test was not broad enough to explain the conduct of people with some mental difficulties. Modern-day psychiatry has come a long way since 1843. So another rule was developed called the "irresistible impulse" test. If, by reason of a mental disease, or abnormal mental state of passion, a defendant is unable to control his actions or impulses to commit the crime, he will be adjudged not responsible. A famous book, *Anatomy of a Murder*, later made into a popular motion picture, used this point of law as the basis for the plot. More than a dozen states recognize this test for insanity in homicide cases.

In 1954, the *Durham Rule* was developed. This ruling was named after the defendant in a case that was tried in Washington, D.C. This rule requires the prosecution to prove that the crime was not a product of a mental disease or defect—that is, any abnormal condition of the mind which substantially impairs behavior control.

Many of our states have adopted still another test which provides that a person is not responsible for criminal conduct if, at the time of his act, as a result of a mental disease or defect, he lacked substantial capacity either to appreciate the criminality of his conduct or to conform his conduct to the requirements of the law.

However, the issue has been complicated by a recent Supreme Court decision. Montana, Idaho and Utah bar the insanity defense, although allowing mental defect or disease. The Montana Supreme Court had ruled that abolishing it did not violate the U.S. Constitution. The Supreme Court agreed. John Hinckley used the defense after shooting President Reagan and Lorena Bobbitt used it to gain acquittal in the famous penis case.

Incest and related crimes

Incest is sexual intercourse, or in some states, merely a marriage, between blood relatives within the degrees where marriage is forbidden. It is a felony. Statutes provide the degree of blood relationship for incest. This may extend as far as uncle and niece. See Chapter 1.

Does incest require the consent of the female? In a case in California, a man was convicted of incest committed upon his young daughter. He based his appeal from this judgment on the assertion that the charge of the trial court to the jury was inaccurate. The trial court had charged that the accused was guilty of the crime of incest whether the intercourse was with or without the consent of the female. His lawyer asserted that the consent of both parties was essential to the crime of incest.

The appellate court held that the trial court's charge was a correct statement of the law and affirmed the conviction.

When incest is committed without consent, it necessarily becomes combined with another crime or crimes. Recently, a father was convicted of incest, assault, and the rape of his own daughter, a child of 14.

Kidnapping as a federal offense

While "kidnapping" means to abduct a person, it also involves the element of force or fraud in the seizure of the victim and connotes that he is carried off against his will.

This distinction was made in a decision affirming the conviction of Arthur Gooch for the kidnapping of two police officers. Gooch and another man, Nix, were at a gas station in Texas, waiting for a tire of their car to be repaired. Two police officers in a patrol car passed the station, became suspicious of the car's owners, and stopped to search it. Inside they found a cache of food, money, automatic shotguns, rifles, and pistols.

They asked Gooch for papers showing his ownership of the car. Gooch, unable to produce them, reached for his gun. The criminals forced the two policemen into the rear seat of the automobile and, covering them with a gun, drove on to Oklahoma, where, after a ride of about 300 miles, they released them six hours later.

A month later, Nix was shot resisting arrest, and Gooch was tried and convicted of the crime of kidnapping. This was more than an offense against a state law (all the states provide severe penalties for kidnapping). Following the Lindbergh kidnapping, a federal statute was enacted which makes any kidnapping a federal offense where the person kidnapped has been taken from one state into another by the criminals. It was under this law, with its heavy penalties, that Gooch was convicted.

The federal statute on kidnapping provides, in substance, that anyone who transports from one state to another anyone who has been unlawfully seized, inveigled, decoyed, kidnapped, abducted, or carried away and held for ransom or reward, shall be punished by death if the kidnapped person has not been liberated unharmed, and if the verdict of the jury recommends this punishment. If the death penalty is not imposed, the guilty person may be imprisoned for life or a term of years.

Anyone who receives or disposes of anything of value which has been delivered as a ransom and knows of that fact is subject to a fine and imprisonment under this statute.

Although in the Gooch case the abductors transported their prisoners a distance of 300 miles, the transporting of an unwilling person over any distance is technically considered kidnapping.

Robbery

Robbery is the felonious taking of personal property belonging to another from his person and against his will, by means of force or fear.

The force or fear is present when the robber is armed or threatens an assault, or does anything that would cause a reasonable person to fear harm if he did not give up his property. This element of compulsion is what distinguishes robbery from larceny, which by and large does not carry as heavy a penalty. The difference is clearly set forth in the following case:

Two men, Rito Ramirez and Jack Murray, were playing cards in an Arizona saloon. Later they left the saloon and were arrested. The police, in searching Ramirez, found a five-dollar gold piece, fifty cents in silver, and some other small coins. During the card game in the saloon, witnesses had seen Ramirez's hand in Murray's pocket. Ramirez was convicted of robbery and sentenced to five years in the penitentiary. When he appealed this conviction, the court set it aside, declaring, "While the evidence might be sufficient to sustain a charge of larceny, there is absolutely no evidence in the record showing, or tending to show, any force used by Ramirez, any fear on the part of Murray, or any intimidation by Ramirez calculated to place Murray in fear." In other words, Ramirez was guilty of picking pockets, which is larceny, whereas he had illegally been condemned for the more serious crime of robbery.

Two kinds of larceny

"Larceny" is the technical legal term for theft. A court decision defines "larceny" as "the felonious taking and carrying away, from any place, of the personal property of another without his consent, by a person not entitled to deprive the owner of the property, and to convert it to the use of the taker or of someone other than the owner." Picking pockets is an example. Some jurisdictions include embezzlement and the obtaining of property under false pretenses within the term "larceny."

The law recognizes two kinds of larceny—*grand larceny*, in varying degrees depending on the state, which is always a felony, and *petit larceny*. The punishment for grand larceny is more severe. The dividing line in terms of the value of the amount stolen varies from state to state. Under the new New York penal law, grand larceny is divided into three degrees.

When a person steals property, he is at least guilty of petit larceny. Petit larceny is a misdemeanor for which a sentence of up to one year can be imposed.

All degrees of grand larceny are felonies. *Grand larceny in the third degree* occurs when property is stolen in a value exceeding $250, or when certain other property, such as a credit card, is stolen, or when the property was taken "from the person of another," regardless of its nature or value. Grand larceny in the third degree is a Class E felony, for which the penalty does not exceed four years in prison. *Grand larceny in the second degree* applies if the value of the property stolen exceeds $1,500. This is a Class D felony, for which the term of imprisonment would not exceed seven years. *Grand larceny in the first degree* applies, regardless of the nature and value of the property, when the property stolen is obtained by frightening the victim into thinking that resistance would result in physical injury to himself or in damage to that property. Grand larceny in the first degree is a Class C felony, for which the penalty could not exceed fifteen years.

It should be noted that the worst degree in crime is that of the first degree. It should also be noted that under the present New York system of classifying felonies, Class A, for which the term is life imprisonment, is the most serious, and as you proceed through the alphabet through Class E, the terms of imprisonment decrease in length. Misdemeanors are divided into Classes A and B. Petit larceny is a Class A misdemeanor.

Criminal and civil libel

To hurt a person's reputation by maliciously printing or writing harmful statements about him is libel. The law in many states punishes libel as a crime when the defamatory statement was published with a malicious intent. This does not necessarily mean that it was made with malice. Legally, the malicious-intent requirement is satisfied if the statement was made willfully and without legal justification. Some states find it a crime if the statement tends to cause a breach of the peace. If the statement is found to be privileged, criminal libel cannot occur. Statements made in judicial proceedings are always privileged. In addition, there is a "qualified privilege" in discussions between people, which depends upon the substance of the remark and the context in which it is made.

Discussions among family members about family matters, for example, enjoy this privilege. Remarks between members of a union about union matters also fall within this protected category. A discussion between people who are unrelated to each other about the family of one of them is not privileged in this "qualified" manner. Defamation, of which civil libel is a part, is discussed further in another chapter.

Narcotics

"That humanity at large will ever be able to dispense with artificial paradises seems very unlikely."

This has become one of the major problems confronting our civilization. The incidence of drug use amongst people of all ages and social strata has reached alarming proportions. There are discussions at all levels of society concerning care, treatment, prevention, education, and punishment. Authorities disagree on all these aspects, as well as on what drugs should be considered harmful and therefore prohibited. Some courts have tried to develop theories which would apply equally to the use of alcohol and narcotics.

What is addiction?

Addiction has been defined by the *World Health Organization* of the United Nations as a state of periodic or chronic intoxication produced by repeated consumption of a drug, natural or synthetic. The characteristics include an overpowering need to continue taking the drug and to obtain it by any means, the tendency to increase the dose, psychological and general physical dependence on the effects of the drug, and an effect detrimental to the individual and to society.

What are narcotics?

The Uniform Narcotic Drug Act regulates and controls the manufacture, distribution, use, and possession of narcotics and has been adopted in most states. The Act designates narcotics as coca leaves, opium, cannabis, which is marijuana, and every other substance neither chemically nor physically distinguished from them. It also includes any other drugs to which federal narcotics laws apply, and any drug found by any state, after reasonable notice and hearing, to have an addiction-forming or addiction-sustaining liability similar to morphine or cocaine. The laws in each state regarding penalties for possession of various drugs cover quite a broad range of severity. Penalties for possession of small amounts of marijuana, for example, have decreased during the last few years, but an Illinois man was recently sentenced to a 20-year prison term for possession of only a few ounces.

Barbiturates

There is a federal *Food, Drug and Cosmetic Act* section which regulates barbiturates and amphetamines. Physicians have known that illness or death can be caused by the combined use of alcohol and barbiturates. However, only recently has that fact been brought home to the public, probably because several well-known personalities were found to have died as a result of such a lethal combination.

An interesting case

A defendant was on trial for murder. Before the trial, he had been nervous and emotional. However, on the day that he testified on his own behalf, he was cool and calculating. He was convicted and sentenced to death. He appealed and his conviction was reversed. It seems that on the morning he was to testify he had been given a sedative which altered his reactions. The court found that a drug-induced change was unfair to the defendant since the jury may have been influenced by his calm manner, thinking he was not sorry for the crime.

A witness who takes drugs

Can his credibility or truthfulness be questioned? The use of drugs is not sufficient for a court in determining a witness is incompetent. It must be shown the witness was under the influence of a drug at the time he witnessed the events in question, or that his habit was such that he could have been under their influence at the time, so that his testimony would probably not be reliable.

What about driving under the influence of drugs?

A California driver's license will be refused to anyone who has been convicted for the possession of narcotics. In Ohio, it is unlawful to operate a motor vehicle while under the influence of alcohol, narcotic drugs, or opiates. In Oklahoma, it is unlawful for a habitual user or anyone under the influence of drugs to a degree which renders him incapable of safely driving to operate a motor vehicle. Many other states have similar provisions.

The Supreme Court and addiction

A California statute made it a misdemeanor for any person to be addicted to the use of narcotics. It made the status of addiction a crime and the offender liable to prosecution at any time while in California. Robinson was picked up although he was not engaged in any antisocial behavior. After conviction under the statute, he appealed. The Supreme Court said, "It is unlikely that any state at this moment in history would attempt to make it a criminal offense for a person to be mentally ill, or a leper, or to be affected with a venereal disease." Therefore, since addiction is an illness, it is unconstitutional and cruel and unusual punishment to convict someone for being addicted. A defendant must commit some overt antisocial act before a crime can be said to have been committed.

What about addiction and insanity?

Generally, the disease of addiction in and of itself does not establish irresponsibility on the part of the drug user. If a person becomes temporarily insane because of his voluntary use of drugs, he will still be considered responsible for his acts. There have been a few exceptions to this rule in trials for premeditated murder. The use of drugs is not considered voluntary if the drugs were taken because of medical need. Also, drug use may not be considered voluntary if the drug is taken due to a physiological dependence on it, even though the user takes the drug with awareness of the consequences.

L.S.D. and other chemicals

The United States has an amendment to the *Food and Drug Act* that makes unlicensed L.S.D. manufacture and sale a felony. A number of states also have legislation on the subject. In New York, the law outlaws the possession of hallucinogenic substances by unauthorized persons and provides for a penalty of up to a year in jail. Recently, the New

York State legislature additionally provided for imprisonment up to four years for possession of hallucinogenics *with intent to sell* by making it a Class E felony.

Perjury

Perjury is an assertion of fact or knowledge by a person under oath when that person knows, or is of the opinion, that what he is swearing to is false. The falsehood, however, must be a material one if it is to count as perjury.

An ordinary lie can become perjury, then, when it is spoken under oath. It is not likely to become perjury if it pertains to some small detail that does not affect the subject of the inquiry one way or the other.

The act of perjury is not necessarily oral. It may be committed in writing, too, as in signing income tax returns or other important papers requiring an oath.

Is having sex a crime?

Some states, such as Virginia, have laws which generally are not enforced until they come to attention, such as in a private lawsuit. In Virginia there is an antifornication statute making premarital sex a misdemeanor punishable by a fine. When a woman sued a former spouse for damages accusing him of giving her herpes before they were married, the Virginia Supreme Court disallowed her action saying her injuries occurred while she was participating in an illegal act.

Courts will not reward anyone who takes part in an illegal act.

Prostitution and the Mann Act

The offense of prostitution, according to an early decision, means "the act of permitting illicit intercourse for hire—an indiscriminate intercourse or what is deemed public prostitution." The definition still holds good today.

The punishment of prostitutes, like that of vagrants, is governed entirely by the statutes of the states or by municipal ordinances. These also provide punishment for keepers of bawdy houses. There is also on the federal statute books a law called the *Mann Act*, also known as the *White Slave Act*, enacted by Congress to prevent commerce in prostitution. This federal statute punishes anyone instrumental in persuading, inducing, enticing, or coercing any woman or girl to go from one place to another in interstate or foreign commerce for the purpose of prostitution or debauchery or for any other immoral purpose, whether with or without her consent. This crime is punishable by a maximum fine of $5,000 and five years' imprisonment.

A typical violation of the Mann Act began when a young girl met a man at a public festival in Virginia. He promised her that, if she would go to New York, he would obtain for her a place of employment with "easy work and plenty of money." After spending the night with her in Virginia, he gave her the money for her transportation to New York.

She was met at the station by the man's wife and another woman. They told her that she could either lead a life of prostitution or starve. For two weeks she plied this age-old trade, then, aided by an elevator boy, she escaped from the hotel where she was confined and returned to Virginia.

She had been induced to cross a state line for an immoral purpose. That she did this of her own free will was not an extenuating circumstance under this federal law, and the man and his accomplices were punished.

Rape and attempt to rape

This crime consists of having vaginal, oral or anal intercourse by force, use of drugs or by placing the victim in fear. It can include penetration by an object or sexual touching by force.

"Attempted rape" is also a crime, even though the rape is not completed. Changes in rape laws have occurred in over forty states. These changes include *shield laws* protecting victims from having their sexual histories raised in court; redefining rape to be gender neutral; and establishing a hierarchy of rape charges so that an attack of short penetration is still a sex offense. Also, several jurisdictions have dropped corroboration requirements, which means that the complainant doesn't have to have other persons or independent evidence to confirm the story of the rape. In many states, the victim need not prove resistance to the attack. New York and Florida prohibit defense attorneys from referring to a complainant's manner of dress in sex crime cases, using it as a motive for an accused's actions.

Statutory rape

This rape is sexual intercourse with a female who is younger than the age set in state law. All states and the District of Columbia have laws forbidding sexual intercourse with a minor. But 26 states and D.C. allow a 16-year-old to consent to the sex. The age of consent is 15 in Colorado and South Carolina and 14 in Hawaii and Pennsylvania. In California it is a felony for a person 3 years older or more to have intercourse with a female of 17 or less. Fraud, ignorance or mistake as to the female's age is no defense. But not every case is prosecuted because of mitigating factors such as a promise to marry.

Rape of males

Statutory rape laws do not, however, apply to protect young males in the same way. Therefore, a female cannot be convicted of statutory rape for having sexual intercourse with a male who is younger than the statutory age of consent that is applied to females. The United States Supreme Court decided that California's statutory rape law does not violate the equal protection clause of the United States Constitution even though only males can be convicted under that law. The Court reasoned, in part, that since only females are susceptible to pregnancy, and the state has a strong interest in preventing teenage pregnancy, the California statute would help to deter males from having sexual intercourse with a female under the statutory age.

No seduction without consent

Seduction is the use by a man of some artifice or promise (such as a promise to marry) or other means by which he induces an unmarried woman to submit to unlawful intercourse with him when she is, and has previously been for a reasonable time, a person of chaste conduct. The promise involved need not be false. If a man seduces a woman by honestly promising marriage, this does not legally excuse him from the crime. In those states where seduction is still considered a crime, the law is seldom enforced.

It should be noted that in legal terms, the act of seduction cannot be committed by a woman against a man.

The woman's consent is essential to this offense. Failing that consent, the case is likely to come under the heading of rape. It does not matter how old the woman is—it is seduction as long as she is able to distinguish between right and wrong and has the capacity to consent. For example, if a man drugs a woman, she loses the capacity to consent, and the court will probably hold that the man who had sexual relations with her when she was in this condition was raping her, not seducing her.

A commonplace case of seduction is one in which a chaste woman agrees to have sexual intercourse with a man because he promises to make her his wife afterward. He then fails to live up to his promise. Her consent has been won—by a promise, in this instance—and so the conditions specified by the statutes exist. Of course, if the man could establish that the woman had habitually had relations with other men, there could be no charge of seduction.

Rape and AIDS

A judge in the District of Columbia would not order a blood test on an alleged rapist to see if he was infected with the AIDS virus, since there was no evidence that he had AIDS. It is a question of the defendant's rights to privacy and presumption of innocence, as against a victim's right to know. AIDS could involve a criminal count of assault with a deadly weapon. Seventeen states have laws allowing for tests in sexual assault cases.

Brutality

The Rodney King police beating case and its aftermath made headlines for months. Excessive force by law enforcement agencies is an on-going complaint. The 9th Circuit Court of Appeals put the burden on local governments and their enforcement agencies to properly train their employees on the limits to the use of force. However, the Supreme Court has limited a municipality's liability for an officer's actions even if he had a prior history of assault. A victim must show "deliberate indifference" by the government, that it consciously disregarded the risk of hiring that person and that the injuries sustained were a plainly obvious consequence of the hiring decision. The officer can be sued individually.

Receiving stolen goods

The offense of receiving property from another, knowing that it has been stolen, is punishable as a crime. This factor of knowledge is an important one. If you buy something that is represented as the lawful property of the seller, and have no reason to think it is stolen property, although that is its actual status, you cannot be charged with a crime.

Threatening the president and other public employees

At common law, a mere threat was not a criminal offense unless it put a reasonable man in fear and unless there was the ability and intent to carry out the threat.

In 1964, after the assassination of President Kennedy, a federal statute was passed making it a crime to threaten the life of the president. The crime exists even though the president may not even know about the threat or if the party involved claims it was only a joke. Pierce was a Navy seaman who got into trouble. While in a Kansas jail, he wrote to Lyndon Johnson that he would kill him the first chance he got. He gave the note to a guard. He was tried and convicted under the 1964 statute. He claimed that he was only joking and that the threat was only idle talk. The serious thing about such a threat, even when made in an offhand way, is that it may plant the seed of crime in the mind of another who may not take it as a joke.

There are also a number of statutes making it a crime to harm others in public life. For instance, it is a crime to assault, kidnap or assassinate a member of Congress or a member elect; it is a crime to kill a U.S. Judge, Assistant U.S. Attorney, U.S. Attorney, U.S. Deputy or Marshal, any employee of the FBI, Postal Service, Secret Service, Drug Enforcement Administration, Internal Revenue, Customs, National Park Service, and employees of most other federal agencies performing their official work. It is also a crime to strike, wound or imprison a foreign official, official guest or an internationally protected person.

Extradition

The United States Constitution provides that any person charged in any state with treason, felony, or other crime (and this can include misdemeanors) who shall flee from justice and be found in another state shall, on demand of the executive authority of the state from which he fled, be delivered up to be removed to the state having jurisdiction of the crime. The object of interstate extradition is to prevent the escape of persons accused of a crime and to secure their return to the state from which they fled.

The *Uniform Criminal Extradition Act* has been adopted in most states, the Virgin Islands and the Panama Canal Zone. Thus far, Louisiana, Mississippi, Nevada, North Dakota, South Carolina, and Washington have not adopted the Act. The Act sets up the procedural rules governing the extradition of fugitives and gives the accused certain rights. He may see the legal papers used as the basis for the extradition proceedings. Sometimes, innocence of the charge can be of importance in creating public pressure to block the return to the demanding state. Other factors which also may be influential are that the punishment in the demanding state does not fit the crime or that the accused has been rehabilitated.

The *Fugitive Felon Act* covers the authority of the federal courts over those who are fleeing to avoid prosecution for certain crimes. Extradition laws between states are not needed in these particular situations.

International extradition is governed by federal treaties with foreign nations. You no doubt have read about criminals fleeing to certain countries, such as Brazil, because the United States has no treaty which can assure their return. Sometimes diplomacy will achieve the result.

Compensation for victims of violence

California and New York are the only states in the United States that have, thus far, enacted legislation to assure some compensation to those who have suffered at the hands of criminals. Proposals have been considered in Oregon, Wisconsin, and Maryland. Among all the rest of the countries of the world, only Great Britain and New Zealand have such compensatory laws.

In New York, the state legislature has provided for *a Crime Victims' Compensation Board* to administer the program of awards to victims and their dependents who may suffer disability, incur financial hardship, or become dependent on public assistance because of crimes. No act involving the operation of a motor vehicle will be considered a crime unless the injury inflicted was done intentionally.

Those eligible for compensatory awards include the victim of the crime, the surviving spouse or children of a dead victim, or any other person dependent upon a dead victim for his principal support. Anyone responsible for the crime, an accomplice, or members of the families of such persons are excluded. Also, no victim who, by his conduct, contributed to the infliction of his own injury may recover.

Because of the importance of this whole process and because the claim form must comply with the board's rules, if you are eligible for an award you should seek counsel at your earliest opportunity. Claims generally must be filed within 90 days after the commission of the crime or 90 days after the death of the victim, although the board may extend the time up to one year. There is a minimum allowable dollar amount for each claim, and the maximum allowance for each award is $15,000.

Each claim is reviewed and investigated, and a hearing is held. Findings must be made that a crime was committed, that personal physical injury or death resulted, that the police records show the crime was reported promptly after it occurred, and that the claimant would suffer serious financial hardship if an award were not made. The decision is sent to the claimant. If he is dissatisfied, he has 30 days to request, in writing, consideration by the full board. Their action is final. The claimant has no right to a review by the courts since all awards are made as a matter of grace by the state.

The awards are not subject to attachment except for expenses resulting from the injury. Awards may be reduced if insurance proceeds or other monies are forthcoming.

The New York law also provides for compensation to persons who have suffered a financial loss because of an attempt, whether or not successful, to prevent a crime or apprehend a criminal. The California law distinguishes between those who are the objects of crime and those who aid in prevention or apprehension of the criminal. Those in the former category must show need before being compensated, but those who assist are indemnified for expenses regardless of financial hardship. The California law also provides that before a victim may be compensated the criminal must be convicted. In New York it does not matter what happens to the criminal. He may even be found not guilty by reason of insanity. The claimant may still be given an award.

Do you have to take the stand?

A person accused of a crime need not take the stand to offer testimony. However, can an inference be drawn from his silence? In 1965, the United States Supreme Court said that the Constitution gives every accused the right to remain silent and no inference of guilt can be raised by the prosecutor because of this silence. At the time this decision was made, five states allowed the prosecutor to comment on the defendant's silence: California, Connecticut, Iowa, Ohio, and New Mexico.

Sometimes, however, a prosecutor can use words which are not a direct comment but are an implied reference. In Florida, a defendant was charged with breaking and entering. He did not testify at his trial. While summing up the case for the state, the prosecutor said that it was uncontroverted that the defendant told a police officer he had committed the crime. This was considered to be an improper reference to the accused's failure to testify. Since the defendant had not testified, it should not have been said that the fact was "uncontroverted."

Beyond a reasonable doubt

In a civil suit, the person establishing a preponderance of evidence wins the case. In a criminal case, for the defendant to be convicted, guilt must be established beyond a reasonable doubt. The presumption of innocence in a criminal trial is one of the basic tenets of our law.

Reasonable doubt

In the usual criminal case, the court will charge the jury at the conclusion, after the summation by the defense and the prosecution, that the defendant is presumed to be innocent, and that the presumption of innocence remains unless and until the defendant is proven guilty beyond a reasonable doubt.

There is no official definition of the phrase beyond a *"reasonable doubt."* That's the term used in the United States Constitution. Some federal circuit courts have recommended that no definition be given to a jury. The Connecticut Supreme Court had no problem with a judge who gave a jury a choice of three definitions.

Older instructions which still are given, use the terms *"moral certainty"* and *"moral evidence."* The Supreme Court in 1994 didn't like those phrases calling them archaic and unhelpful but not unconstitutional. Model instructions were prepared by the Federal

Judicial Center which say "reasonable doubt leaves you firmly convinced of the defendant's guilt and does not leave a real possibility that he is not guilty." Others say it is such as would cause jurors, after careful, candid and impartial consideration of all the evidence, to be so undecided that they cannot say they have an abiding conviction of guilt. It is not a fanciful doubt, a whimsical doubt or a doubt based on conjecture. It is based on reason. In Texas the court said it was "proof of such a convincing character that you would be willing to rely and act upon it without hesitation in the most important of your own affairs."

The burden is on the government to prove that the defendant is guilty beyond a reasonable doubt, not all doubt, or to a scientific certainty. The burden never shifts and the defendant is not required to prove his innocence or to produce any evidence. Unless every element of the charged offense is proved beyond the reasonable doubt, a defendant must be found not guilty.

Deceptive Mailings Prevention Act

Many people have been taken in by offers made through the mail which give the postal patron the idea that the service or product is somehow approved by or even a part of the U.S. Government. This misleads them and gives a false sense of security of the worth and reliability of the service or product.

Now there is a law which penalizes anyone mailing such solicitations. Any nongovernmental entity soliciting through the mail must now prominently display a conspicuous disclaimer if any terms or symbols it uses could reasonably be construed as implying federal government connection, approval or endorsement. If it does not meet these postal regulations for its mailings, it can lose all mailing privileges.

You should always be alert to solicitations which seem to promise more than is reasonable.

Smoke alarms

Although fires are started in a number of ways, including children playing with matches, smoking-related fires cause the most indoor destruction and death. Smoke alarms or detectors could help significantly in reducing the extent of damage. However, although over 80% of homes are equipped with smoke detectors, at least one-third are ill-served because the alarms do not work. Old or missing batteries are the most prevalent reasons for nonfunctional alarms.

Since many children may die in home fires, some jurisdictions are passing laws trying to protect these vulnerable members of society. Maryland, Virginia, and the District of Columbia are among the states which now require all homes to have working smoke alarms. Maryland and Virginia consider it a crime to tamper with a smoke alarm, but local counties issue the regulations. (The federal law on nonsmoking in aircraft also makes it a crime to tamper with the rest room smoke detectors.) In a recent case, a county in Maryland charged the parents of three small children who died in fires with failing to maintain their smoke detectors. They could be fined or sent to prison.

Some regulations require landlords to certify that the smoke detectors in their leased units are working properly. Noncompliance can result in fines. Some regulations also require smoke detectors to have visual signals for the hearing impaired. This will be the case nationally in view of the *Americans with Disabilities Act,* discussed in Chapter 9.

Son of Sam

When a New York murderer sold his story for a large amount of money, the public was outraged. The legislature reacted by passing a law that prevented his receipt of the money. This was the *Son of Sam law,* named after the murderer. However, the U.S. Supreme Court held the law unconstitutional as a violation of the First Amendment's guarantee of free speech.

Now, courts are trying to prevent profit on the part of persons made famous by their crimes and convictions by imposing huge criminal fines. They are guessing that the royalties and interview fees will be offset by the lien on the incomes. But, Tonya Harding and her spouse, Jeff Gillooly, earned more than their fines by exclusive TV appearances. Serial murderer Jeffrey Dahmer hasn't sold his story, as yet, and he has over $100 million in civil judgments pending against him from suits won by the families of his victims. But, his father, Lionel, received a substantial advance for a book, some of which he promised to the families.

Stalking

Stalking someone repeatedly, obsessively waiting, phoning, watching, following. It's frightening. It can be part of domestic violence or conduct of a fan of a celebrity. It can be physical, or done by mail, phone or E-mail, computer message, as was the case recently in Michigan. Many states have not yet addressed electronic stalking.

Legislation on stalking has been a top priority in 48 states. However, many now are amending their laws, broadening the definitions and stiffening the penalties. Now it is not so much the intent of the stalker as how the pattern of action affects the victim. Many prior versions also didn't account for threats to family and friends. The *National Institute of Justice* has a model code being followed by some states, which requires proof that a reasonable person would fear the "course of conduct" and that the stalker knew the actions would cause fear. South Carolina's law was used against an anti-abortion protestor who threatened a clinic director. It may be a tool also to protect abortion providers.

The *Violence Against Women Act,* which makes sex based violence a civil rights violation and allows compensatory and punitive damages and attorney fees, also makes interstate stalking a federal crime. In related action the Congress strengthened it by making interstate stalking and harassment criminal regardless of whether the victim previously had obtained a protective order. Penalties range from up to 5 years in prison for harassment to life for bodily injury.

Sports and other events

26

Chapter 26
Sports and other events

Baseball and antitrust

The issue of baseball's exemption from the operation of the federal antitrust laws, and the various restrictions in the contracts of professional players, have made the subject of law as applied to sports one of more than general interest.

The *Sherman Antitrust Act* passed by the Congress in 1890 provided that there can be no contract in restraint of trade affecting interstate commerce. When the question of the restrictive contracts covering baseball players first reached the United States Supreme Court in 1922, it was held that "the business of professional baseball was not within the scope of the federal antitrust laws because the exhibitions were purely state affairs, were not trade or commerce in the ordinary accepted use of the words, and the interstate transportation of players was merely incidental. . . ."

Of course, in this era of broadcasting and the big business of sports, there is no doubt in anybody's mind that interstate commerce is involved. However, the problem has been that the United States Supreme Court felt that if the rule was to be changed for the business of baseball, it would be up to Congress to make the change. This situation was not the case for various other sports, which were held subject to *the Sherman Antitrust Act*, and so boxing, football, and other sports are not free from the requirements of competition.

Participants in sports and athletic events

A person of sufficient age and understanding who participates in any sport, game, or athletic event, accepts all obvious and necessary dangers in that activity. This applies to those who voluntarily participate, such as umpires, referees, and managers. Nonetheless, you do not assume risks which come solely from the negligence of others.

Assault at a sports event

If you are assaulted while at a sports event, you may not be able to recover from the proprietor or promoter for the injury. A woman in Kansas was hurt by an unknown man while she was on her way to the ladies' room after seeing a wrestling match. She claimed she had not been provided with safe premises. The court agreed that one who gathers together a large number of people for profit must be vigilant to protect them, but the care required is what is ordinary or reasonable; and the proprietor could not, therefore, be liable for this irresponsible and unforeseeable act. In another case, in New York, a fight broke out in Yankee Stadium and a fan was hurt. The court said that ordinary rudeness and jostling is characteristic of crowds at sporting events, and you need something more than that to cause a liability.

Even an umpire may not be successful in his suit for assault. In North Carolina, an umpire was on his way to the lockers when he was hit by a fan. It had been a wild game. One team's manager kept going out to shout at the umpire, and the manager was finally ejected from the game. After the game, the fans came onto the field and cursed the umpire, but no one hit him at that time. He was escorted out by a policeman, and then he was injured. He claimed that the manager was responsible, as well as the fan who hit him. He felt the manager had incited the crowd. The court said the manager did not sow the seeds of the disorder, and that he could not be responsible for the actions of unstable people at games.

A decision like that, when brought to his attention, must have made Leo Durocher feel good after all the years he went storming out to take on the umpires!

We have been discussing the question of the liability of the proprietor or promoter or manager. However, of course, the person who actually did the assault would be liable for such action.

Golf

One court has said that a golf ball is a dangerous missile and can be more dangerous than firing a gun. Danger notwithstanding, more than 8 million people play this game, which has been around in some form since about A.D. 1400. Golfers, as other sportspeople, must assume the ordinary risks of the game, but they do not assume the risk of another's negligent conduct. One of the rules of golf etiquette is that no player should play until a party in front is out of range. Shouting "fore," however, will not save a golfer from the consequences of his other careless acts.

When a player hit a shot through a window, a judge in Kentucky would not give damages to the homeowner since he knew the risk when he built his home next to a golf course. Golfers don't have a duty to hit the ball straight.

In a New York case, an 11-year-old was found negligent when he hit the player ahead with his driven ball. This young man had taken lessons, played regularly, and in fact was playing in adult company at the time of the accident. The court held him to an adult standard of reasonable care. They compared cases involving juveniles driving motorboats, riding watercycles, and operating airplanes. Golf requires skill and involves danger, and infants do not usually partake in such activity, but when one does, the infant must conform to a reasonable level of care.

In another case involving a 14-year-old who was himself injured on a golf driving range, an Iowa court felt the child was not entitled to recover damages. He and a friend had been to the range before. On this day, they were side by side. When some balls spilled over, the 14-year-old bent to get them and was struck by his companion's club. No dangerous condition existed on the range. The accident was caused by a sudden movement and the range management was not held liable.

In a case that went to the highest court in New York, the plaintiff was struck in the eye by the golf ball hit by one of the members of his threesome. The plaintiff had helped the defendant find his ball in the rough to the left of the fairway. He then was walking on the rough between the defendant and the green when the defendant hit the ball without warning and it struck the plaintiff. It was contended that the plaintiff assumed the ordinary risks of the game, including an accident like this. However, the court said the jury was free to find the plaintiff had left a place of safety with the defendant's knowledge in order to help defendant find his ball, and after it was found, was struck without warning when defendant played the recovered ball. The court sustained the jury's finding that defendant was negligent and that the plaintiff was not guilty of contributory negligence and had not assumed the risk.

Female golfers now are suing for the right to play whenever they want. Certain "tee times" traditionally have been reserved for male players. But, a new law prohibiting gender discrimination in these circumstances in states such as California, Maryland, Michigan, Florida, and Massachusetts, can change the way clubs treat their female golfers. They include punishments such as fines, increase in property taxes, removal of liquor licenses and loss of tax deductibility.

Wrestling

Like to watch wrestling on TV? It is probably safer than seeing it in person. In Vermont a spectator at ringside was injured when one wrestler threw the other out of the ring into the spectator's lap. The court in that case held that it was not to be expected that a wrestler would throw his opponent out of the ring, and held for the patron. A court in Georgia, however, came to a different conclusion in a somewhat similar situation. In that case the injury was caused by a wrestler diving through the ropes to get away from his opponent. He hurt the timekeeper, whose job required him to be close to the ring. The Georgia court felt that the experienced timekeeper should have known that wrestlers are thrown, pushed, or fall from the ring, and that being within three feet could be dangerous, and he had assumed the risk. He did not recover for his injury.

Company events

Many companies sponsor programs for their employees as part of their employment packages, such as softball and bowling teams or social activities, such as picnics and Christmas parties. What if an employee is injured at one of these functions? What if a family member or customer is injured? Sometimes company events can be dangerous, such as rock climbing or wilderness treks. Many companies will ask participants to sign a waiver, but just how specific the terms are can make a difference as to liability. Some employees will participate because of pressure to make a good showing despite the potential hazards.

The basic issues for an employee are, did the activity sponsored by the business require their attendance, was the attendance of benefit to the employer, did the employer pay for the event? A court will decide the business connection and whether liability is covered by workers' compensation. Generally, when an accident is job-related, the employer pays medical and disability costs. But, this compensation may be below a negligence law suit recovery and receipt of workers' compensation bars suit against the company for negligence. So, it may be advantageous for the employee to show that attendance was voluntary and any injury suffered would not be covered by workers' compensation.

In Louisiana, two cases which seem similar were decided differently on whether the activity was job-related. In one, a 16-year-old maintenance worker drowned while swimming at a party sponsored by his employer. In another, an adult accountant drowned while swimming during a trip sponsored by his company. The State Supreme Court found in the former that it was job-related since the 16-year-old's supervisor had invited him. In the latter, the court found the trip was a voluntary act for which the employer received no benefit.

In a case in Colorado, a member of a gas and electric club recreation association was not given compensation when he was injured during a softball game. The games were held on public grounds after work, and, although the company furnished the equipment and uniforms, the court felt the employer did not benefit, except indirectly, through the good morale of the employees.

What about when a nonemployee is injured? Workers' Compensation does not apply. In 1983, well-known T.V. newswoman Jessica Savitch died when the car in which she was a passenger went into a canal. She had been to dinner with a *New York Post* newspaper executive. He was driving and the car had been leased by the *Post*. Her estate claimed he was on *Post* business. The paper claimed that the dinner was a social date. They settled the case for more than $7 million.

Drinking at a function

Drinking and driving is a bad combination under any circumstances. For employers hosting a function, it can be very expensive if the attending employee drinks, drives, and kills. An executive of the company that makes Jack Daniels and Southern Comfort whisky drank heavily at a company party and on his way home crashed into another car killing the driver. The widow sued the executive and the company claiming they encouraged their people to drink before driving. The company settled for over $1.5 million.

A similar high recovery occurred even when the drinking was off the company's premises. A salesman got drunk while entertaining clients, and later killed two people in an automobile accident. The company had paid for the salesman's drinks.

Bowling

If you like bowling, you will be interested in two cases which deal with bowling accidents. A woman in Louisiana was acting as a scorekeeper at a bowling tournament for women. She took a coffee break and went to a snack table, which was near a rack where there were spare balls. Just as she was getting up from the table, one of the bowlers came to the rack to test a ball, and as she swung it in her arm, she hit the scorekeeper, who sued the owner claiming that the premises were unsafe. The court said that since there was nothing hidden about the rack, and the plaintiff was familiar with the area and with the fact that bowlers test balls, she had assumed the normal, obvious and ordinary risks of use of the alleys. On the other hand, in Illinois, a male bowler, while attempting to deliver his ball, found his foot stuck to the alley and he was injured. He had been to the men's room and there got some liquid on the bottom of his shoes. The court said that because of the added dangers to bowling patrons from foreign matter on the floors, the alley management should have taken more care to see that the restrooms were kept dry so that liquid would not be brought into the play area.

Roller rink

These cases show that sometimes an owner or occupier of the premises will be held to a slightly higher standard of care for providing safety in the nongame portions of the play area.

If you are a roller rink user, you are entitled to have the premises and equipment maintained with care, consistent with the purposes for use. For instance, if you rent skates they should be able to be used safely. In a case in Massachusetts, a 12-year-old girl, the first customer of the day at the rink, rented some skates. They were dirty and the laces had knots from having been broken and retied. She skated around in them for a few hours and then one lace broke, the shoe came loose, and she fell. The court said the condition of the shoes should have been noted by the person in charge, and that the skater was not herself negligent in accepting the skates. In another case, however, a Louisiana court said that the rink was not responsible when a 14-year-old skated out of the skating area. She went toward a tier of seats where her skate caught on a part of the platform and she fell into a plate-glass window behind the seats. The accident was not a foreseeable one. The court said that hazards must be reasonably expected or else the owner would have to be an insurer of everyone's safety.

Tennis and ping-pong

In cases involving participants in ping-pong and tennis, the courts have relied heavily on two criteria: 1) had an accident occurred before the one in the suit? 2) had the participant been observant? In a New York case, a tennis player was injured when he bumped into a stone wall behind a wire fence on the side of his court. No one had done that in 30 years of playing there. A hotel guest playing in a ping-pong tournament had his arm go through a window in the wall behind him. He had played other games, and the court believed he should have been aware of the space limitations despite his concentration on the game.

Basketball

Basketball is considered the sort of game in which bodily contact is expected. It is not intrinsically dangerous, as has been said of soccer, but accidents can happen. A student at Brooklyn College in New York was playing when he and his opponent knocked heads during a jumpshot. It caused his death, but the New York court held that no one could be blamed. The plaintiff's father alleged that the accident was caused by lack of supervision, but the court reasoned that no referee could have prevented the jumpshot, which is part of the game.

Ski lift

In a case in New York, a plaintiff fell from a ski lift while attempting to dismount, breaking her leg. She contended the ski lift was a common carrier, and that she was accordingly owed the duty of highest care. (On the duty of a common carrier generally, see Chapter 24 on *automobiles and other vehicles*.) She contended that the failure to have an attendant to assist her in getting down from the chair was negligence. The court noted that the chairlift would carry anyone presenting a ticket, and therefore, it could be considered a common carrier. However, the court went on to say that skiing is a dangerous sport, so that if you ride the ski lift up the hill, you should have the same degree of skill for the ride as you propose to employ in skiing down the hill. This means that getting someone to assist you off the chair would make things more difficult, because you would need a clear area in which to land when alighting. Under the circumstances, the carrier was held not liable.

Reckless skiing

Is there an analogy between reckless driving and reckless skiing? There are going to be collisions on the slopes when there are thousands of visitors to ski areas. Most of the suits brought for resulting injuries have been civil in nature to recover for costs and damages. Of late, however, there have been some felony charges filed by the state, including one for manslaughter when a child died after a collision. Authorities think this may help to deter the reckless skier.

Although the state of Colorado, which has a thriving ski industry, enacted a *Ski Safety Act,* it only provides a fine for "hit and run" on the slopes.

Floodlights

Does your town have night ballgames? One community in New York tried to prevent the use of floodlights on the local ballfield for Little League night games. They claimed it would bring noise and traffic to the local neighborhoods, the glare would attract insects, and the serenity of the area would be lost. The courts did not agree and would not enjoin the use as a public nuisance. The lights would be used only on weeknights during the summer till 9:30 P.M. Games had been held in the park regularly and the lights would only be on for an hour or so after dusk. Night Little League games would not change the character of the neighborhood.

Baseball

If you are a spectator at a baseball game and are hit by a foul ball, will you be able to sue the team or the stadium for your injuries? The answer to this question will vary depending on where your suit is brought. In states following the common law rule, a spectator who is hit anywhere in the stadium, except in the most dangerous seats behind home plate, has assumed the risk and is barred from suing.

In states which adopted comparative negligence legislation, such as New York, the answer is less clear. In such jurisdictions, assumption of risk will no longer act as a complete shield against liability, but instead will diminish the amount of any recovery. However, a recent New York decision clouded the picture. They reached the same result that courts had been reaching under the common law for years. The court found that in the exercise of due care, the proprietor of a ball park need only provide screening for the area behind home plate. Therefore, even under their comparative negligence rule, injured spectators, except those behind home plate, are still barred from recovery.

Water ski kiting

If water ski kiting is your sport of choice, you should be aware that, in the event of an accident, you may not be covered by your accident insurance policy. The Supreme Court of Utah recently denied a widow's recovery under her husband's accidental death insurance policy. It excluded coverage for accidents involving aerial navigation devices. The Court found that the water ski kite was a device for aerial navigation within the meaning of the policy's exclusionary clause.

Liability waivers

Until recently, negligence suits in sports injury matters would have been tried. However, if there is a signed waiver or release absolving the potential defendant of liability, more courts are basing decisions on it. In a case of a drowning at a YMCA in Los Angeles, the 19-year-old had signed a waiver and his case was not allowed to go to the jury. In California, Texas and Tennessee, liability suits involving activities such as parachuting, diving and motorcycle racing have been terminated by judges because the plaintiffs signed waivers or releases.

No waiver can absolve a defendant of gross negligence and the waiver will probably not be given much weight if it is signed by a child.

Beaches

Local governments enjoyed immunity to suit when persons swimming at beaches in their jurisdiction were injured because of so-called "natural conditions" such as tides or sandbars. Then the situation changed when some plaintiffs sued and won when they alleged they were misled as to the safety of the area because of lifeguards or lack of warning signs. Now, at least in California, the injured beach frequenter is less likely to prevail. The state legislature decreed that beaches would still be considered "in a natural condition" even when lifeguards are present or other public services are provided. Plaintiffs are also limited from recovering from local governments when they are injured participating in "hazardous recreational activity."

Reducing liability exposure

Some states have worried that lawsuits against their tourist attractions or sports retailers might put them out of business and jeopardize the area's economy. So some have passed laws reducing the liability exposure. In Colorado, companies that guide horses and llama trips aren't liable for risks "inherent" in the activity. Others are considering protecting businesses that rent equipment for water use. But, in Wisconsin a plaintiff injured at a Y camp won because the state's law barring negligence suits against non-profits was poorly written.

Referees

Being a referee or sports official in an amateur sport can be almost as dangerous as the sport involved, particularly your vulnerability to lawsuits. A decision you make may not only be unpopular with the losing team or the hometown fans, but you could find that your decision results in personal liability for damages.

One official was sued by a souvenir company that claimed its inventory was devalued by a call causing a college team to lose a basketball tournament slot. In another case, a bat girl sued the game umpire when she was hit by a bat swung by a batter waiting to hit. A catcher sued an umpire and settled when he was injured because he wasn't wearing a mask. He claimed the umpire should have loaned him his mask. In still another case, a basketball official was sued when a college player broke the jaw of a member of the other team. The injured player sued claiming the game was not properly controlled.

Some states have passed laws limiting sports officials' liability only to situations where they are grossly negligent.

You and your federal government

27

Chapter 27
You and your federal government

False Claims Act

This Act allows the government to sue contractors with whom it does business when they file false claims. It contains a provision called "*qui tam*," which gives employees of the contractor who know about fraud the right to sue for themselves and the United States. It has been used in the health care industry for large recoveries. It forbids employers to retaliate against employees who file complaints. If you know about fraud by government contractors, seek counsel immediately.

Freedom of Information Act

Since many aspects of life are affected by the federal government, the public has increased their demand for information about and from the government. A person's ability to receive such information has been aided in recent years by the federal *Freedom of Information Act (FOIA)*. This act allows the public to request and obtain "records" collected by federal agencies or other establishments in the executive branch of the federal government. The Act, however, does not apply to records under the jurisdiction of the Congress, the federal courts, private corporations or state and local governments. Many states have their own "open records" laws which allow access to records of state and local governments.

Who can use it?

An FOIA request may be made by "any person," which means that all U.S. citizens as well as foreign nationals may use the Act. A request can also be made in the name of a corporation, partnership or other entity, such as a public interest group or newspaper.

Reasonably identifiable records

There are millions of documents already in government files. They can be found on paper, microfilm, or microfiche. The *Freedom of Information Act* applies to these records. If you want information, the government does not have to compile it for you; it just has to retrieve it from its files.

For instance, if you want to know how many handicapped or disabled persons were hired in 1980 by the FBI, if the Bureau does not already have that data in a record, it does not have to go back through personnel or other files to see if it has the information. Nor does it have to interview supervisors or make a survey of all its offices to get information for you.

After President Kennedy was assassinated, the whole world became fascinated with everything and everyone associated with the sad event.

There are still questions which surface and answers which are unsatisfactory. Dr. John Nichols, a pathologist, used the FOIA to pursue his interest in the case. Dr. Nichols, a Kansas physician and professor of pathology, filed requests with the Archivist of the U.S. and the U.S. Navy to obtain the gun used by Lee Harvey Oswald, live and spent ammunition, metal fragments, x-ray films and photos made at the President's autopsy, the written diagnosis and findings made by the radiologist at the Naval Hospital and personal clothing worn by the President. When his requests were denied, he sued the government.

The District Court decided that the materials did not have to be given to Dr. Nichols. The rifle, clothing and bullet fragments were not records and the FOIA did not apply to them. The written materials were covered by the Act but the Court would not release them. On appeal, the Court decided that the items requested were all exempt from disclosure by one of the exemptions to the Act. The exemptions will be discussed in more detail later in this chapter. The exemption that was applied in this case provides that the FOIA does not require release of records if another law states they shall not be released. The law that prevented Dr. Nichols from having his requests honored said that the national interest required the items he wanted to become the possessions of the United States and to be preserved. Therefore, though they could be looked at by certain scholars, they could not be touched.

Make an informal request
Anyone seeking records should first try to obtain them through informal means. The government may readily agree to supply all or part of them. In fact, the information in the records may already be available or in a government publication. If you know what specific records you want and which federal agency has them, call or write to the Public Information or Press Officer of the agency. Agencies are required to have employees assigned to handle freedom of information requests. So, if the press office is not the right office, ask for the "FOIA" officer who may give you the documents you want without the need to file a formal FOIA request.

Formal requests
If the informal approach does not succeed, exercise your rights under the Act by making a formal request in writing to the agency which has the records you want. Put on the envelope that you are making an FOIA request. In your request, describe the documents as best you can, giving names, dates, places, as applicable. They have to answer you in 10 days or ask you to give them an extension of time.

Costs and waiver of fees
The government may charge reasonable fees covering some of their costs in answering your request, mainly for searching for the records and reproducing them. So it can be expensive. They can charge you to search even if none of the records requested can be located. One way to reduce or eliminate costs is to ask the agency to waive or reduce search and reproduction fees. However, you must show that the information you are requesting would benefit the general public and therefore would be in the public interest if released.

Exemptions
Some requests need not be honored. We saw that with Dr. Nichols and the Kennedy file. The Act sets out 9 exemptions and if the records are covered by any of them, the government may refuse to give them to you. The exemptions cover records that relate to

such things as national security, internal agency personnel matters, trade secrets which have been given to the government by businesses, advice and recommendations on government policies written by government employees, personal privacy matters such as health records, law enforcement investigations, federally regulated banks and oil and gas wells records. However, generally, these exemptions are not absolute. The government may decide that they will honor your request since openness in government is important. Also, if you can show that release of the records would be in the public interest, the government may release them to you despite the exemptions. In any event, in documents which contain advice and recommendations, they must separate out from the material that which is factual as compared to advisory.

A bizarre case

The Court of Appeals in Maryland called the Robles case bizarre and illustrative of the ignorance by even scientists of the dangerous properties of radioactive waste materials and the hazards that result from ignorance. In 1950, in Grand Junction, Colorado, a uranium processing plant started giving away its uranium tailings, a sand-like byproduct, for use as fill dirt. In 1966, the hazards incident to use of the tailings was recognized. The Environmental Protection Agency surveyed public structures and approximately 15,000 homes where uranium tailings had been used as fill during construction. The purpose was to ascertain the health hazards due to the resulting background radiation. Homeowners were allegedly assured the results would be kept confidential.

Ms. Robles asked under FOIA for the results of the survey, particularly the data on those structures in which radiation levels exceeded safety guidelines. She also wanted to know the names and addresses of the homeowners or occupiers of the structures. The Environmental Protection Agency agreed to give her the survey but not the names and addresses citing the exemption on personal privacy. The District Court agreed but the Court of Appeals did not. They said there was no way to tell which homeowners had been given the assurance, that there can be no confidentiality for a public building, that the information had already been given out to the Colorado Health Department, and that it could cause more fear for people not knowing.

Rap sheets

A different result occurred in a case which went to the U.S. Supreme Court. The Justices unanimously decided that criminal records, or rap sheets, on individuals need not be released by the Justice Department other than to authorized persons such as banks and licensing officials. This is so even if the information had been publicly available, since it would be an unwarranted invasion of personal privacy. Forty-seven states have laws restricting disclosure of such information. You can find it in searching courthouse files, but you cannot get a government clearinghouse computerized summary.

Direct mail solicitations

A U.S. Court of Appeals decided that the names and addresses of persons stationed at an air force base would have to be released to an inquirer. He wanted them for a direct mail insurance solicitation, but his reason for asking didn't matter. They were not such personnel records as would be exempted from disclosure.

You may appeal

If your formal request is denied, you can appeal to the head of the agency. It is very important to submit a written appeal giving all the reasons why the agency was wrong to deny you the records. You should also indicate that you believe the denial was arbitrary, that is without any good reason. If later on a court finds it was arbitrary, the official who influenced the denial could be reprimanded. The government has 30 days to either give you the records or deny your appeal.

You may want to consult with an attorney before you appeal so that the appeal states your case in the best light. Appeals are usually reviewed carefully by the agency's legal counsel.

FOIA lawsuit

If you lose your appeal, you can bring a lawsuit. You may recover attorneys' fees and court costs if the judge decides that the government improperly withheld some or all of the information you requested.

The Privacy Act

The Privacy Act was passed in 1974. It applies to all agencies in the executive branch but not to the Congress or the federal courts. It deals with information about individuals. Many times requests for records can be made using both the FOIA and the Privacy Act. It has four purposes. It gives an individual the right to see records the federal government has on him or her and to correct any errors in the records; it gives an individual the right to know how information about them is used; it requires the federal agency controlling the records to make sure the information in the records is correct and to prevent misuse of the information; it seeks to assure that no secret records are maintained on any individual. However, on occasion, an individual's right to privacy will be weighed against another important interest, namely, society's need to know the information in question.

What is a record?

A record under the *Privacy Act* is somewhat different from the definition under FOIA. Under the Privacy Act a "record" has three elements. It must contain personal information; you must be able to find it by looking for it by a person's name or social security number; and it must be under an agency's control. The personal information must be something like your home address or your medical history. If you can't find or retrieve the record under your name or social security number, it is not a record under the Act and you can't take advantage of the rights it gives you.

Correction of records

The Act requires that any information about you must be accurate, of records relevant, timely and complete. This is because your rights and benefits may be influenced by what is in the records. You can't color the information according to your own preferences, but you can either have a mistake eliminated or, if there is a dispute, provide data which allows third parties to see both sides. A court can order records corrected if an agency won't do it.

A certain veteran sued the Army to have his medical records corrected. He alleged that he had been discharged based on medical judgments which were erroneous and that because of the errors he was later denied VA benefits. The court agreed that the plaintiff was entitled to seek an amendment of the inaccurate data and the diagnostic conclusions based on that data. The data was ordered deleted. However, the medical judgments were based on observations as well as the data and therefore the court felt they were not sufftciently discredited to require deletion or contradiction. In this case, however, the doctor revised his earlier judgments himself.

System of records

The Act requires each federal agency to put all its records which meet the three criteria in a system of records. This means they must group the records according to the topic or program the records relate to. An example is *"Participants in Experiments, Studies and Surveys"* of the *National Bureau of Standards*. These are people who have voluntarily agreed to serve in experiments conducted by the Bureau, such as how long it takes certain fabrics used in public transportation vehicles to burn.

Some agencies may have 100 systems of records. They are required to publish every year a list of all of them and tell the public where the system is located, what type of individuals are included, what sort of information about them is in the records, and who to contact if you want to see the record about yourself.

You ask for it

Some information on federal employees is available to anyone, such as their name, their salary, their title and their office. Information about you must be disclosed to you if you ask to see it, except if your record comes under exemptions, such as it is investigatory material compiled for law enforcement purposes, it is test material used to determine your qualifications for a position in the government, or it is material to be used to determine your potential for promotion in the armed services.

Others ask about you

Your records may be available to others if you give permission to the agency to disclose them. They may also be available in other situations: For example, if certain officials, such as law enforcement officers, have a need to know, there is a medical emergency and your records can help, or if the system containing your records has been published and you know the routine use the records will be used for and who will be entitled to see them.

Routine use

Routine use is a term from the Act. It means the disclosure of the records is compatible with the purpose for which the information was collected. If you ask your Congressperson to help you with a problem and he or she asks an agency about you, your record in the system of records will be disclosed as a routine use to that member of Congress.

You can sue

You may sue if an agency withholds records from you or discloses records and you are adversely affected. The court may grant damages and reasonable attorney fees and costs if you substantially prevail. You may also collect punitive damages against the government if they acted in an intentional or willful manner. In a recent case, a group of employees in the Wichita office of the Internal Revenue Service sued for damages under the *Privacy Act* because their personnel files were used to pinpoint them as "recalcitrants" who had not pledged to purchase government bonds. They alleged that the Act, which prohibits disclosure of records except in specific circumstances, was designed, in part, to halt the blacklisting of persons who do not always comply with an organization's norms or standards, such as participating in bond drives or charity campaigns. The District Court ruled that the employees had no remedy under the Act but the Court of Appeals disagreed and sent it back for further proceedings. They said that the Treasury Department did not publish savings bond information as a routine use and therefore disclosure of information concerning nonparticipation in this voluntary program for the purpose of soliciting sales was a violation of the Act. They also agreed that the employees did suffer invasion of privacy which could cause mental distress or embarrassment and that management's awareness and participation showed there was willfulness and intentional action.

The Privacy Act is a complicated statute and you will want to consult an attorney if you believe that you have been improperly denied access to your records or that you have been harmed because your records have been disclosed improperly.

Federal Tort Claims Act

At one time, the principle of the divine right of Kings was not questioned. The King could do no wrong and any harm resulting was not actionable. Nowadays, although there are few monarchies and fewer with any real power, the concept of the sovereign's immunity to suit has remained. Many states and cities have it. But the federal government no longer is immune to civil law suits by persons injured by its employees.

The first *Federal Tort Claims Act (FTCA)* was passed in 1946. In 1966, the Act was amended. It is important for you to be aware of your rights under the Act since the activities of the federal government have such a tremendous impact on our daily lives. The federal government employs millions of people and controls a large portion of the land in the country. Its postal vehicles travel daily in our neighborhoods. Its hospitals treat veterans and their dependents. Its employees control traffic at every major airport, report the weather, count the population, maintain the national parks, operate housing developments, authorize the sale of food and drugs, conduct military maneuvers and research.

Negligence

Before the *Tort Act*, the only way you could collect any damages for harm suffered because of federal government activities was through a private relief bill sponsored by your Congressman. The Act provided that claims could be made for injury or loss of property, or personal injury or death caused by the negligent or wrongful act or omission of any employee of the government, if the employee was acting in the scope of his or her office or employment at the time. Now the government can be sued just like any private individual or company. Remember, you sue the United States, not the employee or the agency. You can get damages if you prove three things: the person doing the harm was an employee, he or she was in the scope of employment at the time, and he or she was negligent. Of course, you also have to have an injury.

In discussing negligence it is important to know that, until recently, someone's negligent action had to be the "proximate cause" of the injury, that is "but for" the negligent conduct, the injury would not have happened. Now courts are moving away from that theory of negligence and the California Supreme Court is a prime example. That court has said that a jury should look to whether a defendant's conduct was a "substantial factor" in bringing about the harm and there could be liability even when their behavior was only a contributing factor in the injury. Of course, in *Tort Claims Act* matters, the case is tried in a federal court, but the local law is applied. The California court that said that "one cannot escape responsibility for negligence on the ground that identical harm would have occurred without it" may be speaking for many more courts in the future including the federal bench.

Some examples

An army sergeant used an army vehicle to do a personal favor for his Colonel. This was against regulations so that when he collided with a motorcycle while on the errand his negligence didn't make the U.S. liable to the cyclist. A postman in uniform got off a bus and jostled a woman at the bus stop. She sued the U.S. It was discovered that the postman was off duty and on his way home at the time so the U.S. could not be held responsible. An army truck assigned to a state national guard unit and being driven by a guardsman hit a private auto. The civilian driver sued the U.S. but the Court found that since the national guard unit had not been called up by the president, the unit was not in federal service and the state guard driver was still a state employee. Under all these circumstances, the U.S. could not be held responsible.

What about a case of a soldier on active duty transferring from one duty station to another using his own car? Can he cause the U.S. to become liable for his negligence? A soldier was released from a government hospital and given 15 days leave before reporting to his new duty station. While driving to his new post during the 15 days' leave time he caused an accident. The court found that though he was in the service, he was on vacation at the time of the accident so he could not be considered an employee. In another case however, a serviceman's action did cause the U.S. to be held liable.

Sgt. James Smith unintentionally took home from maneuvers some army explosive devices which simulated the sound of a hand grenade. He put them away in a dresser drawer and they were forgotten. Many months later, while Sgt. Smith was overseas, Mrs. Smith gave one of the devices to a 13-year-old babysitter. He took it home and while playing with it, it exploded and he was injured. His parents sued the U.S. and the court found that the government should be held liable for the sergeant's careless handling of the explosive.

Who can make a claim?

Almost anyone who has been injured by an activity of the federal government may make a claim. You do not have to be a citizen of the U.S. or a resident of any particular state. However, if you are a serviceman, a reservist in training or a government employee, you can't make a claim for an injury sustained while on active duty or on the job. There are special compensation statutes for these people and they are the exclusive remedies for them. A serviceman who was temporarily released from his regular duties to voluntarily participate in the army's chemical warfare testing program and was given LSD without his knowledge, could not sue for physical and mental injuries.

Recovery by family members is barred where the cause of action is derivative of the serviceman's action for his own injury incident to military service. Mr. L., while in the army, allegedly handled radioactive substances and was thereby exposed to radiation. Mrs. L. and the L. children argued that they should be allowed to recover for injuries they had received as a result of Mr. L.'s exposure. Although they had never served in the military and the children were born after Mr. L. had been discharged, the court ruled that they could not recover since "each claim had its 'genesis' in an injury to a serviceman incident to military service."

What about a serviceman who was on a 24-hour pass riding in a friend's car on his way to a quail hunt when he was injured? The accident occurred at Fort Benning and was caused by an army jeep being driven by a pfc. The court decided that the off-duty soldier could sue the U.S. since his injuries were in no way service connected.

Prisoners

A prisoner can make a claim under the Tort Act for the negligence of employees in the prison. Harry Winston was a well-known Communist who was confined to the U.S. penitentiary at Terre Haute. He experienced difficulty with his vision and his problem was diagnosed by government medical personnel at the prison as hypertension. He continued to have problems but was not treated. Eventually an operation was performed, a tumor was removed but his sight could not be saved. Winston sued the U.S. alleging that the negligence of the prison employees was responsible for the delay in treatment and his subsequent blindness. In another prison case, Carlos Muniz was beaten by other inmates causing him to be severely injured. He sued the U.S. alleging negligence and the failure to provide sufficient guards to prevent his assault. The Supreme Court found that both Winston and Muniz could make claims against the U.S. despite their status as federal convicts.

Mickey Cohen, famous for his underworld connections, was confined to the maximum security penitentiary at Atlanta. Also incarcerated there was Berl McDonald who had spent most of his adult life in prisons. He was a known narcotic addict and had had numerous fights while in Atlanta. He had been classified as emotionally unstable. One day while McDonald was in the exercise yard, he scaled a wall and went to a building where Mickey Cohen was working. He assaulted Cohen causing him to suffer severe and permanent injuries. Cohen sued the U.S. under the Tort Act and the court found that the government was negligent in regard to its supervision of McDonald.

A different rule applies to prisoners making claims because of industrial type injuries. There is federal compensation provided to them for such injuries which comes from Federal Prison Industries, Inc., and this compensation law is the exclusive remedy for prisoners who are injured "on the job."

What do you do?

You must first file an administrative claim with the government agency whose employee you allege was responsible for your mishap. If you file your claim with the wrong agency, they will forward it on. There is no ceiling on the dollar amount of your claim. However, you must demand a sum certain. If you demand more than $25,000, the federal agency involved cannot settle with you for anything in excess of $25,000, without first obtaining the approval of the U.S. Department of Justice. Also, whatever amount you claim administratively cannot be increased in a later court action except if there is newly discovered evidence. However, if you have filed a valid claim with a sum certain, it can be amended prior to final action by the agency.

How do you go about making a claim?

It should be done on a Government Form # 95. Written notification can be made in any manner as long as all pertinent information is provided by the injured party or by his or her agent or legal counsel. If the party injured is deceased, a claim may be made by his or her executor, administrator or anyone else the state law recognizes as legally eligible. An insurance company may make a claim. If someone other than the injured party is making the claim, however, he or she must be sure to provide the agency with evidence showing authority to present the claim.

What should you say in your claim?

You must provide the government agency with a good deal of information about your claim if you expect to have it considered favorably. If a personal injury is involved, the agency will want to have statements from your doctor, dentist, or other medical practitioner, in regard to the nature and extent and prognosis of the injury, as well as copies of all bills showing the expenses you incurred, evidence proving any income you may have lost, and information indicating why you believe the United States is responsible for the injury.

If property damage is involved, accompanying the claim statement should be detailed information on your ownership of the property, its value, and any repairs made prior to and as a result of the accident. Again the government will want to know why you believe the United States is responsible for the damage that you have incurred.

If a death resulted from an accident, the claim must be accompanied by details covering the deceased's occupation, income, family responsibilities, physical condition prior to the accident, injuries and pain and suffering sustained as a result of the accident, and all bills related to the accident, subsequent death and burial. Again, you must justify your claim by explaining why the United States should be considered responsible for the death.

Statute of limitations

Statutes of limitations have been discussed elsewhere in the book since they affect all claims of whatever kind. This is a most important aspect of the Tort Act and because of it you should not delay in seeking counsel for your case.

You have two years from the day of the accident or injury to file your mandatory administrative claim. Your disability does not count as an excuse for not filing in time. Thereafter the agency has six months time to consider it. You cannot withdraw it during that time. If your claim is denied at any time during the six months, you may then file suit but you must file not later than six months from the day of the mailing to you of the agency's denial of the claim. If the agency takes longer than six months to act on your claim, you may consider that your claim has been denied and file suit.

When did your claim accrue?

In FICA matters, as in most other negligence cases, you will encounter the problem of when your cause of action accrued. The term *accrued* means the point in time when the wrong was actually done; you need to know this so that you can have the basis for a lawsuit. It may seem easy to pinpoint a date if a postal truck collided with your car at an intersection and your leg was broken. What about a person who has been injured and doesn't find out about it until many years later, when a delayed onset of symptoms ensues? This type of situation is certainly not unusual in medical malpractice cases.

Discovery rule

Mrs. Quinton, while in the hospital on the Larson Air Force Base in Washington state, was negligently given three blood transfusions of improper blood. She had no reaction and didn't know about the error until three years later when she became pregnant. At that time, because of the transfusions of incompatible blood, she gave birth to a stillborn child and was told she could not bear other children without the probability that they would be stillborn, blind or defective.

Mr. Quinton sued the United States and the question of limitations arose. The government said that the suit was brought more than two years after the claim accrued, that is when she received the blood. A United States Court of Appeals decided that Mrs. Quinton could not have known of the negligence prior to her pregnancy and she should not be penalized for "blameless ignorance." They said that in a case of malpractice, a suit could be maintained within two years after the claimant discovered, or, in the exercise of reasonable diligence, should have discovered the existence of the acts of negligence.

Continuous treatment

When a doctor commits an act of malpractice of which you are unaware, but he continues to treat you thereafter, you have a continuing relationship. The court may find that he had a duty all the time he was treating you to remedy the error. If you do not discover his mistake until after he has ceased treating you, you may still be in time to bring a suit. The statute of limitations will only begin to run from the end of the course of treatment. Many times you cannot even discover a physician's malpractice until you go to another physician.

If your claim is denied

If an agency denies your administrative claim, you can generally sue. A Tort Act suit can only be filed in a United States District Court, but it can be brought either in the federal district where you reside or where the accident occurred. Many accidents happen while people are away from home. The Act allows a choice for the sake of the convenience of the injured party. However, the court will apply the law of the state where the accident occurred. For example, if you fall while sightseeing at the Lincoln Memorial and return to your home in Connecticut, you can sue in the District Court in Connecticut. However, the judge will have to look to the law of the District of Columbia to see how the case should be decided and he will decide your case. You are not entitled to a jury in FTCA matters. You must sue the United States not the individual or the agency.

You can't sue in every case

Although the federal government generally has allowed itself to be sued for its civil wrongs, the Act does contain certain exceptions. If you have this type of case, then you don't have any standing to make a claim at all. The reasoning behind most of the exceptions is that the government must remain free to perform some functions and should not be subjected to suit despite even negligent conduct.

Among the exceptions are:

- claims arising out of the loss, miscarriage or negligent transmission of letters or postal matter;
- any claim arising in respect of the assessment of collection of any tax or customs duty or the detention of any goods or merchandise by any officer of customs or excise or any other law enforcement officer;
- any claim for damages caused by the imposition of a quarantine by the United States;
- any claim arising out of the combatant activities of the military or naval forces or the Coast Guard during time of war;
- any claim arising in a foreign country;
- any claim arising from the activities of the Tennessee Valley Authority and
- any claim based upon the exercise or performance or failure to exercise or perform a discretionary function on the part of an employee or agency of the government.

Also, generally, there can't be claims arising out of assault, battery, false imprisonment, false arrest, malicious prosecution, abuse of process, libel, slander, misrepresentation, deceit or interference with contract rights. Except that with regard to acts or omissions of investigative or law enforcement officers of the United States government, such as FBI agents, you can make a claim against the United States arising out of their assaults, batteries, false imprisonment, false arrests, abuse of process or malicious prosecution.

The discretionary function exception

What is the exercise of thought or discretion in planning a government project, what is policy and where does routine begin? These are extremely thorny questions that are faced by our courts frequently, especially in view of the complicated nature of so many governmental operations. One specific case involved Mr. Tilley who was a passenger on a Delta Airlines plane going to Atlanta. While the Delta plane was preparing to take off from Kennedy International Airport, Sabena and Air France planes were also in the vicinity. All three planes were being controlled by the air traffic control tower staffed by employees of the Federal Aviation Agency. Due to instructions from the Tower, the Delta plane made a series of maneuvers and ran off the runway. Mr. Tilley was injured and he sued the United States and Delta Airlines. The government claimed that the traffic controller was exercising discretion in giving the Delta pilot certain emergency instructions and that therefore Mr. Tilley's suit should be barred under the discretionary function exception. The court decided, however, that the Controller's acts were really only operational details and since it was because of his negligence that Mr. Tilley was injured, he could recover as against the United States.

In another case, the children and husband of a woman who had been beaten and brutally murdered by an ex-federal prisoner sued the United States alleging that the prisoner had been released in total disregard of medical reports confirming that he was a homicidal psychotic. The court ruled that the decision to parole is a discretionary function thus excluded from FICA. The plaintiffs, however, were allowed to recover because the government had been negligent in not providing an adequate examination report to the Attorney General prior to the discretionary act.

The Supreme Court ruled unanimously recently in another case that the exception did not apply to government negligence in approving defective or unsafe vaccines for public use. A child had become paralyzed after taking a virulent dose of oral polio vaccine.

Postal exception

The Marine Insurance Company, Inc., a British insurer, insured an air mail package of emeralds going from Switzerland to New York City. The value of the gems was $152,000. About this time, many thefts of valuable packages had been occurring, so when the emeralds arrived at the Mail Division of the U.S. Customs Building in New York City, the government decided to use them as a decoy to trap the thieves. The package was treated with a special powder, put back into the regular mail routine and kept under surveillance. Later, a Custom's employee was arrested for stealing the package, but the gems were not recovered. Marine Insurance paid the insurance on the loss and sued the United States for recovery of that sum. However, the court applied the exception governing claims arising out of the loss, miscarriage or negligent transfer of letters or postal matter and the firm did not recover.

Foreign country exception

Ola Belle Meredith, the wife of a serviceman stationed in Bangkok, Thailand, underwent an eye operation performed in a dispensary in the United States Embassy compound in Bangkok. Later when she returned to California, she sued the United States claiming the operation was negligently performed. She tried to avoid the foreign country exception by saying that since the alleged negligence occurred on Embassy property, it was really a piece of the United States on foreign soil. The court disagreed with her and her suit was dismissed. The reason for this exception is that any suit involving a foreign country would necessarily involve foreign nationals, foreign law and foreign courts, things to be avoided.

However, a claim does not arise where the last event necessary to liability happens but rather where the act or omission of the government employee occurs. In another case a man sought damages for his false arrest and detainment by German officials as a result of an allegedly inaccurate message sent from Washington. The lower court dismissed the government pursuant to the foreign claims exception, because the arrest had occurred in Germany. The Court of Appeals reversed. Since the inaccurate message was sent from the United States, the plaintiff was allowed to recover.

Assault and battery
Mr. Moos went into a government hospital for an operation on his left leg. The operation was performed on his right leg instead. He sued the United States. The court said that since the assault and battery was committed by a government physician the United States could not be sued because of the exception.

Has the government been negligent?
There have been thousands of cases brought under the Act. They vary in as many ways as there are personal incidents in everyone's life.

Slip and fall on wax
Col. Graham's wife had agreed to help in decorating the officer's club at the Robins Air Force Base in Georgia, in preparation for a Strategic Air Command Officers' Wives' luncheon. Some decorating was done the night before and the rest was to be completed prior to the luncheon. Early in the morning of the day of the lunch, the Club's janitor started to wax the tile floor of the dining room as he had done for some years. He had waxed a goodly portion of the room by the time Mrs. Graham arrived to help. She spent some time decorating and then left to cash a check in another part of the Club. It was while she was on her way to do this that she slipped and injured herself. She sued the United States. The court found that the Club had a right to clean and wax its floors and that the time chosen to do so was reasonable. Mrs. Graham should have seen the janitor working in the area and also she should have noted that the room was in various stages of wetness due to the waxing operation. The wax used was slip resistant and no dangerous condition existed. The government was found not responsible for Mrs. Graham's injuries.

Snow
Mrs. Dix slipped while depositing a letter in an outdoor mailbox which was standing on a lawn near the curb in front of the post office in Syracuse, New York. About 43 inches of snow had fallen in Syracuse in the days prior to the accident and it had been snowing lightly until just before her fall. The ground was slippery and banks of snow were piled all around the area. A rough path to the box had been made by people trampling down the snow. Mrs. Dix sued the United States claiming the government was negligent since it had not provided her with a safe means of access to its mailbox. However, the court found that the government's duty in maintaining safe indoor or adjacent premises such as steps or walks could not apply to an area without a regular walk and subject to the elements. "Each mailbox is not a branch post office."

Swimming

Victor Farn was a young enlisted man in the Air Force. One July 4th, he and some buddies decided to spend their free evening swimming in the Cheery Creek Reservoir. The Cheery Creek Dam and Reservoir in Colorado had been constructed by the United States Army Corps of Engineers and thereafter the Reservoir was leased to the Department of Natural Resources of the State of Colorado for a public park and recreational purposes. The State managed the area and on that July 4th swimming was not allowed since no beach facility had been established. Farn and his friends entered the Reservoir from a place along the shoreline known as "The Point." Farn disappeared and drowned about 100 feet from the shore trapped in dense sea weed growing all around. Mrs. Farn sued the United States for the death of her son. The Court held that Victor had gone to the Reservoir for his own purposes and interests, that there was no assurance given to him it was safe to swim and that he had ignored the obvious risk of swimming in a place full of aquatic growth. The government was held not to be liable.

Poison

Lyle Fritz was 15-years-old and lived in North Dakota. One day he and a group of other boys and men gathered to participate in a fox hunt sponsored by the Veterans of Foreign Wars chapter of his town. Prior to the day of the hunt, a mammal control agent of the Fish and Wildlife Service, U.S. Department of Interior, had been requested by a rancher to set up some coyote getters or traps, metal tubes about 7 inches long in which are inserted cyanide pellets. There is a triggering device on the side. The getter is imbedded in the ground and a scented cap is left exposed to attract the coyote. The agent placed caution signs around the ranch warning of the devices. The hunting party went to this ranch and Lyle stepped on one of the trigger mechanisms. The pellet struck him in the right eye causing him to lose it. His father sued the United States. The court found that the coyote getter was like a spring gun and since North Dakota law bars the use of them, the government was negligent in using them at all. Also, the government was held to have given inadequate warning of the presence of the getters.

Water on the floor

Mrs. Dietrich went to a post office in Queens, New York, to mail a letter. It had been raining slightly in the morning and so the postal employees had placed rubber runners on the floor of the post office. Mrs. Dietrich was not wearing rubbers. She walked along part of one mat, but then, intending to take a more direct route to a box in the rear of the post office, she stepped onto the terrazzo floor, slipped, fell and injured herself. The floor was damp but there were no puddles of water. She sued the United States. The court found that the government did not have to provide wall to wall mats nor was there anything negligent in the fact that the floor was slightly damp in view of the weather conditions. The whole thing was just an accident for which no one was responsible.

Who is responsible?

James Barnes was a dealer in used and scrap automotive parts. One day he went to the salvage yard at Fort Benning, Georgia, to purchase scrap parts. While in an outdoor scrap metal bin, he was struck in the eye by some tiny sharp object. It was never found, but because of the object Mr. Barnes lost his eye. Just before the incident a truck nearby had been dumping scrap metal and Barnes contended, in his suit against the United States, that a sliver had snapped and struck him. He also claimed that nothing he had done in the metal bin had caused his injury. The court found that since the object that caused the injury was not found or positively identified, there was no way to determine that the government was, in fact, responsible for it.

Dangerous premises

Sherrie Adams was 10-years-old and was visiting friends camped at Platt National Park in Oklahoma. She and some other children were playing in a natural pool of water in Rock Creek in the park. Someone had tied a rope to a tree limb overhanging the pool and while Sherrie was playing a boy started to swing on the rope and struck her in the head. She died the next day. Her parents sued the United States claiming that the premises were made dangerous by the existence of the rope swing which U.S. Park Service personnel knew or should have known about. The Court found the government operated the park for recreational purposes and that the Rangers knew rope swings were dangerous and had, in fact, prohibited them. The Court also said that the Rangers should have discovered the rope swing at this place frequented by children and eliminated it.

Attorneys' fees

The FTCA provides that your lawyer may receive up to 20% of any administrative settlement and up to 25% of any money you receive from a court in a judgment against the United States.

Federal employees limited

The Supreme Court has ruled that federal employees may not sue their superiors for violations of their constitutional rights stemming from personnel actions. An aerospace engineer at the Marshall Space Center in Alabama, sued after being demoted by NASA for making critical remarks to the media about his superiors. He relied on earlier Supreme Court cases allowing suits against federal agents to deter illegal searches. The Court felt that civil service laws, providing reinstatement and recovery of back pay, already protect federal workers adequately.

In another case, black sailors aboard the USS *Decatur* claimed they were given the worst assignments and were targets of the Klan. The Supreme Court barred them from suing superior officers since such suits undermine the strict discipline between enlisted personnel and their superiors.

Vets win

The Supreme Court has interpreted a 1924 statute to require that the government pay benefits for injuries caused by veterans' hospitals even when there was no negligence or fault. It is compensation to redress injuries from medical or surgical treatment at a V.A. hospital. The law applied to injuries not related to vets' military service. The ruling did not discuss claims pending at the time.

Punitive damages

The FTCA does not allow for payment of punitive damages. In a case involving a patient injured at a V.A. hospital, the issue was what damages could be awarded since he would continue to receive free medical care at the hospital. The lower courts in Wisconsin said that the government's payment for future medical care would duplicate damages and so be punitive. Also, since he was a comatose patient, it would be punitive to award damages for loss of enjoyment.

The Supreme Court, however, in an unanimous opinion, the first written by Justice Clarence Thomas, said that the damages were in a "gray zone," not purely compensation and not punitive aimed to punish misconduct. But the case was returned to the state court for a determination of entitlement under local law as is required by the Act.

Government checks

The *Competitive Equality Banking Act (CEBA)* requires that anyone receiving a government check must cash it within one year of its issue date. If your check is lost or otherwise turns up missing, your claim also must be filed within one year. You may think that people always cash their checks, but you are mistaken. *The Financial Management Services,* a bureau of the U.S. Treasury Department, estimated that there were more than nine million outstanding checks more than one year old. That's the reason for the law, so billions of dollars won't be tied up waiting for what used to be no time limit on government check cashing.

Right to Know Act

In 1986, the Congress passed the *Emergency Planning and Community Right to Know Act (EPCRA),* which was part of the *Environmental Protection Agency's (EPA) Superfund Amendments and Reauthorization Act.* It came about after the tragedy in Bhopal, India, when hundreds died because of a leak of a dangerous chemical from a Union Carbide plant. By the spring of 1989, EPA made available a Toxics Release Inventory, information provided by thousands of companies concerning how much of hundreds of chemicals they have released into the air, dumped on the ground, discharged into water, or disposed of.

Local Emergency Planning Committees in each state must also have in place local emergency response plans including evacuation of an area in the event of a chemical accident.

Call the *EPA's Right to Know Hotline,* (1) 800-535-0202, to obtain the information the companies have given them and also to ascertain who in your state can give you more information on emergency response plans.

Travel

28

Chapter 28
Travel

Right to travel

Among the rights of citizenship is the right to travel. The Supreme Court has held that a statute indiscriminately restricting the right to travel abridges the liberty guaranteed by the Constitution.

However, there are times when states may control your travel rights. In 1983, the United States Supreme Court upheld a Georgia statute, which changed voluntary and willful child abandonment from a misdemeanor for those parents who committed the offense and remained in the state, to a felony for those parents who abandoned their children and then left the state or who abandoned their children after leaving the state.

The Court reasoned that despite the fundamental nature of the right to travel, there are situations in which a state may prevent a citizen from leaving. Among those who might justifiably be detained are convicted criminals and those who committed an offense against state laws.

Travel agents

Travel agents are a font of knowledge and information and can make your trips the dream vacations or business successes you want and need. But you should check out their credentials as you would any contractor with whom you deal. They want to be recognized as professionals. However, along with this recognition comes responsibility. If your vacation or business plans are ruined due to mix ups with your hotel or plane reservations, you may be able to bring a lawsuit against your travel agent to compensate you for your aggravation.

Courts in Illinois, Pennsylvania, and New York have held that travel agents are to be regarded as agents of the traveler and, as such, must fulfill certain recognized duties. Travel agents have a duty to make and confirm reservations. In doing this, the travel agent must independently check the availability and delivery of travel services. If the traveler wants reservations for a specific hotel or flight, the agent must contact the supplier directly and check to see that such services are available.

With package deals promoted by tour operators which feature promised accommodations and services, travel agents must go to the supplier and "independently" establish that what the tour operator is promising is true. Travel agents are also under a duty to investigate the financial stability and reliability of a recommended supplier or tour operator.

The agent must investigate the supplier or tour operator's track record. Consideration must also be given to the traveler's needs and an agent must give advice as is necessary. For example, travel agents have been found liable for failing to tell a traveler about needing a visa to enter a country and for failing to recommend that the traveler take appropriate shots needed to ward off potential illness.

Tour operator default

When *Caribbean Holidays* tour operator went bankrupt, travelers and hotels lost money. How can you protect yourself when your tour operator defaults? Travel insurance policies can help but you must be sure they cover both default and bankruptcy. No travel insurance covers default by travel agencies. You may be able to sue the travel agent who sold you the tour but the relationship between the agent and tour company will govern whether a court will find them liable. If your travel agent participates in a Tour Payment Protection Plan, this plan may repay for traveler losses when a package tour is purchased from an agent member. Finally, if you use a credit card when buying directly from a tour company, if the service is not delivered a refund must be credited to your account.

Common carrier liability for schedules

Some courts have held common carriers, such as bus companies and railroads, liable for failure to meet departure and arrival schedules, and for equipment breakdowns. Using the class action device, consumers have sued railroads on negligence, breach of contract and fraud theories. The plaintiffs have recovered damages and the courts often have rejected disclaimers of liability by the carriers.

Lost luggage

When you travel by air, train, bus, or boat and give your luggage to the agent or check it for delivery at your destination, the carrier to whom you entrusted it is responsible for its delivery. He is liable for its value in almost all cases in which it is lost, provided that you do not contribute to its loss. Exceptions to this rule are for losses resulting from extraordinary incidents as acts of God or from special actions taken by a governmental authority. Even in these exceptional cases, if negligence on the part of the carrier placed the baggage in the position where the loss occurred, the passenger may still be able to recover.

A woman checked her bag and its contents with a bus agent. When she reached the end of her journey, the bag was missing. If the passenger has control of baggage to the exclusion of the carrier, said the court that heard her case, then the railway or bus company is not liable for the loss. But when a passenger delivers a bag or suitcase to a bus agent, as in this instance, the bus company and not the passenger must bear the loss.

Who has control?

The baggage delivered before a passenger has bought his ticket comes under the same rule of law with the same liability of the carrier, unless the carrier lets the passenger know of special liability limitations, such as the fact that it will not become responsible for the baggage until the passenger pays his fare. A passenger normally has the right to deliver his baggage to a bus or railroad in order that he may have a reasonable time before the departure of the train or plane, or before the sailing of a boat, for obtaining a ticket. From the time luggage is delivered to the carrier, responsibility for its safety no longer belongs to the passenger.

The owner of a trunk reserved space on a train from Detroit to Cleveland and left it with the railway baggage agent about six hours before the time of departure. An hour after he left this luggage with the railroad, it disappeared. For the loss of the trunk and its content, the railroad was held liable in the suit brought by the traveler for its value.

On the other hand, if the owner of baggage does not deliver it to the carrier but retains it in his custody, he cannot hold the bus or railroad liable for his loss. A woman boarded a bus at Pulaski, Tennessee, for Birmingham, Alabama. She had with her a bag which she left hanging from an arm of the seat. Later she discovered it was missing. The court held she was not entitled to recover for this loss from the bus company.

In another lost-baggage incident, the bus driver requested the passengers to leave the bus, saying he would hand them their luggage and asking that each passenger identify his bag as it was handed out. When almost all the passengers had received their baggage, one woman was offered a bag not her own—her bag had disappeared.

The court, deciding in her favor, pointed out that, if the driver asked the passengers to leave the bus and to let him distribute their luggage, he assumed control and the company became responsible for any loss.

Different carriers
When baggage is checked for a trip through and over connecting railroad or bus lines and is lost, it is impossible for the owner to know by which bus or railway company the baggage was lost. Under these circumstances, the owner of the baggage can always seek recovery for his loss from the first carrier. Under the law, the initial carrier to which the baggage was delivered, which sold the through ticket and checked the luggage to the destination, is liable for the loss irrespective of where it occurs.

Airline rules
Generally, carriers may limit their liability for failing to perform their contract for safe transportation of a passenger's baggage. Buses and railroads can't do it without passenger consent. Airlines are governed by federal rules mandating compensation, but liability sums are set by individual carriers. For domestic flights they limit baggage liability to $1,250 per passenger and the value is the depreciated value, not a new replacement. There also are varying rules on when a baggage report must be made. Continental requires it in writing within 4 hours of landing. Others give up to 45 days for a claim. United won't be responsible for bags unclaimed more than 30 minutes after landing.

Be aware of items for which airlines won't reimburse: cameras, computers, antiques, software, china, cash, jewelry.

Bumping, which is being turned away because of overbooking, also is regulated by federal law. You can be paid or given a free ticket. Also, the airlines must ask for volunteers to give up their seat (and they make varying offers to them to encourage a volunteer to give up) before bumping anyone.

If the airlines won't voluntarily reimburse you for damages resulting from problems such as late arrival or negligence on board, you should not be too hopeful a lawsuit will be successful.

If you sue in state court, airlines argue that the suit is barred by *the Federal Airline Deregulation Act*, which prohibits states from enforcing rules against airlines relating to "rates, routes or services". Airline suits take years and are expensive. One case that was successful, however, involved a jury award to a handicapped teenager against TWA. They refused to board her. She was covered by the *1986 Air Carrier Access Act*, which bars airlines from discriminating against handicapped persons who are qualified to fly.

If you are a regular air traveler, you should push your regular airline to provide you with a copy of *"Conditions of Contract of Carriage"* so you can be informed on all their rules.

Amusement or theme parks

The public can plan a vacation around a specific theme or amusement park. Tie-ins exist with airlines and local businesses which give visitors discounts. Promotion of these sites is national and international, regular and seasonal. But, legal problems can crop up even at these havens of fun.

They have been sued by their patrons for a variety of things ranging from false arrest to food poisoning to personal injury. On the last, slip and fall cases are the most common. However, it appears unlikely that a patron could win this type of suit at Disneyland because the park has a policy requiring that the whole park be cleaned every fifteen minutes. Therefore, a patron could have difficulty showing that the park was negligent in its upkeep of the property.

A few years ago, a homosexual man claimed that his civil rights were violated when Disneyland refused to let him dance in the park with his boyfriend. His suit was dismissed.

Disneyland was sued for $60 million by relatives of an 18-year-old youth who was stabbed by another patron at a private party at the park. The suit claimed that the park was negligent in admitting someone with a weapon and in failing to provide adequate medical services.

A patron seeking to sue a park in California where there are rides carries a somewhat lighter burden of proving his case than in other places since ride operators there are considered to be common carriers. This means that they must use the utmost care and diligence in making, maintaining and operating the rides. This is a tougher standard than the usual negligence standard of ordinary care.

In states that don't follow the comparative negligence doctrine, where the courts weigh each party's negligence, your suit may be barred because you have assumed a risk of injury. Some parks may even require patrons to sign a release form before they are allowed to participate in activities carrying a higher risk.

Security in a hotel

At old English common law, the innkeeper was regarded as an insurer of the safety of the person and the property of the traveler. The reason for such strict liability was that travel was a risky business, the roads being havens for robbers, thugs and highwaymen.

The obligations of the innkeeper in this country were more relaxed due to the increased safety of our highways. However, in recent years in the United States, crime has increased and hotels located in high crime areas have suffered accordingly. A hotel's liability will be judged according to the incidence of crime at the hotel and in the neighborhood, how the hotel is advertised, and the protective measures employed by the hotel.

The problem of hotel safety is illustrated by a case involving Connie Francis, the singer. In her first engagement after coming out of retirement, Ms. Francis checked into a Howard Johnson Lodge in Westbury, N.Y. After her performance, she returned to her room where she was criminally assaulted by an unknown intruder. Ms. Francis sued, claiming the hotel was negligent and that as a result of the assault she was forced to give up her career. She eventually was awarded $2.5 million in damages against the hotel.

Hotel liability for lost or stolen property

Many jurisdictions hold a hotel proprietor responsible for the safekeeping of the goods of his guests. They make him almost the insurer of the stolen property baggage of those who stay at his hotel, unless the property is lost by an extraordinary incident, such as an act of God, or by the negligence of the guest himself.

The liability, based on the right of the hotel proprietor to charge for the accommodations of guests, is one aspect of those accommodations. Jurisdictions which apply this liability feel that whoever stays at a hotel and pays for a room is entitled to this protection of his property. In other jurisdictions, a hotel owner is only liable for losses if he failed to exercise "adequate" care of the property of his guests. While these jurisdictions demand that less precaution be taken by the proprietor, they will still require that he be extremely careful with the property of his guests before absolving him of liability for any loss.

A sign, displayed either in the room of the guest or in public places about the hotel and which states that the establishment will only be responsible for valuables that are checked with it, may be adequate notice in all jurisdictions to relieve the proprietor of liability for the loss of all valuables that are not checked.

Regulations regarding the depositing of valuables with the proprietor for safekeeping do not apply to the clothing and articles which guests normally use daily, nor do they apply to money in reasonable amounts needed for ordinary expenses. These would normally not be checked and the proprietor may, therefore, still be responsible for them.

Hotel liability for valuables in safe boxes

While hotel safe-deposit boxes are considered more secure than leaving valuables in your room, a hotel's liability for items in a safe is limited in most states. They generally are not liable for items left in a room. Before traveling, if you plan to take jewels or other items of value, check to make sure that your homeowner's policy provides sufficient coverage.

Hotel fire safety

The Hotel and Motel Fire Safety Act should go a long way towards making your stay in a hotel or motel safer, even though its provisions are to protect federal employees who travel on government business. The government will not pay travel expenses to hotels and motels that do not meet fire safety provisions except for buildings three floors or under. The Act will not be fully implemented until 1996, but its provisions have already caused changes.

Every state, the District of Columbia, Puerto Rico, the Virgin Islands, among other places, must give the federal government a list of all their hotels and motels that have sprinklers and smoke detectors in their guest rooms. Eventually 90% of all government employees' nights will have to be in hotels that qualify with sprinklers and detectors. Before you book a room, you should be sure that the hotel or motel you will be using cares about your safety from fire.

Souvenirs

It is a crime to bring many wildlife souvenirs into the country. These can be parts of dead animals such as ivory, coral, furs, feathers of birds or they can be live animals, birds or plants. Because so much wildlife is endangered and exploitation and poaching is rampant, protection against imports is necessary. The laws covering imports include *The Endangered Species Act, The Marine Mammal Protection Act*, and *the Lacey Act*. There is also a wildlife treaty regulating imports of threatened or endangered species of plants and animals.

You must determine the origin of a product and should be aware of the restrictions on its import. Otherwise, you could find it will be refused entry and you will be subject to fine and prosecution. Also, whether endangered or not, plants must undergo inspection by the Department of Agriculture and be documented as free from disease or pests.

If you are uncertain about the legalities, don't buy the souvenir.

When buying overseas, remember all states have compensating use tax laws, like a sales tax, So even a duty free item or one that gets by federal customs may be caught by your state department of taxation looking at customs' records and billings.

Hotel not liable for fear of AIDS

A hotel chain was sued for negligence by a young child's parents when he scratched himself on a needle containing crack cocaine that had been left in the room. A jury did not classify the fear of AIDS as an injury.

Travel and living wills

This topic is discussed in Chapter 12. You should be aware that when you travel abroad, your wishes about care, treatment, resuscitation may not be carried out. Different countries have their own ideas about medical treatment. An elderly woman traveling in Austria suffered a heart attack with consequential brain damage. Despite her wish not to be kept alive when she had no brain function, the hospital put her on machines. Her daughter notified all the medical people and even saw a local attorney but to no avail. She was evacuated at a cost of $15,000 (luckily she had trip insurance to cover it) and died in the U.S. So if you are a traveler, always carry names and numbers of persons to notify, copies of directives, in case they will be honored and have insurance to cover contingencies. This is true for domestic travel also.

Trip insurance

As was discussed in this chapter on the topic of living wills, having a medical evacuation was very costly. Trip insurance covered it.

Years ago when you couldn't take a planned trip, you received a full refund. No more. So you need to buy insurance to cover the contingency.

Just as you would shop around for other insurance, you should be circumspect about trip insurance. You should get the insurance brochure early. The devil is in the details and small print. For example, if your tour company or carrier default, any policy they sold you won't protect you against loss. Most policies cover deposits that would be forfeited because of the cancellation. Some cruise policies provide a credit toward a future cruise. Some policies won't pay benefits if the illness or injury causing the claim was pre-existing. Also, you need to check the coverage period to see if the trip itself is covered, what exclusions there are, particularly as to whose illness or injury can be a trigger, that is only a spouse or does it include parents, children, business partners. You also want to assure yourself that the reimbursement will meet the need, as, for example, medical evacuation costs.

Problems with credit cards abroad

Along with the benefits of not carrying cash and possibly getting a credit on purchases, you should be aware of problems when using a credit card overseas. Your card can mistakenly not be honored or, because you purchased a defective item overseas, your "disputed charge" may be denied by your company.

In the former situation, if your purchases are "out of pattern," the computer may think your card has been stolen or otherwise is being used improperly and your card is blocked. You might want to alert your card company of plans to purchase more expensive items to avoid this possibility.

In the latter case, if a shopkeeper won't repair or replace your merchandise, then his actions are governed by whatever the local law is on the subject, which may be consumer unfriendly. VISA banks now can help cardholders in regard to overseas defective purchases. American Express has a purchase protection plan but with value limits and exceptions. Mastercard also has insurance but only for certain cardholders and with value limits and exceptions.

VAT, value-added tax

Shopping abroad can be cheaper if you take advantage of the refund allowed on purchases. You may get back as much as 20% of the cost of your purchases. You may not have been aware that a sort of sales tax was built in to the price you paid. In France, the VAT is over 15% and in some of Scandinavia it is 20%. Foreign visitors are exempt because they are taking goods out. So you can get a refund of the tax.

To get your refunds you can use *"Tax-free Shopping Service"* when you buy abroad. You keep all the receipts, have them validated at your departure airport customs office and cash them in at the airport's tax-free shopping booth. They'll give you cash, a check or credit on a charge card. There is a fee for their service.

You can avoid fees by using government tax refund forms at the shops, have them validated on departure and then mail them to the stores or a government agency for refunds. According to the country, you may have to spend a minimum amount at their shops. In France, for example, you only get a refund if you spend $370 per store, but given their prices, that shouldn't be difficult.

Storing food in your car

Bears in Yosemite National Park are smart. Many of them have gotten to like people food and they track it down, even in locked cars. There's a federal law which makes it a crime to store food in a car which is parked overnight in Yosemite. Food smells attract the bears, even cubs, and the damage they can do in their efforts to get to it is considerable. They can tear the door off your vehicle or crumple the trunk.

No human being fatalities have been recorded involving bears in the park but cars are another matter. So if you are going to Yosemite, don't have food in your vehicle; carry tightly sealed food containers which are bear resistant and dispose of all leftovers so that nothing will attract bears.

Dictionary of common legal terms

Dictionary of Common Legal Terms

Abortion. Termination of pregnancy by expulsion of a fetus.

Acceptance. Receiving, with the intention of retaining, something offered by another; the act of accepting an offer which results in a binding contract.

Accessory. One who, though not present at the commission of a crime, becomes guilty as a participant.

Acknowledgment. The declaration by a person of the execution of a written instrument as his voluntary act, made to a public officer, such as a notary public, commissioner of deeds, etc.

Action. A proceeding in a court of justice for the enforcement or protection of a right, the redress or prevention of a wrong, or the punishment of a public offense; a case at law.

Actionable. A term used to describe incidents or circumstances that are grounds for instituting a legal action or lawsuit.

Adjudge. To pass on judicially; to decide, settle, or decree, by court decision; to sentence or condemn.

Administration of estates. The management and settlement of the estate of a deceased person.

Administrator. A person appointed by a probate court to administer the estate of a deceased person.

Adoption. The taking of another's child into one's own family and giving that child all the rights and duties of one's own children.

Adult. One who has attained the age of majority, or full responsibility.

Adultery. Voluntary sexual intercourse of a married person with one other than his or her spouse.

Agent. One authorized to represent and act for another in the transaction or management of some business or affair of his.

Alibi. The fact or statement that one was not at the scene of a crime or other happening when it occurred.

Alien. A person who resides in one country and owes allegiance to another a person born outside the jurisdiction of the United States who has not been naturalized under the Constitution and laws of this country.

Alimony. Allowance made by order of the court or by agreement between the parties whereby one spouse receives support in an action for divorce, separation, or annulment, payable in periodic installments or a lump sum.

Allegiance. The obligation of fidelity and obedience owed by an individual to the country in which he lives or of which he is a citizen.

Amortization. The payment of an indebtedness by installments, at stated intervals, for a definite time. The term is usually applied to the payment of bonds, stocks, or mortgages.

Annuity. A specific yearly sum paid to a person for life or for a fixed period.

Annulment action. An action to have a marriage declared void or nonexistent; to be distinguished from a divorce action, which is brought to dissolve an existing marriage.

Appeal. The review of a case by a court of superior jurisdiction. Appellate court. A court having jurisdiction of appeals and reviews.

Apprehension. The seizure, taking, or arrest of a person on a criminal charge. The term is applied exclusively to criminal cases, whereas "arrest" is applied to both criminal and civil proceedings or actions.

Appurtenance. That which belongs to, or is a part of, something else: a barn, for example, is an appurtenance of land.

Arbitration. The investigation and settlement of a matter of contention between opposing parties, by persons or organizations chosen by the parties; government boards also perform this function when the public interest is concerned. The American Arbitration Association is available to act as an impartial administrator for the arbitration of disputes.

Arson. The intentional and malicious burning of a dwelling house or other building, or causing one to be burned.

Assault. An attempt or threat to beat another without touching him; an unlawful offer or attempt with force or violence to commit a bodily hurt upon another.

Assessment. To set a valuation on; the listing and valuation of property and establishment of a rate for the purpose of taxation. Assets. All the property one possesses that may be made available for the payment of debts.

Assign, Assignee. He who receives property from another by assignment, conveyance, devise, descent, or act of law.

Assignment. The transfer to another of real or personal property.

Assignor: He who makes an assignment to another.

Assured. A person indemnified by an insurance company against the loss described in the policy; the insured.

Attachment. The seizure of property by virtue of judicial order or other process.

Attestation. The act of witnessing the signature of an instrument and subscribing it as a witness at the request of the party executing the instrument.

Autopsy. Examination after death of a body.

Award. A judgment, sentence, or final decision.

Bail. The surety or sureties who become responsible for the appearance in court of a person under arrest in return for the release of the prisoner; money pledged for such an appearance.

Bail bond. An obligation signed by the accused with sureties for the performance by the accused of certain acts, generally for his appearance at court at a requited time.

Bailment. The delivery of goods by one person to another for an agreed purpose and to be ultimately redelivered to the owner.

Bankruptcy. Proceedings taken under the bankruptcy statute to have the assets of the bankrupt divided among his creditors.

Bastard. A child born of unlawful intercourse before the lawful marriage of its parents; a child born out of wedlock.

Battery. Any unlawful physical injury inflicted on a person without his consent.

Bench warrant. Process issued by the court or "from the bench" for the arrest of the person named in the warrant.

Beneficiary. One receiving or to receive the benefits, profits, advantages or enjoyments of property by inheritance or under a trust; the person to whom the proceeds of insurance are payable.

Bequeath. To give personal property to another by will; distinguished from devise, which relates to real property.

Bequest. A gift of personal property by will.

Bigamy. The criminal offense of contracting and going through the form of a second marriage while the first marriage still exists.

Blue ribbon jury. A jury chosen for its outstanding qualifications, and used to consider cases of special importance.

Bona fide. Honestly, openly and sincerely; without deceit or fraud.

Bona Fide holder for value. One who takes a negotiable instrument in good faith for a valuable consideration in the ordinary course of business before it is due.

Bona fide purchases. One who buys for a valuable consideration with the belief that the seller has a right to sell and with no knowledge of any impediments to the transfer.

Bookmaking. The recording or registering of bets or wagers.

Bottomry. The contract under which a ship owner borrows money for the use or repair of a vessel.

Breach of promise. Chiefly used to indicate "breach of promise of marriage," or failing to keep one's promise to marry someone.

Breach of the peace. The breaking or disturbing of the public peace by riot or other unlawful action.

Bribery. A payment made to a person to influence his behavior and incline him to act contrary to his duty.

Broker. One whose business is to negotiate purchases and sales.

Capital. The money and other property owned by a person or corporation, used in business.

Capital stock. The sum of money raised by the subscriptions of stockholders and divided into shares.

Carrier: A person or corporation that undertakes to transport persons or property from one place to another by means of a conveyance.

Case. A general term for actions or suits at law or in equity.

Casualty. Accident.

Cause of action. The ground on which a lawsuit can be sustained.

Caveat emptor: Literally, "'Let the buyer beware," a Latin phrase used in the law to indicate that it is the buyer's responsibility to examine, judge, test, and otherwise inspect the article by himself—he is buying at his own risk.

Cestui que trust. He who has a right to and a beneficial interest in an estate of which the legal title is in another.

Chattel mortgage. An instrument giving a lien on personal property as security for a debt or the performance of an obligation.

Chattels. Articles of personal property; property that is not land; goods.

Circumstantial evidence. Facts that establish a condition, or circumstances from which the principal fact is a possible conclusion. Proof of the motive for murder by the accused, with the additional proof of his ownership of the weapon and a failure to account for his whereabouts at the time of the crime, is circumstantial evidence of guilt.

Citation. A writ commanding a person to appear before a named judicial tribunal or officer on a day named.

Citizen. One who under the Constitution and laws of the United States by virtue of birth or naturalization owes allegiance to this country and is entitled to the enjoyment of full civil rights in the United States.

Civil rights. Rights of a nonpolitical kind, secured to citizens by the Thirteenth and Fourteenth amendments to the Constitution of the United States or by various state or federal statutes.

Cohabitation. Living together in the relationship of husband and wife; sexual intercourse.

Collusion. A secret combination, conspiracy, or concerted action between two or more persons for fraudulent, deceitful, or unlawful purposes.

Color of office. The claim or assumption of the right to do an act by virtue of an office.

Co-maker. A person who signs or endorses the promissory note of another before delivery of the note to the payee.

Committee of incompetent. Person or persons invested by order of court with the guardianship of the person or estate of one adjudged an incompetent or lunatic.

Common law. The principles of law derived from the ancient law of England embodied in court decisions; distinguished from statutory law (enacted by the Congress or the state legislatures) and civil law (the law of countries following the Roman or Napoleonic codes, such as we have in the State of Louisiana).

Common-law marriage. A marriage without ceremony created by an agreement between the parties and followed by cohabitation.

Community property. Property owned in common by husband and wife. In community-property-law states, property so owned because acquired by either spouse during marriage.

Comparative negligence. Where the negligence of the parties is weighed and the damage is divided in proportion to the fault of each one.

Complainant. One who applies to the courts for legal redress. Compromise. An arrangement made either in or out of court for the settlement of a dispute.

Concubinage. The act or practice of cohabiting without the sanction of the law or of a legal marriage.

Consanguinity. The relation of persons descended from a common ancestor; blood relationship: kinship.

Constructive. That which is inferred by legal interpretation; that which has not in its own nature the character assigned to it, but acquires such character as a consequence of the way it is regarded in the law.

Contempt. A willful disregard of the authority of a court of justice or legislative body, or disobedience to its lawful orders.

Contract. A promissory agreement between two or more persons that creates, modifies, or ends a legal relation; an agreement creating legal rights enforceable by action.

Contributory negligence. The negligent act of a person claiming damages for injury from negligence of another; this negligent act must also be a genuine contributory cause without which the injury would not have occurred negligence contributing to cause the accident.

Conversion. An unauthorized assumption and exercise of the right of ownership over another's goods.

Convert. To assume or exercise the right of ownership over another's goods without authorization.

Conveyance. The transfer of title to land; a deed.

Conviction. The verdict by a jury of guilty or the final judgment of a court of the criminal guilt of the accused.

Covenant. An agreement by deed, in writing, by which either party pledges himself to the other that something is or will be done, or not done, or stipulates the truth of certain facts.

Coverture. The legal condition or state of a married woman at common law.

Creditor: A person to whom a debt is owed by another person, who is called a debtor.

Crime. An act violating the sanctions of the criminal law, for which the law provides the offender shall make satisfaction to the state by undergoing punishment.

Curtesy. Under common law the life interest a man has at the death of his wife in her real property, when children of the marriage inherit the fee title.

Damages. The money compensation which is recovered in the courts by a person who has suffered a loss, detriment, or injury through the unlawful act of another.

Debtor. A person who owes money.

Decision. The judgment or decree of a court.

Deed. A written instrument by which one person conveys land to another.

Deed poll. A deed which is made by only one person.

Defamation. The offense of injuring a person's character or reputation by false statements.

Defendant. The person against whom an action is brought.

Deportation. The sending back of an alien to the country from which he came.

Descendant. One who is descended from another a child, grandchild, etc.

Descent. Succession to the ownership of property by inheritance.

Devise. A disposition of land by will. See *bequeath*.

Disability. The lack of legal capacity to perform an act.

Discharge in bankruptcy. The release of the bankrupt from the obligations of his debts which were, or might have been, proved in the bankruptcy proceedings.

Disorderly conduct. Any behavior contrary to law, but, more particularly, conduct that tends to disturb the peace or shock the public sense of morality.

Domicile. The true, fixed, and permanent home or residence of a person.

Donee. One to whom property is given.

Donor: The giver of property.

Double indemnify. The provision in an insurance policy that under certain conditions the insurance company will pay to the beneficiary under the policy twice the face amount of the policy.

Dower: The widow's life interest in land her husband owned when he died.

Due process of law. The law in its regular course of administration through the courts of justice.

Easement. A liberty, right to use. or privilege of access which one person may acquire in relation to the land of another.

Eminent domain. The power of the state to take private property for public use, providing a reasonable compensation.

Encumbrance. A claim or lien attached to and binding on real or personal property.

Endorse (also indorse). To write your name on the back of a paper or document; the act of a payee, drawee, or holder of a bill, note, check, or other negotiable instrument in writing his name on the back whereby the property in such instrument is assigned and transferred to another.

Equity. The system of legal rules and principles used in certain areas of jurisdiction not adequately covered by statute and common law; derived from ecclesiastical law to have a fair rather than technical approach to legal matters. "Equity" can also refer to a share or interest in property.

Escrow. Money, property, or a document held by a third person for delivery to the grantee upon the occurrence or performance of certain conditions; title does not pass until the conditions are fulfilled, but the grantor no longer controls the escrow.

Evict. To dispossess or turn out of possession of land or home by process of law.

Execution. A writ issued to a sheriff or other law enforcement officer requiring the execution of a judgment of the court.

Executor: A person appointed by a will to administer the will of a deceased person.

Exemplary damages. Damages increased by reason of the aggravation of a wrong by violence, fraud or malice; punitive damages not limited to actual damaged suffered.

Expatriation. The voluntary act of abandoning one's country.

Extradition. The surrender of a criminal by a foreign state to which he has fled to the state in which the crime was committed, on the demand of the latter state; legal proceedings to obtain this surrender.

False imprisonment. The unlawful arrest, or detention of a person whereby he is deprived of his liberty.

False pretenses. False representations and statements made with the design of obtaining something of value, with intent to cheat.

False representation. An untrue representation willfully made to deceive another to his loss.

Family purpose. The doctrine that the owner of an automobile is liable for damages resulting from the negligent operation of his automobile by members of his family whom he has permitted to use it.

Fee simple. The absolute ownership of land with the unrestricted power of sale or other disposition.

Felony. A crime of a graver nature than a misdemeanor, and more seriously punished.

Fiduciary. A person invested with rights and powers to be used for the benefit of another.

Fixtures. Chattels or goods that, by being annexed to land or attached to a building, become in law a part of it and belong to the owner of the land.

Foreclosure. The court proceedings for the sale of mortgaged land or personal property for the payment of the mortgage, and the disposal of the mortgagor's right to redeem.

Forgery. Falsely making or materially altering any writing with intent to defraud.

Fornication. Sexual intercourse by persons unmarried to each other.

Fourteenth Amendment. An amendment to the Constitution of the United States that became law July 28, 1868. It forbids the making or enforcement by any state of any law abridging the privileges and immunities of citizens of the United States. It secures all persons against any state action by which they may be deprived of life, liberty, or property without due process of law or a denial of the equal protection of the law. This is also known as the "due process" amendment.

Franchise. Authorization granted by an owner to a distributor or dealer to sell the owner's products or services.

Fraud. The deceitful practice or device used to deprive another of his rights or to effect an injury.

Frauds, Statute of. An ancient statute, still in current use, that, among other features, provides that no suit can be maintained on certain contracts unless a note or memorandum in writing has been made and signed by the person sought to be held to the agreement.

Garnishment. A notice to a person holding another's property (for example a bank account) to give the court an accounting of it and not to yield it to the one who holds title to it: a notice to present oneself in court.

Grantee. The person to whom a grant is made.

Grantor: The person by whom a grant is made.

Guaranty. A warranty, given by a third party, of the payment of a debt or other obligation or of the performance of some act.

Guardian. A person invested with the power to, and charged with the duty of, taking care of the person and property of another, usually a minor.

Habeas corpus. A writ or order commanding the person detaining another (generally an officer of the law) to produce him and submit to a decision on the legality of the detention by the court or judge granting the writ of habeas corpus.

Holographic will. A will written by its maker (the testator) entirely in his own handwriting.

Heir. One who inherits property, either real or personal.

Hereditaments. Things capable of being inherited.

Hold over. To retain possession as tenant of leased property after the expiration of the lease.

Homestead. The home, the house, and adjacent land where the head of the family dwells.

Homicide. The killing of one person by another.

Hypothecate. To pledge a thing, generally as security for a loan, without delivering possession to the pledgee or maker of the loan.

Illegitimate. That which is contrary to law, usually applied to bastards or children born out of lawful wedlock.

Impounded. To shut up stray animals or distrain goods in a pound; to seize and hold a fund of money or goods by legal process.

Incest. Sexual intercourse or inbreeding between individuals related within degrees where marriage is prohibited.

Incompetency. The legal status of a parson unable or unfitted to manage his own affairs by reason of insanity, imbecility, or feeblemindedness.

Indemnify. To secure against loss or damage; to make reimbursement to one for a loss already suffered.

Indenture. A deed to which two or more persons are parties, entering into mutual grants and obligations.

Indictment. An accusation in writing, based on the findings of a grand jury, charging that the person named has been guilty of a punishable crime.

Morse (see endorse).

Infancy. The state of a person under the age of legal majority; minority.

Injunction. A writ or order requiring a person to refrain from, or to do, a particular act.

Insemination. The process of introducing male semen into the female genital tract.

Instrument. A written document; a formal or legal document in writing.

Insurable interest. An interest in property or a person's life or health that the beneficiary must have if an insurance policy is to be issued. An insurable interest exists, by and large, if the beneficiary has a serious stake in the life of the person or the safety of the property insured.

Interstate commerce. Traffic, trade, or transportation of persons or property between the states of the United States.

Intestate. Said of one who dies without leaving a will.

Joint tenancy. Where two or mom persons hold concurrent ownership in property and when one dies the. ownership remains in the others.

Judgment. The decision of a court of justice.

Jurisdiction. The power and authority of a judge or magistrate to determine legal causes and carry his determinations into execution; the extent of a court's, state's, country's, or other governmental unit's authority.

Larceny. The wrongful taking and carrying away of the personal goods of another; theft, stealing.

Lawsuit. A suit, action, proceeding or controversy between two or more persons in a court of law.

Legacy. A gift of personal property by a will.

Lemon. An unsatisfactory product.

Levy. The seizure of property by a sheriff, marshal, or other court officer under an execution or attachment.

Libel. Published written or printed matter, or signs, pictures, or other representations calculated to injure the character or reputation of a person by bringing him into ridicule, hatred or contempt. Civil libel is a libel for which damage may be collect & criminal libel-libel punishable as a crime-is that which tends to excite a breach of peace.

License. Permission to do some act that without such authority or permission would be illegal.

Lien. The claim of one person on the property of another as security for a sum due.

LS. The abbreviation for the Latin *focus sigilli*, the place occupied by the seal on a written instrument, as the seal of a public officer, such as a notary. Private persons seldom use a seal nowadays, though legal documents often provide a place for one.

Mandatory. Said of a court order or statute which must be obeyed.

Material. Having bearing on the subject at issue: important, as in the phrase "a material witness."

Mechanic's lien. A lien created by statute in most states in favor of persons who have performed work or furnished material used in the construction of a house or other construction work.

Minority. Infancy; under legal age.

Misdemeanor. A crime that is of a less degree than a felony and distinguished from one by not being punishable by death or imprisonment in a penitentiary.

Mortgage. A pledge of particular property to secure the payment of a debt or the performance of an obligation.

Mortgager. A person who lends money on a property and receives a mortgage on it in exchange.

Mortgages. He who gives a mortgage; the owner of mortgaged property.

Naturalization. The act of adopting an alien into a nation as a citizen and giving him the rights of a natural-born citizen.

Negotiable instrument. A bill of exchange, promissory note, check, or other security, which may be transferred by endorsement and delivery, or only by delivery, so as to give to the endorsee or recipient a legal title and thus enable him to collect pursuant to the terms of the written instrument, or to sue thereon in his own name. A negotiable instrument carries its legal title to the next person by endorsement or delivery, and when transferred before maturity, the transferee has the right to demand the full amount which the face of the instrument calls for. Under the *Uniform Negotiable Instruments Act, a*n instrument to be negotiable must be in writing and signed and contain an unconditional provision or order to pay a certain sum of money on demand or at a fixed or determinable future time; it must be payable to the bearer or to the order of someone.

Nuncuputive will. An oral will or will made by a word-of-mouth declaration.

Pawn. Goods entrusted to a creditor as security for a loan, a pledge, or hypothecation.

Pawnbroker. A person whose business is the loaning of money on the security of personal property deposited in pawn with him.

Pawnee. A person to whom goods are delivered by another in exchange for a loan.

Pawner: A person who pawns goods.

Per capita. By heads, that is, by individuals. Persons taking equal shares each in his own right in the distribution of decedent's estate, in contradistinction to a share for an entire class, which is termed per stirpes.

Per stirpes. Taking property by right of representation is called "succession per stirpes," in opposition to taking in one's own right or as a principal, which is termed per capita: distribution of shares by classes of kindred relations.

Plaintiff A person who brings an action.

Pledge. The deposit of goods with a creditor as security for a debt or obligation; hypothecation.

Posthumous. After death; a term used to describe a child born after the death of his father or (by means of a cesarian operation) after the death of the mother

Power of attorney. An instrument authorizing another to act as one's agent or attorney.

Presumption. A particular inference that is drawn from particular evidence or a state of facts unless and until the contrary of such an inference is proved—for example, a man is presumed to be innocent until proved guilty.

Primogeniture. In ancient law, the supreme or exclusive right possessed by the eldest son to succeed to the entire land of his father to the exclusion of the younger sons.

Principal. The person who constitutes and gives authority to an agent to do some act for him; the person for whom an agent acts.

Probate. The judicial determination which establishes the validity of a will.

Proceeding. Any application to a court for aid in the enforcement of rights, the redress of injuries or other remedial relief: a litigation.

Process. The writ by which a court compels compliance with its demands.

Prosecution. A criminal proceeding for the purpose of determining the guilt or innocence of the person charged with a crime.

Proximate cause. An act or cause of mischief which directly produces or is the. natural and probable consequence of an effect for which someone can be held liable.

Proxy. A person acting as the deputy or agent of another, generally at some meeting; also the instrument by which the person is appointed to act as the deputy for another.

Punitive damages. Damages intended to punish a wrongdoer for violence, fraud, or malice, rather than simply to compensate the victim.

Purchase money mortgage. A mortgage given to secure the unpaid balance of the purchase price on the conveyance of land.

Putative father. The alleged or reputed father of an illegitimate child.

Quiet enjoyment. A covenant or agreement contained in deeds or leases that the grantee or tenant will be permitted to enjoy the premises in peace and without disturbance by the grantor or landlord.

Quitclaim deed. A deed that passes any title, interest, or claim which the grantor has in the property, but contains no warranty of title or representation that the title is valid.

Realty. Land, as distinguished from personal property.

Rebuttable presumption. A legal presumption that may be disproved by evidence.

Remix. To remit or give up.

Representation. The principle by which the descendants of a deceased person inherit the sham of an estate which he would have inherited if living; the taking or inheritance per stirpes.

Res ipsa loquitur. It literally means "the thing speaks for itself." In law, it means that the accident is one that would not have happened in the normal course unless there were negligence, and so the reasonable inference can be made that there was negligence, that the negligence caused the accident, and that it was the defendant's fault. Of course, this inference can only be made where the instrumentality causing the accident was in the exclusive control of the defendant.

Residence. A fixed or permanent home or dwelling place.

Revocation. A recall of some power, authority, or thing granted. Right of action. The right to bring suit.

Right of redemption. The right to free property from a claim or lien by payment of what is due with interest, etc.

Search warrant. An order issued by a judge directed to a sheriff or other peace officer to search specific premises.

Second mortgage. The second lien on property.

Slander. Oral defamation within the hearing of a third party; speaking false words about another person in public, by which his reputation is or may be injured.

Statute. An enactment of the legislature.

Stipulation. A material provision in an agreement; an agreement between attorneys in the conduct of litigation.

Sublease. A lease by a tenant to another person.

Subpoena. A writ requiring one's attendance as a witness.

Subpoena duces tecum. A subpoena requiring a witness to bring with him books or documents in his possession.

Subtenant. An undertenant; one who leases premises from a tenant.

Sufferance. Negative permission by not forbidding; passive consent; a license implied from the omission or neglect to enforce an adverse right.

Summation. In a jury trial, counsel for both sides summarize the evidence already presented to the jury in order to draw its attention to the outstanding points in favor of the side summing up.

Summons. A notice to a parson that an action has been commenced in court against him.

Surety. A person who binds himself for the payment of a sum of money or for the performance of some act by another.

Surrender. A yielding up of an estate by which the lesser estate is merged in the greater by mutual consent; for example, the surrender of a lease to a landlord.

Tenancy at will. The occupation of realty by a person without a lease or after the termination of a lease with neither the agreement nor disagreement of the person in whom is the right of possession; a tenancy ended at the will of either landlord or tenant.

Testamentary. Pertaining to a will.

Testator. One who makes a will.

Things in action. Claims with a money value; judicial proceedings to recover money or personal property.

Title. Ownership; the grounds by which the owner of property has a just possession; a person's right to property.

Tort. A legal wrong committed on a person or property.

Treasure trove. Money, gold, silver, or bullion found hidden, and the owner of which is unknown.

Trespass. An entry on the ground of another without lawful authority.

True bill. The endorsement made by a grand jury on a bill of indictment when it is satisfied with the truth of the accusations.

Trust. A holding of another person's property subject to a duty of employing it according to directions of the person from whom it was derived.

Trustee. A person appointed to execute a trust.

Usury. Interest paid for borrowing of money beyond the maximum rate permitted by law.

Verdict. The decision of a jury after the trial of a case.

Visa. An endorsement on a passport by proper authorities permitting the person who bears it to enter a particular country.

Void. Having no legal force or binding effect.

Waiver. Relinquishment of a known right.

Ward. A person placed by authority of law under the care of a guardian.

Warranty. A representation or promise in a contract.

Will. A legal declaration or testament of a person's wishes for the disposition of his property after death.

Index